Handbook on the Entrepreneurial University

Edited by

Alain Fayolle

Professor of Entrepreneurship and Director, Entrepreneurship Research Centre, EMLYON Business School, France

Dana T. Redford

President of the Platform for Entrepreneurship Education in Portugal, UCP-Porto, Portugal

Edward Elgar
Cheltenham, UK • Northampton, MA, USA

Published by
Edward Elgar Publishing Limited
The Lypiatts
15 Lansdown Road
Cheltenham
Glos GL50 2JA
UK

Edward Elgar Publishing, Inc.
William Pratt House
9 Dewey Court
Northampton
Massachusetts 01060
USA

A catalogue record for this book
is available from the British Library

Library of Congress Control Number: 2013944950

This book is available electronically in the ElgarOnline.com
Business Subject Collection, E-ISBN 978 1 78100 702 0

ISBN 978 1 78100 701 3 (cased)

Typeset by Servis Filmsetting Ltd, Stockport, Cheshire
Printed and bound in Great Britain by T.J. International Ltd, Padstow

Contents

Contributors

Bjørn Willy Åmo is an Associate Professor at Bodø Graduate School of Business, University of Nordland, Norway. He teaches and researches on entrepreneurship.

Vincent Blok is an Assistant Professor with the Social Sciences Group, Wageningen University, the Netherlands. His research interests include knowledge-intensive entrepreneurship, the entrepreneurial university and entrepreneurship education.

Judith Crayford is director for the BA Entrepreneurship programme at Canterbury Christ Church University Business School. Her research interests include student learning transitions into Higher Education and entrepreneurial learning.

Hans Dons is Emeritus Professor Entrepreneurship in the Life Sciences with the Social Science Group, Wageningen University, and Managing Director of BioSeeds b.v., a strategic alliance in molecular plant breeding, located in Wageningen, the Netherlands.

Louise-Jayne Edwards has worked in academia for 14 years, lecturing and researching in enterprise education as well as providing business mentoring. She is currently Head of the Enterprise Education Hub at the University of South Wales (formerly the University of Glamorgan).

Truls Erikson is Professor in Entrepreneurship at the University of Oslo where he serves as the Director of the Centre for Entrepreneurship. Truls received his doctorate from the University of Manchester, UK.

Alain Fayolle is a Professor of Entrepreneurship, and the founder and director of the Entrepreneurship Research Centre at EMLYON Business School, France. In 2013 he won the European Entrepreneurship Education Award.

Colm Fearon is director of both the MSc International Business and MPhil/PhD programmes at Canterbury Christ Church University Business School, UK. He has research focuses on self-/team efficacy and entrepreneurial learning.

Allan A. Gibb, University of Durham, has designed and directed numerous national and international entrepreneurship education programmes at all levels, more recently the UK Entrepreneurial University Leaders Programme.

Peter Groenewegen is Professor of Organization Sciences in the Department of Organization Sciences, Faculty of Social Sciences, VU University Amsterdam. His research concerns the networked character of organizing and entrepreneurship taking place in emergency management organizations, health care and online communities.

Marc Grünhagen is researcher and lecturer in entrepreneurship at the Schumpeter School of Business and Economics at Wuppertal University in Germany. His research focuses on entrepreneurial intentions, enterprise policy and university entrepreneurship.

Maribel Guerrero is a researcher at the Orkestra-Basque Institute of Competitiveness and Deusto Business School in Spain. Her research interests are focused on entrepreneurial activity inside public/private organizations, and its socioeconomic impacts.

Sose Hakhverdyan is a student assistant at the Danish Foundation for Entrepreneurship – Young Enterprise.

Gay Haskins has over 30 years' experience in management development. She has been Dean of Executive Education at the University of Oxford's Said Business School, the Indian School of Business and London Business School.

Willem Hulsink is Associate Professor of Entrepreneurship at RSM Erasmus University, the Netherlands. Previously, he was director/co-founder of its Centre for Entrepreneurship and a Special Professor Innovative Entrepreneurship at Wageningen UR.

Casper Jørgensen, The Danish Foundation for Entrepreneurship – Young Enterprise, is senior analyst undertaking mappings of the spread of entrepreneurship education and analyses of the impact. Casper holds an MSc in Economics.

Nicholas Kalaitzandonakes is Endowed Professor of Agribusiness and Director of the Economics and Management of the Agrobiotechnology Center at the University of Missouri, USA. He publishes on biotechnology industry structure and entrepreneurship.

Christos Kolympiris, Wageningen University, is Assistant Professor in Management. His research revolves around the knowledge economy. His work has appeared, among others, in *Research Policy* and *Small Business Economics* journals.

Thomas Lans is an Assistant Professor in Education and Competence Studies, Wageningen University, the Netherlands. His research interests include assessment and impact measurement in entrepreneurship education and (situated) entrepreneurial learning.

Daniel Leunbach is a PhD Research Fellow at the Centre for Entrepreneurship at the University of Oslo, and he is a doctoral student in the Program in Innovation Management and Innovation Strategy at the Norwegian Research School in Innovation.

Rob Lubberink is a doctoral student in entrepreneurship and responsible innovation in the Social Sciences Group, Wageningen University in the Netherlands.

Niall G. MacKenzie is Lecturer in Entrepreneurship and Family Business at the University of Strathclyde, UK. His interests include entrepreneurship, family business and business history.

Magdalena Markowska is a Post-doctoral Fellow in the Entrepreneurship Institute at ESADE Business School, Spain. She holds a PhD from the Jönköping International Business School in Sweden.

Elisabeth Markussen, is a student assistant at The Danish Foundation for Entrepreneurship – Young Enterprise.

Simon McCarthy is a Senior Lecturer in the School of Law, Accounting and Finance at the University of South Wales.

Kåre Moberg is an industrial PhD Fellow at Copenhagen Business School employed by the Danish Foundation for Entrepreneurship – Young Enterprise and Copenhagen Business School. He is undertaking research on the effects and impact of entrepreneurship education.

Elizabeth J. Muir provides postgraduate supervision, papers and business mentoring at Cardiff Metropolitan University. After 20 years running her own business, Dr Muir returned to academia, establishing the first European Master's programme for women entrepreneurs.

Ernest Samwel Mwasalwiba is a lecturer at the School of Business, Mzumbe University in Tanzania. His research interest is in entrepreneurship education, mainly on educational impact assessment and graduate entrepreneurship in a developing world context.

Onno Omta is Chaired Professor in Business Administration at Wageningen University, Netherlands. He is the author of many scientific articles on innovation management and entrepreneurship in the life sciences.

Gary Packham is Deputy Dean (Research and Enterprise) Lord Ashcroft International Business School at Anglia Ruskin University, UK.

David Pickernell is Professor in Economic Development Policy and Director of the Centre for Enterprise at the University of South Wales (formerly University of Glamorgan).

Dana T. Redford, Platform for Entrepreneurship Education in Portugal and Universidade Católica Portuguesa, is recognized as an international expert in entrepreneurship and public policy. He has worked with the European Commission, OECD, US Department of Commerce and various government and academic institutions worldwide.

Markus Reihlen is Professor of Strategic Management, Vice-President of Leuphana University of Lüneburg, Germany, as well as International Research Fellow at the University of Oxford.

Aidin Salamzadeh is a PhD candidate and a researcher in Entrepreneurship at the University of Tehran. He serves as a member of editorial board on journals such as *Journal of Entrepreneurship, Business and Economics, Journal of Women's Entrepreneurship and Education*, etc.

Ken Schneeberger is Professor of Agricultural Economics and Assistant Dean for Special Programs at the University of Missouri, USA. He has co-authored three books and is active in international economic development.

Mari Saua Svalastog is programme manager for 'Gründerskolen' at the Centre for Entrepreneurship at the University of Oslo. Mari received her Master's degree in informatics from UiO, and she is a former Gründerskolen student.

Susanne Steiner is an entrepreneurship educator at the Technical University of Berlin. Her prior experience encompasses strategy consulting and industry operations. Susanne has been visiting lecturer at ESCP Europe Business School.

David Urbano, Professor in Entrepreneurship at the Autonomous University of Barcelona, UAB, obtained his PhD in Entrepreneurship at UAB and Växjö University, Sweden. His research focuses on the conditioning factors for entrepreneurship in different contexts using the institutional approach.

Elco van Burg, VU University Amsterdam, is an Associate Professor of Entrepreneurship & Organization. His research interests are related to collaboration and imagination in the context of (technology) entrepreneurship.

Wim van Vuuren is director of the Centre for Entrepreneurship and

Innovation at the Canterbury Christ Church University Business School, UK. His research interests include start-ups and entrepreneurial learning.

Gemma van Vuuren-Cassar contributes to various undergraduate and postgraduate programmes in the Faculty of Education at Canterbury Christ Church University in the UK. Her research interests include curricular innovation, learning, assessment and accreditation.

Lene Vestergaard is a teamleader at the Danish Foundation for Entrepreneurship – Young Enterprise working with entrepreneurship education from ABC to PhD. She holds a Master's in Innovation and Leadership.

Christine Volkmann holds the Chair of Entrepreneurship and Economic Development and the UNESCO-Chair of Entrepreneurship and Intercultural Management at the Schumpeter School of Business and Economics at Wuppertal University, Germany.

Ingrid Wakkee is Associate Professor of Entrepreneurship at VU University Amsterdam. Her research focuses on topics like failure and recovery, global start-ups and entrepreneurship education and is published in international peer reviewed journals.

Ferdinand Wenzlaff is research assistant at Leuphana University of Lüneburg, Germany. His research interests cover the change of the Higher Education system, organization theory and economics.

Qiantao Zhang is a doctoral candidate at the Cardiff School of Planning and Geography at Cardiff Metropolitan University. His research interests are in innovation, regional development and knowledge exchange.

Introduction: towards more entrepreneurial universities – myth or reality?

Alain Fayolle and Dana T. Redford

It is clear that universities need to become more entrepreneurial, changing their strategies, their structures and their practices, changing their culture and helping students and faculty members to develop their entrepreneurial mindsets and entrepreneurial actions. But universities are professional bureaucracies focused on core missions and values in relation to education and research. Consequently, their ability/capacity to change and adopt new behaviours seems low. This creates a paradox and tension between what universities are and what they should be to deal with the evolutionary trends and the complexity of the world. At the same time, there is much talk of entrepreneurial universities in both the world of practice/politics and research. Much work has been done on entrepreneurial universities, and this book reflects the rich diversity of such literature. But issues can be raised about the usefulness and applicability of this knowledge. Is there a strong relationship/connection between research on entrepreneurial universities and the needs, the awareness, the policies and the strategies of universities? In other words, is the idea of an entrepreneurial university a myth or a reality? Even if we are convinced that universities must change and become more entrepreneurial, this question must be asked. We believe this book responds to the question, highlighting how universities can conceive of and implement strategic changes to better promote entrepreneurship internally and externally.

This book offers a lens through which to view entrepreneurship promotion and implementation at Higher Education Institutions (HEIs). The book also develops a body of knowledge, research and principles that can be extrapolated from case studies. It addresses issues and questions in relation to entrepreneurship strategies at Higher Education Institutions, relationships between university, industry and government, entrepreneurship education, start-up development from graduate entrepreneurs and researchers as well as the design and implementation of systems and structures dedicated to entrepreneurship.

In the first part of this introductory chapter we discuss the concept of entrepreneurial university before developing, in the second part, the contributions of the book, introducing each of the chapters.

THE CONCEPT OF THE ENTREPRENEURIAL UNIVERSITY

In the classical model of the university, the main missions focus on research and teaching, production and transmission of knowledge within a society. In this model, the researcher is intellectually independent and his or her scientific production is a collective asset. Universities tend to advance universal and objective scientific knowledge.

The modern era acknowledges the importance of a 'Third Mission': the economic and social valorization of knowledge produced by researchers within universities, creating the need for strategies, structures and mechanisms within universities that facilitate and intensify knowledge transfer to the private sector, via various avenues: patents, licensing, and facilitating academic spin-offs and start-ups, among others. Universities also need to develop a more entrepreneurial orientation and culture, and university researchers need to become increasingly entrepreneurial (Etzkowitz and Leydesdorff, 1997). Finally, this new model gives a greater importance to the relationships between three types of stakeholders: governments, universities and businesses.

In the modern knowledge economy the entrepreneurial university is seen as a central force that drives innovation, creativity and economic growth (Audretsch, 1995; Audretsch, et al., 2006; Mueller, 2006). At the core of the entrepreneurial university concept is a connection between the 'ivory tower' and the 'real world'. In Europe, the declarations of Bologna, in 1999, and Lisbon, in 2000, give clear examples of government interest in improving entrepreneurial awareness at all educational levels, and particularly at the university level. More recently both the OECD (2010) and the European Commission (2013) have written about developing strategies for university entrepreneurial support.

There are many definitions of entrepreneurial universities (see, for example, Guerrero and Urbano, 2012). Etzkowitz (2003, pp.111–12) states that 'just as the university trains individual students and sends them out into the world, the Entrepreneurial University is a natural incubator, providing support structures for teachers and students to initiate new ventures: intellectual, commercial and conjoint'. Our intention here is not to debate this question of definition, as we know there is no consensus on it. Rather, we aim to sharpen our view. For us, the entrepreneurial university concept is best utilized if it helps an institution formulate a strategic direction (Clark, 1998), by both focusing academic goals and by converting knowledge produced at the university into economic and social utility (Etzkowitz, 2003). It must not only incorporate entrepreneurship education but also define how start-ups are supported at the university. It must also partner with organizations and champion a vision on how existing infrastructure can be used to sustain entrepreneurial endeavours.

There is clearly a need for more entrepreneurial universities in the sense we view them. The question is: is it an easy path from the classical model to the new one, including the Third Mission? Despite the growing commitment of universities to this strategy of research commercialization and technology transfer in the developed countries (Siegel et al., 2007), there is strong resistance to change in the university world. These involve the difficulty of avoiding conflicts when combining the three missions. The third one, commercialization of knowledge, can be seen quite differently compared to the other two. Have research and education lost their way in being associated with knowledge commercialization? This is a key question both at the individual (researcher) and organizational levels (universities). The principal success factor in this kind of strategy and in developing the entrepreneurial dimension within the universities relates to the capacity of universities to develop 'ambidexterity' at the institutional and individual levels (Chang et al., 2009). Universities, consequently, should change their policies, strategies, structures and organizational rules to allow researchers to engage more easily with university activities in relation to the three missions.

The development of a cross-campus, interdisciplinary approach for the implementation of entrepreneurship initiatives has been gaining momentum as a way to assure quality and build critical mass in fostering graduate entrepreneurship. University strategy, public policy and integrating start-up support are the focus of this book, probing entrepreneurship as a strategy for Higher Education Institutions.

THIS BOOK'S CONTRIBUTION

This book comprises three parts. In Part I, aspects regarding the management and organization of the entrepreneurial university are discussed, as well as country-specific strategies that have been important in improving entrepreneurial university programmes.

The first chapter takes a strategic perspective and examines the ways in which universities need to reconsider their relationships with their stakeholders to become learning organizations. Allan Gibb and Gay Haskins then explore the present and future pressures shaping the entrepreneurial nature of universities and the response to these pressures. Universities act in a specific environment and they have to deal with and negotiate their freedom and autonomy within this environment. This chapter suggests a framework that could be helpful for each university in rethinking and reorienting its development strategies for the future.

Vincent Blok and his colleagues from Wageningen University compare and discuss several entrepreneurship education programmes in Europe, the USA and Canada. They highlight resources and strategies that universities can use in order to manage and improve their entrepreneurial programmes. According to the authors, the adjustment of missions and strategic plans should function as a roadmap to successful implementation of entrepreneurship education programmes at the university level. Bjørn Åmo, in the following chapter, explains why entrepreneurship programmes at the university level need to be adapted to each country's context, and compares the Nordic countries of Finland, Sweden and Norway. He proposes a framework to help the transfer of educational programmes and syllabi and uses data from the Global Entrepreneurship Monitor project to compare the conditions that the potential entrepreneur faces, the actions entrepreneurs take and the outcomes of their actions.

Markus Reihlen and Ferdinand Wenzlaff, in the fifth chapter, explore the institutional change in the German Higher Educational system, from 'professional dominance' to 'federal involvement and democratization', and then to 'managed education'. While the paradigm of managed education is generally a reality in the Anglo-Saxon world, it is argued as key in reconfiguring the German system of Higher Education. The German version of managed education has been locally adapted and has substantial variations in actors and governance compared to its US and UK counterparts.

In calling attention to Tanzania, Mwasalwiba, Groenewegen and Wakkee highlight the need for more entrepreneurial universities to increase effective entrepreneurial activities in developing countries. The authors argue that commitment and investment from governments is required and that proper alignment of teaching context and student profiles as well as educational processes and objectives are necessary. Guerrero, Urbano and Salamzadeh give us further insight into the entrepreneurial university concept in developing countries by discussing the case studies of two universities located in Tehran. They adopt an integrated entrepreneurial university framework that considers the relevance of universities' environmental and internal factors to fulfil their teaching, research and entrepreneurial activities, as well as the socioeconomic impacts generated by these activities.

The section concludes with Niall MacKenzie and Qiantao Zhang evaluating entrepreneurial performance by investigating the regional economic influences in which universities operate. They present findings that provide greater clarity in the push for universities to act as drivers of regional economic development as well as the effects that regional economic influences have on the ability of universities to act entrepreneurially.

Part II offers an overview of entrepreneurship education at the university level and pedagogic strategies to enhance the entrepreneurial university programmes. The first chapter in this section, by Magdalena Markowska, focuses on entrepreneurial university concepts, specifically how to nurture entrepreneurial values and behaviours. The author argues that this sort of mindset requires a different methodology than the one offered by the traditional educational system. Christine Volkmann and Marc Grünhagen continue this section by shedding light on how to get from entrepreneurial intentions to entrepreneurial behaviour. They point out that, due to the non-entrepreneurial tradition of many European universities, entrepreneurship education policy-makers often try to spark the entrepreneurial spirit of institutions through external support instruments and policy initiatives. They look at the potential influence of such measures on entrepreneurial intentions and behaviour through the case study of the German EXIST policy programme.

In 'Boosting entrepreneurship education within the knowledge network of the Dutch agri-food sciences: the new 'Wageningen approach', Willem Hulsink et al. present a programme aimed at stimulating Higher Education Institutions to embed entrepreneurship in their educational programmes. The chapter looks at the origins of the entrepreneurial university, with a special reference to the agricultural and life sciences sectors. It provides a historical overview of entrepreneurship programmes and explains the successful turnaround strategy pursued by the DAFNE network to make the agriculture sector innovative and more internationally competitive.

Susanne Steiner compares teacher profiles from several universities that have different levels of entrepreneurial performance and finds that high-performing institutions usually have a high share of educators with entrepreneurial experience. She suggests that universities with medium levels of entrepreneurial performance might be able to influence their entrepreneurship rating by recruiting more interdisciplinary entrepreneurship education staff.

Truls Erikson, Mari Saua Svalastog and Daniel Leunbach end this section by describing the emergence of Gründerskolen, a Norwegian-based school of entrepreneurship that is a model of inter-university cooperation and works as a 'global entrepreneurship learning lab' designed around internships in start-ups abroad.

Part III focuses on interaction between the entrepreneurial university and enterprises. Simon McCarthy, Gary Packham and David Pickernell discuss intellectual property, university business angels and the potential benefits of university-generated intellectual property. They highlight the potential for universities to engage more closely with business angel networks. Elco van Burg continues this section by reviewing the ethical issues generated by efforts to commercialize research through university spin-offs. He suggests that spin-off creation has three substantial advantages: (1) knowledge utilization, (2) economic growth, and (3) learning from the other 'culture'. He discusses how disadvantages can be mitigated by designing organizational structures that address: (1) the potential change in research directions, (2) the 'anti-commons effect', and (3) the threat to objectivity.

In 'The meandering path: the university's contribution towards the entrepreneurial journey', Elisabeth Muir and Louise-Jayne Edwards bring out the theme of socioeconomic and cultural characteristics of graduate employment. This chapter questions the role of universities in the development of 'future entrepreneurs'. The authors approach this topic from a teaching and learning perspective, proposing that universities must use 'promotional strategies' that enable a student's entrepreneurial journey from university to business. Wim van Vuuren and his collaborators from Canterbury Christ Church University present the IBM 'Universities Business Challenge'. This initiative represented an opportunity for educators and students to reflect and discuss the role of business competition for entrepreneurial learning and the advantages of this type of experience-based form of entrepreneurship education. They also argue that the results strengthen the call for interdisciplinary collaboration and the advantages for taking business competitions beyond the typical business school environment.

To answer the question, 'Where do academic entrepreneurs locate their firms?', Christos Kolympiris, Nicholas Kalaitzandonakes and Ken Schneeberger conducted 16 in-depth interviews with academic entrepreneurs who started life science firms in the USA from 1996 to 2008. They highlight the factors that shaped the firms' location decision and discuss the implications for the regional economic development.

The section ends with a proposal of assessment model for entrepreneurship education, at university level. Kåre Moberg and colleagues from the Danish Foundation for Entrepreneurship – Young Enterprise apply their model of assessment to analyse the strengths and weaknesses of entrepreneurship education in eight Danish universities. By using the model, the authors were able to describe how these universities have developed entrepreneurship education during the past three years. The results suggest that it is important to focus on how to sustain entrepreneurial initiatives at the university, rather than just continuing to invest in new course development.

CONCLUSION

This book makes it clear that the entrepreneurial university is no myth, but it is also not yet a fully realized reality. The current university situations and contexts discussed in this book reveal the complex and challenging journey ahead and suggest ways and strategies to definitively transform universities into more entrepreneurial institutions, in developed and developing countries.

For us, there are two main conditions necessary for this journey to succeed. First, universities should pay close attention to the coherence between them and their environment. They must avoid the 'ivory tower' attitude and take into careful consideration the specificities of their context and the needs of their stakeholders. The second condition relates to the need to change university culture, values and attitudes and promote and broadly diffuse entrepreneurial culture and entrepreneurial values within each university. We know the influence corporate culture may have on a firm's entrepreneurial orientation (Fayolle et al., 2010) and we expect entrepreneurial culture to have a strong impact on university entrepreneurial orientation and the entrepreneurial behaviours of researchers, students and university staff. Turning the traditional university into a more entrepreneurial one is above all a matter of culture and values, and is the essence in role of embedding entrepreneurship education.

REFERENCES

Audretsch, D. (1995), *Innovation and Industry Evolution*, Cambridge, MA: MIT Press, as quoted in Audretsch et al. (2006).

Audretsch, D., M. Keilbach and E. Lehmann (2006), *Entrepreneurship and Economic Growth*, New York: Oxford University Press.

Chang, Y.C., P.Y. Yang and M.H. Chen (2009), 'The determinants of academic research commercial performance: Towards an organizational ambidexterity perspective', *Research Policy*, **38**(6), 936–46.

Clark, B. (1998), *Creating Entrepreneurial Universities: Organizational Pathways of Transformation*, New York: Pergamon Press.

Etzkowitz, H. (2003), 'Research groups as "quasi-firms": The invention of the entrepreneurial university', *Research Policy*, **32**(1), 109–21.

Etzkowitz, H. and L. Leydesdorff (1997), *Universities and the Global Knowledge Economy: A Triple Helix of University–Industry–Government Relations*, London/New York: Pinter.

European Commission (2013), *Entrepreneurship 2020 Action Plan: Reigniting the Entrepreneurial Spirit in Europe*, 9 January, Brussels: EC.

Fayolle A., O. Basso and V. Bouchard (2010), 'Three levels of culture and firms' entrepreneurial orientation: A research agenda', *Entrepreneurship and Regional Development*, **22**(7), 707–30.

Guerrero, M. and D. Urbano (2012), *The Creation and Development of Entrepreneurial Universities in Spain*, New York: Nova Publishers.

Mueller, P. (2006), 'Exploring the knowledge filter: How entrepreneurship and university–industry relationships drive economic growth', *Research Policy*, **35**(10), 1499–1508.

OECD (2010), *From Strategy to Practice in University Entrepreneurship Support*, final report of the project on Strengthening Entrepreneurship and Local Economic Development in Eastern Germany: Youth, Entrepreneurship and Innovation, Local Economic and Employment Development Committee, Paris: OECD.

Siegel, D.S., M. Wright and A. Lockett (2007), 'The rise of entrepreneurial activity at universities: Organizational and societal implications', *Industrial and Corporate Change*, **16**(4), 489–504.

PART I

DIFFERENT PERSPECTIVES OF THE ENTREPRENEURIAL UNIVERSITY

1. Stakeholder management and the entrepreneurial university
Dana T. Redford and Alain Fayolle

There has been rapid growth of entrepreneurship education at colleges and universities throughout the world (Katz, 2003; Kuratko, 2005). Entrepreneurship education is seen as playing a vital role in the development of more and/or better entrepreneurs with greater levels of knowledge, skills and other competencies (Gorman et al., 1997; Pittaway and Cope, 2007; Martin et al., 2013). In this context, entrepreneurial universities play an important role as both knowledge producers and disseminating institutions (Guerrero and Urbano, 2012). Further, in the modern knowledge economy, the entrepreneurial university is seen as a central force that drives innovation, creativity and economic growth (Audretsch, 1995; Audretsch, et al., 2006; Mueller, 2006). At the core of the entrepreneurial university concept is a connection between the 'ivory tower' and the 'real world'. The concept of the entrepreneurial university is a strategy that has been followed by many leading universities around the world (Atlantic Canadian, 2004b) and a strategy pursued by various regional governments (Atlantic Canadian, 2004a). A report from the Global Education Initiative of the World Economic Forum (WEF) in 2009 stated (pp. 7–8):

> [W]hile education is one of the most important foundations for economic development, entrepreneurship is a major driver of innovation and economic growth. Entrepreneurship education plays an essential role in shaping attitudes, skills and culture – from the primary level up. . . . We believe entrepreneurial skills, attitudes and behaviors can be learned, and that exposure to entrepreneurship education throughout an individual's lifelong learning path, starting from youth and continuing through adulthood into Higher Education – as well as reaching out to those economically or socially excluded – is imperative.

The European Commission (2008a) wants to extend entrepreneurship education beyond the 'business school', citing that the most innovative ideas are likely to come from the creative and technical disciplines. Katz (2003) also stated that the growth in entrepreneurship education is likely to come from outside business schools across the globe.

The entrepreneurial university concept can be used to consolidate efforts in entrepreneurship across a university and is best utilized in helping an institution formulate a strategic direction (Clark, 1998). It helps to focus academic goals and convert the knowledge produced at the university into economic and social utility (Etzkowitz, 2003). It can be said that, 'Just as the university trains individual students and sends them out into the world, the entrepreneurial university is a natural incubator, providing support structures for teachers and students to initiate new ventures: intellectual, commercial and conjoint' (ibid., p. 111). In order to achieve this status, the entrepreneurial university needs to become a more entrepreneurial organization with the members of their academic community becoming potential entrepreneurs, and the interaction with their ecosystems needs to follow an entrepreneurial pattern (Röpke, 1998).

'An Entrepreneurial University, on its own, seeks to innovate in how it goes to business. It seeks to work out a substantial shift in organizational character so as to arrive at a more promising posture for the future. Entrepreneurial universities seek to become "stand-up" universities that are significant actors in their own terms'(Clark, 1998, p. 4). As at the heart of any entrepreneurial culture, entrepreneurial universities have to have the ability to innovate, recognize and create opportunities, work in teams, take risks and respond to challenges (Kirby, 2004). An entrepreneurial university 'seeks to work out a substantial shift in organizational character so as to arrive at a more promising posture for the future (Etzkowitz, 2003, p. 111).

MANAGING STAKEHOLDERS IN THE TRIPLE HELIX MODEL

One of the most efficient ways to accomplish collaboration is through the 'Triple Helix' model of university–industry–government interrelationship (Gibbons et al., 1994; Etzkowitz and Leydesdorff, 1998; Ranga and Etzkowitz, 2013). The Triple Helix paradigm proposes a prominent role for universities in the innovation process within an economy. An entrepreneurial university is the keystone of the Triple Helix model, which comprises three basic elements: (1) a more prominent role for the university in innovation, on a par with industry and government in a knowledge-based society; (2) a movement toward collaborative relationships among the three major institutional spheres in which innovation policy is increasingly an outcome of interactions among the spheres rather than a prescription from government or an internal development within industry; and (3) in addition to fulfilling their traditional functions, each institutional sphere also 'takes the role of the other', operating on a vertical axis of their new role as well as on the horizontal axis of their traditional function (Etzkowitz et al., 2008). The Triple Helix explains the creation and consolidation of learning societies, deeply rooted in knowledge production, innovation and dissemination, and in a well-articulated relationship between universities, industry and government.

'The organizing principle of the Triple Helix is the expectation that the university will play a greater role in society', the so-called 'Third Mission' (Etzkowitz and Mello, 2004, p. 161). University–industry–government interaction is key to improving the conditions for innovation in a knowledge-based society. Industry is a key stakeholder for universities, as it represents the locus of production, whereas government is important because it represents the source of interaction with the country's economy and public policies.

A particular community is relevant for an entrepreneurial university if it shares the expectation that a mutually beneficial exchange can take place or that some service can be rendered from their collaboration. The concept of community is thus close to the stakeholder concept at the entrepreneurial university (Jongbloed et al., 2008). In Higher Education, the core community comprises students, internal stakeholders (faculty, staff, administration, etc.) and the most relevant external stakeholder, the government, as the main funder of Higher Education. It therefore follows that the government needs to ensure that Higher Education meets the interests of students and society in general. In point of fact, today's universities interact with many other external domains, such as health, industry, culture, territorial development and the labour market. To this point, Higher Education is not only expected to deliver excellent education and research, but it also has to deliver them in ways and forms that are relevant to the productive process as well as helping to shape the knowledge society, using the perspective of stakeholders rather than just customers (Harrison and Freeman, 1999). Universities need to assume their role in society by engaging with various stakeholders and their communities. Such interconnections and interdependencies relate to the social and economic functions of Higher Education, as well as to the services that universities provide, in terms of teaching, research and knowledge transfer (Jongbloed et al., 2008). Thus, it is axiomatic that, in order to meet its expectations, universities must carefully select and identify the right partners.

The interaction between different organizations and institutions to stimulate innovation introduces a new paradigm of 'open' creativity as opposed to the idea that successful innovation requires control (OECD, 2009b). In the Triple Helix model, the boundary between a university and its environment is more permeable, enabling the flow of knowledge and innovation. Further, opening up to innovation depends on the successful collaboration between government, industry and universities.

UNCOVERING THE RELEVANT STAKEHOLDER GROUPS

Transferring the knowledge generated through innovation at a university to commercial applications creates new market opportunities that fuel job and wealth creation in an economy and enhances a country's competitive advantage. The development of collaborative mechanisms in entrepreneurial universities must therefore also involve the national/regional government in terms of broader vision, policy-making and in the establishment of goals. 'Given the growing significance of universities as agents for promoting innovation and economic transformation, those in academia are faced with different "rules of the game", both internally and externally, to interact with the industrial sector' (Villasana, 2011, p. 43).

By using a stakeholder perspective, the entrepreneurial university creates a powerful tool by intentionally developing a network of social contacts from which resources can be obtained and with whom the university will work to convert these resources into added value. In essence, an entrepreneurial university is a relationship builder that creates a unique configuration of resources through its relationships.

The first step in a potential entrepreneurial situation is to uncover the relevant stakeholder groups involved (Freeman, 1984). While stakeholder relationships are likely to change over time in the university's life cycle, there are two main groups: internal stakeholders (alumni, professors and university staff) and external stakeholders (industry, government and region/local community).

From an entrepreneurial viewpoint, the criteria for determining stakeholder relevance are of practical significance, since entrepreneurs need to decide, either consciously or unknowingly, which are the groups they will need to deal with. Therefore, from a theoretical perspective this seems worthwhile analysing, as well as conceptualizing a framework that may be usefully applied to support this task.

The literature includes many attempts at classifying stakeholders using various criteria (Frooman, 1999; Winn, 2001; Phillips, 2003; Pesqueux and Damak-Ayadi, 2005): primary versus secondary, direct or indirect, generic versus specific, legitimate versus derivative, strategic and moral, core, strategic and environmental stakeholders. Other researchers proposed a classification to inform the managerial process

Table 1.1 Stakeholders grouped by interest groups/roles and functions

Experts	Practitioners	Interest Groups and Organizations
All stakeholders conducting research and compiling data regarding education, skills needs and entrepreneurship: universities, broader research community, public bodies, think tanks	Practitioners in education (school and university): university educators, teachers, headmasters, teachers' unions, awarding bodies, exam boards etc., students, private companies taking over education, NGOs: youth organizations, knowledge centres	Parents, businesses, social partners: labour unions, business associations, employers, employer organizations

Table 1.2 Stakeholder input- and output-related perspectives

Input Perspective	Output Perspective
Who are main contributors to the input to implement entrepreneurship education?	Who are the main interest groups benefiting from educating students for entrepreneurship?
Students, parents, teachers, school management, teachers' unions	Business organizations, trade unions, employer organizations, municipalities, etc.

of stakeholder identification based on power to influence, the legitimacy of each stakeholder's relationship with the organization and the urgency of the stakeholder's claim on the organization (Mitchell et al., 1997; Schlange, 2009). It is also possible to group stakeholders according to specific interest groups/roles and functions, for example, as shown in Table 1.1.

It is also possible to distinguish between interests connected to stakeholder identification, for example, input- and an output-related perspective.

There are, of course, many different classes of stakeholders, from government and civil society to employees and shareholders, each with a specific relationship with an organization. From the point of view of the university, the stakeholder analysis process needs to develop a strategic view between its internal actors and its relevant industry partners, keeping a close relationship with the regional and national government.

ENGAGING INTERNAL AND EXTERNAL STAKEHOLDERS

Managing such relationships, with very different actors, requires specific strategies that cover a multitude of internal and external actions (Table 1.3). First, universities need to create an internal structure for selecting, appraising and rewarding staff and alumni. The internal community may well affect and change the organization of method and substance. Individuals import new ideas and resources into their organization and are instrumental in exporting the ensuing products and services into the environment (Williams, 2009). Universities' strategies indicate the broad responses made to a changing and competitive environment. At the internal level, these are some of the main factors that administrators need to face in managing the internal culture of their university, according to Williams (2009, p. 135):

- 'financial sector' versus general management orientation;
- 'teaching' versus 'learning';
- 'face-to-face' versus 'distance' learning techniques;
- 'teaching/learning' versus 'research';
- 'academic autonomy' versus 'management direction';
- 'moderate' versus 'tight' financial control;
- 'entrepreneurial' versus 'bureaucratic' climate;
- 'departmental' versus 'faculty' structure;
- 'close' versus 'distant' structure for executive education;
- 'maximize student numbers' versus 'quality of student intake';
- 'dependence on parent university' versus 'university autonomy';
- 'state funding' versus 'self-funding'.

Underlying these decisions are choices between old and new paradigms – that is, academic values relating to autonomy, entrepreneurship and knowledge generation and management values relating to competitiveness and financial control. These can be subdivided into four categories: those concerned with the market; those focusing on the individual–university relationship; those concerned with structure; and those affecting the university's autonomy. Most of these dilemmas cannot be resolved by an either/or solution because both choices are legitimate and potentially beneficial to the competitive strength of the institution. It is in balancing these quandaries (given the entrepreneurial mission and objectives of their institution) that universities are expected to provide a lead by initiating and/or supporting appropriate change.

The stakeholder management approach has been extensively elaborated

Table 1.3   Planning, implementing and analysing stakeholder engagement strategy at Higher Education Institutions

	Pre-strategy	Initial Strategy Development	Strategy Implementation and Consolidation	Mainstreaming
Establishing a roadmap	Define aims and objectives of the concrete action	Define agreed aims and objectives of strategy	Define aims and objectives of specific actions to implement	Scaling initiatives to include more participants
Finding common ground	Who has an interest in defined objectives? Who has the power to support the defined objectives?	Who has an interest in defined objectives? Who has the power to support the defined objectives?	Gauge reactions of key actors? From initial experience make adjustments where necessary	From evaluation results make adjustments where necessary. Identify new actors that have emerged
Connecting and implementing	Plan and implement steps to inform, consult, involve, collaborate and empower the stakeholders	Plan and implement steps to inform, consult, involve, collaborate and empower the stakeholders	From initial experience plan steps and implement to inform, consult, involve, collaborate and empower the stakeholders	From evaluation results plan steps and implement to inform, consult, involve, collaborate and empower the stakeholders
Evaluating and reviewing	Evaluate the existing bottom-up processes and collaborations for relevance in implementing new actions	Evaluate early adopters and the activities that have led to a strategy development for stakeholders	Develop continuous monitoring and evaluation of impact for mainstreaming	Develop continuous monitoring and evaluation of impact for review process

on as a key aspect of competitive advantage and socially conscious organizational governance (Freeman, 1984; Friedman and Miles, 2006). Both stakeholder analysis and stakeholder engagement are critical pillars for the stakeholder management. In order to assure the participation of key external stakeholders in the university's strategy it is essential to develop a good engagement plan as part of a broader educational and learning activity. The dominant intention of entrepreneurial universities lies in the creation of value in terms of improving the socioeconomic environment. By engaging external stakeholders, a university can demonstrate its relevance to society. Establishing a stakeholder engagement agenda offers universities a range of citizenship possibilities such as contributing to the social and economic infrastructure, building of social capital, contributing to the resolution of regional difficulties, supporting equity and diversity, and education for democracy (Jongbloed et al., 2008).

In working with relevant stakeholders, there should not only be an analysis of priorities to identify key actors, but also an understanding of the potential barriers to their involvement. Failure to appreciate the dynamics of the relationships that exist between differing actors can lead to barriers that will ultimately have a negative impact upon their collaboration.

In considering the realistic level of participation necessary in designing a specific stakeholder engagement approach the direction and guidance of a cooperative relationship will benefit if the leadership is shared by a cross-section of representatives. This also applies to sharing the decision-making power between the university and external actors. Therefore, in designing an engagement plan, it is advisable to build a team consisting of internal stakeholders (such as teachers) and external stakeholders (such as enterprises and community organizations). The goals of external engagement are therefore based on partnership principles, and should focus on mutual benefits.

Depending on their roles, stakeholders can be involved in differing degrees of activities in the university, such as:

- being informed about the university's directions towards entrepreneurship and entrepreneurial initiatives;
- being consulted as part of the process of developing entrepreneurial mindsets of students;
- collaborating in formulating options and in providing recommendations for developing entrepreneurial initiatives and partnerships at the university;
- participating in the decision-making process and empowering uni-

versities to implement and manage change regarding a more entrepreneurial mindset.

Stakeholder engagement in entrepreneurship education is a phased and developmental process that can be planned, with clear differences in style and purpose of engagement at each stage. By embedding a culture of entrepreneurship through working directly and indirectly with key stakeholders, universities help sustain entrepreneurial activities within their local community and region. Stakeholders that are engaged with entrepreneurial universities start acting in accordance with entrepreneurship values, translating the concept into actions.

According to Gaddefors and Cronsell (2009), there is a collective transition, when entrepreneurship becomes accepted, and turns out to be an expected behaviour within a region. To this effect, all relevant stakeholders at the regional level need to be involved: the local community administration and the region's entrepreneurs as well as civil society institutions. In addition, at the regional level, centrally imposed entrepreneurial standards might be helpful in increasing freedom for entrepreneurial engagement.

GOOD PRACTICE RECOMMENDATIONS IN MANAGING INTERNAL STAKEHOLDERS

'To make the entrepreneurial university successful, it is required to create within its members, especially students, the will and the ability to start their own business' (Röpke, 1998, p. 2). To accomplish this, whether through one course, programme or a degree offered by a university, the curriculum offered must focus on:

- 'the future instead of the past;
- creativity instead of critical analysis;
- insight instead of knowledge;
- active understanding instead of passive understanding;
- emotional involvement instead of absolute detachment;
- manipulation of events instead of manipulation of symbols;
- personal communication and influence instead of written communications and neutrality;
- the problem or opportunity instead of the concept. (Atlantic Canada, 2004b, p. ii)

The development of entrepreneurship support has four phases, according to Etzkowitz and Klofsten (2005):

1   *Inception* – key actors discuss entrepreneurship support and agree on how the university can be at the centre of this development over a long-term effort.
2   *Implementation* – various mechanisms such as support programmes and institutional initiatives are created.
3   *Consolidation and adjustment* – the experiences, results and evaluations of existing mechanisms lead to a change and the establishment of new initiatives.
4   *Self-sustaining growth* – further emphasis placed on supporting actual entrepreneurship rather than cultural change to the culture and less of a need for outside funding for entrepreneurship support structures.

To specifically develop an entrepreneurial university programme several steps need to be taken. These include:

- 'identifying a champion or champions for the program;
- developing a vision and mission statement for the program;
- developing and communicating commitment to the program;
- creating awareness and acceptance for the program;
- facilitating faculty orientation/education in entrepreneurship;
- ensuring a realistic and holistic design program utilizing the most effective teaching methods possible within available faculty resources;
- developing supporting activities;
- creating or fully utilizing available centres for entrepreneurship;
- developing networks with other universities, community partners, private enterprise and funding agencies'. (Atlantic Canada, 2004b, p. 28)

The criteria of good entrepreneurial practices in managing internal stakeholders involve a diversity of strategies, clearly stated in an OECD report (OECD, 2009a). These include:

- conveying a clear understanding of entrepreneurship as a strategic objective of the university;
- making sure there is top-down support for it;
- establishing objectives of entrepreneurship education and start-up support;
- fostering entrepreneurial attitudes, behaviour and skills as well as enhancing both high-tech and low-tech growth-oriented entrepreneurship;
- creating a rewards structure for entrepreneurship educators, profes-

sors and researchers with the measuring of educational outcomes, mentoring potential entrepreneurs, and the sharing of research results.

There are many useful resources that universities can use to accomplish these goals. For instance, financing of staff costs and overheads for graduate entrepreneurship as part of the university budget. The goal would be to achieve internal self-sufficiency of a university's entrepreneurship support. Additional human resource development for entrepreneurship educators and staff involved in start-up support should also be put in place.

When seeking the ideal conditions to build a support infrastructure, universities might want to have dedicated and specific internal academic resources for entrepreneurship (such as a chair, creation of a specific department or support centre). Collaboration, coordination and integration of internal resources support faculty development and foster viable cross-faculty collaboration in teaching and research.

Business incubation, either on the campus or through a close external partnership should be offered. The knowledge transfer can be facilitated through this cooperation between the university, start-ups and external entrepreneurship support organizations. Defining clear roles for all the partners involved can facilitate this relationship.

The overall objective, according to both the OECD (2009a) and European Commission (2008b) is to progressively integrate entrepreneurship education into curricula and advocacy, applying entrepreneurial pedagogies across various parts of the university. Entrepreneurship education offers should be widely communicated, and measures undertaken to increase the take-up rate. As for the courses offered, they must ensure variety, using creative teaching methods tailored to the needs of undergraduate, graduate and postgraduate students. These courses should cover the pre-start-up phase, the start-up phase and the growth phase. To be most effective, certain courses must have the option of active recruitment. The outreach to alumni, business support organizations and firms is also a key component in entrepreneurship education and must be implemented thoughtfully. Finally, it is recommended that the outcomes of entrepreneurship research be integrated into entrepreneurship education messages.

As for the building of start-up support, literature suggests that startups should be closely integrated in entrepreneurship education activities (Gibb, 2007). The emphasis should also be on integrating entrepreneurship education into external business support partnerships and networks. This can be done through maintaining close relationships with firms and alumni. This integration and team-building process can be facilitated by the support of university staff, through networking and the creation of dedicated events. Events connecting access to private financing and start-up support as well as offering specific mentoring sessions with trained professors and entrepreneurs can accelerate this process.

Finally, in evaluating university entrepreneurship activities, the main aspects to take into consideration are: (1) the regular assessment and reassessment of performance measures regarding entrepreneurship support activities; (2) the formalized evaluation of entrepreneurship activities, which includes immediate (post-course), mid-term (graduation), and long-term (alumni and post-start-up) monitoring of their impact.

CONCLUSIONS

Entrepreneurial universities are relevant key actors in shaping communities and societies. Entrepreneurial initiatives are associated with the generation and transference of knowledge, considered a key factor of production and the innovation in today's economy. To foster this, several cultural, educational, institutional and legislative challenges need to be surmounted to be able to successfully cope with the competitive environment that surrounds universities.

The entrepreneurial university is a way through which a talented and prepared workforce can add value to the enterprises and communities of the outside world. 'The university generates ideas and qualified human resources while industry has the economic resources to transform ideas into economically useful products' (Guerrero and Urbano, 2012, p. 56).

By bringing innovation, good practices, strategies, solutions and recommendations to the outside world, the entrepreneurial university also contributes to creating better policies and practices in terms of entrepreneurship education, thus becoming part of a cycle of positive transformation towards a more entrepreneurial society. In this sense, as stated by Guerrero and Urbano (2012, p. 55), 'the university would develop several strategies, structures and a culture oriented to reinforce: (1) better methods of quality education and training based on the personal growth that supports the creativity and entrepreneurial experience; and (2) better strategies for incentives'. Especially in the current economic situation, enterprises also need these improvements to take place in the entrepreneurial universities, in order to better respond to their competitive environment. It follows that a company's strategic advantage lies in its human resources and their ability to use new knowledge and technology.

REFERENCES

Atlantic Canadian Universities Entrepreneurship Consortium (2004a), *Part I: Understanding Entrepreneurs: An Examination of the Literature*, Nova Scotia: The Atlantic Canadian Universities Entrepreneurship Consortium.

Atlantic Canadian Universities Entrepreneurship Consortium (2004b), *Part II: An Examination of Models, Best Practices, and Program Development*, Nova Scotia: The Atlantic Canadian Universities Entrepreneurship Consortium.

Audretsch, D. (1995), *Innovation and Industry Evolution*, Cambridge, MA: MIT Press, as quoted in Audretsch et al. (2006).

Audretsch, D., M. Keilbach and H. Lehmann (2006), *Entrepreneurship and Economic Growth*, New York: Oxford University Press.

Clark, B. (1998), *Creating Entrepreneurial Universities: Organizational Pathways of Transformation*, New York: Pergamon.

Etzkowitz, H. (2003), 'Research groups as "quasi-firms": The invention of the entrepreneurial university', *Research Policy*, **32**(1), 109–21.

Etzkowitz, H. and M. Klofsten (2005), 'The innovating region: Toward a theory of knowledge-based regional development, *R&D Management*, **35**(3), 243–55.

Etzkowitz, H. and L. Leydesdorff (1998), 'Emergence of a Triple Helix of university–industry–government relations', *Science and Public Policy*, accessed 9 November 2012 at http://www.leydesdorff.net/th1a.

Etzkowitz, H. and J.M. Mello (2004), 'The rise of a Triple Helix culture: Innovation in Brazilian economic and social development. *International Journal of Technology Management and Sustainable Development*, **2**(3), 159–71.

Etzkowitz, H., M.L. Ranga, A. Brenner, L. Guarany, A-M. Maculan and R. Kneller (2008), 'Pathways to the entrepreneurial university: Towards a global convergence', *Science and Public Policy*, **35**(9), 681–95.

European Commission (2008a), *Entrepreneurship in Higher Education, Especially Within Non-business Studies: Final Report of the Expert Group*, Brussels: EC.

European Commission (2008b), *Survey of Entrepreneurship in Higher Education in Europe*, Brussels: EC.

Freeman, R.E. (1984), *Strategic Management: A Stakeholder Approach*, Cambridge, UK: Cambridge University Press.

Friedman, A. and S. Miles (2006), *Stakeholders: Theory and Practice*, Oxford: Oxford University Press.

Frooman, J. (1999), 'Stakeholder influence strategies', *Academy of Management Review*, **24**(2), 191–215.

Gaddefors, J. and N. Cronsell (2009), 'Returnees and local stakeholders. Co-producing the entrepreneurial region', *European Planning Studies*, **17**(8), 1191–203.

Gibb, A.A. (2007), 'Creating the entrepreneurial university: Do we need a different model of entrepreneurship?', Chapter 4 in A. Fayolle (ed.) (2007), *Handbook of Research in Entrepreneurship Education*, Vol. 1, Cheltenham, UK and Northampton, MA, USA, pp. 67–104.

Gibbons, M., C. Limoges, H. Nowotny, S. Schwartzman, P. Scott and M. Trow (1994), *The New Production of Knowledge. The Dynamics of Science and Research in Contemporary Society*, London: Sage.

Gorman, G., D. Hanlon and W. King (1997), 'Some research perspectives on entrepreneurship education, enterprise education and education for small business management: A ten-year literature review', *International Small Business Journal*, **15**(3), 56–77.

Guerrero, M. and D. Urbano (2012), 'The development of an entrepreneurial university', *Journal of Technology Transfer*, **37**(1), 43–74.

Harrison, J.S. and R.E. Freeman (1999), 'Stakeholders, social responsibility, and performance: Empirical evidence and theoretical perspectives', *Academy of Management Journal*, **42**(5), 479–85.

Jongbloed, B., J. Enders and C. Salerno (2008), 'Higher Education and its communities:

Interconnections, interdependencies and a research agenda', accessed 21 November 2012 at http://link.springer.com/article/10.1007%2Fs10734–008–9128–2.

Katz, J.A. (2003), 'The chronology and intellectual trajectory of American entrepreneurship education 1876–1999', *Journal of Business Venturing*, **18**(2), 283–300.

Kirby, D.A. (2004), 'Entrepreneurship education: Can business schools meet the challenge?', accessed 10 December 2012 at http://labsel.pesarosviluppo.it/docindexer/Uploads%5C178-Entrepreneurship%20education_Can%20business%20meet%20the%20challange.pdf.

Kuratko, D.F. (2005), 'The emergence of entrepreneurship education: Development, trends, and challenges', *Entrepreneurship Theory and Practice*, **29**(5), 577–97.

Martin, B., J. McNally and M. Kay (2013), 'Examining the formation of human capital in entrepreneurship: A meta-analysis of entrepreneurship education outcomes', *Journal of Business Venturing*, **28**(2), 211–24.

Mitchell, R., B. Agle and D. Wood (1997), 'Toward a theory of stakeholder identification and salience: Defining the principle of who and what really counts', *Academy of Management Review*, **22**(4), 853–86.

Mueller, P. (2006), 'Exploring the knowledge filter: How entrepreneurship and university–industry relationships drive economic growth', *Research Policy*, **35**(10), 1499–508.

OECD (2009a), *Universities, Innovation and Entrepreneurship: Criteria and Examples of Good Practice*, Paris: OECD.

OECD (2009b), *Strengthening Entrepreneurship and Economic Development in East Germany: Lessons from Local Approaches*, OECD Local Entrepreneurship Reviews, March 2009, Paris: OECD.

OECD (2010), *From Strategy to Practice in University Entrepreneurship Support*, final report of the project on Strengthening Entrepreneurship and Local Economic Development in Eastern Germany: Youth, Entrepreneurship and Innovation, Local Economic and Employment Development Committee, Paris: OECD.

Pesqueux, Y. and S. Damak-Ayadi (2005), 'Stakeholder theory in perspective', *Corporate Governance*, **5**(2), 5–21.

Phillips, R.A. (2003), 'Stakeholder legitimacy', *Business Ethics Quarterly*, **13**(1), 25–41.

Pittaway, L. and J. Cope (2007), 'Entrepreneurship education: A systematic review of the evidence', *International Small Business Journal*, **25**(5), 479–510.

Ranga, M. and H. Etzkowitz (2013), 'Triple Helix systems: An analytical framework for innovation policy and practice in the knowledge society, *Research Policy* (forthcoming).

Röpke, J. (1998), 'The entrepreneurial university, innovation, academic knowledge creation and regional development in a globalized economy', Working Paper No. 15 Department of Economics, Philipps-Universität Marburg, Germany, accessed 2 February 2007 at http://www.wiwi.uni-marburg.de/Lehrstuehle/VWL /Witheo3/ documents/entreuni.pdf.

Schlange, L. (2009), 'Stakeholder identification in sustainability entrepreneurship: The role of managerial and organisational cognition', *Greener Management International*, No. 55, 13–32.

Villasana, M. (2011), 'Fostering university–industry interactions under a Triple Helix model: The case of Nuevo Leon, Mexico', *Science and Public Policy*, **38**(1), 43–53.

Williams, Allan, P.O. (2009), 'Leadership at the top. Some insights from a longitudinal case study of a UK business school', *Educational Management Administration and Leadership*, **37**(1), 127–45.

Winn, M. (2001), 'Building stakeholder theory with a decision modelling methodology', *Business and Society*, **40**(2), 133–66.

World Economic Forum (WEF) (2009), *Educating the Next Wave of Entrepreneurs: Unlocking Entrepreneurial Capabilities to Meet the Global Challenges of the 21st Century: A Report of the Global Education Initiative*, Switzerland: World Economic Forum.

2. The university of the future: an entrepreneurial stakeholder learning organization?

Allan A. Gibb and Gay Haskins

INTRODUCTION

This chapter explores the present and future pressures shaping the entrepreneurial nature of universities and the response to these pressures. It eschews the conventional association of entrepreneurship with business and commercialization of university intellectual property.[1] It also goes beyond the concept of the Triple Helix[2] (Etzkowitz, 2008) to a wider stakeholder model, which it explores as 'entrepreneurial'. It is centrally concerned with how universities, using a broader entrepreneurial paradigm, can negotiate their freedom and autonomy in the light of the creation of imposed 'market' conditions and mounting pressure from a wide range of stakeholders. Its central focus is on the dynamics of the Higher Education (HE) environment in the UK, with particular regard to the situation in England.[3] It seeks to use this context to draw out lessons for the way in which the university paradigm, more generally, is changing throughout the world (Brennan and Shah, 2011), and it concludes with a suggested framework that might be used in practice to explore individual university development strategies for the future.

The chapter builds on three earlier contributions that underpinned axioms and contexts that are important to understanding this chapter. The first (Gibb, 2005) sought to clarify the concepts of enterprise and entrepreneurship in an HE context and demonstrate their link to the creation of innovations[4] of all kinds true to the 'idea' nature and tradition of universities as sources of imaginative use of knowledge (Whitehead, 1927; Newman, 2007). The central aim of the paper was to begin to move the debate on the 'entrepreneurial' future of universities away from the narrow focus on commercial exploitation of knowledge and the associated traditional business school corporate approach to entrepreneurship (Gibb, 2002). This view still seems to be responsible for fears that fundamental academic freedoms may be at risk from entrepreneurial and corporate business exposure (Evans, 2002, 2004; Graham, 2002; Collini, 2012). The enterprise and entrepreneurship definitions used are embodied in this chapter. The issue of academic freedom will be explored further below.

The second paper (Gibb et al., 2009) set out more broadly, by way of a substantial review of the literature, the nature of the challenges to leadership of universities arising from changes in the global environment and the implications for the entrepreneurial design of the HE sector. The focus was on the impact of a growing complex and uncertain environment on key areas of university activity and the leadership challenges involved. The paper aimed to provide a strong conceptual base for the development and delivery of the Entrepreneurial University Leaders Programme (EULP).[5] The descriptions of the nature of uncertainty and complexity, the concept of knowledge flows (Nowotny et al., 2003), the Triple Helix model of university (Etzkowitz, 2008), business and government interaction and the concept of public value (Moore, 1995) are all of major relevance to the arguments below.

The third paper (Gibb, 2012) sought to provide a strong basic framework for reviewing the entrepreneurial development capacity of a university by exploration of existing and potential enterprising and entrepreneurial activity in five key areas: strategy, governance, organization and leadership; knowledge exchange; stakeholder relationship development and partnership (local, regional, national and international); enterprise and entrepreneurship education; and internationalization. This was in recognition of the fact that many universities embrace substantial pockets of personal enterprise and organizational entrepreneurial activity that can be fruitfully conjoined (although many activities may not be formally labelled as entrepreneurial). The paper explores the potential for building synergies between the various activities and describes how and why this might be done. The framework, developed into a review tool, has been used in practice and is embraced by the European Union (EU) as a basis for its recommendations on entrepreneurial university development (Bauer, 2012). It provides a basic background for the issues explored below and arguments concerning the entrepreneurial stakeholder model.

The present chapter moves a step further than the earlier articles by examining in some detail the 'specifics' of turbulence in the HE 'task environment'[6] in the UK and England in particular and the immediate challenges these pose for HE institutions. Many universities are currently reviewing their strategic plans (and the very nature of the conventional strategic planning approach) in response to substantially increased levels of uncertainty and complexity in their environment. That the enterprise and entrepreneurial label is frequently used in mission statements[7] and plans is a reflection of the fact that it seems to be increasingly recognized that enterprising behaviour and entrepreneurial organization are both needed and stimulated by turbulence in the environment. The chapter describes how universities are addressing the new challenges and examines the wider issues that are emerging in practice relating to the future positioning of the HE sector in society.

Perhaps the most important issue in this respect is that of preserving academic freedom (and the 'idea' of a university), an issue currently the subject of major controversy in the UK.[8] This chapter will argue that such freedom needs to be negotiated, as has always been the case, but that this stance is of particular importance in coping with the current imposition of 'market' conditions in the HE sector in England and numerous additional external pressures for change. In exploring this issue, the position of the leader of the university is contrasted with that of the independent entrepreneur seeking to maximize organizational autonomy and personal 'independence' in an often uncertain and complex stakeholder relationship task environment (Covin and Slavin, 1991; Namen and Slavin, 1993). Building from this, the chapter explores the repositioning of the university as a broad, pluralistic entrepreneurial stakeholder learning organization, managing numerous interdependencies, and examines what this might mean for the development of future institutional strategies.

PRESSURES SHAPING THE CURRENT UNIVERSITY TASK ENVIRONMENT

Funding, Fees and Competition

The major force contributing to recent environmental turbulence in the English HE sector has been the dramatic shift in the way that universities are financed and the creation of market conditions where funding, substantially and directly, follows student choice. The major rationale for the change, whereby direct public funding of the teaching in English universities has been largely replaced by a student loan system, was set out in the UK government's White Paper of 2011 (UK Department for Business, Innovation and Skills, 2011). The three key objectives were: savings in public expenditure; the creation of market demand for better student experience; and the establishment of HE responsibility for social mobility. Universities in England[9] are now free (within limits) to set their own fees and create associated incentives to influence student choice (with the government still retaining major influence on the direction of student choice via its control of overall student numbers, its capping of fees, and its offer of certain incentives relating to criteria for selection). Traditional methods of public funding of research are largely maintained, as are some programmes to facilitate student engagement and knowledge transfer with industry,[10] although these funds are now somewhat constrained, reflecting the crisis in public finance.

The changes are creating a highly competitive environment in England against a backdrop of falls in student university applications. There are particular concerns about declines in postgraduate applications and the dominance of international students in this area (Higher Education Commission, 2012). New and improved 'national accountability' metrics on student satisfaction, employability, subsequent job quality, salary and social mobility are becoming very important. Price competition and incentives for student choice are emerging signs of a competitive market-place (see below). Competition is being further honed via the encouragement and licensing of private providers, with US companies in particular moving in, and the granting of full degree awarding status to some vocational and former education colleges. The private sector offer leans towards a focus upon professional and vocational degrees but not exclusively so. In contrast, and perhaps a signpost to the future, the UK private New College of the Humanities (NCH), the brainchild of the philosopher Professor Anthony Grayling, offers a new model of Higher Education for the humanities in the UK. NCH students, it is claimed, will have one of the best staff–student ratios in UK Higher Education and will benefit from a high number of contact hours as well as 'engaging and challenging' weekly one-to-one tutorials.[11]

Government Intervention

The creation of a 'market' in the HE sector, particularly in England, has not overly constrained the level of government intervention. There remains a strong UK drive to position the university sector as an engine of future economic growth (Department for Innovation, Universities and Skills, 2007) via the strengthening of university ties with business. This seems to be a view shared by the European Union (European Commission, 2011). The UK government has accepted the findings and recommendations of its commissioned report by Professor Tim Wilson into the relationship of the HE sector to business (Wilson, 2012). The report characterizes universities as a key part of the supply chain for economic development with an emphasis on building networks, applied research, improving the skills of future employees, business collaboration on degree programmes, technology transfer and exchange and skills development of doctoral and post-doctoral research students. There is also substantial emphasis on developing the enterprising and entrepreneurial skills of staff and students, with calls for: the development of innovators who can look beyond their disciplines; the embedding of entrepreneurial learning in all disciplines; internships for all students; and work experience for doctoral students. Particular attention is to be paid to the strengthening of links with small and medium enterprises (SMEs), the engagement of intermediaries in this process and use of volunteering. The report underlines that its recommendations can only be achieved if the university itself is enterprising and entrepreneurial.

Innovation and Business

The Wilson recommendations are to be underpinned by the creation of a National Centre for Universities and Business under the auspices of the Council for Industry and Higher Education (CIHE).[12] The Centre will focus on strengthening the strategic partnership between universities and business, will offer services in this respect and will measure impacts. A major focus will undoubtedly be on innovation in the light of the CIHE's own findings that UK investment in research and development is falling behind key European competitors, particularly with respect to the engagement with SMEs (Hughes and Mina, 2012).

The UK government's support for investment in R&D research processes through a Catapult programme[13] (Technology Strategy Board, 2012) and its concern to emulate the work of the German Fraunhofer system (Hauser, 2010) highlights the pressure for closer university–business collaboration in pursuit of commercial innovation (NESTA undated, Corporate Economic Consultants 2012). Such pressure is also evidenced in the intention to devote 20 per cent (rising eventually to 25 per cent) weighting to the economic and social impact of research in the new university Research Excellence Framework (REF), which is used to determine allocation of public research funding. The pressure for relevance will also be enhanced by the move toward Open Access in publication following a commissioned report (Finch, 2012), which broadly supports this. It is already influencing the terms and conditions for research funding from private foundations[14] and will have major implications for individual university research funding as effectively it transfers much of the costs of publication to the university.

Employability, Employment and Social Mobility

The creation of a 'market' has stimulated the debate on how the sector will in the future provide more 'value for money' for the student.[15] The three key components of the debate are the employability of students, their subsequent progress into employment and the degree to which the sector engineers greater social mobility in society. A distinction is made between employability and employment (Knight and Yorke, 2004).

Employability is seen as creation of 'a set of personal skills, understandings and attributes that make graduates more likely to gain employment' (Pegg et al., 2012, p. 4). The challenge is stated to be one of creating a higher degree of learner autonomy and self-management capacity through the opportunity for the gaining of tacit knowledge and associated 'practical intelligence' (Sternberg et al., 2000). This has clear links with the concept of 'wisdom' discussed below. The UK Commission for Employment and Skills sees employability as being the capacity for: self-management; thinking and solving problems; working together and communicating; and understanding the business/organization (UKCES, 2009).

Employment relates to the transition to work and job futures of graduates. Universities are being asked to produce data on subsequent employment of graduates and their salaries and also to boost up their career advisory services and embed more careers futures responsibility in academic departments. This links in with the official rhetoric for universities to build better academic degree linkages with business and offer more internships (following the Wilson Report recommendations). There is particular concern for part-time students who constitute one-third of the UK Higher Education student population. Applications from mature students, many of whom are part-time, have fallen following the changes in financing arrangements.

The enhancement of social mobility, strongly endorsed officially, has a number of key components. Access to top universities is of major concern. The most advantaged of young people in the UK in terms of social background are reportedly seven times more likely to get into a top university than those at the bottom of the social ladder; and independent private school students are 22 times more likely to achieve this goal (Pearce, 2012). Another key area of concern is the relatively low progression of students into vocational education and through vocational apprenticeships into the HE sector compared with certain major European countries (UKCES, 2010; Dolphin and Lanning, 2011). A challenge to universities in this respect comes from the growth of a programme of Higher Level Apprenticeships supported by government and involving partnerships with companies, enabling progress through apprenticeship to degrees at undergraduate and postgraduate level.[16] The UK government is providing special scholarship support for students from disadvantaged backgrounds and is encouraging consideration of shorter two-year degrees, while also opening up degree awarding powers to selected vocational colleges.

Overall, there are concerns that the pursuit of the above agenda will move the focus of university activity more towards competence-based education and human capital development and away from the broader cultural development of the individual (Grayling, 2012; McGettigan, 2012). Linked with this is the fear that student choice of disciplines to study will be increasingly influenced by related employment pathways and that there will be a move towards greater preference for vocational and professional degrees and away, in particular, from humanities.

Local and Regional Partnership Development

Much has been written about the attempts over the past decade or so to address the disconnect between the universities and their local and regional environment (Williams et al., 2008; Goddard and Vallance, 2011). This challenge has several components: that of engagement of the university with its immediate community, culturally, socially and economically; its relationship with the business economy and particularly its role in innovation and knowledge transfer; its contribution to graduate retention in the locality; and more lately its contribution to social innovation and social enterprise. Much of the official support for this activity in England comes from a Higher Education Innovation Fund (HEIF) aimed at supporting 'Third Mission' activities of universities; this is administered by the publically funded Higher Education Funding Council for England (HEFCE). There are similar financing arrangements in Scotland and Wales. The main thrust is upon knowledge exchange related to research but there is smaller support for local entrepreneurship education, community development initiatives, skills development and use of physical assets. Compared with the total funds flow to universities the sums are small – £601 million is allocated in England for the period 2011–15 – although universities are expected to leverage this amount several times from private, other public and often European sources. Much of the additional public funding has in the past come from regional development agencies but these have been replaced by Local Enterprise Partnerships[17] with smaller budgets available.

The most recent challenges to the UK universities have come for the UK government's 'Big Society' concept,[18] and from the government-commissioned report into growth by Lord Heseltine, a former Deputy Prime Minister.[19] Both of these support the notion of stronger university local links and in the latter case the development of more joint degree ventures with employers. The growth of social enterprise (Universities UK, 2012a) has also presented a new challenge to universities in engaging with local communities in areas of research, knowledge transfer, student project engagement and voluntary support experience – the last mentioned being a key recommendation of the Wilson Report.

Enhancing Student Experience

In the light of the market emphasis placed on student choice, alongside the Wilson recommendations on engagement with SMEs there is considerable pressure upon universities to enhance the student experience. A key UK component of this in the past has been a Knowledge Transfer Partnership programme (KTP) of student project placement in organizations (Regeneris Consulting, 2010). While the number of KTPs involving SMEs has grown substantially in the UK in recent years there remain two major challenges: first, to bring back more of the learning from the KTP experience into the curriculum of university programmes; and second to build ongoing relationships with those companies that have been engaged in the KTP process, thus ensuring that the concept of ongoing knowledge exchange is truly fulfilled (see below).

Building relationships with SMEs also demands closer university ties with the local community and local development agencies. This falls in line with a pressure for the universities to create stronger partnerships with students and between students and local communities while offering them greater ownership of learning. Universities have, for some time, been encouraged to sponsor and engage with an enhanced Academy Schools Programme[20] and are being asked to play a major role in development of the planned new Baccalaureate.[21] The UK government emphasis on improving the student experience will demand a whole new range of measures by universities including provision of more detailed information on: course offers; qualifications required for successful students; student feedback/satisfaction indicators on individual courses; as well as employment and salary data as noted above.

Entrepreneurial Learning

The Wilson Report's emphasis on student entrepreneurial learning has been followed up by the issuing of *Enterprise and Entrepreneurship Education: Guidance for UK Higher Education Providers* by the UK Quality Assurance Agency for Higher Education (QAA).[22] The *Guidance* closely matches the recommendations of Wilson in emphasizing the development of personal qualities and skills relating to innovation, the building of self-efficacy and personal confidence, action orientation and ownership and control of events (QAA, 2012), and the embedding of entrepreneurship pedagogies and curriculum contextually across the whole university.

The challenge to the university in pursuing this agenda has been outlined in an earlier article referred to at the beginning of this chapter

(Gibb, 2012). In summary it embraces a number of key components: clarification of the key personal enterprising attributes to be prioritized in student development; creation of awareness among students and staff of the need for such development; embedding of pedagogical approaches to meet the above and development of capacity within each department to embed them contextually in the curriculum; development of self-employment awareness and self-efficacy programmes open to all students; delivery of start-up programmes for those students and staff wishing to set up their own business immediately; and creation of opportunities for student internships/projects with SMEs in all departments. Several of the above activities can be delivered by strong student entrepreneurial societies, supported where appropriate by university staff and resources. Partnerships with external agencies and businesses will also be a necessary component.

Utilizing New Learning Technologies

Perhaps the greatest challenge in addressing many of the above objectives is that of the utilization of new technologies. The global IT revolution has opened up mass markets for learning and has greatly enhanced the potential for flexible 'self-directed' learning approaches (JISC, 2012). The provision by major US universities of Massive Open Online Courses (MOOCs) is leading the field in this respect (Daniel, 2012). Harvard, MIT, Princeton and Berkeley now offer free online lecture programmes by leading professors and some are joining in delivery consortia of which Coursera is the most visible.[23] In the UK Edinburgh University has joined in Coursera with 12 other international universities to offer online new courses in the arts, computer science, health, mathematics, history, literature and other disciplines.

The associated 'flipped classroom' model, where lectures are delivered online and classroom time is spent in debate and discussion, is attracting substantial attention, particularly in the USA, although approaches of this nature have long been used by the Open University in the UK (Institute of Educational Technology, 2012). They are also a means of attracting mature students particularly when accompanied by flexible credit accumulation and institutional transfer possibilities. This may become of increasing importance in the UK where numbers of full-time mature students have fallen with the rise in tuition fees.[24] They also build upon student competence in the use of social media (Twitter, Facebook and YouTube, among others), which it is argued is outstripping the competency and awareness of many academic staff (Selwyn, 2012).

Programmes of this kind are attracting venture capital as they offer the opportunity for reaching out to many hundreds of thousands of future graduate students. They are also attracting private providers such as Udacity and EdX.[25] Private provision of university education in general is also opening up the debate on two-year, more intensive degrees where there is already public university experience (Foster et al., 2011; Evans, 2012). An outstanding issue in wide delivery of online learning is the link between the offer and assessment and accreditation together with an ability to accumulate credits flexibly in moving to qualification.[26] There are many limitations on this in the present offer.

International Market Dynamics

In general, UK universities are facing increasing international competition and are falling down global rankings.[27] The substantial growth of the HE offer in Asia is symbolic of this (Marginson, 2012b). In particular, the trends in global education delivery through technology have long-term implications for the attraction of foreign students to UK universities. But the substantial international student market for UK HE institutions is also being affected by a number of other factors. Most recently, the impact of stricter immigration controls relating to overseas student study has caused major concern (Universities UK, 2012b). This is against a backdrop of a growing number of UK students now choosing to study abroad.[28] The substantial rise in tuition fees following the changes noted above (with annual fees running between £7000 and £9000) makes English institutions highly uncompetitive on price with many European counterparts.[29] Following the recent changes in funding arrangements, student numbers from abroad are falling.[30] This is happening against a future scenario of a weakening of the pull of the English language appeal to study in the UK, with overseas providers now offering a range of taught degrees in English.[31] There is also a questioning in developing countries of the conventions of the 'colonial' university model of knowledge and learning for its own sake – many developing countries struggle to absorb graduates into graduate-type employment, often leading to the creation of politicized dissident groups.[32]

A Global Curriculum?

The dependency of the university sector on overseas students and consideration of the issues raised above is moving the focus away from income generated by this activity to debate about the kind of intellectual and academic interchange that trans-cultural opportunities to study at our universities should bring (King et al., 2010). Combined with the fact that there is a growing international marketplace for UK graduate employment, there is increasing pressure for enhancing the curriculum in many disciplines to embrace a wider global context (Welikala, 2011). The challenge is seen as one of preparing all students for global citizenship by means of creation of a wider range of programmes that relate more closely to global issues and allow sharing of learning and experience of different cultures (Bourn et al., 2006). Such a challenge has major implications for staff recruitment and development.

The growth of international student mobility is occurring against a backdrop of the pull of higher levels of international research collaboration and publication. One-third of high-level journal publications involve international author partnerships (Bone, 2011).

Summary

The pressures on universities from the 'task environment', summarized above, are numerous and cover all aspects of university activity: discovery, direction of scholarship, teaching and learning, relevance to society, student partnership and community engagement (Figure 2.1).

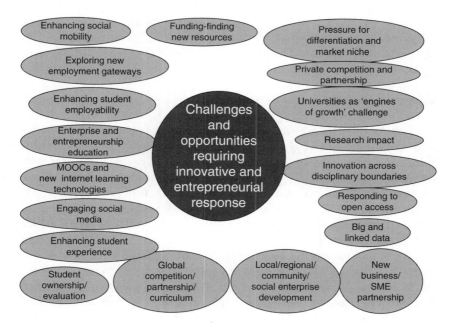

Figure 2.1   Pressures in the university 'task environment'

REVIEWING RESPONSES TO THE ABOVE PRESSURES

Differentiation

Universities in the UK and internationally are pluralistic organizations and vary substantially in terms of their local and regional engagement, overseas initiatives, student recruitment, attitudes to research, development from research, degree of focus upon current real world problems, engagement with business and linkages with the wider stakeholder environment. In Scotland, Wales and Northern Ireland such foci are considerably influenced by the policies of substantially devolved national authorities. Reflecting their origins and traditions, individual universities also have distinctly different modes of governance and indeed cultures. The responses to the pressures outlined above are therefore likely to be highly differentiated. But they are also conditioned, in the UK, by lobbying groups of universities with different agendas relating to the shaping of the sector and particularly competition for resources.[33] Many universities are seeking to position themselves in what is described as blue oceans (Kim and Mauborgne, 2004) of differentiation in applying knowledge, engagement, partnership, learning and enterprise (see also Coiffait, 2012).[34] The work of the HEFCE funded 'Leading Transformational Change' partnership programme led by Plymouth and Teesside Universities[35] provides evidence through case studies and surveys of this activity.

Influencing Student Choice

Notwithstanding the above differences, a common overriding response is to find innovative ways of reaching out to students and all those who influence student choice – parents, schools, NGOs, local government, social networks, the media, potential external investors and sponsors, and sources of funding for educational innovations. Some of the ways in which universities are seeking to influence student choice are shown in Figure 2.2 with a strong focus upon partnership with schools, students[36] and Further Education colleges in the university catchment area.[37] Examples include the setting up of a specific study centre in a school for a particular subject area, the creation of a 'learning passport' system by which students monitor their development in a particular subject area with assistance from the university and the establishment of university staff 'ambassador' links with schools. The messages carried by these means are competitive and differentiated, with different emphases on physical facilities, employ-

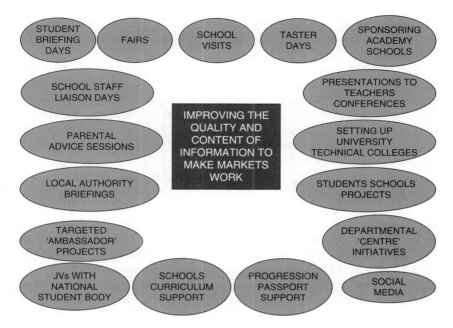

Figure 2.2 The focus of relationship building to influence student choice

ability, employment record, research and teaching excellence and specialization, pedagogy, financial incentives and social life.

Focus Upon Employability and Job Quality

A key competitive focus is upon student employability and subsequent job quality and the enhancement of student experience to these ends. The issue of employability has long been of concern to UK universities (Sternberg et al., 2000; Knight and Yorke, 2004) but has become a major competition issue not only because of market changes but also because of the global economic (and associated employment) crisis. Many UK universities have responded imaginatively to this challenge as described in the Higher Education Academy 'Pedagogy for Employability' paper (Pegg et al., 2012). A major emphasis in many programmes is upon embedding employability issues contextually in the curriculum of each department, backed up by the provision of opportunity for students to gain tacit (experiential) knowledge and thus develop 'practical intelligence' (Butcher et al., 2011). There are also experiments in engaging employers in the development of the curriculum (Tallantyre and Kettle, 2011). The research of the UK National Union of Students (NUS) in partnership with the UK Confederation of British Industry (CBI) documents a variety of examples (2011).

The competition provoked by the enhanced metrics on graduate employment, noted above, has led to a boosted role for careers departments, some being rebranded (for example as 'Futures' or 'Employability' departments), partnerships with private agencies and attempts at embedding employment responsibility contextually in academic departments. It is also boosting pressure for increases in student work experience via short 'sandwich' experience and internships.

Ensuring Wider Access

Social mobility was one of the three major pillars of the UK government's White Paper on Higher Education. The change in the English fee structure has placed extra pressure on the sector to ensure wider access. The Office for Fair Access (OFFA), established alongside the new funding arrangements, has pressured the universities to use more 'contextual' data in entry criteria for universities and will monitor access agreements to be set out by all universities charging fees above the base level. A National Scholarship Programme[38] has been introduced to provide financial help to universities to assist access to poorer students. A 2012 report by the Independent Reviewer on Social Mobility and Child Poverty (Milburn, 2012) called for: greater outreach efforts by the sector; simplified admissions criteria; more foundation programmes; better online provision; and university sponsorship of schools in deprived areas. There is particular challenge to part-time student development, with some universities specializing in this field with flexible evening programmes.[39]

In this respect, and noting the developments in MOOCs discussed earlier, there is likely to be major growth in online learning. A review of the existing UK offer in 2010, funded by HEFCE (White et al., 2010), found 400 course offers, mainly at the postgraduate level, by over 100 Higher and Further Education institutions and a further 175 in partnership with private providers. The major potential for expansion was noted.

Debate on the Use of Knowledge

The employability debate, the pressure for universities to become part of the economic 'value chain' and therefore to focus more upon issues of immediate economic and social relevance to society, and the influence of the vast volume of data on the web, is encouraging wider reflections on the way that universities organize, influence and use knowledge flows (Valima,

2009). This takes a number of directions. Perhaps the most transparent is the intensification of the debate about the value of more focused Mode 2^{40} problem/issue multidisciplinary and transdisciplinary research and teaching (Lyall and Meagher, 2012). A related, very practical and pressing edge to the debate is that of how universities are approaching the issue of the sheer volume of information on the Web – Big Data and Linked Data (McAuley et al., 2012). The former is concerned with the 'philosophical and methodological approach to democratizing data', and the latter is focused upon the cross-correlation of data across cultures, institutions and traditional disciplinary boundaries. In the light of the increasing use by students of such data universities are being forced to consider what this means for the training of staff and students in data literacy.

A deeper philosophical component of the discussion on useful knowledge (somewhat ignited by the current debate on the 'idea' of a university) recalls early philosophical writings that emphasize the role of universities as being concerned with the imaginative and creative use of knowledge and not just knowledge delivery per se (Whitehead, 1927; Newman, 2007). Leading on from this is the reminder that the concept of useful knowledge is not confined to a focus upon 'know how' in the technical sense but refers as much if not more to the need to link the development of student knowledge to values and to broad areas of society's need for development and the carrying forward of culture. This marries up with the concept of wisdom (Maxwell, 1984) as being concerned with the individual's capacity to embrace a combination of experience/knowledge and deeper understanding of a life world of uncertainty and complexity. There is a link here with Grayling's defence of the 'generalist' noted above and the notion of 'practical intelligence' (Sternberg et al., 2000). There is little evidence, however, that this concept (while increasingly debated) has in practice been widely accepted and embodied in university employability agendas.

Enterprise and Entrepreneurial Skills Development

A key component of the employability agenda, as noted above, is the provision of enterprise and entrepreneurial skills and knowledge. There is now wide experience across the UK with many deans and pro-vice-chancellors charged with this responsibility. The UK experience in this respect has been captured by the National Centre for Entrepreneurship in Education (NCEE) in its national surveys[41] and programmes for university staff development in partnership with Enterprise Educators UK.[42] While there is growing evidence of the embedding of entrepreneurship education in individual disciplinary contexts there are relatively few examples as yet of comprehensive coverage across the whole university. There remains, therefore, a major challenge in terms of pedagogical and organization development.

Student Ownership

There is mounting evidence that student bodies can play a major role in entrepreneurship education development. The student-owned National Consortium of University Entrepreneurs (NACUE), set up to support students' entrepreneurship society development is now operating on 120 campuses and embracing 40 000 UK student society members, and with government support it is rapidly expanding. The societies offer start-up programmes and promotions, business connections, in some cases loan schemes and links to venture capital and gateways to experience in SMEs. In many cases they are supported financially by the university.[43]

Building SME Relationships

As in entrepreneurship education there is much experience of universities seeking to build relationships with SMEs. The KTP system noted earlier is one approach that has been substantially developed, though in many cases it has yet to meet a true knowledge exchange criteria of embedding the learning from KTPs into the formal curriculum and developing long-term partnerships.[44] The Shell Technology Enterprise Programme (STEP)[45] was aimed at building opportunities for student project work in SMEs, was highly evaluated (Westhead et al., 1995) but government support has been removed. It also dealt with relatively small numbers. In general, universities find it easier to develop partnerships with small professional service companies rather than the majority of the highly differentiated small firm sector.[46] The focus of much university SME linkage support by government programmes has been upon the narrow high technology and innovation sector. Attempts to widen the base through a government-funded UK Employer Ownership Partner scheme,[47] aimed at creating joint ventures in skill development, appear to be attracting mainly larger firms.

Community Engagement

Local SME engagement can also be viewed through the lens of a university's strategy for community engagement. Many UK universities in recent years have created local community engagement offices and programmes, at times in partnership with other universities.[48] These are not always focused on economic development but also on issues of social deprivation and wider societal problems. They vary in intensity in terms of the degree to which they open up active gateways to engagement across the university for staff and students as opposed to providing information access to the university for local stakeholders.[49] Social enterprise is an area of growing focus. Reflecting this, a National Social Enterprise UEN (University Enterprise Network) was established in 2011 hosted by Plymouth University with founding partners from the private sector including the Co-operative Group and SERCO (a private deliverer of services including education), together with the Social Enterprise Mark Company and the National Centre for Entrepreneurship in Education (NCEE). Its aim is to research, pilot and communicate best practice to help shape national policy, and work with students and staff in the partner institutions to build social enterprises. It will also work with SMEs and existing social enterprises to provide targeted business advice, mentoring and support.

Recent research into university engagement with disadvantaged communities demonstrates substantial and growing involvement across the UK in areas of: collaborative research; outreach education; voluntary work; student project and experience; and institutional commitment in general, including a focus on student recruitment from disadvantaged groups (Robinson et al., 2012).[50] One UK university has deliberately put the understanding and development of social enterprise[51] at the heart of its activity. Many universities have signed up with a National Co-ordinating Centre for Public Engagement.[52]

Innovation and Regional/Local Development

Despite the constraints on funding resulting from the abolition of regional development agencies in England and their replacement by lower resourced Local Enterprise Partnerships (noted earlier) there has remained a strong impetus to university activity in the field of business engagement, innovation and knowledge transfer/exchange. In part this continues to be supported by the Higher Education Innovation Fund (HIEF) and European Community grants but also reflects the pressure for differentiation and need for local engagement and visibility as well as resource acquisition via partnership (University Alliance, 2012).[53] Research demonstrates that in engineering and physical sciences academic engagement has grown, that academics in these disciplinary areas are entrepreneurial and that they perceive the barriers to engagement to be falling (Salter et al., 2010).

Partnerships: Programmes and Curriculum Development

Partnerships between public universities and with private institutions in the education field are also growing as the competitive environment accelerates. There have always been university partnerships in research, some more formalized and longer term than others:[54] one major barrier to collaboration in this respect has been the Research Assessment Exercise, which focuses upon individual university competitive ratings. But these constraints are disappearing as universities seek scale and multidisciplinarity in their research.[55]

Partnerships between UK universities to offer transfers and joint degrees are only slowly emerging and are perhaps more easily managed with overseas institutions once substantial set-up costs are covered. Such partnerships will be important in the future if universities are to follow the Wilson recommendations and offer a wider range of internships and international experience to students. Partnerships with the private sector to deliver available online programmes are well underway.[56] And private companies are actively engaged with universities and colleges in the provision of foundation degrees.[57] Partnerships with large companies to create joint degrees are growing.[58] Private–public collaborations of this nature are likely to further develop, perhaps, on the basis of US experience, towards a model where private providers operate foundation and 'short degrees' and public university partners provide linked Master's and Doctoral programmes. In the UK, however, there are reservations as to whether some of this activity will divorce teaching from accreditation.

The global curriculum pressures noted in the previous section are bringing a new inter-cultural dimension to the partnership concept. UK universities such as Oxford Brookes,[59] Bournemouth (Shiel and Mann, 2005), Leeds and Bristol are, for example, paying particular attention to many of the issues raised by Welikala (2011). This is bringing recognition that addressing issues of global curriculum development goes beyond the design of programme content. It involves partnerships in the creation of: communities of practice between existing student groups; their involvement in more reflexive modes of learning; exchange of experience and resulting experiment on pedagogies; external partnerships for building multicultural modes of learning; and wider democratic approaches to learning.

The Drive for Efficiency and Alternative Revenue

Partnerships of a different nature are emerging in response to the public funding crisis. The private company University Partnerships Programme (UPP), has, for example, partnered extensively with universities in the provision of student accommodation and campus infrastructure.[60] There is also major outsourcing activity in the supply of IT services and an estimated considerable untapped potential in other areas (Massey, 2010) covering not only infrastructure such as playing fields and environment but also marketing, accounting, student relationship development and registration activity. The sharing of services among universities is also growing, with as yet considerable untapped potential.[61] Funding problems are also generating pressure for revenue raising via the selling of services, utilization of spare capacity and consulting and training activity. This can involve the setting up of separate joint venture companies with the private sector and/or the creation of independent service businesses, which can be marketed or franchised to others.[62] There is also estimated untapped potential elsewhere, for example in the expansion of procurement partnerships; such arrangements already account for 15–20 per cent of an estimated £5 billion collective university spend.[63]

Closer engagement with alumni is also being pursued: a recent study for HEFCE found that approximately half of philanthropic revenue for universities came from alumni, with arguably much greater potential at stake (More Partnership, 2012). There is accompanying pressure for all departments to be involved in this role and, in general, to meet revenue-raising targets. In part this may, in the long term, have to be achieved by greater cooperation, and fee sharing arrangements, with business as well as direct fund-raising appeals.[64] Joint private–public ownership is not beyond future possibility. Changes in the legal status of some universities may be pursued to facilitate external investment (Eversheds, 2009).

In the light of the foreseeable resource problems of universities, following the changing financing arrangements, the representative organization, Universities UK, set up a task force to review efficiency in universities, which reported in 2009 (Diamond et al.). The goal was to identify ways in which institutions could work more efficiently and effectively to ensure value for money by developing procurement, streamlining institutional processes, improving the use of data and benchmarking, and supporting better use of shared services and outsourcing (Universities UK, 2010a). A number of Task Groups are working on developments in each of these areas moving towards an implementation phase (Diamond et al., 2011). It is possible that many universities are seeking to increase 'efficiency' by more traditional cost-cutting means, involving larger classes, freezing appointments, use of more adjunct and part-time staff, increasing teaching loads and limiting staff travel (Standard and Poor's, 2008).

Organizational Change

The above challenges are triggering broader organizational change and reflections on the managerialist norms of some existing structures. Several universities have changed or are considering a change in rewards and promotional tracks linked with knowledge exchange and stakeholder development activity as well as teaching and learning excellence. The use of adjunct staff in teaching and mentoring support seems to be growing, with some evidence of greater entrepreneur engagement.[65] Externals, including board and council members, are being used to drive agendas and leverage change. Internally, role models are sought to highlight certain kinds of activity. There may be moves to structure boards of governors in a more 'representative of interest' mode, away from a more traditional composition of disinterested parties from the community, perhaps enhancing the role of alumni and student representation (Gillies, 2011). Official support for student entrepreneur societies is growing.

There is also recognition of the limits of many standard approaches to external relationship development –for example, professionally managed enterprise and technology transfer offices and science and technology parks. There is growing evidence that what is important in technology transfer success is the degree of support and availability of role models at the departmental, bottom up level (Bercovitz and Feldman, 2008): activities overly dominated by professional technology transfer staff may therefore at times weaken the motivation of academic staff to build, independently, external networks of social capital. This process has been identified as key to enhancing a university's capacity for knowledge transfer and exchange. It has been shown that the building of such social capital can also be an important key to innovation. Overall, as noted above, there is evidence of moves to embed issues of employability, external relationship management, knowledge exchange revenue and resource-raising activity more substantially in individual departments. This can lead to some de-layering of levels of management in the organization, which in itself will demand closer professional and academic staff partnership.

THE REBALANCING OF STAKEHOLDER RELATIONSHIPS

Realigning the Interface with the Environment

In the introduction to this chapter, and following from arguments in earlier papers, two key propositions as to the nature of organizations operating in uncertain environments were set out. The first was that contingency organization theory underpins the notion that the distinctive nature and dynamism of the task environment must weigh heavily on organization

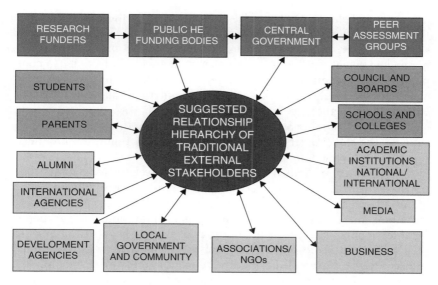

Figure 2.3   University key stakeholders: a shifting balance

design. The second was that it is the level of uncertainty and complexity in the environment that will dictate the need for entrepreneurial behaviour. This chapter, so far, has outlined numerous external pressures on universities in England and the UK, contributing to uncertainty and complexity in their task environment. It is clear from the description of university responses to these major changes that there is now considerable pressure on the sector to engage more fully than hitherto with a wider range of stakeholders, locally, nationally and internationally. UK universities have always interfaced with the broad spectrum of stakeholders as set out in Figure 2.3 but with a strong 'traditional' orientation towards certain groupings.

The traditional stakeholder balance (shaded most heavily in the figure) has been towards the sources of public funding directly through 'independent' conduits (the Higher Education Funding Council for England – HEFCE) and complemented by 'directed' (targeted upon particular desired outcomes) public funding from government, which is often available on a bidding basis. This has been topped up by research grants (public and privately supported), most of which are either dependent upon or influenced to a considerable degree by, peer assessment/review processes.

As a result of new funding and market arrangements in England, the balance of stakeholder dependency patterns is shifting. The emerging dominant stakeholders are students, accompanied by those who influence their choice (shown moderately shaded in Figure 2.3). The government's somewhat determined supply chain view of the role of universities in economic and social development, together with a wider sensitivity to competition, has strengthened the concern of universities to link with external agents at the local, regional, national and international level. There is enhanced motivation to build partnerships both with peer institutions and sources of funding as well as network building to secure sustainable futures. The stakeholders who are lightly shaded in Figure 2.3 are therefore also becoming more prominent.

It is, however, of limited value to explore university stakeholder relationships from a 'total organization' perspective. Every university is a highly pluralistic organization, with each department facing distinctive variations in the stakeholder community mix. 'Traditional' departments/ faculties such as law, medicine, music and divinity have strong links to their associated professions. Many universities now embrace vocational subject areas, for example hospitality, education, tourism, design, nursing and accounting, each with strong associated stakeholder relationships. Humanities departments, at times characterized as having weak external links, are found in practice to be as strong in this respect as departments such as engineering (Hughes et al., 2011).

The Challenge at the Departmental Level

The university challenge in adapting to change in the environment is therefore largely a decentralized one. Each department within the university will face different types and combinations of stakeholders with different levels of uncertainty and complexity. Every department will therefore need to map out its own 'task environment', societal, academic, community and 'practitioner'. A possible stakeholder practitioner scenario of a music department is illustrated in Figure 2.4 and can be described as characterizing the potential future music-related occupational life-world of the student. The challenge for the department can be that of engaging with these 'music world' stakeholders to provide opportunity for students and staff to acquire tacit/experiential knowledge in all of the potential employment contexts: and where possible to build this knowledge and experience into the curriculum and pedagogy. The stakeholders shown can be explored in a local, regional, national and international context. Similar maps could be drawn for each department as the basis for a review of the present position and future potential for tacit learning and the development of practical intelligence.

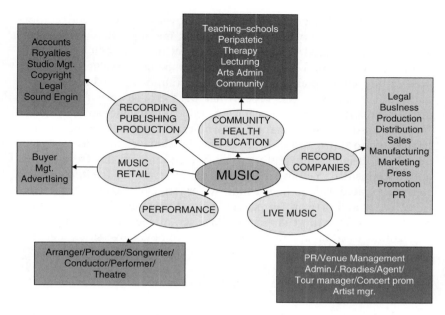

*Figure 2.4   Example: music department stakeholder practitioner
relationship map*

MANAGING MULTIPLE STAKEHOLDER INTERDEPENDENCY: AN ENTREPRENEURIAL CHALLENGE?

This section of the chapter focuses upon the management of multiple stakeholder interdependency as described above. It is argued that to maximize freedom and autonomy in such a milieu requires an entrepreneurial model. The rationale and modus operandi for such a model is explored by borrowing from the manner in which entrepreneurs seek to maintain their independence and organizational autonomy in uncertain, and sometimes, complex environments.

Freedom and Organization Autonomy

It was emphasized at the beginning of this chapter that there are a significant number of academics who feel that their academic freedom and the basic 'idea' of a university and its autonomy are being threatened by the pressures and changes noted above and particularly by the entrepreneurial concept. The academic freedom they refer to was underpinned tradition-ally by systems of public funding that were managed by intermediaries and therefore ensured limited detailed direct accountability to govern-ment. Peer review processes were seen to be the major vehicle for stand-ards setting and accountability to society (although in the UK, as in many other countries, this process has been eroded over the past two decades, in particular by increasing government guidelines and directives). Nevertheless the system enabled academics to enjoy substantial degrees of freedom to think, research, teach and do whatever they deemed to be important. It is the apparently growing constraints on this freedom that are now lamented. Yet, in reality, over many years, this freedom has had to be negotiated with an increasingly wider range of stakeholders seeking to influence and/or work in partnership with universities. The scenario described earlier in this chapter has, however, ratcheted up the imperative to negotiate freedom and raises questions as to how universities in general should respond.

How Entrepreneurs 'Manage' Independence

Almost universally, international research from the beginning of major academic interest since the 1960s has demonstrated that the major per-sonal driver for the establishment of an independent business/organization is not financial reward but the search for individual freedom and inde-pendence (Collins and Moore, 1964). Yet, paradoxically, most would be entrepreneurs are in fact exchanging their dependence upon a single source of income and/or work for a situation of interdependency on a wide range of external stakeholders who they have very limited power to influence. The entrepreneur has, therefore, from the onset, to 'negotiate' his or her desired level of freedom. Consequently, there is, in the process of develop-ment of the business or organization, a constant battle to assert independ-ence in the face of pressures from all the stakeholders whose needs must be met if the organization is to survive (customers, suppliers, financiers, staff, regulators, professional service providers, local government and the Revenue among many others). The art of entrepreneurial management can therefore be described as the management of interdependency in such a way that the desired level of independence and associated freedom is achieved and personal goals are met. It has been argued by one of the present authors that this can only be achieved successfully if the entrepre-neur's organization embraces the model of a porous learning and educat-ing system (Gibb, 1997).

Managing Independence Through Trust-based Relationships

In this model of entrepreneurial stakeholder management the overriding aim is to build mechanisms and motivation at all levels of the organization to negotiate with key stakeholders in the environment to achieve what the entrepreneur and his or her team want (rarely is it just money). The major strategic means to this is the building of trust-based relationships with people and organizations (Aldrich and Zimmer, 1986; Hohmann and Welter, 2005) in order to reduce risk in a task environment over which the entrepreneur has little control. This process of relationship trust building has three key components, each of equal importance. The first is to maximize the organization's capacity at all levels to learn continuously from all stakeholders. This involves ongoing monitoring of changing stakeholder needs; obtaining continuous feedback as to how the entrepreneur's organization is perceived in the environment; and evaluation as to whether it is successful and helpful to stakeholders in meeting their goals.

Optimizing success in building such a trust-based relationship model, however, necessarily involves a two-way process of communication. The second key component is therefore the ongoing education of major stakeholders not only about the capacity of the organization to help them achieve their goals but also proactively to help 'bring forward their futures'. This process demands empathy, some sharing of goals, and at times values, and often, in practice, partnership. The third component is the encouragement of the organization's stakeholders to learn from each other. This demands that the organization constantly strives to influence and help engaged stakeholders to build, between them, partnerships and strong relationships. The strategic aim is to cement the interdependency network of the firm, so that understanding of, and confidence and trust in, the firm is shared. In summary, the entrepreneur and his or her organization are playing the role of builders of social capital and, as knowledge brokers, are often using innovative means to bring forward the future for stakeholders.

Designing an Entrepreneurial Organization to Successfully Manage Interdependence

Successful pursuit of the process described above demands a distinctive entrepreneurial organization design. The key component is maximizing the freedom of individuals in the organization to behave enterprisingly: to take responsibility for building personal stakeholder relationships; to take risks in pursuit of this; be supported in this process; to feel ownership for, and commitment to, seeing things through; and to engage informally in innovation and communication across boundaries laterally and vertically in the organization.

Achieving the above implies a certain kind of organizational culture. Entrepreneurial organizations can be characterized as held together by a shared culture embodied in 'ways of doing, thinking, organizing and communicating things' (Gibb, 2007). The model of trust-based relationship building is as important internally as it is externally and limits reliance upon highly formal control and accountability systems. In such an organization an autocratic leadership style that reserves external stakeholder relationship development to the power elite is inappropriate. A key characteristic of leadership in this cultural climate is that of a role model exemplar 'by doing'. Highly formal strategic planning is replaced by a notion of strategic awareness and orientation where strategy and action are intertwined in constant reflexive mode (Pencarelli et al., 2008).

It is argued below that this model is highly appropriate as a response to the present and most probably future environment of universities (Kitson et al., 2009).

THE UNIVERSITY AS AN ENTREPRENEURIAL STAKEHOLDER LEARNING ORGANIZATION

The model described above characterizes the entrepreneurial institution as a dynamic 'learning organization'[66] meeting two major criteria in this respect. First, that it is porous to learning from stakeholders at all levels of the organization by empowerment of staff in this respect. Second, that its shared culture of internal trust-based relationships facilitates a flow of the knowledge gained across horizontal and vertical boundaries in the organization.

The University as a Knowledge Broker

The traditional university could, perhaps somewhat unfairly, be characterized as a 'learned' rather than 'learning' organization as described above, with its focus upon learning from 'objective', often arms' length, research and scholastic texts. Yet, as argued in an earlier paper (Gibb et al., 2009), universities in the technology-led information age can no longer pretend to be the sole dominant source of knowledge and discovery (Nowotny et al., 2003). They are being pressed to adapt to the international diversity and complexities of knowledge flows as well as to the knowledge and learning needs of a wider range of stakeholders to be engaged (Watson, 2010; Watson et al., 2011).[67] This does not move the university away from its classical role as a focus 'for the imaginative use of knowledge' (Newman, 1852) or from its long established task of discovery, reflection and the carrying forward of the culture of society (Collini, 2012); it does, however, add in the role of 'transformation' (Brennan et al., 2004).

The stakeholder relationship model, as described above, aligns strongly with Mark Moore's conceptualization of the creation of public value via processes of engagement with all key partners in society (Moore, 1995). The model, by its open processes of engagement, meets the criteria of facilitating the pursuit of rich procedural knowledge, rich and tacit factual knowledge and life span contextualization (Marchand, 2003). It therefore clearly addresses the challenge of the 'how' as well as the 'why' in learning and therefore the creation of what Maxwell deems as 'wisdom' (Maxwell, 1984).

Organizing for a Learning Organization

If the concept of the entrepreneurial stakeholder learning organization, as described above, is accepted as appropriate to university development, it has major implications for the redesign of the university to harmonize with a dynamic task environment. The entrepreneurial learning organization model demands the maximizing of the potential and freedom of the individual in the organization to reach out to wider communities of practice, harvest tacit as well as explicit knowledge and innovate across the broad spectrum of institutional. This will demand the empowerment of individual staff members to take risks and be protected and rewarded by the system for their initiative. The most important challenge in pursuing this is that of maintaining academic freedom in a milieu of wider stakeholder demands and competition as described earlier.

There are major implications for the way that communication takes place internally and externally if the benefits from external two-way learning processes are to be optimized. There is substantial evidence that innovation is maximized within a climate of informal networks and social interaction (Obsfeld, 2005). Overall, to be successful, it requires, as noted above, a shared set of beliefs as to the purpose and process of the organization that might be characterized as the appropriate enterprise culture. Some of the major parameters of such an HE organization are summarized in Figure 2.5.

The figure underpins notions of: a decentralized organization designed to empower individuals all the way down the institution; departmental leaders being held responsible for innovation, harvesting resources, and support of risk taking; the breaking down of boundaries within and without the organization; developing strategic partnerships with

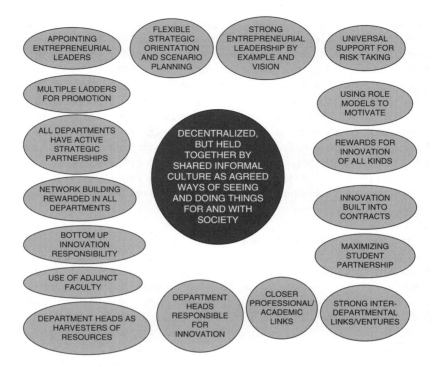

Figure 2.5   Organizing the university for entrepreneurship

stakeholder institutions and engaging them directly through increased use of adjunct faculty; creating new avenues for rewards and promotion; using faculty to act as boundary knowledge brokers; the appointment of entrepreneurial staff in pursuit of these goals; the creation of new forms of partnership with students to maximize their ownership of learning; the use of social media and new technologies to enhance this goal; the full exploitation of synergies across the university as described in an earlier paper (Gibb, 2012); and, above all, strong entrepreneurial leadership by example.

OVERVIEW AND CONCLUSION

The Challenge of Differentiation and Strategic Partnership Building

It has been constantly emphasized in this chapter that enterprising behaviour and entrepreneurial organization are contingent phenomena most needed when operating under dynamic conditions of uncertainty and complexity. The nature and scale of pressures for change in the HE task environment have been described above, along with the challenge to organization design. The sheer volume of change pressures in the environment provides numerous opportunities as well as threats demanding entrepreneurial response. It has been argued that the opportunities lie in the ability of institutions to adopt an entrepreneurial organization model; strategically assess the stakeholder environment; identify appropriate responses; seek to bring forward stakeholder futures alongside their own vision; build upon views of the long-term HE environment; match it to their own organization strengths and weaknesses; and develop a discovery, learning, educational and relationship agenda accordingly. This means moving substantially beyond a Triple Helix concept, confined to tripartite government/business/university partnership, to a model of much wider stakeholder and societal culture engagement. There have been attempts to move the Triple Helix model into fourth or fifth dimensions to cover wider aspects of a civil society (Carayannis and Campbell, 2012) but the stakeholder model allows strategies covering the totality of knowledge flows, relationships and cultural/global challenges.

Such strategies are already emerging, with institutions choosing distinctive key local, regional, national and/or international areas of focus. Entrepreneurial organizations seek to differentiate themselves. Almost certainly many of the strategies will demand more fluid internal cross-boundary relationships and the building up of strong external strategic partnerships. They will also necessitate continuous reflection on the foci of teaching and learning and its relationship to research (Prince et al., 2007), particularly in the light of the growing debate on 'wisdom' and 'practical intelligence'. Scholarship stands apart from research, and the concept of wisdom in turn demands an intellectualism that goes beyond scholarship. A focus on the broad concept of wisdom is also a reminder that the supreme stakeholder for the university is society itself and that the sum total of the stakeholder relationship parts may not truly represent the whole.

In addressing the learning agenda and the issue of differentiation, the key 'discovery' aspect of university activity may need to be an area for reflection. It does not necessarily follow that good teaching follows from good research (Jenkins, 2004). As Jenkins points out, effective approaches to teaching and learning can stand apart from formal research. The increasing demands (of both business and other organizations) for a wider range of personal transferable and entrepreneurial skills to be developed in graduates create major new pedagogical challenges for learning and teaching (QAA, 2012). These challenges are being intensified by advances in technologies for learning. The new dynamics of the task environment provide many opportunities for niche differentiation in the discovery and learning process. Example abound: the University of Plymouth brands itself as 'enterprise led', the University of Northampton as the university for employability, and Strathclyde University as a university for 'useful learning'.

It has been argued that a major challenge in creating greater public value will be that of aligning, appropriately, the university with the future for key stakeholders and beyond, for society (the transformational role). As noted above, much of the detail of the challenge in this respect will be at the departmental level with each department mapping out its own 'task environment', academic, community and practitioner. Overall, closer engagement with stakeholders will demand a more flexible approach to strategic planning, the flexibility being determined by the dynamics of the learning relationships. As in an entrepreneurial company there will be stronger pressure to seek to lower uncertainty by the building of trust-based relationship partnerships. Drawing down from the strategic partnership literature (Mohr and Spekman, 1994) some key guidelines in this respect might include:

- a careful search for multiple partnerships with longer term horizons;
- a sharing of vision and objectives with selected strategic partners;
- more open exchanges and a move away from isolated development processes to greater joint activity and problem solving;
- maximizing gateways to ongoing informal social relationship building with stakeholders across the university as a key to stimulating innovation;
- moving away from limited one-off contact points to more ongoing engagement;
- associated greater empathy with stakeholder values and a willingness to share these;
- an associated movement from fragmented development projects to networked approaches and more joint technical development processes with a sharing of costs and benefits;
- an enhanced understanding of professional stakeholder standards and ways of doing things;
- greater cooperation with HE competitors rather than the taking of adversarial stances.

Although this chapter has focused substantially upon the UK and England, it is clear that many of the issues raised are relevant to the future of universities across the globe (Kwiek, 2009, Marginson, 2012a). At the core of an entrepreneurial academic response to environmental change is the preservation of freedom. It has been argued in this chapter that such freedom needs to be negotiated with an ever wider range of stakeholders. The adoption of the broadly defined entrepreneurial approach to managing relationships described in this chapter might enhance the capacity of a university to move away from short-term reactive 'market' tactics, strengthen its ability to influence social and cultural change in society and at the same time enhance, negotiate and maintain key areas of academic independence and freedom.

NOTES

1. For an academic defence of this stance see Gibb (2002).
2. A model of government, business and university interaction.
3. Wales and Scotland in particular have their own policy control over university finance and development and have not chosen to pursue the student-led market approach to funding as in England.
4. Embracing innovations, for example, in: programme design, development, curriculum and pedagogy, stakeholder relationship development and partnerships (local, regional, national and international); research design and development; research impact; funding and resource acquisition; trans-disciplinary approaches to research and teaching; inter-departmental and cross-boundary collaborations in general; internationalization; and organization development.
5. See www.eulp.co.uk. A pioneering executive development programme for senior university leaders, now run annually through the National Centre for Entrepreneurship in Education and Universities UK.
6. The task environment constitutes the institutions and forces with whom the organization interfaces in pursuit of its activity. It is a concept that has influenced organization development theory for many years, initially explored by the Tavistock Institute. See, for example, William (1958) and Lawrence and Lorsch (1986).
7. See the Enterprising Universities website http://www.enterprisinguniversities.co.uk/ for a review of missions.
8. Leading to the establishment of a Council for the Defence of British Universities by high-profile academics and writers.
9. The funding changes apply only to England, with the Scottish and Welsh governments able to make their own HE funding decisions.
10. See reference to the Higher Education Innovation Fund (HEIF) below.
11. New College of the Humanities (NCH) is a private for-profit college in London, the creation of which was announced in June 2011 by the philosopher Anthony Grayling, its founder and first master. Disciplines covered are economics, English, history, law and philosophy.
12. See http://www.hefce.ac.uk/news/newsarchive/2012/name,73447,en.html, accessed 27 July 2013.
13. The Catapult programme is a network of centres publically primed, aimed at bridging the gap between universities and business focused on high-value manufacturing, cell therapy, offshore renewable energy, satellite applications, connected digital economy, future cities and transport systems; see http://www.innovateuk.org/deliveringinnovation/catapults.ashx, accessed 27 July 2013.
14. See, for example, Wellcome Trust on Open Access at http://www.wellcome.ac.uk/About-us/Policy/Policy-and-position-statements/wtd002766.htm, accessed 27 July 2013.

15. See, for example, Shaheen (2011).
16. The UK government's £25 million Higher Apprenticeship Fund aims to support a progression through vocational training to undergraduate and postgraduate degrees in partnerships with companies. It already covers accounting, professional services, hospitality, management, manufacturing and public relations, and in future will aim more widely at science and technology.
17. Thirty-nine LEPs cover the whole of England. LEPs bring local business and civic leaders together with the aim of stimulating vision and leadership to drive sustainable economic growth and create the conditions to increase private sector jobs in their communities.
18. This has led to a growth of university/local voluntary and 'pro bono' activities across the country. See *The Guardian*, 9 November 2010 for a review by Lucy Tobin at http://www.guardian.co.uk/education/2010/nov/09/students-advise-charities, accessed 27 July 2013.
19. Heseltine (2012).
20. A government programme designed to, in theory, increase the independence of former state schools.
21. See 'Michael Gove plans Baccalaureate shakeup of A levels', *The Guardian*, 17 October 2012, accessed 27 July 2013 at http://www.guardian.co.uk/politics/2012/oct/17/michael-gove-baccalaureate-a-levels.
22. The QAA is an independent body that reviews the performance of universities and colleges of Higher Education. Its audit reports are available online – www.qaa.ac.uk.
23. See https://www.coursera.org.
24. See 'Compare tuition fees schemes in Europe', accessed 27 July 2013 at http://www.studyineurope.eu/tuition-fees.
25. See www.udacity.com; https://www.edx.org/.
26. There are initiatives in the USA funded by the Gates Foundation and supported by the American Council on Education to overcome some of the accreditation problems.
27. 'University rankings: UK risks "global mediocrity"', *Daily Telegraph*, 3 October 2012, accessed 27 July 2013 at http://www.telegraph.co.uk/education/universityeducation/9584022/University-rankings-UK-risks-global-mediocrity.html.
28. See Iles (2012).
29. See 'Compare tuition fees schemes in Europe', op cit.
30. See Financial Times, July 9, 2012.
31. See, for example, International University of Japan at www.iuj.ac.jp.
32. This issue, provoked by the Minister for Higher Education, was debated at the Policy Dialogue Higher Education in Sri Lanka and UK on the theme of the Entrepreneurial University. See report by Eranda Ginige British Council Sri Lanka British Council June 2008.
33. There are four distinct university mission/pressure groups in the UK: two brand themselves as research-intensive institutions (the Russell Group and the 1994 Group); one represents universities that are largely teaching focused with an emphasis on social inclusion (Million+); and one represents universities that are research led and business engaged (Alliance). Not all Higher Education Institutions within the UK belong to a mission group.
34. See http://www.enterprisinguniversities.co.uk/.
35. 'Leading, governing and managing universities', accessed 27 July 2013 at http://www.hefce.ac.uk/whatwedo/lgm/landg/lgmf/leadingtransformationalchange/.
36. The Newcastle University PARTNERS Programme links the university with schools across the North of England offering a wide range of activities for students and parents as well as guarantees for places at the university linked with various pre-university courses and activities. See http://www.ncl.ac.uk/partners/about/events/studentfinance/therealdeal.htm, accessed 27 July 2013.
37. The University of Derby has an extensive national and international partnership programme in particular providing strong links between Further and Higher Education. See http://www.derby.ac.uk/lei/uk-partnerships/be-a-partner, accessed 27 July 2013.

38. See http://www.hefce.ac.uk/whatwedo/wp/currentworktowidenparticipation/national scholarshipprogramme/, accessed 27 July 2013.
39. For example, Birkbeck College London with its 'learning cafés' in East London, an area with very low HE participation.
40. See an earlier paper 'Leading the entrepreneurial university' (Gibb, 2009) for a brief discussion of the Mode 2 concept.
41. Enterprise and Entrepreneurship in Higher Education 2010 National Survey; see www. ncge.com/EE_Survey, accessed 27 July 2013.
42. International Entrepreneurship Educators Programme for university staff from any department wishing to lead entrepreneurship and enterprise education; see www.ncee. org.uk/entrepreneurship_education/ieep, accessed 27 July 2013.
43. See www.nacue.com.
44. The KTP evaluation study of 2010 (Regeneris Consulting) focused substantially on a knowledge transfer as opposed to knowledge exchange process with KTPs and has little to say about the bringing of knowledge gained back into the university or the building of longer term partnerships with business.
45. Originated at Durham University Small Business Centre in partnership with Shell UK in 1986 and expanded across the UK via a process of local partnerships. It ran for over 20 years.
46. See, for example, the Huddersfield University Partners in Law and Partners in Accountancy programmes working with groups of local firms. See http://www.hud. ac.uk/courses/supporting/law/businessprofessional/, accessed 27 July 2013.
47. Launched in November 2011 with government funding to drive enterprise, jobs and growth within a sector, supply chain or locality. See http://www.bis.gov.uk/assets/ biscore/further-education-skills/docs/e/12–1026-employer-ownership-of-skills-pilot-state-aid-application.pdf, accessed 27 July 2013.
48. Funded by HEFCE, the South East Coast Communities Partnership (2008–11) involved nine universities in the South East of England working collaboratively with members of the local community in the area in order to build their capacity to meet their health and well-being needs. See http://www.coastalcommunities.org.uk/, accessed 27 July 2013.
49. See De Montford University Square Mile Project as an example of wide staff, student and stakeholder engagement. See http://www.innovationunit.org/blog/201209/ de-montfort-university%E2%80%99s-square-mile-project-university-local-public-good, accessed 27 July 2013.
50. See also Universities UK (2010b).
51. See University of Northampton at http://www.northampton.ac.uk/social-enterprise, accessed 27 July 2013.
52. The National Co-ordinating Centre for Public Engagement consists of a network of six beacons that are university-based collaborative centres that help support, recognize, reward and build capacity for public engagement work.
53. This booklet provides a variety of perspectives on, and examples of, English university activity.
54. For example, the N8 Research Partnership involves collaboration between the Universities of Durham, Lancaster, Leeds, Liverpool, Manchester, Newcastle, Sheffield and York, aimed at exploiting the research and industrial strengths of the North of England. Centres have been established that focus on areas of future growth in the economy, such as regenerative medicine and molecular engineering, each working to create collaboration between industry and academia. See http://www.n8research.org. uk, accessed 27 July 2013.
55. See, for example, the Francis Crick Institute to be launched in 2015, focused upon multidisciplinary medical research through partnerships between public and private research councils and three leading London universities; http://www.crick.ac.uk, accessed 27 July 2013.
56. See, for example, Liverpool University's partnership with Laureate International

offering a wide range of Master's and Doctoral degrees to several thousand students worldwide. See http://www.liverpool-degrees.com/, accessed 27 July 2013. Also, Resource Development International (RDI) partners with several UK universities to provide a broad portfolio of degrees, Master's and MBA programmes online, which it markets and delivers worldwide. See http://www.rdi.co.uk/about-rdi/, accessed 27 July 2013.

57.   For example, retail company Tesco and the travel company TUI have their own tailored UK foundation degrees. Manchester Metropolitan University is in partnership with MacDonald's in a foundation degree. See also http://www.ucas.ac.uk/students/choosingcourses/choosingcourse/foundationdegree/, accessed 27 July 2013.\

58.   The UK Open University is a lead UK institution in actively engaging in degree provision with a range of large private companies. See http://www.open-university.co.uk/ou-for-your-business.php/, accessed 27 July 2013.

59.   See Oxford Brookes Centre for Curriculum Internationalisation at http://www.brookes.ac.uk/services/cci/index.html, accessed 27 July 2013.

60.   See http://www.upp-ltd.com/about/, accessed 27 July 2013. UNITE, another private company, manages Higher Education facilities and accommodation for over 50 universities with over 40 000 bedrooms in 20 cities in the UK. See http://www.unite-group.co.uk/our-customers/universities.go, accessed 27 July 2013.

61.   The HEFCE Shared Services Advisory Group estimates that successful use of shared services can yet produce cost savings of 20–30 per cent in the public sector. An HEFCE Modernisation Fund provides a small financial incentive to increase efficiency. See http://www.hefce.ac.uk/whatwedo/invest/funds/umf/, accessed 27 July 2013.

62.   For example, Unitemps, a Warwick University company is an online recruitment service that provides temporary staffing to leading universities and commercial businesses across the UK and globally. See https://www.unitemps.co.uk/, accessed 27 July 2013.

63.   See HEFCE report at http://www.hefce.ac.uk/pubs/rdreports/2006/rd15_06/rd15_06.pdf, accessed 27 July 2013.

64.   De Montfort University has, for example, issued £110 million in bonds to raise cash for modernization of facilities.

65.   The University of Plymouth is, for example, advertising for an Entrepreneur in Residence with responsibility for 'curricular and extra-curricular interventions'.

66.   Defined as an organization that collects information and creates knowledge about the relevant environment, both the internal environment and the external environment. An organization that manifests learning is not necessarily a learning organization. The above process must be an omnipresent thread in the organizational fabric. Interdependence is an essential feature of a learning organization as is the capacity of the organization members to 'absorb'. (Taken from Xin An Lu literature review [undated] 'Surveying the Concept of the Learning Organisation' Southern Illinois University, accessed 27 July 2013 at http://www.leadingtoday.org/weleadinlearning/xaoct04.htm).

67.   See also Watson (2002), 'What is a university for?', accessed 27 July 2013 at http://www.guardian.co.uk/education/2002/jan/15/highereducation.news.

REFERENCES

Aldrich, H.E. and C. Zimmer (1986), 'Entrepreneurship through social networks', University of Illinois at Urbana-Champaign's Academy for Entrepreneurial Leadership, Historical Research Reference in Entrepreneurship.

Bauer, P. (2012), 'Developing entrepreneurship and entrepreneurial universities in Europe', presentation to Conference on Universities, Münster, 26–27 April, European Commission.

Bercovitz, J. and M. Feldman (2008), 'Academic entrepreneurs: Organizational change at the individual level', *Organization Science*, 19(1), 69–85.

Bone, Sir Drummond (2011), 'Internationalization 2011: An overview', Balliol College Oxford, *Higher Learning Research Communications*, **1**(1), 4–9 June.

Bourn, D. A. McKenzie and C. Shiel (2006), 'The global university: The role of the curriculum', Development Education Association.

Brennan, J. and T. Shah (eds) (2011), 'Higher Education and society in changing times: Looking back and looking forward', Centre for Higher Education Research and information, Open University UK.

Brennan, J., R. King and Y. Lebeau (2004), *The Role of Universities in the Transformation of Societies. An International Research Project*, Synthesis Report, Association of Commonwealth Universities and Centre for Higher Education Research and Information, Open University.

Butcher, V., J. Smith, J. Kettle and L. Burton (2011), 'Review of good practice in employability and enterprise development', Centres for Excellence in Teaching and Learning, a report for HEFCE by the Higher Education Academy.

Carayannis, E.G. and D.F.J. Campbell (2012), 'Mode 3 knowledge production in quadruple helix innovation systems', *SpringerBriefs in Business*, **7**, 1–63.

Coiffait, L. (ed.) (2012), *Blue Skies: New Thinking About the Future of Higher Education*, a collection of short articles by leading commentators, UK, pearsonblueskies.com.

Collini, S. (2012), *What Are Universities For?*, London: Penguin Books.

Collins, O.F. and D.G. Moore (1964), *The Enterprising Man*, East Lansing, MI: Michigan State University.

Covin, J.G. and D.P. Slevin (1991), 'A conceptual model of entrepreneurship as firm behavior', *Entrepreneurship, Theory and Practice*, **16**(1), 7–25.

Daniel, Sir John (2012), 'Making sense of MOOCs: Musings in a maze of myth, paradox and possibility', accessed 27 July 2013 at ime.open.ac.uk/jime/article/view/2012–18.

Department for Innovation, Universities and Skills (2007), *Academies, Trusts and Higher Education*, London: DIUS.

Diamond, I. et al. (2009), *Efficiency and Modernization in Higher Education*, a report by the Universities UK Efficiency and Modernization Task Group, Universities UK.

Diamond, I. et al. (2011), *Efficiency and Modernization in Higher Education. Phase 2. Implementation Plan*, Universities UK.

Dolphin, T. and T. Lanning (2011), *Re-thinking Apprenticeships*, London: Institute for Public Policy Research (IPPR).

Etzkowitz, H. (2008), *The Triple Helix. University–Industry–Government, Innovation in Action*, London: Routledge.

European Commission (2011), 'Supporting growth and jobs: An agenda for the modernization of Europe's Higher Education system', Communication from the Commission to the European Parliament, the Council, the European Economic and Social Committee and the Committee of the Regions, Brussels COM 2011 567 final.

Evans, G.R. (2002), *Academics and the Real World*, Milton Keynes: Open University Press.

Evans, M. (2004), *'Killing Thinking. The Death of the University*, London and New York: Continuum 2004.

Evans, A. (2012), 'The role of private universities', presentation to the Higher Education Conference Workshop, BPP University College.

Eversheds (2009), *Developing Future University Structures. New Funding and Legal Models*, report for Universities UK, accessed 27 July 2013 at http://www.universitiesuk.ac.uk/highereducation/Pages/FutureUniversityStructures.aspx.

Finch, J. (2012), *Accessibility, Sustainability, Excellence: How to Expand Access to Research Publications*, report of the Working Group on Expanding Access to Published Research Findings, Department for Business Innovation and Skills, June.

Foster, W., L. Hart and T. Lewis (2011), *Costing Study of Two-year Accelerated Honours Degree*, Liz Hart Associates for HEFCE.

Gibb, A.A. (1997), 'Small firms' training and competitiveness. Building upon the small business as a learning organization', *International Small Business Journal*, **15**(3), 13–29.

Gibb, A.A. (2002), 'Creative destruction, new values, new ways of doing things and new combinations of knowledge. In pursuit of a new enterprise and entrepreneurship paradigm', *International Journal of Management Reviews*, **4**(3), 233–68.

Gibb, A.A. (2005), 'Towards the entrepreneurial university. Entrepreneurship education as a lever for change', National Council for Graduate Entrepreneurship (NCGE) Policy Paper, accessed 25 July 2013 at http://www.ncee.org.uk/publication/towards_the_entrepreneurial_university.pdf.

Gibb, A.A. (2007), 'Entrepreneurship: Unique solutions for unique environments. Is it possible to achieve this with the existing paradigm?' *International Journal of Entrepreneurship Education*, **5**, 93–142.

Gibb, A.A. (2009), 'Leading the entrepreneurial university: Meeting the entrepreneurial development needs of Higher Education Institutions', Saïd Business School, University of Oxford.

Gibb, A.A. (2012), 'Exploring the synergistic potential in entrepreneurial university development: Towards the building of a strategic framework', *Annals of Innovation & Entrepreneurship*, **3**, 1–24

Gibb, A.A., G. Haskins and I. Robertson (2009), 'Leading the entrepreneurial university. Meeting the entrepreneurial development needs of Higher Education Institutions', a National Council for Graduate Entrepreneurship (NCGE) Policy Paper, accessed 27 July 2013 at http://www.ncee.org.uk/publication/leading_the_entrepreneurial_university.pdf.

Gillies, M. (2011), 'University governance. Questions for a new era', a personal view from the Vice Chancellor of London Metropolitan University, accessed 27 July 2013 at http://www.hepi.ac.uk/files/UniversityGovernance.pdf.

Goddard, J. and P. Vallance (2011), 'The civic university and the leadership of place', Centre for Urban and Regional Development Studies (CURDS), Newcastle University UK.

Graham, G. (2002), *Universities. The Recovery of an Idea*, Exeter: Imprint Academic UK.

Grayling, A.C. (2012), 'Higher humanities education in the 21st century', Chapter 2 in L. Coiffait (ed.) (2012), *Blue Skies: New Thinking About the Future of Higher Education*, a collection of short articles by leading commentators, UK, pearsonblueskies.com.

Hauser, H. (2010), *The Current and Future Role of Technology and Innovation Centres in the UK*, report for Lord Mandelson, Secretary of State Department of Business, Innovation and Skills.

Heseltine, Lord Michael (2012), *No Stone Unturned. In Pursuit of Growth*, London: Cabinet Office.

Higher Education Commission (2012), *Postgraduate Education: An Independent Inquiry by the Higher Education Commission*, London: HEC.

Hohmann, H. and F. Welter (eds) (2005), *Trust and Entrepreneurship. A West East Perspective*, Cheltenham, UK and Northampton, MA, USA: Edward Elgar Publishing.

Hughes, A., M. Kitson, J. Probert and I. Milner (2011), *Hidden Connections: Knowledge Exchange Between the Arts and Humanities and the Private, Public and Third Sectors*, Cambridge, UK: Arts and Humanities Research Council and Centre for Business Research.

Hughes, A. and A. Mina (2012), *The UK R&D Landscape*, reprinted and revised, March, London, Cambridge: Council for Industry and Higher Education and UK Innovation Research Centre.

Iles, J. (2012), 'Investigation: British students flock overseas. Recent statistics show a sharp increase in British applications to American and European universities', *Cherwell*, 27 April 2012, accessed 27 July 2013 at http://www.cherwell.org/news/oxford/2012/04/27/investigation-british-students-flock-overseas.

Institute of Educational Technology (2012), 'Future learning systems', http://www8.open.ac.uk/iet/main/learning-teaching/our-learning-teaching-programmes/future-learning-systems, Open University

Jenkins, A. (2004), *A Guide to the Research Evidence on Teaching–Research Relations*, Higher Education Academy UK.

JISC (2012), *Learning in a Digital Age. Extending Higher Education Opportunities for Lifelong Learning*, London: HEFCE.

Kim, W.C. and R. Mauborgne (2004), 'Blue ocean strategy', *Harvard Business Review*, October.

King, R., A. Findlay and J. Ahrens (2010), *International Student Mobility Literature Review*, report to HEFCE and co-funded by the British Council, UK National Agency for Erasmus, accessed 27 July 2013 at http://www.britishcouncil.org/hefce_bc_report2010. pdf.

Kitson, M. J. Howells, R. Braham and S. Westlake (2009), 'The connected university. Driving recovery and growth in the economy', NESTA UK.

Knight, P. and M. Yorke (2004), *Learning, Curriculum and Employability in Higher Education*, London: Routledge Falmer.

Kwiek, M. (2009), 'The changing attractiveness of European Higher Education. Current developments, future challenges and major policy issues', Chapter 7 in B.M. Kehm, J. Huisman and B. Stensaker (eds) (2009), *The European Higher Education Area. Perspectives on a Moving Target*, Rotterdam: Sense Publishers.

Lawrence, P.R. and J.W. Lorsch (1986), *Organization and Environment: Managing Differentiation and Integration*, Cambridge, MA: Harvard Business School Classics.

Lyall, C. and L. Meagher (2012), 'A masterclass in interdisciplinarity: Research into practice in training the next generation of interdisciplinary researchers', Innogen Working Paper No. 95, ESRC Genomics Network, Economic and Social Research Council.

Marchand, H. (2003) 'An overview of the psychology of wisdom', accessed 27 July 2013 at http://www.wisdompage.com/AnOverviewOfThePsychologyOfWisdom.html.

Marginson, S. (2012a) 'Resurrecting public good(s) in Higher Education', presentation to British Education Research Association Manchester September Conference on 'Privatization in Tertiary Education: The Good, the Bad and the Ugly', 4–6 September.

Marginson, S. (2012b), 'A more plural Higher Education world: Global implications of the rise of East Asia systems', paper to the AC21 Conference University of Adelaide Australia, accessed 27 July 2013 at http://www.cshe.unimelb.edu.au/people/marginson_ docs/Marginson_keynote_AC21_13June2012_paper.pdf.

Massey, A. (2010), 'Higher Education in the age of austerity: Shared services, outsourcing and entrepreneurship', Policy Exchange Research Note, accessed 27 July 2013 at http://www.po licyexchange.org.uk/publications/category/item/higher-education-in-the-age-of-austerity-shared-services-outsourcing-and-entrepreneurship.

Maxwell, N. (1984), *From Knowledge to Wisdom: A Revolution in the Aims and Methods of Science*, Oxford: Basil Blackwell.

McAuley, D., H. Rahemtulla, J. Goulding and C. Souch (2012), 'How open data, data literacy and linked data will revolutionise Higher Education', in Pearson Blue Skies 2012 Asia, accessed 29 July 2013 at http://pearsonblueskies.com/category/ editions/2012-asia-pacific/.

McGettigan, A. (2012), 'Academics and standards: Avoiding market failure', Chapter 3 in L. Coiffait (ed.) (2012), *Blue Skies: New Thinking About the Future of Higher Education*, a collection of short articles by leading commentators, UK, pearsonblueskies.com.

Milburn, A. (2012), *University Challenge: How Higher Education Can Advance Social Mobility*, a progress report by the Independent Reviewer on Social Mobility and Child Poverty, London: Cabinet Office.

Mohr, J. and R. Spekman (1994), 'Characteristics of partnership success: Partnership attributes, communication behavior, and conflict resolution techniques', *Strategic Management Journal*, 15(2), 135–52.

Moore, M.H. (1995), *Creating Public Value: Strategic Management in Government*, Cambridge, MA: Harvard University Press.

More Partnership (2012), *Review of Philanthropy in UK Higher Education*, UK Higher Education Funding Council (HEFCE) September.

Namen, J.L. and D.P. Slavin (1993), 'Entrepreneurship and the concept of fit: A model and empirical tests', *Strategic Management Journal*, 14(2), 137–53.

NESTA (undated), 'Doing the business. University–business links and innovation', NESTA UK.

NESTA UK Public and Corporate Economic Consultants Cambridge (2012), 'Strengthening the contribution of English Higher Education Institutions to the innovation system: Knowledge exchange and HEIF funding', an executive summary for HEFCE UK.

Newman, J.H. (1852), 'Knowledge, learning and professional skill', in R.M. Alden (ed.) (1917), *Readings in English Prose of the 19th Century*, Cambridge, MA: Cambridge Press, pp. 418–39.

Newman J.H. in Newman Reader (2007), 'Discourse 6. Knowledge viewed in relation to learning', The National Institute for Newman Studies.

Nowotny, H., P. Scott and M. Gibbons (2003), '"Mode 2" revisited: The new production of knowledge', *Minerva*, **41**(3), 179–94.

NUS and CBI (2011), *Working Towards Your Future*, National Union of Students and Confederation of British Industry.

Obsfeld, D. (2005), 'Social networks, the tertius iungens orientation, and involvement in innovation', *Administrative Science Quarterly*, **50**(1), 100–30.

Pearce, N. (2012), 'How can students best be served. Mature policies for Higher Education access', Section 5 in L. Coiffait (ed.) (2012), *Blue Skies: New Thinking About the Future of Higher Education*, a collection of short articles by leading commentators, UK, pearsonblueskies.com.

Pegg, A., J. Waldock, S. Hendy-Isaac and R. Lawton (2012), *Pedagogy for Employability*, Higher Education Academy UK.

Pencarelli, T., E. Savelli, S. Splendiana (2008), 'Strategic awareness and growth strategies in small sized enterprises', 8th Global Conference on Business and Economics, 18–19 October, Florence.

Prince, M.J., R.M. Felder and R. Brent (2007), 'Does faculty research improve undergraduate teaching? An analysis of existing and potential synergies', *Journal of Engineering Education*, **96**(4), 283–94.

Public and Corporate Economic Consultants Cambridge (2012), 'Strengthening the contribution of English Higher Education institutions to the innovation system: Knowledge exchange and HEIF funding', an executive summary for HEFCE UK.

Quality Assurance Agency for Higher Education (QAA) (2012), *Enterprise and Entrepreneurship Education: Guidance for UK Enterprise Education Providers*, accessed 27 July 2013 at ww.qaa.ac.uk/Publications/InformationAndGuidance/Documents/enterprise-guidance.pdf.

Regeneris Consulting Limited (2010), *Knowledge Transfer Partnerships Strategic Review*, Cheshire, UK: Technology Strategy Board.

Robinson, F., I. Zass-Ogilvie and R. Hudson (2012), 'How can universities support disadvantaged communities?', accessed 29 July 2013 at Durham University http://www.dur.ac.uk/StChads/prg/JRF%20Universities%20and%20Communities%20pre-full%20publication.pdf, accessed 27 July 2013.

Salter, A., V. Tatari, P. D'Este and A. Neely (2010), *The Republic of Engagement. Exploring Academic Attitudes to Collaborating with Industry and Entrepreneurship*, Advanced Institute of Management Research (AIM) and Innovation Research Centre UK.

Selwyn, N. (2012) 'Social media in Higher Education', The Europa World of Learning Online, www.worldoflearning.com.

Shaheen, F. (2011), *Degrees of Value. How Universities Benefit Society*, Universities UK, University Partnerships Programme, New Economics Foundation.

Shiel, C. and S. Mann (2005), 'A global perspective at Bournemouth University. Education for global citizens and sustainable development', Global Perspectives Group, Bournemouth University.

Standard and Poor's (2008), *Revenue Diversification and Sustainability: A Comparison of Trends in Public Higher Education in the UK and US*, The Council for Industry and Higher Education, UK.

Sternberg, R.J., G.B. Forsythe, J. Hedland, J.A. Horvarth, R.K. Wagner, W.M. Williams, S.A. Snook and E.L. Grigorenko (2000), *Practical Intelligence in Everyday Life*, Cambridge, UK: Cambridge University Press.

Tallantyre, F. and J. Kettle (2011), *Learning From Experience in Employer Engagement*, Higher Education Academy UK.

Tatlow, P. (2012), 'Gove needs to put a brake on A level reforms', *The Guardian*, 11 September.

Technology Strategy Board (2012), *Catapult Update. Shaping the Network of Centres*, accessed 27 July 2013 at https://www.innovateuk.org/documents/1524978/2138994/Catapult+update+-+shaping+the+network+of+centres/b869d3da-606b-4e86-beeb-4ffab6031511.

UK Commission for Employment and Skills (2009), *The Employability Challenge*, London: UKCES.

UK Commission for Employment and Skills (2010), *Progression from Vocational Applied Learning to Higher Education*, University Vocational Awareness Council for UKCES, London: UKCES.

UK Department of Business Innovation and Skills (2011), *Higher Education. Students at the Heart of the System*, Command 8122 June.

Universities UK (2010a) 'Efficiency and effectiveness in Higher Education', a report by the universities efficiency and modernization task group. Efficiency and modernization in Higher Education, Phase II, Implementation Plan.

Universities UK (2010b), 'Universities engaging with local communities', accessed 27 July 2013 at http://www.universitiesuk.ac.uk/highereducation/Pages/EngagingLocalCommunities.aspx.

Universities UK (2012a), *Universities Enabling Social Enterprise. Delivering Benefits for All*, London: Universities UK.

Universities UK (2012b), *Universities UK Response to the Student Immigration System – A Consultation*, accessed 27 July 2013 at http://www.universitiesuk.ac.uk/highereducation/Documents/2011/ResponseToTheStudentImmigrationSystem.pdf.

University Alliance (2012), *Growing the Future: Universities Leading, Changing and Creating the Regional Economy*, accessed 27 July 2013 at http://www.unialliance.ac.uk/site/2011/09/19/growing-the-future-universities-leading-changing-and-creating-the-regional-economy/

Valima, J. (2009), 'The relevance of Higher Education to knowledge society and the knowledge-driven economy: Education, research and innovation', Chapter 2 in B.M. Kehm, J. Huisman and B. Stensaker (eds) (2009), *The European Higher Education Area. Perspectives on a Moving Target*, Rotterdam: Sense Publishers, pp. 23–41.

Watson, D. (2010), 'Universities' engagement with society', in B. McGaw, P. Peterson and E. Baker (eds), *The International Encyclopedia of Education*, 3rd edition, Oxford: Elsevier.

Watson, D., R.M. Hollister, S.E. Stroud and E. Babcock (2011), *The Engaged University. International Perspectives on Civic Engagement*, New York: Routledge.

Welikala, T. (2011), 'Rethinking international Higher Education curriculum: Mapping the research landscape', Universitas 21, accessed 27 July 2013 at http://www.universitas21.com/news/details/32/rethinking-international-higher-education-curriculum-mapping-the-research-landscape.

Westhead, P., D.L. Storey and F. Martin (1995), 'Outcomes reported by students who participated in the 1994 Shell Technology Enterprise Programme', University of Nottingham Institute for Enterprise and Innovation.

White, D., N. Warren, S. Faughnan and M. Marian (2010), *Study of UK Online Learning*, report to HEFCE by the Department of Continuing Education, University of Oxford.

Whitehead, A.N. (1927), 'Universities and their function', address to the American Association of the Collegiate Schools of Business, Harvard University.

William, R.D. (1958), 'Environment as an influence on managerial autonomy', *Administrative Science Quarterly*, **2**(4), 409–43.

Williams, L., N. Turner and A. Jones (2008), *Embedding Universities in Knowledge Cities*, London: Work Foundation UK.

Wilson, T. (2012), *A Review of Business–University Collaboration*, London: Department for Business Innovation and Skills.

3. Managing the improvement of entrepreneurship education programmes: a comparison of universities in the life sciences in Europe, USA and Canada

Vincent Blok, Rob Lubberink, Thomas Lans and Onno Omta

INTRODUCTION

A central feature of the transition towards an entrepreneurial university is the development of an entrepreneurship education programme. Following Etzkowitz's definition of the entrepreneurial university as a 'natural incubator, providing support structures for teachers and students to initiate new ventures' (Etzkowitz, 2003, p. 112), entrepreneurship education can be seen as one of its three key missions (cf. Guerrero, 2008). Furthermore, the development and implementation of entrepreneurship courses and other activities that favour student attitudes towards entrepreneurship can be seen as factors that potentially facilitate the development of entrepreneurial universities (Kirby et al., 2011).

In this chapter we contribute to the literature on the entrepreneurial university by focusing on research-based interventions to implement or improve the entrepreneurship education programme. To this end, a benchmark study is executed in a specific domain of the life sciences in Europe, USA and Canada: the agri-food sciences. The focus on entrepreneurship in a specific domain is important, because learning is generally thought to be domain or context specific (Brown et al., 1989; Rae, 2006).

Benchmarking is a method that is developed in order to determine the best practices and analyse the similarities and differences in activities that lead to higher or lower performance (Jackson and Lund, 2000). Because we focus on managerial interventions to implement or improve the entrepreneurship education programme at universities, the benchmark method is not primarily applied to *rank* entrepreneurship education programmes in the life sciences, but in order to learn from practice which interventions are able to improve the performance of the education programme (cf. Freytag and Hollensen, 2001). The research question of this chapter is: what kind of research-based educational interventions can be formulated for managers at universities in the life sciences who want to start with or improve their (high-tech) entrepreneurship education programme? Contrary to previous benchmark studies on entrepreneurship education programmes (FORA, 2004; NIRAS et al., 2008; cf. Hoffmann et al., 2008), where recommendations were given for policy-makers at the national and European level, we focus primarily on the management perspective of life science universities.

The main results of this study are that six dimensions of entrepreneurship education are identified – based on the FORA and NIRAS reports – and further developed through a literature review. These dimensions are: strategy, resources, institutional infrastructure, education, outreach and development. Based on the literature review and the benchmark study, specific educational interventions for each dimension of entrepreneurship education could be identified and described. These interventions enable managers of life science universities to start with or improve their entrepreneurship education programme.

PERFORMANCE INDICATORS AND DIMENSIONS OF ENTREPRENEURSHIP EDUCATION

One of the complexities with regard to entrepreneurship education concerns the definition of the concept and its consequences for the education programme. For example, if an entrepreneur is defined as a business owner or as an initiator of a new venture, then the educational programme of the university should focus primarily on the education of these new self-employed entrepreneurs (starters). However, if entrepreneurship is conceived as an inborn characteristic that is impossible to develop, then the education programme should primarily focus on interventions that make it easier for entrepreneurial students to start their own business.

Over the last three decades, research in entrepreneurship has convincingly shown that entrepreneurial experience (Baron and Ensley, 2006) and entrepreneurial education (Pittaway and Cope, 2007) have positive effects on entrepreneurial success. Furthermore, it has been shown that the identification and pursuit of business opportunities is a distinctive feature of entrepreneurship (Shane and Venkataraman, 2000; Gaglio and Katz, 2001), as well as the capacity to build and establish social networks (Arenius and Clercq, 2005). The development of these entrepreneurial competencies is not only necessary if someone wants to start a new venture, but is also needed within smaller or larger companies (intrapreneurship or corporate entrepreneurship) (Lans and Gulikers,

2010). Entrepreneurship education programmes therefore primarily focus on the development of entrepreneurial competencies (cf. FORA, 2004; NIRAS et al., 2008); the knowledge, skills and attitudes that enable successful task performance and problem solving with respect to real-world entrepreneurial problems, challenges and opportunities (Lans and Gulikers, 2010).

After the dissemination of entrepreneurship in education curricula in the United States (Kuratko, 2005), it also became widespread in Europe (NIRAS et al., 2008). This has led to an increasing diversity of different entrepreneurship education programmes at universities in Europe. After the implementation of first generation programmes, the question arose how to distinguish between good and bad entrepreneurship education programmes and how to improve the quality of the entrepreneurial curricula at European universities.

Vesper and Gartner developed a first framework of dimensions important for entrepreneurship education: the *education* itself, the *development* of the programme and the *outreach* or the links with external stakeholders were seen as important drivers for the quality of entrepreneurship education programmes (Vesper and Gartner, 1997).

One of the first European benchmark studies on entrepreneurship education, commissioned by the OECD (FORA, 2004), focused on five dimensions of entrepreneurship education: educational set-up, educational scope, institutional characteristics, outreach and evaluation. In the FORA study, however, the selection of best practice universities was not based on specific performance indicators for entrepreneurship education, but on the average score of all dimensions. In a study by NIRAS et al. (2008), commissioned by the European Commission, the conceptual model of Vesper and Gartner (1997) and FORA (2004) was further improved by including specific performance indicators for entrepreneurship education on the one hand and by identifying six dimensions of entrepreneurship education programmes on the other: strategy, resources, institutional infrastructure, teaching and learning, outreach and development. Based on this improved model, hundreds of Higher Education Institutions (HEIs) in Europe were benchmarked and policy recommendations were given on how to improve entrepreneurship education in Europe.

In our benchmark study, we combine the results of the FORA and NIRAS reports in order to identify performance indicators and dimensions of entrepreneurship education programmes. Because both reports differ with regard to the indices for the dimensions of the programmes, a literature review was first conducted in order to identify specific activities for each dimension, which are able to improve the performance of the programme.

Performance Indicators

Because it is expected that an entrepreneurial mind-set, entrepreneurial competence and the transfer of knowledge all have a positive impact on economic growth in general and new venture creation, innovation and wealth in particular, the NIRAS report identified three specific performance indicators:

- Entrepreneurial students through education, measured by the share of students enrolled for entrepreneurship courses as percentage of the total amount of students. This measures to what extent the entrepreneurial mind-set and entrepreneurial competencies are disseminated in a university.
- Knowledge transfer to society, measured by the number of patents, external funding (contract research and consultancy) and peer-reviewed studies conducted by the universities' staff. Knowledge transfer measures to what extent universities (and its staff) perform entrepreneurial behaviour and to what extent courses and extra-curricular activities are *state of the art*.
- Entrepreneurial students through practice, measured by the number of executive education attendants and the number of students participating in extra-curricular activities. It measures to what extent the entrepreneurial mind-set and entrepreneurial skills are developed in a university.

Dimensions of Entrepreneurship Education

Because universities cannot be seen solely as 'breeding grounds' for new venture creation (FORA, 2004) but rather as places where an entrepreneurial mind-set is fostered, entrepreneurial competencies are developed and behaviour is encouraged, the dimensions of entrepreneurship education programmes exceed the basic activity of entrepreneurship lecturing. Based on the FORA and NIRAS reports we identified six dimensions of entrepreneurship education. Each dimension consists of a variety of activities universities are engaged in to provide entrepreneurship education. These dimensions are further developed through a literature review.

Strategy
This dimension concerns the question whether and in what way universities embed the entrepreneurship education programme in their strategy (NIRAS et al., 2008). Specific activities related to this dimension are (1) the mission and strategy or the *goals* of the university, and (2) the

(operational) *policies* arising from these goals in order to improve the entrepreneurship education programme. The mission and strategy is important to reflect the adaptation to the rapidly changing environment of the entrepreneurial university (Sporn, 2001). Goals with regard to entrepreneurship education should be (3) embedded at different management levels within the university, that is, in policies of all departments (Potter, 2008) and should function as a road map for implementing entrepreneurship education programmes (Vesper and Gartner, 1997).

According to Sotirakou (2004), not only the governance structure but also the leadership style at universities should create a context in which entrepreneurship education can prosper. This implies that the entrepreneurship education programme should not only be supported by the educational staff but also by the senior management and the programme directors of the university (Mortimer, 1995). Although the dimension strategy involves aspects that only indirectly stimulate entrepreneurship education (Pittaway and Cope, 2007), Vesper and Gartner (1997) argue that these three aspects of the dimension strategy are highly important for high quality entrepreneurship education.

Resources
The resources dimension focuses on the financial resources available for the development and execution of the entrepreneurship education programme (NIRAS et al., 2008). Specific activities related to this dimension are improvements of (1) the allocated resources, (2) the types of resources available and (3) the self-generated income of the university, for example, by consultancy or admission fees for seminars and workshops. Various researchers have pointed to the importance of financial resources for the development and execution of entrepreneurship education programmes, which is impossible without dedicated funds (McMullan and Long, 1987; Vesper and Gartner, 1997; Wilson, 2008 in Potter, 2008).

Besides the size of the budget, also the type and availability of resources over time have an impact on the sustainability of entrepreneurship education programmes (Wilson, 2008 in Potter, 2008). Sporn (2001), for instance, warns about complete dependency on state funding, because it decreases the ability to adapt to changes in the educational environment. The diversification of types of resources will decrease the vulnerability of universities (Williams, 1995; Clark, 1998) and increase the sustainability of the programmes (Potter, 2008; Wilson, 2008).

One way of diversifying the types of resources is via activities of the university that generate income. It is expected that the availability of financial resources for the entrepreneurship education programme will lead to higher performances of the university, because entrepreneurship education programmes with larger budgets available are able to invest in facilities, extra-curricular activities and training of staff.

Infrastructure
The institutional infrastructure dimension involves the facilities offered to support the entrepreneurship education programme. It not only involves the structures established at the university to support the programme (NIRAS et al., 2008), but also specific activities to develop and improve (1) facilities such as incubator facilities for (graduated) students or centres of entrepreneurship and (2) research in entrepreneurship. Garavan and O'Cinneide (1994) showed the general importance of facilities that are conducive to learning for entrepreneurship, and Etzkowitz (2003) also acknowledged the importance of facilities that stimulate knowledge valorization (cf. Siegel and Phan, 2004). Menzies (1998) showed that centres of entrepreneurship not only stimulate entrepreneurship within the university but also enhance the entrepreneurial exchange and knowledge transfer between university and society. Rasmussen and Sørheim (2006) pointed at the essential roles incubator facilities and mentors play for students who want to start their own businesses, during or directly after their study (cf. Klofsten, 2000). An infrastructure that facilitates research in entrepreneurship is important, because state of the art knowledge generated by research can be used to improve teachers' and students' knowledge of entrepreneurship in general and the education programme in particular (Wilson, 2008).

Because entrepreneurship education is multidisciplinary by nature (Martinez et al., 2010), (3) activities that improve the multidisciplinarity of the entrepreneurship education programme belong to this dimension. The programme should not only be available for different disciplines within the university (Potter, 2008), but multidisciplinarity should also be encouraged by minimizing institutional barriers. Wiese and Sherman (2011) argued that a multidisciplinary approach results in cross-fertilization of ideas among students. Also, Hynes (1996) and Potter (2008) mention the importance of teamwork and Wilson (2008) stresses the importance of multidisciplinarity and the cross-fertilization of ideas within the programme, instilling creative and innovative entrepreneurial thinking.

Education
The education dimension covers the educational activities within the entrepreneurship education programme, the type of didactics and pedagogical methods that are employed. Specific activities related to this dimension are improvements of (1) the scope of the education programme and (2) the educational set-up of the programme (NIRAS et al., 2008).

Entrepreneurship education not only has a direct impact on students' knowledge about entrepreneurship (Souitaris et al., 2007) but should also foster their attitude (Lepoutre et al., 2010), intentions towards and inspiration for entrepreneurship (Souitaris et al., 2007). Kolvereid and Isaksen (2006) mention a positive correlation between entrepreneurial intentions and entrepreneurial behaviour (cf. Fayolle et al., 2006).

Courses in entrepreneurship are the most important driver for successful entrepreneurship education programmes (Vesper and Gartner, 1997). Vesper and Gartner state that the success of the entrepreneurship education programme is not only dependent on the quantity of available entrepreneurship courses, but also on their logic, coherency and efficacy. Furthermore, Lans and Gulikers (2010) and Pittaway and Cope (2007) mention that the application of suitable didactic methods, including assessments, is a necessary condition to stimulate the development of an entrepreneurial mind-set for students. In this respect, most authors agree that effective entrepreneurship education has characteristics of experiential learning (Corbett, 2005), action learning (Clarke et al., 2006), authentic learning (Nab et al., 2009) and opportunity-centred learning (Rae, 2003). Although the exact emphasis on these types of learning approaches might be slightly different, they have in common that entrepreneurial learning is characterized by learning by doing in a specific context – (Dana, 1987; NIRAS et al., 2008; Walter and Dohse, 2009). Various studies showed that entrepreneurship education is more successful when experiential hands-on approaches are employed (Solomon et al., 2002; Aronsson and Birch, 2004; Izquierdo, 2008; Lepoutre et al., 2010).

Outreach
The outreach dimension covers the mutual influence and networks between the entrepreneurship education programme of the university and the wider (business) environment. Linkages with the business environment provide students opportunities to gain practical experience with entrepreneurship and, in the end, to develop an entrepreneurial mind-set (NIRAS et al., 2008). Specific activities related to this dimension are the involvement of (1) external stakeholders and (2) alumni in the programme. Souitaris et al. (2007) and Pittaway and Cope (2007), among others, have shown the importance of stakeholder involvement. Stakeholders like local entrepreneurs and entrepreneurial employees, but also representatives of government and industry can facilitate the development of entrepreneurial competences by confronting students with real-life entrepreneurship (e.g., by offering opportunities for practical experience, guest lectures, business visits, etc.). Hynes and Richardson state that 'the added value of the linkages lies in the ability to provide technical support, business support and

skills development for both the student and the owner/manager' (Hynes and Richardson, 2007, p. 736). Furthermore, the knowledge of stakeholders like business people and entrepreneurs can be helpful to keep the education programme up to date (Rasmussen and Sørheim 2006).

A specific class of stakeholders are alumni of the university. Like other stakeholders, they can be helpful in the development of the entrepreneurial activities of universities (Standish-Kuon and Rice, 2002; NIRAS et al., 2008), for example, by providing guest lectures and internships (Matlay, 2011).

In addition to the involvement of external stakeholders and alumni in the education programme, activities for (3) community engagement and knowledge transfer to society should also be developed. These align the education programme with the dynamics of the wider environment of the university in general, and enhance the commercialization of research and technology by universities (Etzkowitz, 2003).

Development
The dimension of development concerns the evaluation of the entrepreneurship education programme in order to improve its quality and adapt it to the changing needs of students and stakeholders involved in the programme. By continuously improving the programme, it can better satisfy the needs and wishes of the actors involved (Vesper and Gartner, 1997; NIRAS et al., 2008). Specific activities related to this dimension are the (1) frequent evaluation of the programme with internal and external stakeholders and (2) the implementation of user-driven improvements of the programme.

The evaluation of the programme by students, staff and external stakeholders makes it possible to improve the education programme (Rossi et al., 2004). Whitely (1995) pointed at the importance of self-evaluation by lecturers for improvement of the education programme in the long run. Because students are the main users of the programme, they are also able to evaluate its performance. The combined information of students, staff and external stakeholders can be helpful to improve the programme.

In addition to the evaluation of the programme, (3) the investments in the human resources involved in entrepreneurship education can also improve its quality. Entrepreneurship education is different from regular education – experiential learning, multidisciplinarity and so on – and therefore needs lecturers who have specific skills for entrepreneurship education. Sorgman and Parkison (2008) state that lecturers starting with entrepreneurship education are often unprepared for the shift towards more experiential forms of learning, because most of them are originally mono-disciplinary educated. Therefore, training in project management skills and basic business knowledge is important for entrepreneurship education. According to Hytti and O'Gorman (2004), there is an emerging consensus that action-learning approaches are the starting point for entrepreneurship education. In action learning, students work independently and teachers concentrate on monitoring and evaluation. For this reason, teachers need to be trained in balancing teaching and coaching activities.

MATERIALS AND METHODS

In order to answer the research question, it is necessary to compare entrepreneurship education programmes and more specifically the activities in the best practice universities. First, we executed a literature review in order to identify and develop the relevant dimensions of entrepreneurship education programmes. Based on the report of the European Commission (NIRAS et al., 2008) and the literature review, we were able to identify three performance indicators and develop six dimensions of life science entrepreneurship education programmes: strategy, resources, institutional infrastructure, education, outreach and development (cf. §2). The assumption is that the performance of the best practice universities is a result of well-managed inputs with regard to these six dimensions of entrepreneurship education programmes.

In this chapter, we apply the benchmark method to identify best practice entrepreneurship education programmes in Europe, USA and Canada and analyse the activities they are engaged in. As a first step, we selected universities in the life sciences, which are indicated as best practices in the report of the European Commission (NIRAS et al., 2008) or are top ranked in the QS World University Rankings of Biological Sciences. Cornell University (16) and the University of Wisconsin Madison in the US (49) are among the top 50 life sciences universities in the world. The Ludwig Maximilians Universität München in Germany and the Wageningen University in the Netherlands rank between 51 and 100 of the life sciences universities. The other universities are Aarhus University in Denmark (101–150) and the University of Guelph (201–250). This sample is assumed to provide valuable insights into entrepreneurship education programmes because of their homogeneity in the type of research – agri-food sciences as a specific domain of the life sciences – and their heterogeneity in university culture and structure.

To measure the performance and the activities of these entrepreneurship education programmes, interviews were conducted with the head of the entrepreneurship education programme and, if possible, with a (senior) lecturer involved in entrepreneurship education. In order to prevent the tendency of respondents to provide answers that would give their programme the highest ranking, we communicated upfront that the results of this study would be presented anonymously.

Next, a secondary data analysis was executed. A content analysis of the mission statement and the strategic plan of the university was executed in order to assess the strategic importance of the different entrepreneurship education programmes at the university. The annual financial plans of the universities were consulted to calculate the third flow of funds. A content analysis of course manuals was executed to assess the didactic methods of entrepreneurship courses. Based on this analysis, we were also able to assess whether real-life examples of entrepreneurship are included in the programme.

Based on the primary and secondary data collection, we were able to measure the performance of the participating universities. Every performance indicator is measured by several aspects scored on a scale reaching from 1 (lowest score) to 5 (highest score) with all questions having equal weight. Subsequently, the average score on the indicator was calculated.

Based on the primary and secondary data collection, we were able to analyse the activities related to each dimension of the entrepreneurship education programme and to identify specific activities that were expected to lead to higher performance of entrepreneurship education programmes. However, what are more important for this chapter are the case descriptions of best practice universities and successful interventions to improve the entrepreneurship education programmes.

RESULTS

In this section the results of the benchmark study will be presented. Based on the performance of the participating universities, first the best practice entrepreneurship education programmes will be identified. Next, the activities will be presented for each dimension of the entrepreneurship education programme. Because of the low number of participating universities in this benchmark study and the focus on educational interventions for managers, we focus on the qualitative description of the activities the best practices are engaged in. Activities of the other education programmes will only be described if they correspond with the set of activities presented in section 2.

The Best Practice Entrepreneurship Education Programmes

In this section, we first present the overall scores of the entrepreneurship education programmes on the performance indicators (Table 3.1).

Table 3.1   Scores on performance

	Knowledge Transfer	Entrepr. Through Education	Entrepr. Through Practice	Performance
A2098	4	5	2	3.67
B1846	3.67	2	5	3.56
E8935	2.67	2	2	2.22
C0542	2.67	2	2	2.22
D8552	1.33	1	3	1.78
H0892	1.67	1	2.5	1.72

Subsequently, we explain and select the best practice education programmes.

Two entrepreneurship education programmes clearly outperform the other programmes on the performance indicator knowledge transfer: A2098 and B1846. Although both programmes score relatively high on all three measurements, the difference between high and mediocre performers on knowledge transfer – E8935 and C0542 – is mainly due to the amount of patents. B1846 scores relatively low on the number of peer-reviewed studies, which is explained by the strategic focus of this university on the education of students.

On the performance indicator entrepreneurial students through education, A2098 received the highest scores. In absolute and relative numbers, it outperforms the mediocre performers B1846, E8935 and C0542. On the performance indicator entrepreneurial students through practice, B1846 received the highest scores. All other education programmes scored low on the number of executive education attendants compared with B1846, while all programmes scored between 3 and 5 on the number of students participating in extra-curricular activities. This last measurement explains the difference between relatively low and mediocre performers on the performance indicator entrepreneurial students through practice.

Overall, two entrepreneurship education programmes clearly outperform the other programmes: A2098 and B1846. Both programmes have the highest scores on the performance indicator knowledge transfer. A2098 shows the highest score on entrepreneurial students through education and B1846 shows the highest score on entrepreneurial students through practice. These two programmes are selected as best practice education programmes in this benchmark study.

The Relation Between Performance and the Dimensions of Entrepreneurship Education Programmes

Based on a sample of 198 entrepreneurship education programmes, the NIRAS et al. report (2008) shows a solid positive correlation between the scores on the dimensions of education programmes and its overall performance. This positive correlation is partly supported by this benchmark study.

Best practice programme B1846 also received the highest scores on five out of six dimensions of entrepreneurship education programmes. Best practice programme A2098 received high scores on the institutional infrastructure (position 2), education (position 2) and outreach (position 2) dimensions. Nevertheless, the programme received also low scores on the strategy (position 5), resources (position 5) and development (position 4) dimensions. The same ambiguity holds for the lowest overall performer H0892, which scored relatively low on four out of six dimensions, but relatively high on the strategy (second position) and resources (third position) dimension.

Because of the low number of participating entrepreneurship education programmes in this benchmark study, we do not analyse the correlation between performance and the dimensions of entrepreneurship education programmes but concentrate on the activities the best practice education programmes are engaged in (cf. conclusions and recommendations).

The Relation Between Performance and the Dimensions of Entrepreneurship Education Programmes

In this section, the activities will be presented for each dimension of the entrepreneurship education programme.

Strategy

Although it is clear from literature that activities with regard to strategy stimulate the development of entrepreneurship education programmes (cf. §2), the participating universities in this benchmark study pay relatively little attention to this dimension of the education programme compared with the other dimensions. While best practice B1846 received the highest score on this dimension (Table 3.2), A2098 received the lowest score. This discrepancy (which also holds for cases in the NIRAS report; see NIRAS et al., 2008, p.95) is explained by the fact that entrepreneurship education is not given strategic priority at a corporate level at A2098, while various departments of the university are involved in the execution

Table 3.2   Scores on strategy

University	Goals	Policy	Embeddedness	Strategy
B1846	1.5	3.33	4	2.94
H0892	2	3.67	3	2.89
E8935	2	2.33	3	2.44
C0542	2.5	3.33	1.5	2.44
A2098	2.5	1	1.5	1.67
D8552	Missing	1.33	1	Missing

of entrepreneurship education and support extra-curricular activities like business competitions.

With regard to activities related to this dimension, entrepreneurship is not or only implicitly communicated in the mission statement and strategies or *goals* of most universities. Positive exceptions are found in the cases of A2098 and C0542. Several aspects such as the entrepreneurial identity of the university are, for instance, communicated in the strategic plan of A2098:

> Many words have been used to describe the nature of this institution as a whole: complex, creative, entrepreneurial, eminent, and engaged. . . . the tradition of public engagement and impact, along with faculty creativity, academic entrepreneurialism and international visibility are promising capabilities upon which to build. (From the strategic plan of the university)

Although A2098 and C0542 are positive exceptions compared with the other participating universities, the role of entrepreneurship is still quite implicitly formulated in the mission statement and strategy of these universities.

Because this benchmark study does not provide good examples of how to include entrepreneurship in the mission statement and strategic plan, we refer to a good example of a European high-tech university, which is not included in this benchmark study:

> The focus of *** is on coherent education, research and knowledge valorisation in the field of engineering, science and technology. . . . In the field of knowledge valorisation, *** is committed to ensure that its research results are translated into successful innovations and new companies. . . . *** encourages students and staff to be entrepreneurial. . . . *** offers both students and staff an international and academic, intellectually stimulating climate of study and work. This inspires broad personal development, societal and cultural engagement as well as an entrepreneurial outlook. . . . On its campus, *** encourages the location and cooperation of Higher Education institutes, research institutes and

(new) high-tech enterprises. (Quote from the mission statement in the strategic plan of the university)

These quotes provide clear examples of how various aspects of entrepreneurship education – fostering entrepreneurial attitudes among students and staff, the focus on knowledge transfer, the university as entrepreneurial university and so on – can be communicated in mission statements and strategic plans.

When we look at the indicator policies, B1846, H0892 and C0542 score relatively high because the strategy of the university is operationalized in entrepreneurship education plans for the various departments. In C0542, departments are relatively autonomous in making their own policies. This university has clearly written entrepreneurship education policy plans and 80–100 per cent of the departments have their own entrepreneurship policy plans.

With regard to the embeddedness of the education programme at different management levels within the university, B1846, H0892 and E8935 score relatively high. This is because the highest management levels of the university – rector, chancellor, board of directors – are strategically responsible for entrepreneurship education and/or high-level managers function as entrepreneurship champion within the university. An example is the dean of a department that provides entrepreneurship education at B1846, who intensively cooperates with the deans of other departments in order to promote the exchange of students between departments in general and with regard to entrepreneurship education in particular.

Resources
The results show clearly (Table 3.3) that most programmes score relatively well on this second dimension of entrepreneurship education and have at least sufficient resources available for maintaining and developing their education programme. Negative exceptions are again best

Table 3.3   Scores on resources

University	Allocation	Types of Resources	Self-generated Income	Resources
B1846	4	4	5	4.33
C0542	5	3.5	3	3.83
H0892	4	4.5	3	3.83
E8935	4.5	3.5	1	3
A2098	1.5	2	2	1.83
D8552	1	1.5	3	1.83

practice A2098 and D8552. The relative low score of A2098 can be explained by the fact that entrepreneurship education is not given strategic priority at the corporate level. The budget available is insufficient to realize the high ambitions of the people involved in the education programme, although sufficient funds are available to maintain the current programme.

With regard to activities related to this dimension, it becomes clear that various education programmes diversified their sources of income. Some programmes are mainly funded by institution and government funds (A2098, E8935, C0542). Although governmental funds are important for programmes that have just started, it is acknowledged that governmental funding often stops after the development of the education programme. This is the main reason for diversifying the sources of income, as one of the respondents explained:

> We were funded by governmental money but only till [the] summer of last year. . . . Now we have to make our own money with fundraising.

Some universities are already mainly funded by other benefactors (H0892, B1846), as becomes clear from the next quote:

> Bottom line: our grant from Kauffman for the five-year effort ending June 2012 is just under $3 million. We are also expecting to show an investment of $16–17 million in matching funding through donations, in-kind time and expenses and other programme funding contributions that all go toward the goal of creating a campus-wide culture open to entrepreneurial thinking and actions. All that is across the five-year period. This suggests on average the Kauffman grant has provided $600k per year while matching funds provide about $3 million per year. What I cannot answer is how big a percentage that is relative to the total entrepreneurship activity here on campus.

Furthermore, they receive a biannual budget from the state. In this way, B1846 diversified the sources of income that are available for different periods of time.

In order to diversify sources of funding, several examples of successful interventions to obtain multiple sources of income are found. At B1846 for instance, students and staff are free to choose between the technology transfer office (TTO) of the university or a private equivalent. Because the TTO has to compete with private organizations in a competitive market, they provide an incentive to attract their clients:

> [The TTO] is a stand-alone organization.. . . But it does have fee income from inventions and things arising from the university. . . . it also gives money back to the university. Every year it writes a check of 16 or 17 million US dollars back to the [university].

They [the TTO] try to create an incentive for our faculty staff and students to work with them because that money comes back to the university. Some of it goes back to the department you work in, some to the school or college you work for and the rest goes to [the] campus. And the campus used some of that money to invest in entrepreneurship . . . on a periodic basis.

The education programme at H0892 also has multiple sources of income. The majority of their budget is based on five-year gift agreements with benefactors, which are long-term agreements. Other sources of income are continuously received.

Self-generating income activities are also possible ways to diversify the sources of funding. Some programmes ask a fee for seminars and workshops they organize (B1846, C0542, H0892, D8552). An example is the housing fee B1846 raises for students who participate in the entrepreneurship residential community. Other programmes provide services and consultancy (B1846, C0542) or raise donations from companies and alumni (B1846, H0892, D8552, A2098). University A2098 shows that a programme can be financed by resources obtained from alumni with the absence of a strategic foundation. The alumni play an essential role in this as the top-down support from the university board is not there.

Respondents say that alumni organizations play an essential role in fundraising and that close cooperation between the alumni organizations and university funds are also important to receive endowments from alumni. Best practice B1846, for instance, involves alumni in entrepreneurship courses as guest lecturers or facilitators and attracts large amounts of money from alumni to fund individual entrepreneurship education projects.

Institutional infrastructure
The institutional infrastructure dimension involves the facilities provided by the university such as incubators and TTOs, the research done by the institute and the multidisciplinarity of the programme. The best practice education programmes B1846 and A2098 outperform the mediocre performers E8935 and H0892 on this third dimension of entrepreneurship education (Table 3.4).

With regard to the activities related to this dimension, it becomes clear that most universities provide incubator facilities and technology transfer offices. B1846, for instance, developed an entrepreneurial residential learning community. Students from different study programmes but with entrepreneurial intentions live together here and are taught how to put their ideas into action. Furthermore, B1846 provides a student business incubator that offers office space, materials and business training services. The student incubator facilitates hands-on learning in a supportive environment in order to enable students to start their own company. Findings indicate

Table 3.4   Scores on institutional infrastructure

University	Facilities	Research	Multidisciplinarity	Institutional Infrastructure
B1846	3	3.5	5	3.83
A2098	3	2.5	3	2.83
E8935	3	1.5	2.67	2.39
H0892	3	1	3	2.33
D8552	3	1	1.67	1.89
C0542	1	2	2.33	1.78

that facilities such as an entrepreneurship café, a meeting place for entrepreneurial students or any building where students, teachers and business people can meet are essential for entrepreneurship education. Also, E8935, D8552 and H0892 provide a meeting place for students, which enhances the exchange of entrepreneurial ideas and nurtures entrepreneurship.

With regard to research, only A2098 has a specific entrepreneurship chair group. This suggests that entrepreneurship is more accepted here as an academic discipline than in the other institutions. This is also confirmed by their highest score on the number of peer-reviewed studies. Efforts by champions of entrepreneurship and alumni have led to great results like this. Having a chair group and that it also generates income is essential to becoming more embedded in a university where there is little support by the university board. The other best practice education programme (B1846) has no entrepreneurship chair group, although many professors are involved in entrepreneurship education. Furthermore, there seems to be no strict relation between the number of professors involved in the education programme and the number of peer-reviewed publications. B1846, for instance, scores relatively low on publications, which suggests that their education programme mainly focuses on educating students. At E8935, D8552 and C0542, it seems to be the other way around.

With regard to the multidisciplinarity of the education programme, it becomes clear that many more disciplines are involved in entrepreneurship education in the best practice education programmes. At B1846 and A2098, multiple disciplines like management, law, engineering, agriculture and life sciences are involved in the execution of the education programme for students with various backgrounds/disciplines. Furthermore, at B1846 multiple departments are also involved in the development of new elements of the education programme. Another example is C0542, where the law, management and education and competencies departments join forces to develop new entrepreneurship courses.

Table 3.5   Scores on education

University	Education Scope	Education Set-up	Education
B1846	3.5	3.8	3.65
A2098	3	2.2	2.6
C0542	2	2.9	2.45
D8552	1	3.2	2.1
H0892	1	3.2	2.1
E8935	1.5	2.2	1.85

Education

The fourth dimension of entrepreneurship education involves the scope and the educational set-up of the education programme (Table 3.5). The best practice education programmes B1846 and A2098 outperform the mediocre performer C0542 on this fourth.

With regard to the education set-up, all education programmes provide individual courses in entrepreneurship and most programmes also provide a BSc minor in entrepreneurship. Most education programmes focus entirely on undergraduate students. Only B1846 provides an MSc minor in entrepreneurship. B1846 and C0542 provide also a PhD trajectory in entrepreneurship.

With regard to the education set-up, the education programmes show an interesting variety in experimental education methods and ways of confronting students with real-life entrepreneurship problems. Based on a content analysis of the course syllabi, at least 28 per cent of the entrepreneurship courses are provided by guest lectures. An example is D8552:

> We think it is important that students get to know the people who work in their field of education and to hear from them how they do and how exciting it is. . . . We also have two events here. We have lecture series called 'leading entrepreneurs' where we invite successful entrepreneurs to come to the university to speak to the students, and also an event called 'idea jamming' where students talk about new ideas and a speaker holds a very short speech. That is very important to us. We always invite our students to the lectures.

All education programmes seem to acknowledge the importance of practical and experimental didactic methods for entrepreneurship education. The champions of entrepreneurship education at A2098 fully believe in the educational approach to confront students with real-life entrepreneurial problems, because it increases their interest and understanding of the theory too; they become aware that they need certain knowledge in order to deal with complex tasks and get excited when they experience the relevance of entrepreneurship education for their lives, whether they want to start their own business or not. The programme not only focuses on entrepreneurial skills but more importantly on the way students can add value and create their own competitive advantage. In this respect, entrepreneurship education helps them to get focus in their career. This idea is realized without a university-wide strategy, but by champions of entrepreneurship education who are convinced of this approach.

Another example is the education programme of H0892, which confronts students with real-life entrepreneurship in an interesting way. Entrepreneurship courses have to be understood as business opportunities and every class as a business meeting. From this perspective, wearing a business outfit is highly appreciated and missing a meeting is unacceptable. Furthermore, students have to sign a team contract that contains the expectations, policies, procedures, and so forth. In this way, the university confronts students with real-life entrepreneurship.

Outreach
The fifth dimension of entrepreneurship education involves the role of the university in the wider (business) environment. In general, the education programmes seem to experience few problems in creating and maintaining a network of external stakeholders. The best practice education programmes B1846 and A2098 outperform the mediocre performer C0542 on this fifth dimension of entrepreneurship education (Table 3.6).

With regard to the involvement of external stakeholders, B1846 and C0542 have clear links with governmental organizations, foundations and investors, entrepreneurs and companies. At C0542, for instance, the patent office (government) provides guest lectures for students and representatives of science parks provide coaching for postgraduates who want to start a new venture. The links with external stakeholders provide a 'combination of money, knowledge and expertise' to the education programme. A2098 has relatively few links with external stakeholders, because they are

Table 3.6   Scores on outreach

University	External Stakeholders	Community	Alumni	Outreach
B1846	4.33	4.75	2.5	3.86
A2098	2	3.5	5	3.5
C0542	4	3	3	3.33
H0892	4	2	3	3
D8552	3.33	2.25	1.5	2.36
E8935	2.33	2.75	2	2.36

situated in an isolated location without 'centres of commercialization like Boston or Palo Alto' in the neighbourhood. However, this is not a problem according to this university, because entrepreneurial students are often involved in entrepreneurial activities in later stages in their career.

With regard to alumni, A2098 outperforms the mediocre performers C0542 and H0892. As the university board is less involved in entrepreneurship education, they depend more on the alumni and champions of entrepreneurship education who are not in the highest management levels of the university. A2098 has 250 alumni involved in their entrepreneurship education programme, which is many more than the other programmes:

> There is a very extensive alumni affairs and development office that follows all kind of alumni [this is done by the university]. We [the Centre of Entrepreneurship] work on keeping track of the number of ventures started. . . . Other reasons [to involve alumni] would be for raising funds. . . . A large percentage of the funding at A2098 comes from alumni, both from endowments . . . and annual giving.

Just like A2098, C0542 and H0892 also keep contact with alumni, keep track of their career and the number of ventures they started.

Alumni are not only useful for raising funds but they are also useful for the development of entrepreneurship activities and for providing linkages with the business environment. Furthermore, they can act as guest lecturers and can offer positions for practical experience. One can choose to outsource alumni management to an external organization. The results indicate that both options can work out well under the condition that it receives a high priority within the university.

With regard to knowledge transfer, B1846 and A2098 clearly outperform the other programmes with regard to the number of patents and the third flow of funding. B1846 has the highest number of patents (429 according to the WIPO database) while most other universities have between 26 and 65. Their application for patents is outsourced to a TTO. The TTO can take up some tasks often carried out by a centre of entrepreneurship and is sometimes involved in the development of the stakeholder network, advisory services for entrepreneurs and so on. Besides the best practice universities, E8935 and C0542 also receive high scores on the percentage of third flow of funding (between 32.5 per cent and 37.5 per cent of the total turnover of the university). A third flow of funding is mainly contract research and is not necessary related to entrepreneurship.

Development

The sixth dimension of entrepreneurship education concerns the evaluation of the education programme in order to improve its quality and adapt

Table 3.7   Scores on development

University	User-driven Improvement	Evaluation	Human Resources	Development
C0542	5	5	2	4
B1846	2	5	2.33	3.11
D8552	2	3	Missing	2.5
A2098	2	3	2	2.33
H0892	2	3	2	2.33
E8935	2	2	1.33	1.78

it to the changing needs of students and stakeholders (Table 3.7). The best practice education programme B1846 outperforms the other education programmes, just as C0542 does. Best practice A2098 shows that it is hard to manage the development dimension without a strategic foundation, as development involves a long-term view and the assessment of goals and strategies. With the lack of a strategic focus on entrepreneurship, this can only be done at executive level and by initiatives of champions of entrepreneurship education.

With regard to the evaluation of the programme, most education programmes apply self-evaluation by the teacher, and student evaluations as a method for user-driven improvements. In the case of C0542, peer reviews and executive staff evaluations are also applied. Furthermore, the effect of the education programme on students' careers and stakeholders' needs are evaluated. Formal and informal stakeholder meetings are organized to evaluate whether stakeholder needs are met.

With regard to the investment in human resources, we may conclude that this aspect doesn't receive priority. One of the best practice education programmes offers teachers training in order to become an entrepreneurship teacher. Some programmes encourage entrepreneurship education by providing grants and/or fellowships to develop new initiatives. Other programmes focus more on recognition for achievements in entrepreneurship education, for instance an award for entrepreneurship teachers.

CONCLUSIONS AND RECOMMENDATIONS

In this benchmark study, we identified and further developed six dimensions for entrepreneurship education programmes at life science universities and provided specific managerial interventions for each dimension. In this section, we summarize these interventions to start with or improve the entrepreneurship education programmes of life science universities and discuss some directions for future research.

With regard to the dimension strategy, we can conclude that the adjustments of the mission and strategy of the university and the (operational) policies arising from these goals can be seen as important interventions to improve the entrepreneurship education programme. Nevertheless, the example of best practice A2098 suggests that the implementation of entrepreneurship education is possible without its implementation at a strategic level. Instead of a clear strategic focus, the programme is more dependent on efforts by champions of entrepreneurship education and alumni. They seize opportunities for the further development of the programme and manage self-generating income activities, while the university management primarily plays a coordinating role. The involvement of champions and alumni enabled the further development of the education programme, independent from a sound strategic foundation.

The example of A2098 shows, however, that future research is needed on the relation between the performance of the education programme and the implementation at the strategic level. There are also other reasons to question the necessity of implementation of the education programme at the strategic level. There are, for instance, examples of universities who have chosen to remove the word 'entrepreneurship' from the mission statement because of the negative or unscientific connotations of the term. On the other hand, the literature review made clear that the adjustment of missions and strategic plans can function as a road map for implementing successful entrepreneurship education programmes. Several aspects of entrepreneurship education can be included in the mission statement or strategy of the university, like the entrepreneurial identity of the university itself, the importance of enhancing the entrepreneurial attitude of students and staff, the importance of knowledge transfer towards society, knowledge valorization, the encouragement of public–private partnerships, the development of science parks in the environment of the campus and so on. B1846 is a clear example of a high-performing education programme that is operationalized in clearly written entrepreneurship education policy plans that are implemented in the various departments of the university. Furthermore, it is recommended that the highest management levels of the university should be strategically responsible for the programme and that entrepreneurship champions are involved in the development and dissemination of the programme.

With regard to the dimension resources, it is clear that sufficient resources should be available to develop and maintain the entrepreneurship education programme. It is recommended that universities who want to start with or improve their programme should not only provide sufficient resources for its development, but also pay attention to the diversification of the sources of income. The best practice education programmes provide clear examples of how resources can be diversified, for instance by attracting grants from benefactors other than government funds, by attracting funding from organizations that are dependent on the entrepreneurship education programme like TTOs, by self-generating income activities like seminars, workshops, consultancy, and so forth. With regard to private funding by companies and alumni, it should be taken into account that these interventions are only in a limited way applicable in the European context, mainly due to differences in tax systems.

With regard to the dimensions institutional infrastructure, education, outreach and development, we can conclude that the best practice education programmes received the highest scores on these dimensions. Universities in the life sciences who want to start or improve their entrepreneurship education programme should therefore implement educational interventions related to these four dimensions.

With regard to infrastructural facilities, one can think of (student) incubator facilities, TTOs, centres of entrepreneurship and a meeting place for students. In the case that universities have a strategic focus on research, one can think of an entrepreneurship chair group. Such a chair group is not necessary in the case of universities with a clear focus on education, although the facilitation of research is highly recommended; it generates state of the art knowledge, which is useful to improve teachers' and students' knowledge on entrepreneurship in general and the education programme in particular. With regard to the multidisciplinarity of the education programme, it is recommended that institutional barriers to interdisciplinary and inter-departmental cooperation should be minimized and multidisciplinary cooperation should be encouraged. With regard to education, it is recommended that courses and minors at BSc *and* MSc Level are developed. Universities with a clear strategic focus on research could also implement PhD trajectories in entrepreneurship.

Furthermore, the use of experimental didactic methods for entrepreneurship education and confronting students with real-life entrepreneurial problems are recommended. In entrepreneurship education, multidisciplinary groups of students should work on interdisciplinary assignments. This means that students from different disciplines should work together, each with their specific background, to reach a common goal. This creates serious challenges in Higher Education. While in education in general many factors influence the quality of teaching, the teacher has a crucial role in entrepreneurship education. European research suggests, for instance, that entrepreneurship education requires other roles and didactics of teachers (Nab et al., 2010). However, most teachers in Higher Education have a disciplinary background (e.g., biology, chemistry) with little prior knowledge in educational science and often no entrepreneurial hands-on experience. Both teachers and students experience boundary crossing (Akkerman and Bakker, 2011); they are confronted with disciplines that are not part of their specialization and therefore less familiar to them. Offering a boundary object, like training, will enable teachers to educate in entrepreneurship education as they learn to build bridges between their specialization, entrepreneurship education and the real-life entrepreneurial world. Surveys show that European graduates have a poor opinion of Higher Education as a contributor to their entrepreneurial skills (Allen and van der Velden, 2009) and research indicates that teachers are considered to be a weak link in effectively introducing entrepreneurship education (McCoshan et al., 2010). However, until now little is known about the roles and competencies of teachers in entrepreneurship education. More research in this field is clearly needed.

With regard to outreach, building a network with external stakeholders like governmental organizations, investors and entrepreneurs is recommended. They can provide funding, knowledge and expertise, which is useful for entrepreneurship education. The same holds for alumni, who facilitate knowledge transfer in general and can offer guest lectures and practical experience in particular.

With regard to development, implementing methods for user-driven improvements of the education programme is recommended, like self-evaluations by the teacher, student evaluations, executive staff evaluations and peer reviews. This last form of evaluation also enhances the exchange of ideas, methods and approaches among teachers. Furthermore, evaluating the effect of the education programme on students' careers and stakeholders' needs, for instance by formal and informal stakeholder meetings, is also recommended. As stated, because most teachers are originally mono-disciplinary educated and the interdisciplinary character of entrepreneurship education involves experimental didactic methods, it is highly recommended to invest in human resources, for instance by attracting teachers with business experience or by providing specific training in business skills and entrepreneurial learning methods.

With these recommendations for educational interventions to start up or improve entrepreneurship education programmes, we do not imply that all interventions can be applied one by one on other universities. Rather, the best practices show actual activities that may inspire managers of other life science universities to develop and implement comparable interventions, in which the specific culture, institutional structure and strategic focus of the university is taken into account.

REFERENCES

Akkerman, S. and A. Bakker (2011), 'Boundary crossing and boundary objects', *Review of Educational Research*, **81**(2), 132–69.

Allen, J. and R. van der Velden (2009), *Competencies and Early Labour Market Careers of Higher Education Graduates*, Ljubljana, Slovenia: University of Ljubljana, Faculty of Social Sciences.

Arenius, P. and D.D. Clercq (2005), 'A network-based approach on opportunity recognition', *Small Business Economics*, **24**(3), 249–65.

Aronsson, M. & D. Birch (2004), 'Education matters: But does entrepreneurship education? An interview with David Birch', *Academy of Management Learning & Education*, **3**(3), 289–92.

Baron, R.A. and M.D. Ensley (2006), 'Opportunity recognition as the detection of meaningful patterns: Evidence from comparisons of novice and experienced entrepreneurs', *Management Science*, **52**(9), 1331–44.

Brown, J.S., A. Collins and P. Duguid (1989), 'Situated cognition and the culture of learning', *Educational Researcher*, **18**(1), 32–42.

Clark, B.R. (1998), *Creating Entrepreneurial Universities: Organizational Pathways of Transformation. Issues in Higher Education*, New York: Elsevier.

Clarke, J., R. Thorpe, L. Anderson and J. Gold (2006), 'It's all action, it's all learning: Action learning in SMEs', *Journal of European Industrial Training*, **30**(6), 441–55.

Corbett, A.C. (2005), 'Experiential learning within the process of opportunity identification and exploitation', *Entrepreneurship Theory and Practice*, **29**(4), 473–91.

Dana, L.P. (1987), 'Towards a skills model for entrepreneurs', *Journal of Small Business and Entrepreneurship*, **5**(1), 27–31.

Etzkowitz, H. (2003), 'Research groups as "quasi firms": The invention of the entrepreneurial university', *Research Policy*, **32**(1), 109–21.

Fayolle, A., B. Gailly and N. Lassas-Clerc (2006), 'Assessing the impact of entrepreneurship education programmes: A new methodology', *Journal of European Industrial Training*, **30**(9), 701–20.

FORA (2004), *Entrepreneurship Education at Universities – a Benchmark Study*, Background Report for the Entrepreneurship Index 2004.

Freytag, P. V. and S. Hollensen (2001), 'The process of benchmarking, benchlearning and benchaction', *The TQM magazine*, **13**(1), 25–34.

Gaglio, C.M. and J.A. Katz (2001), The psychological basis of opportunity identification: Entrepreneurial alertness', *Small Business Economics*, **16**(2), 95–111.

Garavan, T.N. and B. O'Cinneide (1994), 'Entrepreneurship education and training programmes: A review and evaluation – Part 1', *Journal of European Industrial Training*, **18**(8), 3–12.

Guerrero, M. (2008), 'The creation and development of entrepreneurial universities in Spain. An institutional approach', PhD thesis, Autonomous University of Barcelona.

Hoffmann, A., N.M. Vibholt, M. Larsen and M. Lindholt Moffet (2008), 'Benchmarking entrepreneurship education across US, Canadian and Danish universities', in J.G. Potter (ed.), *Entrepreneurship and Higher Education*, Paris: OECD, pp. 139–64).

Hynes, B. (1996), 'Entrepreneurship education and training – introducing entrepreneurship into non-business disciplines', *Journal of European Industrial Training*, **20**(8), 10–17.

Hynes, B. and I. Richardson (2007), 'Entrepreneurship education: A mechanism for engaging and exchanging with the small business sector', *Education and Training*, **49**(8/9), 732–44.

Hytti, U. and C. O'Gorman (2004), 'What is "enterprise education"? An analysis of the objectives and methods of enterprise education programmes in four European countries', *Education+ Training*, 46(1), 11–23.

Izquierdo, E.E. (2008), 'Impact assessment of an educational intervention based on the constructivist paradigm on the development of entrepreneurial competencies in university students', unpublished dissertation, Ghent: Ghent University.

Jackson, N. and H. Lund (2000), *Benchmarking for Higher Education*, Florence: Taylor & Francis.

Kirby, D.A., M. Guerrero and D. Urbano (2011), 'Making universities more entrepreneurial: Development of a model', *Canadian Journal of Administrative Sciences*, **28**(3), 302–16.

Klofsten, M. (2000), 'Training entrepreneurship at universities: A Swedish case', *Journal of European Industrial Training*, **24**(6), 337–44.

Kolvereid, L. and E. Isaksen (2006), 'New business start-up and subsequent entry into self-employment', *Journal of Business Venturing*, **21**(6), 866–85.

Kuratko, D.F. (2005), 'The emergence of entrepreneurship education: Development, trends, and challenges', *Entrepreneurship Theory and Practice*, **29**(5), 577–98.

Lans, T. and J. Gulikers (2010), 'Assessing entrepreneurial competence in education and training', in A. Fayolle (ed.), *Handbook of Research in Entrepreneurship Education*, Vol. 3, Cheltenham, UK and Northampton, MA, USA: Edward Elgar.

Lepoutre, J., W. van den Berghe, O. Tilleuil and H. Crijns (2010), 'A new approach to testing the effects of entrepreneurship education among secondary school pupils', Vlerick Leuven Gent Management School Working Paper Series.

Martínez, A.C., J. Levie, D.J. Kelley, R.J. T. Sæmundsson and Schøtt (2010), *Global Entrepreneurship Monitor Special Report*.

Matlay, H. (2011), 'The influence of stakeholders on developing enterprising graduates in UK HEIs', *International Journal of Entrepreneurial Behaviour & Research*, **17**(2), 166–82.

McCoshan, A. et al. (2010), *Towards Greater Cooperation and Coherence in Entrepreneurship Education: Report and Evaluation of the Pilot Action High Level Reflection Panels on Entrepreneurship Education Initiated by DG Enterprise and Industry and DG Education and Culture*.

McMullan, W. and W.A. Long (1987), 'Entrepreneurship education in the nineties', *Journal of Business Venturing*, **2**(3), 261–75.

Menzies, T.V. (1998), 'An exploratory study of university entrepreneurship centres in Canada: A first step in model building', *Journal of Small Business and Entrepreneurship*, **15**(3), 15–38.

Mortimer, K. (1995), 'Enterprise in Higher Education: Reflections from the chair', *Education + Training*, **37**(9), 20–24.

Nab, J., A. Pilot, S. Brinkkemper and H.T. Berge (2009), 'Authentic competence-based learning in university education in entrepreneurship', *International Journal of Entrepreneurship and Small Business*, **9**(1), 20–35.

NIRAS, FORA, ECON Pöyry (2008), *Survey of Entrepreneurship in Higher Education in Europe*, European Commission, Directorate-General for Enterprise and Industry.

Pittaway, L. and J. Cope (2007), 'Entrepreneurship education', *International Small Business Journal*, 25(5), 479–510.

Potter, J.G. (2008), *Entrepreneurship and Higher Education: Future Policy Directions*, Paris: OECD.

Rae, D. (2003), 'Opportunity centred learning: an innovation in enterprise education?' *Education + Training*, **45**(8–9), 542–9.

Rae, D. (2006), 'Entrepreneurial learning: A conceptual framework for technology-based enterprise', *Technology Analysis and Strategic Management*, **18**(1), 39–56.

Rasmussen, E.A. and R. Sørheim (2006), 'Action-based entrepreneurship education', *Technovation*, **2**(26), 185–94.

Rossi, P.H., M.W. Lipsey and H.E. Freeman (2004), *Evaluation: A Systematic Approach*, London: Sage.

Shane, S. and S. Venkataraman (2000), 'The promise of entrepreneurship as a field of research', *Academy of Management Review*, **25**(1), 217–26.

Siegel, D.S. and P.H. Phan (2004), 'Analyzing the effectiveness of university technology transfer: Implications for entrepreneurship education', in G. Libecap (ed.), *University Entrepreneurship and Technology Transfer: Process, Design, and Intellectual Property*, Oxford: JAI Press, pp. 1–38.

Solomon, G.T., S. Duffy and A. Tarabishy (2002), *The State of Entrepreneurship Education in the United States: A Nationwide Survey and Analysis.*

Sorgman, M. and K. Parkison (2008), 'The future is now: Preparing K-12 teachers and students for an entrepreneurial society', *Journal of Entrepreneurship Education*, **11**, 75–86.

Sotirakou, T. (2004), 'Coping with conflict within the entrepreneurial university: Threat or challenge for heads of departments in the UK Higher Education context', *International Review of Administrative Sciences*, **70**(2), 345–72.

Souitaris, V., S. Zerbinati and A. Al-Laham (2007), 'Do entrepreneurship programmes raise entrepreneurial intention of science and engineering students? The effect of learning, inspiration and resources', *Journal of Business Venturing*, **22**(4), 566–91.

Sporn, B. (2001), 'Building adaptive universities: Emerging organisational forms based on experiences of European and US universities', *Tertiary Education and Management*, **7**(2), 121–34.

Standish-Kuon, T. and M.P. Rice (2002), 'Introducing engineering and science students to entrepreneurship: Models and influential factors at six American universities', *Journal of Engineering Education*, **91**(1), 33–9.

Vesper, K.H. and W.B. Gartner (1997), 'Measuring progress in entrepreneurship education', *Journal of Business Venturing*, **12**(5), 403–21.

Walter, S.G., D. Dohse and U.K.I. f. Weltwirtschaft (2009), *The Interplay Between Entrepreneurship Education and Regional Knowledge Potential in Forming Entrepreneurial Intentions*, Institute for the World Economy.

Whiteley, T. (1995), 'Enterprise in Higher Education – an overview from the Department for Education and Employment', *Education + Training*, **37**(9), 4–8.

Wiese, N.M. and D.J. Sherman (2011), 'Integrating marketing and environmental studies through an interdisciplinary, experiential, service-learning approach', *Journal of Marketing Education*, **33**(1), 41–56.

Williams, G. (1995), 'The "Marketization" of Higher Education: Reforms and potential reforms in Higher Education finance' in D.D. Dill and B. Sporn (eds), *Emerging Patterns of Social Demand and University Reform: Through a Glass Darkly*, Oxford: Pergamon Press.

Wilson, K. (2008), 'Entrepreneurship education in Europe', in J.G. Potter (ed.), *Entrepreneurship and Higher Education*, Paris: OECD, pp. 119–38.

4. Entrepreneurship in Finland, Sweden and Norway: transferability of entrepreneurship educational programmes

*Bjørn Willy Åmo**

INTRODUCTION

This chapter compares conditions for and manifestations of entrepreneurship in Finland, Sweden and Norway. It does so as educational programmes and syllabuses are often transferred between countries and implemented without a theoretically based framework for considerations regarding local adjustments. This chapter then discusses the need for such adjustments and proposes a framework for local adjustments. The chapter presents an outline of antecedent, process and output when discussing conditions and perceptions leading to entrepreneurial behaviour. The chapter utilizes data from the Global Entrepreneurship Monitor research programme in order to compare the conditions the potential entrepreneur faces, the actions of entrepreneurs and the outcome of these entrepreneurial actions. The chapter then discusses how entrepreneurship programmes at university level have to be adjusted to the different settings for entrepreneurship in the local countries as the entrepreneurs experience it to be, and the entrepreneurs' corresponding entrepreneurial actions.

Entrepreneurship is considered to be an important mechanism for economic development through employment, innovation and welfare effect (Schumpeter, 1934; Acs and Audretsch, 1988). This understanding has led to a growing appreciation of the relevance of entrepreneurship education as a tool to gain such benefits (Fayolle and Kyrö, 2008). Higher Education Institutions have a responsibility for providing necessary competence for people wanting to develop their own business ideas into a successful enterprise or wanting to be able to help others develop and craft ideas into a viable business. The purpose of an entrepreneurship programme in universities should be to contribute to the development of the students' ability to discover/identify business opportunities and their ability to exploit these opportunities (Landström, 2000). In the search for educational programmes serving the students' need for entrepreneurship skills and the societies' need for entrepreneurs, universities look for best practice in entrepreneurship education at other universities in order to copy these practices.

According to Klyver and Bager (2012) some precautions have to be taken when trying to copy best practice, as there always has to be local adjustments when adopting innovations. The right phrase is translation of innovation instead of transfer of best practice. Likewise, best practice for some implies perfection, or at least being as close to perfection as possible. In the real world there is always room for improvements even for practice that works, even for practice that works well. Instead of transfer of best practice, what often happens is an effort to translate good practice. This chapter addresses how to translate good practice within entrepreneurship education.

The presumption of translating good practice is that what works for one is working for the other. It is well known in innovation research that there is always a bit invention in the adoption of innovations (Rogers, 1995). An innovation has to be adjusted to the local situation in order to be successful, and the more insightfully this adjustment is made, the better results the adoption delivers. When an innovation, such as an educational programme in entrepreneurship, is to be copied by an institution, some adjustments have to be made. The adjustments needed depend on the purpose of the adoption, the complexity of the innovation, the complexity of the adopting organization and how the environment differs for the copied and the copying institution.

This chapter addresses the need for adjustments in educational programmes regarding entrepreneurship. The chapter investigates the conditions for entrepreneurship in Finland, Sweden and Norway. It also reveals differences between the countries in entrepreneurship activity and their corresponding entrepreneurial results. The chapter links to current research streams when it discusses how these differences influence the need for entrepreneurship education and how this entrepreneurship education should be shaped to fit the unique challenges the three countries face (Hytti, 2008).

The study presents an antecedent, process and output outline when discussing conditions and perceptions leading to entrepreneurial behaviour. Antecedents consist of the environment as the entrepreneur faces it, the process represents the tools that the government has in hand and how it utilizes it and the outcome is the entrepreneurial result. The discussion in this chapter links to governmental policies and the business context that are found to relate to entrepreneurial behaviour. The overall outcome of entrepreneurship education is capable entrepreneurs – the skilled business act, which could be manifested in several ways: either as business start-up, as business renewal or as support for people who act entrepreneurially. Entrepreneurship is required for its ability to create jobs for people, providing them with salaries. The population in general may want entrepreneurship because it provides them with new products and services to make life easier. The government may want entrepreneurship and innovation as it strengthens industry, which secures its tax revenues and provides the inhabitants in that area with access to needed jobs, products and services.

The chapter is organized as follows: the theoretical perspectives discuss how entrepreneurship is defined, how people act when they are entrepreneurial and it presents the Global Entrepreneurship Monitor (GEM) model of entrepreneurship along with a description of the GEM project. This is then followed by a method section discussing the data describing the three countries regarding entrepreneurship. The findings present a comparison of the entrepreneurial conditions, the actions and their results. The conclusion section argues why and how these factors influence how entrepreneurship education programmes could be translated from one university to another.

THEORETICAL PERSPECTIVES

The economic progress of northernmost Europe is dependent on the development of entrepreneurship and innovativeness in the region. Its culture, its resources and industries based on these resources enable competitive businesses as far as the people in the region have competences and capabilities to utilize these possibilities. It is a stated goal that such local competences and capabilities should be strengthened (Nordland Fylkeskommune, 2005, 2006). To respond to this challenge, entrepreneurship education in the northern regions needs new ideas (Kunnskapsdepartementet, 2006). The present education at universities in entrepreneurship is matured and fully grown (Katz, 2008), but still results are falling (Kolvereid and Åmo, 2007). This might be due to the continuing globalization of the economy and the rising number of competent competitors providing entrepreneurship education or training. In order to take a new lead, local universities need to rearrange and rethink entrepreneurship education. Many universities then should engage in efforts to learn from best practices in order to meet this challenge.

Entrepreneurship is often defined as an individual acting upon an opportunity in order to create a benefit. Entrepreneurship education is then the processes that aim to enable an individual to assimilate and develop knowledge, skills, values and an understanding that allows a broader range of problems to be addressed (Hynes, 1996). Business opportunities have to be perceived before one can act upon them. There is a discussion in the entrepreneurship literature regarding whether business opportunities are created or discovered. Even so, the business opportunity exists in the nexus between the individual and the environment (Shane and Venkataraman, 2000). Research evidences that different institutional structures influence entrepreneurship differently across countries (Spencer and Gómez, 2004). Structuration theory shows how cues from the environment of the entrepreneurial action influence the actors. Sarason et al. (2006) offer structuration theory as a lens to comprehend the nexus of opportunities and individuals. Structuration theory puts forward that the actor and the social system co-evolve in an environment where social structures both constrain and enable entrepreneurial activity (Giddens, 1976, 1979). The actor is viewed as a reflexive agent engaging in purposeful action. In structuration theory, the agent is viewed as having the ability to choose whether or not to intervene in the world, and the agent usually has a full range of resources in hand to pursue his or her goal. Structuration theory has led to considerations concerning how cues from the environment may influence the entrepreneur's action and how he or she wants to represent these actions. Furthermore, the entrepreneur with his or her human capital is both enabled and constrained by the socio-economic context, as the structural properties of a social system consists of the habitual arrangements and the means that guide people's everyday life (Dowling, 2005). This implies that entrepreneurship education has to fit into the cultural and industry context (Hytti, 2008).

Such a fit is not necessarily always present. Klyver and Bager (2012) refer to neo-institutional theory when they discuss how entrepreneurship policy recommendations emerge and develop. Neo-institutional theory discusses three mechanisms that explain why ideas as policy recommendations within entrepreneurship and entrepreneurship education are similar also in countries that differ significantly. DiMaggio and Powell (1983) label these forces as coercive, mimetic and normative isomorphism. Coercive forces stem from formal and informal pressure to act in a given way, mimetic isomorphism stems from a standardized response to uncertainty rooted in shared understandings, while normative isomorphism is often associated with normative rules shared and developed among members of a profession. Klyver and Bager (2012) argue that policy recommendations regarding entrepreneurship are similar in Denmark and in Australia even if the conditions for entrepreneurship differ significantly in these two countries. They show how coercive, mimetic and normative isomorphism forces could lead to a danger of reproducing and imitating initiatives across nations that inconstantly fit with the local context.

The Global Entrepreneurship Monitor research programme describes the conditions for entrepreneurship, the entrepreneurial processes and the entrepreneurial results in different countries. GEM is a research project that started in 1999 with ten participating countries, including Finland. Sweden and Norway joined the GEM project in 2000. Throughout the GEM project's duration more than 60 countries have engaged in it. The GEM project responds to a significant gap in the international entrepreneurship research by engaging in yearly in-depth inquiries into the dynamics leading to entrepreneurial activity. The main objectives of GEM is to create an annual assessment of (1) the level and nature of entrepreneurial activity across countries, (2) the factors within countries that give rise to systematic differences in entrepreneurship rates, and (3) national outcomes of entrepreneurship (De Clercq and Crijns, 2008). The Global Entrepreneurship Monitor defines entrepreneurship as 'Any attempt to create a new business enterprise or to expand an existing business by an individual, a team of individuals, or an established business' (Zacharis et al., 2000, p. 5).

Entrepreneurship is a socioeconomic phenomenon. The Global Entrepreneurship Monitor model (Bosma et al., 2008) links the individual's perception of the opportunity, the conditions for entrepreneurship as provided by the societal structures, and the established business structure with the entrepreneurial action. At the individual level, people act upon cues from the environment as they perceive these to be (Ajzen, 1991). Furthermore, Ajzen (ibid.) models that the individual takes into consideration both how others value the action, how the individual values the action and if the individual believes in mastering the tasks needed for fulfilling the action, when deciding whether to undertake an action. This implies that the potential entrepreneur considers how others value entrepreneurship, if entrepreneurship is suitable for him- or herself, and how capable he or she is of succeeding as an entrepreneur when deciding whether or not to respond to a perceived business opportunity (Stewart Jr. and Roth, 2007). In addition to this, an individual makes a cost/benefit analysis of an innovation before adopting the innovation (Rogers, 1995). With regard to entrepreneurship, the individual will then evaluate the potential business in order to judge if acting upon the perceived business opportunity is beneficial or not. Such a decision to act could be regarded as an intention to act. Concerning entrepreneurship as a complex and time-consuming task, the intention to act may differ from the actual experienced action, this because the individual has to show persistency over a length of time to fulfil his or her intentions. During this time the individual interacts with the institutional structures and other actors and may change their intention as a result of this influence (Fayolle and Degeorge, 2008). The GEM model assumes that institutional characteristics, demography, entrepreneurial culture and the degree of economic welfare all shape a country's entrepreneurial landscape (Bosma et al., 2009). Entrepreneurial activity rates may differ across countries for cultural, institutional, economic and demographic reasons (Levie and Hunt, 2004).

This study discusses how the social, cultural and political contexts influence entrepreneurship education and how entrepreneurial education again influences entrepreneurship activity, attitudes and aspirations. The GEM model allows each country to have its own growth trajectory regarding entrepreneurship. The trajectory depends upon its starting point and how the actors in sum choose to interpret and act upon these cues. Differences in entrepreneurial activity levels may be specific to regional economic, demographic and cultural contexts and may be composed of entrepreneurs who may vary in type and aspiration (Bosma et al., 2008). This discussion leads to the following proposition:

Proposition: Finland, Sweden and Norway differ regarding entrepreneurship, thus adjustments in educational programmes are needed when translating good practices in entrepreneurship education between the three countries.

METHODOLOGY

The Global Entrepreneurship Monitor (GEM) project utilizes three different data sources for its analysis. These are the Adult Population Survey data (APS), the National Expert Survey (NES) data and indicator data. The data used in this chapter consist of APS data from 2007, NES data from 2004 and indicator data from 2008. These are the latest data sources available that contain comparable data from Finland, Sweden and Norway. Finland and Norway have conducted APSs and NESs each year since they joined the research project. Sweden participated last time in GEM in 2007 and the last time NES data was collected in Sweden was in 2004.

The Adult Population Survey (APS) addresses a minimum of 2000 randomly selected respondents in each country. The APS addresses the adult population aged 18 to 64 and investigates the respondent's relationship to entrepreneurship. Besides asking how the individual perceives the conditions for entrepreneurship to be, GEM asks the respondent if they currently are trying to start a business, or have started a business during the last 42 months. It also asks whether the respondent owns a business. GEM measures entrepreneurship by different means. A nascent entrepreneur is an individual who is actively starting a business, owns part of or all of the business, but the business has not yet paid wages to the founder(s). Baby businesses are established businesses that have paid wages to their owners for a period shorter than 3.5 years. Early stage entrepreneurs (TEAs) consist of nascent and baby businesses. Established businesses have paid wages to their owners for more than 3.5 years. The APS data from Finland represent 2005 adults aged between 18 and 64; in Sweden it represents 1712 while the Norwegian data represent 1541 adults. The APS data are dichotomous. This means that the APS numbers listed in the tables in this study represent percentages of the population responding 'Yes' to a given topic.

The National Expert Survey (NES) addresses 36–50 experts in entrepreneurship, asking them to state how they perceive conditions for entrepreneurship in their country to be. The national experts were asked to give their opinion on a multitude of subjects related to conditions for entrepreneurship. The items were represented by a five-point Likert scale with the additional option of 'Don't know' or 'Does not apply/Refuse to answer'. Based upon all NES data from all GEM countries, GEM provides a principal component analysis (PCA) combining the items in variables describing certain aspects of the national conditions for entrepreneurship. The numbers in the tables in this study then represent a PCA of the expert's responses to multiple items addressing each entrepreneurial condition. The higher the value on the PCA, the more the expert agrees that the conditions are favourable for entrepreneurship in their home country. Further information on the GEM research project and the methodology can be found in Reynolds et al. (2005). We were able to retrieve the full APS and NES datasets from Finland and Norway. Hence we could compare the values for the Finnish and the Norwegian items using independent samples *t*-tests. For the Swedish data we were only able to obtain the mean value for the items. This implied a one-sample *t*-test where we compared the Swedish mean for the given variable with the values from the Finnish or the Norwegian full dataset.

The third data source GEM uses are indicators at a national level gathered from multiple official sources. Examples of such could be GDP or demographical data. The data in the tables in this study then represent actual numbers or actual occurrences of a phenomenon per 1000 inhabitants. The data from the third data sources are all actual numbers representing the full population. This implies no variation, hence all differences are statistically significant. Whether the difference is meaningful rests on the arguments in the discussion.

FINDINGS

The institutional structures represent the national environment for entrepreneurship. The structural factor influencing entrepreneurial activity is, among others, the size of internal markets in a country. In the long run the government is able to shape some of the structure for entrepreneurship. It could improve its institutional structures for entrepreneurship by putting into effect programmes supporting entrepreneurship, that is, finance, infrastructure or education. Another antecedent to entrepreneurship is how suitable the population finds entrepreneurship as a tool for themselves in improving their living conditions or realizing other personal goals. The institutional structure for entrepreneurship manifests itself in conditions for entrepreneurship, as perceived by the potential entrepreneur.

Table 4.1 describes the antecedents to entrepreneurial activity by displaying among others the size of the home markets of Finland, Sweden and Norway. The table shows that Sweden is the country with the most inhabitants, while Norway has the fewest. The number of inhabitants in a country gives an indication of the domestic market size and thus might give indications on the likelihood for firms to address export markets. The table reveals the opinion of the national experts regarding how the conditions in their country support entrepreneurship. The table shows that in the experts' opinion, the governmental emphasis on improving conditions for entrepreneurship is higher in Finland and Norway than in Sweden and that these conditions are evaluated to be most supportive in Finland. Furthermore, in the view of the experts, the presence of adequate governmentally instituted entrepreneurship programmes is higher in Finland and Sweden than in Norway.

The figures in Table 4.1 based upon APS data show that there is a bigger share of the population in Finland and Sweden who perceive there to be better conditions to start a business in the area where they live, than in Norway. Likewise, the data indicate that the Swedes are more confident that they possess the necessary knowledge and skills for starting a business than do the Norwegians. Even so, Norwegians and Finns agree more often that entrepreneurship is a good career choice than do Swedes.

The entrepreneurial process is an enactment of the institutional structures for entrepreneurship. The entrepreneurial process at the national level could manifest itself among others as expenditures on research and development. The motivation and the capacity for entrepreneurial deeds among the population is also a sign of how the institutional structures are converted to entrepreneurial activity. The conditions for entrepreneurship are interpreted and acted upon at the individual level. This perception is then translated to motivation and intentions toward entrepreneurship. As there are different conditions for entrepreneurship across countries, the entrepreneurial processes are then different. These differences in entrepreneurial action reveal themselves as differences in start-up aspirations, number of owners necessary for handling the complexity in the institutional structures, and in purpose and motivation for the entrepreneurial action.

Table 4.1 *The antecedents for entrepreneurship in Finland, Sweden and Norway*

Entrepreneurial Antecedents	Finland	Sweden	Norway	Finland vs Sweden	Finland vs Norway	Sweden vs Norway
National characteristics						
Total population, all ages, 2008	5 244 749	9 045 389	4 644 457	n.a.	n.a.	n.a.
Expert data						
Governmental emphasis on improving conditions for entrepreneurship	3.17	1.84	2.15	***	***	n.s.
The presence of adequate governmental entrepreneurship programmes	3.23	2.33	2.83	***	n.s.	***
Adult population survey						
YES: Good conditions to start business in the next six months in area I live, % of population aged 18–64	52.96	50.33	46.29	n.s.	**	**
YES: Has the required knowledge/skills to start business, % of population aged 18–64	39.73	41.65	36.23	n.s.	n.s.	***
YES: People consider starting business as good career choice, % of population aged 18–64	37.48	52.38	54.95	***	***	n.s.

Note: Level of statistical significance: *** indicates $p < 0.01$, ** indicates $p < 0.05$, * indicates $p < 0.10$, n.s. indicates not significant, n.a. indicates significance not applicable.

Source: Author.

Table 4.2 displays some of the processes the government is in control of and that influence the entrepreneurial climate in a country. The table indicates that the total expenditure on research and development per capita is higher in Sweden than in Finland, and that the expenditure is lowest in Norway. Research and development is a vital source of innovations. Moreover, Table 4.2 indicates that the Finnish population is more capable and motivated to engage in entrepreneurial opportunities than are the Norwegian and the Swedish populations, according to the national experts. The items building the capacity index are several. Among the items are 'Many people know how to start and manage a high-growth business', 'Many people have experience in starting a new business' and 'Many people have the ability to organize the resources required for a new business'. A country needs inhabitants with these abilities for there to be entrepreneurial activity.

Table 4.2 further reveals some of the entrepreneurial processes of individuals in Finland, Sweden and Norway. The table shows that 10.4 per cent of the Swedish population expects to start a new business within the next three years, and that this interest is lower in Norway (8.9 per cent) and Finland (8.65 per cent). Further, the number of expected owners per business start-up is higher in Norway and Sweden than in Finland. Norway has the highest number of owners per start-up (2.39), Sweden the second highest (2.26) whiles Finland has the lowest (1.89). The higher number of owners is associated with higher growth intentions (Kolvereid et al., 2008). Table 4.2 indicates that the Norwegian entrepreneurs in general have more prior entrepreneurial experience than do the Swedish and Finnish entrepreneurs. Likewise, there are more serial entrepreneurs in Norway. The purpose of establishing the business is also influencing the survival and growth trajectory of the firm. The Finnish entrepreneurs have more serious intentions regarding their business than do the Swedish and the Norwegian entrepreneurs; we see that in the percentage of the entrepreneurs that intend to work full-time in their business. Moreover, the table shows that the Finnish entrepreneurs start their business because they want more independence more often than do their Swedish and Norwegian counterparts. The Norwegian entrepreneurs are more concerned with increasing or maintaining their income than are the Finnish and the Swedish entrepreneurs.

The entrepreneurial process provides results both nationally and for the entrepreneurs themselves. The research and development process may result in patents and a successful patent may lead to royalties. Another entrepreneurial output is the share of the population starting up a new business, owning a business or supporting others' businesses. Due to societal structures and entrepreneurial processes there might be age and

Table 4.2   Entrepreneurship processes in Finland, Sweden and Norway

Entrepreneurship Processes	Finland	Sweden	Norway	Finland vs Sweden	Finland vs Norway	Sweden vs Norway
National characteristics						
Total expenditure on research and development per capita, US$ in 2006	1372.5	1609.4	1074.4	n.a.	n.a.	n.a.
Expert data						
The entrepreneurial capacity of the population	2.85	1.91	2.46	***	**	***
How motivated the population are to engage in entrepreneurial opportunities	3.11	2.49	2.99	***	n.s.	***
Adult population survey						
YES: Expects to start a new business in the next three years, in % of the population aged 18–64	8.65	10.36	8.9	***	n.s.	*
Average number of expected owners in the new firm	1.87	2.26	2.39	***	*	***
Among those in the process of starting a business or owning a business younger than 3.5 years: started and managed a different business before this one	37.56	38.87	39.67	n.s.	n.s.	n.s.
Among those in the process of starting a business or owning a business younger than 3.5 years: full-time involved	58.36	45.8	44.32	***	***	n.s.
Among those in the process of starting a business or owning a business younger than 3.5 years: opportunity type: independence	59.66	51.01	43.5	*	**	n.s.
Among those in process of starting a business or owning a business younger than 3.5 years: opportunity type: maintain income	3.57	3.39	17.14	n.s.	***	***

Note: Level of statistical significance: *** indicates $p < 0.01$, ** indicates $p < 0.05$, * indicates $p < 0.10$, n.s. indicates not significant, n.a. indicates significance not applicable.

Source: Author.

gender differences in this entrepreneurial output. Likewise, the entrepreneurial output in a country is hallmarked by which production process and products the entrepreneur addresses their selected markets with. These entrepreneurial outputs are a result of how the entrepreneur judges the structural arrangements supporting entrepreneurship and the entrepreneur's own human and social capital.

Table 4.3 reveals some national-level output from entrepreneurial activity among inhabitants in the country. Such an innovative behaviour could be manifest in patents securing the commercial value of the innovation. The table reveals that the inhabitants in Sweden and Finland secure most patents abroad and receive far the highest royalty and licence fees compared to Norway. The Finns file most patents in their home country.

Table 4.3 also exposes the entrepreneurial activity in Finland, Sweden and Norway and compares these individual-level outputs. One entrepreneurial output is employees contributing in establishing business spin-offs. Spin-offs have better access to resources and so enhanced opportunity for growth and survival compared to independent start-ups. The table shows that a larger part of the population is engaged in business spin-offs in Norway and Finland than in Sweden. In the GEM terminology, start-up attempts that have not paid wages to their founders are nascent entrepreneurs. These are business start-up attempts that have not been realized yet. There are proportionally more nascent entrepreneurs in Finland than in Norway and Sweden. Baby business owners are those start-ups that pay wages to the founders, but not so for more than 3.5 years. These are business start-up attempts that still have not faced the reality of the market fully. The table hints that there are more baby business owners in Norway than in Finland and Sweden proportionally. The early stage entrepreneurial activity (TEA) measure consists of persons that are either nascent or baby business owners. The table shows that there is more early stage entrepreneurship in Finland and Norway than in Sweden. The TEA rate in Finland is 6.9, Sweden 4.2 and Norway is 6.5 for 2007. TEA is early stage entrepreneurial activity and measures those presently making efforts to start a new business including those owning a new business not older than 42 months. There is also more female entrepreneurship in Finland and Norway than in Sweden. Males are more engaged in entrepreneurship than are females in all three countries. The Finnish and the Norwegian entrepreneurs expect more often that the business they start will hire employees during the next five years than do the Swedes. Even so, high-growth entrepreneurs as measured as intending to have 20 or more employees in five years from start-up are more common in Norway and Sweden than in Finland.

Table 4.3 Entrepreneurial output in Finland, Sweden and Norway compared

Entrepreneurial Output	Finland	Sweden	Norway	Finland vs Sweden	Finland vs Norway	Sweden vs Norway
National characteristics						
Number of patents secured abroad by country residents in 2005, per million aged 18–64.	643.4	665.5	335.9	n.a.	n.a.	n.a.
Patent applications filed by residents in 2005, per million aged 18–64	552.6	452.2	395.8	n.a.	n.a.	n.a.
Royalty and licence fees receipts in US$ millions, per million aged 18–64	452.0	713.5	263.3	n.a.	n.a.	n.a.
Adult population survey						
YES: Currently involved in business start-up (SU), as part of normal job, in % of the population aged 18–64	2.67	1.97	3.04	*	n.s.	**
Baby business owner (BB): owns-manages business with income < 3.5 years, in % of the population aged 18–64	2.71	2.38	2.77	n.s.	n.s.	n.s.
TEA involvement: setting up firm or owner of young firm (SU or BB), in % of the population aged 18–64	6.91	4.15	6.47	***	n.s.	***
TEA (male): setting up firm or owner of young firm (SU or BB), in % of the male population aged 18–64	8.96	5.78	8.59	***	n.s.	***
TEA (female): setting up firm or owner of young firm (SU or BB), in % of the female population aged 18–64	4.81	2.47	4.28	***	n.s.	**

Table 4.3   (continued)

Entrepreneurial Output	Finland	Sweden	Norway	Finland vs Sweden	Finland vs Norway	Sweden vs Norway
Adult population survey						
TEA – any jobs now or in five years	4.7	3.34	4.32	*	n.s.	*
TEA – expects more than 19 jobs in five years	0.41	0.74	0.77	**	**	n.s.
Products new to all customers, in % of those within TEA	12.19	15.57	7.62	n.s.	***	***
Uses very latest technology (only available since last year), in % of those within TEA	14.17	8.68	25.27	*	**	***
% within TEA, no customers outside country	67.73	65.23	50.9	n.s.	**	***
% within BB, no customers outside country	64.56	68.55	42.06	n.s.	***	***
YES: Provided funds for new business in past three years exclusive of stocks & shares, in % of the population aged 18–64	3.31	3.74	3.87	n.s.	n.s.	n.s.

Note: Level of statistical significance: *** indicates $p < 0.01$, ** indicates $p < 0.05$, * indicates $p < 0.10$, n.s. indicates not significant, n.a. indicates significance not applicable.

Source: Author.

The entrepreneurs in Finland, Sweden and Norway are addressing markets differently. The Swedish entrepreneurs in general offer products that are new to customers more often than do entrepreneurs from Finland and Norway. Norwegian entrepreneurs rarely report offering new products to the intended customer. Even so, Norwegian entrepreneurs tend to use newer technology than do entrepreneurs in Finland and Sweden. Norwegian entrepreneurs and business owners more often address foreign markets than do Swedes and Finns. The data might indicate that there are more business angels per capita in Norway than in Sweden and Finland. Business angels are those investing in other persons' firms.

CONCLUSIONS AND DISCUSSIONS

The chapter presents antecedent, process and output of entrepreneurship and compares institutional structures and individual perceptions leading to entrepreneurial behaviour in Finland, Sweden and Norway. As indicated by previous research (Hytti, 2008) and suggested by GEM data, there are differences regarding antecedents to the process of and the output of entrepreneurship between the three countries: Finland Sweden and Norway. The first part of the proposition, that there are differences in entrepreneurship between Finland, Sweden and Norway is then confirmed. Antecedents consist mostly of the environment as the entrepreneur faces it, the process is the tools that the government has to hand and how they utilize it and the outcome is the entrepreneurial result.

As indicated by the displayed data, there are institutional structures regarding antecedents of entrepreneurship that differ between Finland, Sweden and Norway. These differences are influencing how suitable the inhabitants find entrepreneurship as a tool for themselves. This results in differences in how people in Finland, Sweden and Norway perceive entrepreneurial opportunities and act upon these opportunities. The data revealed that Sweden has a larger home market than Finland and Norway. According to the national experts the Finnish government is more engaged in improving the conditions for entrepreneurs than are the Norwegian and the Swedish governments. Sweden has the largest number of its population agreeing that they feel confident that their knowledge and training is sufficient for starting a firm, while Finns believe less often that entrepreneurship is a suitable career path for them. There are more perceived business opportunities in Finland per capita than in Norway and Sweden.

Looking at the entrepreneurship process indicators, Sweden is more focused on research and technology development than are Finland and Norway. Even so, both entrepreneurship motivation and capacity is stronger in Finland than in Norway and Sweden. The data also show that there are comparatively more Swedes expecting to start a business in the next three years, while the Finns are more determined to start a full-time business than are Swedes and Norwegians. There are remarkable differences in entrepreneurship motivation among the three countries as well. The Finns are more concerned with achieving independence while the Norwegians are more concerned with increasing or maintaining their income.

Likewise, there are important differences in entrepreneurial outcomes. The Swedes and the Finns are more eager to formalize their research achievements into commercial commodities than are their Norwegian counterparts. The entrepreneurial output differs in several other ways across the three countries as well. The Swedes are less engaged in entrepreneurship than are Norwegians and Finns, both as employees in an established firm trying to found a spin-off company, or as independent entrepreneurs trying to establish something for themselves. The data indicate that this is true for both genders. Norwegians are more convinced that their start-up effort will result in a big company with many employees, and the start-up teams are bigger than the Swedes' and the Finns'. The Norwegians' start-up is based upon more recent technology than are the Finns' and the Swedes'. Even so the Norwegians are not introducing new products to the markets to the same extent as the Swedes and the Finns. The Norwegians are more export oriented than are the Finns and the Swedes.

IMPLICATIONS FOR ENTREPRENEURSHIP EDUCATION

This chapter hinges around the assumption that different challenges across countries regarding entrepreneurship need different educational matters and forms. As the data indicate that there are differences in how entrepreneurship manifests itself in Finland, Sweden and Norway, there are then differences in the challenges universities offering entrepreneurship programmes faces.

In order to be inspired by good practice, good practice has to be recognized as such. A good practice is regarded as a success measured by the goals of the activity. Regarding entrepreneurship education at universities, this implies a discussion of the goals of entrepreneurship education at the specified universities. An educational institution has to relate to the present situation and can only to a certain extent try to change the direction of the established industry, this as the industry is founded upon a growth trajectory based on and evolved from the local adjustments to the local resource base and the global requirements. Good practice in entrepreneurship education is then serving the needs of the industry while aligning with the institutional structures shaping the entrepreneurial opportunity.

There are many entrepreneurs in Finland, they tend to start full-time firms, and they tend to start their firms to achieve independence. Even so, entrepreneurship is not recognized as a good career choice in Finland. Finns do not invest in others' businesses as business angels to the same extent. Finns start their firms alone more often than in Sweden and Norway. The GEM data indicate that Finnish entrepreneurs that start in teams, more often than those starting alone, succeed as business owners. The high TEA rate in Finland indicates a high level of entrepreneurship in Finland. Even so, the data point to some challenges for Finnish entrepreneurs. They tend to start firms with low growth ambitions and they tend to involve fewer people in the start-up process. Involving more people in the start-up process allows diversity in human capital; such a multitude of human capital could induce higher growth ambitions. Finns tend to see entrepreneurial opportunities but do not trust their own entrepreneurial capabilities (Stenholm et al., 2008). Finnish universities offering entrepreneurship programmes could respond to this challenge in order to ensure more successful entrepreneurs. Finnish universities could then engage students to work in diversified groups and challenge them to combine their skills in order to develop high-growth business ideas. This could inspire the students to start growth-oriented businesses based upon diverse human capital.

In Sweden, the entrepreneurs are fewer than in Norway and Finland, even though the Swedes perceive there to be good business opportunities and have adequate skills for responding to these opportunities. There is an untapped potential for entrepreneurship in Sweden, this is evidenced by the GEM data. There are more Swedes expecting to start a firm in the next three years than in Norway and Finland. Even so, the entrepreneurial capacity is lower in Sweden. The Swedish government does not focus on entrepreneurship to the same extent as do the Finnish and the Norwegian governments. Even though Swedes see themselves as entrepreneurs, they do not act as entrepreneurs. From the data, it seems that the Swedish challenge is to release entrepreneurial potential. Entrepreneurship education in Sweden could be directed toward motivating the students to start their own businesses, and it could be directed toward understanding how the government could strengthen the institutional framework for entrepreneurship in Sweden. Swedish universities could engage students to start and run student businesses, allowing the students to master the entrepreneurial challenge, potentially inspiring them to take the leap and become entrepreneurs as graduates.

The entrepreneurs in Norway tend to start firms with high-growth ambitions using new technology, addressing foreign markets with well-known products. The challenges for Norwegian entrepreneurs are related to improving their business idea in such a way that the growth ambition is fulfilled; securing that the circumstances around the new technology are taken into consideration in such a way that the implementation and use of it is successful and at the same time that their well-known products are welcomed by the market. Securing the property rights to their technological inventions is also a problem in Norway. Entrepreneurship education in Norway could be directed toward strengthening the business plan process by focusing on the commercialization of technology and market knowledge. Universities could arrange business plan competitions where securing property rights to intellectual property is one of the elements. Another element could be to show how the technical solution relates to a real customer need.

These analyses indicate that the second part of the proposition also has to be accepted. The differences present between Finland, Sweden and Norway regarding entrepreneurship imply that care has to be taken when copying entrepreneurship education programmes. When searching for educational programmes, syllabuses or educational elements to take from other universities, considerations about the purpose of the education should be made. The suggestion condensed from this research is then for the universities translating good practice within entrepreneurship education to investigate which needs this good practice serves, and compare these needs with the needs the copying university is to serve. When the needs are similar, the chances are that the provided solutions will also work for the copying university. It is also useful to bear in mind that different needs may require different projected aims for different audiences with different pedagogical matters and forms (Hytti, 2008).

The findings presented here regarding differences in conditions for entrepreneurship between Norway, Sweden and Finland could be interpreted in several ways. It could be interpreted as if the present status is the best position possible, given the countries' specific mix of resources and their paths of initiatives to utilize these; hence no improvements are possible. Another option is to take a more normative approach and suggest improvements based upon an informed judgement. Most of the textbooks in entrepreneurship education used in Norway are produced in the USA as a response to problems and challenges important in a

US context. The conditions for entrepreneurship, the entrepreneurial process and the entrepreneurial outcome differ between the USA and Norway (Noies et al., 2010). This present research report similarly indicates there to be important differences between Norway, Sweden and Finland, providing this informed judgement on how such differences should influence changes in educational offerings related to entrepreneurship.

In the long run governments are able to change the growth trajectory of the country by introducing development programmes and incentives for industry change. To move in a forward direction in the evolving industry structure, a solid understanding of the present position is needed. This chapter provides a basis for such an understanding of the present situation for entrepreneurship in Finland, Sweden and Norway. How the Finnish, Swedish and Norwegian governments could utilize the analysis and the findings presented in this chapter represents challenges for future research.

NOTE

* The author would like to thank the Finnish GEM team represented by Professor Anne Kovalainen for providing access to the Finnish GEM data. Our use of their data is our responsibility solely. The author also would like to thank Nordland Fylkeskommune and Interreg IVA for funding this research.

REFERENCES

Acs, Z.J. and D.B. Audretsch (1988), 'Innovation in large and small firms: An empirical analysis', *American Economic Review*, **78**(4), 678–90.
Ajzen, I. (1991), 'The theory of planned behavior', *Organizational Behavior and Human Decision Processes*, **50**(2), 179–211.
Bosma, N. et al. (2008), *Global Entrepreneurship Monitor: 2007 Executive Report*, London: London Business School.
Bosma, N. et al. (2009), *Global Entrepreneurship Monitor, 2008 Executive Report*. Santiago, Chile and Babson Park, MA: Global Entrepreneurship Research Consortium.
De Clercq, D. and H. Crijns (2008), 'Entrepreneurs and education in Belgium: Findings and implications from the Global Entrepreneurship Monitor', in A. Fayolle (ed.), *The Handbook of Research in Entrepreneurship Education, Vol. 2: Contextual Perspectives*, Cheltenham, UK and Northampton, MA, USA: Edward Elgar Publishing, pp. 169–84.
DiMaggio, P.J. and W.W. Powell (1983), 'The iron cage of institutional isomorphism and collective rationality in organizational fields', *American Sociological Review*, **48**(2), 147–60.
Dowling, S. (2005), 'The social construction of entrepreneurship: Narrative and dramatic processes in the coproduction of organizations and identities', *Entrepreneurship Theory & Practice*, **29**(2), 185–204.
Fayolle, A. and J.M. Degeorge (2008), 'Attitudes, intentions and behaviour: New approaches to evaluating entrepreneurship education', in A. Fayolle and H. Klandt (eds), *International*

Entrepreneurship Education: Issues and Newness, Cheltenham, UK and Northampton, MA: Edward Elgar Publishing, pp. 74–89.
Fayolle, A. and P. Kyrö (2008), 'Conclusion: Toward new challenges and more powerful dynamics', in A. Fayolle and P. Kyrö (eds), *The Dynamics between Entrepreneurship, Environment and Education*, Cheltenham, UK and Northampton, MA, USA: Edward Elgar Publishing, pp. 289–326.
Giddens, A. (1976), *New Rules of Sociological Method*, London: Hutchinson.
Giddens, A. (1979), *Central Problems in Social Theory*, Berkeley, CA: University of California Press.
Hynes, B. (1996), 'Entrepreneurship education and training – introducing entrepreneurship into non-business disciplines', *Journal of European Industrial Training*, **20**(8), 10–17.
Hytti, U. (2008), 'Enterprise education in different cultural settings and at different school levels', in A. Fayolle, and P. Kyrö (eds), *The Dynamics between Entrepreneurship, Environment and Education*, Cheltenham, UK and Northampton, MA, USA: Edward Elgar Publishing, pp. 131–48.
Katz, J.A. (2008), 'Fully mature but not fully legitimate: A different perspective on the state of entrepreneurship education', *Journal of Small Business Management*, **46**(4), 550–66.
Klyver, K. and E. Bager (2012), 'Entrepreneurship policy as institutionalized and powerful myths', *International Journal of Entrepreneurial Venturing*, **4**(4), 409–26.
Kolvereid, L. and B.W. Åmo (2007), 'Entrepreneurship among graduates from business schools: A Norwegian case', in A. Fayolle (ed.), *Handbook of Research in Entrepreneurship Education, Vol. 2: Contextual Perspectives*, Cheltenham, UK and Northampton, MA, USA: Edward Elgar Publishing, pp. 207–18.
Kolvereid, L., E. Bullvåg, and B.W. Åmo (2008), *Entreprenørskap i Norge 2007*, Bodø, Norway: Bodø Graduate School of Business.
Kunnskapsdepartementet (2006), *Se mulighetene og gjør noe med dem! – strategi for entre-prenørskap i utdanningen 2004–2008*, Oslo: Kunnskapsdepartementet.
Landström, H. (2000), *Entreprenörskapets rötter*, 2nd edition, Lund: Studentlitteratur.
Levie, J. and S. Hunt (2004), 'Culture, institutions and new business activity: Evidence from Global Entrepreneurship Monitor', in S.A. Zahra et al. (eds), *Frontiers of Entrepreneurship Research*, Babson, MA: Babson College, pp. 519–533.
Noies, E., B.W. Åmo and I.E. Allen (2010), 'Entrepreneurship and conditions for entrepreneurs: Norway and the USA compared', in C.G. Brush, R. Sørheim, L.Ø. Widding and L. Kolvereid (eds), *The Life Cycle of New Ventures: Emergence, Newness and Growth*, Cheltenham, UK and Northampton, MA, USA: Edward Elgar, pp. 13–23.
Nordland Fylkeskommune (2005), *Fylkestingssak 28–2005. Et felles løft for barn og ungdom – innovasjon og entreprenørskap i utdanning og opplæring i Nordland*, Bodø, Norway: Nordland County.
Nordland Fylkeskommune (2006), *Fylkestingssak 37–2006. Oppfølging av FT-sak 28/05: Handlingsplaner*, Bodø, Norway: Nordland County.
Reynolds, P. et al. (2005), 'Global Entrepreneurship Monitor: Data collection, design and implementation 1998–2003', *Small Business Economics*, **24**(3), 205–31.
Rogers, E.M. (1995), *Diffusion of Innovation*, 4th edition, New York: The Free Press.
Sarason, Y., T. Dean and J. Dillard (2006), 'Entrepreneurship as the nexus of individual and opportunity: A structuration view', *Journal of Business Venturing*, **21**(3), 286–305.
Schumpeter, J.A. (1934), *The Theory of Economic Development*, Cambridge, MA: Harvard University Press.
Shane, S. and S. Venkataraman (2000), 'The promise of entrepreneurship as a field of research', *Academy of Management Review*, **25**(1), 217–26.
Spencer, J.W. and C. Gómez (2004), 'The relationship among national institutional structures, economic factors and domestic entrepreneurial activity: A multicountry study', *Journal of Business Research*, **57**(9), 1098–107.
Stenholm, P. et al. (2008), *Global Entrepreneurship Monitor 2008 Report, Finland*, Turku, Finland: Turku School of Economics.
Stewart, W.H. Jr and P.L. Roth (2007), 'A meta-analysis of achievement motivation differ-

ences between entrepreneurs and managers', *Journal of Small Business Management*, **45**(4), 401–21.

Zacharis, A., W. Bygrave and D. Shepherd (2000), *Global Entrepreneurship Monitor: National Entrepreneurship Assessment, United States, 2000*, executive report prepared for the Kauffman Center for Entrepreneurship and the Ewing Kauffman Foundation, Kansas City, KS: Ewing Kauffman Foundation.

5. Institutional change in the German Higher Education system: from professional dominance to managed education

Markus Reihlen and Ferdinand Wenzlaff*

INTRODUCTION

Institutional changes in the German system of Higher Education are remarkable. Within the last 60 years, the system of professional dominance inspired by the Humboldtian model of a rule-governed community of scholars (Scott, 2006; Olsen, 2007) based on values of free inquiry, academic autonomy and self-regulation has gradually transformed to a new regime of managed education (Münch, 2011). With the rise of mass education in the late 1960s and 1970s coupled with more fundamental reforms in university governance, the model of professional dominance was already unsettled. Federal control and democratization of Higher Education became guiding pillars of a new era that displaced the initial logic of professional dominance. After three decades of internal democracy and federal control, the system was again challenged by declining student numbers, a low degree of international visibility and the general demand for the reorganizing of public services in the name of competition, innovativeness and cost-efficiency. The typical public universities in Germany encountered a demand–response imbalance (Clark, 1998) as with the limited resources outstanding research and high standards in teaching became difficult to realize. The seeds were created for the rise of a new system of managed education with the entrepreneurial university as the emerging organizational form.

The hallmarks of managed education are threefold (Münch, 2011). First, based on a market ideology the education system has been reformed in the name of competition, excellence and efficiency. Universities have been given greater degrees of autonomy, resulting in a stratification of elite and non-elite or central and peripheral educational institutions that differ in both their scale and reputation (Münch, 2007). This development is rather new for the German educational field, which traditionally rather equalized than fostered differences (Münch, 2011). Second, the new market discourse is coupled with the rise of an audit society (Power, 1997), in which organizational life is subject to an institutionalization of quantification and evaluation. Third, the rise of New Public Management established a new remote-controlled approach for managing educational institutions whose funding becomes dependent on how the university 'is assessed on the basis of its effectiveness and efficiency in achieving political purposes' (Olsen, 2007, p. 31). Managed education has strong implications for the role of the state, which plays an active role in orchestrating competition between educational institutions in the name of academic excellence and efficiency (Münch, 2007, 2011).

These trends are manifested in the new institutional logic of the educational field, which is sometimes referred to as the commercialization of Higher Education (Bok, 2003), academic capitalism (Slaughter and Leslie, 1997; Slaughter and Rhoades, 2004), or the Triple Helix that interlinks Higher Education, the state and the market (Etzkowski et al., 1998). Managed education unfolds strong isomorphic pressures that forces universities to comply with these shared rules and norms of the Higher Education field. Instead of being passive adopters or victims of this new educational regime, scholars have suggested an entrepreneurial response as represented by Clark's (1998) 'entrepreneurial university' or more recently by Wissema's (2009) 'third generation university'.

While the existing literature on the German Higher Education system deals with a number of detailed developments on the macro-level such as the emergence of New Public Management (Lange, 2008; Schmoch and Schubert, 2010), the new Excellence Initiatives by the federal government (Kehm and Pasternack, 2008; Leibfried, 2010; Sieweke, 2010), or the impact of Bologna reforms on German universities (Hanft and Müskens, 2005; Witte, 2006; Bührmann, 2008), very little research exists that synthesizes these existing findings into a broader, longitudinal analysis of the institutional changes that have unfolded during the postwar period. In order to understand the nature of the unique setting of the German Higher Education system, which created a path dependency with distinctive institutional pressures to change, we build on earlier work by Scott et al. (2000) and adopt their framework to the organizational field of Higher Education. It is composed of three main components that are of particular importance for understanding institutional change: institutional logics, institutional actors and governance systems.

We present a chronological and historical analysis of the German Higher Education field starting with the postwar period and going right up to the more recent changes in the institutional environment. The purpose of this research and our contribution is to develop a better understanding of the societal and managerial issues associated with the transition and change on the macro level from an era of professional dominance to managed education affecting the micro level with its transition from the Humboldtian towards the entrepreneurial university.

INSTITUTIONAL CHANGE IN THE GERMAN HIGHER EDUCATION SYSTEM

The idea of an era is that the composition of actors, their interaction and governance system is given coherence and orientation by an underlying institutional logic, which allows the production and reproduction of stable patterns of actions over time. We distinguish three eras of Higher Education systems in postwar Germany: professional dominance (1945–68); federal involvement and democratization (1968–98); managed education (from 1998) (see Webler, 1983; Oehler, 1989 for similar conceptions of German postwar eras until the 1980s). Universities have a far more ancient history in Germany. Nevertheless in 1945 the governmental and Higher Education system reconstituted itself and therefore provides an adequate starting point for our analysis. The German constitution organized the German Republic as a federation and responsibility for culture and education was transferred to the states. The victorious allies connected the emergence of the Nazi regime to the authoritarian education system and wanted to allow a re-education based on freedom and democracy by means of a decentralized Higher Education system (Burtscheidt, 2010). In principle, universities were designed according to the Humboldtian ideal (Jessen, 2010) and the Higher Education system of the Weimar Republic era preceding the Nazi regime was restored.

The Era of Professional Dominance

Institutional logic
Following institutional theory we argue that each era has a distinct logic that organizes the interaction of institutional actors. The institutional logic of professional dominance is based on two general but important ideas associated with the concept of professionalism (Freidson, 1970, 2001) and the republic of science (Polanyi, 1962). Professionalism means that academics enjoy a large degree of autonomy and feel loyal to their discipline rather than their employment organization (Baldridge and Deal, 1983; Clark, 1983). The republic of science is based on the belief that scientific work is so specialized that it is inaccessible to those lacking the required training and experience. In addition, it is built upon the belief that this work involves fresh judgement and discretion that cannot be

standardized, rationalized or commodified. Scientific expertise depends on a stock of academic knowledge, which accomplishes two basic functions (Abbott, 1988). First, the academic stock of knowledge is subject to a considerable amount of research activity. It was Wilhelm von Humboldt's basic idea 'to appoint the best intellects available, and to give them the freedom to carry on their research wherever it leads' (Fallon, 1980, p. 19 in Scott, 2006). The logic of professional dominance is modelled around the Humboldtian principles of (1) the unity of research and teaching and (2) academic freedom involving *Lernfreiheit* (freedom to learn) and *Lehrfreiheit* (freedom to teach) (Scott, 2006). Higher Education was perceived as an activity of 'human and personality building'. In order to offer them choices for general education, students enjoyed study programmes that were less dense (Rektorenkonferenz, 1961, p. 44).

Finally, academic knowledge is a source of legitimacy of the scientist's claim of having esoteric knowledge (Veblen, 1918) that goes beyond the ordinary and is, in a fundamental sense, the basis of scientific authority. In the service of free inquiry and scholarly education, scientists should be autonomous; they should have full control over their work, while scientific ethics claims to be independent of any particular interest groups such as the state, private enterprise, or the general public (Polanyi, 1962; Freidson, 2001). As a consequence, the primary logic associated with professional dominance, corresponding to Brint's (1994) idea of the professionals as 'social trustees', is the quality of research and teaching as determined exclusively by scholarly rules and norms.

Important institutional actors
Universities were organized according to the ordinaria system, where the ordinarius (full professor) constituted the 'germ cell' of the university and enjoyed great academic freedom and autonomy on a scale never reached before (Teichler and Bode, 1990; see Pasternack and Wissel, 2010 for a brief characterization and further references), but also reflected an elitism and personality cult (Burtscher and Pasqualoni, 2004). They were in charge of a specific knowledge field, directed an 'institute', and were supported by a number of academic and non-academic staff. Furthermore, the institute was directly funded by the ministry (Scott, 2006).

State ministries of education were the main source of funding for science and scholarship. Academic associations determined scholarly standards and norms in various research fields; journals and books were the dominant outlets of scholarly work disseminated by academic publishers who perceived their work less as a business than as a profession (Thornton and Ocasio, 1999).

In order to coordinate Higher Education several actors emerged. Already in 1949 the Rectors' Conference (Westdeutsche Rektorenkonferenz) as a voluntary association of the universities was founded (Teichler and Bode, 1990). On the federal level, in 1955 the Nuclear Ministry was established and in 1962 transformed into the Science Ministry (since 1994 Ministry of Science and Education). In 1957 the Science Council (Wissenschaftsrat) with representatives from politics, academia and the public was founded as a regulative body in addition to the Conference of Education Ministers. The motive was to overcome the failures of decentralized planning and to enable coordination between governmental bodies and the universities across different states (Teichler and Bode, 1990; Scott, 2006; Burtscheidt, 2010).

Governance system

After 1945, academics demanded the highest possible independence in order to avoid political instrumentalization. The autonomy and freedom of science and scholarship was codified in the new German constitution. Academics claimed a corporate autonomy through the legal form of the university as a public body and financial autonomy through having the senate drafting the budget (*Haushaltsplan*) as well as academic freedom in the sense of the power to make appointments (Burtscheidt, 2010). To a great extent, the state embraced these demands and professors gained a degree of power never reached before (Teichler and Bode, 1990). This was reflected in the governing structure, in which decision-making power was largely decentralized to the ordinaria who controlled their work through academic self-regulation basically following the collegial model. But the governance system remained a hybrid of autonomy and state control, since Higher Education was dependent on public funding (Teichler and Bode, 1990; Scott, 2006; Burtscheidt, 2010).

Precursors of change

Through the reconstitution of the ordinaria of the nineteenth century the chance to restructure the Higher Education system was missed (Burtscheidt, 2010). The emerging demands for democratization of society in general and university structures in particular led to student revolts in the late 1960s, with demands for equal access to Higher Education, the abolition of elites and wide-ranging participation in academic matters (Teichler and Bode, 1990). The movement reflected an extension of the social-democratic concept of a social state, in which capitalist interests were held in check by a democratic order, to the Higher Education field (Nitsch, 1983).

A second driver for change was the continuously increasing number of student enrolments. A growing middle class was sending students to universities and industry demanded highly skilled labour (Oehler, 1989). The rise of mass education itself was a phenomenon across developed countries at the time (Schofer and Meyer, 2005). In Germany, the rise of mass education was encountered with regional expansion and hiring of existing universities, but funding was not sufficient, leading to a perceived decline in academic quality (Teichler and Bode, 1990; Hödl and Zegelin, 1999; Binswanger, 2010; Burtscheidt, 2010; Münch, 2011). Already in the late 1950s, the ideal of universal education (*Bildung*) had to give way to the idea of specialized academic training (*Ausbildung*) in order to facilitate the 'second industrial revolution' (Brandt, 1957 cited in Jessen, 2010, p. 263). The Humboldtian ideal of the unity of teaching and research could not be practised with masses of students to be trained in highly specialized fields (Jarausch, 1999). Students also became less interested in general education, but developed an 'instrumental orientation' in search of an academic qualification that would raise their value on the labour market (Oehler, 1989; Lullies, 1996). It became more apparent that the existing logic of professional dominance with decentralization and academic self-organization could neither deal with the increasing 'professional utilitarianism' (Jessen, 2010) and massification, nor serve the new demands for democratic reforms. A new institutional logic surfaced in which the federal government stepped in and took an active role as planner and regulator of Higher Education at the cost of an emerging regime that coupled the university more tightly to the interests of the state, precisely what was feared by the victorious allies and academics when the system was first set up. This increasing role of the state was coupled with wide-ranging reforms for the democratization of universities.

The Era of Federal Involvement and Democratization

Institutional logic
In the section on precursors of change we indicated two major forces of change, which correspond to two interacting logics characterizing the era of federal involvement and democratization. The first underlying institutional logic of this era was marked by a massive expansion in Higher Education financed by the government, equality of access to Higher Education was stressed, and the state played an increased regulatory role (Teichler and Bode, 1990). This logic of democratization of Higher Education won over the incompatible logic of academic self-regulation and professorial collegiality, as now non-professorial academic staff and students took part in defining the quality of Higher Education.

The second logic was guided by the idea of making Higher Education for masses more effective by central coordination and planned development (ibid.) and can be labelled as the institutional logic of central planning or bureaucratic control. Professional self-regulation seemed to be incompatible with democracy as well as with massification and was thus replaced by this new double logic.

New actors
The growing need to manage Higher Education for the masses in Germany was accompanied by a rapid proliferation of new federal and state agencies and commissions engaged in coordinating, planning and controlling various aspects of the Higher Education system. For instance, the Education Council (Bildungsrat, 1966–75), the Joint Commission of the States and the Federal Government for Education Planning (Bund-Länder-Kommission für Bildungsplanung, 1970), and the Federal Ministry of Education and Science (1970) all served the primary purpose of a centrally coordinated system of Higher Education (Jessen, 2010).

As a consequence of mass education, financial problems of the states and pressures of the '68' student movement, the federal government gained influence on state legislation by establishing framework legislative powers (*Rahmengesetzgebungskompetenz*) for itself in the field of Higher Education in 1969. Since then coordination in Higher Education has been anchored in the constitution and the transfer of far-reaching responsibilities to the federal level was legalized. The peak of centralized federal involvement was reached with the Higher Education Framework Law (Hochschulrahmengesetz) of 1976. The idea was to homogenize the diversity in the German Higher Education system by regulating in detail the structure of university personnel and committees as well as academic domains (study programmes, course contents, exams).

In addition, new agencies were created to deal with the rising number of students. For instance, already in the 1960s the Rectors' Conference founded a central registry (*zentrale Registrierstelle*) for allocating study places at medical schools based on school-leaving grades. In 1972 the successor agency (ZVS) of the registry was founded, which centrally distributed students mainly on the basis of school-leaving grades to universities for several subject areas including medicine, business administration, psychology and law. With such a federal control agency, the supply of Higher Education programmes was centrally coordinated with the demand for places. This marriage of federal control and mass education initiated the period of supply-oriented study programmes (Witte and Stuckrad, 2007).

Student associations have a long tradition in Europe, but the student movement that emerged in the late sixties (for the history see Habermas, 1969; Bauß, 1977; Schmitthenner, 1986; Becker and Schröder, 2000; Koch, 2008) was highly politicized, aiming at influencing university governance and thus becoming an important actor within the field. However, the student revolts were not the cause of the Higher Education reform but an important catalyst of an existing societal consensus for a necessary reform of the ordinaria system (Rohstock, 2009).

Governance system

The governance system had an internal and an external dimension. Internally, democratization as well as homogenization was reflected by the following main structural changes (Teichler and Bode, 1990). Despite objections to university democratization and fears of a negative impact on the freedom of teaching and research by professors (Schmidt and Thelen, 1969), the ordinaria university was replaced by a new organizational type, the committee or group university (*Gremien- or Gruppenuniversität*) (see Pasternack and von Wissel, 2010 for a brief characterization and further references); academic careers were shortened and autonomous research was facilitated for academic staff who had not reached professorial rank; duration of the rector was extended from one to two to four to eight years; without strengthening the position of the dean, some decision areas that addressed the interests of professors were transferred from the ministerial to the faculty level.

Besides the reorganization of the university's internal governance, the relationship to the state changed in the direction of more intensive financial and educational regulation and control. The reasoning behind this was to provide equal opportunities for university applicants and to cap costs. The newly created cost containment regimes of the early 1970s were supply driven. This is well represented by the capacity regulation (KapVO), which was a follow-up of a contract between the states and the federal government of 1972 (Seeliger, 2005). The idea of the capacity regulation regime was to balance conflicting interests between university applicants and the scarcity of teaching capacity (ibid.). As a consequence, the number of admissions into a study programme under the capacity regulation regime was standardized on the basis of the available teaching capacity. Universities were not allowed to set any admission restrictions or university-specific student selection criteria. Since they were required to exhaust their capacity, which 'froze' the number of incoming students, universities operated permanently at their limit and this weakened the position of state universities in an emerging Higher Education market, which now included domestic private and foreign public and private competitors (Kluth, 2001). Furthermore, study programmes/curricula (Witte and von Stuckrad, 2007) as well as budgeting were highly regulated and subject to a control philosophy (Nickel et al., 2009).

In this era, the state model of governance was strengthened by the new role of the state and especially by the federal role in regulating and coordinating Higher Education. At the same time, the call for more democracy shifted internal university governance from a collegial to a democratic model.

Precursors of change

In 1977 the state launched a policy of 'Opening Universities' (*Öffnung der Hochschulen*) as a response to the predicted baby boomer generation. This policy aimed at ensuring equal chances for Higher Education, albeit without committing the financial resources needed for an expansion in educational infrastructure. As a result, universities had to overstretch their capacities, at least until the baby boomer generation graduated (Teichler and Bode, 1990). The 'crisis' of the German Higher Education system was driven by the burden of mass education coupled with chronically underfinanced universities and ineffective regulation and administration, resulting in a considerable decline of the education quality (Hödl and Zegelin, 1999).

Study duration in Germany was considered as excessive and graduates were perceived as too old in comparison with other EU countries. Probably unparalleled in any other country an extension of regular study duration had tradition and was regarded as an academic freedom (Teichler and Bode, 1990). Furthermore, the often politicized internal governance accompanied by time- and resource-consuming struggles in committees – 'organized irresponsibility', as the rector of the Frankfurt University once described the committee governance regime within universities – and the detailed bureaucratic regulation of academic and financial affairs by the state became barriers for improving the quality of research and teaching (Hödl and Zegelin, 1999; Burtscheidt, 2010).

The first amendment of the Higher Education Framework Law in 1985 initiated the first reforms aiming at deregulation. Nevertheless, reforms in the 1980s remained cautious and far less drastic than in earlier decades (Teichler and Bode, 1990).

Until the early 1980s only 20 per cent of all research activities were directly funded by external sources such as governmental funding programmes and funding agencies. In 1983 the Federal Ministry of Education and Science labelled the emerging changes in Higher Education with the slogan 'Differentiation and Competition'. In the following years, an increasing consensus formed, namely that the competitiveness of educational institutions would be reached by increased competition for external funding and engagement in entrepreneurial activities, and be assessed based on rankings, reputation and performance indicators of universities and their faculties (ibid.).

In the 1990s an OECD study brought to light the deficits of the German Higher Education system and the pressure for change rose. The OECD agenda was regarded as a main driver for the new definition of the role of universities as promoters of innovations and economic growth; accordingly, universities were elevated to the status of entrepreneurial actors in the worldwide competition for innovation (Münch, 2011).

These emerging trends made the contradictions of the era of federal involvement and democratization more visible. Universities that were considered as the central actors in the global competition for innovation had very little strategic choices to improve their own competitiveness. Attracting highly talented students was confined by the state-controlled supply plans, which made it difficult to develop a differentiated and attractive educational profile (for an overview of the discussion at the end of the era of federal involvement see Meyer and Müller-Böling, 1996). The situation was similar for attracting qualified academics who would contribute to a specific research and teaching profile; universities lacked the required financial autonomy to pay competitive and flexible salaries for highly qualified professors. In summary, the demand for competition and differentiation as new policy measures in the Higher Education field was incompatible with the centralized state control model of the era of federal involvement and democratization. Expected benefits of competition can only be harvested if universities are given greater autonomy in matters of resource allocation, student selection, hiring policies, educational programme development and strategic positioning. As the turning point into the new era of managed education, we chose the federal parliament's adoption of the amendment to the Framework Act in 1998, which abolishes the previous 'immunity' external evaluation by providing the legal basis of deregulation, performance orientation and incentive creation.

The Era of Managed Education

Since Europe intends to become the 'most competitive and dynamic knowledge-based economy' (European Council, 2000), Germany's Higher Education system was required to become more effective in producing useful knowledge and skilled labour to support the necessary innovations at company, regional and national level (Warning, 2007). Additionally, a more effective and efficient utilization of resources was requested that would allow cutting costs in Higher Education in order to meet fiscal constraints (Kluth, 2001). What we recognize is an emerging worldwide structure of Higher Education that unfolds isomorphic forces. As an effect, academics, universities and even countries are becoming more alike in the way they encourage, incentivize and manage Higher Education.

Global competition in science increasingly follows an economic rationale in which countries, universities and researchers compete on a global education market for reputation and market share. Germany was a late mover in the reaction to diffusing use of indicators, evaluations and rankings (Weingart and Maasen, 2007). The Anglo-American model serves as an intellectual source for a market model of Higher Education by the German government and educational experts (Kühler, 2006) in their attempts to gain stronger visibility by scoring higher in global benchmarks and moving up in global rankings, and derives its legitimacy from the successful positions of Anglo-American universities in global rankings, despite the articulated critique of how these rankings are constructed (Münch, 2011). In search of a more competitive educational regime the market model reveals strong legitimacy for the restructuring of Higher Education. Interestingly, the marketization of the US Higher Education system was incremental and led by non-governmental initiatives, while in the case of the EU the model is engineered by governments and the supranational organizations (Slaughter and Cantwell, 2011). Notably, the transformation of the system from professional dominance to democratization and federal involvement was carried out in the glare of publicity, whereas the institutional change to managed education has rarely been noticed at least in the early stages (Küpper, 2009).

Institutional logic
With the rise of managed education a new interpretive scheme based on three main pillars emerged. First, the centralized planning approach to Higher Education invented in the 1970s was gradually replaced by a market logic. This move required new policy measures such as increasing deregulation of Higher Education, especially granting universities greater autonomy in selecting their own students, hiring their own academic staff and allocating their own financial resources for the development of a strategic profile in competitive educational markets. The role of students also changed gradually from socialized and cultivated learners to sovereign consumers in search of a human investment (Gumport, 2000; Ritzer, 2004). As Gumport (2000, p. 79) points out: 'The conceptual shift elevates consumer interests as paramount considerations in the restructuring of academic programs and the reengineering of academic services'.

The application of market logic to research was facilitated by the emergence of research productivity indicators such as the social sciences citation index and various research rankings (Münch, 2007; Adler and Harzing, 2009; Frey and Osterloh, 2010) that gradually formed the belief among university administrators and some educational experts that research output can be measured and reasonably quantified. This created the impression that even non-experts can access the quality and productivity of research by simply counting the number of publications, weighted, for instance, by the quality of the journal. The market logic turns the highly uncertain venture of research into a commodity. As Bunge (1998b, p. 253) writes, from a market perspective:

> scientists produce commodities namely problems, concepts, hypotheses, data, and methods – that can be imputed shadow prices; that they trade these commodities among themselves; that they sell them to universities, business firms, or governments; that every scientist attempts to maximize his utilities by producing the largest possible quantity of papers . . .; that scientific creativity is market-driven.

Second, new auditing practices (Power, 1997) became a prerequisite and a reinforcing mechanism of the new competitive regime of managed education. In order to organize Higher Education as a competition within quasi-markets (Bartlett and Le Grand, 1993; Binswanger, 2010), audits and evaluations serve as a substitute for purchase decisions in private goods markets (Meier and Schimank, 2009). Audits and evaluations, whether of teaching or research, establish feedback mechanisms that aim to raise quality, but at the same time create 'a measure of uniformity and homogeneity' (Larson, 1977, p. 40). As Power (1997, p. 14) argues, with the rise of the audit society, auditing becomes a ritualized practice of verification whose technical efficacy is less clear than its role in the creation of organizational legitimacy.

Third, the market model is combined with a managerialist ideology based on the belief that the external university relation to the state can best be managed by a New Public Management (NPM) approach. NPM was developed in the 1980s and became the dominant managerial model for public organizations (Lane, 2000; Gruening, 2001) based on the perceived lack of accountability and declining trust in the quality and efficiency of public services (Nixon, 2004). The German version of NPM was formalized as the New Control Model (*Neues Steuerungsmodell*) by the newly founded institution Municipal Association for Administration Management (KGSt, 2012). A guiding idea of NPM is that decentralized decisions with organizational and financial freedom result in more effective outcomes and more efficient use of scarce resources than the former centralized planning approach of public administrations (Ziegele, 2002). Instead of regulating processes, a main characteristic of the era of federal involvement, NPM defines educational policy missions and derives specific objectives for research and teaching that are further broken down to individual universities, faculties and departments. The financial support of the state then depends largely on the attainment of negotiated objectives (Nickel, 2007).

The internal dimension of the managerialist ideology is reflected in new roles and practices of academic managers. Principles of academic autonomy and self-governance have been perceived as less effective for adapting the academic enterprise to changing market needs (Wissema, 2009). As in many other professions, more corporate models based on managerial authority and corporate control have attracted interest and have been legitimized as superior for the enterprising university (Clark, 1998). The hallmarks of this new institutional logic are well summarized by Frey and Osterloh (2010, p. 3), '"More market" and "strong leadership"'.

New and transforming actors

For all participating European countries, the Confederation of EU Rectors' Conferences became an influential actor after the Bologna Declaration in 2000. This new actor initiated restructuring processes for the development of Higher Education (Hanft and Müskens, 2005; Witte, 2006; Nickel, 2007; Bührmann, 2008). The general idea of the 'action programme' of the Confederation of EU Rectors' Conferences can be summarized as convergence, competition and international competitiveness, higher quality, and efficiency (Confederation of EU Rectors' Conferences, 2000). The implementation of a set of convergence instruments to restructure Higher Education aims to 'enhance the employability and mobility of citizens' and 'to compete more resolutely than in the past for students, influence, prestige, and money in the worldwide competition of universities.' (Confederation of EU Rectors' Conferences, 2000, p. 4).

In 1994, the Centre for Higher Education (Centrum für Hochschulentwicklung, CHE) was designed as a partner for ministries and Higher Education Institutions to support restructuring projects and to offer training programmes. The CHE is free from directives of its funding organizations, publishes ongoing studies, and since 1999 has developed a national university ranking.

Throughout all eras, publications, associations and conferences have been the institutions of communication, exchange and networking for academics. In the past, communication and quality control of publications were more or less decentralized in the hands of academics. Managed education is characterized by the emergence of central organizations as intermediaries between the state and academics to govern science and scholarship by allocating resources and reputation as well as controlling research agendas (Meier and Schimank, 2010). The most important authorities are citation indices such as the Social Sciences Citation Index, the hegemony of American high-impact journals, and university rankings such as the Shanghai-Ranking (Frey and Osterloh, 2010; Münch, 2011). The narrowing of publication preferences results in a devaluation of monographs, book chapters, research reports or policy recommendations and a loss of originality, resulting from the limitations of the peer review process (Münch, 2011).

Since study programmes are no longer approved by the ministries, national and international accreditation agencies supervised by a national accreditation council founded in 1998 appeared (Meyer, 2010). These new actors became important players in the quality control of the university's teaching programmes and may improve quality assurance and reduce the inefficiency of 'traditional' state bureaucracy (Schwarz and Westerheijden, 2004); however, the auditing practices of accreditation agencies may involve new problems such as a new bureaucratization of universities and an increasing standardization and homogenization of teaching programmes as well as ignorance of non-measurable quality properties (Münch, 2011). With the establishment of the European Consortium for Accreditation (ECA) in order to mutually recognize accreditation decisions, control and bureaucratization seem to be reintroduced on a higher level.

The logic of managed education demands a division of labour on the lines of teaching, research and management of academic affairs, and results in new groups or actors. In Germany this trend is becoming visible, even though Germany is still lagging behind in hiring professional full-time presidents or deans (Kirchgessner, 2011), and some academics are critical about the division of teaching and research contradicting the Humboldtian ideal of their unity (Meier and Schimank, 2009; Münch, 2009).

While we recognize different responses to managed education by German universities, the most wide-ranging response is the emergence of a new archetype – the entrepreneurial university. Entrepreneurial universities are opportunity-seeking and opportunity-exploiting regimes that respond strategically to challenges in their core domains of research, teaching and commercialization of academic knowledge in order to fulfil their mission. The entrepreneurial university (Guerrero-Cano and Urbano, 2010) strives for the 'capitalization and commercialization of knowledge' (Slaughter and Leslie, 1997), the 'contribution to local economic development' (Röpke, 1998), and the 'development of an entrepreneurial culture', both within and around the university (Clark, 1998; Kirby, 2005).

Governance system
The changes in institutional logics were accompanied by a move from the state to the market model of governance. The new system of governance is reflected in an internal reorganization and managerialization (Blümel et al., 2011) of the university and new external relationships to the state and other actors in the field such as intermediaries.

The internal governance system of universities has been changed by strengthening the rights of university administrators while reducing the participation rights of academic and non-academic members. The withdrawal of democratic rules was manifested in the following structures:

Shifting power structure – from a rectoral to a presidential constitution   The introduction of councils goes hand in hand – at least ideally – with a strengthening of the executive committee and a weakening of the senate by reducing the latter's competencies in academic matters (Kluth, 2001; Meyer-Guckel et al., 2010).

Emergence of university councils (boards of trustees)   Behind the diversity of state laws of Higher Education, three commonalities can be identified: the council is an additional managing body to the traditional organs of rectorate and senate; in most states, the majority of its members or all of the trustees are to be non-university members, the idea being to make university leadership more sensitive and responsive to the broader demands of society; inspired by NPM, councils are taking over supervision and control functions, which had previously been performed by state bureaucrats; university managers should be more professionalized and take the managerial practices from the corporate world as an important reference point (Kluth, 2001; Bogumil et al., 2007; Burtscheidt, 2010; Meyer-Guckel et al., 2010).

Shifting incentives   In the past, professors could negotiate initial endowments and resources were fixed for the duration of their tenure (Burtscheidt, 2010). In managed education, academics increasingly are paid for their performance in research, teaching, and other university-relevant domains, as measured by such indicators like the acquisition of external funding, number and quality of journal publications as well as specific objectives that bring academics into line with the university's strategy (Osterloh and Frey, 2008).

Mergers of Higher Education institutions for cost efficiency and strategic profile development   Whereas mergers in Higher Education have been widespread in the USA, UK, Australia and the Netherlands since the 1970s (Harman and Meek, 1988; Goedegebuure, 1992; Skodvin, 1999; Harman and Harman, 2003) in Germany mergers are a fairly new phenomenon. Motives for these mergers are profile development, quality improvement, raising visibility, economies of scale, and synergy effects to improve the position in competitive education markets (Battke and Cremer-Renz, 2006; Weber, 2009; Pruisken, 2012). Empirically, the majority of the few mergers in Germany still reflect state-decreed cost reduction policies (Pruisken, 2012).

The reforms of external governance were designed to encourage competition among universities and enhanced an increasing degree of autonomy. However, the autonomy gained is ambivalent: the 4th amendment of the Higher Education Framework Law in 1998 was an important legal step towards achieving the universal desire for increased university autonomy by deregulating internal and external organization, administration and the budgeting process. Following NPM, input control was replaced by output control, that is, funding was now related to outputs through goal attainments, controlling, reporting and auditing systems based on performance indicators (Nickel, 2007). Cameralism in the era of managed education was disappearing, to be replaced by global budgets, where the state only provides few aggregated items (in the extreme case two items: investments and current expenditures). In practice, the degree of financial autonomy of universities varies by state law and in most cases a 'minimal cameralism' remains (Ziegele, 2002). Generally, universities have gained a new degree of autonomy over their resources, especially financial resources, and they can allocate inputs themselves in order to accomplish specific outputs. These changes have brought universities an increasing autonomy, which is the necessary condition for creating profiles and striving for excellence by becoming entrepreneurial (Meier and Schimank, 2010; Weingart, 2010). However, in practice it has not stopped the states from cutting university funding (Behrens et al., 2006) and maintaining influence (Knobloch, 2010).

Substitution of basic funding through competitive funding programmes   Funding agencies in the form of transnational organizations such as the World Bank or the European Union, national research foundations such as the Deutsche Forschungsgemeinschaft (DFG), Volkswagenstiftung and programmes offered by federal, state and local government agencies are important actors in shaping research. In Germany, the percentage of total funding accounted for by so-called third party funds is increasing continually (DESTATIS, 2009). Funding agencies develop research programmes ranging from the future of production (BMBF)[1] to Joint Ventures for Caucasian railways (EU). More recently, the most prominent of these competitive funding programmes is the federal Excellence Initiative, which is having a considerable impact on restructuring the German Higher Education system into a competitive, incentive-driven, and demand-oriented service system (Kehm and Pasternack, 2008; Leibfried, 2010; Sieweke, 2010). Typically, these programmes initiate interaction within the academic community and, depending on the programme, even facilitate inter-disciplinary discourse. The institutional function of these programmes is at least twofold. First, they offer specific research services for the beneficiaries. Second, programmes trigger innovations in the scientific system. As studies on innovation problems of research groups show, research teams have a tendency to stabilize the status quo and therefore demonstrate conservative behaviour patterns (Krohn and Küppers, 1989). Krohn and Küppers (ibid., p. 89) argue that this situation leads to an interesting paradox. In those areas where science can be practised autonomously, we can recognize a tendency of research groups to do the same thing over and over again, while in areas where they have to attract external funding substantial greater innovating activities can be recognized. In this respect, funding agencies perform an important cognitive function for the scientific community. These programmes are constructions of future knowledge and considerably affect the cognitive orientation of researchers (Braun, 1998). Competitive funding is subject to criticism, for it restricts knowledge creation, especially in times when basic funding for independent research by professors is being reduced, leads to a stratification of universities (Münch, 2009), and creates inefficient resource allocation because of declining economies of scale (Binswanger, 2010; Münch, 2011).

CONCLUSION

The key motivation for writing this chapter was the growing awareness that the Higher Education system in Germany and in most other Western countries is undergoing a fundamental institutional change. This change is redefining the rules of the game of science and scholarship; and hence the roles played by universities and scholars as well as the state within this emerging institutional context of managed education. While managed education is a far more tangible reality in the Anglo-Saxon world, it has also become the key reconfiguring force for the German system of Higher Education (Rhoades and Sporn, 2002; Münch, 2007, 2011; Burtscheidt, 2010). However, the German version of managed education is not simply a transfer of practices that have been implemented elsewhere, especially in the UK and the USA. It turns out to be a locally adapted form with substantial variations in actors and governance systems. Since all education systems have a history of creating a path dependency, our aim was not simply to reconstruct the current state of affairs of the German system of Higher Education. Rather, we wanted to understand how the institutional changes have unfolded over time and emerged into systems of beliefs, norms and practices in the postwar period. As a result, we developed a typology of institutional eras composed of a unique interplay of logics, actors and governance systems. The German system of Higher Education, we argue, departed in the postwar period from an era of professional dominance (1945–68), which was replaced by an era of federal involvement and democratization (1968–98) until more recently managerialism and marketization became guiding principles for the new archetype of managed education (since 1998). With managed education a new type of university – the entrepreneurial university – emerged as a strategic response to the institutional pressures.

We argue that the evolution of the institutional system of Higher Education not only in Germany, but also in many other Western countries, swung like a pendulum between the two extreme systems' designs: one fostering individual freedom of scientific autonomy and one emphasizing the instrumental character of science for national educational agendas. Both extremes describe a fundamental tension: is the role of the education system geared towards the values and norms of the republic of science (Polanyi, 1962) or is Higher Education designed to serve predetermined educational interests and goals of the state? As Olsen (2007) points out, 'institutional change is often seen as driven by perceived failure' (p. 52), which undermines the legitimacy of institutions and is followed by processes of de-institutionalization (Greenwood et al., 2002). The rise of the student movement and the desire of the federal government for central planning of the education system had led the Higher Education system to swing from one that emphasized scientific autonomy to the other extreme. Only during the third era of managed education has it started to return to a more balanced position.

In managed education, policy-makers orchestrate autonomy of research and teaching with the need to coordinate these decentralized policies by promoting cooperation and competition at different levels within and across universities and regions. Orchestrating the Higher Education system becomes a balancing act for policy-makers. New Public Management and wide-ranging auditing and control practices can be applied to over-manage the system. The faith of policy-makers in the use of quantitative goal attainments, evaluations and rankings as control instruments of the Higher Education system can undermine professional self-regulation (Freidson, 2001) and may even foster professional disintegration (Broadbent et al., 1997). On the contrary, fostering too much competition and relying predominantly on market forces facilitate the commodification of science (Bunge, 1998a). Some of the dysfunctional effects of the marketization of science, such as rising student consumerism (Riesmann, 1998; Gumport, 2000), intellectual prostitution (Frey, 2003), the undermining of scientific creativity (Heinze et al., 2009), and a loss of intrinsic motivation (Osterloh and Frey, 2008; Binswanger, 2010) are well documented.

Future research should therefore investigate in-depth the consequences of managed education and different policy approaches. To this end we propose a multi-level analysis (Reihlen, et al., 2007; Reihlen and Werr, 2012). Such an analysis entails first the level of the Higher Education field, involving actors, logics and governing systems, as well as processes of change; second the level of the university, and in our case especially the emerging archetype of the entrepreneurial university and its transformation processes; and third the level of the individual scholar, socialized and embedded in this new institutional setting. The guiding research question is: how does managed education affect the reconfiguration of the Higher Education field, the strategic choices and structures especially of universities, and the motivation and behaviour of scholars? Shedding more light on these issues and developing sustainable policy measures are crucial for the future governing practices of academia and consequently for its usefulness and relevance to society.

NOTES

*   We greatly appreciate the funding of this research by a grant from the German Federal Ministry of Education and Research (Grant No. 01PW11018B).
1.   BMBF: Bundesministerium für Bildung und Forschung (German Federal Ministry of Education and Research).

REFERENCES

Abbott, A. (1988), *The System of Professions: An Essay on the Division of Expert Labor*, Chicago: University of Chicago Press.
Adler, N.J. and A.W. Harzing (2009), 'When knowledge wins: Transcending the sense and nonsense of academic rankings', *The Academy of Management Learning and Education – ARCHIVE*, **8**(1), 72–95.
Baldridge, J.V. and T.E. Deal (eds) (1983), *The Dynamics of Organizational Change in Education*, Richmond, TX: McCutchan.
Bartlett, W. and J. Le Grand (1993), *Quasi-Markets and Social Policy*, Houndmills, Basingstoke: Macmillan.
Battke, K. and C. Cremer-Renz (eds) (2006), *Hochschulfusionen in Deutschland: Gemeinsam stark?!* Bielefeld: UVW.
Bauß, G. (1977), *Die Studentenbewegung der sechziger Jahre in der Bundesrepublik und Westberlin: Handbuch*, Köln: Pahl-Rugenstein.
Becker, T.P. and U. Schröder (eds) (2000), *Die Studentenproteste der 60er Jahre: Archivführer, Chronik, Bibliographie*, Köln: Böhlau.
Behrens, T., M. Leszczensky, C. Mück and A. Schwarzenberger (2006), 'Flexibilisierung und Globalisierung der Hochschulhaushalte der Bundesländer im Vergleich', HIS Projektbericht.

Binswanger, M. (2010.), *Sinnlose Wettbewerbe: Warum wir immer mehr Unsinn produzieren*, Freiburg: Herder.
Blümel, A., K. Kloke and G. Krücken (2011), 'Professionalisierungsprozesse im Hochschulmanagement in Deutschland', in A. Langer and A. Schroer (eds), *Professionalisierung im Nonprofit Management*, Wiesbaden: VS, pp. 105–31.
Bogumil, J., R.G., Heinze, S. Grohs and S. Gerberg (2007), 'Hochschulräte als neues Steuerungsinstrument? Eine empirische Analyse der Mitglieder und Aufgabenbereiche', Düsseldorf: Hans-Böckler-Stiftung.
Bok, D. (2003), *Universities in the Marketplace: The Commercialization of Higher Education*, Princeton, NJ: Princeton University Press.
Braun, D. (1998), 'The role of funding agencies in the cognitive development of science, *Research Policy*, **27**(8), 807–21.
Brint, S. (1994), *In an Age of Experts: The Changing Role of Professionals in Politics and Public Life*, Princeton, NJ: Princeton University Press.
Broadbent, J., M. Dietrich and J. Roberts (eds) (1997), *The End of the Professions? Restructuring of Professional Work*, London: Routledge.
Bührmann, A.D. (2008), 'Der Bologna-Prozess: seine Risiken und Nebenwirkungen', in K. Zimmermann, M. Kamphans and S. Metz-Göckel (eds), *Perspektiven der Hochschulforschung*, Wiesbaden: VS, pp. 215–30.
Bunge, M. (1998a), *Social Science Under Debate*, Toronto: University of Toronto Press.
Bunge, M. (1998b), *Social Science Under Debate: A Philosophical Perspective*, Toronto: University of Toronto Press.
Burtscheidt, C. (2010), *Humboldts falsche Erben – Eine Bilanz der deutschen Hochschulreform*, Frankfurt a.M.: Campus.
Burtscher, C. and P.-P. Pasqualoni (2004), 'Demokratie im Universitätsbetrieb?' in W.G. Weber, P.-P. Pasqualoni and C. Burtscher (eds), *Wirtschaft, Demokratie und soziale Verantwortung: Kontinuitäten und Brüche*, Göttingen: Vandenhoeck and Ruprecht, pp. 347–76.
Clark, B.R. (1983), *The Higher Education System: Academic Organization in Cross-national Perspective*, Berkeley, CA: University of California Press.
Clark, B.R. (1998), *Creating Entrepreneurial Universities: Organizational Pathways of Transformation*, Oxford: Pergamon Press.
Confederation of EU Rectors' Conferences (2000), 'The Bologna Declaration on the European Space for Higher Education: An explanation', accessed 5 August 2013 at http://ec.europa.eu/education/policies/educ/bologna/bologna.pdf.
DESTATIS (2009), 'Hochschulstandort Deutschland 2009. Ergebnisse aus der Hochschulstatistik', accessed 5 August 2013 at https://www.destatis.de/DE/Publikationen/Thematisch/BildungForschungKultur/Hochschulen/Hochschulstandort5213101099004.pdf.
Etzkowski, H., A. Webster and P. Healey (1998), *Capitalizing Knowledge: New Directions of Industry and Academe*, Albany, NY: Suny Press.
European Council (2000), 'Presidency conclusions. Lisbon strategy', 23 and 24 March 2000.
Fallon, D. (1980), *The Germany University: A Heroic Idea in Conflict with the Modern World*, Boulder, CO: Colarado Associated University Press.
Freidson, E. (1970), *Professional Dominance*, Chicago: Aldine.
Freidson, E. (2001), *Professionalism: The Third Logic*, Cambridge, UK: Polity.
Frey, B.S. (2003), 'Publishing as prostitution? Choosing between one's own ideas and academic success', *Public Choice*, **116**(1), 205–23.
Frey, B. and M. Osterloh (2010), 'Academic rankings and research governance', University of Zurich, CREMA Working Paper.
Goedegebuure, L. (1992), *Mergers in Higher Education. A Comparative Perspective*, Utrecht: Lemma.
Greenwood, R., R. Suddaby and C.R. Hinings (2002), 'Theorizing change: The role of professional associations in the transformation of institutionalized fields', *Academy of Management Journal*, **45**(1), 58–80.

Gruening, G. (2001), 'Origin and theoretical basis of New Public Management', *International Public Management Journal*, **4**(1), 1–25.

Guerrero-Cano, M. and D. Urbano (2010), 'The development of an entrepreneurial university', *The Journal of Technology Transfer*, **37**(1), 43–74.

Gumport, P.J. (2000), 'Academic restructuring: Organizational change and institutional imperatives', *Higher Education*, **39**(1), 67–91.

Habermas, J. (1969), *Protestbewegung und Hochschulreform*, Frankfurt a.M.: Suhrkamp.

Hanft, A. and I. Müskens (eds) (2005), *Bologna und die Folgen für die Hochschulen*, Bielefeld: UVW.

Harman, G. and K.M. Harman (2003), 'Dissemination of the findings of educational research', in J.P. Keeves and R. Watanabe (eds), *International Handbook of Educational Research in the Asia Pacific Region*, Dordrecht: Kluwer Academic Publishers, pp. 1137–50.

Harman, G.S. and V.L. Meek (1988), *Australian Higher Education Reconstructed? Analysis of the Proposals and Assumptions of the Dawkins Green Paper*, Armidale, NSW: Dept. of Administrative and Higher Education Studies, University of New England.

Heinze, T., P. Shapirabm, J.D. Rogers and J.M. Senkerd (2009), 'Organizational and institutional influences on creativity in scientific research', *Research Policy*, **38**, 610–23.

Hödl, E. and W. Zegelin (1999), *Hochschulreform und Hochschulmanagement. Eine kritische Bestandsaufnahme der aktuellen Diskussion*, Marburg: Metropolis.

Jarausch, K.H. (1999), 'Das Humboldt-Syndrom: Die Westdeutschen Universitäten von 1945–1989. Ein akademischer Sonderweg?', in M.G. Ash (ed.), *Mythos Humboldt. Vergangenheit und Zukunft der deutschen Universitäten*, Wien: Böhlau, pp. 58–79.

Jessen, R. (2010), 'Massenausbildung, Unterfinanzierung und Stagnation. Ost- und Westdeutsche Universitäten in der siebzigern und achtziger Jahren', in M. Grüttner, R. Hachtmann, K.H. Jarausch and J. John (eds), *Gebrochene Wissenschaftskulturen: Universität und Politik im 20. Jahrhundert*, Göttingen: Vandenhoeck and Ruprecht, pp. 261–78.

Kehm, B.M. and P. Pasternack (2008), 'The German "Excellence Initiative" and its role in restructuring the national Higher Education landscape', in D. Palfreyman and T. Tapper (eds), *Structuring Mass Higher Education. The Role of Elite Institutions*, London: Routledge, pp. 113–27.

KGSt (2012), *Das Neue Steuerungsmodell. Begründung, Konturen, Umsetzung (B 5/1993)*, Köln: Municipal Association for Administration Management [Kommunale Gemeinschaftsstelle für Verwaltungsmanagement (KGst)].

Kirby, D.A. (2005), 'Creating entrepreneurial universities in the UK: Applying entrepreneurship theory to practice', *Journal of Technology Transfer*, **31**(5), 599–603.

Kirchgessner, K. (2011), 'Der Dekan als Manager', *Zeit Online*.

Kluth, W. (2001), *Nachfrageorientierte Steuerung der Studienangebote. Rechtsgutachten*, Gütersloh: CHE Centrum für Hochschulentwicklung.

Knobloch, C. (2010), *Wir sind doch nicht blöd! Die unternehmerische Hochschule*, Münster: Westfälisches Dampfboot.

Koch, H.-A. (2008), *Die Universität: Geschichte einer europäischen Institution*, Darmstadt: WBG.

Krohn, W. and G. Küppers (1989), *Die Selbstorganisation der Wissenschaft*, Frankfurt a.M.: Suhrkamp.

Kühler, L.L. (2006), *Hochschulreform in Deutschland nach amerikanischem Vorbild: Chancen, Möglichkeiten und Grenzen*, Saarbrücken: VDM.

Küpper, H.-U. (2009), 'Effizienzreform der deutschen Hochschulen nach 1990 – Hintergründe, Ziele, Komponenten', *Beiträge zur Hochschulforschung*, **31**(4), 50–75.

Lane, J.-E. (2000), *New Public Management*, London, New York: Routledge.

Lange, S. (2008), 'New Public Management und die Governance der Universitäten', *er moderne staat – Zeitschrift für Public Policy, Recht und Management*, **1**(1), 235–48.

Larson, M.S. (1977), *The Rise of Professionalism*, Berkeley, CA: University of California Press.

Leibfried, S. (ed.) (2010), *Die Exzellenzinitiative. Zwischenbilanz und Perspektiven*, Frankfurt a.M.: Campus.

Lullies, S. (1996), 'Rückblick und Wertung. I. Der Hintergrund der 68er-Bewegung', in K. Strobel and G. Schmirber (eds), *Drei Jahrzehnte Umbruch der deutschen Universitäten*, Vierow: SH-Verlag, pp. 226–8.

Meier, F. and U. Schimank (2009), 'Matthäus schlägt Humboldt? New Public Management und die Einheit von Forschung und Lehre', *Beiträge zur Hochschulforschung*, **31**(1), 42–61.

Meier, F. and U. Schimank (2010), 'Mission now possible: Profile building and leadership in German universities', in R. Whitley, J. Gläser and L. Engwall (eds), *Reconfiguring Knowledge Production*, Oxford: Oxford University Press, pp. 211–36.

Meyer, H.J. and D. Müller-Böling (eds) (1996), *Hochschulzugang in Deutschland – Status quo und Perspektiven*, Gütersloh: Bertelsmann.

Meyer, S. (2010), 'Akkreditierung als kooperatives Verwaltungsverfahren. Gewährleistung von Qualität, Transparenz und Vielfalt oder verfassungswidrige Einschränkung der Lehrfreiheit?' in S. Meyer and B. Pfeiffer (eds), *Die gute Hochschule. Ideen, Konzepte und Perspektiven*, Berlin: Sigma, pp. 143–58.

Meyer-Guckel, V., M. Winde and F. Ziegele (2010), *Handbuch Hochschulräte. Denkanstöße und Erfolgsfaktoren für die Praxis*, Essen: Stifterverband.

Münch, R. (2007), *Die akademische Elite*, Frankfurt a.M.: Suhrkamp.

Münch, R. (2009), 'Entkopplung, Kolonialisierung, Zielverschiebung. Wissenschaft unter dem Regime des Exzellenzwettbewerbs zwischen Universitäten', *Bulletin*, **136**(Dezember), 8–11.

Münch, R. (2011), *Akademischer Kapitalismus: Über die politische Ökonomie der Hochschulreform*, Frankfurt a.M.: Suhrkamp.

Nickel, S. (2007), *Partizipatives Management von Universitäten: Zielvereinbarungen, Leitungsstrukturen, staatliche Steuerung*, München: Rainer Hampp.

Nickel, S., T. Zdebel and D.F. Westerheijden (2009), 'Joint degrees im europäischen Hochschulraum. Hindernisse und Chancen transnationaler Studiengangskooperationen am Beispiel der EUREGIO Deutschland-Niederlande', CHE Centrum für Hochschulentwicklung, CHEPS Center for Higher Education Policy Studies, Euregio.

Nitsch, W. (1983), 'Hochschule als Organisation', in L. Huber (ed.), *Ausbildung und Sozialisation in der Hochschule*, Stuttgart: Klett: pp. 141–50.

Nixon, J. (2004), 'Education for the good society: The integrity of academic practice', *London Review of Education*, **2**(3), 245–52.

Oehler, C. (1989), *Hochschulentwicklung in der Bundesrepublik Deutschland seit 1945*, Frankfurt: Campus.

Olsen, J.P. (2007), 'The institutional dynamics of the European university', in P. Maassen and J.P. Olsen (eds), *University Dynamics and European Integration*, Hamburg: Springer, pp. 25–54.

Osterloh, M. and B.S. Frey (2008), 'Anreize im Wissenschaftssystem', CREMA Research Paper, Universität Zürich.

Pasternack, P. and C. von Wissel (2010), 'Programmatische Konzepte der Hochschulentwicklung in Deutschland seit 1945', Arbeitspapier No. 204, Düsseldorf: Hans-Böckler-Stiftung.

Polanyi, M. (1962), 'The republic of science: its political and economic theory', *Minerva*, **38**(1), 1–21.

Power, M. (1997), *The Audit Society: Rituals of Verification*: Oxford: Oxford University Press.

Pruisken, I. (2012), 'Institutionelle Erneuerung durch Fusion? Vergleich von Hochschulfusionen in Deutschland und Großbritannien', in T. Heinze and G. Krücken (eds), *Institutionelle Erneuerungsfähigkeit der Forschung*, Wiesbaden: VS.

Reihlen, M. and A. Werr (eds) (2012), *Handbook of Research on Entrepreneurship in Professional Services*, Cheltenham, UK and Northampton, MA, USA: Edward Elgar.

Reihlen, M., T. Klaas-Wissing and T. Ringberg (2007), 'Metatheories in management studies: Reflections upon individualism, holism, and systemism', *M@n@gement*, **10**(3), 49–69.

Rektorenkonferenz, W. (ed.), (1961), *Dokumente zur Hochschulreform*, Wiesbaden: Franz Steiner.
Rhoades, G. and B. Sporn (2002), 'New models of management and cost production: Europe and the United States', *Tertiary Education and Management*, **8**(1) 3–28.
Riesmann, D. (1998), *On Higher Education. The Academic Enterprise in an Era of Rising Student Consumerism*, New Brunswick, NJ: Transaction Publishers.
Ritzer, G. (2004), *The Globalization of Nothing*, Thousand Oaks, CA: Pine Forge Press.
Rohstock, A. (2009), *Von der 'Ordinarienuniversität' zur 'Revolutionszentrale'?: Hoch schulreform und Hochschulrevolte in Bayern und Hessen 1957–1976*, München: Oldenbourg.
Röpke, J. (1998), 'The entrepreneurial university. Innovation, academic knowledge creation and regional development in a globalized economy', Department of Economics, Philipps-Universität Marburg.
Schmidt, L. and D. Thelen (1969), *Hochschulreform. Gefahr im Verzuge?* Frankfurt a.M.: Fischer.
Schmitthenner, W. (1986), 'Studentenschaft und Studentenvereinigungen nach 1945', in W. Doerr (ed.), *Semper Apertus. Sechshundert Jahre Ruprecht-Karls-Universität Heidelberg. 1386–1986*, Berlin: Springer, pp. 569–616.
Schmoch, U. and T. Schubert (2010), 'Strategic steering of research by New Public Management in German universities: A looming state–science conflict?' *Research Evaluation*, **19**(3), 209–16.
Schofer, E. and J.W. Meyer (2005), 'The worldwide expansion of Higher Education in the twentieth century', *American Sociological Review*, **70**(6), 898–920.
Schwarz, S. and D.F. Westerheijden (eds) (2004), *Accreditation and Evaluation in the European Higher Education area*, London: Springer.
Scott, J.C. (2006), 'The mission of the university: Medieval to postmodern transformations', *The Journal of Higher Education*, **77**(1), 1–39.
Scott, W.R., M. Ruef, P.J. Mendel and C.A. Caronna (2000), *Institutional Change and Healthcare Organizations: From Professional Dominance to Managed Care*, Chicago: University of Chicago Press.
Seeliger, B. (2005), 'Leitfaden zur Anwendung der Kapazitätsverordnung', Planning Department of Hamburg University.
Sieweke, S. (2010), 'Die Wirkungen der Exzellenzinitiative auf die deutsche Hochschul-landschaft', *die hochschule*, **2**, 120–39.
Skodvin, O.-J. (1999), 'Mergers in Higher Education – success or failure?' *Tertiary Education and Management*, **5**(1), 65–80.
Slaughter, S. and B. Cantwell (2011), 'Transatlantic moves to the market: The United States and the European Union', *Higher Education*, **63**(5), 583–606.
Slaughter, S. and L.L. Leslie (1997), *Academic Capitalism: Politics, Policies, and the Entrepreneurial University*, Baltimore, MD: Johns Hopkins University Press.
Slaughter, S. and G. Rhoades (2004), *Academic Capitalism and the New Economy: Markets, State, and Higher Education*, Baltimore, MD: Johns Hopkins University Press.
Teichler, U. and C. Bode (1990), *Das Hochschulwesen in der Bundesrepublik Deutschland*, Weinheim: Deutscher Studien Verlag.
Thornton, P.H. and W. Ocasio (1999), 'Institutional logics and the historical contingency of power in organizations: Executive succession in the Higher Education publishing industry, 1958–1990', *American Journal of Sociology*, **105**(3), 801–44.
Veblen, T. (1918), *The Higher Learning in America*, New York: B.W. Huebsch.
Warning, S. (2007), *The Economic Analysis of Universities. Strategic Groups and Positioning*, Cheltenham, UK and Northampton, MA, USA: Edward Elgar.
Weber, W. (2009), 'Hochschulfusionen als strategische Maßnahme: Nutzung von Ergebnissen der Fusionsforschung', in T. Wrona (ed.), *Strategische Managementforschung – Aktuelle Entwicklungen und internationale Perspektiven*, Wiesbaden: Gabler, pp. 127–48.
Webler, W.-D. (1983), 'Geschichte der Hochschule seit 1945', in L. Huber (ed.), *Enzyklopädie Erziehungswissenschaft*, Stuttgart: Klett, pp. 169–92.

Weingart, P. (2010), 'Die "unternehmerische Universität"', in D. Gugerli (ed.), *Universität*, Zürich: Diaphanes, pp. 55–72.

Weingart, P. and S. Maasen (2007), 'Elite through rankings: The emergence of the enterprising university', in R. Whitley and J. Gläser (eds), *The Changing Governance of the Sciences. The Advent of Research Evaluation Systems*, Dordrecht: Springer Netherlands, pp. 75–99.

Wissema, J.G. (2009), *Towards the Third Generation University: Managing the University in Transition*, Cheltenham, UK and Northampton, MA, USA: Edward Elgar.

Witte, J.K. (2006), *Change of Degrees and Degrees of Change: Comparing Adaptations of European Higher Education Systems in the Context of the Bologna Process*, CHEPS, Center for Higher Education Policy Studies.

Witte, J.K. and T. von Stuckrad (2007), 'Kapazitätsplanung in gestuften Studienstrukturen. Vergleichende Analyse des Vorgehens in 16 Bundesländern', CHE Working Paper No. 89.

Ziegele, F. (2002), 'Reformansätze und Perspektiven der Hochschulsteuerung in Deutschland', *Beiträge zur Hochschulforschung*, **24**(3), 106–21.

6. University entrepreneurship education in Tanzania: introducing entrepreneurship education in a context of transition

Ernest Samwel Mwasalwiba, Peter Groenewegen and Ingrid Wakkee*

INTRODUCTION

In Africa, the education of entrepreneurial graduates is equated with the future prosperity of the nation (Kenway et al., 2004; Morley et al., 2009). This purported economic role of entrepreneurs in Africa (Bigsten and Söderbom, 2006) and the apparent link between an entrepreneur's level of education and the quality of business innovation, growth and success increased the demand for entrepreneurship education (Robinson and Sexton, 1994; Kuzilwa, 2005). In Tanzania, the increase in the number of enterprising graduates thus has been a major policy priority (Kaijage, 2001; Kristiansen, 2001; Wedgwood, 2007). Yet, surprisingly, self-employment among graduates has recently been reported to be falling (Al-Samarrai and Bennell, 2003; Mukyanuzi, 2003). Therefore, the conundrum of the effectiveness of teaching entrepreneurship in this specific context provides an interesting focus.

This study has two aims. First, it aims at understanding the steps in the process of entrepreneurship education and the need for more entrepreneurial universities that might lead to an increase in high-value entrepreneurial activities in developing countries. Second, it extends instructional design theories to the domain of entrepreneurship education, thereby answering the call to exploit already developed and empirically established educational theories to the field of entrepreneurship education (Béchard and Grégoire, 2005). To that end, the following research questions were formulated:

1 What are the objectives, methods and general teaching context of Tanzanian academic entrepreneurship education?
2 To what extent do Tanzanian universities actually support the introduction of academic entrepreneurship education and how is this

reflected in the way in which they have created an infrastructure that actually supports entrepreneurial education, entrepreneurial students and staff?

3 What are the general entry-level profiles, career interests and learning expectations of academic entrepreneurship students in Tanzania?

4 To what extent does academic entrepreneurship education in Tanzania meet students' expectations? And to what degree does it influence students' interest towards a career in entrepreneurship?

5 What is the state of alignment between the teaching contexts, methods and students' profiles? Does this explain the current level of achievement and the decreasing number of graduate entrepreneurs?

In developing a theoretical framework to guide our empirical research, the Biggs 3P model (Biggs, 2003) is connected to the concept of the entrepreneurial university as it has been defined by Clark (1998, 2004) and Schulte (2004). Clark (2004) and Schulte (2004) argue that in addition to training future entrepreneurs, an entrepreneurial university also has to develop an entrepreneurial spirit amongst all students and staff members and establish connections to the regional environment to facilitate actual entrepreneurial activities by students and staff members via the training of staff, the allocation of funding, the alignment of courses with the overall entrepreneurial agenda and continuous evaluation of teaching in terms of its quality and relevance (European Commission, 2008). The empirical study was based on a mixed method design, including qualitative and quantitative sources of information collected from four Tanzanian universities where semester-long courses on entrepreneurship are offered.

The remainder of this chapter is structured as follows. First, a conceptual framework is presented in which we relate the concept of the entrepreneurial university to the Biggs 3P model of instructional design (Biggs, 2003). This framework will form the basis of the empirical analysis. Next, the methodology is described, followed by the results. This chapter ends with a discussion and conclusion in which implications for policy-makers and educators in Tanzania and beyond are presented.

CONCEPTUAL ISSUES

The concept of the entrepreneurial university has received significant attention since the publication of Clark's book in 1998. According to Clark, universities around the world were increasingly confronted with changes that led to demands that increasingly ask too much of the response capacity of these institutions. These demands include the rise in the number and diversity of students, future employer expectations, cost reductions and knowledge production. Clark (1998, 2004) argued that becoming more entrepreneurial, as an institution, would form the answer to this challenge. In Western countries, earning revenues via commercialization of research outputs has become the dominant model of the entrepreneurial university (Slaughter and Leslie, 2001; Markman et al., 2008) Yet, this techno-economic paradigm may be in conflict with the broader social purpose of Higher Education and its contribution towards the public good, social renewal and basic development (Subotzky, 1999). In the African context, where this social purpose of Higher Education is more pronounced than in developed countries, and where commercially valuable research output is scarcer, models of the entrepreneurial university that focus on education rather than on research are needed. This idea is in line with current ideas of what academic entrepreneurship entails according to the European Commission. Besides training future entrepreneurs, becoming an entrepreneurial university involves the development of an entrepreneurial spirit amongst all students and staff members and the establishment of connections to the regional environment to facilitate actual entrepreneurial activities by students and staff members via the training of staff, the allocation of funding, the alignment of courses with the overall entrepreneurial agenda, and continuous evaluation of teaching in terms of its quality and relevance (European Commission, 2008).

In Africa, including Tanzania, universities were initially founded to train civil servants and thus have little to no experience in educating entrepreneurs (Juma, 2005). Resource shortages leave narrow space for innovation. Therefore, building a teaching model that is properly aligned for this purpose is essential.

While originally aimed at the individual lecturer rather than at the institutional level, we argue that the Biggs 3P model of instructional alignment (Biggs, 1996, 2003) offers a useful model to analyse the extent to which universities are en route towards becoming more entrepreneurial. His model has been widely employed by course developers and evaluators in their efforts to assure a 'proper alignment' within their educational systems (Freeth and Reeves, 2004; Reeves, 2006); it consists of three components: presage, process and product (Figure 6.1).

First, *presage* refers to both the teaching context including the teaching objectives, the profile of the lecturers, the means of assessment and the general teaching environment or climate, as well as to a number of student-related factors including their background and expectations. Second, the *process* refers to the activities that are undertaken so that students can actually learn to the extent that objectives and expectations are met. Finally, the *product* refers to the outcomes of these activities both

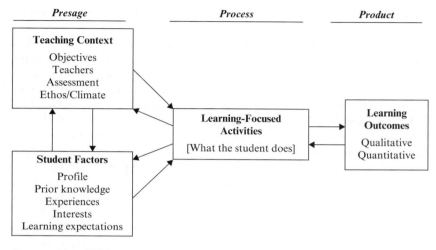

Source: Biggs (1996).

Figure 6.1   3P model of instructional design

in quantitative and qualitative terms. In an aligned instructional system, the presage and process interact to produce the product in service to a common goal, while imbalances in the system will lead to poor teaching and superficial learning. Non-alignment is reflected in inconsistencies, unmet expectations, and practices that contradict what is taught (Biggs, 2003).

When relating this model to the notion of the entrepreneurial university, a number of issues come to the fore. First, because entrepreneurship education is a relatively new arrival in the academic field, few senior lecturers are actually educated in entrepreneurship themselves. Consequently, entrepreneurship is often taught by lecturers who have sometimes forcibly switched from their original (more or less related) specializations to entrepreneurship without having the necessary theoretical understanding (Low, 2001; Kuratko, 2005). Such ill-prepared lecturers are more likely to misunderstand student profiles and this can lead to misdirected teaching approaches and failure to achieve teaching objectives (Ferguson, 2003). Furthermore, while there is growing consensus amongst entrepreneurship scholars that entrepreneurship can be taught (Kuratko, 2005) many individuals from outside the domain continue to doubt this stand (Hindle, 2007). If the newly assigned lecturers share such doubts and voice these in the presence of students, the legitimacy of the education and thereby its impact are compromised. Finally, the lack of sufficiently trained lecturers may lead to overcrowded classes and limited opportunities for small-scale interactive or action-based education.

Second, while most (university) policy-makers continue to focus solely on stimulating students to become self-employed (Fayolle and Gailly, 2008), entrepreneurship education does not have to be limited to producing future self-employed people but it can also be focused on future intrapreneurs or even a variety of professionals like policy-makers and bankers who can support entrepreneurs (Mwasalwiba, 2010). The inclusion of different combinations of objectives clearly poses different requirements for course designs.

Third, as Tanzanian society has only recently begun to favour entrepreneurship (Wedgwood, 2007), considerable variety is likely to exist amongst university students in terms of their entry profiles. The effects of these differences may be reinforced by the changing employers' preferences (Henderson and Robertson, 1999). Different experiences, values and career expectations shapes students' expectations about the course, in terms of what benefits will be achieved by attending the course (Gigliotti, 1987). Lecturers who recognize this can make the learning process as responsive as possible to learners' differing goals and starting points (Freeth and Reeves, 2004).

Fourth, little consensus exists regarding how entrepreneurship should be taught and some even argue that current teaching methods are inadequate as they are still based on traditional approaches used by business schools (Hindle, 2007). A relevant distinction is made by Biggs (1999) who distinguishes teacher-focused and student-focused strategies. Teacher-focused strategies involve transmission of information from the teacher (expert) to the student (inexpert), the focus lies on what the teacher does, that is, getting it across. According to Hindle (2007) a teacher-focused strategy is more appropriate for teaching a class *about* entrepreneurship as economic or socio-cultural phenomena or its impact on development. A student-focused approach aims at bringing about a conceptual change in students' understanding of the world. According to Biggs (1999) learning is foremost a result of students' learning-focused activities which are engaged in by students due to both their own perception and inputs and the teaching context. Thus, what matters is not what the lecturer does, rather *what the student does* to learn. A combination of teacher-centred and student-centred strategies would be appropriate when students are prepared for becoming entrepreneurs themselves. In this case, the students need to first understand the theoretical side of entrepreneurship, and later using a student-centred approach, need to gain the mastery of entrepreneurial competencies by being exposed to practical issues of entrepreneurship.

Finally, assessing outcomes (product) is highly challenging because of the complexity in establishing a direct cause-and-effect link between students' attendance in a course with their future actions. This is particularly the case with entrepreneurship as evidence suggests that graduates only start their first business between ten and 15 years after graduation and success may come much later still (Galloway and Brown, 2002). Therefore, measuring impact in terms of students' change of perception or behavioural attitude towards entrepreneurship (Pittaway and Cope, 2007) or in terms of the extent to which the programme has met the expectations of its students seems more sensible (Vesper and Gartner, 1997).

METHOD

Tanzania has a total of 33 institutions of higher learning, which includes: eight publicly funded universities, 13 publicly funded polytechnics/specialized colleges, and 12 privately funded universities or colleges (SARUA, 2009), with over 55 000 students being enrolled in 2005/06 (UNESCO, 2007; Morley et al., 2009). Four of these institutions participated in this study. A mixed methods approach including both (policy and educational) document analysis, semi-structured interviews with ten lecturers teaching undergraduate entrepreneurship courses in the fall of 2010, and a survey amongst students participating in entrepreneurship courses in this same period, was used to perform the empirical research (Table 6.1).

Semi-structured interviews and document analysis were used to identify the objectives, methods and general teaching context and to determine the extent to which the participating universities actually support the introduction of academic entrepreneurship education. Also, lecturer views on student entry profiles, career interests and learning expectations and how these reflect a broad definition of entrepreneurship were assessed in this way. The analysis of the qualitative data consisted of systematic recording of themes and issues from the ten interviews, and to link them together (Burnard, 1991). These common themes were captured from specific quotations in the interview transcripts and were then used to support the findings. The survey was used to assess student profiles, to determine the extent to which courses meet students' expectations and how it influences their career interests. All sources were combined to determine the state of alignment between the teaching contexts, methods and students' profiles.

A survey instrument was developed to collect students' related data both before teaching commenced ($t = 0$) and at the end ($t = 1$) of a course. The target participants were undergraduate students taking an entrepreneurship course in the four universities. A total of 1124 students were

Table 6.1   Overview of the data sources and connection to the research issues addressed

Method/Data Source	N	Type of Data Collected	Research Issue Addressed
1. Semi-structured interviews (lecturers)	10	1. Teaching objectives 2. Perception of students 3. Perceptions on how entrepreneurship should be taught 4. Applied teaching methods 5. Ever run a business? 6. Educated in entrepreneurship? 7. Original area of specialization?	1. Profile of entrepreneurship lecturers 2. Teaching objectives as per the lecturers 3. Their perceptions on the teachability of entrepreneurship 4. Their perceptions on the type of students they teach
2. Documentary reviews	5	Government policy documents: 1. The Tanzania Development Vision 2025 (1999) 2. National Strategy for Growth and Reduction of Poverty-NSGRP/MKUKUTA (2005) 3. SME Development Policy (2002) 4. National Trade Policy (2003) 5. National Higher Education Policy (1999)	1. Essence and general context of UEE 2. Policy drivers towards the adoption of UEE 3. Objectives of UEE at the national-level 4. State of entrepreneurial environment
	4	University course outlines: 1. Sokoine University of Agriculture: • AEA 210: Agri-business and Entrepreneurship Development 2. Mzumbe University: • BUS 270: Small Business Management and Entrepreneurship Development	1. Course objectives and expected learning outcomes 2. Prescribed teaching methods

3. Institute of Finance Management:
- MG 361: Entrepreneurship and
- PENT 101: Entrepreneurship
4. College of Business Education:
- HD 14: Entrepreneurship Development

4 University final examination results:
- For the above courses (i.e., AEA 210, BUS 270, MG 361 and HD 14)

1. To relate students' performance with their general feedback on how the course has/not met their learning expectations

3. Survey before/after the course (students) — 437

1. Mean students age
2. Gender
3. Percentage of students who ever run a business
4. Percentage of students with one or two parents who ever run a business
5. Students' mean scores on level of attraction towards entrepreneurship/self-employment (before and after)
6. Students' mean scores on learning expectations before the course (about, in, for)
7. Students' mean scores on how course met learning expectations (about, in, for) after the course

1. General student profile, their learning expectations, and interest towards entrepreneurship
2. Students' view/feedback on how the course has met their learning expectations
3. Change in students' interest towards self-employment/entrepreneurship

143

enrolled in entrepreneurship courses given during that semester. Of these, 932 students (82.9 per cent) participated in the first round of the survey and 706 students (62.8 per cent) in the second round. After matching the two datasets ($t = 0$ and $t = 1$) using students' registration numbers, 433 students (38.5 per cent) were found to have participated in both rounds and were included in our analysis (College of Business Education $n = 85$, 19.6 per cent; Institute of Finance Management, $n = 122$, 28.2 per cent; Mzumbe University $n = 20$; 4.6 per cent; and Sokoine University of Agriculture $n = 206$; 47.6 per cent). The respondents were on average 25.2 years old, 58.2 per cent were males ($n = 252$) and 35.8 per cent were females ($n = 155$), and 6 per cent of the students ($n = 26$) did not answer the gender question. The surveyed students have diverse specializations with the highest numbers of the students coming from (1) accounting and (2) rural development courses, followed by (3) agricultural economics and (4) agribusiness. ANOVA analysis indicated that no significant demographic differences could be observed across the four institutions. Non-response was mainly due to non-attendance on the day that the questionnaires were administered; those who were present participated. Students had no prior knowledge of the exact date and time at which the questionnaire was to be administered, hence non-response was purely by chance rather than intentional.

Survey questions were formulated following the earlier discussed generic teaching/learning objectives/expectations. Students were asked to indicate, on a seven-point Likert scale, their learning expectations using questions like: 'To what extent do you expect that this course will develop you in each of the following areas: (1) to obtain a general understanding about entrepreneurship; (2) to obtain necessary abilities to work as an entrepreneurial employee; (3) to obtain the necessary abilities and skills in starting your own business venture?' Students were also asked to indicate their level of attraction to both salaried employment and entrepreneurship. The post-course questionnaire included the same questions, but also asked the students to indicate the level at which their learning expectations were achieved in the course. The career interest question remained the same for the purpose of observing how students will change their responses after the course.

RESULTS AND FINDINGS

Tanzania is emerging from its own type of socialism, the *Ujamaa Na Kujitegemea* (socialism and self-reliance). During the *Ujamaa* era, entrepreneurship was actively discouraged. Major political changes started to take place in the late 1980s, when the government embarked on trade liberalization in which entrepreneurship became a key to the country's development, and was now to be inculcated in the society's cultures (URT, 1999a).

In Tanzania, the role of education as a culture-influencing tool is well recognized. In the socialist era, education was used as major tool for building a socialist society. Students, at all levels of education, were instructed in subjects based on political education. Today, entrepreneurship education has almost completely replaced the former socialist-based topics (Kristiansen, 2001). Nevertheless, as reflected in a number of policy statements, policy-makers are unsatisfied about the ability of universities to train entrepreneurial graduates. In the Trade Policy of 2002, Higher Education Institutions were categorically blamed for their tendency to create employment seekers rather than job creators (URT, 2002). This, among other issues, prompted the requirement to incorporate training in entrepreneurship (URT, 1999a, 1999b, 2003).

It was, however, not only politics that led to the introduction of academic entrepreneurship education in Tanzania. The *Policy on Entrepreneurship Development* of the University of Dar es Salaam (UDSM, 2001) shows that individual universities also had their own motivation for the teaching of entrepreneurship. Following outcries from employers about the poor quality and lack of innovative skills of graduates, the universities felt the need to improve the general competitiveness of their graduates in the labour market. Indeed, at Sokoine University, introducing entrepreneurship education was a response to the difficulties that their agriculture graduates faced in the labour market after the government had stopped its automatic employment policy. This is explained by Interviewee 10: 'we found out that there were employment problems among our graduates . . . we realized that our graduates lacked practical skills in commercializing what they have learnt at university . . . we realized they lacked entrepreneurial skills . . . there was a need for our students to have the ability to become self-employed'.

Entrepreneurship centres were established at all four participating universities as well as at many other universities across the country. Via these centres, universities are trying to develop structures that enable lecturers to establish linkages with local business via Community Engagement Programmes. Most notably the Entrepreneurship Center of the University of Dar es Salaam is investing in entrepreneurial training, business advice and incubation services for small-scale alumni entrepreneurs. Also, these centres are responsible for teaching entrepreneurship to students either as electives or as a mandatory part of the curriculum.

While good lecturers are central in achieving learning objectives,

Table 6.2   Overview of lecturers' backgrounds

Interviewee	University	Educational Qualifications
1	College of Business Education	MSc Entrepreneurship
2	Mzumbe University	MSc Management Studies – Strategy and Innovation; BBA Entrepreneurship
3	University of Dar es Salaam	PhD MBA Business Administration; BCom
4	College of Business Education	MBA Corporate management; BSc Economics
5	Tumaini University College	BBA – Accounting; Diploma in Education – Science
6	Sokoine University	MSc Forestry
7	Mzumbe University	MA Marketing Management; BA Education
8	Institute of Finance Management	MBA Marketing; Advanced Diploma in Materials Administration; Certified Supplies Profession
9	Sokoine University	PhD Agriculture, MSc Agriculture. Econ; BSc Agriculture
10	Sokoine University	MBA – Agribusiness; BSc Agronomy; Diploma in Banking

Tanzanian universities had to follow government policy directives, and hence had to hastily adopt entrepreneurial subjects, with little regard to or review of the availability of appropriately educated staff. As one interviewee recalled: 'No specific person was prepared for the subject. . . . [there was] no lecturer with appropriate education . . . the subject had to be thrown to somebody to teach it' (Interviewee 7). In most cases, university policy-makers considered entrepreneurship to be related to business studies or marketing and thus could be taught by any one of those departments. Indeed, only two out of ten lecturers are formally educated in the domain of entrepreneurship, six lecturers have a background in somewhat related management domains but two lecturers of Sokoine University are educated only in the field of forestry and agriculture (Table 6.2).

While the current situation is far from optimal, evidence shows that Tanzanian universities have begun to invest in teaching capacity through both new recruitment and sending more faculty members for further studies in entrepreneurship: 'There was an offer to lecturers to apply for two PhD scholarships in entrepreneurship. So me and my other colleague are specifically trained to promote entrepreneurship at this university'

(Interviewee 6). Yet, as most lecturers who are (now being) educated in the field of entrepreneurship are rather young, they lack actual teaching experience. Despite their lack of formal education in the field of entrepreneurship, the data do not provide any evidence that any of the lecturers actually questions the teachability of the topic of entrepreneurship. Rather, the fact that they all indicate that their course aims to prepare future entrepreneurs suggests the contrary.

When asked about their expectations regarding their students' entry profiles, lecturers generally expect that students will come into the class with a negative attitude towards entrepreneurship and self-employment and that their career aspirations are towards salaried jobs. For instance, Interviewee 6 said: 'The problem with our students is with their attitudes and mindsets towards entrepreneurship' while Interviewee 4 indicates that 'Our students' attitudes are copied from the older generation'. Also, lecturers believe that students neither have awareness nor practical experience on the subject matter and that they have had limited exposure to entrepreneurial role models (e.g., parents, or important others).

Remarkably, these expectations about students' entry profiles are in sharp contrast with the self-reported profiles from the students. Many respondents (i.e., 65.1 per cent, $n = 259$) have parent(s) who had started or run own businesses. Moreover, 23 per cent of the students ($n = 99$) had started and operated businesses of their own. Also, students indicated that they were indeed attracted to entrepreneurship to a higher extent than towards salaried employment. As shown in Table 6.3, having an entrepreneurial parent has a significant link with students' past attempts to start or run own businesses ($r = 0.164$, $p < 0.05$), which is in line with the conventional wisdom that children from entrepreneurial parents are more likely to become entrepreneurial themselves (Scherer et al., 1989; Crant, 1996; van Auken, et al., 2006). Yet, as no significant relationship between parents' entrepreneurial status and students' attraction to entrepreneurship as a future career is found the entrepreneurial role model thesis is not fully supported. This may imply that while a student may attempt to start a business (to follow a parent's example) this may not necessarily be a response to the attractiveness of entrepreneurship as a career, especially when the student is exposed to other career possibilities.

In Tanzania, official course objectives are directly derived from national education policies and agendas and formulated by university administrators. From the analysis of official course outlines a common set of objectives appears across all four institutions: (1) to create a general understanding about entrepreneurship among students; (2) to produce graduates with the skill, ability and intention to become entrepreneurs/self-employed; and (3) to create an enterprising workforce of graduates.

Table 6.3 Correlations between entry profiles, career interest and learning expectations

	Mean	1	2	3	4	5	6	7	8
1 Gender	0.61								
2 Ever started a business	1.77	−0.074							
3 Parents ever started own firm	0.65	−0.003	0.164*						
4 Attracted to salaried job	4.59	−0.029	0.079	−0.106*					
5 Attracted to entrepreneurship	5.99	0.027	−0.044	−0.030	0.048				
6 Obtain knowledge about entrepreneurship	6.05	0.066	−0.134*	−0.017	0.055	0.218**			
7 Learn to work innovatively	5.27	−0.040	−0.046	−0.055	0.270**	0.125*	0.297**		
8 Learn abilities to become an entrepreneur	6.17	−0.034	−0.135*	0.028	−0.067	0.364**	0.418**	0.198**	

Note: **Correlation is significant at the 0.01 level (2-tailed); *correlation is significant at the 0.05 level (2-tailed).

While the ambitions formulated in the official outlines are moderate, from the interviews it becomes apparent that the lecturers interpret these objectives in an overly ambitious way. Perhaps due to their own lack of insight in the matter, they seem to be blind to the limitations of the teaching process. They are rather rhetorical in talking about their own objectives and desire to impart students with skills and abilities for self-employment as is shown from the following quotes: 'to develop entrepreneurial spirit and culture . . . a positive attitude towards entrepreneurship. Our students to become innovative even when employed' (Interviewee 4). And 'The objective is to give them ability to start own business . . . and be innovative and creative even when employed. But our main focus is to develop a graduate who will go into self-employment' (Interviewee 7). Yet, despite the strong focus on educating future entrepreneurs the interviewees agree that there is first a need to create awareness of the role and function of entrepreneurship and that this requires not only skills but also knowledge. This is clearly in line with the lecturers' expectations that, in general, students know little about entrepreneurship and have rather negative perceptions about it. Furthermore, the lecturers all recognize that the entrepreneurial skills obtained through the course may equally be relevant for future intrapreneurs as for future self-employed people.

Students' level of attraction to a career in entrepreneurship correlated significantly with all the learning expectations (see Table 6.3). This is in line with Henderson and Robertson (1999) who argued that when entering a course, a student's expectations are at least partially dependent on what they want to learn in light of their current career ambitions. Following the same logic, students who were more interested in salaried employment also indicated higher expectations regarding learning how to work more innovatively. Interestingly, the findings suggest that students with prior experiences in running their own business tend to have somewhat lower learning expectations compared to those without previous entrepreneurial experience. This might either suggest that they believe they already have developed some knowledge and skills in this area or that they are less convinced than other students that you can learn entrepreneurship at university. Combining the interview and survey findings suggests that despite the misalignment between the expected and the observed student entry profile, lecturers and students at least seem to be in agreement regarding the desired learning objectives.

As shown in Table 6.4, in order to reach these objectives, a variety of teaching methods ranging from lectures to interactive seminars and practical assignments were originally prescribed. Consistent with their intentions to train future entrepreneurs, lecturers furthermore indicated that they preferred the use of vocational methods including the involvement

Table 6.4   Teaching methods: prescribed vs applied and lecturers' views on methods

University	Prescribed Methods	Envisaged Methods by Lecturers	Applied Methods
Mzumbe University	Lectures and seminars	To involve practitioners	Lectures
Sokoine University	Practical assignments and seminars on selected topics	Practical-based methods	Lectures
College of Business Education	Not prescribed in course outline	The way carpenters are trained	Lectures and group discussions
Institute of Finance Management	Not prescribed in course outline	To involve local entrepreneurs	Handouts and lectures

of practitioners. In practice, however, lecturers had to revert to far less interactive and hands-on methods such as lectures and the use of handouts. While some connections to local entrepreneurs had been established, entrepreneurship lecturers rarely invited them into their class to share experiences with the students. Notably, attempts to do so at Sokoine University were rather unsuccessful due to the inability of the university to compensate these entrepreneurs for their time and efforts, while few entrepreneurs were willing to do so voluntarily. Testing was based on multiple choice and open-ended questions rather than on the originally preferred practical assignments. Large class sizes and lack of resources and contacts were mentioned as the main reason for this.

To assess the outcomes of these efforts we again combined various types of information. An immediate outcome of any course is the examination score. Unfortunately, lecturers were unwilling or unable to provide us with a list of the examination results per student but they are willing to show us the distribution of the results (Table 6.5). The marks suggest relatively good performance with the large majority of the students passing the courses. These findings are an indication that learning objectives have at least been met in the short term.

Next, we examined the extent to which the courses met student expectations and caused a change in future career aspirations. As mentioned, using teacher-centred methods is useful for transferring knowledge about entrepreneurship but is less appropriate for training future entrepreneurs. Indeed, lecturers were unsatisfied with their own achievements:

Table 6.5   *Overall student performance at the end of semester*
entrepreneurship exams

Grade	Number of Students	Percentage
A	73	6.8
B+	210	19.4
B	365	33.8
C	373	34.5
D	59	5.5
N/A	14	–
Total	1094	100

'we have not succeeded in achieving our objectives . . . all of them are in salaried employment; we fail to give them the confidence of going out and wanting to try. The problem with them is not on the procedures of how to start a business, the problem is their ability to see opportunities which our courses have failed to develop in our students' (Interviewee 2). Also, it is not surprising that students indicated that while the courses did meet their expectations with respect to learning about entrepreneurship, they fell short of their expectations when it came to learning skills and abilities to become an entrepreneur as is shown in Table 6.5 ($t = -0.284$, $p < 0.00$). While the theory would suggest that more student-centred teaching methods are more appropriate for this purpose, students indicated that the courses met their expectations regarding how to work more innovatively. Finally, the results show that immediately after the courses, students' attraction towards salaried employment had significantly been lowered ($t = -0.320$, $p < 0.05$) while attraction to entrepreneurship had significantly increased ($t = 0.457$, $p < 0.05$) (see pair 4 and 5 in Table 6.6). This suggests that even though the courses did not bring the students as much as they had expected in terms of development of skills and abilities, what they had learned during the course gave the students more confidence about entrepreneurship as a potential career or it simply raised their awareness of the possibilities.

Finally, to explore potential differences in learning outcomes across universities we conducted some ANOVA analysis. Results in Table 6.7 indicated that at $t = 0$ there were no significant differences in attraction to entrepreneurship as a future career and expectations to learn the necessary abilities for that between students from the four participating universities. At $t = 0$, significant differences were observed in relation to attraction to salaried employment and expectations to learn *about* entrepreneurship and to learn to work more innovatively. After participating in the course

Table 6.6   Paired samples results: students' expectations and changed career attractions

		Mean	St. Dev.	T	Df	Sig. (2-tailed)
Pair 1	Obtain knowledge about entrepreneurship	−0.041	1.385	−0.582	393	0.561
Pair 2	Learn to work innovatively	0.102	1.867	1.079	393	0.281
Pair 3	Learn abilities to become an entrepreneur	−0.284	1.493	−3.779	393	0.000**
Pair 4	Attraction to salary employment $t1 - t0$	−0.320	2.634	−2.410	393	0.016*
Pair 5	Attraction to entrepreneurship $t1 - t0$	0.457	3.900	2.325	393	0.021*

Note: ***Correlation is significant at the 0.000 level (2-tailed), **correlation is significant at the 0.01 level (2-tailed); *correlation is significant at the 0.05 level (2-tailed).

($t = 1$) no significant differences regarding attraction to either salaried employment or entrepreneurship could be established across universities. Significant differences were found to exist across universities in terms of the extent to which students indicated they had actually learned. In particular, students from Sokoine University reported the highest learning outcomes in all three areas, while they also reported the highest (though non-significant) attraction towards becoming entrepreneurs themselves. When it came to meeting students' expectations regarding learning abilities for becoming an entrepreneur themselves, the other three institutions underperformed.

DISCUSSION AND IMPLICATIONS FOR PRACTICE

This study sought to characterize entrepreneurship education at four Tanzanian universities, in terms of what they are attempting to achieve and ways in which this objective is being implemented. This research was informed by the observation of the apparent paradox that increased attention for entrepreneurship education at universities was matched by lower rather than higher levels of graduates starting their own ventures. While set in Tanzania, the insights derived from this investigation equally apply to other countries both in the developing and developed world as globally educators are struggling to achieve higher levels of entrepreneurial graduates.

Table 6.7 Comparison of learning outcomes across universities

Variable	University	t = 0				t = 1			
		N	Mean	F	Sig.	N	Mean	F	Sig.
Obtain	CBE	82	5.598			80	5.838		
knowledge	IFM	115	6.209			107	5.869		
about entre-	Mzumbe	20	6.200			18	5.667		
preneurship	Sokoine	176	6.131			192	6.281		
	Total	393	6.046	4.944	0.002	397	6.053	7.454	0.000
Learning how	CBE	82	4.695			80	5.075		
to work	IFM	115	5.183			107	5.140		
innovatively	Mzumbe	20	4.650			18	5.000		
	Sokoine	176	5.591			192	5.573		
	Total	393	5.237	7.224	0.000	397	5.330	4.296	0.005
Learning	CBE	82	6.159			80	5.638		
abilities to	IFM	115	6.026			107	5.617		
become an	Mzumbe	20	6.400			18	5.833		
entrepreneur	Sokoine	176	6.284			192	6.151		
	Total	393	6.188	1.431	0.233	397	5.889	7.174	0.000
Attraction to	CBE	82	4.171			80	4.300		
salary-	IFM	115	4.304			107	4.131		
employment	Mzumbe	20	3.750			18	4.278		
	Sokoine	176	5.000			192	4.464		
	Total	393	4.560	5.220	0.002	397	4.332	0.784	0.503
Attraction to	CBE	82	5.963			80	6.150		
entrepre-	IFM	115	5.887			107	6.140		
neurship	Mzumbe	20	5.700			18	5.944		
	Sokoine	176	6.080			192	6.781		
	Total	393	5.980	0.636	0.593	397	6.443	1.059	0.366

Note: Listwise $N = 384$.

When contemplating why learning achievements fell short of learning expectations, one only has to consider the state of alignment among the main components of the academic entrepreneurship education in Tanzania. Importantly, educating for entrepreneurship was close to a mission impossible due to a mismatch between the teaching objective and the applied methods. Teaching methods failed to engage the students in learning activities that build the skills and capacities for start-up. This was reaffirmed by the lecturers' doubts on achievements. In contrast, the courses motivated students in terms of understanding the possibility of an entrepreneurial career, hence explaining the proper alignment between the less demanding objectives of the subject, with the more theoretical teaching methods (lecturers and group discussions). Other factors contributed to these current effects including the lecturers' profiles, teaching facilities and the (limited) links with local industry.

Our findings show that the introduction of academic entrepreneurship education in Tanzania was driven by extensive governmental pressures and strategic responses of universities to student and employer demands. Evidence shows that while stakeholders seem to be in agreement that entrepreneurship, particularly in the form of self-employment, has beneficial effects on economic development, parties do not agree on what entrepreneurship really means and which educational models can be used to stimulate it. Conflicting pieces of information and a lack of (human) resources have resulted in a situation where universities struggle to translate overambitious goals into their curriculum.

Our findings show that lecturers feel they need to prepare students for a career in self-employment and thus to impart them with the necessary skills and abilities. Yet, at the same time these lecturers think their students are ill-prepared for this and will have negative, if any, perceptions about entrepreneurship. Consequently, lecturers consider that their courses should also have more basic objectives such as transferring knowledge about entrepreneurship and raising awareness about entrepreneurship as a future career path. While combining such different types of learning objectives is complicated everywhere, in the Tanzanian context this struggle is complicated by factors like the diversity of students' specializations, limited course duration, limited financial and human resources, poor teaching facilities, crowded classes and a less than optimal external entrepreneurial climate.

Furthermore, it is clear that many lecturers are ill-prepared for the job as they themselves lack a thorough basis in entrepreneurship education. Lecturers are overly ambitious in their objectives, have faulty assumptions about their students' profiles and are unsatisfied with the achievements of their courses. Providing lecturers with the opportunity to obtain a Master's degree or even a PhD in entrepreneurship, as some participating institutions do seems to be a promising, yet costly step towards building a better equipped teaching staff. A less profound, but equally less costly, approach may be to arrange for international 'traineeships' so that lecturers have the opportunity to experience and learn from how entrepreneurship education is arranged elsewhere.

Likewise, both national and institutional policy-makers may consider shorter-term study trips abroad to exchange ideas and experiences with their peers across the world to obtain insights into best practices and to develop a more realistic perspective on what is attainable given the current stage of development. Formulating more realistic objectives at the national and institutional level in light of the available resources and knowledge level would also help to avoid disappointments in terms of attainable learning achievements for students.

At the same time, lecturers and policy-makers should realize that the local context does play a significant role in what should be taught and how it should be taught. Transferring a programme and teaching materials from developed countries, even from other developing countries, without adapting them to the Tanzanian context may do more harm than good. Consequently, institutions also have to invest in developing teaching activities and materials that fit the local environment. For this it is essential that institutions and individual lecturers foster connection with local industry, something that is currently missing.

Previous research has shown that establishing such connections proves difficult for educators around the world (e.g., Hynes and Richardson, 2007). Hynes and Richardson (2007) argue that offering courses to local SME managers may be a useful instrument for achieving this. In the Tanzanian context, offering specific courses might be too expensive but opening up the courses or a number of specific sessions to local business people may be a step in that direction. Furthermore, while entrepreneurs may find it too costly to give presentations and lectures about their experiences during the day time for a very small fee or even for free, inviting them to talk to students about their business in the evening hours may be more appealing to them, especially if the university is able to arrange some publicity about these sessions in a way that raises the entrepreneur's reputation. Furthermore, besides local entrepreneurs, local bankers and accountants may be invited to talk to the students about what they can and cannot do for starting entrepreneurs. While their stories may not necessarily show a positive picture of the entrepreneurial climate in Tanzania it will help students to obtain a more realistic understanding of the environment in which they have to work.

A third way in which connections with local industry may be fostered is via the offering of traineeships with local entrepreneurs. While the number of students participating in entrepreneurship courses is simply too large to make this an integral part of entrepreneurship education at this stage, providing such opportunities to a small group of promising students as an extra-curricular and CV-building activity helps to build connections and develop more insight into the real-world struggles of entrepreneurs. Particularly, consultancy-based approaches as recently described by Ohe and Tih (2012) based on cases from Asia, where students can tap into both their recently acquired knowledge about entrepreneurship and into the knowledge from their academic major (e.g., marketing, accountancy, procurement) could be appealing to lecturers and students, as well as the receiving SMEs. Reports resulting from such traineeships may eventually be used to develop local case study materials that lecturers can use in their classes instead of the current European and American examples.

A final way to bring local industry into the classroom is possibly the easiest way. Our data show that many students either have been active as an entrepreneur themselves or have one or two parents who have operated as entrepreneurs. This actually means that students themselves should be more actively invited during the course to reflect on these activities. An easy approach could be that during the first five to ten minutes at the beginning of each lecture a (self-selected) student would talk about how the topic of that lecture connects to their own experience. The lecturer can then refer back to this personal story during the remainder of this session. Students who deliver these personal accounts as well as the other students in the audience will become more engaged in the material in this way. Such approaches to align presage and process in the classroom environment could work equally in other developing countries and developed countries around the world.

While it is clear that both the institutions and the individual lecturers already recognize that more interactive student-centred teaching methods are needed in order to reach their own teaching objectives, lack of resources, facilities and knowledge mean that in practice teaching methods are used that are inadequate for these goals, such as lectures and handouts (Biggs, 1999; Hindle, 2007). Testing is based on exams that can only assess the level of knowledge that is acquired by the students rather than the attitudes and the skills they need for entrepreneurship (Hynes, 1996; Vesper and Gartner, 1997; Charney and Libecap, 2000). At the very best the exam scores may be viewed as an indicator of students' interest in the topic (Schiefele et al., 1992), which may in turn be a first step towards a future career in entrepreneurship. Unfortunately, in this study, we were not able to match individual exam scores with self-reported learning achievements and therefore it remains unclear to what extent this would be the case here. When linking these findings to the self-reported achievements however, the examination marks may also be interpreted as a sign that the courses were too *easy* for the students as their entry profile exceeded the lecturers' expectations. Examining the quality of the exams was beyond the scope of this study, yet in order to gain a better understanding of the meaningfulness of examination marks, future research should incorporate evaluations of exams in order to determine their usefulness for measuring learning outcomes.

It is remarkable how far apart the perception of the student-entry profiles of lecturers and the self-reported entry profiles of students actually are. Lecturers typically expect negative attitudes and a lack of knowledge of and experience with entrepreneurship. Therefore, they devote considerable attention to raising awareness and building positive attitudes. Yet, students show exceptionally entrepreneurship-friendly entry profiles and, prior to the course, most indicate they are very much attracted to the idea of becoming self-employed; they also have very high learning expectations. Given the rather difficult entrepreneurship climate in Tanzania (Wedgwood, 2007) and the fact that the surveyed entrepreneurship courses form a mandatory part of the students' curriculum, this finding is rather surprising. In fact, the results might suggest a response bias, in light of the government's campaign to foster entrepreneurship or in order to show respect to their lecturers. In order to check for such response biases the principal investigator also talked to a number of students in a more informal setting about these issues and these conversations yielded similar positive mind-sets with regard to a future entrepreneurial career and high learning expectations based on their enthusiasm for the topic. The fact that many students have actually started a business in the past (22 per cent), and almost all of them have entrepreneurs amongst their close friends (83 per cent) is further evidence of the students' sincerity. Consequently, while lecturers spent considerable time on building awareness and motivations through lectures and classroom discussions, students were waiting for skill building through more active forms of teaching. Consequently, students reported that they had learned less than they had expected to learn when entering the course. These findings show that entrepreneurial universities and lecturers have to invest in getting to know their students better. While the necessary means to offer more small-group or individual teaching activities may not be available there are many other ways for universities to engage in conversations with their students including the use of pre-entry surveys or panel discussions with class representatives. Such interactions with students will enable lecturers to direct their teaching efforts so that they match student profiles. Also, while currently it may not be able to meet all of the students' expectations such interaction might also help to formulate and communicate more realistic teaching and learning expectations to avoid disappointment among students. While considerable research shows that in general pre-entry and induction activities help to reduce dropout levels in academic programmes (e.g., Shobrook, 2004; Crosling et al., 2009), further research is required to see to what extent and in which way pre-entry feedback from students can actually be used in the alignment of presage and process of entrepreneurship education. Taking pre-entry information seriously may require lecturers to have a broader portfolio of teaching topics and activities prepared than they may be used to, so that they can pick and choose those issues that fit their current student profile best.

A further way to measure learning outcomes is to look at the change in students' career intentions (Fayolle et al., 2006; Souitaris et al., 2007). The findings show that across the four universities, academic entrepreneurship education in Tanzania significantly influences students' interests in entrepreneurship, and respectively lowering their interest in salaried employment. Given that the share of students that were attracted to entrepreneurship prior to entering the courses was already large, this result is pleasing and may be better than expected. Yet, at the same time, the results should not lead to over-optimistic expectations. The increase in attraction to entrepreneurship was reached without meeting the students' learning expectations. This might be a warning signal that the awareness and attraction effects might be only temporary or that they will not be translated into actions, that is, starting a business in the future unless students know where and how to develop additional knowledge and skills. Indeed, recent studies have shown that sometimes participating in a single entrepreneurship course can actually lower students' intentions and behaviour towards starting their own firm as they become more aware of their own shortcomings and lack of skills in this area (Oosterbeek et al., 2010). If students become frustrated by not having learned what they expected to learn the same might happen here as well.

To conclude, the current model of the Tanzanian academic entrepreneurship education may be appropriate for raising students' general entrepreneurial intentions by inspiring them to seriously consider entrepreneurship as a future career. Also, by transferring knowledge about the nature, diversity, role and function of entrepreneurship the current academic entrepreneurship education may actually be used to educate future public or private sector officials about its importance and hence shaping them into entrepreneur-friendly decision-makers who will facilitate entrepreneurial activities by contributing to an entrepreneurial climate and infrastructure. Whether graduates will occupy such positions in the future remains yet to be seen but should be a focus of future research. Yet, while it is on top of the agenda of policy-makers in Tanzania, currently universities are not sufficiently equipped to actually educate future graduate entrepreneurs via the development of skills and other abilities they will need when dealing with the sub-optimal entrepreneurial environment in the country. Even considering these drawbacks, the changed educational content and the large number of students shows a shift to an entrepreneurial university attitude in the making, while at the same time reflecting the manner in which local idiosyncrasies need to be taken into account in order to understand the form entrepreneurial education develops.

This study has implications to both policy-makers and educators. First, significant commitment and investments and continued dedication at all levels (governments, universities and lecturers) needs to be combined in order to develop a sustained effort to work towards a more advanced stage of educating future entrepreneurs. This may include stronger collaboration with entrepreneurship educators from abroad where entrepreneurship education is more advanced. Stakeholders should, however, be acutely aware that the local environment in which graduate entrepreneurs operate forms a significant input in developing courses. As mentioned, transferring ideas and building blocks from other (more entrepreneurially developed) countries will not work, while even a system in early development may lead to positive results. Initial connections with existing businesses need to be advanced and developed in the near future, and to some extent the student population itself shows connections that might be exploited.

Clearly, stimulating graduate entrepreneurship requires more than teaching entrepreneurship at university. The solution to the ultimate academic entrepreneurship education effectiveness is not only dependent on offering more entrepreneurship training, but also on both re-aligning the current academic entrepreneurship model with the policy needs, teaching context, students' profiles, teaching, assessment methods and other enabling/inhibiting factors outside the university. Therefore, Tanzanian universities need to direct research efforts to the assessment of contextual factors that shape graduates' decisions to enter into entrepreneurship. Such studies could benefit from extended qualitative analysis of graduates' experiences and their perceptions. Until that time, it is unlikely that graduate entrepreneurship levels will rise significantly.

NOTE

* Another version of this chapter is included in the doctoral dissertation of Ernest Mwasalwiba: Mwasalwiba, E.S. (2012), 'University entrepreneurship education in Tanzania: Teaching context, students' profile, expectations and outcome', VU University, Amsterdam, Chapter 4.

REFERENCES

Al-Samarrai, S. and P. Bennell (2003), 'Where has all the education gone in Africa?: Employment outcomes among secondary school and university leavers', Institute of Development Studies, University of Sussex.
Béchard, J.P. and D. Grégoire (2005), 'Entrepreneurship education research revisited: The case of Higher Education', *Academy of Management Learning and Education*, **4**(1), 22–43.
Biggs, J. (1996), 'Enhancing teaching through constructive alignment', *Higher Education*, **32**(3), 347–64.
Biggs, J. (1999), 'What the student does: Teaching for enhanced learning', *Higher Education Research and Development*, **18**(1), 57–75.
Biggs, J. (2003), 'Aligning teaching and assessing to course objectives', in *Teaching and*

Learning in Higher Education: New Trends and Innovations, University of Aveiro, pp. 13–17.

Bigsten, A. and M. Söderbom (2006), 'What have we learned from a decade of manufacturing enterprise survey in Africa?' *The World Bank Research Observer*, **21**(2), 241–56.

Burnard, P. (1991), 'A method of analysing interview transcripts in qualitative research', *Nurse Education Today*, **11**(6), 461–6.

Charney, A. and G. Libecap (2000), *Impact of Entrepreneurship Education*, Kansas City, MO: Kauffman Center for Entrepreneurial Leadership.

Clark, B.R. (1998), 'The entrepreneurial university: Demand and response', *Tertiary Education and Management*, **4**(1), 5–16.

Clark, B.R. (2004), 'Delineating the character of the entrepreneurial university', *Higher Education Policy*, **17**(4), 355–70.

Crant, J.M. (1996), 'The proactive personality scale as a predictor of entrepreneurial intentions', *Journal of Small Business Management*, **34**(3), 42–9.

Crosling, G., M. Heagney and L. Thomas (2009), 'Improving student retention in Higher Education', *Australian University Review*, **51**(2), accessed 4 August at http://educational policy.org/pdf/AUR_epitoday_090917.pdf.

European Commission (2008), *Survey of Entrepreneurship in Higher Education in Europe*, Brussels: European Commission.

Fayolle, A. and B. Gailly (2008), 'From craft to science: Teaching models and learning processes in entrepreneurship education', *Journal of European Industrial Training*, **32**(7), 569–93.

Fayolle, A., B. Gailly and N. Lassas-Clerc (2006), 'Assessing the impact of entrepreneurship education programmes: A new methodology', *Journal of European Industrial Training*, **30**(9), 701–20.

Ferguson, K. (2003), 'Becoming a string teacher', *Bulletin of the Council for Research in Music Education*, 38–48.

Freeth, D. and S. Reeves (2004), 'Learning to work together: Using the presage, process, product (3P) model to highlight decisions and possibilities', *Journal of Interprofessional Care*, **18**(1), 43–56.

Galloway, L. and W. Brown (2002), 'Entrepreneurship education at university: A driver in the creation of high growth firms?' *Education + Training*, **44**(8/9), 398–405.

Gigliotti, R.J. (1987), 'Expectations, observations, and violations: Comparing their effects on course ratings', *Research in Higher Education*, **26**(4), 401–15.

Henderson, R. and M. Robertson (1999), 'Who wants to be an entrepreneur? Young adult attitudes to entrepreneurship as a career', *Education + Training*, **41**(5), 236–45.

Hindle, K. (2007), 'Teaching entrepreneurship at university: From the wrong building to the right philosophy', in A. Fayolle (ed.), *Handbook of Research in Entrepreneurship Education*, Vol. 1, pp. 104–26.

Hynes, B. (1996), 'Entrepreneurship education and training – introducing entrepreneurship into non-business disciplines', *Journal of European Industrial Training*, **20**(8), 10–17.

Hynes, B. and I. Richardson (2007), 'Entrepreneurship education: A mechanism for engaging and exchanging with the small business sector', *Education + Training*, **49**(8/9), 732–44.

Juma, C. (2005), 'We need to reinvent the African University', *Science and Development Network*, accessed 3 August 2013 at http://www.scidev.net/global/capacity-building/opinion/we-need-to-reinvent-the-african-university.html.

Kaijage, E. (2001), 'Knowledge and skills of B.Com graduates of the faculty of commerce and management of the University of Dar es Salaam in the job market', Research Paper, Accra, Ghana: Association of African Universities.

Kenway, J., E. Bullen and S. Robb (2004), *Innovation and Tradition: The Arts, Humanities, and the Knowledge Economy*, New York: Peter Lang Pub Inc.

Kristiansen, S. (2001), 'Promoting African pioneers in business: What makes a context conducive for small-scale entrepreneurship?' *The Journal of Entrepreneurship*, **10**(43), 43–69.

Kuratko, D.F. (2005), 'The emergence of entrepreneurship education: Development, trends, and challenges', *Entrepreneurship Theory and Practice*, **29**(5), 577–98.

Kuzilwa, J.A. (2005), 'The role of credit for small business success: A study of the National Entrepreneurship Development Fund in Tanzania', *Journal of Entrepreneurship*, **14**(2), 131–61.

Low, M.B. (2001), 'The adolescence of entrepreneurship research: Specification of purpose', *Entrepreneurship Theory and Practice*, **25**(4), 17–26.

Markman, G.D., D.S. Siegel and M. Wright (2008), 'Research and technology commercialization', *Journal of Management Studies*, **45**(8), 1401–23.

Morley, L., F. Leach and R. Lugg (2009), 'Democratising Higher Education in Ghana and Tanzania: Opportunity structures and social inequalities', *International Journal of Educational Development*, **29**(1), 56–64.

Mukyanuzi, F. (2003), *Where Has all the Education Gone in Tanzania: Employment Outcomes Among Secondary School and University Leavers*, Dar es Salaam: DfID.

Mwasalwiba, E.S. (2010), 'Entrepreneurship education: A review of its objectives, teaching methods, and impact indicators', *Education + Training*, **52**(1), 20–47.

Ohe, T. and S. Tih (2012), 'Consulting-based entrepreneurship education: Regional cases', in H. Thomas and D. Kelley (eds), *Entrepreneurship Education in Asia*, Cheltenham, UK and Northampton, MA, USA: Edward Elgar Publishing, pp. 168–82.

Oosterbeek, H., M. van Praag and A. Ijsselstein (2010), 'The impact of entrepreneurship education on entrepreneurship skills and motivation', *European Economic Review*, **54**(3), 442–54.

Pittaway, L. and J. Cope (2007), 'Entrepreneurship education', *International Small Business Journal*, **25**(5), 479–510.

Reeves, T.C. (2006), 'How do you know they are learning? The importance of alignment in Higher Education', *International Journal of Learning Technology*, **2**(4), 294–309.

Robinson, P.B. and E.A. Sexton (1994), 'The effect of education and experience on self-employment success', *Journal of Business Venturing*, **9**(2), 141–56.

SARUA (2009), *Towards a Common Future: Higher Education in the SADC Region – Regional Country Profiles*, Johannesburg: South Africa Southern African Regional Universities Association, accessed 3 August 2013 at http://www.sarua.org/files/countryreports/Country_Report_Tanzania.pdf.

Scherer, R.F., J.S. Adams, S.S. Carley and F.A. Wiebe (1989), 'Role model performance effects on development of entrepreneurial career preference', *Entrepreneurship Theory and Practice*, **13**(3), 53–71.

Schiefele, U., A. Krapp and A. Winteler (1992), 'Interest as a predictor of academic achievement: A meta-analysis of research', in K.A. Renninger, S. Hidi and A. Krapp (eds), *The Role of Interest in Learning and Development*, Hillsdale, NJ: Lawrence Erlbaum, pp. 183–212.

Schulte, P. (2004), 'The entrepreneurial university: A strategy for institutional development', *Higher Education in Europe*, **29**(2), 187–91.

Shobrook, S. (2004), 'The role of pre-entry practices and induction strategies in relation to student retention', Strategy Guide Resource of the PROGRESS Project, The University of Hull, accessed 4 August at http://www.heacademy.ac.uk/assets/documents/subjects/engineering/role-pre-entry-practices.pdf.

Slaughter, S. and L.L. Leslie (2001), 'Expanding and elaborating the concept of academic capitalism', *Organization*, **8**(2), 154–61.

Souitaris, V., S. Zerbinati and A. Al-Laham (2007), 'Do entrepreneurship programmes raise entrepreneurial intention of science and engineering students? The effect of learning, inspiration and resources', *Journal of Business Venturing*, **22**(4), 566–91.

Subotzky, G. (1999), 'Alternatives to the entrepreneurial university: New modes of knowledge production in community service programs', *Higher Education*, **38**(4), 401–40.

UDSM (2001), *Policy on Entrepreneurship Development*, Dar es Salaam: University of Dar es Salaam.

UNESCO (2007), *Global Education Digest 2007: Comparing Education Statistics Across the World*, Montreal: UNESCO Institute of Statistics.

URT (1999a), *National Higher Education Policy*, Dar es Salaam: Ministry of Science, Technology and Higher Education.

URT (1999b), *Tanzania Development Vision 2025*, Dar es Salaam: Planning Commission.
URT (2002), *Small and Medium Enterprises Development Policy*, Dar es Salaam: Ministry of Industry and Trade.
URT (2003), *National Trade Policy*, Dar es Salaam: Ministry of Industry and Trade.
van Auken, H., P. Stephens, F.L. Fry and J. Silva (2006), 'Role model influences on entrepreneurial intentions: A comparison between USA and Mexico', *International Entrepreneurship and Management Journal*, **2**(3), 325–36.
Vesper, K.H. and W.B. Gartner (1997), 'Measuring progress in entrepreneurship education', *Journal of Business Venturing*, **12**(5), 403–21.
Wedgwood, R. (2007), 'Education and poverty reduction in Tanzania', *International Journal of Educational Development*, **27**(4), 383–96.

7. Evolving entrepreneurial universities: experiences and challenges in the Middle Eastern context

*Maribel Guerrero, David Urbano and Aidin Salamzadeh**

INTRODUCTION

Despite great differences in economic conditions and resource availability, social structures, cultural settings and historical backgrounds, Higher Education systems in most countries face similar challenges: maintaining research capacity, combining elite with mass Higher Education, offering lifelong education and providing society with a space for the development and maintenance of critical knowledge, independent thinking, social identity and values. This fact becomes more relevant during recessionary times and has gained the attention of academics, governments and policymakers around the world. Particularly, these efforts have been encouraged because entrepreneurial universities become important catalysts for regional, economic and social development (Guerrero and Urbano, 2011; Kirby et al., 2011). The existing literature on entrepreneurial universities provides insights about the entrepreneurial transformation process of universities in developed countries (e.g., the United States by O'Shea et al., 2005, 2007; and Link and Scott, 2005; and Europe by Clark, 1998; Klofsten and Jones-Evans, 2000; Kirby, 2006; Wright et al., 2007; Grimaldi, et al., 2011; and Guerrero and Urbano, 2011, 2012) and current efforts to explore it in developing countries (e.g., Iran by Sooreh et al., 2011; Farsi et al., 2012). The studies evidenced that usually in developing countries the first measures implemented to fostering entrepreneurship within universities are entrepreneurship educational programmes. The main explanation is the positive relationship between entrepreneurship education and entrepreneurial activity (Coduras et al., 2008). However, the low prevalence rate of formal and informal entrepreneurship education in developing countries (i.e., Uruguay, Latvia, Peru, Chile, Iran, Argentina and Mexico) clearly evidenced the need of other support measures for entrepreneurs starting business within universities (Coduras et al., 2010). Therefore, in developing countries, the literature on entrepreneurial universities is somewhat limited or, more accurately, rare (Etzkowitz and Mello, 2004).

Based on these previous arguments, our purpose is to contribute to a better understanding of the entrepreneurial transformation process of entrepreneurial universities in developing countries. To accomplish this objective, theoretically we adopted an integral entrepreneurial university framework that considers: (1) the relevance of universities' environmental and internal factors to fulfil their teaching, research and entrepreneurial activities (Guerrero and Urbano, 2011, 2012) and (2) the socioeconomic impacts generated by these activities (Urbano and Guerrero, 2013). To accomplish this objective, we focus on Iran, which is a lower-middle-income economy and one of the most important countries in the Middle East region (World Bank, 2009). Methodologically, we explore case studies of two universities located in Tehran:[1] University of Tehran (UT)[2] and Sharif University of Technology (SUT).[3] Following this introduction, this study comprises four main sections: the entrepreneurial universities framework, the multiple case study design, the experience of Iranian entrepreneurial universities, and conclusions.

ENTREPRENEURIAL UNIVERSITIES FRAMEWORK

Kirby et al. (2011) state that an entrepreneurial university is a natural incubator that endeavours to simultaneously fulfil its missions (teaching, research and entrepreneurial activities) while providing an adequate atmosphere in which the university community (academics, students and staff) can identify, explore and exploit innovative and creative ideas that could be transformed into new ventures. Based on the literature review, Figure 7.1 shows an integral entrepreneurial university framework and a brief description of each construct of this framework.

Environmental Factors (EF)

The institutional approach draws attention to institutional or contextual – cultural, social, political and economic – factors as determinants of entrepreneurship (Veciana and Urbano, 2008; Thornton et al., 2011). In general terms, North (1990, p. 3) explains how institutions affect economic and social development: 'Institutions are the rules of the game in a society, or more formally, institutions are the constraints that shape human interaction'. Specifically, institutions can be either formal (with political rules, economic rules and contracts) or informal (with codes of conduct, attitudes, values, norms of behaviour and conventions – essentially, the

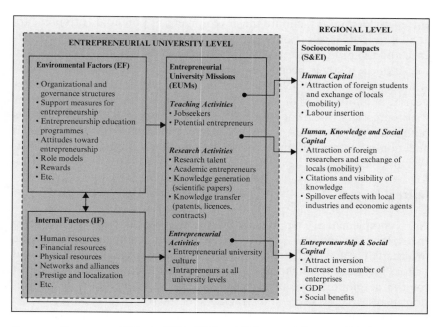

Sources: Guerrero and Urbano (2011, 2012) and Urbano and Guerrero (2013).

Figure 7.1   Entrepreneurial university framework

culture of a specific society). In this context, the institutional approach provides a better understanding about the environmental factors of entrepreneurial universities. According to previous investigations, the key environmental factors of entrepreneurial universities include: (1) a flexible organizational and governance structure with innovative forms to help reduce the levels of bureaucracy and to support a fluid language with other agents in the region's entrepreneurial ecosystem to allow for the interaction and the definition of policies and practices to achieve their missions (O'Shea et al., 2007; Wood, 2009); (2) measures integrated by different instruments and mechanisms developed by universities to support internal and external new firm creation as centres of small-university businesses, research facilities, research groups or quasi-firms, liaison offices, technology transfer offices and incubators (Grandi and Grimaldi, 2005; Link and Scott, 2005); (3) adequate educational pro-grammes, for both students and academics, that provide a wide variety of situations, aims and methods oriented toward improving students' skills, attributes and behaviours to develop both creative and critical thinking (Kirby, 2004); (4) community members' favourable attitudes toward entrepreneurship to facilitate the development of potential entrepreneurs at all university levels (Louis et al., 1989; Liñán et al., 2011); (5) the existence and the diffusion of successful entrepreneurs, who will become new role models to their peers, demonstrating that entrepreneurial success is more than a theory (Venkataraman, 2004) and influencing entrepreneurial intentions (Liñán et al., 2011); and (6) adequate reward systems that represent strategic actions intended to promote an enterprise that is both monetary (bonuses, use of corporate resources, profit-sharing, etc.) and non-monetary (promotion and recognition systems) (Kirby, 2006; Wright et al., 2007).

Internal Factors (IF)

As a complementary approach, the resource-based view (RBV) helps to explain the internal factors that generate a competitive advantage (Wernerfelt, 1995) within an entrepreneurial university. The main internal factors include: (1) human resources, which are the most critical element for the development of educational quality and generation of innovation in research (Powers and McDougall, 2005); (2) financial resources from diversified sources of income (e.g., government, research contracts, campus services, student fees, and others) (Clark, 1998) are relevant to obtain positive and statistically significant relationships between research and development (R&D) expenditures and spin-off activities (Powers and McDougall, 2005); (3) physical resources that delimit the old boundaries between the university and the external world through infrastructure designed to satisfy social demands (Clark, 1998) and that create a fertile environment for innovation and new ventures (Guerrero and Urbano, 2011); (4) strong networks/alliances that support entrepreneurial universities' activities by attracting the financial resources required for innovation and new venture creation (O'Shea et al., 2007); and (5) status and prestige representing the uniqueness of historical conditions, whereby firms as intrinsically historical and social entities can be the basis for sustained competitive advantage (O'Shea et al., 2005) and can also attract investments, networks and access to public funding (O'Shea et al., 2007).

Entrepreneurial University Missions (EUMs)

The entrepreneurial university must fulfil three missions simultaneously that otherwise might be at odds with one another: teaching, research and entrepreneurship (Schulte, 2004). A university's primary function has always been to teach, which provides society with graduates who become both jobseekers and job creators. Its secondary function has been to conduct research, which, within the new knowledge-based economy, not only generates published academic findings but also innovations for new companies. Now, entrepreneurial activities link research results to their practical implications for society. Knowledge spillover appears to transmit university research via several conduits (Audretsch, 2007). Based on that, new companies are generated by the commercialization of research outputs of multidisciplinary research (Schulte, 2004).

Socioeconomic Impacts (S&EI) at the Regional Level

To understand how an economy works, it is necessary to know the political, social and cultural factors that establish its organizational dynamics, including its system of beliefs and decision-making processes (North, 2005). Particularly, following the influence of each entrepreneurial university's factors on academic entrepreneurship, the entrepreneurial university makes it possible to generate several direct outcomes from teaching, research and entrepreneurial activities. Outcomes could be transformed into determinants of economic development or factors of production function such as human capital (Lucas, 1988), knowledge capital (Solow, 1956; Romer, 1986), social capital (Coleman, 1988), and entrepreneurship capital (Audretsch and Keilbach, 2004), which later could produce positive impacts on the economy and society of a specific region (Urbano and Guerrero, 2013).

METHODS

This chapter adopts a multiple case study approach to explore the contemporary phenomenon of an entrepreneurial university within a real-life context (the Middle East), where the boundaries between phenomenon and context are complex, underexplored and not clearly evident (Yin, 1984; Eisenhardt, 1989). Etzkowitz and Mello (2004) assert that in developing countries, the entrepreneurial university is often viewed as a normative as well as an analytical concept; a goal to be sought rather than a reality to be investigated. Thus, multiple case studies are generally more robust than single case studies because they provide the observation and the analysis of the phenomenon in several settings as well as allow the logical replication in which the cases are treated as a series of independent experiments (Eisenhardt, 2007). Therefore, a convenience sampling was used in this chapter, in particular, two universities (one that is broad-based and one that is technological) in the Middle East. Nevertheless, a preliminary inquiry was carried out in order to identify the universities more entrepreneurially. The criteria considered to select these universities were: (1) universities located in regions characterized by higher levels of entrepreneurship measured by the number of new enterprises (Audretsch and Lehmann, 2005); (2) universities that promoted an entrepreneurial culture in their strategic actions that allows adaptation to environmental changes (Clark, 1998); (3) universities that showed self-instituting efforts to change their general character, developing entrepreneurial initiatives (Guerrero and Urbano, 2011, 2012) with outcomes such as patents, licences, spin-offs and research agreements (Klofsten and Jones-Evans, 2000); and (4) universities in the first-position rankings such as Webometrics (Guerrero and Urbano, 2011, 2012). Based on these criteria, the University of Tehran (UT) and Sharif University of Technology (SUT), both in Tehran, were selected. The main data of the universities analysed in this research are presented in Table 7.1. To triangulate the case findings and enhance the validity and reliability of the study (Yin, 1984), during more than six months, data were collected based on Clark's (1998) research methods (semi-structured interviews [SI] and secondary sources of data [SS]). With this data, we expect to understand the evolution, experiences and challenges of entrepreneurial universities in the Iranian context.

The semi-structured interviews (SI) were based on previous studies that gathered the perspectives from the top directive teams involved in universities' entrepreneurial transformations (Clark, 1998; Guerrero and Urbano, 2011, 2012; Kirby et al., 2011). The reliability requirement was covered using a standard protocol. In this investigation, the interviews were planned and realized during 2011. At UT and SUT, respectively, 12 interviewees and 11 interviewees (people such as officials, professors and science park managers) provided evidence about environmental and internal factors, university missions and socioeconomic impacts. The length of the interviews ranged from 30 minutes to 120 minutes, with a previous contextualization about the research. Almost all conversations were recorded,[4] and a second interviewer not actively involved in the interview process took detailed notes. It should be noted that in an effort to gather the required data, some interviewees were interviewed more than twice. The secondary sources of data (SS) were collected from other internal and external sources. Internal sources include records and media published by each university, such as university magazines, bulletins, memoires, annual reports and websites. External sources include records and media published by official organizations and associations associated with Higher Education, technology transfer, innovation and entrepreneurship.

Regarding data analysis, a research database was created with the results obtained, which increased the reliability of the entire study (Yin,

Table 7.1 General information of universities selected

	University of Tehran (UT)	Sharif University of Technology (SUT)
Founded	1934	1966
Founder	Dr Sayyed Mahmoud Hessaby	Dr Mohammad Ali Mojtahedi
Type	Broad-based	Technical
Area of University	554 647 square metres	20 hectares
Campuses	8 (Kargar Shomali, Agriculture and Natural Resources – Karaj, Qom, Abourihan, Kish Int. Campus, Aras Int. Campus, Caspian Sea)	2 (Tehran, Kish Island)
Academic and research structures	39 faculties, 120 departments, 40 research centres and 512 labs	14 faculties, 14 departments, 17 research centres and 15 labs
Scientific journals	89 (64 scientific-research, 25 others)	12
Membership in international associations/ unions and international agreements	*International associations* International Associationof Universities (IAU), Federation of the Universities of the Islamic World (FUIW), American Universities Admission Programs (AUAP), International Union of the History and Philosophy of Science (IUHPS), Internet Socio Consortium (ISC), Committee on Spatial Research	*International associations* International Association of Universities (IAU), the International Center for Theoretical Physics (ICTP) and the Third World Academy of Sciences (TWAS), among others

Table 7.1 (continued)

	University of Tehran (UT)	Sharif University of Technology (SUT)
	(COSPAR), International Gas Union (IGU), Global Entrepreneurship Monitor (GEM), World Trade Organization (WTO), and International Union of Geodesy and Geophysics (IUGG), among others *International Agreements*: more than 232	*International Agreements* Nuclear Suppliers Group (NSG), TOKTEN programme and universities from Malaysia, Japan, Indonesia, Italy, Spain, Hong Kong, Canada, France, Singapore and Sweden, among others
Statistics (2010)	1492 full-time faculty members 34 691 students (3559 PhDs, 11 492 Master's, and 19 640 Bachelor's) 2359 administrative staff 1800 graduates	426 full-time faculty members, approximately 430 part-time faculty members 10056 students (769 PhDs, 3287 Master's, and 6000 Bachelor's) 800 administrative staff 1800 graduates
Ranking	Webometrics (2010), 899 and 528 world position QS World (2011), 501–550	Webometrics (2010), 1404 and 1038 world position QS World (2011), 601+

Sources: Based on National Higher Education reports; Ministry of Science, Research and Technology; online official resources and university websites; documents; and interviews with officials and academics.

1984). First, the qualitative data were categorized and analysed according to the key informants that provided the basis for delineating themes and aggregate dimensions through the comparison of key events. Later, evidence obtained from both interviews and secondary data was examined by adopting an inductive approach (Eisenhardt, 1989).

EXPERIENCE OF IRANIAN ENTREPRENEURIAL UNIVERSITIES

In Iran,[5] governmental policies supporting entrepreneurial activities and education led to a flow of investments toward entrepreneurship at different levels. Regardless of this influx, however, Iranian universities are still challenged to operate more entrepreneurially (Tanha et al., 2011). According to Baerz et al. (2011), the Iranian government has developed several actions to foster entrepreneurship, knowledge and technology transfer, and innovation, including: (1) coordinating, supervising and evaluating the creation of a national system for managing science and technology; (2) supporting and providing resources for knowledge transfer (new venture creation) and the commercialization of innovations; and (3) promoting policy-making and macro-programming with regard to university–industry interactions.

In this context, Higher Education organizations implemented several strategies to anticipate and respond effectively to the dramatically changing environments. Generally, based on a SWOT (strengths, weakness, opportunities and threats) analysis, universities defined the mission, vision and objectives in order to select and implement strategies for teaching, research and entrepreneurship (Alashloo et al., 2005). In the case of Iran's universities, Table 7.2 summarizes the actions and programmes implemented by the government to support teaching, research and university–industry interaction. As can be seen, during this transformation process, the main impediments were: the lack of a national strategy, lack of incentive systems, lack of enough motivation among the managers and employees, and lack of employee commitments.

Iranian Entrepreneurial Universities

In this section, we present a brief description of each case study selected as well as the timeline of the main entrepreneurial actions implemented during the last three decades. In general terms, the evolutionary process of both universities has been influenced by government actions. A brief summary is presented in Table 7.3.

Table 7.2 *Role of government in the entrepreneurial actions*

Issues	Previous	1930–61	1962–82	1983–95	1995–2002	2002–04	2005–09
Evolution of Higher Education Institutions	Was an exclusive right for nobility	Establishing the Ministry of Education and councils Foundation of Tehran University (role model)	Establishing the Ministry of Culture and Higher Education (1967) Essential educational reforms	Medical education Reformed in four sciences groups: engineering, literature and humanities, arts, and business	Increased number of universities (22 in 1978 to 98 in 2000) Paid attention to research and postgraduate degrees	Reforms: science and technology strategies Develop postgraduate programmes (improve research) Research projects	Contribution to economic development
University–industry interaction		Based on education	Importing technologies	Based on research tasks	New basis for relation	Provide the necessities for a sustainable development	Based on knowledge and technology transfer
Social influences	Dynasty		Iran's Islamic revolution closed universities for two years	Reopened and restructuring	Centralized		Promoting entrepreneurial culture through providing financial and non-financial incentives

Sources: Based on Alashloo et al. (2005), Rasian (2009) and Baerz et al. (2011).

Table 7.3 Timeline of UT and SUT (Iranian entrepreneurial universities)

	Regional Actions	University's Actions	
		UT (1934)	SUT (1966)
60s	University–industry interaction was based on education		Industry Linkage Office was established
80s–90s	Knowledge, technology and innovation. Therefore, looking to establish scientific towns or parks	Office of Research Planning and Control (previously known as Industry Linkage Office)	Graduate School of Management and Economics
2000	KARAD national plan for improving entrepreneurship in universities was launched		Entrepreneurship Center (EC) was established
2001	National document of entrepreneurship development in Iran	Entrepreneurship Center was established	
2003	Ministry of Science, Research and Technology became responsible for integrating the country's	Authorization of the Ministry to establish the Technology Incubator	Pardis Technology Park (PTP) was established
2005	entrepreneurship Higher Education administrative affairs and scientific system policy-making. Also definition of tasks	Science and Technology Park of the UT with three centres (the Incubator Center of Technology Units, the Entrepreneurship Center, the Center of the Studies and the Development of Ideas and Futures Studies)	Sharif Advanced Technologies Incubator (SATI) was established
2007	Expand knowledge-based commodities' market, research commercialization and increase the role of private and cooperative sectors	Faculty of Entrepreneurship in UT and also GEM Iran office is established in this faculty Entrepreneurship Master's	

Table 7.3 (continued)

	Regional Actions	University's Actions	
		UT (1934)	SUT (1966)
2008	Build a competitive regimen of science, technology and innovation to design policies and strategies (Constitutional law's clause 124) Coordination canons for educational-research centres, cooperation and industries Definition of macro-plans Definitions of legal personalities to knowledge transfer	Entrepreneurship e-Learning Center established and online Master's degree programmes started Three new centres (the Intellectual Properties and Commercialization Center, the Technology Transfer Center, the Professional Industry and Entrepreneurship Consultation Center – the Industry and Entrepreneurship Polytechnic)	Technological Affairs Office was established
2010	Preparation of country scientific map of science and technology General policies to development of science, innovation and technology;	UNESCO Chair in Entrepreneurship	Sharif Fund for Research and Technology Export was established
2011	streamlining infrastructures; synergized collaborations; promotions	PhD in Entrepreneurship in the Faculty of Entrepreneurship	Dr Mojtahedi Innovation Award

Sources: Based on the universities' official sources, Alashloo et al. (2005) and Baerz et al. (2011).

University of Tehran (UT)

Founded in 1934, UT is the symbol of Higher Education in the country. UT comprises the following fields of study: Humanities, social sciences, behavioural sciences, technical and engineering, basic sciences, agriculture, arts and new sciences. UT also provides Islamic instruction, meritorious professors and other staff who produce scientific theories to fulfil the intellectual and scientific needs of society. UT's main missions are: (1) to preserve science and scientists' dignity, considering justice and to provide equal opportunities for the development of scientific and technical talents in the country; (2) to attempt to become the first-ranking comprehensive university in the Islamic world; (3) to train well-educated and scientifically powerful individuals and to produce knowledge, innovation and new technologies in order to gain pride and success for Iran and the Islamic world in the present and future. In addition, UT collaborates multilaterally with other universities at national and international levels and considers the university as an appropriate environment in which to think liberally and critically based on Islamic principles and to train thoughtful individuals, researchers and experts to collaborate, synergize and disseminate new thoughts in order to improve individual and social life. UT also collaborates with executive organizations of the country; trains experts in scientific, technological, economic and social fields; and considers leading fundamental research and supplying the scientific and practical needs of the society at all levels as its tasks.

Sharif University of Technology (SUT)

Founded in 1966, SUT was established in order to train and supply a part of required expert human resources of the country on an equal level to credible universities of the world. Compared with other worldwide universities, it is a young and growing pioneer in both basic and applied sciences. The main aims of SUT are: (1) to create an organization where students can be instructed in both theoretical and applied sciences, with special emphasis on the particular needs of Islamic society; (2) to teach students the advanced knowledge and techniques required to participate in the fields of engineering and technology and to cultivate them into creative engineers, good scientists and innovative technologists; and (3) to educate engineers who are ready to be employed, who contribute significantly to their jobs, and who have a strong sense of public responsibility and a desire to continue to learn. The emphasis is placed on the promotion of multidisciplinary research at the graduate and doctoral levels. Based on that, SUT provides a scientific and dynamic environment for those who are trying to gain knowledge. In other words, SUT is a place for those who are trying to understand and comprehend scientific realities and facts, and are trying to convey those to others.

Environmental (EF) and Internal (IF) Factors of Iranian Entrepreneurial Universities

Entrepreneurial organization and governance structure (EF1)

A flexible organizational and governance structure generates fluid interaction with other agents of the region's entrepreneurial ecosystem (O'Shea et al., 2007; Wood, 2009). At UT, governance includes the president, who is also the CEO and the top manager appointed through a proposal by the Minister of Science, Research and Technology that is approved by the High Council of Cultural Revolution. The governance structure also includes the secretariat of the president, the secretariat of the board of trustees (senate) and the Document Center. The board of trustees has the highest position in UT and overlooks the university's educational expansion, financial projections and other major plans. In this case, the university's internal governance follows a collegium pattern and has a strong link to the government (McNay, 1995). Similarly, SUT is managed by a board of trustees, which appoints a president. The president enjoys two supporting positions as Dean of International Relations and Director of Public Relations. Vice-presidents, department heads and educational and research centres are under the president's direct supervision. A relevant issue is that all SUT presidents have been highly educated scholars from well-known universities such as MIT, UC Berkeley, and so on. Based on that, SUT follows an entrepreneurial organization, especially after establishing the Entrepreneurial Center. The entrepreneurial structure of SUT is based on its entrepreneurial entities and organizations, which play their role as support measures. The SUT guides and improves entrepreneurial activities through these channels. UT follows an enterprise and managerial governance structure (ibid.) used to embrace internal structures, decision-making, and leadership roles (Middlehurst, 2004).

Support measures for entrepreneurship (EF2)

Both Iranian universities have implemented several mechanisms to support their activities and missions. UT has established various support measures during the last decade. For example, an Entrepreneurship Center (EC) with the aim of fostering an entrepreneurial culture in the university community toward teaching (e.g., courses, seminars, conferences, proposing entrepreneurial curriculum, etc.), knowledge transfer (e.g., consultancy services, motivating entrepreneurial minds and academics, industry linkage programmes, etc.), and research (e.g., publications in journals and newsletters, research funding, etc.). Other infrastructures include the Incubator of Technology Unit (ITU), which is the most successful example of a university incubator in the country; the Science and Technology Park

(STP), which is used to transfer knowledge into wealth, commercialize research gains and create a technological connection between university and industry; and the Small Business Development Center (SBDC) and UNESCO Chair in Entrepreneurship, which reinforce networking and create liaisons between universities and industry.

Similarly, since its founding, SUT has gained valuable experience with respect to entrepreneurship, innovation and knowledge transfer. It has established support measures similar to UT, such as the Industry Linkage Office, the Entrepreneurship Center, the KARAD plan initiated by the Ministry of Science Research and Industry, the Pardis Technology Park (PTP), the Sharif Advanced Technologies Incubator (SATI), the Technological Affairs Office, and the Sharif Fund for Research and Technology Export. The evidence from both universities corroborates the same instruments observed in the literature (Link and Scott, 2005; Grandi and Grimaldi, 2005).

Entrepreneurship education programme (EF3)
Complementary to the education programmes provided as support measures for academics, UT has implemented specific programmes for students, such as the Entrepreneurship Management Master's in 2007 and the Entrepreneurship PhD in 2011. Similarly, SUT's Entrepreneurship Center (EC) holds courses for affiliated firms and spin-off members while its Graduate School of Management and Economics holds courses in line with the academics' and students' needs, such as the MSc in Management (Entrepreneurship) and MBA (Entrepreneurship). The recent implementation of entrepreneurship education programmes in both universities that focus on the necessities of students and academics is a key element for improving their skills, competences, attributes and behaviour toward becoming entrepreneurs (Kirby, 2004).

Favourable Attitudes toward Entrepreneurship (EF4)
In the 1980s, at UT, the establishment of the Office of Research Planning and Control (previously known as the Industry Linkage Office) was the first step toward entrepreneurial culture. In 2001, a new era commenced at UT with the addition of the EC, ITU and STP to bolster entrepreneurial culture. Similarly, after establishing entrepreneurial support organizations, SUT experienced its own era of linking to industries and developing its contracting activities in order to improve the entrepreneurial intentions of students. Although, based on the GEM report (Razavi et al., 2012), Iran stands between the factor-driven economies,[6] UT and SUT try their best to be the pioneers of the transition toward efficiency-driven economies and to make substantial impacts on the formation of attitudes toward entrepreneurship at the regional and national levels.

Entrepreneur role models (EF5)
The diffusion of role models is one of the best strategies to foster entrepreneurship because it provides evidence to potential entrepreneurs that there are real students and academics who have experimented with being entrepreneurs within the university (Venkataraman, 2004). UT acknowledges its entrepreneurial role models, including students, faculty members and even graduates, at a variety of events. For example, each year successful student entrepreneurs are selected and awarded. As well, SUT, as a leading university in Iran, tries to get closer to the market and industry. For this reason, there are numerous academic and student entrepreneurs. Each year, the EC and the SATI of SUT hold an Entrepreneurship Festival in which entrepreneurial role models of the university are introduced and acknowledged. Also, the entrepreneurial faces of the university are documented in SUT reports.

Reward systems (EF6)
Adequate rewards systems, both monetary and non-monetary, are a strong incentive for recognizing the entrepreneurial efforts of the university community (Kirby, 2006; Wright et al., 2007). Following this perspective, both Iranian universities have implemented several monetary rewards. For example, UT has a system for students that includes financial aid, funding and awards; academic faculty receive career promotions and financial awards; university businesses (spin-offs) are awarded free equipment, financial aid, tax exemptions (based on university notification to government), and free services; and affiliate businesses enjoy an ease of collaboration and consultation services. Similarly, SUT developed an annual Entrepreneurship Festival that grants rewards (around €17 060.72, according to some Financial Aids and Loans, Privileges and Certificates of Appreciation from the 2011 Festival) to entrepreneurial academics, students, spin-offs established at SUT, and innovative business plans. Spin-offs are also encouraged through government, the EC, the SATI, and other previously mentioned entrepreneurial entities at SUT. But reward systems can be non-monetary as well. For example, in June 2010, SUT held the Dr Mojtahedi Innovation Award ceremony to recognize the innovation in research and education promoted by the university community.

Human resources (IF1)
Human resources are the most critical element in the entrepreneurial transformation process (Powers and McDougall, 2005); for this reason, an entrepreneurial university requires that it must be characterized by higher qualifications (Guerrero and Urbano, 2011). In the Iranian context,

according to the Official National Reports, in 2011 the top 500 students of the undergraduate Iranian National Examinations preferred SUT (68 per cent), UT (29 per cent), and other universities (3 per cent). UT, as the best and most well-known general university in Iran, each year attracts the top students in different fields of study as well as prominent world-class scholars and academics from around the globe. However, no clear statistics support this claim because invitations and collaborations are based on faculty needs and departmental arrangements (based on interviews and evidences, less than 5 per cent). At SUT, the undergraduate admission is limited to the top 5 per cent of students. Thus, a golden opportunity and a valuable amount of brilliant human capital are designated annually to SUT. Also, each year SUT students achieve honours at both national and international levels (e.g., in Olympiads, scientific contests, robotics, etc.). SUT has a high rate of brain drain (between 12 per cent to 25 per cent in different years). For these reasons, SUT has focused on attracting the most talented and well-trained faculty members available, and each faculty member is required to spend at least one year in a research organization anywhere on the globe. Faculty members are mostly graduates of well-known universities such as MIT, UC Berkeley, UCLA, Illinois Institute of Technology, Columbia University, University of Waterloo, Sharif University of Technology, University of Tehran, and so on. However, one of the deficiencies in Iranian universities is the lack of faculty members from other countries. Yet, a significant number of graduates come back to Iran and participate in the Iranian universities.

Financial resources (IF2)
Entrepreneurial universities are characterized by diverse sources of funding (e.g., government, research contracts, campus services, student fees and others) (Clark, 1998). Traditionally, both Iranian universities in this study have been financed mainly by governmental funds and budgets. In the past decade, however, a significant number of other financial sources have become available to them. According to the Ministry of Science, Research and Technology in 2011, UT is the first university allocated in the government budget, with approximately €134 442 169,[7] while SUT is the fourth university allocated in the budget, with €46 909 215. In addition, SUT has other sources of funding, such as the turnover of the 40 top firms in Iran (€293 010 053) and contracts with private sectors (€49 631 175), among others.

Physical resources (IF2)
In the entrepreneurial transformation process, UT has invested in several physical resources to build a variety of entities such as the Faculty of

Entrepreneurship, Entrepreneurship Center, Incubator of Technology Unit, Science and Technology Park, Small Business Development Center, and UNESCO Chair in Entrepreneurship. At the same time, SUT has also made valuable investments in infrastructures supporting entrepreneurial activities. Technological innovations and techno-entrepreneurship take place in such SUT centres as the Industry Linkage Office, Entrepreneurship Center, Pardis Technology Park, Sharif Advanced Technologies Incubator, Technological Affairs Office, and Sharif Fund for Research and Technology Export. SUT research centres play a significant role in the technological affairs of the university. In summary, all this evidence reveals the commitment for an expansion in physical resources (Clark, 1998).

Networks and alliances (IF3)

UT has a wide range of networks and alliances with: (1) more than 200 universities worldwide, such as Germany, Sweden, Malaysia, France, Afghanistan and India, among others; (2) Iranian ministries such as the Ministry of Science, Research and Technology and the Ministry of Health and Medical Education; and (3) international organizations and associations (see Table 7.1). Similarly, SUT has a wide range of networks and alliances with: (1) universities from Iran, Malaysia, Japan, Indonesia, Italy, Spain, France, UK and Canada; (2) Iranian ministries such as the Ministry of Science, Research and Technology and the Ministry of Health and Medical Education; (3) national institutions and bodies such as the Energy Productivity Organization of Iran, National Iranian Drilling Company, and so on; (4) international associations; and (5) affiliate companies such as Samsung, LG, Sony, System Group, Iran Khodro, among others.

Status and prestige (IF4)

It is crystal clear that UT (also known as 'the mother University of Iran' or the 'symbol of Iran's Higher Education') is the most well known and the oldest university in Iran, both traditionally and academically. Although SUT, as a technical university, still strives to compete with UT, no other university in the country has the ability to compete with UT in other fields. Also, based on QS ranking data, it is evident that SUT and UT are respectively ranked as 264th and 235th in Engineering and IT. In UT, less than the top 1 per cent of students who pass the National Exam will be admitted to the Faculty of Engineering. During the last few years, UT has ranked as the first university in the country. Similarly, SUT is a high-status university in Iran. According to ISC ranking (2010), it stands as the first technical university in Iran.

Table 7.4   Iranian universities' outcomes (2010)

	UT	SUT
Teaching activities		
Graduate students	4248	1800
Research activities		
Papers indexed in ISI Web of science	11 732	6589
Average citations	445	n.a.
Patents and licences	n.a.	More than 25 patents recorded by the SATI
Research contracts	With the industry through STP, more than €71 344 815 With only the industry, around €49 631 175 With government bodies, around €37 223 381	With the industry, more than €49 631 175 With government bodies, around €1 861 169 088
Entrepreneurial activities		
Spin-offs	On average, 16	More than 100
New enterprises	70 knowledge-based companies	More than 85 companies

Source: Both universities' official sources.

Socioeconomic Impacts of Iranian Entrepreneurial Universities

Table 7.4 summarizes the main outcomes obtained by each university's teaching, research and entrepreneurial activities. In general terms, this table shows that UT has better results associated with teaching and basic research, while SUT has better results associated with applied research (e.g., patents, research contracts) and entrepreneurial activities. These results are not surprising because they are linked to the nature of each university, but they will be critical if we analyse in-depth the relationship between the cost and the benefit related to R&D investment and entrepreneurship. Based on that, it is possible to associate these results with the socioeconomic impacts of these universities in the region.

The first impact is attracting foreign investment and entrepreneurship capital. In this context, UT attracts a variety of investments from governmental firms and international bodies as well as innovative ideas and plans to be made collaboratively through its infrastructures. Similarly, based on its nature, SUT has signed several contracts of around €1 240 779 with China in 2010. In addition, an increase of enterprises located around

SUT, with €8 065 066 sales on average, has been observed in 2010. Fifty-two firms are now working under SUT's support and supervision. The second impact is associated with human capital. To some degree, barriers such as language and financial restrictions limit UT's ability to attract international human resources. However, at the same time, UT welcomes international faces to attend different events, and some faculties employ foreign human resources (according to interviews, less than 5 per cent of human resources are foreign in origin). Similarly, SUT annually invites international faces of technology from different countries. But, unfortunately, because of limitations, the obvious presence of international human resources, especially as faculty members, is not significant. Finally, UT plays a significant role in the region and the country. This fact is evident in statistics and the news. Everyday, UT officials appear in the national news. Contracts with industrial sectors, governmental bodies and international companies are other issues to consolidate this reasoning. Also, according to its entrepreneurial directions, UT strives to be the first academic entity in the country to direct entrepreneurship. In order to do so, the Faculty of Entrepreneurship was established to play its role as a link between governmental and regulatory bodies and private sector firms. Similarly, SUT, as a leading technical university in Iran, plays a paramount role in the economic growth of the whole country. SUT and UT are the country's main sources for companies looking for excellent human resources. SUT graduates are preferred in employment tests and are privileged. At the national level, SUT renders a variety of services to governmental bodies and large industries, ranking first in providing scientific and industrial services to businesses.

CONCLUSIONS

Although the analysis of entrepreneurial universities in developing countries is different from what one might find in the existing literature, there are some good examples of universities in these countries that are moving toward this generation of universities. Iran, as a developing country, experiences the entrepreneurial transformation process in its Higher Education organizations. In this study, we concentrated on two of the top, most well-known and well-respected universities of Iran. As we mentioned earlier, UT is a broad-based university while SUT is a technical one. According to its nature, SUT exhibits more visible entrepreneurial movements and activities. While it could be noted that UT's technical faculty also acts more entrepreneurially based on the nature of its studies, there are other similarities between the technical faculty of UT and that of SUT. Regarding environmental factors of entrepreneurial universities in Iran, we found several similarities associated with the governance structure and support measures for entrepreneurship. For example, broad-based universities follow a collegium pattern and have a strong link to the government while technological universities overlook their future educational expansion, financial projections, and other major plans like an enterprise with a managerial governance structure used to embrace internal structures, decision-making and leadership roles. Also, Iranian universities present similar strategies about support measures for entrepreneurship and entrepreneurial education programmes. The main difference is related to the existence of favourable attitudes toward entrepreneurship. Iranian universities try their best to make a substantial impact on the formation of attitudes toward entrepreneurship at the regional and national levels.

Proposition 1: In developing countries with comparable social, economic and political situations, entrepreneurial universities could present similarities in environmental conditioning factors related to governance structures, support measures and entrepreneurial education programmes as well as present differences related to attitudes toward entrepreneurship.

With regard to internal factors of entrepreneurial universities, human resources are the most critical element in the entrepreneurial transformation process because one of the deficiencies in Iranian universities is the lack of talent and well-trained faculty members. On the other hand, the main similarity is in financial terms because, traditionally, the Iranian universities have been financed mainly by government funds and budgets. In particular, technological universities have been the first allocated in the government budgets.

Proposition 2: In developing countries with comparable social, economic and political situations, entrepreneurial universities could present similarities in internal conditioning factors related to financial resources as well as present differences related to human capital.

Concerning the socioeconomic impacts of entrepreneurial universities, not surprisingly Iranian technological universities have better results associated with entrepreneurial activities while broad-based organizations have better results associated with teaching and research. In this sense, the main socioeconomic impact is associated with foreign investment and entrepreneurship capital because technological universities attract a variety of investments from governmental firms and international bodies. But, unfortunately, this is conditioned by the lack of human resources.

Proposition 3:   In developing countries with comparable social, economic and political situations, the differences in environmental factors (governance structures, attitudes toward entrepreneurship and rewards systems) and internal factors (human capital) directly conditioned the outcomes/outputs related to entrepreneurial activities.

In summary, in Iran, as in the majority of developing countries, there is a lower demand from industry because 70 per cent of industry is state run and the 30 per cent of industry that is privately run shows weak efforts to invest in research. Because this region has a strong economic dependence on oil profits, there is no need for R&D, as all needs can be met from outside sources. Still, there are so many fast-growing companies in the country that are trying to meet the market needs and companies that are exporting their competitive goods and services to other countries. Thus, the Iranian culture advocates individual work or family aggregations.

Under this scenario, the main challenges and implications for universities interested in becoming more entrepreneurial are: (1) to promote the entrepreneurial culture in society, (2) to reinforce entrepreneurial attitudes, (3) to build a stronger relationship with national or international industry; and (4) to pave the way for universities to become more entrepreneurial through reinforcing the required rules and regulations and improving the business environment of the country. Last but not least, a lack of sufficient databases and a lack of integrity among the available reports are considered the most paramount limitations of the present study. Therefore, we believe that further empirical research could be undertaken, first to analyse individually the leadership that has significant relevance in different regions (Young et al., 2008). Second, a focus on outreach activities (e.g., aimed at industry and primary and secondary school pupils) is critically important for universities to sustain their competitive positions with respect to core missions. Our study found a variety of activities that regional universities have adopted and in doing so contributed to entrepreneurial societies and regions (Audretsch, 2007). Third, insights about the socioeconomic output of entrepreneurial universities are necessary to evaluate the real-world effect in the long term of adopting ideas from endogenous growth theory, such as those 'related to productive factors' (Salter and Martin, 2001) as well as analysing the cost–benefit ratio of government investment (e.g., in all restructuring and entrepreneurship programmes) with the socioeconomic impacts of universities.

NOTES

* The authors wholeheartedly appreciate the brilliant comments and ideas of the collaborators in this research, including all the interviewees. Maribel Guerrero recognizes the support of Mexico's National Council of Science and Technology (CONACYT). David Urbano acknowledges financial support from Projects ECO2010–16760 (Spanish Ministry of Science and Innovation) and 2005SGR00858 (Catalan Government Department for Universities, Research and Information Society).
1. The capital of Iran has a population of approximately 12 000 000 (2011). According to the National Bureau of Statistics, in 2006, 28.3 per cent was active population, 6.1 per cent was the unemployment rate (out of the active population), 54 per cent of the population had social security, 25 per cent share in the gross domestic product (GDP), and the main share of sectors in GDP were Services (78 per cent), Industries (14 per cent) and Agriculture (8 per cent).
2. The University of Tehran – the country's oldest university – is called 'the mother university of Iran'. It enjoys an old tradition of education dating back to the Jondishapour in the Sassanid period (224–651 AD) and in seminaries 700 hundred years ago.
3. Established in 1966 as the Aryarmehr University of Technology – which included 54 faculty members and 412 students, who were selected by national examination – it was renamed the Sharif University of Technology in 1980.
4. Because of lack of consent and other limitations, some of the interviews were not recorded.
5. With a population of 70 million, Iran is the most populous country in the region and one of the most densely populated countries in the world. According to OPEC, Iran is the second largest oil producer and the second largest server of gas.
6. Perceived opportunity: 32.0; perceived capabilities: 46.4; fear of failure: 32.7; entrepreneurial intentions: 29.9; entrepreneurship as a good career choice: 61.1; high status to successful entrepreneurs: 72.7; and media attention for entrepreneurship: 58.4.
7. 1 Euro = 16 115 Rials (as of 2011).

REFERENCES

Alashloo, F., P. Castka and J. Sharp (2005), 'Towards understanding the impeders of strategy implementation in Higher Education (HE): A case of HE institutes in Iran', *Quality Assurance in Education*, **13**(2), 132–47.

Audretsch, D. (2007), *The Entrepreneurial Society*, New York: Oxford University Press.

Audretsch, D. and M. Keilbach (2004), 'Entrepreneurship capital and economic performance', *Regional Studies*, **38**(8), 949–59.

Audretsch, D. and E. Lehmann (2005), 'Does the knowledge spillover theory of entrepreneurship hold for regions?' *Research Policy*, **34**(8), 1191–202.

Baerz, A., T. Abbasnejad, A. Rostamy and A. Azar (2011), 'The role of governmental policies in improving national innovation systems: A case study of Iran', *Middle-East Journal of Scientific Research*, **7**(4), 625–33.

Clark, B.R. (1998), *Creating Entrepreneurial Universities*, Oxford: Pergamon.

Coduras, A., D. Urbano, A. Rojas and S. Martínez (2008), 'The relationship between university support to entrepreneurship with entrepreneurial activity in Spain: A GEM data based analysis', *International Advances in Economic Research*, **14**(4), 395–406.

Coduras, A., J., Levie, D. Kelley, R. Sæmundsson and T. Schøtt (2010), *Global Entrepreneurship Monitor Special Report: A Global Perspective on Entrepreneurship Education and Training*, Babson Park, MA: Babson College.

Coleman, J.S. (1988), 'Social capital in the creation of human capital', *American Journal of Sociology*, **94**(Supplement), 95–120.

Eisenhardt, K. (1989), 'Building theories from case study research', *Academy of Management Review*, **14**(4), 532–50.

Eisenhardt, K.M. (2007), 'Theory building from cases: Opportunities and challenges', *Academy of Management Journal*, **50**(1), 25–32.

Etzkowitz, H. and J. Mello (2004), 'Rise of the Brazilian Triple Helix', *International Journal of Technology Management and Sustainable Development*, **2**(3), 159–71.

Farsi, J.Y., N. Imanipour and A. Salamzadeh (2012), 'Entrepreneurial university conceptualization: Case of developing countries', *Global Business and Management Research: An International Journal*, **4**(2), 193–204.

Grandi, A. and R. Grimaldi (2005), 'Academics' organizational characteristics and the generation of successful business ideas', *Journal of Business Venturing*, **20**(6), 821–45.

Grimaldi, R., M. Kenney, D. Siegel and M. Wright (2011), '30 years after Bayh-Dole: Reassessing academic entrepreneurship', *Research Policy*, **40**(8), 1045–57.

Guerrero, M. and D. Urbano (2011), *The Creation and Development of Entrepreneurial Universities in Spain: An Institutional Approach*, New York: Nova Science Publishers, Inc.

Guerrero, M. and D. Urbano (2012), 'The development of an entrepreneurial university', *Journal of Technology Transfer*, **37**(1), 43–74.

Kirby, D.A. (2004), 'Entrepreneurship education: Can business schools meet the challenge?' *Education + Training*, **46**(8/9), 510–19.

Kirby, D.A. (2006), 'Creating entrepreneurial universities in the UK: Applying entrepreneurship theory to practice', *Journal of Technology Transfer*, **31**(5), 599–603.

Kirby, D.A., M. Guerrero and D. Urbano (2011), 'The theoretical and empirical side of entrepreneurial universities: An institutional approach', *Canadian Journal of Administrative Sciences*, **28**(3), 302–16.

Klofsten, M. and D. Jones-Evans (2000), 'Comparing academic entrepreneurship in Europe: The case of Sweden and Ireland', *Small Business Economics*, **14**(4), 299–310.

Liñán, F., D. Urbano and M. Guerrero (2011), 'Regional variations in entrepreneurial cognitions: Start-up intentions of university students in Spain', *Entrepreneurship and Regional Development*, **23**(3), 187–215.

Link, A. and J. Scott (2005), 'Opening the ivory tower's door: An analysis of the determinants of the formation of U.S. university spin-off companies', *Research Policy*, **34**(7), 1106–12.

Louis, K.S., D. Blumenthal, M.E. Gluck and M.A. Stoto (1989), 'Entrepreneurs in academe: An exploration of behaviours among life scientists', *Administrative Science Quarterly*, **34**(1), 110–31.

Lucas, R. Jr. (1988), 'On the mechanics of economic development', *Journal of Monetary Economics*, **22**(1), 3–42.

McNay, I. (1995), 'From the collegial academy to corporate enterprise: The changing cultures of universities', in T. Schuller (ed.), *The Changing University?*, Milton Keynes: Open University Press, pp. 105–15.

Middlehurst, R. (2004), 'Changing internal governance: A discussion of leadership roles and management structures in UK universities', *Higher Education Quarterly*, **58**(4), 258–79.

North, D.C. (1990), *Institutions, Institutional Change and Economic Performance*, Cambridge, UK: University Press.

North, D.C. (2005), *Understanding the Process of Economic Change*, Princeton, NJ: Princeton University Press.

O'Shea, R., T.J. Allen, A. Chevalier and F. Roche (2005), 'Entrepreneurial orientation, technology transfer and spin-off performance of US universities', *Research Policy*, **34**(7), 994–1009.

O'Shea, R.P., T. J. Allen, K.P. Morse, C. O'Gorman and F. Roche (2007), 'Delineating the anatomy of an entrepreneurial university: The Massachusetts Institute of Technology experience', *R&D Management*, **37**(1), 1–16.

Powers, J. and P.P. McDougall (2005), 'University start-up formation and technological licensing with firms that go public: A resource-based view of academic entrepreneurship', *Journal of Business Venturing*, **20**(3), 291–311.

Rasian, Z. (2009), 'Higher education governance in developing countries. Challenges and recommendations. Iran as case study', *Nonpartisan Education Review*, **5**(3), 1–18.

Razavi, S.M., M. Reza, N. Faghih, M. Ahmadpur, A. Kordnaeij, J. Yadulahi and L. Sarfaraz (2012), *Monitoring Entrepreneurship in Iran: GEM-based Data 2008*, national report, accessed 5 August 2013 at http://www.gemconsortium.org/docs/download/2260.

Romer, P. (1986, 'Increasing returns and long-run growth', *The Journal of Political Economy*, **94**(5), 1002–37.

Salter, A.J. and B.R. Martin (2001), 'The economic benefits of publicly funded basic research: A critical review', *Research Policy*, **30**(3), 509–32.

Schulte, P. (2004), 'The entrepreneurial university: A strategy for institutional development', *Higher Education in Europe*, **29**(2), 187–91.

Solow, R. (1956), 'A contribution to the economic growth theory', *The Quarterly Journal of Economics*, **70**(1), 65–94.

Sooreh, L.K., A. Salamzadeh, H. Safarzadeh and Y. Salamzadeh (2011), 'Defining and measuring entrepreneurial universities: A study in Iranian context using importance–performance analysis and TOPSIS technique', *Global Business and Management Research: An International Journal*, **3**(2), 182–200.

Tanha, D., A. Salamzadeh, Z. Allahian and Salamzadeh (2011), 'Commercialization of university researches and innovations in Iran: Obstacles and solutions', *Journal of Knowledge Management, Economics, and Information Technology*, **1**(7), 126–46.

Thornton, P., D. Ribeiro-Soriano and D. Urbano (2011), 'Socio-cultural factors and entrepreneurial activity: An overview', *International Small Business Journal*, **29**(2), 105–18.

Urbano, D. and M. Guerrero (2013), 'Entrepreneurial universities: Socioeconomic impacts of academic entrepreneurship in a European region', *Economic Development Quarterly*, DOI: 10.1177/0891242412471973.

Veciana, J.M. and D. Urbano (2008), 'The institutional approach to entrepreneurship research: An introduction', *International Entrepreneurship and Management Journal*, **4**(4), 365–79.

Venkataraman, S. (2004), 'Regional transformation through technological entrepreneurship', *Journal of Business Venturing*, **19**(1), 153–67.

Webometrics (2010), 'Methodology of ranking: Web of university rankings in the world', accessed 5 August 2013 at http://www.webometrics.info/.

Wernerfelt, B. (1995), 'The resource-based view of the firm: Ten years after', *Strategic Management Journal*, **16**(3), 171–4.

Wood, M. (2009), 'Does one size fit all? The multiple organizational forms leading to successful academic entrepreneurship', *Entrepreneurship Theory and Practice*, **33**(4), 929–47.

World Bank (2009), *Middle East and North Africa Region. Economic Developments and Prospects. Navigating through the Global Recession*, Washington, DC: The World Bank.

Wright, M., B. Clarysse, P. Mustar and A. Lockett (2007), *Academic Entrepreneurship in Europe*, Cheltenham, UK and Northampton, MA, USA: Edward Elgar Publishing.

Yin, R. (1984), *Case Study Research, Design and Methods*, Beverly Hills, CA: Sage.

Young, B., N. Hewitt-Dundas and S. Roper (2008), 'Intellectual property management in publicly funded R&D centres. A comparison of university-based and company-based research centres', *Technovation*, **28**(8), 473–84.

8. A regional perspective on the entrepreneurial university: practices and policies

Niall G. MacKenzie and Qiantao Zhang

INTRODUCTION

The role of universities has evolved dramatically in recent years in both advanced economies and developing nations. Once largely focused on teaching and research within 'ivory tower' settings, universities now undertake a variety of additional knowledge transfer activities with commercial benefit to them and have consequently become more entrepreneurial (Etzkowitz and Leydesdorff, 1997, 2000; Etzkowitz, 1998; Gibb et al., 2009). This change reflects a major shift in expectations to their role as economic drivers that should make an active contribution to regional development and engage with the wider society on various scales (Chatterton and Goddard, 2000; Goddard, 2009). Entrepreneurship is becoming more integrated into the general education agenda of universities in order to build an entrepreneurship-friendly culture, which could improve the entrepreneurial performance of institutions, and in consequence serve the wider economy. In the aftermath of the world financial and economic crisis, an increasingly important role ascribed to universities is converting knowledge and scientific breakthroughs into economic success, in order to promote recovery from recession (Kitson et al., 2009). This is by no means a straightforward task and much of the extant discourse tends to focus on the examples of best practices, that is, extraordinary universities in competitive regions, while other analyses have examined the development of entrepreneurial universities in a specific region (Jauhiainen and Suorsa, 2008; Saad and Zawdie, 2011). There is, however, a lack of recognition of the difficulty of transplanting the models of engagement with business in successful regions to weaker regions and from stronger universities to weaker universities. To this end, this chapter focuses on the questions of whether or not the regional profile has a direct bearing on the potential for success or failure in developing entrepreneurial universities and if it should be a consideration when seeking to design policies to encourage changes in Higher Education institutions. Our intention in doing so is to shed further light on the development of entrepreneurial universities through the prism of competitive and uncompetitive (or weaker) regions using the case of the UK, focusing on regional divergence, institutional difference and government policies.

In the UK context, the ineffectiveness of the translation of scientific work into business innovation was famously espoused by Marshall in the early twentieth century, stating 'the small band of British scientific men have made revolutionary discoveries in science; but yet the chief fruits of their work have been reaped by businesses' (Marshall, 1919, p. 102). Towards the last decade of the twentieth century, UK government policy began emphasising the inter-relatedness of research and economic benefit (Hewitt-Dundas, 2012). With the introduction of the 1993 Realising Our Potential Awards, the UK government showed an increased focus on the impact of university–business interactions (Abreu et al., 2008). The 1998 Government White Paper – *Our Competitive Future* – argued that the crucial factor in building the knowledge-driven economy is about 'the more effective use and exploitation of all types of knowledge' (DTI, 1998), of which knowledge created by the university sector accounts for an important share. In a 2000 White Paper titled *Excellence and Opportunity*, the government proposed a number of initiatives and programmes to create clusters of innovation that draw universities and businesses together, and to ensure that excellence in science was turned into products and services (DTI, 2000). The UK Science and Innovation Investment Framework for the period 2004–14 further embedded the notion of translating the knowledge base more effectively into business and public service innovation (HM Treasury, 2004).

While the significance of converting scientific progress into economic success was being highlighted by national policies, the UK government also launched a series of funding schemes to boost knowledge transfer activities in the university marketplace. In 1999 the Higher Education Funding Council for England (HEFCE) established the Higher Education Reach-out to Business and the Community Fund (HEROBC) for the purpose of enhancing the contribution that universities make to the economy and society (HEFCE, 2000). The Higher Education Innovation Fund (HEIF) succeeded this in 2001, and the current incarnation of the fund runs from 2011 to 2015 (HEFCE, 2011; PACEC, 2012). In 2004, the Higher Education Funding Council for Wales (HEFCW) founded its Third Mission (3M) Fund and has recently renamed it the Innovation and Engagement (I&E) Fund (HEFCW, 2009, 2011). Northern Ireland runs an adaptation of HEIF in England, while Scotland offers its own Knowledge Transfer Grant (KTG) (SQW, 2009; DELNI, 2010).

Published by the HEFCE on behalf of all UK Higher Education

Institutions (HEIs) and the national funding bodies, the Higher Education–Business and Community Interaction Survey (HE-BCI) has been collecting data related to knowledge transfer activities in UK universities since the academic year 1999–2000. Analysis in this chapter draws on the 2009 HE-BCI survey, referring to the academic year 2007–08, which reports data for 160 universities across the UK (out of 165 HEIs). First, it evaluates the divergence of university entrepreneurial performance between competitive and uncompetitive regions. Second, it examines how research intensity of universities is reflected in the scale of entrepreneurial activity they undertake. Third, it considers the differences between institutions in terms of age and the effect the regional economic context in which they operate has on them.

The following section considers some missing elements in the conventional wisdom of the entrepreneurial university. Section 3 outlines the data and methods used in the analysis, followed by section 4, which reports the main findings. The section that follows states some future work to be completed, while the last section concludes with implications for policy for entrepreneurial universities, which argue for a more tailored approach regarding regional divergence and institutional difference.

THE ENTREPRENEURIAL UNIVERSITY: MISSING ELEMENTS IN THE LITERATURE

Institutional Difference

When evaluating the technology transfer process of universities, the literature has tended to do so by examining the aspects of academic spin-off activities (Di Gregorio and Shane, 2003; Pirnay et al., 2003; Clarysse et al., 2005); patenting and licensing (Mowery and Shane, 2002; Mowery and Ziedonis, 2002; Thursby and Thursby, 2003; Geuna and Nesta, 2006); science parks (Cabral and Dahab, 1998; Kihlgren, 2003; Phan et al., 2005; Vaidyanathan, 2008); and the effects universities have on companies (Audretsch et al., 2005, 2011). Little attention has been paid to institutional differences between universities and how entrepreneurial performance of an institution may be related to its own features such as research intensity and mission statements as well as the regional characteristics of its locale. Some nationwide surveys within this realm, including the AUTM survey in the USA and the HE-BCI survey in the UK, mainly show the progress of 'Third Mission' activities in the university sector compared to their performance in the previous investigation period and draw conclusions on an aggregated basis. That is to say, although the survey results reveal how entrepreneurial activities have improved in the country, it remains unclear how the individual universities have contributed to that improvement.

The desire for transferring 'best practice' has resulted in myriad analyses of the successful stories of a number of universities, many of whom represent the 'gold standard' in the field, such as MIT, Columbia, Stanford and the University of Wisconsin (Page, 2007). While we acknowledge the impressive performance of these institutions, and agree with their significant role in developing the academic field in technology transfer, it is necessary to bear in mind that the stories of these universities are not the norm – they are recognized globally as being exceptional; implicit in this then should be the recognition that their success is not easily transferable to other institutions. For example, Thursby and Thursby (2003) investigated the case of licensing in their study and found that about one-third of respondents (university central administrations) received no royalty income at all. Licensing is not the only area where universities are found to differ in their performance, however. The study by Di Gregorio and Shane (2003) shows that spin-off activity is increasing worldwide, but with considerable variations at the individual institutional level. In particular, spin-offs tend to be created by the more research-intensive universities, suggesting that institutional difference can be helpful in explaining the fact that not all universities could harvest the fruits of entrepreneurial activities, at least not on the same level.

The differentiation in the university sector and knowledge transfer activity was recently acknowledged by, among others, a 2007 review of UK government's science and innovation policy (HM Treasury, 2007). It highlighted the necessity of a diversity of excellence, 'with research universities focusing on curiosity-driven research, teaching and knowledge transfer, and business-facing universities focusing on the equally important economic mission of professional teaching, user-driven research and problem-solving with local and regional companies' (HM Treasury, 2007). This recognition of the varieties of knowledge transfer and exchange is an important distinction. Equally, recognizing the differing intensities amongst universities in Third Mission activities and designing policy accordingly is important.

Within a regional innovation system, the interactions between institutions innovating through creation, storage and transfer of knowledge will largely decide the competitiveness of that region (Cooke et al., 1998; Cooke, 1998, 2004; Charles, 2003). Universities, as well as other innovation actors such as government laboratories, public research organizations and industrial research centres, are generally regarded as principal components of those institutions. Whilst linkages among these components would always co-exist at multiple levels (such as international, national and regional), it has been suggested that a regional perspective seems more appropriate to examine the roles of universities, since they are more able to shape regional network typologies, compared to their role as pathways linking other actors and recipients of systems at national level (Arbo and Benneworth, 2004), and by virtue of the fact that they are often semi-permanent physical fixtures in their respective locales.

Regional Divergence

It is often competitive regions, accompanied with the presence of world-leading Higher Education Institutions, that have attracted the attention of academic researchers and policy-makers. The stories of Silicon Valley in California (Saxenian, 1994; Kenney, 2000; Lee et al., 2000), Route 128 in Massachusetts (Saxenian, 1994), and the Research Park Triangle in North Carolina (Link and Scott, 2003) have been repeatedly told and in substantial detail. In Europe, the case of Cambridge in the UK has been identified as particularly influential in its success in transforming the economy of the surrounding region (SQW, 1985). Being 'a geographic area of intense high-technology innovation activity encompassing the City of Cambridge as its heart and sub-regional Greater Cambridge hinterland of approximately 25 miles radius', Cambridge Technopole is said to have significantly benefited from the presence, and more importantly, the embeddedness of the three main universities within the area: University of Cambridge, Anglia Ruskin University and the Open University (Herriot and Minshall, 2008, p. 1).

The studies on these successful areas emphasize the crucial role of risk-taking cultures, highly educated workforces, leading universities and strong local and regional innovation networks in building an entrepreneurial region. In each case, universities became actively engaged in regional (as well as international) innovation networks as ways of seeking technological potential for research findings, translating them into use, and deploying the consequent commercial value. These regions represent the 'totemic sites' of the knowledge-based economy however, where an abundant supply of academics meet vast demands from industry, and equally, if not more, importantly, high absorptive capacity of firms in the region (Cohen and Levinthal, 1990). Compared to these symbolic regions, there are more numerous less successful regions or less favoured regions (LFRs), as defined by Benneworth (2006). These regions contain 'few favourable background conditions such as cultures, economic structures and institutional arrangements', which might provide explanations for the decline of old industrial regions (Benneworth, 2006, p. 2). Indeed, when comparing the economic and innovation contribution of universities in the context of UK regions, Huggins and Johnston (2009, p. 14) found that Wales was the least competitive region in the UK, which could partly be explained by 'a lack of demand from firms within the region for the type of knowledge that Welsh universities are capable of supplying'. A later study by Huggins et al. found evidence that for those uncompetitive regions, an urgent task 'would be to focus on alleviating demand-side weakness by educating and facilitating firms in how to effectively engage with universities' (Huggins et al., 2012, p. 495), suggesting that the problem may not lie so much with universities in uncompetitive regions, but instead with the demand for their products and services. In a report prepared for NESTA, Benneworth (2007) termed regions without the extraordinary assets of Silicon Valley as 'ordinary' regions and implied that it might be impossible for those areas to make the leap from an old-economy paradigm to one based on innovation in services and high-technology industries, suggesting that regional divergence is a factor that should be considered when discussing the entrepreneurial performance of any region, and by extension, any university.

A further question to consider then is whether universities, in competitive and weaker regions, may follow distinctive pathways when they advance their entrepreneurial activities and engage with regional economic development. The work by Boucher et al. (2003) argued that structural, institutional and social factors interact to shape the participation of most European universities in regional development. Whilst more careful empirical analyses are required for a better understanding of specific roles of universities in their region, it is apparent that policies aimed at boosting the entrepreneurial performance of universities should be cognisant of the particular conditions present in each region within both the Higher Education sector as the supplier of goods and services, and the business sector as the demand side. Furthermore, it is also apparent that an understanding of the capabilities of the universities themselves should also be recognized for their distinctiveness, both positive and negative, in the formulation and implementation of such policies.

DATA AND METHODOLOGY

This chapter draws on the 2009 HE-BCI survey results, which show entrepreneurial performance in terms of engagement with the community and business and commercial revenues raised by 159 UK universities and HEIs. From the academic year 2002–03 onward, the data were collected through two pathways: one for strategic and infrastructure data and the other one for financial, numeric (time-bound) data. The HE-BCI survey considers that universities interact with business and the community in a wide range of activities, including intellectual property (IP) channels such as patenting, licensing and spin-offs, as well as collaborative research, contract research, consultancy, facilities- and equipment-related services, and so on. This is in line with the approach of other studies, which have argued that the importance of IP activities has been overestimated (Abreu et al., 2008), and that focusing narrowly on the IP activities underestimates the comprehensive role of universities (Abreu, et al., 2009). The entrepreneurial activities of universities are defined by the category of knowledge transfer activities set out by the HE-BCI survey that assess the performance of universities in measures of collaborative income, contract research income, consultancy income, facilities- and equipment-related services income as well as income from professional courses and IP activities.

Two typologies are employed with the purpose of capturing institutional difference and regional divergence within the UK context, respectively. First, we use the classification of regions defined by Huggins's UK Competitiveness Index 2010, which comprehensively assesses the relative economic competitiveness of the 12 UK regions. The South East, London and East of England were categorized by the report as competitive regions, while the remaining nine regions were categorized as being uncompetitive (Huggins and Thompson, 2010). It is on this basis that this study moves on to examine whether universities in the two types of regions perform differently in building entrepreneurial engagements, that is, how the regional context impacts on the scale and scope of knowledge transfer between universities and their stakeholders.

Second, in terms of the categorization of UK universities, prior studies have usually grouped them according to factors such as research intensity and mission statements (Abreu et al., 2009; Hewitt-Dundas, 2012; Huggins et al., 2012). Abreu et al. (2009) compared the entrepreneurial performance of the Russell Group (research-intensive UK group of universities akin to the US Ivy League), other established universities (formed before 1992 but not Russell Group), post-1992 universities (mainly ex-polytechnics), and others (mainly art schools and agricultural colleges). The Further and Higher Education Act 1992 ended the 'binary divide' in the UK by granting university status to Higher Education Institutions that had previously been known as polytechnics, which are usually called post-1992 universities or New Universities. Huggins et al. (2012, p.481) acknowledged the diversity of UK HEIs, and in particular found that 'more established universities tend to be more research focused and may have a greater attraction for external organisations'. With this in mind, we follow Huggins et al.'s classification of UK HEIs and compare the entrepreneurial performance of established (pre-1992) and new (post-1992) universities. In order to control for the difference of size of UK universities, we used the number of academic full-time equivalents (FTEs) in 2007–08 drawn from the Higher Education Statistics Agency (HESA). Consequently our findings are based on the analysis of activities of the two different types of university – new and established – within the two different types of region – competitive and uncompetitive.

FINDINGS

Entrepreneurial activity income of UK universities by type of university, per academic FTE, 2007–08

Our findings showed that established universities tend to generate much higher income from knowledge transfer activities than their new counterparts do per full-time employee, suggesting that established universities are more capable of turning their research into tangible economic outcomes (Table 8.1). Given that established universities are more research intensive and carry out more research as well as committing more funds to it, their stronger performance in knowledge exchange is perhaps unsurprising. Our results also showed that the two groups of universities are significantly different (at the $p < 0.01$ level) in generating income from collaborative research, contract research and IP activities. We found that in all measures the established HEIs outperform their new counterparts. Being more research focused, again it is unsurprising to find that established universities are more actively engaged in collaborative research and contract research projects with both firms and public sector organizations. Furthermore, the European Union (EU) funding secured by established universities is four times more than that which flows to new universities, indicating a substantial difference between them. Relatively less significant difference was found between the two groups in income generated from business courses and facilities- and equipment-related services. Consultancy is the only sort of activity where new universities were seen to perform at a similar level to established institutions suggesting that although each group possesses different levels of research intensity, they may provide comparable quantity of consultancy services.

UK government departments were found to be the most important collaborative income source for new universities, while OST (Office of Science and Technology) research councils are the most important source for established ones. Non-SME commercial companies, compared with SMEs and non-commercial companies, appear to be major partners of established universities, whilst new universities secure most income from

Table 8.1   Entrepreneurial activity income of UK universities by university group, per academic FTE, 2007–08

	University Group				
	Established universities $N = 78$		New universities $N = 81$		
	Mean	Median	Mean	Median	
Collaborative research income (£000s)					
OST research councils	2.6	1.1	0.6	0.1	**
Other UK government departments	1.8	1.0	1.3	0.4	**
EU government	1.6	1.1	0.4	0.0	**
Other	0.6	0.1	0.3	0.0	*
Total collaborative income	6.6	4.7	2.7	1.3	**
Contract research income (£000s)					
SMEs	0.4	0.2	0.1	0.0	**
Non-SME commercial	2.5	2.0	0.6	0.1	**
Non-commercial	4.0	2.7	1.2	0.8	**
Total contract income	6.9	6.1	2.0	1.2	**
Consultancy income (£000s)					
SMEs	0.4	0.2	0.5	0.1	
Non-SME commercial	0.9	0.3	0.8	0.2	
Non-commercial	1.4	0.6	1.5	1.0	
Total consultancy income	2.7	1.3	2.8	1.7	
Facilities- and equipment-related services income (£000s)					
SMEs	0.4	0.1	0.3	0.0	*
Non-SME commercial	0.3	0.0	0.2	0.0	**
Non-commercial	0.3	0.1	0.3	0.0	
Total F&E income	1.0	0.5	0.8	0.2	†
Income from courses for business and community (£000s)					
SMEs	0.4	0.1	0.4	0.1	
Non-SME commercial	4.9	0.2	1.0	0.1	
Non-commercial	1.7	0.8	2.6	1.2	†
Individuals	1.4	0.6	2.2	0.6	
Total income from courses	8.3	2.6	6.1	4.6	*
IP income (£000s)					
SMEs	0.1	0.0	0.1	0.0	**
Non-SME commercial	0.3	0.0	0.1	0.0	**
Non-commercial	0.0	0.0	0.2	0.0	**
Sales of share in spin-offs	0.1	0.0	0.0	0.0	**
Total IP income	0.5	0.2	0.3	0.0	**
Total knowledge exchange activity income (£000s)					
Total income	26.0	21.6	14.7	11.9	**

Note: Mann-Whitney test was used to test whether the two samples were independent for each variable. † $p < 0.10$, * $p < 0.05$, ** $p < 0.01$.

Source: Author's calculation from HEFCE (2009).

non-commercial partners indicating that there may be an attraction for larger companies to partner with more established seats of learning.

Entrepreneurial activity income of all UK universities by type of region, per academic FTE, 2007–08

A further question we sought to answer was how the competitiveness of a region in which a university is located impacts on its entrepreneurial activity income. To determine this we compared the entrepreneurial performance of 66 universities in competitive locations with 93 universities in less competitive regions (Table 8.2). We found no significant difference between the two groups in total entrepreneurial activity income, suggesting that, on average, academics in each type of region generate similar income from engaging in entrepreneurial activities. When breaking down the income into the six sub-groups of collaborative research, contract research, consultancy, facilities- and equipment-related services, courses and IP, we found no significant difference in all but one type of activities: facilities- and equipment-related services (F&E). Universities in competitive regions reported higher income from F&E-related services than those in less competitive areas (statistically significant at the $p < 0.05$ level). Nevertheless, income from F&E-related services accounts for only a modest share of total income for universities in both types of regions, meaning it is a relatively minor factor that does not determine the overall pattern. For universities in competitive regions, most income is generated from courses for business and the community, which account for 44 per cent of the total income. Collaborative research contributes 27 per cent of the total income for universities in uncompetitive regions. These two figures should be treated with caution, however, as there is suggestion that the results might be biased towards a few outperformers as the median value is much lower than the mean value.

Universities in competitive regions secure more income from OST research councils than their counterparts in uncompetitive areas (though not statistically significant at the $p < 0.10$ level). Non-commercial organizations emerge as the major partners of universities in both competitive and uncompetitive regions. For those universities located in competitive areas, non-commercial organizations account for the main income source of contract research and consultancy, while they are the main contributors in contract research, consultancy, facilities- and equipment-related services and business courses for universities in less competitive regions.

Having found that the competitiveness of the region had no significant impact on the entrepreneurial activities of universities as a whole, we then sought to determine if there was any impact of regional competitiveness on the types of university we identified, starting with established universities.

Table 8.2   Entrepreneurial activity income of all UK universities by region group, per academic FTE, 2007–08

	Region Group			
	Universities in competitive regions $N = 66$		Universities in uncompetitive regions $N = 93$	
	Mean	Median	Mean	Median
Collaborative research income (£000s)				
OST research councils	1.7	0.1	1.5	0.5
Other UK government departments	1.6	0.4	1.5	0.8	*
EU government	1.0	0.0	1.0	0.4
Other	0.6	0.0	0.3	0.1
Total collaborative income	5.0	2.1	4.3	2.3
Contract research income (£000s)				
SMEs	0.2	0.0	0.3	0.1
Non-SME commercial	1.9	0.2	1.3	0.4
Non-commercial	2.9	1.3	2.4	1.3
Total contract income	5.0	2.3	3.9	2.4
Consultancy income (£000s)				
SMEs	0.4	0.1	0.5	0.2	†
Non-SME commercial	1.1	0.2	0.6	0.3
Non-commercial	1.7	0.7	1.3	0.8
Total consultancy income	3.2	1.2	2.4	1.8
Facilities- and equipment-related services income (£000s)				
SMEs	0.5	0.1	0.2	0.0	**
Non-SME commercial	0.3	0.0	0.2	0.0
Non-commercial	0.3	0.1	0.3	0.0	*
Total F&E income	1.1	0.4	0.8	0.2	*
Income from courses for business and community (£000s)				
SMEs	0.6	0.0	0.2	0.1
Non-SME commercial	6.3	0.1	0.5	0.1
Non-commercial	2.3	0.7	2.0	1.2
Individuals	2.5	0.6	1.3	0.6
Total income from courses	11.6	3.2	4.1	3.1
IP income (£000s)				
SMEs	0.1	0.0	0.1	0.0
Non-SME commercial	0.2	0.0	0.1	0.0
Non-commercial	0.2	0.0	0.0	0.0
Sales of share in spin-offs	0.1	0.0	0.0	0.0
Total IP income	0.5	0.1	0.3	0.0
Total knowledge exchange activity income (£000s)				
Total income	26.5	15.9	15.9	15.2

Note: Mann-Whitney test was used to test whether the two samples were independent for each variable. † $p < 0.10$, * $p < 0.05$, ** $p < 0.01$.

Source: Author's calculation from HEFCE (2009).

Entrepreneurial activity income of established universities by type of region, per academic FTE, 2007–08

Analysing the entrepreneurial performance of established universities per different region type yielded a set of results that suggest that regional competitiveness does not significantly impact on established universities' entrepreneurial performance (Table 8.3). Again, this is perhaps unsurprising as established universities have, by their nature and by virtue of their age and longevity, a developed (and probably mature) set of business and community networks and relationships both within and outside their respective regional locales, including worldwide partnerships, to facilitate knowledge exchange. Consequently, these types of relationships probably inure them against the negative impacts their regional situations could otherwise have. Significant differences were, however, found in a few indicators, including collaborative research income from other UK government departments, consultancy income from SMEs and facilities- and equipment-related services income from non-SME commercial.

Having ascertained that established universities were not affected by the regional competitiveness of their locales, we then analysed the impact of the regional dimension on the entrepreneurial activities of new universities.

Entrepreneurial activity income of new universities by type of region, per academic FTE, 2007–08

In this analysis we found that new universities are affected by regional competitiveness (at $p < 0.10$ level). Most significant differences between the two samples were found in the level of facilities- and equipment-related services income (Table 8.4). More specifically, we found that new universities in competitive regions perform better than their counterparts in uncompetitive regions. Given that we asserted earlier that established universities often have connections that go beyond their regional locales, this finding could imply that the regional profile has a stronger influence on new universities that, in the absence of an established reputation and mature relationships, may be more dependent on regional collaborations. Certainly, in terms of where the priorities lie for new universities, as the HE-BCI survey also reveals, a higher percentage of them (46.91 per cent) identify meeting regional skills needs as a priority than their more established counterparts (22.78 per cent), a figure likely influenced by the strong vocational origins of many new universities in the UK.

For established universities, major industrial and business partners are often large companies. Compared with SMEs, large companies, especially multinational enterprises, are less sensitive to proximity and generally search worldwide for the best academics and knowledge (Huggins et al., 2010b). Earlier empirical studies have confirmed the positive relationship

Table 8.3   *Entrepreneurial activity income of established universities by region group, per academic FTE, 2007–08*

	Region Group				
	Established universities in competitive regions $N = 34$		Established universities in uncompetitive regions $N = 44$		
	Mean	Median	Mean	Median	
Collaborative research income (£000s)					
OST research councils	2.5	0.8	2.6	1.5	
Other UK government departments	1.1	0.5	2.1	1.5	*
EU government	1.5	1.0	1.6	1.2	
Other	0.8	0.1	0.5	0.1	
Total collaborative income	6.2	3.7	6.8	5.4	
Contract research income (£000s)					
SMEs	0.3	0.1	0.4	0.2	
Non-SME commercial	2.5	1.0	2.5	2.5	
Non-commercial	4.2	1.7	3.8	3.3	
Total contract income	7.0	5.0	6.8	6.4	
Consultancy income (£000s)					
SMEs	0.2	0.1	0.5	0.2	**
Non-SME commercial	1.0	0.2	0.7	0.4	
Non-commercial	1.6	0.4	1.4	0.8	
Total consultancy income	2.8	1.0	2.6	1.8	†
Facilities- and equipment-related services income (£000s)					
SMEs	0.6	0.1	0.2	0.0	
Non-SME commercial	0.3	0.0	0.3	0.1	†
Non-commercial	0.3	0.1	0.4	0.0	
Total F&E income	1.2	0.4	0.9	0.5	
Income from courses for business and community (£000s)					
SMEs	0.5	0.0	0.2	0.1	
Non-SME commercial	10.5	0.2	0.6	0.1	
Non-commercial	2.0	0.6	1.5	1.0	
Individuals	1.8	0.6	1.1	0.6	
Total income from courses	14.8	2.5	3.4	2.7	
IP income (£000s)					
SMEs	0.1	0.0	0.1	0.0	
Non-SME commercial	0.3	0.0	0.3	0.0	
Non-commercial	0.1	0.0	0.0	0.0	
Sales of share in spin-offs	0.2	0.0	0.1	0.0	
Total IP income	0.6	0.0	0.4	0.2	
Total knowledge exchange activity income (£000s)					
Total income	32.6	20.2	20.9	21.9	

Note: Mann-Whitney test was used to test whether the two samples were independent for each variable. † $p < 0.10$, * $p < 0.05$, ** $p < 0.01$.

Source: Author's calculation from HEFCE (2009).

Table 8.4   *Entrepreneurial activity income of new universities by region group, per academic FTE, 2007–08*

	Region Group				
	New universities in competitive regions $N = 32$		New universities in uncompetitive regions $N = 49$		
	Mean	Median	Mean	Median	
Collaborative research income (£000s)					
OST research councils	0.9	0.0	0.5	0.1	
Other UK government departments	1.9	0.3	1.0	0.5	
EU government	0.4	0.0	0.4	0.1	†
Other	0.4	0.0	0.2	0.0	
Total collaborative income	3.6	1.0	2.1	1.3	
Contract research income (£000s)					
SMEs	0.2	0.0	0.1	0.0	
Non-SME commercial	1.2	0.1	0.2	0.0	
Non-commercial	1.4	0.9	1.1	0.8	
Total contract income	2.9	1.3	1.4	1.0	
Consultancy income (£000s)					
SMEs	0.5	0.1	0.6	0.1	
Non-SME commercial	1.3	0.2	0.4	0.2	
Non-commercial	2.0	1.1	1.3	1.0	
Total consultancy income	3.7	1.6	2.3	1.7	
Facilities- and equipment-related services income (£000s)					
SMEs	0.4	0.1	0.3	0.0	**
Non-SME commercial	0.3	0.0	0.1	0.0	**
Non-commercial	0.4	0.2	0.3	0.0	†
Total F&E income	1.1	0.4	0.6	0.0	**
Income from courses for business and community (£000s)					
SMEs	0.7	0.1	0.2	0.1	
Non-SME commercial	1.8	0.0	0.5	0.1	
Non-commercial	2.7	0.8	2.5	1.6	
Individuals	3.2	0.6	1.5	0.6	
Total income from courses	8.3	5.6	4.7	4.1	
IP income (£000s)					
SMEs	0.0	0.0	0.1	0.0	
Non-SME commercial	0.1	0.0	0.0	0.0	
Non-commercial	0.3	0.0	0.1	0.0	
Sales of share in spin-offs	0.0	0.0	0.0	0.0	
Total IP income	0.5	0.0	0.2	0.0	
Total knowledge exchange activity income (£000s)					
Total income	20.1	14.0	11.3	11.0	†

Note: Mann-Whitney test was used to test whether the two samples were independent for each variable. † $p < 0.10$, * $p < 0.05$, ** $p < 0.01$.

Source: Author's calculation from HEFCE (2009).

between the number of links to large R&D-intensive firms and the levels of research income of UK universities (Huggins et al., 2010a). In contrast, new universities generate most knowledge transfer activity income from non-commercial organizations, mainly government departments.

LIMITATIONS OF THE STUDY AND FUTURE WORK

This study found that new universities seeking to develop their entrepreneurial activities are at a disadvantage compared with established universities when they find themselves located in uncompetitive regions based on analysis of the 2009 HE-BCI survey data. By virtue of the fact that the analysis is cross-sectional, that is, represents only a snapshot in time, it should not be considered a comprehensive analysis, but instead a first attempt at marrying the established measures of regional competitiveness with survey data on university entrepreneurial activities. The UK Competitiveness Index dates back to 2002 and the HE-BCI survey to 2001, allowing for future work on longitudinal analysis of any changes in the relationship between university entrepreneurial activities and regional competitiveness and a greater understanding of the development of the two and any changes over the period. Other data could also be considered, such as the HE-BCI survey data on the universities' responses to questions concerning their strategies for knowledge transfer and the amount of resources in personnel terms they dedicate to realizing these ambitions, which are only briefly touched upon in this chapter due to constraints of time and space. Further work needs to be completed in order to more fully understand the relationship between regional competitiveness and universities' entrepreneurial activities, but the initial findings are heartening and suggest that there may be merit in doing so, not least in terms of informing policy to that end.

Another direction that future work could follow is the transferability of this research by comparing the entrepreneurial performance of universities in, for instance, the European Union countries. Efforts in this way shall extend the implications this research might have in a broader sense. One of the main difficulties that currently impede this process is the availability of comparable data of entrepreneurial activities across nations. Whilst many surveys have been developed in European countries to collect data on the commercialization of public science, as shown in a 2009 report published by the European Commission, metrics used in those surveys differ significantly in measured type of activity, targeting sample and response rate (European Commission, 2009). Should a pan-European survey be carried out along the lines of the Community Innovation Survey where countries are comparable due to the consistency of metrics and data used then comparability and consistency of data across transnational boundaries will be required.

CONCLUSION

Whilst acknowledging efforts made by previous studies either to explore spatial difference in certain types of knowledge transfer activity or to compare institutional difference across a range of university–business engagements, there is still a gap in the literature that marries these aspects together, that is, to examine a full spectrum of knowledge transfer activities, and in the meantime, to compare performance across regions and institutions. This chapter has attempted to fill this gap somewhat to better inform our understanding of the interrelationships between research intensity, regional profile and entrepreneurial performance of universities with a view towards establishing a methodology for doing so in order to open up future research avenues.

Drawing upon the HE-BCI survey data for the academic year 2007–08 and the UK Regional Competitiveness Index 2010, this study examined the performance of UK universities in Third Mission – entrepreneurial – activities with a special focus on the impacts of research intensity and regional competitiveness on the performance of universities. We compared the performance of two university groups (established and new universities) and in two region groups (competitive and uncompetitive regions). Overall, more established universities outperform their younger counterparts in generating income from knowledge transfer activities, demonstrating more active involvement in their entrepreneurial missions. More relevantly, we also found that new universities were negatively impacted when located within uncompetitive regions in their entrepreneurial activities suggesting that a possible policy intervention may be needed in order to redress this issue.

The complexity of the UK Higher Education sector has been largely absent in innovation policy agendas until recently. Results from our analysis show that both established and new universities are of importance to regional economic development, albeit in different areas and in different ways. Given that most knowledge transfer policies and programmes ignore the specific individual characteristics of universities, it may be hard to expect all of them to make the same progress. Nonetheless, that does not mean that policy should remain as a broad brush attempting to catch all. For example, new universities often come from a vocational/training-focused background and are to an extent playing catch up with their more established peers in research terms and the higher value aspects of Third Mission activities. Consequently, recognition of the different roles they play within their regional situation and the Third Mission activities they are most concentrated in would help them improve their engagement levels. Specially tailored policies are thus required to maximize the potential of universities to contribute to economic development in their various locations that recognize the differences within the broad range of institutions that comprise the sector and thus enable them, irrespective of their age, to contribute more effectively in Third Mission activities.

REFERENCES

Abreu, M., V. Grinevich, A. Hughes and M. Kitson (2009), *Knowledge Exchange Between Academics and the Business, Public and Third Sector*, Cambridge, UK: UK-Innovation Research Centre.

Abreu, M., A. Hughes, V. Grinevich, M. Kitson and P. Ternouth (2008), *Universities, Business and Knowledge Exchange*, Cambridge, UK: Centre for Business Research, and London: Council for Industry and Higher Education.

Arbo, P. and P. Benneworth (2004), *Understanding the Regional Contribution of Higher Education Institutions: A Literature Review*, Paris: OECD.

Audretsch, D.B., M. Hulsbeck and E.E. Lehmann (2011), 'Regional competitiveness, university spillovers, and entrepreneurial activity', *Small Business Economics*, **39**(3), 587–601.

Audretsch, D.B., E.E. Lehmann and S. Warning (2005), 'University spillovers and new firm location', *Research Policy*, **34**(7), 1113–22.

Benneworth, P. (2006), 'The role of university spin-off firms in strengthening regional innovation systems in weaker places', paper presented at the Sixth European Urban and Regional Studies Conference, 21–24 September, 2006, Roskilde, Denmark.

Benneworth, P. (2007), *Leading Innovation: Building Effective Regional Coalitions for Innovation*, London: NESTA.

Boucher, G., C. Conway and E. van der Meer (2003), 'Tiers of engagement by universities in their region's development', *Regional Studies*, **37**(9), 887–97.

Cabral, R. and S. Dahab (1998), 'Science parks in developing countries: The case of BIORIO in Brazil', *International Journal of Technology Management*, **16**(8), 726–39.

Charles, D. (2003), 'Universities and territorial development: Reshaping the regional role of UK universities', *The Journal of the Local Economy Policy Unit*, **18**(1), 7–20.

Chatterton, P. and J. Goddard (2000), 'The response of Higher Education Institutions to regional needs', *European Journal of Education*, **35**(4), 475–96.

Clarysse, B., M. Wright, A. Lockett, E. van de Velde and A. Vahora (2005), 'Spinning out new ventures: A typology of incubation strategies from European research institutions', *Journal of Business Venturing*, **20**(2), 183–216.

Cohen, W.M. and D.A. Levinthal (1990), 'Absorptive capacity: A new perspective on learning and innovation', *Administrative Science Quarterly*, **35**(1), 128–52.

Cooke, P. (1998), 'Introduction: Origins of the concept', in H. Braczyk, P. Cooke and M. Heidenreich (eds), *Regional Innovation Systems*, 1st edition, London: UCL Press, pp. 2–25.

Cooke, P. (2004), 'Evolution of regional innovation systems – emergence, theory, challenge for action', in P. Cooke, M. Heidenreich and H. Braczyk (eds), *Regional Innovation Systems*, 2nd edition, London: Routledge.

Cooke, P., M.G. Uranga and G. Etxebarria (1998), 'Regional systems of innovation: An evolutionary perspective', *Environment and Planning A*, **30**(9), 1563–84.

DELNI (2010), *Evaluation of the Northern Ireland Higher Education Innovation Fund 2 (NI HEIF 2)*, Belfast: DELNI.

Di Gregorio, D. and S. Shane (2003), 'Why do some universities generate more start-ups than others?' *Research Policy*, **32**(2), 209–27.

DTI (1998), *Our Competitive Future: Building the Knowledge Driven Economy*, London: Stationery Office.

DTI (2000), *Excellence and Opportunity – A Science and Innovation Policy for the 21st Century*, London: Stationery Office.

Etzkowitz, H. (1998), 'The norms of entrepreneurial science: Cognitive effects of the new university–industry linkages', *Research Policy*, **27**(8), 823–33.

Etzkowitz, H. and L. Leydesdorff (eds) (1997), *Universities and the Global Knowledge Economy: A Triple Helix of University–Industry–Government Relations*, London: Cassell Academic.

Etzkowitz, H. and L. Leydesdorff (2000), 'The dynamics of innovation: From national systems and "Mode 2" to a Triple Helix of university–industry–government relations', *Research Policy*, **29**(2), 109–23.

European Commission (2009), *Metrics for Knowledge Transfer from Public Research Organisations in Europe*, Brussels: European Commission.

Geuna, A. and L. Nesta (2006), 'University patenting and its effects on academic research: The emerging European evidence', *Research Policy*, **35**(6), 790–807.

Gibb, A., G. Haskins and I. Robertson (2009), *Leading the Entrepreneurial University: Meeting the Entrepreneurial Development Needs of Higher Education Institutions*, Birmingham: National Council for Graduate Entrepreneurship.

Goddard, J. (2009), *Reinventing the Civic University*, London: NESTA.

HEFCE (2000), *Higher Education Reach-out to Business and the Community Fund, Second Round Funding Allocations*, Bristol: HEFCE.

HEFCE (2009), *Higher Education–Business Community Interaction Survey 2007–08*, Bristol: HEFCE.

HEFCE (2011), *Higher Education Innovation Funding 2011–12 to 2014–15*, Bristol: HEFCE.

HEFCW (2009), *Evaluation of HEFCW's Third Mission Fund 2004/05 to 2006/07*, Cardiff: HEFCW.

HEFCW (2011), *Innovation and Engagement Funding Arrangements 2011/12 to 2013/14*, Cardiff: HEFCW.

Herriot, W. and T. Minshall (2008), *Cambridge Technopole Report Spring 2008: An Overview of UK's Leading High-technology Business Cluster*, Cambridge, UK: St John's Innovation Centre.

Hewitt-Dundas, N. (2012), 'Research intensity and knowledge transfer activity in UK universities', *Research Policy*, **41**(2), 262–75.

HM Treasury (2004), *Science and Innovation Investment Framework 2004–2014*, London: Stationery Office.

HM Treasury (2007), *The Race to the Top: A Review of Government's Science and Innovation Policies*, London: Stationery Office.

Huggins, R. and A. Johnston (2009), 'The economic and innovation contribution of universities: A regional perspective', *Environment and Planning C: Government and Policy*, **27**(6), 1088–106.

Huggins, R. and P. Thompson (2010), *UK Competitiveness Index 2010*, Cardiff: University of Wales Institute.

Huggins, R., A. Johnston and C. Stride (2012), Knowledge networks and universities: Locational and organisational aspects of knowledge transfer interactions', *Entrepreneurship and Regional Development*, **24**(7/8), 475–502.

Huggins, R., H. Izushi and D. Prokop (2010a), University–industry networks: Interactions with large R&D performers', paper presented at the DRUID Summer Conference 2010, 16–18 June, 2010, Imperial College London Business School, UK.

Huggins, R., H. Izushi, N. Clifton, S. Jenkins, D. Prokop and C. Whitfield (2010b), *Sourcing Knowledge for Innovation: The International Dimension*, London: NESTA.

Jauhiainen, J.S. and K. Suorsa (2008), 'Triple Helix in the periphery: The case of Multipolis in northern Finland', *Cambridge Journal of Regions, Economy and Society*, **1**(2), 285–301.

Kenney, M. (2000), *Understanding Silicon Valley: The Anatomy of an Entrepreneurial Region*, Stanford. CA: Stanford University Press.

Kihlgren, A. (2003), 'Promotion of innovation activity in Russia through the creation of science parks: The case of St. Petersburg (1992–1998)', *Technovation*, **23**(1), 65–76.

Kitson, M., J. Howells, R. Braham and S. Westlake (2009), *The Connected University: Driving Recovery and Growth in the UK Economy*, London: NESTA.

Lee, C.M., F.M. William and S.R. Henry (eds) (2000), *The Silicon Valley Edge: A Habitat for Innovation and Entrepreneurship*, Stanford, CA: Stanford University Press.

Link, A.N. and J.T. Scott (2003), 'The growth of Research Triangle Park', *Small Business Economics*, **20**(2), 167–75.

Marshall, A. (1919), *Industry and Trade*, London: Macmillan and Co.

Mowery, D. and S. Shane (2002), 'Introduction to the special issue on university entrepreneurship and technology transfer', *Management Science*, **48**(1), v–ix.

Mowery, D. and A. Ziedonis (2002), 'Academic patent quality and quantity before and after the Bayh-Dole Act in the United States', *Research Policy*, **21**(3), 399–418.

PACEC (2012), *Strengthening the Contribution of English Higher Education Institutions to the Innovation System: Knowledge Exchange and HEIF Funding*, Cambridge, UK: PACEC.

Page, N. (2007), 'The making of a licensing legend: Stanford University's office of technology licensing', in A. Krattiger, R.T. Mahoney and L. Nelson (eds), *Intellectual Property Management in Health and Agriculture Innovation: A Handbook of Best Practice: 1719–1728*, Oxford: MIHR.

Phan, P.H., D.S. Siegel and M. Wright (2005), 'Science parks and incubators: Observations, synthesis and future research', *Journal of Business Venturing*, **20**(2), 165–82.

Saad, M. and G. Zawdie (2011), 'Introduction to special issue: The emerging role of universities in socioeconomic development through knowledge networks', *Science and Public Policy*, **38**(1), 3–6.

Pirnay, F., B. Surlemont and F. Nlemvo (2003), 'Towards a typology of university spin-offs', *Small Business Economics*, **21**(4), 355–69.

Saxenian, A. (1994), *Regional Advantage: Culture and Competition in Silicon Valley and Route 128*, Cambridge, MA: Harvard University Press.

SQW (1985), *The Cambridge Phenomenon: The Growth of High Technology Industry in a University Town*, Cambridge, UK: Cambridge University Press.

SQW (2009), *Evaluation of the Knowledge Transfer Grant (KTG)*, London: SQW Limited.

Thursby, J. and M. Thursby (2003), 'University licensing under Bayh-Dole: What are the issues and evidence?', accessed 6 August 2012 at http://opensource.mit.edu/papers/Thursby.pdf.

Vaidyanathan, G. (2008), 'Technology parks in a developing country: The case of India', *The Journal of Technology Transfer*, **33**(3), 285–99.

PART II

PEDAGOGIC PRACTICES IN ENTREPRENEURIAL EDUCATION

9. 'The apple doesn't fall far from the tree': the entrepreneurial university as nurturer of entrepreneurial values
Magdalena Markowska

INTRODUCTION

Entrepreneurship has been in vogue for the past 30 years. During that time, entrepreneurship education gained a permanent home at many business schools and universities. Despite a growing understanding that entrepreneurship is a practice and a mindset, the majority of entrepreneurship curricula still focus on teaching *about* and not *in* entrepreneurship. Educating in entrepreneurship requires a different epistemology and different methodology of transferring entrepreneurial values to individuals and their organizations. It is much more about instilling entrepreneurial intentions, competences and capabilities than knowledge in and of itself. Extant research exploring the triggers of entrepreneurial competence development and the acquisition of entrepreneurial values stresses four different mechanisms that facilitate this process (cf. Markowska, 2011). These triggers – action-control beliefs, development of entrepreneurial identity, access and interaction with entrepreneurial role models and ability to set adaptive goals – can be developed and strengthened through a supportive context. The role of an entrepreneurial university is thus to create conditions that foster the development of an entrepreneurial mindset.

More specifically, the importance of practical examples that increase entrepreneurial propensity has been emphasized in the literature (Bandura, 1986; Davidsson and Honig, 2003). In order to be able to effectively instil entrepreneurial values in others, universities need to become entrepreneurial themselves (Etzkowitz, 2003; Mueller, 2006). They need to adopt and live by entrepreneurial values. Crucial in this process is the translation of the concept of entrepreneurship to everyday practice, for example its meaning to an university's International Office or programme managers. Furthermore, while entrepreneurship is generally considered desirable by national governments, research shows that individuals do not always ascribe positive value to entrepreneurship (Down and Warren, 2008). Thus, entrepreneurial universities through their actions should strive to show what it means to be entrepreneurial and that entrepreneurial values are positive and desirable.

In this chapter, I briefly present each of the four triggers and illustrate how each of them can be embodied within an entrepreneurial university and how the university can help facilitate their development amongst all its stakeholders (valuable learning activities are presented after each subsection). Finally, I offer policy recommendations.

TRIGGERS TO ENTREPRENEURIAL COMPETENCE

The importance of entrepreneurial competence development in entrepreneurial action is well established (e.g., Bird, 1995; Markowska, 2011). Research suggests that competence reflects the ability to effectively interact with the environment (Johannisson, 1991; Skinner, 1995). This presupposes the ability to produce desired and to avoid undesired events. Intentional use of abilities reflects individuals' agency. Agency is the embodiment of endowments, belief systems, self-regulatory capabilities and functions through which personal influence is exercised (Bandura, 1986); it also allows formulation and realization of intended actions (Emirbayer and Mische, 1998). Thus, what an entrepreneur pursues reflects his or her values, goals, strategies and visions (Mintzberg, 1988). Adopting and living entrepreneurial values requires an ability to sense and adapt to uncertainty, allowing entrepreneurs to become dynamic, flexible and self-regulated (Haynie and Shepherd, 2009).

Competence encompasses knowledge, skills and abilities (Argyris, 1993). In an entrepreneurship context, the knowledge, skills and abilities relate to building the capacity to successfully create new means-ends frameworks (Sarasvathy, 2001). More specifically, gaining entrepreneurial competence requires entrepreneurs to gain the ability to identify and pursue new and unique opportunities and the ability to acquire and use the resources that will allow them to do so successfully (Johannisson, 1993; Chandler and Hanks, 1994; Erikson, 2002).

Already Johannisson (1991, 1993) postulated that knowledge (know what) and skills (know how) are not sufficient to develop an entrepreneurial competence; the process requires the development of appropriate attitudes and motives (know why), social skills (know who) and insights (know when). A well-developed know-when competence gains value in dynamic environments. Embeddedness in an entrepreneurial context, for example, of an entrepreneurial university is likely to foster competence acquisition by indirectly instilling entrepreneurial intentions and motivations.

This means that competence can be acquired and developed (Bird, 1995; DeTienne and Chandler, 2004; Baron and Ensley, 2006). Baron and Ensley (2006) found that experienced entrepreneurs were able to recognize more seemingly unrelated patterns than novices and that these were more closely related to the actual business operations. This suggests that, with experience, entrepreneurs develop skills in pattern recognition and learn how to be clearer and more specific. The ability to learn is independent of the initial predisposition to innovate (DeTienne and Chandler, 2004) and feedback enhances this process (Bird, 1995). The socialization process plays an important role both in developing perceptions of ability and in obtaining actual knowledge (Aldrich and Martinez, 2007). This is why entrepreneurial universities that are able to embody entrepreneurial values are more effective in transmitting these values to their stakeholders, in general, and to students, in particular.

Aldrich and Martinez (2007) identified three common sources of entrepreneurial knowledge: previous work experience, advice from experts, and imitation and copying. While work experience gives direct feedback on the level of acquired competence, advice from experts provides clues on how to improve it. Additionally, observation of how others behave shapes individuals' attitudes and beliefs and thus indirectly influences their perceptions of desirability and the feasibility of their intended actions. In particular, prior encounters with role models predispose individuals to consider entrepreneurial action and affect their willingness to develop entrepreneurial skills (Duncan, 1965). Social sources of knowledge and skills become increasingly important when acquiring tacit knowledge as its acquisition is often difficult (Sternberg, 1994), yet it is also crucial to the development of competence (Horvath, 1999). In other words, own experience and social example facilitate acquisition of entrepreneurial competence.

The development of entrepreneurial competence is crucial for entrepreneurial action, but the acquisition of knowledge alone is insufficient and has to be followed by the ability to use it and the belief that one has access to it. Positive beliefs provide a feeling of being in control. This perceived control reflects the generalized expectancy of internal control of reinforcements (Lefcourt, 1982) enabling agency and stimulating action (Bandura, 1982). Individuals need to perceive their experiences as the result of their own actions, otherwise the ways in which one sees the world and consequently the way one functions cannot be changed. Perceived control thus motivates individuals to engage in intentional action (Bandura, 1986). Bandura argues that agency, with its power to originate an action for given purposes, is the fundamental element of personal control.

The model developed by Markowska (2011) suggested that the

constellation of four factors – increasing action-control beliefs and entrepreneurial identity as well as access to proximal role models and appropriate goal orientation – is crucial in fostering the development of entrepreneurial competence (see Table 9.1), because indirectly they strengthen perceived control. Such growing entrepreneurial competence can result in increased levels of creativity and economic growth. Translating these findings into the context of Higher Education Institutions (hereafter: HEIs) requires that actions aimed at building up entrepreneurial identity and increasing levels of agency amongst staff and faculty members are undertaken; that the core values of entrepreneurship – the emergence of *new* economic (and social) value (Davidsson, 2004) are disseminated in a way that each of the individuals can translate what this new activity and value mean in their respective cases. Such action has potential to result in transforming the staff and faculty as well as the university to be more entrepreneurial. Moreover, in becoming an entrepreneurial university,[1] the university also becomes a role model for the students who can easily relate to what it means to be entrepreneurial. By being entrepreneurial, new solutions, new partnerships (with various stakeholders) and new reconfigurations of resources can help generate new means-end frameworks (Sarasvathy, 2008) that can be utilized to promote and support entrepreneurship and venturing in new ways. Two examples from Jönköping University (Sweden) and ESADE (Spain) will be used to illustrate this.

The perception of entrepreneurial competence and the willingness to grow this competence are shaped by beliefs, goal orientation and contextual embeddedness (Markowska, 2011). Social cognitive theory (Bandura, 1986) postulates that an individual's behaviour is shaped by a triadic reciprocal interaction between his or her cognitive characteristics – including beliefs and intentions, the cues from the environment, and his or her behaviour. To guide their behaviour, entrepreneurs tend to engage in developing belief systems that they use as a working model of the world (Dimov, 2007). These belief systems signal the attractiveness through various actions and influence the formation of intentions (Bird, 1988; Ajzen, 1991). The perceived attractiveness depends on values and norms present in an individual's context. It has been shown that embeddedness in local structures and interactions with relevant others affect the individuals' intentions and behaviour by promoting and encouraging behaviours that are consistent with prevalent values and norms (e.g., Davidsson and Wiklund, 1997; Davidsson and Honig, 2003). Therefore, understanding how individuals develop their beliefs is important, as such beliefs play a fundamental role in what individuals perceive as relevant, how they react to different stimuli and whether the new knowledge will or not be available to them (Feltovich et al., 2006; Krueger, 2007). Beliefs are partially

Table 9.1 Triggers nurturing entrepreneurial competence development (examples from JIBS, Sweden)

Triggers	Role	Example
Action-control beliefs	Facilitating the belief of the ability to create new means-ends frameworks and having access to resources that would enable this; increasing perceived propensity to achieve entrepreneurial goals	A programme manager notices growing demand for family business and realizes the potential to offer a course in it (*means-ends beliefs*). Knowing that there is faculty researching this topic, she decides to approach the person to discuss the idea (*agent-means beliefs*). Having developed other programmes in the past, the programme manager feels that she can successfully realize the project (*agent-ends beliefs*)
Entrepreneurial identity	By changing the perception of who I am and providing content to what it means to be entrepreneurial, there is an increased propensity to live by entrepreneurial values	Traditionally the International Office dealt mainly with incoming and outgoing students, but having adopted entrepreneurial identity and values, the IO engaged with discussions with both faculty members and partner universities to create a new product leveraging the in-house competencies and demand from partner universities
Role models	The role of example, a guideline. Encourages individuals and illustrates what entrepreneurial behaviour may involve	The focus on entrepreneurship and internationalization from early on has shaped the everyday practices at JIBS. The university has actively looked for role models that it could follow both in teaching, research and community engagement. As a result the organization remained flexible and adaptable to the changing conditions; bottom-up actions are possible. And entry surveys show that many students choose this university exactly because they see that it enables them entrepreneurial practice
Goals	Flexibility and adaptability to emerging possibilities; acting on them	Engagement in the local community has been important for JIBS. In order to achieve this goal the university has engaged in developing a number of initiatives to learn different ways of interacting with local community, now that some of them proved to be working, the nature of the goals changed from learning to performance and ways to improve the efficiency and effectiveness of these initiatives are in vogue

formed through personal experience and observation of others but are also partially influenced by the rules and expectations present in different structures in which the individual is embedded (i.e., Davidsson and Wiklund, 1997; Davidsson and Honig, 2003).

Subsequently, deeply held beliefs, goals and contextual embeddedness are important to understand the motives of engaging in entrepreneurial action and competence development activities, and they will be discussed below, in more detail.

Increasing Action-control Beliefs

Beliefs are the deeply held, strong assumptions underpinning individuals' decision-making, which help them organize their perceptions of how the world works, giving meaning to experience (Dweck, 1999; Krueger, 2007). Individuals develop their beliefs into meaning systems that help them to guide their thinking, feeling and acting. Beliefs gain additional importance in the context of entrepreneurship due to the inherent uncertainty of entrepreneurial endeavours. Entrepreneurs cannot be sure about the value and meaning of the different resources they have at hand (i.e., knowledge, contacts), the imagined outcomes for these resources or even their own capability to reach their goals, and as such need to rely on their beliefs and outcome expectancies to motivate their action (Bandura, 1982, 1997).

Extending the view that self-efficacy is the most important belief, Skinner et al. (1988) proposed that intentional goal-directed behaviour was a function of three interrelated action-control beliefs: strategy beliefs, control beliefs and agency beliefs. These beliefs are built upon perceptions of relationships between the entrepreneur and the opportunities that they believe they can potentially pursue. More specifically, the *strategy beliefs* (means-ends relationship) presuppose that particular causes produce outcomes (e.g., the ingredients in the fridge influence what can be cooked from them) and the *control beliefs* (agent-ends relationship) are expectations about one's desire of reaching the ends (e.g., am I able to execute this task?). Finally, the *agency beliefs* (agent-means relationship) are accessed when there is the need to assure availability of the required resources (e.g., do I have access to the means?). This framework seems extremely appropriate to understand entrepreneurial action, as inherent to it is the perception of new means-ends frameworks, capacity and willingness to bring business ideas into fruition. Furthermore, as emphasized by Skinner and her colleagues (Chapman and Skinner, 1985; Skinner, 1995), action-control beliefs are organized around interpretations of prior interactions and they are flexible and likely to change over time. Adopting this framework is therefore helpful in explaining why expert entrepreneurs are more likely than novices to be successful in their pursuit of entrepreneurial action (Krueger, 2007, 2009).

More specifically, strategy beliefs can be seen as reflecting the ability of an individual to see how different inputs can lead to different outputs. For example, how knowledge about databases brought in by a new recruit could be used to build up a new information system about the alumni that could be later used as a source of information on possible host companies (JIBS) and/or guest speakers (ESADE). The wider the means-ends beliefs, the more possible strategies become available to the entrepreneur, subsequently extending his or her portfolio of possible new means-ends frameworks.

It has been shown that often, even if novices possess knowledge, they may neither be aware of it nor be able to see how it can be applied, which supports the importance of developing strategy beliefs and agency (capacity) beliefs (Feltovich et al., 2006). The strategy beliefs are crucial in generating ideas about future means-ends frameworks and the agency beliefs are important in realizing the access to the required means that will enable the achievement of the desired ends. This observation is in line with the arguments developed by Sarasvathy et al. (2003) who argued that in order to be able to speak about opportunities, entrepreneurs not only need to have new ideas, but they also need to believe that they can turn these ideas into their imagined means-end frameworks and be able to sell them in the market. Finally, control beliefs reflect the belief that an individual will be able to attain anticipated results; implicitly emphasizing the degree of agency and the subsequent willingness to act. Increasing the beliefs about action-control is likely to influence the level of effort and persistence that individuals exert in the face of adversity (Dweck, 1986). Therefore, it is important that entrepreneurial HEIs offer possibilities to their stakeholders to try out and engage in action. As argued by Bandura, direct experience is the best way to increase control beliefs. For example, at JIBS the students taking the entry-level course in entrepreneurship are required to start and run their own venture for the duration of the course. This includes designing the value proposition, identifying the market, producing their product and/or service, often acquiring funding, selling as well as making accounts for the operations.

Summing up, instilling entrepreneurial values requires agency from the individual. The beliefs and the willingness to undertake action in the expectation of future returns are what drive entrepreneurial behaviour. Developing broad interests and openness for new knowledge facilitates building of the strategy beliefs. The interdisciplinary nature of some courses clearly offers a possibility for students to not only gain entrepreneurial knowledge, but also to engage in the co-creation of new knowledge, through the interaction with other participants of the programme. On the other hand, the agency beliefs increase the resourcefulness of individuals and their perception of what they can achieve, given the means they have at hand (also through their social networks). Finally, control beliefs can be strengthened through the engagement in practice; by engaging in a number of versatile activities, individuals are able to increase their perception of self-control and control over the environment, and feel capable of entrepreneurial action. To exemplify this approach, a selection of learning activities valuable to educators in teaching entrepreneurial competence is presented below.

Valuable learning activities

- To strengthen means-ends beliefs it is useful to work with different kinds of creativity and brainstorming assignments where the participants are required to generate new applications for certain resources, use analogies to come up with new or improved functionality of a product, and so forth.
- To strengthen agency beliefs all sorts of networking exercises will be helpful. In particular, exercises in creating partnerships to get access to resources, including knowledge, technology, market, and so on.
- To strengthen control beliefs tasks involving mastery (direct) experience will be useful, for example performing the different elements of entrepreneurial task (identifying appropriate market, getting investors onboard, etc.) as well as tasks that expose students to a dynamic environment (for example, simulation of a project management task with built in interaction with the project client, changing requirements or other environmental interruptions).

Developing Entrepreneurial Identity

Role identity beliefs have a pivotal role in understanding entrepreneurs' actions (Krueger, 2007). Entrepreneurs make decisions based on the behavioural expectations that are prevalent in their role identity. Therefore, an understanding of how they perceive themselves and their own role is required, in order to understand their behaviour. Identity is composed by self-views that emerge from identification with particular roles (for example, what it means to be a student, a business owner, a professional and/or a mother). The identification is influenced by the role's relative position in the social structure. The identities are manifested in an individual's goal-directed practices; they result from agency and embeddedness in social structures. Being embedded in different groups and playing different roles results in individuals developing multiple identities (James, 1890; Mead, 1934). Furthermore, the interrelatedness of the different spheres means that the personal identity, role identity and the social identity are intimately and inevitably linked (Watson, 2009).

Role identity can be described by the goals, values, beliefs, norms, interaction styles and time horizons typically associated with the role (Ashforth, 2001). Exhibiting a particular role identity means acting to fulfil the expectations of the role partners, and manipulating the environment to control the resources in which their role has responsibility (Baker and Faulkner, 1991). In this view, an identity is a cognitive belief created by internalization of the role into the self-concept and answering the question 'Who am I?' (Stryker and Serpe, 1982). The roles are the 'positions' that represent relatively stable components of the social structure. They carry the shared behavioural expectations whose meaning is negotiated between the role-taker and the surrounding society. Thus, beliefs about the self emerge through the interaction within the role-making and role-taking process, which involves negotiating, modifying, developing and shaping each role's expectations. In this way, each person's beliefs about their self are uniquely shaped by both their experiences and their interactions with others.

Consequently, individuals' beliefs about who they are depend on their perceptions of their own role in society as well as their degree of identification with different social groups. Moreover, membership or embeddedness in different contexts is likely to result in adopting more easily certain beliefs about self than others. To help develop the entrepreneurial identity, a selection of valuable learning activities is presented below.

Valuable learning activities

- To strengthen entrepreneurial identity exercises where individuals learn about and/or interact with entrepreneurs are helpful. For example, finding out what it means to these individuals to be an entrepreneur, how they see their role, how has the perception changed over time?
- Reflect and discuss in a group what it means to be an entrepreneur in your community? Think about entrepreneurs you know or have heard about, do they fit into this picture (the perceptions and values ascribed to entrepreneurs)? If they are different, what could be a reason for this?

Identifying Inspiring Role Models

A role model is a person providing an example in a broader context that includes both professional and personal aspects of life (Levinson et al., 1991). The value of role models in the development of individuals' values and aspirations as well as in their career advancement has long been recognized (Mead, 1934; Stryker, 1980). More specifically, in an academic setting, research shows that junior faculty members who have mentors or role models publish more articles (Bland and Schmitz, 1986), feel more confident in their capabilities and are more satisfied overall with their career than those without mentors (Reich, 1986). In the context of gourmet restaurants, it has been found that individuals who served their apprenticeship with renowned chefs who they saw as role models subsequently develop higher aspirations for their own careers (Johnson et al., 2005). It can therefore be argued that the identification of, and interaction with, role models positively influences individuals' motivation to develop specific competences and increases their levels of aspiration.

In the entrepreneurship context, Mitchell and Chesteen (1995) have found that access and interaction with expert role models contributes to the acquisition of expert scripts and subsequently the usage of superior strategies. In a series of experiments they were able to show that students who observed expert role models and discussed with them about their strategies were subsequently able to adopt more effective solutions. Thus, expert role models provide not only behavioural cues but also have the potential to influence changes in the knowledge structures of the individuals with whom they interact and share practices.

As individuals we search for people we admire and would like to be similar to; people who are our heroes and models. Apart from the active side of searching for such role models, we are also likely to be influenced by the culture that surrounds us. Therefore, to be able to instil entrepreneurial values in stakeholders, universities should display these values themselves. If individuals see that individual action is possible and encouraged throughout the university, it may be easier for them to realize that living by these values is possible and they may feel more encouraged to engage in such entrepreneurial action by themselves, as well. For example, at ESADE the Entrepreneurship Institute has created EEI Forum, organizes workshops and invites entrepreneurs (particularly alumni entrepreneurs) to tell their stories and inspire the students and share with them the everyday practice. Below learning activities linked to identification of entrepreneurial role models are presented.

Valuable learning activities

- Identify a role model and find out what drives the person, what helped the person to become who he or she is right now? What characteristics, traits or skills of this person do you admire?
- What it is that you would like to learn from that person? How can you go about acquiring the same characteristics by yourself?

- If you were to be a role model, what traits and capabilities would you like that other people admire in you? Why? How could you go about developing these capabilities even further?

Adapting Goals

Goals are an inherent aspect of intentional goal-directed behaviour. The extant literature on goals affirms that they can be used by individuals as a self-management technique to arrive at aspired outcomes (Bandura, 1977; Latham and Locke, 1991). Goals reflect the achievement motivation of entrepreneurs (Skinner, 1995) and are set based on utility judgements (Latham and Locke, 1991). Two general goal orientations have been identified – learning goal orientation and performance orientation (Elliott and Dweck, 1988). These differing goal orientations reflect two basic needs: the need to validate/protect one's intelligence, and the need to challenge oneself and learn something new (Dweck, 1986). While the learning orientation assumes that ability and thus competence are flexible and that failure does not negatively reflect on intelligence, the performance orientation treats intelligence as an entity and is more focused on protecting existing beliefs about level of intelligence than on developing them further. In general, both orientations are present in life and both are valuable.

The learning goal orientation is more effective for achieving task mastery (Noel and Latham, 2006), while performance goals, which require attainment of a specific level of performance on the task itself, are effective in stirring motivation but not necessarily in strategy generation (Earley and Erez, 1991). Thus, learning goals are better when the task at hand is complex, as is usually the case in entrepreneurship or when the outcomes are unknowable (Seijts and Latham, 2001; Noel and Latham, 2006). Setting specific and difficult learning goals draws attention in the development of specific ways to perform well, rather than on a specific level of performance that is to be attained. Seijts and Latham (2001) reported that learning goals helped to generate strategies that had positive effect on performance. Latham et al. (1994) found that group discussion of strategies resulted in a large pool of effective strategies. Hence, it has been shown that learning orientation allows individuals to treat failures as challenges and learn from them, while performance orientation is beneficial in situations where results are expected. Individuals with learning orientation search for challenges and learning opportunities and are not afraid of experimenting and trying new things because their focus is on attaining more competence and more skills (Dweck and Elliott, 1983; Dweck and Leggett, 1988; Wood and Bandura, 1989). On the other hand, individuals who set performance goals are more inclined to refrain from trying new, often challenging tasks, because they want to remain within their perception of intelligence. They see new challenges as threatening their identity and their perception of capability (Dweck and Elliott, 1983; Wood and Bandura, 1989). Thus, to see entrepreneurs grow and develop their entrepreneurial competencies requires that they have a learning approach that sees failures and obstacles as challenges and opportunities to learn. Individuals with a preference for performance goals are likely to avoid engagement in novel activities, because such engagement could mean that they would not be able to verify their ability, putting their self-worth at risk.

In general, most organizations focus on performance goals because they help to achieve higher levels of efficiency; however, in order to be able to identify and exploit emerging ideas and opportunities, there needs to be space for learning goals and opportunities to learn. This often requires a change in the culture of the organization. For example, individuals will not be willing to engage in new trial and error behaviours unless they are convinced that their efforts will not be negatively evaluated by the organization. This does not mean that there should not be a process guiding the endeavour, but that the environment is supportive of this kind of activity. Becoming and remaining entrepreneurial requires the ability to adapt goals to emerging opportunities, that is, to co-create the future based on interaction with different stakeholders, but also more generally the ability to switch between performance and learning goals, depending on the requirements of the task. An entrepreneurial university ought to encourage individual action and setting learning goals that result in new opportunities being identified and exploited. Below is an example of learning activity directed towards developing flexibility in formulating goals.

Valuable learning activities

- For example, formulate a performance goal that you strive for; write down both the positive and the negative aspects of formulating the goal as a performance goal.
- Now repeat the same exercise reformulating the goal into a learning goal; what are the potential advantages and/or disadvantages of formulating goals as learning goals?

POLICY RECOMMENDATIONS

The demand for entrepreneurial universities reflects the general need for an enterprising society. Entrepreneurial values are important for driving the economy forward, innovating and increasing its competitiveness. To be able to fulfil this role it is crucial that universities become entrepreneurial and that every member of an HEI lives these values in their daily work.

This requires that both faculty and staff of the university feel not only efficacy but also responsibility for identifying and exploiting emerging opportunities, and that the organization develops a culture that encourages and rewards such behaviour. Encouraging entrepreneurial action means enabling open communication and sharing of knowledge, a feeling of belonging and passion for work, providing an arena for bottom-up initiatives, identifying and making accessible positive role models both within and outside the organization. Finally, this also requires the management team of HEIs to be open and flexible to the emerging possibilities and willing to engage in learning activities.

CONCLUSIONS

This chapter discusses ways in which universities can develop an entrepreneurial approach and thereby nurture entrepreneurial values in society. I have argued that development of entrepreneurial competence and values can be facilitated by strengthening of action-control beliefs, development of entrepreneurial identity, search and interaction with role models and appropriate goal setting that opens up learning experiences. These four factors reflect individuals' agency and perceived control as drivers for entrepreneurial behaviour. The chapter offers some policy recommendations and examples of how entrepreneurial values can be expressed in everyday practices throughout the entrepreneurial university.

NOTE

1. Entrepreneurial university is defined as a producer of new knowledge that is convertible into economic and social utility (Etzkowitz, 2003).

REFERENCES

Ajzen, I. (1991), 'The theory of planned behavior', *Organizational Behavior and Human Decision Processes*, **50**(2), 179–211.

Aldrich, H.E. and M.A. Martinez (2007), 'Many are called, but few are chosen: An evolutionary perspective for the study of entrepreneurship', in Á. Cuervo, D. Ribeiro and S. Roig (eds), *Entrepreneurship*, Berlin and Heidelberg: Springer, pp. 293–311.

Argyris, C. (1993), *Knowledge for Action: A Guide to Overcoming Barriers to Organizational Change*, San Francisco, CA: Jossey Bass Publishers.

Ashforth, B.E. (2001), *Role Transitions in Organizational Life: An Identity-based Perspective*, Mahwah, NJ: Lawrence Erlbaum Associates.

Baker, W. and R. Faulkner (1991), 'Role as resource in the Hollywood film industry', *American Journal of Sociology*, **97**(2), 279–309.

Bandura, A. (1977), 'Self-efficacy: Toward a unifying theory of behaviour change', *Psychological Review*, **84**(2), 191–215.

Bandura, A. (1982), 'Self-efficacy mechanism in human agency', *American Psychologist*, **37**(2), 122–47.

Bandura, A. (1986), *Social Foundations of Thought and Action*, Englewood Cliffs, NJ: Prentice Hall.

Bandura, A. (1997). *Self-efficacy: The Exercise of Control*, New York: Freeman.

Baron, R. and M. Ensley (2006), 'Opportunity recognition as the detection of meaningful patterns: Evidence from comparisons of novice and experienced entrepreneurs', *Management Science*, **52**(9), 1331–44.

Bird, B. (1988), 'Implementing entrepreneurial ideas: The case for intention', *Academy of Management Review*, **13**(3), 442–53.

Bird, B. (1995), 'Towards a theory of entrepreneurial competency', in J.A. Katz and R.H. Brockhaus (eds), *Advances in Entrepreneurship, Firm Emergence and Growth*, Greenwich, CT: JAI Press, pp. 51–72.

Bland, C. and C. Schmitz (1986), 'Characteristics of the successful researcher and implications for faculty development', *Journal of Medical Education*, **61**(1), 22–31.

Chandler, G. and S. Hanks (1994), 'Founder competence, the environment, and venture performance', *Entrepreneurship Theory and Practice*, **18**(3), 77–89.

Chapman, M. and E.A. Skinner (1985) 'Action in development/development in action', in M. Frese and J. Sabini (eds), *Goal-directed Behavior: The Concept of Action in Psychology*, Hillsdale, NJ: Erlbaum, pp. 199–213.

Davidsson, P. (2004), *Researching Entrepreneurship*, New York: Springer.

Davidsson, P. and B. Honig (2003), 'The role of social and human capital among nascent entrepreneurs', *Journal of Business Venturing*, **18**(3), 301–31.

Davidsson, P. and J. Wiklund (1997), 'Values, beliefs and regional variations in new firm formation rates', *Journal of Economic Psychology*, **18**(2/3), 179–99.

DeTienne, D.R. and G. Chandler (2004), 'Opportunity identification and its role in the entrepreneurial classroom: A pedagogical approach and empirical test', *Academy of Management Learning and Education*, **3**(3), 242–57.

Dimov, D. (2007), 'From opportunity insight to opportunity intention: The importance of person–situation learning match', *Entrepreneurship Theory and Practice*, **31**(4), 561–83.

Down, S. and L. Warren (2008), 'Constructing narratives of enterprise: Clichés and entrepreneurial self-identity', *International Journal of Entrepreneurial Behaviour and Research*, **14**(1), 4–23.

Duncan, O. (1965), 'Social origins of salaried and self-employed professional workers', *Social Forces*, **44**(2), 186–9.

Dweck, C. (1986), 'Motivational processes affecting learning', *American Psychologist*, **41**(10), 1040–48.

Dweck, C. (1999), *Self-theories. Their Role in Motivation, Personality, and Development*, Philadelphia, PA: Taylor and Francis.

Dweck, C. and E. Elliott (1983), 'Achievement motivation', in E. Hetherington (ed.), *Socialization, Personality, and Social Development*, New York: Wiley.

Dweck, C. and E. Leggett (1988), 'A social-cognitive approach to motivation and personality', *Psychological Review*, **95**(2), 256–73.

Earley, P.C. and M. Erez (1991), 'Time-dependency effects of goals and norms: The role of cognitive processing on motivational models', *Journal of Applied Psychology*, **76**(5), 717–24.

Elliott, E. and C. Dweck (1988), 'Goals: An approach to motivation and achievement', *Journal of Personality and Social Psychology*, **54**(1), 5–12.

Emirbayer, M. and A. Mische (1998), 'What is agency?' *American Journal of Sociology*, **103**(4), 962–1023.

Erikson, T. (2002), 'Entrepreneurial capital: The emerging venture's most important asset and competitive advantage', *Journal of Business Venturing*, **17**(3), 275–90.

Etzkowitz, H. (2003), 'Research groups as "quasi-firms": The invention of the entrepreneurial university', *Research Policy*, **32**(1), 109–21.

Feltovich, P., M. Prietula and K.A. Ericsson (2006), 'Studies of expertise from psychological perspectives', in K.A. Ericsson, N. Charness, P. Feltovich and R. Hoffman (eds), *The Cambridge Handbook of Expertise and Expert Performance*, Cambridge, UK: Cambridge University Press, pp. 41–68.

Haynie, J.M. and D. Shepherd (2009), 'A measure of adaptive cognition for entrepreneurship research', *Entrepreneurship Theory and Practice*, **33**(3), 695–714.

Horvath, J. (1999), 'Tacit knowledge in the profession', in R. Sternberg and J. Horvath (eds), *Tacit Knowledge in Professional Practice. Researcher and Practitioner Perspectives*, Mahwah, NJ: Lawrence Erlbaum Associates.

James, W. (1890), *Principles of Psychology*, Vol. 2, New York: Holt.

Johannisson, B. (1991), 'University training for entrepreneurship: Swedish approaches', *Entrepreneurship and Regional Development*, **3**(1), 67–82.

Johannisson, B. (1993), 'Entrepreneurial competence and learning strategies', in R. Larsson, L. Bengtsson, K. Eneroth and A. Malm (eds), *Research in Strategic Change*, Lund: Lund University Press, pp. 77–99.

Johnson, C., B. Surlemont, P.F. Nicod and F. Revaz (2005), 'Behind the stars. A concise typology of Michelin restaurants in Europe', *Cornell Hotel and Restaurant Administration Quarterly*, **46**(2), 170–87.

Krueger, N. (2007), 'What lies beneath? The experiential essence of entrepreneurial thinking', *Entrepreneurship Theory and Practice*, **31**(1), 123–38.

Krueger, N. (2009), 'The microfoundations of entrepreneurial learning and education: The experiential essence of entrepreneurial cognition', in G.P. West, E. Gatewood and K. Shaver (eds), *Handbook of University-wide Entrepreneurship Education*, Cheltenham, UK and Northampton, MA, USA: Edward Elgar Publishing, pp. 35–59.

Latham, G. and E. Locke (1991), 'Self-regulation through goal setting', *Organizational Behavior and Human Decision Processes*, **50**(2), 212–47.

Latham, G., D. Winters and E. Locke (1994), 'Cognitive and motivational effects of participation: A mediator study', *Journal of Organizational Behavior*, **15**(1), 49–63.

Lefcourt, H. (1982), *Locus of Control. Current Trends in Theory and Research*, 2nd edition, Hillsdale, NJ: Lawrence Erlbaum Associates.

Levinson, W., K. Kaufman, C. Brinton and S.W. Tolle (1991), 'Mentors and role models for women in academic medicine', *West Journal of Medicine*, **154**, 423–6.

Markowska, M. (2011), 'Entrepreneurial competence development. Triggers, processes and consequences', JIBS Dissertation Series, No. 071, Jönköping: Jönköping International Business School.

Mead, G.H. (1934), *Mind, Self, and Society*, Chicago: University of Chicago Press.

Mintzberg, H. (1988), 'The simple structure', in J.B. Quinn, H. Mintzberg and R.M. James (eds), *The Strategy Process: Concepts, Contexts and Cases*, Englewood Cliffs, NJ: Prentice Hall, pp. 532–9.

Mitchell, R.K. and S. Chesteen (1995), 'Enhancing entrepreneurial expertise: Experiential pedagogy and the entrepreneurial expert script', *Simulation and Gaming*, **26**(3), 288–306.

Mueller, P. (2006), 'Exploring the knowledge filter: How entrepreneurship and university–industry relationships drive economic growth', *Research Policy*, **35**(10), 1499–508.

Noel, T.W. and G.P. Latham (2006), 'The importance of learning goals versus outcome goals for entrepreneurs', *Entrepreneurship and Innovation*, **7**(4), 213–20.

Reich, M. (1986), 'The mentor connection', *Personnel*, **63**(2), 50–56.

Sarasvathy, S. (2001), 'Causation and effectuation: Toward a theoretical shift from economic inevitability to entrepreneurial contingency', *Academy of Management Review*, **26**(2), 243–63.

Sarasvathy, S. (2008), *Effectuation. Elements of Entrepreneurial Expertise*, Cheltenham, UK and Northampton, MA, USA: Edward Elgar.

Sarasvathy, S., N. Dew, S. Velamuri and S. Venkataraman (2003), 'Three views of entrepreneurial opportunity', in Z.J. Acs and D. Audretsch (eds), *Handbook of Entrepreneurship Research: An Interdisciplinary Survey and Introduction*, New York: Kluwer, pp. 141–60.

Seijts, G. and G. Latham (2001), 'The effect of distal learning, outcome, and proximal goals on a moderately complex task', *Journal of Organizational Behavior*, **22**(3), 291–307.

Skinner, E.A. (1995), *Perceived Control, Motivation, and Coping*, Vol. 8, Thousand Oaks, CA: Sage Publications.

Skinner, E.A., M. Chapman and P.B. Baltes (1988), 'Control, means-ends, and agency beliefs: A new conceptualization and its measurement during childhood', *Journal of Personality and Social Psychology*, **54**(1), 117–33.

Sternberg, R.J. (1994), 'Allowing for styles of thinking', *Educational Leadership*, **52**(3), 36–41.

Stryker, S. (1980), *Symbolic Interactionism: A Social Structural Version*, Menlo Park, CA: Benjamin Cummings.

Stryker, S. and R.T. Serpe (1982), 'Commitment, identity salience, and role behavior: Theory and research example', in W. Ickes and E.S. Knowles (eds), *Personality, Roles and Social Behavior*, New York: Springer Verlag, pp. 199–218.

Watson, T.J. (2009), 'Entrepreneurial action, identity work and the use of multiple discursive resources: The case of a rapidly changing family business', *International Small Business Journal*, **27**(3), 251–71.

Wood, R.E. and A. Bandura (1989), 'Impact of conception of ability on self-regulatory mechanisms and complex decision making', *Journal of Personality and Social Psychology*, **56**(3), 407–15.

10. Integrated support for university entrepreneurship from entrepreneurial intent towards behaviour: the case of the German 'EXIST' policy programme
Christine Volkmann and Marc Grünhagen

PURPOSE AND IMPLICATIONS OF THE CHAPTER

Traditionally, European universities have pursued tasks other than producing entrepreneurial output, however now entrepreneurial activities are increasingly on the agenda (Wissema, 2009; Hofer and Potter, 2010). Due to this long-ranging non-entrepreneurial tradition of the European university, entrepreneurship, education and research policy-makers often try to spark entrepreneurial spirit in Higher Education Institutions (HEIs) through external support instruments and policy programmes on the path towards the entrepreneurial university. In this chapter we discuss some ideas with regard to the potential influences of such measures on entrepreneurial intentions and behaviour of university members towards starting and pursuing academic venture projects.

In our case study we analyse the German EXIST policy programme (www.exist.de) on the basis of secondary data from recent evaluation reports of the programme (see Becker et al., 2011; Kulicke, 2011; Kulicke et al., 2011). EXIST aims to support and promote start-up creation by faculty as well as students and graduates from German universities. The EXIST programme was first established in 1998 for selected German universities to build an initial entrepreneurial infrastructure for high-technology and knowledge-intensive start-ups. The programme presents an interesting case study as it spans more than ten years from initial steps to introduce elements of entrepreneurship up to the current phase EXIST IV, which aims to develop organization-wide cultures in universities to become entrepreneurial institutions. In Table 10.1 we provide an overview of the different phases of the EXIST programme with their specific aims, approximate budget volumes and exemplary policy instruments (for further information on the programme see the case discussion in section 4 below).

As a long-term entrepreneurship policy programme that aims to integrate support measures for university organizations to become more

Table 10.1 Overview of the German EXIST entrepreneurship policy programme

	EXIST I 'Model Regions'	EXIST II 'Transfer'	EXIST III 'Specific Projects'	EXIST IV 'Entrepreneurial Universities'
Time frame	1998–2001	2002–04/05	2006–11	2010–18
Budget volume (in million euros)	14	11	40	46
Aims and main scope of programme phase	Explore initial support infrastructure for university entrepreneurship in five German regions; regional network approach	Knowledge transfer from EXIST I regions to other regions; funding of additional support infrastructure at universities	Furthering of existing support frameworks for university entrepreneurship; implementation of specific support instruments individual to the applicant universities; exploration of novel approaches to policies for university entrepreneurship (beyond EXIST I and II)	Establishment of entrepreneurial cultures at EXIST universities; sustainability of organization-wide support for entrepreneurship at universities
Example measures	Institutionalization of entrepreneurship chairs; collaboration projects with business development	Institutionalization of entrepreneurship support in new EXIST II transfer regions;	Development of incubators for science-based start-ups; establishment of support programmes for	Sponsoring of new entrepreneurship study programmes and degree courses; measures to

	agencies, investors, external consultants and local communities	support of collaboration projects and partnerships with EXIST I regions	entrepreneurial opportunity identification in exploitation in tech-entrepreneurship	implement entrepreneurship at top management and admin level of universities
Direct support to start-up projects	EXIST-Seed/ Gründerstipendium (coaching, mentoring and funding of academic start-up projects; use of university resources and infrastructure)	EXIST-Seed/ Gründerstipendium	EXIST-Seed/ Gründerstipendium and EXIST-Forschungstransfer (focus on elite research-based ventures; more specific coaching and financial support, including grants for capital expenditure)	EXIST-Seed/ Gründerstipendium and EXIST-Forschungstransfer

Source: Based on Kulicke (2011).

entrepreneurial as well as direct support to academic start-ups, the most significant characteristic of EXIST is its breadth of policy instruments embracing academic entrepreneurship. Therefore, EXIST is a study case not so much about the functioning of an individual policy measure but rather interesting in terms of different policies working in concert to promote entrepreneurship at university. However, in their study of a sample of EXIST academic entrepreneurs, Patzelt and Shepherd (2009) stress that still little is known in entrepreneurship research about the effects of multiple policy support measures, in particular throughout the process of venture emergence and establishment after academics show an initial interest in starting up.

To shed further light on this, we use a theory of planned behaviour framework to make suggestions of selected policy influences on academics' intentions to initiate *and* proceed with entrepreneurial behaviour. In particular we explore (1) perceived measures to reduce opportunity costs for academic entrepreneurs and communicated benefits of knowledge commercialization, (2) perceived university-wide encouragement and acceptance by university peers, and (3) perceived infrastructure, financial and other material support through EXIST policies at universities. Particular challenges for policy initiatives to establish entrepreneurial universities appear to be twofold: first, to appreciate the sector and founder-person heterogeneity of venture projects and academic entrepreneurs, and second, to embrace the entire process from stimulating self-employment preferences and the formation of initial start-up intentions towards continued efforts to build and develop academic start-up projects. After outlining a point of departure in the following section we will briefly establish the entrepreneurial intentions frame. In the fourth section we explore the EXIST case and in section 5 some policy implications will be discussed.

POINT OF DEPARTURE: THE ENTREPRENEURIAL UNIVERSITY AND ITS ACADEMIC ENTREPRENEURS

In an earlier volume of this *Handbook* series, Gibb (2007) asked whether new avenues of entrepreneurship will be needed in the evolution towards the entrepreneurial university. Further exploration of this important question requires entrepreneurship research to improve our understanding of factors that influence entrepreneurial behaviour by the members of universities and other Higher Education Institutions. And there may be a plethora of potential influence factors that could make a university entrepreneurial. In their categorization of university-level entrepreneurship

Jusof and Jain (2010) define a wide range of external and internal elements of entrepreneurial universities based on the earlier works of Clark (1998), Sporn (2001), Etzkowitz (2004), Kirby (2006), Rothaermel et al. (2007) and others. 'These key elements should provide a basis for the identification of factors or antecedents which may determine or influence university-level entrepreneurial activities' (Jusof and Jain, 2010, p. 85). There seems to be a central challenge for research into university entrepreneurship with regard to identifying these factors. The university members as those actors who develop intentions and actually engage in entrepreneurial behaviour have frequently been disregarded in the literature in the past (Goethner et al., 2009). Rather, a perspective that focuses on scientists' and/or students' intentions and behaviour towards entrepreneurship will contribute to the development of policy recommendations for the management of universities (and other Higher Education Institutions) and entrepreneurship policy support (cf. Fayolle, 2005).

In this chapter we take a people-orientated perspective towards policy support for entrepreneurship at universities, particularly for faculty and students. To facilitate future research, we will discuss selected university support and other organizational influence factors for potential university entrepreneurs in terms of entrepreneurial intentions, and actual behaviour to start and continue developing a new venture. The idea of our exploration follows the spirit of the GUESSS – Global University Entrepreneurial Spirit Students' Survey – studies (Sieger et al., 2011), which have investigated a range of university context and education impact factors on students' entrepreneurial intentions, as well as the groundwork of Fayolle (2005) and Welter et al. (2008) who have suggested comparing entrepreneurship policy instruments directed at Higher Education Institutions with studies of entrepreneurial intentions in the university context. Empirically, in an illustrative case study of the German EXIST policy initiative, we follow this path, exploring selected support instruments for universities to bring about entrepreneurial behaviour among its members. In the next section we will sketch out the conceptual framework for this.

ENTREPRENEURIAL INTENTIONS AND BEHAVIOUR OF UNIVERSITY MEMBERS

The formation of entrepreneurial intent and behaviour among university members implicitly takes a process view on new venture creation within the university. And the university is itself embedded in a context of regional institutions and collaboration networks (e.g., companies, business

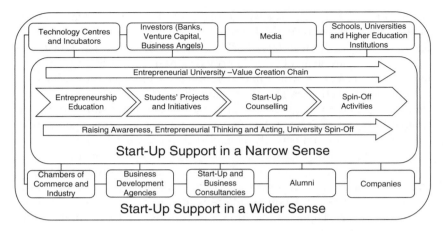

Source: Own illustration.

Figure 10.1   Example of an embedded support chain for student entrepreneurial activities

development agencies, or venture capital firms), which may impact entrepreneurial processes within the university organization (Rothaermel et al., 2007; see Figure 10.1).

Many support functions around and within the university alongside the above example process of student entrepreneurial activities may be conceivable. We will focus on support through external entrepreneurship policy initiatives for entrepreneurship in the narrower sense of the formation of high-technology and knowledge-intensive start-ups by university members.

For the case of university members Sieger et al. (2011) recently explored the influence of individual factors and university support offers on students' occupational goals and intended entrepreneurship as well as nascent entrepreneurial action and start-up establishment. And Goethner et al. (2012) found a significant relationship between entrepreneurial intentions and actual behaviour in scientists in research institutions. This suggests that exploring influences on intent formation will be valuable for our understanding of initial scientific start-up emergence, which itself plays an important role in further venture development (Vohora et al., 2004). This development is embedded in the university organization including possible catalysing as well as inhibiting influences (e.g., Rasmussen and Borch, 2010). Here, models of entrepreneurial intentions enable the analysis of individual as well as organizational and policy influences on university members' entrepreneurial intent and subsequent behaviour (Walter and Dohse, 2009). Intentions models based on Ajzen's

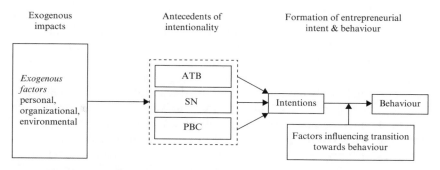

Figure 10.2   Basic entrepreneurial intentions model

theory of planned behaviour (TPB) have been very widely used and tested in entrepreneurship, in particular student entrepreneurship, but much less so with regard to scientists' entrepreneurial intentions (Ajzen, 1991; for an overview see the recent discussion of TPB intentions models in Engle et al., 2010 or Moriano et al., 2012; for entrepreneurship education and student entrepreneurship see, for example, Kuehn, 2008 and Mueller, 2011; for scientist entrepreneurship see Scholten et al., 2004 and Goethner et al., 2012).

Basically, the TPB model posits that any exogenous personal, situational/organizational, or environmental factors will influence (entrepreneurial) intentions only indirectly, mediated by shaping attitudes of the individual towards the target behaviour to found one's own business and continue to develop it (e.g., Shepherd and Krueger, 2002). As depicted in Figure 10.2, these immediate antecedents of intent are the perceived attractiveness (personal attitude towards the target behaviour; ATB), the social acceptability of venture creation decisions by personal reference groups (subjective norms; SN), and the individual's assumed controllability of the behaviour (perceived behavioural control; PBC) (Linan, 2008). On the right-hand side the relationship between intentionality and target behaviour may be moderated by further precipitating, facilitating, or inhibiting factors (Fayolle, 2005).

Building on the principal model of entrepreneurial intentions, we will explore potential influence factors of elements of the entrepreneurial university and policy measures on the three core antecedents of entrepreneurial intent, that is, individuals' attitudes towards the attractiveness of being an entrepreneur (ATB), perceived support and acceptance from important others (SN), and perceived behavioural control (PBC).[1] Broadly speaking, earlier research on entrepreneurial intentions amongst students and scientists indicates that there may be influences on entrepreneurial intentions and its antecedents in terms of the environment of education and research institutions (e.g., scientists' group identification within their research institution; Goethner et al., 2009) and entrepreneurship education itself (Fayolle et al., 2007; Kailer, 2007; Souitaris et al., 2007; Mueller, 2011). Within the entrepreneurial university not only intra- and extra-curricular entrepreneurship education courses but also organizational facilitation and resource support (e.g., support from university's administration or practical coaching and consulting) will be relevant. With regard to the latter the next section explores the role of external entrepreneurship policy activities to support the university start-up process from entrepreneurial intent to academic entrepreneurs founding businesses. The above TPB framework offers a suitable framework for this exploration, since it will be the university members themselves who take up and engage in founding behaviour and external policy measures will likely effect university entrepreneurship through these individuals and their entrepreneurial intentionality.

POLICY SUPPORT FOR THE ENTREPRENEURIAL UNIVERSITY: THE CASE OF THE GERMAN 'EXIST' PROGRAMME

Overview: The EXIST Study Case

As we have briefly noted above, the German entrepreneurship policy programme 'EXIST – University-based Business Start-ups' (see www.exist.de) constitutes an integrated support programme for potential and actual university entrepreneurs particularly from science and engineering but also from other academic fields. Initiated and run by the German Federal Ministries of Education and Research and, later, of Economics and Technology, it covers a wide range of support areas, in particular awareness raising, entrepreneurship education, generation of business ideas from science and research, consulting and counselling, financial and infrastructure resources, networking and the overall development of academic entrepreneurial culture (Kulicke et al., 2011). The support areas have been developed over time through four different phases of EXIST policies (EXIST I to IV). From 1998 to 2005 EXIST I and II concentrated on the development of basic entrepreneurial infrastructures at universities in five model regions and transferring the experiences made in the first phase to more than 30 other university regions (with a total funding of approximately 25 million euros). In EXIST III more specific individual projects were supported with 40 million euros of funding in order to close gaps in the infrastructure landscape built throughout the first two phases (Becker et al., 2011). Since 2010, EXIST IV aims at developing true '*Gründerhochschulen*' ('entrepreneurial universities') with a further scheduled funding volume of around 45 million euros (Kulicke, 2011).

The two main policy instruments in terms of direct individual support to nascent academic entrepreneurs and start-ups within the EXIST policy framework are 'EXIST-Forschungstransfer (EFT)' and 'EXIST-Gründerstipendium (EGS)' or formerly EXIST-SEED, which – as the name denotes – promote academics already in the seed phase before founding a venture. The former (EFT) has a narrower focus on high-technology research and development work and the commercial exploitation of excellent research results or inventions (Becker et al., 2011). The latter instrument (EGS) is broader in scope, also promoting the initial development and business planning phase of knowledge-intensive business start-ups, for example grounded on business ideas from diploma or PhD thesis projects (Kulicke et al., 2011).

The following case discussion is based on independent secondary data on the EXIST programme, which have been gathered by the Fraunhofer Institut für System- und Innovationsforschung (ISI; Institute for Systems and Innovation Research).[2] The Fraunhofer ISI has been tasked by the German government with the continuous analysis and evaluation of EXIST and has developed a differentiated and extensive set of reports alongside the different phases and elements of the programme (see e.g., Kulicke, 2011 for an overview). The evaluation reports allow a fairly broad exploratory analysis of the policies directed at (potential) nascent entrepreneurs. A case-based approach seems to be suitable for such an exploration, which features a rich policy context in a process perspective in an area where entrepreneurship lacks proven theoretical models (that is, the perception of policy support instruments by academic entrepreneurs; see Patzelt and Shepherd, 2009 for this and Pauwels and Matthyssens, 2004 as well as Yin, 2003 for the suitability of case studies in this respect).

Case Discussion

We will discuss support instruments and actions taken by EXIST university institutions in relation to the above three categories inspired by entrepreneurial intentions models: potential policy and organizational influences on the attitudes towards and personal attractiveness of engaging in entrepreneurship (ATB), the perceived subjective normative acceptability (SN) and the perceived behavioural controllability (PBC).

EXIST policies and university members' perceived attractiveness of entrepreneurship

The overall attitude towards entrepreneurial behaviour captures the extent of consistently positive and respectively negative evaluations (generally Ajzen, 1991). These appraisals include both evaluative and affective aspects of starting and developing a new business, for example the perceived benefits of becoming an academic entrepreneur (Kolvereid, 1996; Linan, 2008). Consequently, it has been suggested that university members may be more inclined to engage in start-up behaviour if it is considered stimulating and promises monetary benefits (e.g., Gulbrandsen, 2004).

In her regular evaluation of the EXIST programme, Kulicke (2011) reports that the local EXIST initiatives at the universities and research institutions unfold a range of activities aimed at sensitizing and raising awareness for the possibilities of self-employment as an attractive occupational choice for academics (for example, information fairs, networking events, press releases, entrepreneurial business simulations etc.). This is considered by the EXIST initiatives as a part of public relations and marketing 'groundwork' at the grassroots level. In this broad sense it would be exaggerated to argue that such public relations groundwork generally propels the perceived attractiveness of entrepreneurship in the eyes of university members (at the most more extensive entrepreneurship education instruments may have lasting positive effects on ATB; Souitaris et al., 2007). However, more focused support activities with regard to research commercialization and related business idea generation may be more relevant. In the following we address two possible impacts, the potential impact of perceived benefits of knowledge commercialization and policy instruments in EXIST to reduce the supposedly high opportunity costs of academic entrepreneurs at university.

The attractiveness of acting entrepreneurially may be impacted by the perceived promises and benefits of utilizing one's knowledge gained at university for students and graduates as well as employed staff in terms of their research. This may be related to a specific technology, which may be commercialized, or ideas for products and complex services to be developed. Such benefits may be both evaluative and material (e.g., in terms of economic return) but also expectations of reputation, enjoyment and control seem to play a role in commercialization efforts (e.g., Göktepe and Mahagaonkar, 2009 and Goethner et al., 2009). Here, the EXIST universities are reported to have lined up a host of activities in view of the fact that the entrepreneurial utilization of academic and scientific knowledge is not yet a regular routine at German universities and research institutions. Therefore, the EXIST initiatives aim to show the potential of and assist in the generation of business ideas, for example, from science and engineering through instruments such as technology and innovation scouting, idea competitions and early-stage product development workshops (Kulicke et al., 2011).

Engaging in the entrepreneurial exploitation of opportunities in the university context is not without alternatives for researchers as well as for students and graduates. Policies to build entrepreneurial universities in the sense that the people within them act entrepreneurially need to address the potentially negative impact of *opportunity costs* on the perceived attractiveness of and attitudes towards entrepreneurial behaviour. In particular, for university faculty in Europe it has been argued that the prospect of stable life-long employment in the public sector may be detrimental to entrepreneurship (Chiesa and Piccaluga, 2000). In addition, an entrepreneurial exploitation of results from research or university work (be it via patent disclosure, licensing or business foundation) may not rank very highly in faculty members' minds (Hemer et al., 2010). With regard to (high-potential) students and graduates, Wiklund et al. (2004) discussed that opportunity costs of entrepreneurship may be relatively high for those with a lot of accumulated human capital to be utilized in the labour market. Empirically, it has been observed that while the extent of entrepreneurial intentionality amongst first year students may be higher, it appears to decline to lower levels in higher semesters and closer to graduation where final year students typically learn about employment and career options (Brockhoff and Tscheulin, 2001). Of course, becoming an entrepreneur is only one of many career options for faculty and graduates, and universities are tasked with ensuring general employability in their education programmes. However, entrepreneurship policy may aim at lowering the costs of trying out entrepreneurship both for faculty and students at university.

In the experimental, high-risk stage at the beginning of the entrepreneurial process, EXIST offers financial and other material support to university members. This support through the EGS and EFT instruments is directed particularly at the pre-founding stage, and EXIST explicitly aims to support the initial development of business ideas, preliminary R&D and product development work (particularly in EFT) and the preparation of business plans in the seed phase (Kulicke et al., 2011). The financial support covers living expenses of the nascent entrepreneurs ranging between 800 and 2500 euros per month (Becker et al., 2011). Having enough money to support oneself and one's family is a concern to university members and Becker et al. argue that EXIST most notably provides a time window for researchers and students to pursue their business idea full-time while living expenses are compensated (ibid.). Such instruments may help to address the immediate operative opportunity costs while trying to evaluate the business idea and building a business in the first place. The perceived strategic opportunity costs in terms of choosing a future career path may also have to do with the perceived acceptance of engaging in entrepreneurship in the university context. This will be discussed in the next section.

EXIST policies and university members' perceived normative acceptance of entrepreneurship

The subjective normative acceptance of engaging in entrepreneurship captures perceived 'social pressure to perform or not to perform the behavior' (Ajzen, 1991, p. 188). Such pressure may be felt by university members both from broader societal norms and the more personal demands from important reference people. TPB argues that it is the latter *subjective* norms constituted by one's relatives, friends, and work or study fellows that are relevant in forming behavioural intentions (Rivis and Sheeran, 2003). In terms of the university organization that may be the target of entrepreneurship policies we are going to discuss two important aspects for engaging in entrepreneurial activity: (1) perceived acceptance by university peers and (2) perceived university-wide acceptance and encouragement. In terms of the relevance of these factors Stuart and Ding (2006) found that scientists who believe that entrepreneurial activity is acceptable in their organization show more frequent involvement in research commercialization.

The supportiveness of and approval by one's faculty and student peers may be inferred from the actual behaviour of these reference people. That is, the probability of start-up behaviour may be higher in contexts where these local university peers also act as entrepreneurs themselves (George et al., 2006). Here, Becker et al. (2011) highlight that the EXIST programme has been (and is still) running for many years and that earlier entrepreneurial pioneers at the EXIST universities are important in encouraging academic followers, sometimes acting as role models or showcases with their start-up businesses in EXIST activities. George et al. (2006) discuss that in addition to the entrepreneurial activity of colleagues or work fellows, generally entrepreneurship-friendly departments and institutional norms may also facilitate entrepreneurship. For the case of university faculty members Bercovitz and Feldman (2008) found that such local faculty norms may be more important than personal norms developed through individual socialization. However, the subjective norms variable has often been found to only weakly explain entrepreneurial intentions. Goethner et al. (2009) have therefore suggested explicitly including perceived group identity as an important moderating variable to differentiate the relationship in university entrepreneurship, which may be explored in future research.[3]

The overall university-wide encouragement of entrepreneurial activity may, for example, be judged from a university organization's mission and stated strategic objectives (e.g., O'Shea et al., 2007 for the MIT case), but also facilitative organizational rules may be instrumental. The fourth phase of the EXIST programme currently focuses on these aspects under the roof of the *Gründerhochschule* sub-programme. In particular, the programme outline by the Federal Ministry of Economics and Technology considers the development of adequate organizational rules and procedures ('*Regelwerke*'), entrepreneurship-driven organizational strategies, and consistent monitoring of quality as important strategic ingredients to further catalyse entrepreneurship in German Higher Education Institutions (see www.exist.de and also Hemer et al., 2010 for institutional rules and practices concerning new venture and spin-off creation at German universities). EXIST IV is just in its initial rounds of concept development by universities aiming to participate in the programme, therefore there are no detailed operational results available yet. However, for example, the strategies and concepts reported by three universities from the first round (the technical universities of Berlin, Braunschweig and Munich) indicate the focus on committing to the establishment of entrepreneurship at all levels of the university organization as a part of their university's organizational and EXIST project missions (compare Clark, 1998 for a strategic mission and leadership core as one of the ingredients of the entrepreneurial university). However, the most salient point may be to flesh out such organization-wide support concepts and to put them into practice in terms of assisting academic entrepreneurs. And towards this end, there seems to be room for further improvement in establishing entrepreneurship in universities' organizational missions and strategies. For example, an OECD report focusing on universities and Higher Education Institutions in the Berlin and Rostock regions in East Germany summarized that while substantial bottom-up efforts have been made to offer entrepreneurship education and support to students and graduates, a strategically anchored and coordinated approach, which is endorsed and encouraged by the universities' top management, is still often lacking (OECD, 2010, p. 9). Doubts about the commitment of university leadership to entrepreneurship may not only undermine the engagement of university personnel involved in running entrepreneurship support offers, but also hamper academics' own plans to become entrepreneurial.

EXIST policies and university members' perceived behavioural control of entrepreneurship
While becoming an entrepreneur may seem an attractive career option to students and university researchers (Linan, 2008; Goethner et al., 2009),

at the same time academics may face considerable start-up barriers such as a potential lack of capital and relevant knowledge or the financial risks involved in founding a business (Welter et al., 2008). This may hamper the perceived behaviour control of start-up behaviour as the 'perceived ease or difficulty of performing a behavior' (Ajzen, 1991, p. 188). In particular, PBC entails personal beliefs about the adequacy of one's capabilities with regard to the task and the availability of required resources. In terms of strengthening these perceptions, universities and policy instruments may take on different roles relating to a range of support options. Rasmussen (2011) explored the relationships between universities and their spin-offs throughout their founding and establishment process and identified the following university roles: use of research and physical admin facilities, advisory and business services as well as technology transfer support, and university resources to support the spin-off. Within the EXIST programme similar sources of support are channelled through its EGS and EFT instruments. We will explore three principal areas in this respect: (1) infrastructure support, (2) information and advice, and (2) financial and other material support.

First of all, elements of physical infrastructure offered to potential university entrepreneurs may come with perceived overall responsiveness of administrative staff (George et al., 2006), which may not only make founding a business seem acceptable in the university organization, but which may also make it seem more feasible. This is since the provision of laboratory or office space (as well as other forms of support discussed further below) is likely to facilitate the immediate preparatory steps to founding a business (Kulicke et al., 2011). Becker et al. (2011) emphasize the obligation of the EXIST universities to give the nascent entrepreneurs sponsored by EXIST access to research and office facilities as well as to provide mentoring and start-up coaching. In addition to physical infrastructure support, personal advice and information access may also be instrumental to making the start-up process more manageable.

Providing *information and advice* through mentoring, consulting and coaching to assist potential academic entrepreneurs is important because of the diagnosed knowledge and information gaps about entrepreneurship at university (Achleitner et al., 2004; Isfan et al., 2005; Kulicke 2011). In the EXIST EGS and EFT policies mentors and coaches are furnished to each entrepreneurial project. Becker et al. (2011) have asked nascent entrepreneurs in the programme for their choices of mentors, and the most important criteria seem to be the research and technological expertise of the mentor, his or her contact network to investors and research partners, and his or her entrepreneurial management competences. In terms of overall information support and assistance through mentors, coaches, and the local EXIST networks the sponsored entrepreneurs make use of advice in the following areas: assistance in developing the business idea, in market analysis, in crafting business and financing strategies, and in initiating contacts to future investors and customers (ibid.). It becomes clear in Becker et al.'s survey (2011) that the support offers are used more intensively in the EGS programme than in the EFT programme, which supports more complex, high-technology start-up projects. The authors suppose that this may be because the latter need (and make use of) much more specific advice offers (e.g., in patenting strategies). This relates to the general observation that university entrepreneurs may require competence building, support and advice on an individual basis to back up general information and qualification offers channelled through entrepreneurship education at the group level (Welter et al., 2008; see also Rothaermel et al. 2007).

In addition to infrastructural and advisory support, financial and other material resource support may have a positive influence on academics' perceived feasibility and controllability of successfully seeing through the venture formation process, not least because the feared lack of capital and corresponding financial risks may be a barrier to start-up behaviour. Supposed financing obstacles by potential academic entrepreneurs likely relate to the capital market conditions for seed and early stage finance; and for this segment of the capital market a funding gap is often discussed – including state intervention to address potential market failure (e.g., OECD, 2009). The EXIST programme also offers funding sources to academic founders. In their study Becker et al. (2011) looked in detail at the perceived appropriateness of financial support offers in EXIST both in the EGS and EFT instruments. The capital grants range between 800 and 2500 euros gross per person (depending on academic status) to cover living expenses. Moreover, in EGS, the nascent entrepreneurs receive capital expenditure and consulting budgets between 15000 and 20000 euros; in EFT there is a budget of 60000 euros that may be used to found a business. Once a business has been established, EXIST offers non-repayable funding of up to 150000 euros in a second grant period of EFT. The time frame of EXIST support is one year in the EGS scheme and a two-stage support period of 18 months each in EFT. Becker et al. (ibid.) summarize that financial and material support in EXIST predominantly provide potential academic entrepreneurs with resources to commit full-time to the venture project. The authors further stress that this is particularly important for demanding and complex start-up ideas in university and high-technology entrepreneurship. With this is mind it is interesting to see how the sponsored nascent entrepreneurs evaluate the financial support in EXIST.

Around two-thirds of sponsored EGS and EFT entrepreneurs agreed that the granted financing to cover living expenses is adequate. The appropriateness of the budgets for capital expenditure, consulting and other start-up costs is rated slightly less positively. In this regard and also with regard to the time frame of support there are more pronounced critical evaluations by the responding entrepreneurs. In EGS the one-year time period of support is considered appropriate by less than a quarter of respondents and more than one-quarter do not agree with the statement that the time (for which EGS support is granted) is adequate. Similarly, in particular the time period of the second support stage in EFT is evaluated as being too short. Those who viewed the time frame and budgets of the instruments negatively were asked for their ideas for improvements. Becker et al. (2011) report that most respondents suggested 18 to 24 months as an adequate time span. Budgets to cover start-up costs, necessary investments and needs for consulting ought to be increased to 100 000 euros and the grant in EFT II to 200 000 euros. Beneath this, there also seem to be sector differences in the evaluation of the appropriateness of support measures. The data indicate that entrepreneurs with (potentially smaller) venture projects located in the internet and software sectors consider the volume and time length of financial support less negatively than founders, for example, in the life sciences, engineering and material sciences sectors (ibid.). This is not surprising because the latter often have higher needs for start-up investments and up-front R&D expenditure as well as considerably longer time horizons to break even.

Overall, these results point at two related challenges that may be typical for direct measures of entrepreneurship policy-making (Grünhagen et al., 2005; Shane, 2005). First, on the one hand entrepreneurship policy-makers rightly focus on the need for self-sustainability of new ventures that should not be pampered for too long with tax-payers' money. On the other hand, enterprise policy does not want to withdraw support too early, hampering or derailing the perceived feasibility and controllability of founding a business at university and, in turn, entrepreneurial intentions and efforts, in particular in cases of potential market failure to provide the necessary resources, for example through capital rationing of seed and early-stage start-ups. And even in cases of legitimate state intervention policy-makers should always appreciate the long-term need for sustainability of entrepreneurship support infrastructures as external support should not be granted ad infinitum in order to create true entrepreneurial universities. This is also still a challenge in the EXIST programme, which initiated such external and policy-induced entrepreneurship support. This also seems to be a problem to be solved with regard to public entrepreneurship policy at German universities more generally. An OECD report indicated that support structures for entrepreneurship in East German universities are typically only funded on a temporary basis (e.g., through public project funding) with a lack of sustainable 'in-house' funding of entrepreneurship instruments and personnel (e.g., education courses) through the universities' budgets themselves (OECD, 2010).

Second, a further challenge will be the considerable heterogeneity in start-up projects across sectors and founder-persons in terms of their financing and other support needs and the time horizons in which self-sustainability may be expected. And in OECD (2010) it is suggested that within EXIST (but also elsewhere in entrepreneurship policy) the financial and coaching support instruments are not always sufficiently flexible to serve the individual needs of academic business starters from different backgrounds and disciplines. This suggests that there will be no universal 'one-size-fits-all' policy instrument to support academic entrepreneurs from different disciplines but rather policy programmes with different support measures. Here, the study on EXIST entrepreneurs by Patzelt and Shepherd (2009) suggests that multiple simultaneous policy measures are perceived most favourably by entrepreneurs for the development of their start-up projects. These general challenges for crafting support policies in university entrepreneurship should be kept in mind when implications for developing entrepreneurial universities through policy instruments such as the EXIST programme will be highlighted in the final section.

RESEARCH AND POLICY IMPLICATIONS

The evaluation figures and data that have been collected in the immediate context of an enterprise policy programme should be handled carefully. And the EXIST reports do not indicate detailed quantitative analysis on why exactly start-up projects have been initiated and why they have been continued or terminated during the support process. However, it can be said that the reports present a mixed bag of implications. On the one hand, there are reasons for university members to engage in entrepreneurship as well as reasons for giving it up during the start-up process that may be beyond the influence of policy instruments. On the other hand, the EXIST instruments appear to be important in a number of ways: (1) as a potential trigger for people with latent entrepreneurial motives to actually initiate start-up behaviour, (2) in speeding up the venturing process, and (3) possibly facilitating the process by addressing start-up barriers and keeping some of the nascent entrepreneurs on track. The latter aspects are also pointed out by Patzelt and Shepherd (2009) who put forward the idea that policy programmes may be useful in motivating entrepreneurs from university to put substantial effort into potential entrepreneurial opportunities, which would otherwise not always be the case. For future research the tasks that follow from this are threefold.

First, broadly speaking we need to explore further where exactly policy instruments aimed at building the entrepreneurial university take effect, for example in the development of entrepreneurial start-up preferences, in the formation of entrepreneurial intentions, or in catalysing actual behaviour and efforts to develop academic businesses. Regarding the transition from influences on intended entrepreneurial activity towards actual start-up behaviour the model of academic entrepreneurship proposed in Goethner et al. (2012) offers good starting points for this as the authors analyse external influences on both intentions and behaviour.

Second, since such influences will presumably affect entrepreneurial cognitions at the attitude level (Krueger, 2003), entrepreneurship research may delve further into the role of ATB, SN and PBC in mediating between exogenous influences and focal intentionality and behaviour. This has been the focus of this chapter and we have made some suggestions as to possible factors that may be explored further for their impact on academics' intentions throughout the venturing process:

- *ATB*: perceived benefits of knowledge commercialization; perceived measures to reduce opportunity costs of academic entrepreneurship;
- *SN*: perceived supportiveness and approval by one's university peers; perceived university-wide acceptance and organizational encouragement;
- *PBC*: physical infrastructure support; provision of information and advice; financial and other material resource support.

There will surely be many more influence factors, particularly in terms of entrepreneurship education measures and the pedagogical characteristics of such instruments. However, our aim in this chapter has been to discuss possible factors within policies for the entrepreneurial university surrounding core instruments of entrepreneurship education (for an integrated view of supporting high-growth university start-ups see Volkmann, 2009).

Third, keeping in mind that in the entrepreneurial university many factors may affect its entrepreneurial outputs, it will be useful to evaluate the effects of policies in university entrepreneurship with regard to other influence factors in the context of the progression from university start-up preferences and the formation of entrepreneurial intentions towards actual start-up behaviour and venture continuation and growth intentions (see Bönte and Jarosch, 2010 and Rasmussen, 2011 for these stages). In particular, for pivotal entrepreneurial intentionality it has been stressed that intent will be person- and situation-specific (e.g., in Krueger, 2003), and research on and evaluations of policy measures to build the entrepreneurial university will need to appreciate the specific context of university organizations and academics' work and study life.

In addition to the substantial heterogeneity of venture projects across different sectors and science disciplines, the situation- and person-specific character of entrepreneurial processes at university may help entrepreneurship policy-makers in identifying realistic influence factors, but this also poses limits to creating entrepreneurial universities deliberately. Along this line Becker et al. (2011) remind us, and be it only for the case of the EXIST programme, that policy-makers should not rely too heavily on pull instruments that attract academics to entrepreneurship (e.g., through extensive marketing measures and prospects of ample and generous financial grants). Rather, they stress that self-selection by students and faculty themselves also appears to do a good job in the retention of credible venture projects from university. This may also help to keep at bay the problem of the opportunistic free-riding of those who would have founded a venture anyway or who do not really intend to found a business from academia. Kulicke (2011) reports a figure of less than one-tenth of EGS-sponsored entrepreneurs who would have founded their business irrespective of EXIST policy support. The important aspect to note is that this does not mean that support policies for university entrepreneurs are redundant. Rather, this suggests that motivating university members to engage in entrepreneurship is not the only starting point for support policies. The discussion above has pointed to some important roles of policy programmes to be played beyond initial motivation of academics to become entrepreneurs. These roles are in supporting and removing barriers for nascent academic entrepreneurs, who make the effort and try to establish a new business from their research and study work at university. This requires the entrepreneurial university and policy initiatives to appreciate the whole breadth of the entrepreneurial process and the individuality and heterogeneity of academic founder-persons and their ventures.

NOTES

1. Our analysis is not meant to present a complete list of influences on the entrepreneurial process at universities. In particular, we will not discuss detailed impacts of different characteristics of entrepreneurship courses here since this has been done elsewhere and readers are referred to the literature sources cited below.
2. Since the authors belong to one of the EXIST university regions, we did not collect primary field data to avoid data collection and interviewing biases.

3. The data in the evaluation reports of EXIST do not include information on organizational commitment or identity.

REFERENCES

Achleitner, A.K., C.W. Kaserer, N. Poech, A. Brixner, M. Buchner and A. Moldenhauer (2004), 'Charakteristika und Erfolgsmerkmale junger deutscher Unternehmen – Schwerpunkt Finanzierung', CEFS Working Paper Series No. 2004-07, Munich: Technische Universität München.

Ajzen, I. (1991), 'The theory of planned behavior', *Organizational Behavior and Human Decision Processes*, **50**(2), 179–211.

Becker, C., T. Grebe and T. Lübbers (2011), *Evaluation der Fördermaßnahmen, 'EXIST-Gründerstipendium' und 'EXIST-Forschungstransfer'*, Endbericht für das BMWi.

Bercovitz, J. and M. Feldman (2008), 'Academic entrepreneurs: Organizational change at the individual level', *Organization Science*, **19**(1), 69–89.

Bönte, W. and M. Jarosch (2010), 'Mirror, mirror on the wall, who is the most entrepreneurial of them all?' Schumpeter Discussion Paper No. 2010-009, Schumpeter School of Business and Economics, Wuppertal, Germany.

Brockhoff, K. and D. Tscheulin (2001), 'Studentische Einstellung zum Unternehmertum', *ZfB*, **71**(3), 345–50.

Chiesa, V. and A. Piccaluga (2000), 'Exploitation and diffusion of public research: The case of academic spin-off companies in Italy', *R&D Management*, **30**(4), 329–39.

Clark, B.R. (1998), *Creating Entrepreneurial Universities: Organizational Pathways of Transformation*, New York: Pergamon.

Engle, R.L., N. Dimitriadi, J.V. Gavidia, C. Schlägel, S. Delanoe, I. Alvarado, X. He, S. Buame and B. Wolff (2010), 'Entrepreneurial intent – a 12-country evaluation of Ajzen's model of planned behavior', *International Journal of Entrepreneurial Behavior & Research*, **16**(1/2), 35–57.

Etzkowitz, H. (2004), 'The evolution of the entrepreneurial university', *International Journal of Technology and Globalization*, **1**(1) 64–77.

Fayolle, A. (2005), 'Evaluation of entrepreneurship education: Behavior performing or intention increasing?' *International Journal of Entrepreneurship and Small Business*, **2**(1), 89–98.

Fayolle, A., B. Gailly and N. Lassas-Clerc (2007), 'Toward a new methodology to assess the entrepreneurship teaching programmes', in A. Fayolle (ed.), *Handbook of Research in Entrepreneurship Education*, Vol. 1, Cheltenham, UK and Northampton, MA, USA: Edward Elgar, pp. 187–97.

George, G., J. Sanjain and M.A. Maltarich (2006), 'Academics or entrepreneurs? Entrepreneurial identity and invention disclosure behavior of university scientists', paper presented at Academy of Management Conference, 11–16 August 2006, Atlanta, USA.

Gibb, A. (2007), 'Creating the entrepreneurial university: Do we need a different model of entrepreneurship', in A. Fayolle (ed.), *Handbook of Research in Entrepreneurship Education*, Vol. 1, Cheltenham, UK and Northampton, MA, USA: Edward Elgar, pp. 67–104.

Goethner, M., M. Obschonka, R.K. Silbereisen and U. Cantner (2009), 'Approaching the agora: Determinants of scientists' intentions to pursue academic entrepreneurship', Jena Economic Research Papers in Economics No. 2009-079, Friedrich-Schiller-University Jena, Max-Planck-Institute of Economics, Germany.

Goethner, M., M. Obschonka, R.K. Silbereisen and U. Cantner (2012), 'Scientists' transition to academic entrepreneurship: Economic and psychological determinants', *Journal of Economic Psychology*, **33**(3), 628–41.

Göktepe, D. and P. Mahagaonkar (2009), 'Inventing and patenting activities of scientists: In the expectation of money or reputation?' *Journal of Technology Transfer*, **34**(4), 401–23.

Grünhagen, M., L.T. Koch and S.P. Saßmannshausen (2005), 'Kooperation in EXIST-Gründungsförderungsnetzwerken – eine explorative Untersuchung zur Bedeutung von Promotorenfunktionen', in A.K. Achleitner, H. Klandt, L.T. Koch and K.I. Voigt (eds), *Jahrbuch Entrepreneurship – Gründungsforschung und Gründungsmanagement 2004/2005*, Berlin/Heidelberg: Springer, pp. 319–38.

Gulbrandsen, M. (2004), 'But Peter's in it for the money – the liminality of entrepreneurial scientists', paper presented at the 4S Conference, 26–28 August 2004, Paris.

Hemer, J., F. Dornbusch, M. Kulicke and B. Wolf (2010), *Beteiligungen von Hochschulen an Ausgründungen*, Endbericht für das BMWi.

Hofer, A.R. and J. Potter (2010), *University Entrepreneurship Support: Policy Issues, Good Practices and Recommendations*, OECD Report, accessed 16 August 2012 at http://www.oecd.org/dataoecd/50/34/46588578.pdf.

Isfan, K., P. Moog and U. Backes-Gellner (2005), 'Die Rolle der Hochschullehrer für Gründungen aus deutschen Hochschulen-erste empirische Erkenntnisse', in A.K. Achleitner, H. Klandt, L.T. Koch and K.I. Voigt (eds), *Jahrbuch Entrepreneurship 2004/05. Gründungsforschung und Gründungsmanagement*, Berlin/Heidelberg: Springer.

Jusof, M. and K.K. Jain (2010), 'Categories of university-level entrepreneurship: A literature survey', *International Entrepreneurship Management Journal*, **6**, 81–96.

Kailer, N. (2007), 'Evaluation of entrepreneurship education: Planning problems, concepts and proposals for evaluation design', in A. Fayolle (ed.), *Handbook of Research in Entrepreneurship Education*, Vol. 2, Cheltenham, UK and Northampton, MA, USA: Edward Elgar, pp. 221–42.

Kirby, D.A. (2006), 'Creating entrepreneurial universities in the UK: Applying entrepreneurship theory to practice', *Journal of Technology Transfer*, **31**(5), 599–603.

Kolvereid, L. (1996), 'Prediction of employment status choice intentions', *Entrepreneurship: Theory & Practice*, **21**(1), 47–57.

Krueger, N.F. (2003), 'The cognitive psychology of entrepreneurship', in Z.J. Acs and D.B. Audretsch (eds), *Handbook of Entrepreneurship Research – An Interdisciplinary Survey and Introduction*, Boston: Kluwer, pp. 105–40.

Kuehn, K.W. (2008), 'Entrepreneurial intentions research: Implications for entrepreneurship education', *Journal of Entrepreneurship Education*, **11**(6), 87–98.

Kulicke, M. (2011), 'Wirkungen des Förderprogramms EXISTGründerstipendium aus Sicht von Geförderten Ergebnisse der Befragung 2010 und Gegenüberstellung mit EXIST-SEED', Arbeitspapier der wissenschaftlichen Begleitforschung, 'EXIST – Existenzgründungen aus der Wissenschaft', Karlsruhe.

Kulicke, M., F. Dornbusch and M. Schleinkofer (2011), *Maßnahmen und Erfahrungen der EXIST III geförderten Gründungsinitiativen in den Bereichen Ideengenerierung, Beratung, Qualifizierung, Sensibilisierung, Inkubation und Alumni-Einbindung Bericht der wissenschaftlichen Begleitforschung*, 'EXIST – Existenzgründungen aus der Wissenschaft', Karlsruhe.

Linan, F. (2008), 'Skill and value perceptions: How do they affect entrepreneurial intentions?' *International Entrepreneurship Management Journal*, **4**(3), 257–72.

Moriano, J.A., M. Gorgievski, M. Laguna, U. Stephan and K. Zarafshani (2012), 'A cross-cultural approach to understanding entrepreneurial intentions', *Journal of Career Development*, **39**(2), 162–85.

Mueller, S. (2011), 'Increasing entrepreneurial intention: Effective entrepreneurship course characteristics', *International Journal of Entrepreneurship and Small Business*, **13**(1), 55–74.

OECD (2009), *Local Entrepreneurship Reviews: Strengthening Entrepreneurship and Economic Development in East Germany: Lessons from Local Approaches*, final report prepared by the OECD, Paris.

OECD (2010), *From Strategy to Practice in University Entrepreneurship Support, Final Report of the Project on Strengthening Entrepreneurship and Local Economic Development in Eastern Germany: Youth, Entrepreneurship and Innovation*, Local Economic and Employment Development Committee, Paris: OECD.

O'Shea, R.P., T.J. Allen, K.P. Morse, C. O'Gorman and F. Roche (2007), 'Delineating the anatomy of an entrepreneurial university: The Massachusetts Institute of Technology experience', *R&D Management*, **37**(1), 1–16.

Patzelt, H. and D. Shepherd (2009), 'Strategic entrepreneurship at universities: Academic entrepreneurs' assessment of policy programs', *Entrepreneurship: Theory & Practice*, **33**(1), 319–40.

Pauwels, P. and P. Matthyssens (2004), 'The architecture of multiple case study research in international business', in R. Marschan-Piekkari and C. Welch (eds), *Handbook of Qualitative Research Methods for International Business*, Cheltenham, UK and Northampton, MA, USA: Edward Elgar, pp. 125–43.

Rasmussen, E. (2011), 'Understanding academic entrepreneurship: Exploring the emergence of university spin-off ventures using process theories', *International Small Business Journal*, **29**(5), 448–71.

Rasmussen, E. and O.J. Borch (2010), 'University capabilities in facilitating entrepreneurship: A longitudinal study of spin-off ventures at mid-range universities', *Research Policy*, **39**(5), 602–12.

Rivis, A. and P. Sheeran (2003), 'Descriptive norms as an additional predictor in the theory of planned behaviour: A meta-analysis', *Current Psychology*, **22**(3), 218–33.

Rothaermel, F.T., S.D. Agung and L. Jiang (2007), 'University entrepreneurship: A taxonomy of the literature', *Industrial and Corporate Change*, **16**(4), 691–791.

Scholten, V., R. Kemp and O. Omta (2004), 'Entrepreneurship for life: The entrepreneurial intention among academics in the life sciences', paper prepared for European Summer University 2004, Twente, Netherlands.

Shane, S. (2005), 'Government policies to encourage economic development through entrepreneurship: The case of technology transfer', in S. Shane (ed.), *Economic Development Through Entrepreneurship, Government, University and Business Linkages*, Cheltenham, UK and Northampton, MA, USA: Edward Elgar, pp. 33–49.

Shepherd, D.A. and N.F. Krueger (2002), 'An intentions-based model of entrepreneurial teams' social cognition', *Entrepreneurship: Theory & Practice*, **27**(2), 167–85.

Sieger, P., U. Fueglistaller, U. Zellweger (2011), *Entrepreneurial Intentions and Activities of Students across the World: International Report of GUESSS 2011*, Schweizerisches Institut für Klein- und Mittelunternehmen an der Universität St. Gallen, St. Gallen: Switzerland.

Souitaris, V., S. Zerbinati and A. Al-Laham (2007), 'Do entrepreneurship programmes raise entrepreneurial intention of science and engineering students? The effect of learning, inspiration and resources', *Journal of Business Venturing*, **22**(4), 566–91.

Sporn, B. (2001), 'Building adaptive universities: Emerging organizational forms based on experiences of European and US universities', *Tertiary Education and Management*, **7**(2), 121–34.

Stuart, T.E. and W.W. Ding (2006), 'When do scientists become entrepreneurs? The social structural antecedents of commercial activity in the academic life sciences', *American Journal of Sociology*, **112**(1), 97–144.

Vohora A., M. Wright and A. Lockett (2004), 'Critical junctures in the development of university high-tech spinout companies', *Research Policy*, **33**(1), 147–75.

Volkmann, C. (2009), 'Entrepreneurship in Higher Education', in World Economic Forum – Global Education Initiative (ed.), *Educating the Next Wave of Entrepreneurs – Unlocking Entrepreneurial Capabilities to Meet the Global Challenges of the 21st Century*, WEF: Geneva, pp. 42–79.

Walter, S.G. and D. Dohse (2009), 'The interplay between entrepreneurship education and regional knowledge potential in forming entrepreneurial intentions', working paper, Kiel: Institute for the World Economy.

Welter, F., K. Althoff, A. Pinkwart and M. Hill (2008), 'Vom Studium zur Gründung-eine typisch deutsche Hochschulkarriere? – Bestandsaufnahme und Perspektiven der Gründungsförderung an Hochschulen', in P. Letmate, J. Eigler, F. Welter, D. Kathan and T. Heupel (eds), *Management kleiner und mittlerer Unternehmen: Stand und Perspektiven der KMU-Forschung*, Wiesbaden: Dt. Univ.-Verl., pp. 97–116.

Wiklund, J., F. Delmar and K.S. Jönköping (2004), 'Entrepreneurship at any expense? The effect of human capital on high-potential entrepreneurship', in S.A. Zahra, C.G. Brush, P. Davidsson, J. Fiet, P.G. Greene, R.T. Harrison, M. Lerner, C. Mason, D. Shepherd, J.E. Sohl, J. Wiklund and M. Wright (eds), *Frontiers of Entrepreneurship Research 2004*, Babson Park, MA: Babson College, pp. 109–23.

Wissema, J.G. (2009), *Towards the Third Generation University – Managing the University in Transition*, Cheltenham, UK and Northampton, MA, USA: Edward Elgar.

Yin, R.K. (2003), *Case Study Research – Design and Methods*, 3rd edition, Thousand Oaks, CA: Sage.

11. Boosting entrepreneurship education within the knowledge network of the Dutch agri-food sciences: the new 'Wageningen' approach*

Willem Hulsink, Hans Dons, Thomas Lans and Vincent Blok

INTRODUCTION

The last decade has seen a dramatic rise in the number and status of entre-preneurship programmes in universities across North America, Europe, South America and Asia. The popularity of entrepreneurship courses at universities has increased dramatically among both graduate and under-graduate students, especially those located in the management and busi-ness schools. In North America, university alumni, local benefactors and state legislators not only provided additional resources earmarked for research but were also supportive of the development of entrepreneurship programmes over the last decades. In fact, in many instances it has been the demands of these constituencies that have led to the creation or expan-sion of entrepreneurship programmes within these schools. In Europe, with less of a tradition of private universities, fundraising and alumni involvement in the university's policy, national or regional governments took the lead to promote and support the development of entrepreneur-ship education within universities and colleges through applying a variety of policy instruments (NIRAS et al., 2008). This chapter addresses the politics that have put the concept of the entrepreneurial university and the promotion of entrepreneurialism on the agenda of one particular university, namely Wageningen University and Research Centre (and its associated Higher Education Institutions) through the development of a new collaborative teaching and extension programme.

Also in the Netherlands it was recognized that stimulation of entrepre-neurship at universities was needed to guarantee economic growth in the future. Although scientific research was at a high-quality level, the transla-tion of research results into innovative products processes lagged behind, known as the Dutch (or European) Paradox (Ministry of Economic Affairs, 2003). To promote the entrepreneurial spirit of the future generation as a stimulant for its economy, in 2007 the Dutch government initiated the 'Partnership in Entrepreneurship Education'. This programme was aimed to stimulate Higher Education Institutions to embed entrepreneurship in their various educational programmes and boost the number of students showing entrepreneurial behaviour and eventually starting a new business within five years (Partnership Leren Ondernemen, 2007). More than 26 million euros in total, with 12 million euros provided by the Dutch government, have been invested in the creation of so-called Centres of Entrepreneurship (CoEs) at Dutch universities and higher vocational education institutions.

The model for stimulating the creation of Centres of Entrepreneurship through a call for tender by the Dutch government in 2007 has been taken from the USA where leading universities benefited from grants and subsidies of the Kauffman Foundation through its Campuses Initiative. The Kauffman Foundation has funded more than a dozen institutions between 2003 and 2006 to a maximum of $5 million each to infuse their entire university or college with entrepreneurial activities, courses and approaches (Streeter et al., 2011). The Campuses Initiative aimed at transforming the way entrepreneurship education is taught in the nation's colleges and universities by making entrepreneurship education available across their campuses, enabling any student, regardless of field of study, to access entrepreneurial training. In two rounds, 14 universities were selected to develop and host a university-wide Kauffman Campus; in total about $50 million was awarded to entrepreneurial universities.[1]

Among the shortlisted and granted proposals for establishing CoEs in the Netherlands, the DAFNE[2] programme (the Dutch Agri-Food Network of Entrepreneurship) was unique since its aim was to create a dynamic network involving all agri-food Higher Education Institutions in the Netherlands, coordinated and led by Wageningen UR. This DAFNE programme was chosen by the Dutch government in 2007 as one of the six Centres of Entrepreneurship for promoting entrepreneurship education and stimulating the entrepreneurial attitude of students, teachers and researchers within universities. The other granted proposals for establishing CoEs were either regionally based (e.g., the cities of Amsterdam, Rotterdam and Maastricht) or sector-based (e.g., the creative industry in the Utrecht region and the agri-food business in the north-east of the country).

This contribution concentrates on the joint approach of the Dutch agri-food sector to make their dedicated university, research institutes and universities of applied sciences in this specific domain more entrepreneurial. It assesses the impact and the lessons learned from implementing the DAFNE programme and seeks answers to the following research questions: (1) How did the process of establishing an entrepreneurial university evolve in the specific 'Wageningen' setting? (2) What was the impact of the new entrepreneurship promotion programme DAFNE and what were its learning experiences?

We will operationalize the overarching research question by critically evaluating a number of projects that were part of the DAFNE programme. Subsequently, we will evaluate what they have contributed to the entrepreneurial curriculum of the partners and the larger support structure for innovation, technology transfer and new business. The chapter is structured as follows. First, we start by shedding light on the origins of the entrepreneurial university with special reference to the agricultural and life sciences sectors. Second, we will provide an historical overview of entrepreneurship programmes that were predominantly launched by American universities, with special attention on the curriculum, strategies to establish an entrepreneurship centre and policies for getting support from external stakeholders. Third, the chapter focuses on the organization of the Dutch agri-food sector, the crisis it found itself in during the 1980s and 1990s and the successful turnaround strategy it pursued to make the sector innovative and internationally competitive again. Fourth, we focus on the transition of Wageningen University as an entrepreneurial university and the promotion of entrepreneurialism by the Higher Education Institutions. Subsequently, the focus of attention will shift towards the DAFNE programme by looking into its development and in more detail by discussing the content and the merits of all the individual projects. Finally, the impact of the DAFNE programme, in terms of tangible results, and merging it into the new Startlife initiative, will be discussed in the concluding sections.

THE ENTREPRENEURIAL UNIVERSITY

The established university system in North America and Europe is facing a number of daunting challenges, such as fast-rising student numbers, turning Higher Education into a commodity and leading to an increase of bureaucracy, internationalization of research and education and cross-university competition at all levels for the best academics, students and research grants (Wissema, 2009). Furthermore, the rise of interdisciplinary research, the increase of collaboration between university and industry (co-financed by the government), the emergence of special research institutes, and the ever-increasing cost of cutting-edge research, put a real strain on the organization of Higher Education and academic research. Today's universities are increasingly seen by policy-makers as cradles of new economic activity and as strategic players in a local innovation hub. In addition, to continue carrying out cutting-edge scientific research and providing academic education, most universities have adopted the commercial exploitation of their knowledge and know-how as their third task. They have started to look for alternative funding and have established incubators to commercialize their technologies by selling or licensing them to existing large firms or fresh start-up or spin-off firms (ibid.)

Equipped with this new role for the university as a network broker or catalyst to stimulate regional growth, Wissema (2009) and Youtie and Shapira (2008) refer to the Third Generation or Mode 3 university respectively. While the First Generation or medieval university was basically a storehouse or accumulator of knowledge where income for the university would come from property, fees from students and grants from wealthy princes and clergy, the Second Generation university is more of a knowledge factory, looking forward and transforming inputs into outputs (for an overview of the three generations of universities, see Table 11.1). The Second Generation university was equipped with two objectives: research

Table 11.1   Comparing First, Second and Third Generation universities

	Characteristics		
	First Generation university	Second Generation university	Third Generation university
Objective	Education	Education and research	Education, research and know-how exploitation
Role	Defending the truth	Discovering nature	Creating value
Method	Scholastic	Modern science, monodisciplinary	Modern science, interdisciplinary
Creating	Professionals	Professionals and scientists	Professionals, scientists and entrepreneurs
Orientation	Universal	National	Global
Language	Latin	National languages	English
Organization	Nationes[a], faculties, colleges	Faculties	University institutes
Management	Chancellor	(part-time) academics	Professional management

Note: [a] Institutions comprised of students and academics from the same region in the first generation university. They live on in an informal way in certain students' associations.

Source: Wissema (2009, p. 23).

(scientific breakthroughs and publications) and education (teaching and training bright students); it is basically financed by the state through government subsidies and research grants (allocated through research funding agencies) and through fees from students. The Third Generation university has knowledge exploitation as its third objective. Now the university has an economic development role advancing innovation and entrepreneurship and function as a thriving knowledge hub and actively contributing to the development of local technology clusters. This modern university has a cosmopolitan outlook and relies upon obtaining international know-how, resources and partnerships to prepare itself for global competition. The Third Generation university is (more) disentangled from the state; in addition to income through fees from students and research grants, it relies upon third party funding (e.g., through contract research) and endowments (e.g., donations from wealthy individuals or organizations).

In the US system of Higher Education, universities have a tradition where entrepreneurship education, research and offering extension and consultancy services to local/regional constituencies are highly developed. In establishing this system both the federal and the state governments played a key role. The first provided seed funds, grants for basic research and support for student aid. The latter facilitated the establishment and growth of public universities in their home base by providing basic financial support and a commitment to low tuition fees for their indigenous students. The legal framework of these support-oriented state universities and support institutions included the 1862 Morill Act, which gave federal land to the states establishing colleges that offered programmes in agriculture, mining and engineering, hence the term 'land grant universities'; the Hatch Act of 1887, which provided for agricultural experiment stations; and the 1914 Smith-Lever Act, which made cooperative extension available (Geiger, 1986). These dedicated land grant colleges were committed to the economic and social development of its state by assisting local farmers and manufacturers through the provision of agricultural and urban extension services (e.g., additional training and research related to the application of new business methods and technologies). The land grant universities successfully fostered the high productivity of the American farm through the teaching of food production skills. Practical solutions to agricultural problems emerged from research at these universities that was spurred by the specific needs of the local agricultural community (through university-affiliated agricultural experimental stations and extension services). Land grant universities like Wisconsin University, Cornell University and MIT were among the first to align themselves with daily life, local business assistance and regional socioeconomic development, through providing extension services, running experimental stations and offering consultancy activities (Kerr, 1995).

Historically, involvement of American universities in knowledge transfer has come through the training of students who transfer what they have learned to the commercial sector, the publication of the results of research for use by the scientific and industrial communities, and the services of faculty and other staff members consulting with industry (Etzkowitz, 2007). From the early 1970s onwards, universities began to become more active in commercializing research and promoting relations with industry through patent and technology licensing offices, investment in start-up companies, research partnerships with industry, technical assistance programmes and the establishment of business incubators and research parks.

A couple of decades later, entrepreneurship, innovation and knowledge transfer have become important for nearly all universities and public research laboratories in Europe too. In addition to their traditional roles in advancing research and teaching the new generation, these knowledge institutes now have a 'Third Mission', namely knowledge valorization. This is a new Euro-English term that refers to the ambition but also to the public duty to give social and economic value to the knowledge generated by universities and public laboratories. In addition to the traditional definition of academic research as pursuing curiosity-driven science and advancing knowledge with less attention for societal impact and commercial applications of discoveries and new technologies and financial pay-offs of the academic endeavour. In the new entrepreneurial university commercialization and commodification have become important too. The first refers to custom-made education and training programmes, the offering of consultancy and extension services and the establishment of public–private partnerships in R&D (universities working together with industry, co-financed by governments). The second refers to claiming particular inventions through patents and licensing them out to established companies and/or university spin-off firms (Jacob et al., 2003). Entrepreneurship, fund raising and wealth/impact creation are now prominent elements in their plans and activities in the domains of education and research. While still bringing their research to the public domain (e.g., by publishing), now researchers and R&D managers seriously look into the promises and pitfalls of bringing their inventions and skills to the market place (e.g., by consulting, patenting, licensing and/or creating spin-off firms). In the following section we will discuss the transition towards the Third Generation university and the emergence of entrepreneurship education, first in the USA, followed a couple of decades later in Europe and elsewhere.

ENTREPRENEURSHIP EDUCATION: THE USA AS A MODEL

Until the 1970s few universities in the USA offered teaching programmes in entrepreneurship. The exception was Harvard Business School, which since 1926 offered an entrepreneurship course in disguise, called 'Manufacturing Industries', taught by General Georges Doriot, and since 1947 it offered a full-blown entrepreneurship elective in its curriculum (Cruikshank, 2005). Other universities followed suit after World War II: Peter Drucker introduced entrepreneurship courses to the curriculum of New York University in 1953, Babson College started to offer the first undergraduate major in entrepreneurship in 1968, and in 1971 the University of Southern California launched the first Master's/MBA programme in entrepreneurship. Other pioneers in the design and diffusion of entrepreneurship programmes were the agricultural schools of the land grant universities, which, in close collaboration with the university extension services and experimental stations, already since the 1920s offered small business management and training programmes for local farmers (Katz, 2003, 2008). Similarly, engineering schools offered a blend of entrepreneurship, innovation management and other business subjects in their programmes, seeking to provide an overview of the whole company (Vesper, 1982). For instance, in 1958, Dwight Baumann, an engineering professor at MIT was among the first to introduce an entrepreneurship course at the institutes of technology and the engineering schools across the United States (McMullan and Long, 1987).

The real growth of small business and entrepreneurship education came in the 1970s and 1980s. At the beginning of the 1970s only 16 universities in the USA offered courses related to entrepreneurship; by the early 1980s 300 universities were reporting courses in entrepreneurship and small business. By the 1990s the number of schools offering such courses had grown to more than 1000 in 2001 and 1600 in 2005 (Kuratko, 2005; Solomon, 2007). This exponential growth in the number of schools was to a large extent accomplished by non-entrepreneurship colleges, like the engineering, art, law and medical schools and science and technology development programmes (Solomon, 2007; Katz, 2008).

Several studies have shown how the emergence, growth and institutionalization of entrepreneurship education have taken shape over the last 50 years in the United States (Katz, 2003, 2008; Kuratko, 2005; Solomon, 2007). First of all, there is the evolution of the curriculum from a couple of courses with a few pedagogies at a small number of universities and colleges, to fully integrated entrepreneurship courses and programmes with a variety of pedagogies across the curriculum and offered by a multitude of universities across the country (Solomon, 2007). Second, one can see a substantial growth of Centres of Entrepreneurship over the last 50 years, starting on a small scale by a group of pioneering universities involving adjunct professors with business experience, to a plethora of centres with different models, domains and strategies, searching for prominence in teaching, research and/or outreach/extension (Finkle et al., 2006). Third, there is the evolution of entrepreneurship education via funding all these activities and obtaining support from within the larger university, local business communities and regional governments; this is visible by the increase in the number of endowed professorships in entrepreneurship and sponsored centres in this field (Katz, 2003, 2008).

As Streeter et al. (2002) have observed, there are various approaches to integrating entrepreneurship education at universities. In their conceptual framework they distinguish between two: first of all there is the focused approach and second, there is the unified or university-wide approach. In the focused approach faculty students and staff are situated exclusively in the academic area of business, or in the combined areas of business and engineering. Harvard is an example of the focused model: its entrepreneurial programmes are targeted exclusively to Harvard Business School students (students from other faculties may apply, but only a limited number will be admitted). The focus in the unified or university-wide approach is broader, targeting students outside the realms of business schools as well, including courses aimed at those in arts and sciences, or in physical sciences. Over the past ten years the trend toward university-wide entrepreneurship education has been strong and is gaining momentum. Streeter et al. (2002) found that approximately 74 per cent offered university-wide programmes. There are three versions of the unified approach: the magnet model (66 per cent), the radiant model (7 per cent) and a mixed mode (28 per cent). In the magnet model students are drawn from a broad range of majors. Entrepreneurial activities are offered by a single academic entity but attended by students from all over the university. All resources and skills are united into a single platform that helps facilitate the coordination and planning of entrepreneurial activities. This approach has been applied at MIT where entrepreneurship programmes are administered by the Sloan School of Management (highly centralized, a locus for funding, students and all activities). In the radiant model individual institutes and faculties are responsible for facilitating the integration and visibility of entrepreneurship activities; entrepreneurship activities can therefore be adjusted to the specific structure of individual faculties. Cornell University has applied this model; there the teaching of entrepreneurship education takes place in nine schools and colleges (highly decentralized, every unit has independent sources of funding, students, faculties and activities).

THE DUTCH AGRI-FOOD SECTOR

In the post-World War II period, between 1950 and 1980, the large majority of the Dutch agri-food sector consisted of small business owners – most of them family businesses and self-employed farmers. In that period only a few large and international-oriented agro-chemical and food companies (e.g., Heineken, Unilever) and agricultural cooperatives (e.g., Friesland, Campina) developed. In a world economy where companies largely focused on domestic markets until the 1980s, the Dutch agri-food producers were among the pioneers selling their products abroad. To this day, the Netherlands is the largest agricultural exporter in the European Union with leading positions in flowers and plants, potato production, pig farming and milk production (De Bont and van Berkum, 2004; Snijders et al., 2007).

For many decades, until 2010, the agri-food sector in the Netherlands was the responsibility of a specific Ministry of Agriculture, Nature Management and Food Quality (LNV). Not only policy-related issues concerning the agri-food sector but also research, innovation and knowledge transfer, and education concerning the agri-food domain, were funded and governed predominantly through that ministry. Together with a number of semi-public corporatist institutions, representing the farmers, growers and food companies, LNV was quite influential in directing research and knowledge development, that is, the Ministries of Education and Economic Affairs played second fiddle in those matters. The private and the public sectors in the agri-food sector cooperated in agenda setting and policy-making for research and education; also the financial burden is shared by the agricultural community and the public sector. The centre of the public knowledge network of the agri-food industry in the Netherlands is Wageningen University and Research Centre (Wageningen UR); this is where the greater part of fundamental as well as applied research takes place. Since 2010 the Ministry of Agriculture (LNV) merged with the Ministry of Economic Affairs hereby creating the new Ministry of Economic Affairs, Agriculture and Innovation (EL&I). Initially, the unique status of education, research and innovation in the agri-food domain was continued in the new setting. With the new Dutch government coming into office in 2012, the name of the ministry changed again into the new and old 'Ministry of Economic Affairs', marginalizing the special position of agriculture in policy-making and politics even further. The consequences of bringing the Ministry of Agriculture under the control of the Ministry of Economic Affairs and its effects on the current research, education and innovation practices and polices have yet to be seen.

The success of the Dutch agri and food clusters in general and their active export orientation was the result of an effective innovation system, which was based on the Research, Extension and Education (REE) triptych (in Dutch: *OVO drieluik*) (van den Ban, 1987; van den Ban and Bauwens, 1988; Dons and Bino, 2008). This REE triptych is a classic example of a linear innovation model where research creates and develops new knowledge; extension disseminates the knowledge among farmers and growers, who are trained by educational institutes and therefore able to effectively absorb the new knowledge. Research was conducted by the agricultural university and some other (general) universities, governmental research institutes, experimental stations and private R&D laboratories of corporations and cooperatives. Education was organized by specialized Higher Education Institutions (HEIs) and vocational schools. Extension is technical assistance to practising farmers and growers, which is provided by an elaborate system of experimental stations and public and private service or consultancy agencies. Although the basic purpose of (cooperative) extension is to bring relevant innovations to the attention of farmers and growers, the other objective of bringing the problems and challenges facing farmers and growers to the attention of research and education has traditionally been less prominent (Postlewait et al., 1993; De Groot, 2003).

Despite its active export orientation, the agricultural sector in the Netherlands was traditionally inward looking, supply oriented and focused on incremental innovation. This approach was appropriate and relatively successful after World War II when the environment was relatively stable and predictable, with increasing food security being the main policy objective. Especially in animal husbandry, fisheries, arable farming, horticulture and food processing the Netherlands was internationally competitive till the early 1990s. The system was based on the production of commodities for the food industry (e.g., dairy, meat) and/or sales through auctions (flowers and vegetables), and focused entirely on efficiency and the increase of productivity, which did not provide the right set of incentives for farmers and growers to innovate and change (Diederen et al., 2000). From the 1980s onwards it became clear that the large-scale production of bulk products and integrated supply chains no longer guaranteed a strong competitive advantage of the Dutch agri-food business. Consumers increasingly appreciated high-quality and new original products, and thus provided responsive and flexible agri-food producers with demand for differentiated products in the up market segment.

In addition, in the early 1990s strong regulations addressing growing food safety concerns and the ongoing exploitation of natural resources (e.g., sea, soil vegetation and livestock) made adjustments in the existing Dutch agri-food value chain unavoidable, which in some cases even meant looking for alternative forms of production. The Dutch flower cluster managed to survive relatively easily, using the stagnation in demand to stir up its R&D effort and churn out differentiated and better products. Most of the Dutch agricultural sector, however, was severely in crisis, signals from shifts in the market (e.g., away from bulk products and regular productivity increases) with more segmentation and proliferation of newly emerging market segments had been ignored. As expressed in the title of an influential government-commissioned consultancy study by AT Kearney (1994), the Dutch agri-food community had 'missed the market'. Key policy-makers started to realize that the sector was locked into a production system based on economies of scale, process innovation and output maximization and that a new system based on diversified quality production, with an emphasis on economies of scope, quality, flexibility and innovative entrepreneurship was required.

From the late 1990s onwards the sector has become increasingly dynamic, both in a positive and in a negative sense. In addition to numerous firm exits and business transfers, we have seen new entrants and re-born agricultural firms with alternative approaches and competencies, pursuing new product, process and service concept innovations (Rutten and van Oosten, 1999). Now the Ministry of LNV finds the key to structural change among innovative entrepreneurs, who bring in creativity and variety to the agri-food sector by pursuing all kinds of opportunities traditional farmers and firms have never considered (LNV, 2001, 2005). For that purpose some of those 'new farmers' and 'agro-entrepreneurs' have even formed study clubs and alternative networks sharing information and best practices. It is a change that has opened the door to experiments with alternative farming methods (e.g., multifunctional agriculture, land-scaping, rural tourism), new products (e.g., functional foods and products from organic farming); and innovations in business processes and distribution (e.g., tracking and tracing systems and value-added logistics, and so on) (Lans et al., 2011; Verhees et al., 2012).

TOWARDS AN ENTREPRENEURIAL UNIVERSITY, FROM AN 'OLD' TO 'NEW' WAGENINGEN APPROACH

In the 1980s public spending for agricultural research and education diminished and the public agricultural extension services were privatized. The traditional REE triptych started to fall apart: extension became a commercial service, research became more market driven and the knowledge resulting from public–private projects was no longer available for free extension, becoming more difficult to access and use in education. The traditional close collaboration between education, extension and research became subject to market negotiations. Increasingly, words like innovation and entrepreneurship emerged in all kinds of policy documents, and became buzzwords in the corridors of the Ministry of Agriculture, Wageningen University and the R&D labs and headquarters of agrifood companies. The linear innovation chain became gradually replaced by a more open and organic network in which universities, agricultural entrepreneurs, firms and vocational education institutes are more loosely coupled in generating and sharing knowledge (De Groot, 2003; Dons and Bino, 2008).

If we look at the history of Wageningen University and the Netherlands Foundation for Agricultural Research (DLO) (including the Ministry of Agriculture's research laboratories, extension services and experimental stations) both institutions were founded in Wageningen. The State Agricultural School that preceded the Agricultural University was established in 1876, and the first experimental station in the country, which later evolved into the DLO Foundation, was formed a year later. Over more than a century these organizations formed the heart of the agricultural knowledge system and 'Wageningen' became an internationally recognized centre of knowledge and expertise in agriculture. But over the past 20 years the organization of agricultural research has changed dramatically. As a reaction to all changes in the agri-food sector and in research, education and extension, mentioned before, the Agricultural University had to change into a more entrepreneurial university. The whole process of transforming Wageningen University into an entrepreneurial university started at the end of the 1980s, when the university also changed its focus from agricultural research and education to life sciences. It changed its name from Wageningen Agricultural University into Wageningen University of Life Sciences. But this was just the beginning of large changes in the organization. In 1997, more than a century after the founding of the university, the Ministry of LNV decided to join forces and to merge Wageningen University and DLO to establish Wageningen University and Research Centre (Wageningen UR) (Peper, 1996). In 2003 the Van Hall Larenstein (VHL) University of Applied Sciences merged into Wageningen UR. The whole integration process from a complex array of organizations to one large organization took almost 15 years (Dons and Bino, 2008). The organization now houses the whole range from fundamental, strategic, application-oriented, applied and practical research. While the university conducts the more fundamental, curiosity-driven research, the DLO institutes carry out strategic and application-oriented research, and practical research is carried out by the experimental stations, jointly financed by government and farmers and growers involved. There is a full integration of these different types of research in five science groups: plant sciences, animal sciences, agro-technology and food sciences, environmental sciences and social sciences.

Wageningen UR is unique among Dutch universities in a number of ways: (1) the university specializes almost exclusively in the domains of agri-food and environment (2) because of the aforementioned integration at various science levels, Wageningen UR is recognized as an important actor in technology transfer and economic development in its domain; (3) the student/staff ratio is almost 1.5 to 1, with about 10 000 students (including approximately 1500 PhDs) and 7000 professional staff (about 4000 of whom work as researchers in associated research institutes); (4) Wageningen UR has performed well in fundraising and obtaining national and European research grants and private funds from industry; (5) the university's activities are not strictly confined to its home city Wageningen but also include major research centres and experimental stations throughout the Netherlands

In the transformation process towards an entrepreneurial university, Wageningen UR sought to address the issues of commercializing research and transferring knowledge and technologies to the market. This has been established in several ways. The most important one was a dramatic change in the formulation and financing of research programmes by the establishment of so-called public–private partnerships (PPPs) in which (large) research programmes were developed in a concerted action between industry and Wageningen UR, stimulated by grants from the Dutch government. These initiatives intensified the collaboration with industry and put more focus on research that could more easily result in innovation and application. In fact, instead of the linear knowledge transfer via the REE system, these PPPs form a more integrated model in which co-innovation and direct knowledge transfer take place (Dons and Bino, 2008). The various types of research have their own financial structure, with increasing budgets from industrial partners depending on opportunities for application. The fundamental research of university groups at Wageningen UR depends predominantly upon first stream funding from its sponsoring ministry (163 million euros in 2011), with additional research grants acquired in the second stream (mainly Dutch research funds and EU grants) and an increasing amount of money obtained through contract research (third stream money 96 million euros). The strategic research of the DLO institutes is funded mainly via open/competitive contract research (152 million euros in 2011) and captive contract research for the ministry (144 million euros), with additional incomes among others from patents and licences, strategic business expertise, and other output sales (57 million euros). Finally, the revenue stream of Van Hall Larenstein is also dominated by the government's contribution (31 million euros), with additional funds from tuition fees (8 million euros) and third stream income (around 11 million euros).

Another option is to valorize the commercial value of university's intellectual property (IP) more actively. However, neither the university nor the DLO Foundation had a long tradition of patenting, and were heavily dependent on the people involved, their drives and predominant financing mechanisms (Jongen et al., 2004). Although the university hired its first technology transfer official in 1981, patenting remained a marginal activity. Early in 2000, when the university and DLO were busy implementing the merger, a clear need was felt to commercialize the abundantly available knowledge and to start a number of new activities (Wageningen UR, 2003). As a response Wageningen formulated a set of goals: (1) pursuing an active IP policy aimed at generating revenue and creating a scouting and support infrastructure for that purpose; (2) launching new spin-off businesses and actively promoting, supporting and acquiring new knowledge-intensive businesses; (3) creating a commercial awareness among researchers and lecturers and encouraging them to look for opportunities for consultancy, contract research and new products; (4) stimulating entrepreneurship among students and staff members. The idea was to centralize these activities through the creation of Wageningen Business Generator (WBG). WBG became responsible for the exploitation of the patent portfolio of Wageningen UR, to start-up new ventures together with entrepreneurial scientists and to stimulate awareness for valorization within the organization. WBG was active in the period 2005–08. Although several new companies were created based on research results of scientists from Wageningen UR, the Board of Wageningen UR decided that it would be more efficient to decentralize these activities and to have the individual Sciences Groups to take the responsibility for valorization within their own group. This also shows that it is not easy for universities to find the right approach, organization and management structure in their development towards an entrepreneurial university.

It is important to note that the Dutch universities, including Wageningen UR, in all their efforts to become more entrepreneurial were supported to a great extent by governmental policy since 2000. Many initiatives were taken for the stimulation of entrepreneurship, more specifically the creation of start-up companies. The central governments launched large subsidy programmes, for example, BioPartner and TechnoPartner, to stimulate various aspects of entrepreneurship. In four years BioPartner was supporting over 100 new start-ups and also created five incubators for life sciences industries, one in Wageningen. There are several other Dutch government programmes for the financial support of the first phase of the founding of new ventures, for example, Foundation for Knowledge Exploitation (SKE) and the Preseed Fund of the Netherlands Genomics Initiative.

Wageningen UR was not alone in gradually beginning to feel strongly about encouraging innovation and entrepreneurship in the agro-food and life sciences. This also applies to Food Valley, a well-known ecosystem for agri-business and food research in Europe, centred around Wageningen University. Food Valley wants to attract major R&D centres to its home base, establish R&D-based companies and create new innovative projects. In terms of the availability of public and private research laboratories, there is the Top Institute for Food and Nutrition (TIFN), which is a powerful alliance of European food corporations such as Unilever, DSM Nutrition and Friesland Dairy and the public food research laboratories, including Wageningen UR and, within close range, NIZO Food Research (Ede) and TNO Food (Zeist).

Adjacent to the university and the private research labs of Numico and Campina DMV, there is a concentration of dynamic and innovative companies that work together with leading players in the life sciences and agri-food industry, including Keygene, Noldus, N-sure, Bfactory and Checkpoints. Another example is research in plant breeding for which large public–private partnerships have been developed, for example, Technological Top Institute Green Genetics (TTI-GG) and the Centre for BioSystems Genomics (CBSG) in which the top players in the Dutch seed industry work together with top plant scientists (Dons and Bino, 2008). The newly established dairy giant FrieslandCampina, as a merger of the Friesland and Campina cooperatives will establish a knowledge and innovation centre in Food Valley of about 350 R&D workers.

As mentioned before, there is also the BioPartner Centre Wageningen, which acts as an incubator for new ventures (such as Easygene, Microdish and Genetwister) and new innovation centres (e.g., Campina Innovation). The municipality of Wageningen and the regional development agency of the province of Gelderland have played a supportive and proactive role in real estate development by working together with the university in developing the Agro-Science Park Wageningen in the early 1990s. All these developments over the past ten years clearly show that around Wageningen UR a real ecosystem within the agri-food sector is being developed, in which a number of research and education centres collaborate intensively with various established industries, new biotech companies, consultancies in various fields. It also shows that the transition of Wageningen UR towards a Third Generation university is complex. Today it is recognized that stimulation of innovation, knowledge valorization and entrepreneurship, which are key elements for an entrepreneurial university, requires the education of students, staff and management of the organization. With this purpose Dutch government initiated an education programme via Centres of Entrepreneurship. Also Wageningen UR with its partners established such a centre, the DAFNE programme, which will be described in detail in the next section.

DESCRIPTION AND ASSESSMENT OF THE VARIOUS PROJECTS OF THE DAFNE PROGRAMME

As explained, the Netherlands has acquired a leading position in the agri-food domain through a combination of innovation, entrepreneurship and salesmanship, successfully using the knowledge generated by the knowledge institutes (Wals et al., 2011). To maintain its leading position, the Netherlands was in need of a new wave of activities and a new generation of graduates with a dynamic set of competencies: enterprising researchers, researching entrepreneurs and entrepreneurial managers. Because there was a strong desire to encourage entrepreneurship through the ongoing development of an entrepreneurial culture at the research institutes of Wageningen UR and the agri-food sector, Wageningen UR invested in intensive and interactive collaboration with the business community and public–private partnerships, also in the field of entrepreneurship education. The objective of Wageningen UR was (1) to encourage entrepreneurial behaviour among its students, postgraduates and staff members; (2) to encourage knowledge valorization, and (3) to promote the development of new businesses. This was not an easy task since the link between scientific research and effective commercialization was not automatic, and the percentage of students who saw entrepreneurship as a career option was very small (approximately 5 per cent) (KLV, 2005; Hu, 2007). Although 50 per cent of the 25 000 alumni work in the private sector, it is estimated that only 5 per cent of the total population was self-employed or owned a business (KLV, 2005). In a recent survey among 445 alumni-entrepreneurs conducted to measure their level of interest in becoming involved in start-up, spin-off and business generation activities, it turned out that most of them (almost 80 per cent) were active in the areas of consultancy, catering and trading, with only 15 per cent working in production. The population of Wageningen-educated entrepreneurs is very small and most of them operate in low-innovation and service-oriented sectors.

For this reason the DAFNE programme fitted nicely into the policy of Wageningen UR. It focused on the improvement and extension of the entrepreneurship education programme and was developed in a bottom-up process. From 2006 on, a sense of urgency has been experienced by most of the teachers, researchers, entrepreneurs, students and incubation managers within Wageningen UR, who were all actively involved in promoting, encouraging and organizing innovation, knowledge transfer and entrepreneurship to make the university more entrepreneurial. In a network of approximately 20 people – informally called 'Entrepreneurship@ Wageningen' (also known as Waeghals) brought together by the two part-time professors of entrepreneurship – the main groups in the areas of orientation, education, research and new entrepreneurship were represented, including Wageningen Business School, Wageningen Business Generator, Management Studies Group, Education and Competence Studies, Student Entrepreneur Centre (StOC), Agricultural Economic Research Institute (LEI), the Royal Netherlands Society for Agricultural Sciences (KLV), Van Hall Larenstein and BioPartner Centre Wageningen. One of the major areas of discussion – or it should be said, confusion – was on the definition of entrepreneurship, that is, small business and family firms in the agricultural sector versus academic entrepreneurship/ entrepreneurship in the life sciences (i.e., knowledge transfer between universities and start-up and spin-out firms). Eventually Waeghals became an effective platform where the entrepreneurship professionals within Wageningen UR got to know each other and prepared the groundwork for mobilizing the resources and commitment needed for launching the DAFNE programme. The whole DAFNE programme consisted of a number of projects, all concerning education in entrepreneurship in one way or another. Several projects focused on a broad range of students at Bachelor's, Master's and PhD level. Others also targeted researchers, staff and managers. The various projects were grouped according to the three main themes of the DAFNE programme: (1) improvement of the entrepreneurial mindset; (2) development of skills and competences, (3) knowledge valorization and intellectual property. Table 11.2 summarizes the various projects within the three themes and indicates the type of activity and the target groups.

Improvement of the Entrepreneurial Mindset

The aim of these projects was to bring students, researchers and staff of the various universities and research institutes in contact with the interesting and stimulating world of successful entrepreneurs. The use of role models is an established way to create awareness and enthusiasm for entrepreneurship (Gibb and Hannon, 2006; Wilson, 2008). So-called 'champions of entrepreneurship' can convince the management that entrepreneurship education is important, which in turn is beneficial to the embeddedness of entrepreneurship education throughout the institution. Besides the

Table 11.2   Summary of DAFNE's entrepreneurial activities, its contents, and target groups, activity/project

	Contents/Aim	Target Group
Improving the entrepreneurial mindset		
Database of entrepreneurs	A database of entrepreneurs affiliated to Wageningen University to be approached for guest lectures	Students
Master in Entrepreneurship	Series of video-clips of successful entrepreneurs to be used by students or in class	Students, teachers
Schilperoort Lectures	Lectures by entrepreneurial scientists, serving as role models	Students, teachers, staff of universities
Cases on entrepreneurship	Cases on successful companies and/or entrepreneurs to be used in education programmes	Students, teachers
Business challenges and games	'Pressure cooker' experiences on aspects of business plans	All students
Entrepreneurial route planner	Interactive route planner to support young entrepreneurs to find the way to courses, coaches, finances etc.	All students
Development of skills and competences		
Professional BSc	Assessment, personal development plan, minor entrepreneurship	BSc students universities of applied sciences
Professional Master's	Master's in agri-business development	Students from universities of applied sciences
Top-class Entrepreneurship	Special education for real student entrepreneurs	BSc students from universities of applied sciences
Academic Master Cluster	Entrepreneurship module in Modular Skills Programme	MSc students Wageningen University
BSc minor Innovation and Entrepreneurship	Minor with beta-gamma integration	BSc students Wageningen University
New venture creation	Development of business plan, pitching	MSc students Wageningen University

Table 11.2   (continued)

	Contents/Aim	Target Group
Development of skills and competences		
Go West	Exchange programme with US universities	MSc students Wageningen University
Entrepreneurial Boot Camp	Summer school on entrepreneurship at Wageningen University and Wisconsin University	PhDs from Dutch universities and American PhDs and post-docs
Knowledge valorization and intellectual property		
Chair knowledge valorization and IP management	Founding of a new chair to close the knowledge gap on IP at the university	Students, teachers, staff of Wageningen University
MSc course IP	Course on the basics of intellectual property in the agri-business	MSc students
IPR in the Seed Business	Course on plant breeders' rights and patent rights in the plant seed business	Professionals in the agri-food sector

improvement of the institutional infrastructure of the participating HEIs, like the establishment of chair groups/lectureships in entrepreneurship, incubator facilities, technology transfer offices and meeting places for students (cf. Lubberink et al., 2012), several specific and innovative projects were developed in which the experience of successful entrepreneurs was used.

A database of entrepreneurs

To facilitate the search for entrepreneurs who are willing to participate in education and share their experience with students, a database of entrepreneurs has been developed with entrepreneurs who are enthusiastic to share their experience within their alma mater. Within the alumni-portal of Wageningen UR, a matching tool 'Entrepreneurs for Entrepreneurs' was created with 300 entrepreneurs who are active in various sectors. By using this tool, entrepreneurial students were able to contact one or more experienced entrepreneurs in order to share their ideas, ask for advice and so on. The objective to also connect the other DAFNE partners to the database has not been achieved, partly due to technical difficulties and partly due to privacy reasons (Rutten and van Oosten, 1999).

Video-clips 'Master in Entrepreneurship'
Twenty successful entrepreneurs in the agri-food sector were extensively interviewed and video-taped on various aspects of entrepreneurship. This has resulted in 175 short clips about several entrepreneurial aspects like the motivation to start your own business, attracting investors, finding a launching customer, family businesses and so on.

The Schilperoort Lectures
A series of lectures by entrepreneurial scientists was named after the entrepreneurial professor Rob Schilperoort, who was one of the first entrepreneurial professors in the life sciences in the Netherlands. The focus of these lectures was on a combination of biographical information about the entrepreneurial development of the entrepreneurial scientists and their research, which was shared with students and researchers. The strength of this format was the very personal way in which these successful entrepreneurial scientists explain how they were able to bring the results from their scientific research to society, via commercialization or other means. The format of the lectures was such that interaction between participants and lecturers was stimulated via networking drinks after the lectures and a 'dinner with the speaker'. During the project, over 1000 students and staff members have attended the lectures.

Cases on entrepreneurship
Cases on entrepreneurship in the agri-food sector have been described by researchers and entrepreneurs to support entrepreneurship education. Apart from cases of successful established companies in the agri-food sector, special attention was paid to SMEs and start-up companies. In total 13 case studies have been developed, with a variety of companies within the agri-food sector.

Business challenges and games
In order to positively influence the attitude of current agri-food students towards entrepreneurship, fast games and simulations are developed. The 'business challenge' is a 'pressure cooker experience' in which a business plan has to be developed in one day. During such challenges, small teams of students are coached by experienced entrepreneurs during the development of the business plan, which has to be presented in front of a jury. The business challenge is applicable in different situations and at various levels of experience (BSc, MSc, PhD, staff members). The entrepreneurship

game XLX has been developed in order to simulate various aspects of entrepreneurship. Nowadays, the game is still used at one of the agri-food HEIs in the Netherlands during the second year of the Bachelor's programme.

Development of Skills and Competences

The development of skills and competencies was one of the major goals of the DAFNE programme, in which new courses in the field of entrepreneurship have been developed for the various categories of students. Although the curriculum at universities is quite definite with little room for changes, most of these courses were successfully implemented. The education programmes on innovation, valorization of knowledge and entrepreneurship at the participating HEIs have been extended considerably. For students at BSc, MSc and PhD level, the opportunities to improve their skills and competences in the field of entrepreneurialism and entrepreneurship have been improved significantly, by the development and implementation of various new courses in the curriculum and by various activities in entrepreneurial learning outside the formal curriculum (see below for details). Nowadays at the four HEIs participating in the DAFNE programme, a varying number of 150 to 560 students per HEI per year receive entrepreneurship courses, from five to 25 ECTS[3] programmes (Lubberink et al., 2012). Besides individual courses, of which a selection will be described briefly below, most HEIs offer their students a BSc minor and full Bachelor's in entrepreneurship. One HEI offers a major in agricultural entrepreneurship and Wageningen UR offers also a PhD trajectory in entrepreneurship. This guarantees continuity in entrepreneurial learning for the future.

Professional BSc
At the professional BSc level, the focus was on the optimization of entrepreneurial ambitions of students. This was realized by an assessment of entrepreneurial skills, a personal development plan, the implementation in the study programme of a minor on entrepreneurship and an associate degree in entrepreneurship. All students participating in this education programme are measured using the Entrepreneurship Scan online psychometric assessment tool (cf: www.vhlondernemers.nl).

Professional Master's
At the professional Master's level, CAH Dronten has implemented a new Master's programme on agri-business development (International Corporate Entrepreneurship). This is a programme of one year and will

result in Master's graduates who have the skills to become an entrepreneur or an entrepreneurial manager in companies within the international agri-food sector. The programme was developed in close interaction with CEOs from the international agri-food business. A number of companies are involved as 'Master Companies' and offer opportunities for students to gain experience in the challenges in industry. As an illustration of the importance of this Master's programme, a new chair (lectorate) on entrepreneurship and society was established at this HEI in 2010, responsible for the further development and implementation of it.

Top-class Entrepreneurship

This programme is executed by HAS Den Bosch, based on a fully tailor-made educational concept in which the education programme is adapted to the entrepreneurial ambitions and opportunities of the individual student. Only students who have developed a convincing and realistic business plan are selected for this specific programme. Approximately 15 students per year join the Top-class, which is highly successful and highly appreciated by the selected students (van der Heijden, 2008).

Academic Master Cluster

This module is integrated in the Modular Skills Programme of Wageningen UR. This short course (40 hours) does not focus on theories about entrepreneurship or writing of a business plan, but on the development of an 'entrepreneurial attitude' and an 'entrepreneurial way of living'. The course offers students the opportunity to learn and practice their personal entrepreneurial theory, skills and attitudes. Through provided literature, skills training, guest lectures and the reflection on their personal development, students become aware of their own entrepreneurial behaviour and attitude. Basically, this module is an appetizer for students who are thinking about an entrepreneurial career, have heard about it or just want to know whether it is something they might consider for the future. The course functions as a gateway to other entrepreneurship courses, minors and activities offered at the university. Students work on three themes: (1) personal qualities and entrepreneurship, (2) generation of ideas and (3) pitching and networking. The evaluation of the course shows that participating students represent all education domains of Wageningen UR, including the natural sciences. Furthermore, the students represented 27 nationalities in total. An evaluation of the results of the course with more than 100 students shows that students in all domains scored lowest on their intention to inherit or take over a family firm (i.e., alternative intentions), while the intrapreneurial intentions scores were the highest for students from all study programmes. Although there are differences between the study programmes, students from the social sciences seem to be a bit more entrepreneurial (e.g., classic intention to start up a new firm and overall), although none of these differences were found to be significant.

BSc minor Innovation and Entrepreneurship

At the academic level, Wageningen UR has developed a new minor in Innovation and Entrepreneurship, in which an interesting natural sciences and social sciences interaction was realized at the crossroads of life sciences, innovation and entrepreneurship. This creates opportunities for students in plant, animal and food sciences to become familiar with aspects of innovation and entrepreneurship. As a BSc minor, this programme is officially integrated in the curriculum of Wageningen University. Here is an overview of the programme (total ECTS for this minor is 24 [4 × 6 ECTS]):

Three compulsory courses:

- Introduction in Management and Marketing;
- Basics of Entrepreneurship;
- Enabling the Transfer and Commercialization of Science and Technology.

And a choice of one of the following courses:

- Innovation Management and Cross-disciplinary Design;
- Strategic Change Management and Innovation;
- Agricultural Business Economics;
- Financial Business Management.

Two of the three compulsory courses are dedicated to entrepreneurship: 'Basics of Entrepreneurship' and the newly developed course 'Enabling the Transfer and Commercialization of Science and Technology'. This minor has an interdisciplinary set-up, with lecturers affiliated to five different disciplines. Because the teaching staff was fully occupied by existing education programmes, it was necessary to attract additional staff for the minor. Although it is very difficult to create capacity for permanent positions, nowadays two full-time assistant professors are responsible for the execution of entrepreneurship education programme at Wageningen UR. Since the start of the programme, an increasing number of students have participated in it. This programme at BSc level also gives a good basis for follow-up courses at MSc level, for example, 'New Venture Creation' in which students learn to develop a sound business plan.

Go West

In order to stimulate the exchange of students at BSc and MSc level, the programme 'Go West' was developed. The idea behind this programme was the observation that at universities in the USA the development of entrepreneurial skills and competences is already structurally embedded in the curricula. Also in the natural sciences at BSc and MSc level, much attention is paid to the societal and economic relevance of scientific research. This offers great opportunities for Dutch students to experience the entrepreneurial attitude at American universities. Cornell University was selected as partner in this exchange programme, which fits well in the current ELLSNA programme (Euroleague for Life Sciences and North American Universities) in which both Wageningen UR and Cornell University participate. Through this Go West project, the possibilities for exchange of students are improved. Unfortunately, the available positions are restricted since these programmes are dependent on the matching an equal number of students from each university.

Entrepreneurial Boot Camp

Researchers and especially junior researchers working on their PhD thesis are strongly focused on the scientific content of their research. This is important, but it might also lead to a lack of awareness about the societal and economic impact of their research. Together with the Business School at Wisconsin University in Madison USA, DAFNE developed a so-called Entrepreneurial Boot Camp.[4] This is a course of two weeks – one week in Madison and one week in Wageningen – for PhD students and young post-docs. In an intensive programme the participants learn skills and competences in entrepreneurship. In the four years of the DAFNE programme 67 PhDs and post-docs have participated from the Dutch side. Several research disciplines were involved and the population was very international. The presence of many nationalities was very stimulating and as an extra spin-off it allowed the participants to create an international network. Twenty-one of the Dutch participants indeed started their own company.

With the projects Go West and the Entrepreneurial Boot Camp, Wageningen UR also had the opportunity to develop an international collaboration with Cornell University and the Business School at Wisconsin University. The DAFNE programme used the existing expertise in both renowned universities in the USA extensively, together with Professor Bill Lesser (Cornell University), a visiting professor at Wageningen UR, and two successful conferences were organized.

Knowledge Valorization and Intellectual Property

It is well known that the number of disclosures and patent applications based on research at Dutch universities is not in line with the high quality of the academic research (The 'Dutch Paradox'). Therefore it is very important to create much more awareness among students, teachers and scientists for the value of the results of research. On the one hand, valuable results of fundamental research should be applied in more practical 'contract' research and on the other hand, this intellectual property should be protected. Wageningen UR is acknowledged as an important actor in technology transfer and economic development in its domain and as a source of basic knowledge, technical solutions and a skilled workforce that have contributed to Dutch society. An indication is the third flow of income of Wageningen UR, which is approximately 32 per cent of the turnover (Lubberink et al., 2012). Other participants of the DAFNE programme implemented training facilities for entrepreneurs, advice centres for entrepreneurs, open entrepreneurial events and so on in order to transfer knowledge from the HEIs towards society (ibid.). Within the DAFNE programme, attention is also paid to the protection of intellectual property:

Chair for knowledge valorization and IP management
One of the initiatives was to consider the establishment of a new extraordinary chair on 'knowledge valorization and IP management'. That was seen as an important step to improve the awareness and knowledge about intellectual property rights (IPRs) in general and for the Wageningen domains specifically. The industry in one of these domains (plant breeding) had made available the financial resources. Unfortunately due to long-lasting discussions about the research and education programme of this chair the DAFNE programme did not succeed is establishing the chair.

MSc course on IPRs
In the Law and Governance department of Wageningen UR, a new Master's course on IPRs was developed. The course addresses the operation of IPRs, how to use patents and related rights and what their impact is in society. IPRs are increasingly important for researchers and for public and private research organizations, for generating revenue and as a strategic tool in partnerships, and as a source of scientific information. The course provides a solid basis for natural scientists and future business managers to realize the value and limitations of IPRs in their daily work, and to know different views in society about these roles. IPRs are a tool in innovation policies and in trade and development policies.

IPRs in the Seed Business
In recent years the need for more education and research in the field of intellectual property has increased considerably. Especially in the plant breeding and seed industry a worldwide intensive discussion started on the interaction between plant breeder's rights and patent rights in relation to the introduction of new plant varieties. On behalf of the Dutch government a working group under the lead of Wageningen UR made a report on this issue that was published (Louwaars et al., 2009). Based on this report, Wageningen Business School (part of Wageningen UR) took the decision to develop a master class 'IPR in the Seed Business' with the aim to enhance the knowledge on IPRs in this industrial sector. Another example is the collaboration between DAFNE and the Centre for BioSystems Genomics (CBSG) in order to improve the awareness and knowledge about the importance of the valorization of the research output. Together they developed a number of courses for the scientists of CBSG on specific topics such as intellectual property protection. In 2011, all Centres of Entrepreneurship have been evaluated, including the DAFNE programme. An extensive evaluation among students who participated revealed that they are satisfied by the education programmes offered. They are much more aware of the advantages of entrepreneurship and an entrepreneurial attitude. In general, they are more positive about entrepreneurs and about their own opportunities to become an entrepreneur. Furthermore, students indicate that they have a much better idea of their own competences.

With all these projects, the DAFNE programme has strongly stimulated the Wageningen entrepreneurial ecosystem. The DAFNE network included many partners: Wageningen Business Generator (WBG), Wageningen Business School (WBS), Royal Agricultural Society (KLV), Student Entrepreneur Centre (StOC), Consortium of Agricultural Entrepreneurship, public–private cooperatives (TTI-GG, TIFN, FND, CBSG2012), Food Valley Society and BioPartner Centre Wageningen, and so on. In the evaluation, a number of specific remarks have been made with regard to the DAFNE programme. Not all students studying at Wageningen UR see commercial entrepreneurship as an interesting option. However, the Wageningen students are more interested in entrepreneurship if it is seen in the context of sustainability and societal development. The evaluation report also concludes that scientific disciplines that might have impact on entrepreneurial learning, for example, psychologists and education specialists, are usually not involved in the education. Wageningen UR is seen as an exception, because researchers and teachers from the Education and Competences Studies Group are also involved in the development of the programme.

CONCLUSION AND DISCUSSION

To conclude, in this chapter we have described the historical underpinnings of the entrepreneurial university in general and in the agri-food sector of the Netherlands in particular. The developments within the agri-food sector show the movement from a linear knowledge and innovation system with clear separated functions for research, extension and agricultural practice towards a more dynamic, co-constructive model of knowledge generation and diffusion, commercialization and training/education. Wageningen University and Research Centre has gradually shifted in this knowledge system towards becoming a Third Generation university in which advancing innovation and entrepreneurship have become increasingly important. Accordingly we have described the actions and impact of the so-called DAFNE programme, which was put more recently in place to further strengthen entrepreneurial education and create a dynamic network involving not only Wageningen UR, but all the higher agri-food educational institutions in the Netherlands. The 'Wageningen approach' – encouraging entrepreneurship in a specific domain, throughout the entire higher educational chain – was at the time of conceptualization around 2005–06 virtually new. Looking back, the Wageningen approach could be seen as a unique networked version of the university-wide radiant approach towards entrepreneurship education (as described earlier).

The introduction of DAFNE had its share of successes and lessons to be learned as well. Without pretending to be conclusive, we would like to highlight three major learning points for further discussion. First, the transformation towards entrepreneurial (applied) universities has initially led to confusion among the different partners in DAFNE. Sharing espoused theories and theories-in-use on entrepreneurship within the Wageningen approach and between the established entrepreneurship in the primary sector (agro-entrepreneurship) and the emerging entrepreneurship in the life sciences, was necessary to sharpen the focus of developing an entrepreneurial mindset, strengthening entrepreneurial competencies and knowledge valorization activities. The Waeghals initiative mentioned earlier, as well as the appointment of two part-time entrepreneurship professors around 2000 facilitated this process. Second, the DAFNE programme was successful in terms of introducing entrepreneurship courses to the curriculum, which followed a traditional route of course and curriculum development, even though the system is tight and conservative (one course in means one course out). However, other 'educational experiments' that fit well with ideas about entrepreneurial learning (e.g., cases, personal development plans, guest lectures) were less successful and ended up in the extracurricular programme. Such projects are difficult to maintain and therefore less sustainable because of their dependence on external inputs. One of the reasons these projects were not integrated in the curriculum was the fact that they have been developed separately by different DAFNE stakeholders, and not part of an overarching, shared vision on entrepreneurial pedagogy and didactics. Although there was consensus about key characteristics of entrepreneurial learning (e.g., action oriented, experiential) among the partners, a clear translation towards didactics (e.g., role of the teacher, type of learning activities, learning environment, assessment strategies) was not formulated explicitly in the DAFNE programme. Third, if Higher Education Institutions move to an entrepreneurial (applied) university, internal human resource practices should evolve in this direction as well; for instance, by fostering soft factors such as willingness to change rather than focusing on classic hard factors such as time and money. In general there is a large gap between policy and practice in school organizations (Runhaar, 2008). Managers and teachers operate in separate zones and have different needs. The current introduction of the 'tenure track system' is an example of this.

Thanks to all the activities to promote entrepreneurship within and outside the curriculum as described and assessed in this chapter, it can be concluded that, compared to five to ten years ago entrepreneurship has finally become a serious policy item at Wageningen University and its partnering Higher Education Institutions. The valorization of knowledge and the creation of spin-off activities has become an important third aim of Wageningen University. Especially for Wageningen University with its slogan 'Science for Impact', it is/was important to have a strong programme on research and education in the field of innovation, valorization and entrepreneurship. An important new step is the new Startlife programme where for another time Wageningen UR, Food Valley and other partners in the agri-food sector have taken the initiative in 2011 to work together in the field of entrepreneurial learning and valorization, incubation and new venture creation. This programme, which will run till 2016 replacing and integrating the DAFNE and the Regional Knowledge Exploitation platform, received substantive financial backing from the national and regional governments.

NOTES

* The authors would like to thank all project leaders of the programme for their contributions, with special thanks to Gitte Schober, managing director of the DAFNE programme and Startlife and Professor Onno Omta, academic director of the DAFNE programme. This investigation was a collaboration of the Management Studies Group (Blok, Dons and Hulsink [till 2011]) and the Education and Competence Studies Group of Wageningen University (Lans).

1. For more information about the Kauffman Foundation's Campuses Initiative and its recent history, see http://www.kauffman.org/entrepreneurship/kauffman-campuses. aspx.
2. Funded by the Dutch Ministry of Economic Affairs.
3. European Credit Transfer and Accumulation System (ECTS) is a standard for comparing the study attainment and performance of students of Higher Education across the European Union and other collaborating European countries.
4. An agreement was reached for collaboration with two leading American universities in the domain of teaching entrepreneurship, with Cornell University, Ithaca, NY, which already had an extensive entrepreneurship education programme and spin-off policy, and with Wisconsin University, Madison, which is a top class university in the areas of entrepreneurship education, knowledge valorization and IP management.

REFERENCES

Cruikshank, J.L. (2005), *Shaping the Waves. A History of Entrepreneurship at Harvard Business School*, Cambridge, MA: Harvard Business School Press.

De Bont, C.J.A.M. and S. van Berkum (eds) (2004), *De Nederlandse landbouw op het Europese scorebord*, Report No. 2.04.03, The Hague: LEI/Wageningen UR.

De Groot, S.A. (2003), *Van OVI naar VOVI. Nieuwe institutionele arrangementen voor kennisverwerving en – ontwikkeling van agrarische ondernemers*, The Hague: LEI/Wageningen UR.

Diederen, P., H. van Meijl and A. Wolters (2000), *Eureka! Innovatieprocessen en innovatiebeleid in de land- en tuinbouw*, The Hague: LEI/Wageningen UR.

Dons, H. and R.J. Bino (2008), 'Innovation and knowledge transfer in the Dutch horticultural system', in W. Hulsink and H. Dons (eds), *Pathways to High-tech Valleys and Research Triangles*, New York: Springer Verlag.

Etzkowitz, H. (2007), *MIT and the Rise of Entrepreneurial Science*, London: Routledge.

Finkle, T.A., D.F. Kuratko and M.G. Goldsby (2006), 'An examination of entrepreneurship centers in the United States: A national survey', *Journal of Small Business Management*, **44**(2), 184–206.

Geiger, R. (1986), *To Advance Knowledge: The Development of American Research Universities, 1900–1940*, New York: Transaction Publishers.

Gibb, A. and P. Hannon (2006), 'Towards the entrepreneurial university', *International Journal of Entrepreneurship Education*, **4**(1), 73–110.

Hu, H. (2007), 'Wageningen and entrepreneurship: De ervaringen van een ondernemende alumnus', Presentation, 16 November 2006, Wageningen UR.

Jacob, M., M. Lundqvist and H. Hellsmark (2003), 'Entrepreneurial transformations in the Swedish university system: The case of Chalmers University of Technology', *Research Policy*, **32**(9), 1555–68.

Jongen, W., M. Kleter, P. Steverink and H. van der Meer (2004), *Wageningen UR en kennisvalorisatie: Wageningen Business Generator*, Report WBG/Wageningen UR.

Katz, J. (2003), 'The chronology and intellectual trajectory of American entrepreneurship education 1876–1999', *Journal of Business Venturing*, **18**(2), 283–300.

Katz, J. (2008), 'Fully mature but not fully legitimate: A different perspective on the state of entrepreneurship education', *Journal of Small Business Management*, **46**(4), 550–66.

Kearney, AT (1994), *De markt gemist? Door beperkte marktgerichtheid dreigt somber perspectief voor de Nederlandse agrosector*, Amsterdam: AT Kearney.

Kerr, C. (1995), *The Uses of the University*, 4th edition, Cambridge, MA: Harvard University Press.

KLV (2005), *Wagenings Ondernemerschap. KLV onderzoek 2005 naar ondernemerschap bij Wageningse afgestudeerden en hun mogelijke inzet bij starters and spin-offs in de Life Sciences*, Wageningen: KLV.

Kuratko, D.F. (2005), 'The emergence of entrepreneurship education: Development, trends, and challenges', *Entrepreneurship: Theory and Practice*, **29**(5), 577–97.

Lans, T., J.A.A.M. Verstegen and M. Mulder (2011), 'Analysing, pursuing and networking: Towards a validated three-factor framework for entrepreneurial competence from a small-firm perspective', *International Small Business Journal*, **29**(6), 695–713.

LNV (2001), *Innovatie. Sleutel tot vernieuwing. LNV Innovatiebeleid voor Voedsel en Groen*, The Hague: Ministerie van Landbouw, Natuurbeheer en Visserij.

LNV (2005), *Kiezen voor landbouw. Een visie op de toekomst van de Nederlandse agrarische sector*, The Hague: Ministerie van Landbouw, Natuurbeheer en Visserij.

Louwaars, N. and H. Dons et al. (2009), *Breeding Business, the Future of Plant Breeding in the Light of Developments in Patent Rights and Plant Breeders' Rights*, Report No. 2009–14, Centre for Genetic Resources (CGN) Wageningen UR.

Lubberink, R., F. Simons, V. Blok and O. Omta (2012), *Benchmarking Entrepreneurship Education Programmes. A Comparison of Green Higher Education Institutes in Belgium and the Netherlands*, Wageningen UR.

McMullen, W.E. and W.A. Long (1987), 'Entrepreneurship education in the nineties', *Journal of Business Venturing*, **2**(3), 261–75.

Ministry of Economic Affairs (2003), *The Innovation Letter: Action for Innovation*, White Paper, The Hague: Ministry of Economic Affairs.

NIRAS, FORA, ECON Pöyry (2008), *Survey of Entrepreneurship in Higher Education in Europe*, European Commission, Directorate-General for Enterprise and Industry.

Partnership Leren Ondernemen (2007), *Leren ondernemen van basisschool tot universiteit. Samenvatting van de sectorraamwerken ondernemerschap en onderwijs*, The Hague: Partnership Leren Ondernemen.

Peper, B. (1996), *Duurzame kennis, duurzame landbouw. Een advies aan de Minister van Landbouw, Natuurbeheer en Visserij over de kennisinfrastructuur van de landbouw in 2010*, The Hague: Ministerie van LNV.

Postlewait, A., D.D. Parker and D. Zilberman (1993), 'The advent of biotechnology and technology transfer in agriculture', *Technological Forecasting and Social Change*, **43**, 271–87.

Runhaar, P. (2008), 'Promoting teachers' professional development', unpublished PhD thesis, Universiteit Twente, the Netherlands.

Rutten, H. and H.J. van Oosten (eds) (1999), *Innoveren met ambitie. Kansen voor agrosector, groene ruimte en vissector*, Report No. 99/17, The Hague: NRLO.

Snijders, H., H. Vrolijk and D. Jacobs (2007), *De economische kracht van agrofood in Nederland*, The Hague: SMO.

Solomon, G. (2007), 'An examination of entrepreneurship education in the United States', *Journal of Small Business and Enterprise Development*, **14**(2), 168–82.

Startlife (2011), *Start life. Kennisvalorisatie voor agro, food en leefomgeving*, Wageningen.

Streeter, D.H., J.P. Jaquette Jr and Hovis, K. (2002), 'University-wide entrepreneurship education: Alternative models and current trends', Working Paper Department of Applied Economics and Management, Ithaca, NY: Cornell University.

Streeter, D.H., R. Kher and J.P. Jaquette (2011), 'University-wide trends in entrepreneurship education and the rankings: A dilemma', *Journal of Entrepreneurship Education*, **14**(5), 75–92.

van den Ban, A.W. (1987), 'Communication systems between agricultural research and the farmers: The Netherlands way', *Journal of Extension System* **3**(June), 26–35.

van den Ban, A.W. and A.L.G.M. Bauwens (1988), 'Small farmer development: Experiences in the Netherlands', *Quarterly Journal of International Agriculture*, **27**, 215–27.
van der Heijden, Y. (2008), 'Ondernemen en afstuderen', *Het Financieele Dagblad*, 9 January 2008, 12.
Verhees, F.J.M., T. Lans and J.A.A.M. Verstegen (2012), 'The influence of market and entrepreneurial orientation on strategic marketing choices: The cases of Dutch farmers and horticultural growers', *Journal on Chain and Network Science*, **12**(2), 167–80.
Vesper, K.H. (1982), 'Research on education for entrepreneurship', in C.A. Kent, D.L. Sexton and K.H. Vesper (eds), *Encyclopedia of Entrepreneurship*, Englewood Cliffs, NJ: Prentice-Hall. pp. 321–43.
Wageningen UR (2003), *Strategisch plan '03–'06*, Wageningen.
Wals, A.E.J., T. Lans and H. Kupper (2011), 'Blurring the boundaries between vocational education, business and research in the agrifood domain', *Journal of Vocational Education and Training*, **64**(1), 1–21.
Wilson, K. (2008), 'Entrepreneurship education in Europe', Chapter 5 in OECD (ed.), *Entrepreneurship and Higher Education*, Paris: OECD, pp. 119–38.
Wissema, J.G. (2009), *Towards the Third Generation University. Managing the University in Transition*, Cheltenham, UK and Northampton, MA, USA: Edward Elgar.
Youtie, J. and P. Shapira (2008), 'Building an innovation hub: A case study of the transformation of university roles in regional technological and economic development', *Research Policy*, **37**(8), 1188–204.

12. Not just the what and how, but also the who: the impact of entrepreneurship educators

Susanne Steiner*

At an entrepreneurial university, teachers and instructors of entrepreneurship should be important intermediaries to raise awareness of entrepreneurship and to link academia to business in the long run.

(Günther and Wagner, 2008, p. 403)

INTRODUCTION

The profile of entrepreneurship educators is as unexplored as it is diverse. While many studies in entrepreneurship education (EE) look at students and their entrepreneurial learning process (e.g., Peterman and Kennedy, 2003; Fayolle et al., 2006; Pittaway and Cope, 2007; Müller, 2009), they have so far paid little attention to the profiles of educators.

Educators' profiles, however, might play a key role in the quality of delivery of EE. This study therefore aims at filling this research gap by analysing educator profiles and their potential impact. This interdependency has become all the more important in the course of striving towards the 'entrepreneurial university' (Clark, 1998). National policy-makers have increasingly set the target of developing entrepreneurial profiles for their Higher Education Institutions (HEIs) (cf. Potter, 2008; Schleinkofer and Kulicke, 2009). But building and driving entrepreneurial universities will require faculties with suitable competencies, for example, building networks between universities and external players.

Why look at e-educator profiles? What could be their impact on EE? As the major carrier of these competencies, the entrepreneurship educator (e-educator) is not only one of the wide range of EE-stakeholders (cf. Matlay, 2010), but also plays the central role in meeting the requirements of an entrepreneurial university. 'Academic autobiography' is known to influence teaching style (Fiet, 2001a, p. 4). Moreover, differences in EE course design can result from an educator's 'unwillingness or inability to view the world through other lenses' (ibid.). A 'competency trap' (Shepherd, 2004, p. 284) may result from this, and may affect quality and effectiveness of entire EE-programmes. Therefore, this chapter analyses the profiles of e-educators and their impact on EE curricula and teaching methods as suggested by Shepherd (2004).

Existing academic publications on e-educators mostly deal with EE-programmes and methodologies, but not with educators. Little research has gone into 'the systematic assessment' of e-educators, as Kabongo and McCaskey (2011, p. 28) have recently pointed out. Furthermore, the few publications on e-educators are based on case studies. The study by Hills (1988) is a prominent example of case-study-based research on EE-programmes: his survey of 15 leading e-educators in the USA evaluates the EE-programmes and their underlying objectives, but not the interviewed educators' profiles (cf. Henry et al., 2005).

The few and heterogeneous references to educators themselves do not draw a coherent picture, reflecting the wide range of characteristics that e-educators currently show (Robbers, 2010; Neck and Greene, 2011). This apparent lack of consistency calls for the development of an occupational profile to 'reduce arbitrariness' while preserving the 'highly desirable and inevitable pluralism' among educator profiles (Robbers, 2010, p. 2). Meanwhile, the trend towards an increasingly wide range of EE-teaching and -learning content both increases educator pluralism and reinforces the need for systematization, for example, an EE-typology (Haase and Lautenschlaeger, 2012).

Existing literature on e-educators reveals two further knowledge gaps. First, most published studies are US focused (cf. Hills, 1988; Finkle, 2007; Finkle et al., 2007; Kabongo and McCaskey, 2011). However, US-based results might not be applicable to Europe because EE might differ between the USA and Europe. This would inevitably lead to geographical differences in educator profiles. Second, the few publications on European EE deal only marginally with the entrepreneurship educator (cf. Halbfas, 2006). Research on German-speaking countries only discusses EE-staff as a side aspect to the trend towards entrepreneurship chairs (Klandt, 2004; Schleinkofer and Kulicke, 2009). In sum, there is little information available on German educators other than full-time professors.

Our study fills some of the above-mentioned gaps by analysing the profiles of a sample of e-educators at German universities and their impact on EE-courses, exploring the following research questions and along the following structure:

1   What is already known about the profiles of current actors in EE?
2   How do e-educators at universities in Germany compare, and does a university's overall entrepreneurial performance have an impact on the profile of its e-educators?

3   Does an e-educator's profile have an influence on teaching contents of EE, and if so, how?

IN SEARCH OF CLARITY: WHO IS THE ENTREPRENEURSHIP EDUCATOR?

The earliest reference to the term 'entrepreneurship educator' was made by Hills (1988, p. 112), followed by Katz and Green (1996, p. 371) and Fiet (2001b, p. 103). 'Entrepreneurship scholar' was more often used (e.g., Fiet, 2001a, p. 2), referring to both researchers and/or instructors. A multitude of reference terms, as illustrated by Table 12.1, reflects the diversity of individuals as well as the lack of a common occupational profile.

The heterogeneity of existing literature makes it necessary to investigate in depth the findings that they have in common. We focus on select aspects that may contribute to an educator's mindset and teaching approach and thus may affect EE, starting with aspects of the educator profile, and with the best-researched profile of EE practitioners. As a result we derive a working definition of the term 'e-educator' for the present study.

To What Extent are Practitioners Being Used in EE?

Several scholars mention the use of practitioners – as full- or part-time adjunct faculty – to be an important part of entrepreneurship education (Plaschka and Welsch, 1990; Brockhaus, 1992; Katz, 1995, 2003). In the USA, practitioners were originally involved in EE to compensate for a lack of tenured entrepreneurship faculty (Katz, 1995).[1] The involvement of practitioners has since become widely accepted, 'reflected in the high percentages of adjunct (i.e., non-tenure track, part-time) faculty' (Katz, 2003, p. 297). This observation is questioned in a recent study by Kabongo and McCaskey (2011) who show a share of only 17 per cent of adjunct/part-time staff (p. 35) and suggest that their share might have been decreasing. Notwithstanding this possible decline, EE also involves practitioners as guest speakers (Solomon, 2007). While the EE-element of guest speakers is valued for 'bringing the real world to class' (Gartner and Vesper, 1994, p. 187), their 'erratic' speaking quality has led some US EE-programmes to give up this input (ibid., p. 183).

In addition to the real-world input there are two main reasons for the use of practitioners: the increase in EE-offerings and the resulting need for educators (Brush et al., 2003), and the finding that the introduction

Table 12.1 Examples of literature on management and/or entrepreneurship educators

Authors (Journal)	Year	Term Used	Focus On	Region	Methodology
Hills (*J ournal of Business Venturing*)	1988	Entrepreneurship educator	EE-programmes	USA	Interviews with leading scholars/ case studies of EE-programmes
Katz and Green (*Simulation and Gaming*)	1996	Entrepreneurship scholar	Publication track records	USA	Quantitative study
Fiet (*Journal of Business Venturing*)	2001a	Entrepreneurship scholar	Teaching approaches	Global	Content analysis of EE-syllabi
Fiet (*Journal of Business Venturing*)	2001b	Entrepreneurship educator	The teacher's role; teaching strategies	Global	Conceptual paper
Doh (*Academy of Management Learning and Education*)	2003	Management educator	Teaching approaches	USA	Interviews with leading scholars
Brush et al. (*Journal of Management*)	2003	Entrepreneurship scholar	Career paths	USA	Method mix (interviews and survey)
Elmuti (*Management Decision*)	2004	Management educator	Educator types (career academic vs educator with previous business experience)	USA	Interviews with leading scholars

Finkle (*Journal of Entrepreneurship Education*)	2007	Entrepreneurship scholar	Faculty recruitment (candidates and open positions)	USA	Quantitative study
Sarasvathy (book, Edward Elgar Publishing)	2008	Entrepreneurship instructor	Teaching methods	USA	Conceptual paper (based on interviews with founders)
Günther and Wagner (*European Journal of International Management*)	2008	Teachers and instructors of entrepreneurship	Cooperation between e-educators and technology transfer activities	Europe	Quantitative study of technology transfer institutions
Robbers (IntEnt-conference paper)	2010	Entrepreneurship educator	Status of the e-educator's professional field of practice	Germany	Qualitative study
Kabongo and McCaskey (*Journal of Small Business and Enterprise Development*)	2011	Entrepreneurship educator	Academic qualification, primary teaching areas, research interests and journal publications	USA	Quantitative study

of entrepreneurial role models to the curriculum is an effective element to raise EE-participants' intention to start up (Müller, 2009).

What Academic Qualification is Required for Teaching EE at Universities?

Entrepreneurship faculty can have an academic or a business background, or both. But what entrance qualification for teaching in academia exists, and to what extent do full-time and part-time faculty differ? Both in the USA and in Europe a PhD is the prevalent degree among e-educators, with the majority of PhDs in business/economic sciences. The US-based sample of e-educators assessed by Kabongo and McCaskey (2011) features 60 per cent of e-educators holding a PhD degree or equivalent (p. 34). The majority of these are full-time staff, whilst only 2 per cent were adjunct/part-time staff (p. 35). In Germany, 'entrepreneurship professors generally hold a PhD' (Schleinkofer and Kulicke, 2009, p. 30). We have not found published data on academic qualifications that other German e-educators currently hold.

An Interdisciplinary Arena – Reflected by Diverse Educational Backgrounds?

German entrepreneurship professors have much more diverse educational backgrounds than their US colleagues. Whether this is also the case for non-professorial staff in Europe and in the USA remains open. Reflecting the high expectations for e-educators 'to know everything about every field' (Neck and Greene, 2011, p. 56), the profession of educators in this interdisciplinary field holds a wide spectrum of backgrounds and experience. These profiles encompass 'academics, entrepreneurs, consultants, investors, full-time, part-time, academically qualified, and professionally qualified' (ibid.). Further, there is ongoing debate within EE on two opposed teaching approaches: the 'specialist' and the 'generalist' approach (cf. Béchard and Grégoire, 2005, p. 24). Both approaches lead to respective e-educators' profiles: the individual educator as 'specialist' (e.g., teaching start-up finance) or 'generalist' (e.g., teaching business planning, encompassing financial aspects).

As to educational backgrounds (incl. study degrees), existing research shows that entrepreneurship faculty in the USA reflect the interdisciplinary nature of the field, holding degrees in disciplines as varied as management, psychology, anthropology or engineering (Brush et al., 2003; Katz, 2003). With the increase in EE-offerings, the diversity of educational backgrounds grows even further: according to Kabongo and McCaskey (2011), 'educators from diversified disciplines such as industrial technology, psychology, art, music, engineering and the sciences have been invited to develop and teach entrepreneurship courses' (p. 29).

Among German entrepreneurship professors at HEIs, the spectrum of educational backgrounds has broadened into more diverse social sciences, for example psychology and sociology (cf. Klandt, 2004), but with a considerable majority of PhD holders in business or economic sciences (Schleinkofer and Kulicke, 2009; 86.1 per cent). Schleinkofer and Kulicke (2009) also found that 11 per cent of German entrepreneurship professors hold double degrees in business/economic sciences and engineering/technical studies (p. 45).

Incorporating Theory and Practice – Does the Ideal Profile Exist?

Published research in EE has repeatedly brought up the requirement for and difficulties in deploying educators who can bring their own entrepreneurial experience to the classroom (cf. Hills, 1988; Rabbior, 1990). McMullan and Long (1987) refer to the ideal of bringing both academic and entrepreneurial experience to the classroom as 'not . . . as unlikely in the entrepreneurship field as [in] many others' (p. 268). The e-scholar and e-educator Fiet (2001b) proves that this ideal does indeed exist, recounting his own (multiple) start-up experiences (p. 104). Nonetheless, due to the prerequisite of faculty's academic training, this requirement, however justified, proves to be difficult to fulfil in reality.

In their study on entrepreneurship tenure requirements at US Higher Education schools and universities, Finkle et al. (2007) assess the share of tenured faculty members with start-up experience and find that 50 per cent of all faculty members who have earned tenure have experience in starting at least one business (p. 109). More recently, Kabongo and McCaskey (2011) report that even 80 per cent of US e-educators claim entrepreneurial experience outside of the classroom (p. 38). The authors note that these activities encompass a 'wide variety' of entrepreneurial experience, such as experience as consultant to start-ups (41 per cent), as business owner (36 per cent), as corporate executive and director of institutions (29 per cent), as entrepreneur (19 per cent) and in venture capital (5 per cent) (ibid.).

Klandt et al. (2008, p. 39) report an equally high share of 76 per cent of entrepreneurship professors with entrepreneurial activities for Germany. The authors give details of these activities, which feature business start-ups alone or in a team as leading activity (61 per cent), followed by holding a stake in a company (36 per cent), corporate take-over (11 per cent) and running a family-owned business (8 per cent).

A direct comparison of these findings is not possible, due to inconsistent and overlapping terminology on entrepreneurial activities in the two surveys on the US and Germany.

Working Definition of 'Entrepreneurship Educator'

In summary, actors in the field of EE form a 'rich and diverse pool of collaborative educators . . . with a common understanding that entrepreneurship education is important' (Neck and Greene, 2011, p. 56). The present study builds on Neck and Greene's (2011) understanding. For the purpose of our study we refer to the term 'e-educator' as follows:

> An *e-educator* can be any person[2] in charge of running and/or managing an entrepreneurship course, independent of status and position at the university. An e-educator can thus be a professor, a teaching assistant, or an external lecturer. The e-educator is not necessarily involved in the design of the EE-course or of the whole programme. His/her roles not only include that of the teacher and trainer, but also increasingly that of the facilitator, e.g. when involving guest speakers (cf. Solomon, 2007). In this study the category of guest speakers is not considered as e-educators, but rather as a content component of EE.

METHODOLOGY

This study builds on a survey carried out at German private and public universities in 2010.

Sample

In order to obtain our sample of entrepreneurship educator profiles, we identified over 500 EE-offerings at 76 universities. We applied simple random sampling with a stratified element (individual courses only, no complete EE-programmes), combined with a systematic element (curricular courses only, with Credit Points allocated). Special Master's programmes in Entrepreneurship or pure academic offerings were not included in the sampling. The result is a sample of 76 curricular EE-offerings, with one EE-course each per university. We then contacted the 76 entrepreneurship scholars in charge of running the respective course and received 45 valid survey questionnaires, which corresponds to a response rate of 58 per cent.

Categorization of Responding Universities' 'Entrepreneurial' Performance

As part of the evaluation of our sample, we categorized the responding universities according to their 'entrepreneurial' performance. We followed the existing ranking by Schmude and Heumann (2011) and its underlying criteria. The 'Schmude-ranking' is conducted regularly and published every two to three years. It measures the performance of German universities in the following eight areas: (1) EE, (2) extra-curricular qualification and support, (3) external network, (4) framework set by Higher Education policies, (5) cooperation and coordination, (6) communication, (7) mobilization of target groups, (8) start-up activity. Schmude and Heumann (2011) have defined three performance categories that they highlighted in different colours (pp. 10–11). (1) 'green area' (= founder area): universities with comparably good to very good offerings and services were awarded 200+ points in the survey; (2) 'yellow area': universities with offerings and services of overall 'comparably average' were awarded 100–199 points in the survey; and (3) 'red area': universities offering 'comparably bad' to 'very bad' conditions for potential entrepreneurs obtained up to 99 points.

Based on this ranking our sample is composed of a 'green' majority of universities of 'high entrepreneurial performance' (dark grey shading in Figure 12.1) (53 per cent), a 'yellow' share of universities of 'medium entrepreneurial performance' (medium grey shading in Figure 12.1) (25 per cent) and of 22 per cent private universities (light grey shading in Figure 12.1) that have the reputation of being universities of high entrepreneurial performance, but are not included in the 'Schmude-ranking'. We will therefore assess this group separately. This categorization of German entrepreneurial universities based on established criteria allows

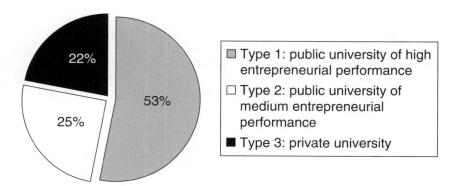

Figure 12.1   Distribution of universities by entrepreneurial performance in the sample

us to compare educator profiles for the different types of universities in our sample.

Data Analysis

In order to compare our findings to the largely US-based published findings, we first evaluated the respondents' mean percentages in the following three content categories: academic qualification, educational background and potential own entrepreneurial experience brought to the classroom. We compared the differences in the mean percentages across the three responding types of educators: the full-time tenured professors, teaching assistants and adjunct/part-time instructors. This initial analysis of the entire sample allows us to fill the existing knowledge gap on e-educator profiles across German universities.

To determine whether the reported differences are significant, we conducted a non-parametric statistical test after having tested the sample for normal distribution, which led to the rejection of the normal distribution hypothesis (cf. Janssen and Laatz, 2008, p. 254). In order to test for normal distribution we assessed skewness and kurtosis. While the tests for skewness were within acceptable boundaries, the results for kurtosis were both below minus 1, indicating a distribution with an abnormal peak (compressed). In addition, we ran a Shapiro-Wilk test, recommended for samples with under 50 observations (cf. Janssen and Laatz, 2005, p. 242). All tests showed that the distribution observed in the sample most likely does not stem from a normally distributed population. The non-parametric statistic (2-tailed) for each category was evaluated to determine if the difference was significant at the levels of $p < 0.10$, $p < 0.05$ respectively.

In a next step we introduced the three above-mentioned categories of universities. Finally we compared the mean percentages in each of the five content categories across e-educators for each of the three groups of universities identified in the sample (inter-group comparison). We tested these results for significance through a non-parametric statistical test to determine if the differences between groups were significant at the levels of $p < 0.10$, $p < 0.05$ respectively.

We want to point out that we intend this university grouping only to provide additional information on e-educators' profiles. We cannot draw conclusions from the individual educator level to the level of the corresponding university, as our sample encompasses only one respondent per university.

In order to assess the possible impact of an e-educator's profile on teaching contents of EE, we evaluated the frequency with which the respondents apply a range of teaching contents. Finally, we assessed the significance of our findings based on the respective non-parametric statistical value for each of the teaching contents.

FINDINGS

Educator Profiles in Germany

The analysis of the 45 educators in our sample confirms that there is no consistent educator profile at German universities. Based on an evaluation of the three content categories of academic qualification, educational background and potential own entrepreneurial experience, the profiles in our sample are characterized as follows:

1   Academic qualification of external e-educators is high

External/adjunct educators display a polarization of academic qualifications: while only 30 per cent of them do not have a PhD, 43 per cent of them show a qualification equivalent to the prerequisite to apply for a chair ('Habilitation', cf. endnote 1) (Figure 12.2).

The literature on e-educators reviewed for comparison includes little information on the academic qualifications of external instructors in the

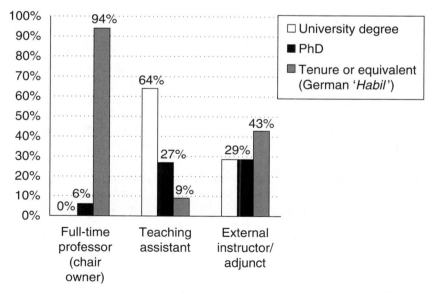

Figure 12.2   E-educators in the sample and their academic qualifications

USA. Kabongo and McCaskey (2011) mention that '[out] of 195 entrepreneurship faculty who held a PhD in [our] sample, about 3.08 per cent were adjuncts' (p. 35). We therefore assume that in Germany, adjunct e-educators require considerably higher academic qualifications than their US counterparts. This assumption has to be tested in a separate, more detailed, study, but is supported by the fact that German regulations require honorary professors to hold a PhD.

2   E-educators predominantly have educational backgrounds in business/ economic sciences

The vast majority of German academic e-educators have an educational background in business and economic sciences (89 per cent), including both pure management degrees (67 per cent) and degrees of non-business studies combined with management/business studies (22 per cent). The most frequent combination was business and technical studies (11 per cent), followed by business and social sciences (9 per cent). Emphasizing the interdisciplinary character of EE, some educators have multiple educational backgrounds, such as creative/business/social sciences (4 per cent), business/natural sciences (2 per cent) as well as social sciences/handicraft (2 per cent).

3   62 per cent of e-educators bring their own entrepreneurial experience to the classroom

A remarkable share of all three groups of e-educators, both full- and part-time, demonstrates own entrepreneurial experience (62 per cent). Eighty-eight per cent of responding professors (chair holders), 71 per cent of responding external instructors and even 41 per cent of teaching assistants can draw on own entrepreneurial experience (Figure 12.3).

Overall, every other e-educator with entrepreneurial experience in our sample held a professorship (chair). This is in line with a study on full-time professors by Finkle et al. (2007, p. 109) who found that half (50 per cent) of all tenured faculty members had started at least one business.

Inter-group Comparison of Educator Profiles in Germany

Our inter-group comparison of e-educator profiles at German universities of different entrepreneurial performance shows a distinct mix of faculty for each category:

- Universities of *high* entrepreneurial performance host the biggest mix of educational backgrounds, often in combination with a business/economic sciences degree (88 per cent).

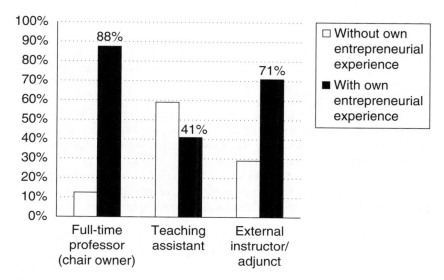

Figure 12.3   *E-educators in the sample and their own entrepreneurial experience*

- Universities of *medium* entrepreneurial performance exclusively feature EE-staff with a business/economics background (100 per cent). A third of them show a combination with another background in technical studies.
- *Privately funded* universities show the highest share of educators with own entrepreneurial experience (90 per cent), followed by universities of high performance (60 per cent) and then medium performance (50 per cent). Like universities of medium performance, all educators at private universities have a background in business/ economic sciences. However, they combine this with a wide range of other backgrounds, including social sciences (30 per cent) and the arts (10 per cent).[3]

There was a statistically significant difference between the university groups (chi-square = 5.315, $p = 0.070$), with a mean rank of 18.00 for universities of medium performance, 22.50 for universities of high performance and 29.25 for private universities. This underlines that privately funded universities in Germany have a statistically higher share of e-educators with own entrepreneurial experience, which is in line with their reputation.

Potential Impact of E-educators on EE

To assess the potential impact of e-educators on the contents of EE, we focused on an analysis of the role of an educator's own entrepreneurial experience. To this end we asked the respondents to what extent their respective EE-course contained one or more of 16 different teaching elements. The list encompassed teaching methodologies and contents. Based on the average values of respondents' answers for every teaching element, we added to our analysis whether the responding educators had entrepreneurial experience or not. These two groups differ considerably in four content elements (cf. italic values in table below). A Pearson's chi-square test confirmed the use of three EE-content elements by educators with entrepreneurial experience to be of statistical significance.

E-educators with start-up experience have an impact on teaching contents of EE, by preferring (1) the element of participants establishing their own network ($X^2 = 12.56$, $p = 0.002$, hence $p < 0.01$); (2) the element of encouraging participants to critically reflect/question ($X^2 = 8.20$, $p = 0.017$, hence $p < 0.05$), and (3) interdisciplinary elements ($X^2 = 6.88$, $p = 0.032$, hence $p < 0.05$).

Our findings show that the profile of e-educators at German universities can have both a direct and an indirect impact on EE:

- It can directly influence the actual teaching contents. In our sample, an educator's own entrepreneurial experience led to the significant preference for three teaching elements.
- In addition, it can indirectly affect the actual effectiveness of EE. Müller (2009) has, for example, identified enabling participants to 'build their own network' as an 'effective' element to raise course participants' intentions to start up.[4]
- Finally, publicly financed universities of high entrepreneurial performance and privately funded universities seem to put particular emphasis on the employment of teaching staff with start-up experience who are likely to train these effective elements.

Overall, the study's findings show a significant diversity of educational backgrounds among e-educators at universities of high performance. This evidence suggests that such a profile mix contributes to the success of an institution's strive towards an entrepreneurial university.

Table 12.2   *Comparison of mean values EE-content elements used between e-educators with and without own entrepreneurial experience in the sample (confirmed elements in italic and underlined)*

Activity	E-educator with Own Entrep. Experience	N	Average	SD
Discussion elements among participants (1)	No	17	2.71	0.588
	Yes	28	2.86	0.448
Business planning elements (2)	No	17	2.47	0.874
	Yes	28	2.64	0.731
Action-oriented elements (3)	No	17	2.53	0.717
	Yes	28	2.75	0.585
Interaction with practice (4)	No	17	2.41	0.870
	Yes	28	2.61	0.685
Mentoring elements (5)	No	17	*1.71*	0.849
	Yes	28	*2.11*	0.875
Establishing own network (6)	No	17	*1.53*	0.874
	Yes	28	*2.43*	0.790
Critical reflection/questioning (7)	No	17	*2.24*	0.903
	Yes	28	*2.86*	0.448
Building a team (8)	No	17	2.24	0.903
	Yes	28	2.50	0.839
Role models resp. founder idols (9)	No	17	2.00	0.791
	Yes	28	2.25	0.844
Lecture elements (10)	No	17	2.71	0.588
	Yes	28	2.50	0.694
Interdisciplinary elements (11)	No	17	*2.06*	1.029
	Yes	28	*2.43*	0.790
Simulation (e.g., training game) (12)	No	17	1.76	0.970
	Yes	28	1.68	0.905
Own start-up during seminar (13)	No	17	1.59	0.870
	Yes	28	1.93	0.900
Internship in a start-up (14)	No	17	1.29	0.588
	Yes	28	1.32	0.612
Training in negotiation skills (15)	No	17	1.35	0.606
	Yes	28	1.39	0.685
Video case study (16)	No	17	1.35	0.702
	Yes	28	1.18	0.548

CONCLUSIONS AND IMPLICATIONS

Our literature review has demonstrated that instead of a coherent picture of e-educators a plethora of rather 'patchy' details currently exists. With regard to e-educators in Germany, we have only few references to compare our findings to, and the results are:

1   As in the USA, there is no common e-educator profile yet in Germany.
2   In Germany, the level of academic qualification is considerably higher for external e-educators than in the USA.
3   More than in the USA, a background in business/economic sciences is still the 'educational background number one' among e-educators in Germany, either as only degree (70 per cent), or combined with a second degree (20 per cent). The potential effects of such a 'monocultural' element on an interdisciplinary field are controversial.
4   The German entrepreneurship professors in our sample have as much experience in real-world entrepreneurship as their US-counterparts.

In addition, our findings allow for several new insights into different e-educator profiles, especially into those other than of full-time professors. In particular, a high percentage of e-educators in our sample have start-up experience, especially the external instructors (70 per cent), but also the teaching assistants (40 per cent).

The inter-group comparison of e-educator profiles across different university categories shows a distinct mix of faculty for each category. Most notably, universities of medium entrepreneurial performance feature a considerably higher share of EE-staff with a business/economics background. Compared to the best-performing universities, they run the risk of a business 'mono-culture' among their e-educators. Both privately funded universities and universities of high performance show high shares of educators with entrepreneurial experience. Universities of medium performance, on the other hand, might be able to influence their entrepreneurship rating by recruiting more interdisciplinary EE-staff.

Most importantly, our study has confirmed that the profile of an e-educator does have an impact on EE. This impact is not only a direct one, by way of influencing the actual teaching contents; it can also be an indirect one, by contributing to EE-effectiveness.

Overall, the above findings have implications at different levels: for EE in general, as well as for faculty and EE-offerings in the context of the entrepreneurial university in particular. According to a series of studies, the following implications equally apply to EE in Germany and in Europe (EU, 2003, 2006 and 2008; Hofer et al., 2010).

General implications for entrepreneurship education

1 In the interdisciplinary field of entrepreneurship, educator profiles are heterogeneous, and this has positive effects on entrepreneurship teaching quality. Given the heterogeneity of e-educators in the USA and in Germany, an introduction of standardized profiles would not only be difficult, but also counterproductive. As Neck and Greene (2011) point out, EE 'requires teaching a *method*.. . . The method is people dependent [sic] but *not* dependent on a type of person' (p. 57, emphasis added).

2 Entrepreneurship education offerings could be improved by a common additional qualification of e-educators, rather than by an overall profile 'standardization'. Such a common qualification would have to address current and future teaching staff. It should encompass the academic foundations of entrepreneurship as well as the practical foundations of teaching. Both new coherent doctoral programmes in entrepreneurship (Brush et al., 2003) and a common basic (teaching) qualification for e-educators could deliver this. Well-known programmes in this area are Babson College's Modules for Entrepreneurship Educators (MEE) in the USA as well as the qualification suggested by the international Network for Teaching Entrepreneurship (NFTE). However, there are also successful initiatives in Europe, as illustrated by the national Observatory of Pedagogical Practices in Entrepreneurship in France and the International Master of Entrepreneurship Education and Training in Denmark (OECD, 2010). In the longer term, the development of an occupational profile for e-educators might allow for quality assurance.

3 Faculty profile is a key success factor. High-performing universities show faculty with more diverse educational profiles and entrepreneurial experience. It is thus critical for universities to attract and keep the 'right' type of educator. As this process might currently be hindered by a lack of mobility of educators across the EU, the coming years will see EU initiatives to promote and support such mobility (EU, 2006).

4 It is not just the *what* and the *how* that matter, but also the *who*. In particular, e-educators' own entrepreneurial experience not only enhances the reputation of a university's entrepreneurship programme (Kabongo and McCaskey, 2011), but also contributes indirectly and significantly to the effectiveness of EE in terms of raised start-up intentions by students.

Implications for faculties and EE-offerings in the context of the entrepreneurial university

On a university level, the implications of our findings for the composition and recruitment of EE-faculty lead to four recommendations:

1   *Embrace and leverage diversity.* Our findings point out the potential of educator profiles to improve the quality of EE. This study thus supports Jones (2010) in his call for 'appreciating the nature of heterogeneity in our classrooms' (p. 71). In a European context, this can be further enabled by HEIs introducing 'cross-discipline structures' (NIRAS et al., 2008).

2   Assess the current composition of EE-faculty. In order to leverage their potential to attract 'the right kinds of educators – both academics and practitioners' (McMullan and Long, 1987, p. 272), universities first have to understand the 'make-up' of their faculties. An initial assessment of EE-faculty with own entrepreneurial experience is only one example and a first step. We recommend a more comprehensive way of how universities can evaluate their teacher profiles, based on the concept of 'the entrepreneurial leader' by Gibb et al. (2009). Building on literature including Clark's design of the entrepreneurial university organization (1998 and 2004) the authors present ten criteria (Gibb et al., 2009, Figure 6, p. 23), against which the profile of EE-faculty could be assessed.

3   Define the aspired EE-faculty composition. We recommend recruiting individual e-educators according to a university's desired EE-team composition. This might include balancing 'specialist' and 'generalist' staff as well as academically and practically experienced staff. At HEIs across the EU, e-educators with own entrepreneurial experience do 'not seem very widespread' (NIRAS et al., 2008, p. 6). This is not restricted to the EU, as reflected by a set of recommendations issued by the World Economic Forum (WEF) to all academic institutions: they encompass the guidance to 'look to recruit professors and teachers who have entrepreneurship experience' (WEF, 2009, p. 26).

4   Never underestimate the power and effectiveness of role models. One of the effects of e-educators on EE is based on an educator's existing own start-up experience, as 'educators serve as role models. There are many academics who would not make good role models for future entrepreneurs' (McMullan and Long, 1987, p. 268). The present study shows *how* role models affect EE.

Recommendations for future research
We have evaluated a snapshot of e-educator profiles on a national level and their implications for content and effectiveness of EE. The shortcomings of this design lead to three directions for complementary research. (1) It would be of interest to assess the effects of educator profiles on German EE with a longitudinal design, and to expand the current single-informant design with one e-educator per university to a multi-informant one. (2) Including different organizational levels within a university (staff level – chair level – department level – head of university) would shed light on a university's EE-strategy and resource allocation. (3) Finally, comparative studies between regions or countries are a further research area. In this context, it would be of interest to apply a different and more cross-national approach to the evaluation of a university's entrepreneurial profile. Whilst we decided to follow an existing ranking that is established in Germany, there is a range of other potential criteria for evaluation. However, examples like the traditional criteria for assessment of any kind of education organisation by the Malcolm Baldrige National Quality Award in the USA (cf. Vesper and Gartner, 1997) as well as those by NIRAS et al. (2008), applied for a European benchmark of university performance in EE, do not account for the requirements of an entrepreneurial organization. For further research beyond Germany we therefore suggest using ten aspects of specific organizational design – published by the British National Council for Graduate Entrepreneurship (NCGE) – as evaluation criteria (cf. Gibb et al., 2009, p. 17), and apply a Likert-scale.

Several other knowledge gaps have arisen throughout our research. A first promising area for future research would be the entrepreneurial university's staff: what exactly are faculty's entrepreneurial competencies, how can they be defined, and what do they contribute to the overall performance of the university? In addition, it is of interest to obtain detailed information on the current composition of EE-faculties (teams). This would allow for a better understanding of current EE-teams as well as for the comparison between universities of different entrepreneurial performance.

NOTES

*   The author of this study gratefully acknowledges the support of the German Association for Entrepreneurship-Research, -Education and -Policy (*Förderkreis Gründungs-Forschung e.V. Entrepreneurship Research* [FGF e.V.]) in the process of data collection.
1.   In the Anglo-American Higher Education system the term 'tenure' commonly refers to an academic position for life.

2. Sarasvathy (2008) also refers to the respective educating institution as an 'e-educator' (p. 310). For the purpose of this study such 'institutional e-educators' are not encompassed by the term.
3. A test for significance of the share of educators with business/economic background in our sample showed no statistically significant differences between the different types of German universities.
4. Müller (2009) identifies 'options for building up networks' by course participants as one of 'seven educational variables . . . which can positively influence the antecedents of entrepreneurial intention' (p. 1).

REFERENCES

Béchard, J. and D. Grégoire (2005), 'Entrepreneurship education revisited: The case of Higher Education', *Academy of Management Learning and Education*, **4**(1), 22–43.
Brockhaus, R.H. (1992), 'Entrepreneurship education: A research agenda', in H. Klandt and D. Müller-Böling (eds), *Internationalizing Entrepreneurship Education and Training: Proceedings of the IntEnt 92 Conference*, Dortmund, 23–26 June 1992, Dortmund: Förderkreis Gründungs-Forschung: FGF-Entrepreneurship-Research-Monographien, 3–7.
Brush, C., I. Duhaime, W. Gartner, A. Stewart, J.A. Katz, M. Hitt, S. Alvarez, G.D. Meyer and S. Venkataraman (2003), 'Doctoral education in the field of entrepreneurship', *Journal of Management*, **29**(3), 309–31.
Clark, B.R. (1998), *Creating Entrepreneurial Universities: Organizational Pathways of Transition*, Oxford: IAU Press/Elsevier.
Clark, B.R. (2004), 'Delineating the character of the entrepreneurial university', *Higher Education Policy*, **17**(4), 355–70.
Doh, J.P. (2003), 'Can leadership be taught? Perspectives from management educators', *Academy of Management Learning and Education*, **2**(1), 54–67.
Elmuti, D. (2004), 'Can management be taught?' *Management Decision*, **42**(3/4), 439–53.
EU Commission of the European Communities (2003), *Green Paper: Entrepreneurship in Europe*, Brussels: EU, COM (2003) 27 final.
EU (2006), *Entrepreneurship Education in Europe: Fostering Entrepreneurial Mindsets through Education and Learning*, final proceedings of the Conference, Oslo, 26–27 October, European Commission.
Fayolle, A., B. Gailly and N. Lassas-Clerc (2006), 'Assessing the impact of entrepreneurship education programmes: A new methodology', *Journal of European Industrial Training*, **30**(8/9), 701–20.
Fiet, J.O. (2001a), 'The theoretical side of teaching entrepreneurship', *Journal of Business Venturing*, **16**(1), 1–24.
Fiet, J.O. (2001b), 'The pedagogical side of entrepreneurship theory', *Journal of Business Venturing*, **16**(2), 101–17.
Finkle, T.A. (2007), 'Trends in the market for entrepreneurship faculty from 1989–2005', *Journal of Entrepreneurship Education*, **10**, 1–24.
Finkle, T.A., P. Stetz and M. Mallin (2007), 'Perceptions of tenure requirements and research records of entrepreneurship faculty earning tenure: 1964–2002', *Journal of Entrepreneurship Education*, **10**, 101–25.
Gartner, W.B. and K.H. Vesper (1994), 'Executive forum: Experiments in entrepreneurship education: successes and failures', *Journal of Business Venturing*, **9**(3), 179–87.
Günther, J. and K. Wagner (2008), 'Getting out of the ivory tower – new perspectives on the entrepreneurial university', *European Journal of International Management*, **2**(4), 400–417.
Gibb, A., G. Haskins and I. Robertson (2009), *Leading the Entrepreneurial University. Meeting the Entrepreneurial Development Needs of Higher Education Institutions*, pub-

lished by The National Council for Graduate Entrepreneurship (NCGE) and Saïd Business School, University of Oxford.

Haase, H. and A. Lautenschlaeger (2013), 'The ATMO-Matrix: A typology for entrepreneurship education at universities', in A. Fayolle et al. (ed.), *Handbook of Research in Entrepreneurship Education, Vol. 4, Entrepreneurial University Handbook*, Cheltenham, UK and Northampton, MA, USA: Edward Elgar (forthcoming).

Halbfas, B.G. (2006), 'Entrepreneurship education an Hochschulen – Eine wirtschaftspädagogische und -didaktische Analyse', dissertation, Bergische Universität Wuppertal, Paderborn: Eusl.

Henry, C., F. Hill and C. Leitch (2005), 'Entrepreneurship education and training: Can entrepreneurship be taught? Part I', *Education + Training*, **47**(2), 98–111.

Hills, G.E. (1988), 'Variations in university entrepreneurship education: An empirical study of an evolving field', *Journal of Business Venturing*, **3**(1), 109–22.

Hofer, A. et al. (2010), 'From strategy to practice in university entrepreneurship support: Strengthening entrepreneurship and local economic development in Eastern Germany: Youth, entrepreneurship and innovation', OECD Local Economic and Employment Development (LEED) Working Papers, 2010/09, OECD Publishing.

Janssen, J. and W. Laatz (2005), *Statistische Datenanalyse mit SPSS für Windows 5, neu bearbeitete und erweiterte Auflage*, Berlin/Heidelberg/New York: Springer-Verlag.

Jones, C. (2010), 'Accounting for student/educator diversity: Resurrecting coactions theory', in A. Fayolle (ed.), *Handbook of Entrepreneurship Education, Vol. 3, International Perspectives*, Cheltenham, UK and Northampton, MA, USA: Edward Elgar, pp. 71–85.

Kabongo, J.D. and P.H. McCaskey (2011), 'An examination of entrepreneurship educator profiles in business programs in the United States', *Journal of Small Business and Enterprise Development*, **18**(1), 27–42.

Katz, J.A. (1995), 'Managing practitioners in the entrepreneurship class', *Simulation and Gaming*, **26**(3), 361–75.

Katz, J.A. (2003), 'The chronology and intellectual trajectory of American entrepreneurship education 1876–1999', *Journal of Business Venturing*, **18**(2), 283–300.

Katz, J.A. and R.P. Green (1996), 'Academic resources for entrepreneurship education', *Simulation and Gaming*, **27**(3), 365–74.

Klandt, H. (2004), 'Entrepreneurship education and research in German-speaking Europe', *Academy of Management Learning and Education*, **3**(3), 293–301.

Klandt, H., L.T. Koch, J. Schmude and U. Knaup (2008), *FGF-Report 2008. Entrepreneurship-Professuren an deutschen Hochschulen: Ausrichtung, Organisation und Vernetzung*, Bonn/Germany: FGF – Förderkreis Gründungs-Forschung e.V.

Matlay, H. (2010), 'Stakeholder participation in, and impact upon, entrepreneurship education in the UK', in A.A. Fayolle (ed.), *Handbook of Entrepreneurship Education, Vol. 3, International Perspectives*, Cheltenham, UK and Northampton, MA, USA: Edward Elgar, pp. 110–21.

McMullan, W.E. and W.A. Long (1987), 'Entrepreneurship education in the nineties', *Journal of Business Venturing*, **2**(3), 261–75.

Müller, S. (2009), 'Encouraging future entrepreneurs: The effect of entrepreneurship course characteristics on entrepreneurial intention', dissertation, Universität St. Gallen, Switzerland.

Neck, H.M. and P.G. Greene (2011), 'Entrepreneurship education: Known worlds and new frontiers', *Journal of Small Business Management*, **49**(1), 67–68.

NIRAS et al. (2008), *Survey of Entrepreneurship in Higher Education in Europe*, October 2008, requested by the European Commission, Directorate-General for Enterprise and Industry, accessed 13 August at http://ec.europa.eu/enterprise/policies/sme/files/support_measures/training_education/highedsurvey_en.pdf.

Peterman, N. and J. Kennedy (2003), 'Enterprise education: Influencing students' perceptions of entrepreneurship', *Entrepreneurship Theory and Practice*, **28**(2), 129–35.

Pittaway, L. and J. Cope (2007), 'Entrepreneurship education: A systematic review of the evidence', *International Small Business Journal*, **25**(5), 479–510.

Plaschka, G.R. and H.P. Welsch (1990), 'Emerging structures in entrepreneurship education: Curricular designs and strategies', *Entrepreneurship Theory and Practice*, **14**(3), 55–71.

Potter, J. (ed.) (2008), *Entrepreneurship and Higher Education*, Paris: OECD Publications.

Rabbior, G. (1990), 'Elements of a successful entrepreneurship/economics education program', in C.A. Kent, (ed.), *Entrepreneurship Education. Current Developments, Future Directions*, New York: Quorum Books, pp. 53–65.

Robbers, I. (2010), 'Pedagogical professionalism of the entrepreneurship educator', paper presented at the Conference Internationalizing Entrepreneurship Education and Training (IntEnt), 5–8 July 2010, at the HAN University of Applied Sciences, Arnhem [unpublished].

Sarasvathy, S.D. (2008), *Effectuation. Elements of Entrepreneurial Expertise*, Cheltenham, UK and Northampton, MA, USA: Edward Elgar Publishing.

Schleinkofer, M. and M. Kulicke (2009), *Entrepreneurship Education an deutschen Hochschulen – Studie der wissenschaftlichen Begleitforschung zu 'EXIST – Existenzgründungen aus der Wissenschaft'*, Stuttgart: Fraunhofer Verlag.

Schmude, J. and S. Heumann (2011), *Vom Studenten zum Unternehmer: Welche Universität bietet die besten Chancen*, published by the Lehrstuhl für Wirtschaftsgeographie und Tourismusforschung der Ludwig-Maximilians-Universität, Munich.

Shepherd, D. (2004), 'Educating entrepreneurship students about emotion and learning from failure', *Academy of Management Learning and Education*, **3**(3), 274–87.

Solomon, G. (2007), 'An examination of entrepreneurship education in the United States', *Journal of Small Business and Enterprise Development*, **14**(2), 168–82.

Vesper, K.H. and W.B. Gartner (1997), 'Measuring progress in entrepreneurship education', *Journal of Business Venturing*, **12**(5), 403–22.

World Economic Forum (2009), *Educating the Next Wave of Entrepreneurs. Report on Entrepreneurship Education, Executive Summary*, accessed 13 August 2013 at http://www3.weforum.org/docs/WEF_GEI_EducatingNextEntrepreneurs_ExecutiveSummary_2009.pdf.

13. Global start-up internships as a source of experiential learning

Truls Erikson, Mari Saua Svalastog and Daniel Leunbach

INTRODUCTION

To prepare students for the realities of today's ever-changing, hyper-competitive and global marketplace, new forms of academic–industry collaborations need to be explored and developed. In fact, EU and national policies are gradually becoming more focused on the role of universities in job creation. This has led to increased focus on academic–industry collaborations (Etzkowitz, 1998), and not least, entrepreneurship education.

During the 1980s, the atmosphere for academic institutions changed as new disciplines such as biotechnology and ICT developed remarkably quickly (Iversen et al. 2007). The Bayh-Dole Act in the USA created debates in many Western countries, including Norway, and a comparable law was introduced in 2003. This law extended the societal role of Norwegian universities to include the 'Third Mission'. In practice, the law abolished professors' long-held privilege regarding ownership of his or her inventions (ibid., p. 398), and it smoothed the progress of the Technology Transfer Offices. It was during these formative days that Gründerskolen emerged, and the programme's emergence can be seen in light of these Third Mission debates. As such, we consider Gründerskolen as a response to these wider societal changes.

The emphasis of Gründerskolen is on international technology entrepreneurship, and the curriculum reflects the workload of a full semester. The programme, which is carefully designed around experiential learning, is, of course, experience-based as students work on real projects, not only as part of their course assignments, but also as part of a 12-week start-up internship abroad. As such, it is one way of facilitating academic–industry collaborations.

EXPERIENCE AS THE SOURCE OF LEARNING

Those familiar with experiential learning theory (ELT) will know that among the six propositions currently shared by ELT scholars, the most central is the notion that learning is best conceived as a process and not in terms of outcomes (Kolb and Kolb, 2009). Consistent with this line of reasoning, ELT advocates that learning and knowledge creation should be viewed as an endless ubiquitous process of grasping and transforming experience: 'Knowledge results from the combination of grasping and transforming experience' (Kolb, 1984, p. 41), where 'the process and goal of education are one and the same thing' (Dewey, 1897, p. 9). Depending on their field of origin, we suspect that readers unfamiliar with this literature will vary in their 'knee-jerk' reaction to this open disregard for outcomes. The whole field of strategic management for example, is arguably structured around the shared practice of developing explanations for variance in organizational outcomes, most notably performance (Barney and Clark, 2007). Confounding as it may sound, the proposition is nonetheless key to understanding what Kolb and Kolb (2005, p. 193) described as 'above all a philosophy of education'. Building on the work of twentieth-century scholars John Dewey, Kurt Lewin, Jean Piaget and others, ELT upholds that experience should play a fundamental role in theories of human development and learning. Experiential learning theorists define learning as 'the process whereby knowledge is created through the transformation of experience' (Kolb, 1984, p. 38). The experiential learning cycle (Figure 13.1) provides a useful model of ELT. As indicated by this holistic model, concrete experience (CE) and abstract conceptualization (AC), each represent two dialectically related means of grasping experience; similarly, reflective observation (RO) and active experimentation (AE) each represent two dialectically related means of transforming experience.

This idealized learning cycle suggests a learning process where the learner undergoes a continuous process of experiencing, reflecting, thinking and acting. As pointed out by Little (1993), the model provides a suitable framework for creating a theoretical basis for internships, as 'internships are virtually a point-by-point application of the essential activities of this model' (p. 444). Surprisingly, this is the only published study known to us that has used ELT as a theoretical foundation for studying internships. This is less strange, however, if one considers the scarcity of internship research in general. In fact, a recent review, Narayanan et al. (2010) found only 22 published studies (none of which looked at internship-based entrepreneurship programmes). It has been estimated that about 75 per cent of US college students complete an internship before graduation (Coco, 2000). The majority of these internships, however, take place in addition

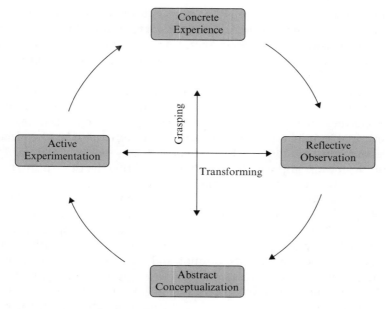

Source: Adapted from Kolb and Kolb (2008).

Figure 13.1   Experiential learning cycle

to, and outside of, any formal learning experience (D'Abate et al., 2009). Despite the wide prevalence of internship participation and the growing integration of internships into the formal learning experience, little is still known about the effectiveness of such educational initiatives and about the value of internships in general. Furthermore, few of the studies that exist are explicitly grounded in a conceptual model. Narayanan et al. (2010, p. 62) summarize this quite succinctly 'Simply put, the literature on internship experiences is largely descriptive and anecdotal'. Considering this lack of theoretical grounding, two legitimate questions emerge. First, how can we justify our use of internships? In other words, how are we to respond to those who claim that our experiential learning initiatives are 'founded on sand'? The need for a better theoretical foundation was emphasized by Little two decades ago:

> Theoretical principles are necessary to the people working with internships and other experiential activities so that they can articulate persuasively the necessity for, and the benefits of, such experiences for students at a level beyond the first-hand testimonials most of us seem to rely on to justify such experiential activity for academic credit. (Little, 1993, p. 447)

Second, assuming, like Little (1993), that our intuitions are correct, that internships and other experiential activities represent useful and valuable learning tools; how can we design these learning experiences so as to maximize their effectiveness? These are some of the questions we consider in this chapter.

So, why should we bother with internships in the first place? In an amusing attempt to deal with this question, McCormick (1993), provides the following analogy: 'The difference between classroom learning and experiential learning in an internship is like the difference between learning about roller coasters watching one from across the street and learning about them while gripping the front handrail during the ride' (p. 261).

Luckily, we do not have to rely on personal anecdotes and colourful analogies alone when justifying our use of internships. For instance, based on their survey of 144 alumni from a public university in the USA, Gault et al. (2000) reported a significant relationship between early career success and past participation in an undergraduate internship. Advantages included less time to obtain first position and increased monetary compensation, as well as greater overall job satisfaction. A recent review by Liu et al. (2011) lists additional benefits, including job-related skill enhancement, and emphasizes that internships offer students a valuable chance to apply classroom knowledge to practical problems (Clark, 2003; D'Abate et al., 2009; Liu et al., 2011), and help ease students' role transition by exposing them to the realities of the business world (Taylor, 1985, 1988; Knouse et al., 1999; Gault et al., 2000; Liu et al., 2011). Referring to the Cooperative Education Program at the University of Cincinnati, Gault et al. (2000) call attention to the fact that college-endorsed employment programmes have been recorded as early as 1906 and assert that 'Despite nearly 100 years of offering credit for internships, existing higher-education assessment research has focused primarily on the effects of classroom instruction' (p. 46).

While the literature does not provide conclusive support, the limited empirical research that does exist is essentially supportive of internships as a means to facilitate student learning. Besides, simply pointing out that the literature is scattered and under-developed, is, of course, not a convincing argument against the use of internships in itself. Considering the widespread call to formally integrate internships into academic curricula (D'Abate et al., 2009) and the aforementioned popularity of internship participation (Coco, 2000), a phenomenon that has existed for at least 105 years, we are arguably better off spending our limited resources investigating ways to improve our experiential initiatives.

Next, we elaborate on Gründerskolen as a case. As a research method we have relied on years of participative observation, archival data, interviews and recent surveys. We have structured the presentation to first start with the programme's emergence, we then elaborate on its structure and underlying philosophy. Thereafter we report on a survey on internship job and environmental characteristics. The underlying assumption is that these job and environmental characteristics contribute in shaping valued learning experiences.

CASE DESCRIPTION: GRÜNDERSKOLEN

Emergence

The very first initiative behind Gründerskolen was taken by professor Nils D. Christophersen from the Department of Informatics at the University of Oslo (UiO), Norway. During the fall of 1997, Professor Christophersen had a sabbatical period at Stanford University in the USA. Noticing the much tighter connection and collaboration between the university and the industry compared to his experiences in Norway, he started thinking about how Norway could get more of the same fruitful collaborations.

In the fall of 1998, back in Norway, Christophersen was elected head of his department. In his new position he brought with him his ideas of finding a way to strengthen academic–industry collaboration. He was soon convinced that a good way to do so might be to send aspiring young students abroad to places like Silicon Valley so that they could experience the many possibilities such collaborations could provide, such as the commercialization of research through licensing or the establishing of new ventures. He wanted students three years into their university degrees to experience internships in high-tech start-ups, in addition to following an entrepreneurship course at a university abroad to help bridge practice and theory.

Professor Christophersen shared his ideas with colleagues and other potential partners, but the main feedback he received was that the internship component did not fit very well with the traditional teaching practices at the university. This component would also be a problem for the State Education Loan Fund in Norway, which provides substantial financial support to Norwegian students studying in Norway and abroad. It was not until a meeting with representatives from the Norwegian Trade Council's (NTC) office in San Francisco that the ball started rolling. The NTC's work involves supporting Norwegian industry in getting access to the US market and vice versa. The people at NTC were eager to support an exchange programme to foster an entrepreneurial mindset among Norwegian students, and were willing to take on the responsibility of organizing everything abroad: a relatively complex task that included identifying potential intern-hosting start-up companies in the Silicon Valley area, follow-up of companies and students, securing agreements with a university partner in the USA to issue student visas and provide a relevant course, securing housing for the students, as well as being the students' main point of contact while abroad. The involved parties also agreed that the students should have some basic knowledge on the subject of entrepreneurship before travelling abroad to prepare them for their internships during the summer. Since UiO did not have a business school, an agreement was made with the BI School of Management (BI) in Oslo that students from UiO could attend a typical business plan course at BI during the spring semester. Having the stay abroad during the summer was important in getting the programme approved by the university, as it would not interfere with the students' main studies.

Six students of informatics were recruited to participate in the pilot programme in 1999. The programme was named Gründerskolen, from the German word '*Gründer*', which means one who is running his or her own business and '*skolen*' which means 'the school' in Norwegian. The name was intended to reflect the hands-on and practical nature of the study programme. When the first six students got back from the USA in the fall of 1999, they formally presented their experiences and learning outcomes to faculty, staff and students. It was obvious from their convincing professional presentations that the students had matured over the summer. The students had clearly caught some of the US inspiration, self-confidence and belief in entrepreneurship as a way of realizing the potential of academic research. Following the success of the initial pilot, a conscious decision was made to attract students from different academic backgrounds into the programme, this included recruiting students from the Norwegian University of Science and Technology (NTNU) in Trondheim, another region in Norway, and business students from BI. It was arranged so that the students from NTNU could follow an introductory course at their local university, similar to the course provided by BI in Oslo. This allowed the NTNU students to fulfil the introductory course requirements locally in Trondheim rather than travelling to Oslo. Twenty-one students completed the programme in 2000, and the programme grew rapidly in the years that followed, as shown in Table 13.1 and in Figure 13.2.

Current Programme Structure, Status and Success Factors

While the programme has developed considerably in terms of student numbers and national and international partners, the initial ideas for the

Table 13.1   The table summarizes the growth of Gründerskolen with regard to the number of students who have completed the programme every year, and when new destinations abroad were added. Some destinations have been terminated, for various reasons.

Year	No. of students	Programme Destinations						
		Silicon Valley*	Boston	Singapore	Shanghai	South Africa**	London	Houston
1999	6	✓						
2000	21	✓						
2001	49	✓						
2002	60	✓	✓	✓				
2003	67	✓	✓	✓				
2004	131	✓	✓	✓	✓			
2005	139	✓	✓	✓	✓	✓		
2006	144	✓	✓	✓	✓	✓	✓	
2007	98	✓	✓	✓	✓	✓		
2008	137	✓	✓	✓	✓	✓		
2009	143	✓	✓	✓	✓	✓		✓
2010	146	✓	✓	✓		✓		✓
2011	150	✓	✓	✓		✓		✓
2012	163	✓	✓	✓		✓		✓

Note: * San Jose and/or San Francisco; ** Johannesburg or Cape Town.

programme have been kept intact over the years. A summary of the most important programme characteristics is given below:

- The programme teaches technology entrepreneurship.
- The aim is to inspire students to start their own businesses or work with entrepreneurship and innovation in other ways, and increase their chances of success by equipping them with relevant theory, experience and networks.
- The main part of the programme is a 12-week stay abroad, where the students work full-time in start-up companies and follow an entrepreneurship course during evenings/weekends.
- Before the stay abroad the students follow an introductory course in entrepreneurship.
- In preparation for their stay abroad, all the accepted students attend a common seminar that is specifically designed to prepare them for their stay abroad, both practically and mentally. Lectures on cross-cultural understanding, reflective practices and leadership are

No. of students
180
160
140
120
100
80
60
40
20
0
1999
2000
2001
2002
2003
2004
2005
2006
2007
2008
2009
2010
2011
2012
Year

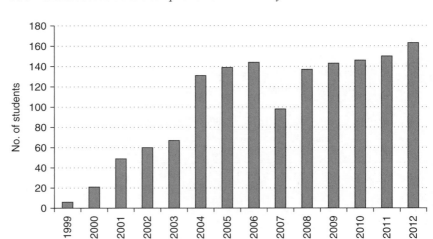

Figure 13.2 *The figure provides a graphical illustration of the growth of Gründerskolen with regard to the number of students who have completed the programme every year. The significantly lower number in 2007 was mainly caused by an extremely preferable (to the students) employment market, which caused many more students than usual to prioritize work instead of education.*

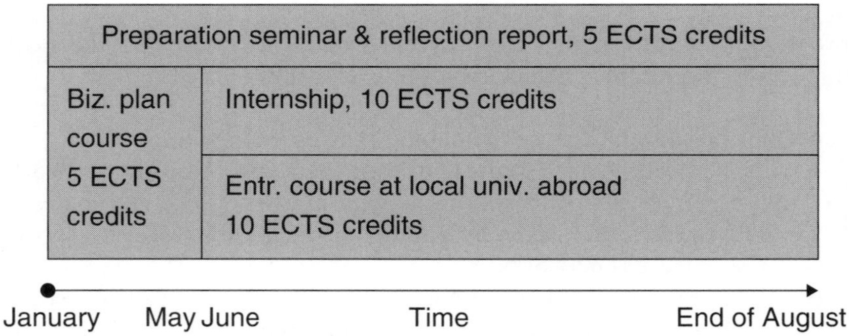

Preparation seminar & reflection report, 5 ECTS credits
Biz. plan course 5 ECTS credits
Internship, 10 ECTS credits
Entr. course at local univ. abroad 10 ECTS credits
January
May June
Time
End of August

Figure 13.3 *The figure shows the Gründerskolen programme structure*

typical topics covered. While abroad, the students reflect on and record their experiences in diary format and they hand in a reflection report at the end of their stay. Figure 13.3 summarizes the structure of the programme.

- For every student cohort, there are typically 30–40 students at each destination.
- The programme is open to students from all disciplines; the aim of the programme is that one-third of the accepted students have a background within disciplines such as engineering, natural sciences or medicine, one-third from disciplines within management, economics and marketing, and one-third from other disciplines.
- The programme consists of 30 ECTS[1] credits at Master's level, as the minimum admission requirement is a completed Bachelor's degree or equivalent.
- The programme's current destinations abroad and the university partners there are San Francisco (UC Berkeley), Boston (Boston University), Singapore (National University of Singapore), Houston (Rice University) and Cape Town (University of Cape Town). It should be noted that in 2009 the Cape Town programme was changed into a programme focusing on social entrepreneurship, but still with the internship experience as a key component.

The Gründerskolen programme has been acknowledged with two prizes. In 2006, it was awarded 'Best Learning Environment' at the University of Oslo. In 2007 the programme was awarded by the Norwegian Agency for Quality Assurance in Education, which emphasized the thorough planning and execution of the stay abroad. In 2011, 86 per cent of the students said that they would recommend the programme to other students, and 70 per cent of the 2012 applicants said they knew someone who had previously attended the programme. Some of the positive outcomes highlighted by former students include the experience of personal growth from having dealt with many challenges and the new network of highly competent and ambitious people from a lot of different disciplines.

There are three main factors that we believe have been crucial for the establishment and growth of the Gründerskolen programme. First, it could not have been done without a partner like the NTC offices abroad with their local industry knowledge, network and ability to deal with all sorts of issues that arise with young students abroad. All new destinations have been established in cities where entrepreneurship activity levels are considered higher than in Norway and where NTC has an office. It should be noted that from 2004, NTC was included in a new organization called Innovation Norway (IN), which is the Norwegian government's most important instrument for regional industrial development. Innovation Norway is also the government's official trade representative abroad, and these trade offices are typically located at, or near, the Norwegian embassies and consulates.

Second, the close collaboration between higher learning institutions in Norway has been crucial for scaling the programme to its current student number. The careful yet resource-demanding recruitment and interviewing process is distributed across many different learning institutions throughout Norway. Former students help out at their school together with local staff. These institutions also offer introductory courses required before the stay abroad for the locally accepted students.

Third, the State Educational Loan Fund, which was sceptical about supporting the internship component of the programme, as this was something very different than what it usually supported, were convinced to do so in the end, although there is still an ongoing debate regarding whether it should do so or not. So far the government has instructed it directly to continue with the support, which is given to the students as grants and loans. This helps making the tuition fees abroad affordable to most Norwegian students. The group of facilitating actors in the programme and how they affect each other is shown in Figure 13.4. As governmental policies encourage learning institutions in Norway to collaborate and also strive for more student exchanges this motivates further cooperation around a programme such as Gründerskolen.

Next, we turn to the last part of this chapter. Since we know so little about what really works and what does not work with regard to international start-up internships we have chosen an explorative 'fact-based' research design (Hambrick, 2007) where we seek to tap into what really makes this a good learning experience for the students. For this, we build on the D'Abate et al. (2009) study.

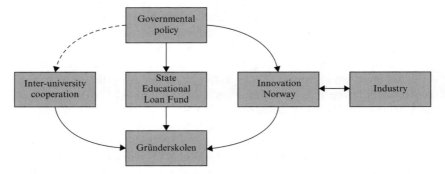

Figure 13.4   The group of facilitating actors in the programme and how they affect each other

Table 13.2   Survey details

	Stratified Study Samples	
	2010 cohort	2010 and the 2011 cohort
Average completion time	Approx 15 min.	Approx 14 min.
Panellist count	132	265
Saw e-mail	76	128
Clicked through	52	104
Partial completes	1	6
Reached end	38	70
Total responded	39	76

EXPLORING THE INTERNSHIP CHARACTERISTICS THAT SHAPE VALUED EXPERIENTIAL LEARNING

As part of this study, we collected survey data from both the 2010 and the 2011 cohort. The most recent alumni were contacted by e-mail during April and May 2012. The survey had 45 questions, and was live for two weeks, with one reminder. Among those 265 alumni, 128 saw the e-mail, 104 clicked through. As seen in Table 13.2, 76 of the responses are usable, which reflects a response rate of 60 per cent based on those who saw the e-mail, or an effective response rate of 29 per cent considering the whole sample frame. Table 13.2 illustrates the details from the data collection.

In this study, we replicate the D'Abate et al. (2009) study. D'Abate and colleagues researched Bachelor's students in management, and focused on what job characteristics, work environment characteristics and other contextual characteristics were associated with internship satisfaction. In our work, we address Master's-level students with diverse backgrounds minoring in entrepreneurship, and we control for several contextual factors.

D'Abate and colleagues build their study on the insights from Steers and Porter (1991), and not least, Hackman and Oldham's (1975, 1980) seminal work. In the current study, we seek to explore which factors are associated with valued experiential learning. In this context, we operationalize valued experiential learning with internship satisfaction. Next, we elaborate on the dependent and the independent variables of this internship study.

Dependent variable: internship satisfaction
We used a version of the job satisfaction scale based on Hackman and Oldham (1975, 1980) to measure satisfaction with the internships. These are the same measures as D'Abate and colleagues employed. The three

items read as the following: 'Generally speaking, I was very satisfied with my internship', 'I frequently thought of quitting my internship/or changing the internship company' (reversed), and 'I was generally very satisfied with the kind of work I did at my internship'. Here we employed a seven-point Likert scale.

Independent variable: job characteristics

Here, we built on Hackman and Oldman's (1980) Job Characteristics Model that highlights the following job-related factors: skill variety, task identification, task significance, autonomy at work and on-the-job feedback – the same measures as D'Abate and colleagues employed in their study:

Skill variety captures how varied the job tasks are. It was measured with the following items: 'How much variety was there at your internship?' (That is, to what extent did the internship require you to do many different things at work, using a variety of your skills and talents?), 'The internship required me to use a number of complex or high-level skills', and 'The internship was quite simple and repetitive (reversed)'.

Task identification captures the wholeness of a task, as an identifiable piece of work, and was measured with the following items: 'To what extent did your internship involve doing a "whole" and identifiable piece of work? That is, was the internship a complete piece of work that had an obvious beginning and end? Or was it only a small part of the overall piece of work, which was finished by other people or automated machines?', 'The internship was arranged so that I did not have the chance to do an entire piece of work from beginning to end', The internship provided me the chance to completely finish the pieces of work I began'.

Task significance is the extent a job has an impact on other people. It is measured by means of the following three items: 'In general, how significant or important was your internship? That is, were the results of your work likely to significantly affect the lives or well-being of other people?', 'The internship itself was not very significant or important in the broader scheme of things', 'This internship was one where a lot of other people could be affected by how well the work got done'.

Autonomy is the amount of freedom the intern is given at the workplace. We measured it by means of the following three items: 'How much autonomy was there in your internship? That is, to what extent did your internship permit you to decide on your own how to go about doing the work?', 'The internship gave me considerable opportunity for independence and freedom in how I did the work', 'The internship denied me any chance to use my personal initiative or judgement in carrying out the work'.

Feedback is the amount of information that the intern is given about their effectiveness. It is measured by means of the following three items: 'To what extent did doing the internship itself provide you with information about your work performance? That is, did the actual work itself provide clues about how well you were doing – aside from any "feedback" co-workers or supervisors may provide?', 'The internship itself provided very few clues about whether or not I was performing well', 'Just doing the work required by the internship provided many chances for me to figure out how well I was doing'. We applied five-point Likert scales to all these items.

Basically, these factors capture what an intern does at work (Steers and Porter, 1991, p. 22; D'Abate et al., 2009). In practice, we measure here a set of job-related factors that may contribute to shape valued learning experiences. Table 13.3 shows that these factors are highly correlated with internship satisfaction (the first numbered column).

Independent variable: work environment characteristics
Work environment characteristics differ from job characteristics in the way that they are indirectly shaping learning experiences as they relate to the affect-based characteristics of the environment. Extant research points to five such characteristics: learning opportunities, career choice alternatives, supervisory support, co-worker support and satisfaction with the choice of internship company. Next, we elaborate on these in turn.

Learning opportunities are considered a significant prerequisite for experiential learning. This variable is meant to capture the richness of learning opportunities. The three items read as: 'My internship taught me a lot of things that I would never have been able to learn elsewhere', 'My internship did not help me learn anything new (reversed)', and 'My internship provided me with a chance to learn a lot more about entrepreneurship'.

Career choice alternative: this variable captures the attractiveness of the type of work they did. The three items read as: 'My internship helped me determine that this was a field I was interested in for a career'. 'My internship helped me decide that this was not a field I would want to work in (reversed)', and 'My internship provided me with opportunities to examine a potential career field'.

Supervisory support is normally considered to be a vital ingredient in learning. We measured it by means of the following three items: 'My internship supervisor helped make my internship a pleasant experience', 'My internship supervisor acted as a mentor to me while I was interning', and 'My internship supervisor did not provide me with enough support while I was doing my internship'.

Co-worker support may also be associated with a good practice. The three items read as: 'My internship co-workers helped to make my internship a good experience', 'I really liked the people that I worked with at

Table 13.3　Descriptive statistics and Pearson's correlations (2-tailed)

	Mean	SD	1	2	3	4	5	6
1 Internship satisfaction	16.06	3.66	1.00					
2 Age	26.46	2.53	−0.016	1.00				
3 Gender	0.58	0.50	−0.122	−0.054	1.00			
4 Firm size	19.71	34.75	0.195	−0.030	−0.227	1.00		
5 Flexibility at work	6.55	2.36	0.173	0.027	0.314	0.042	1.00	0.929
6 Long commute to work	7.13	3.32	0.150	−0.224	0.042	−0.134	0.125	1.00
7 Socialize with cohort	10.13	3.07	−0.097	−0.128	−0.016	0.003	−0.005	0.054
8 Skill variety	9.94	3.03	0.688	0.229	−0.141	0.045	−0.012	0.101
9 Task identification	19.99	2.75	0.403	−0.011	0.030	0.155	0.129	0.150
10 Task significance	9.49	2.79	0.616	0.008	−0.220	0.150	0.006	0.025
11 Autonomy at work	11.82	2.49	0.456	0.074	0.064	0.082	0.341	0.017
12 On-the-job feedback	9.64	2.92	0.524	0.000	−0.045	0.095	0.036	0.228
13 Learning opportunities	11.57	2.79	0.596	−0.025	−0.169	−0.029	0.019	0.083
14 Career alternative	10.43	3.18	0.617	0.032	0.075	0.037	0.132	0.169
15 Supervisory support	10.59	3.41	0.568	−0.160	−0.070	0.200	0.055	0.216
16 Co-worker support	12.92	2.30	0.440	−0.105	−0.051	−0.071	0.067	0.269
17 Company satisfaction	8.24	2.09	0.705	−0.165	0.012	0.029	0.024	0.244

Note:　$* p < 0.05.$ $** p < 0.01.$ $*** p < 0.001.$ Cronbach's alphas are reported crosswise, except for internship satisfaction (0.759) and firm satisfaction (0.925).

my internship', 'I did not get along with the people I worked with at my internship'. We applied five-point Likert scales to all these items as well.

Satisfaction with the choice of company may also be a viable factor when assessing the success of an internship. The two items we employed read as: 'I really liked the company that I did my internship with', 'I did not like the company that I worked for while doing my internship' (reversed).

7	8	9	10	11	12	13	14	15	16	17
0.841										
1.00	0.728									
−0.115	1.00	0.818								
−0.016	0.514	1.00	0.791							
−0.144	0.667	0.400	1.00	0.734						
−0.161	0.533	0.375	0.319	1.00	0.814					
−0.054	0.571	0.463	0.633	0.243	1.00	0.793				
−0.031	0.568	0.209	0.506	0.231	0.421	1.00	0.796			
−0.144	0.548	0.334	0.527	0.378	0.463	0.504	1.00	0.724		
−0.056	0.465	0.251	0.401	0.335	0.532	0.458	0.357	1.00	0.837	
0.073	0.379	0.241	0.254	0.0341	0.416	0.484	0.332	0.455	1.00	0.794
−0.034	0.437	0.175	0.464	0.323	0.513	0.504	0.405	0.0667	0.558	1.00

Control variables

In addition, we included some contextual control variables such as age, gender, firm size, flexibility at work, long commute to work, and the perceived role of the study cohort (that is, to what extend did they also learn from debating and benchmarking their internships with their study peers). Flexibility at work was measured by means of the following two items: 'I was allowed to set my own hours at my internship', and 'My internship had flexible hours'. Here we used a five-point Likert scale.

RESULTS FROM THE QUANTITATIVE SURVEY ANALYSIS

Table 13.3 gives us a first insight to the explored relationships. It basically shows that internship satisfaction is moderately to strongly correlated with all the factors sub-grouped to both internship job characteristics, and work environmental characteristics. However, if we control for the effects of other related variables, we obtain a more refined insight. From Table 13.4, we see that flexibility at work is important for internship satisfaction. Moreover, we see that skill variety is a key success factor. Internships that facilitate the use of a number of complex, or high-level

Table 13.4   Job and environmental characteristics shaping internship satisfaction

	Model 1	Model 2	Model 3	Model 4
Control variables				
Intercept	14.00*	9.17†	3.01	3.40
Age	−0.001	−0.122	0.043	−0.040
Gender	−0.151	−0.039	−0.140+	−0.118
Size of the start-up	0.155	0.107	0.109	0.101
Flexibility at work	0.190	0.161†	0.155*	0.182*
Long commute to work	0.156	0.047	−0.025	−0.038
Socialize with cohort	−0.106	−0.013	−0.020	−0.014
Independent variables				
Job characteristics				
Skill variety		0.511***		0.360**
Task identification		−0.043		0.076
Task significance		0.191		−0.018
Autonomy at work		0.064		−0.037
On-the-job feedback		0.087		−0.071
Work environment characteristics				
Learning opportunities			0.165†	0.050
Career alternative			0.314***	0.210*
Supervisory support			0.026	−0.035
Co-worker support			−0.036	−0.044
Company satisfaction			0.496***	0.500***
Adjusted R^2	0.034	0.517***	0.640***	0.698***
F	1.450	8.396	13.261	11.961
N	76	76	76	76

Note: † $p < 0.1$; * $p < 0.05$; ** $p < 0.01$; *** $p < 0.001$. Missing values are replaced with means.

skills, and that require a variety of skills and talents are apparently key to internship satisfaction. It is noteworthy that this is the only significant finding among the identified job characteristics.

From the work environment characteristics section in Table 13.4, we also see that those satisfied with the internship are those who have been able to determine whether entrepreneurship is feasible as a career path. This variable captures what Clarysse et al. (2011) point out, that regardless of whether the experience was a positive or negative one the learning outcome may be deemed as a positive one. Finally, satisfaction with the choice of company appears to be the most important factor contributing to internship satisfaction. It basically means that the selection of the company is key to a good internship programme, but it also means that it is important that potential internship students are open to a variety of types of firms. That is, the narrower the choice preferences, the lesser the likelihood for satisfaction with their choices.

The variance inflation factors are all well within acceptable ranges (1.36–3.89), so multicollinearity is not an issue. However, this analysis gives us a brief overview into some of the tentatively key factors that matters with regard to valued experiential learning, but it does not provide evidence of any mediating or moderating effects (Siegel and Bowen, 1971), only direct effects. Future studies should therefore seek to uncover the more complex relationships between the factors that contribute to experiential learning. For instance, future studies could seek to capture the complexity by comparing different experiential learning styles with factors contributing to internship satisfaction or its effectiveness, because people with various learning styles may value internship characteristics differently. Future studies could also address the more complicated mediating or moderating effects that obviously are in play, as most of the positive correlates to internship satisfaction in Table 13.3 disappeared in Table 13.4. This indicates that there may be many complex patterns of mediating and/or interacting effects involved. Employing a fact-based analysis allows us to discover and explore such patterns that yield insight to our research questions. As our study here shows, at least flexibility at work, skill variety, the chance to determine whether this is a feasible career path, and the choice of company, seem to be vital factors in developing experiential based learning programmes in entrepreneurship.

Internship directors may play an important organizing role, as pointed out by Little (1993). In other words, the organizers and other facilitators of internships are key to successful experiential learning. A good indicator of this assertion is the strong relationship between internship satisfaction and the choice of companies. That is, facilitators and organizers need to be aware of their role as 'co-creators' in the experiential learning process.

CONCLUSION

We have in this chapter shown that internships provide a useful learning vehicle in entrepreneurship education, and experiential learning theory appears useful in understanding how students acquire and not least transfer information from experience. Future studies could look into how experiential learning theory relates to entrepreneurship education in general, not only how experiential learning theory relates to ideation (Gemmel et al., 2011), opportunity identification (Corbett, 2005, 2007) or to cross-cultural learning (Yamasaki and Kayes, 2004).

We have in this chapter also illustrated the emergence, and the partial functioning of 'global learning labs' in entrepreneurship. These experiential learning labs represent promising playgrounds for students, and are instrumental in nurturing students' entrepreneurial abilities and in strengthening their entrepreneurial mindsets. We have also been able to identify a few key characteristics that contribute in shaping valued learning experiences; these include satisfaction with the choice of company, skill variety in the assignment and the opportunity to elucidate whether entrepreneurship is a viable future career option.

In moving their institutions into a more entrepreneurial mode, university staff are frequently faced with the universal challenge of structural inertia, especially when designing experiential learning for which there are limited theoretical foundations. With hindsight, it seems evident that Gründerskolen provides a noteworthy and well-documented example of university entrepreneurship; our hope is that this chapter has provided some clues to how internships (whatever form they may take) can contribute to bridging academic–industry collaborations.

NOTE

1. European Credit Transfer and Accumulation System (ECTS) is a standard for comparing the study attainment and performance of students of Higher Education across the European Union and other collaborating European countries.

REFERENCES

Barney, J.B. and D.N. Clark (2007), *Resource-based Theory: Creating and Sustaining Competitive Advantage*, Oxford: Oxford University Press.
Clark, S.C. (2003), 'Enhancing the educational value of business internships', *Journal of Management Education*, **27**(4), 472–84.
Clarysse, B., V. Tartari and A. Salter (2011), 'The impact of entrepreneurial capacity, expe-

rience, and organizational support on academic entrepreneurship', *Research Policy*, **40**, 1084–93.

Coco, M. (2000), 'Internships: A try before you buy arrangement', *S.A.M. Advanced Management Journal*, **65**(2), 41–4.

Corbett, A.C. (2005), 'Experiential learning within the process of opportunity identification and exploitation', *Entrepreneurship Theory and Practice*, **29**(4), 473–91.

Corbett, A.C. (2007), 'Learning asymmetries and the discovery of entrepreneurial opportunities', *Journal of Business Venturing*, **22**(1), 97–118.

D'Abate, C.P., M.A. Youndt and K.E. Wenzel (2009), 'Making the most out of an internship: An empirical study of internship satisfaction', *Academy of Management Learning and Education*, **8**(4), 527–39.

Dewey, J. (1897), 'My pedagogic creed', *The School Journal*, **LIV**(3), 77–80.

Etzkowitz, H. (1998), 'The norms of entrepreneurial science: Cognitive effects of the new university–industry linkages', *Research Policy*, **27**(8), 823–33.

Gault, J., J. Redington and T. Schlager (2000), 'Undergraduate business internships and career success: Are they related?' *Journal of Marketing Education*, **22**(1), 45–53.

Gemmel, R.M., R.J. Boland and D.A. Kolb (2011), 'The socio-cognitive dynamics of entrepreneurial ideation', *Entrepreneurship Theory and Practice*, September, 1–21.

Hackman, J.R. and G.R. Oldham (1975), 'Development of the job diagnostic survey', *Journal of Applied Psychology*, **60**(2), 159–70.

Hackman, J.R. and G.R. Oldham (1980), *Work Redesign*, Reading, MA: Addison-Wesley Publishing Company.

Hambrick, D.C. (2007), 'The field of management's devotion to theory: Too much of a good thing?' *Academy of Management Journal*, **50**(6), 1346–52.

Iversen, E.J., M. Gulbrandsen and A. Klitko (2007), 'A baseline for the impact of academic patenting legislation in Norway', *Scientometrics*, **70**(2), 393–414.

Knouse, S.B., J.T. Tanner and E. Harris (1999), 'The relation of college internships, college performance, and subsequent job opportunity', *Journal of Employment Counseling*, **36**(1), 35–43.

Kolb, D.A. (1984), *Experiential Learning: Experience as the Source of Learning and Development*, Englewood Cliffs, NJ: Prentice Hall.

Kolb, A.Y. and D.A. Kolb (2005), 'Learning styles and learning spaces: Enhancing experiential learning in Higher Education', *Academy of Management Learning and Education*, **4**(2), 193–212.

Kolb, A.Y. and D.A. Kolb (2009), 'Experiential learning theory: A dynamic, holistic approach to management learning, education and development', in S.J. Armstrong and C. Fukami (eds), *Handbook of Management Learning, Education and Development*, London: Safe Publications.

Little, S.B. (1993), 'The technical communication internship: An application of experiential learning theory', *Journal of Business and Technical Communication*, **7**(4), 423–51.

Liu, Y., J. Xu and B.A. Weitz (2011), 'The role of emotional expression and mentoring in internship learning', *Academy of Management Learning and Education*, **10**(1), 94–110.

McCormick, D.W. (1993), 'Critical thinking, experiential learning, and internships', *Journal of Management Education*, **17**(2), 260–62.

Narayanan, V.K., P.M. Olk and C.V. Fukami (2010), 'Determinants of internship effectiveness. An exploratory model', *Academy of Management Learning and Education*, **9**(1), 61–80.

Siegel, J.P. and D. Bowen (1971), 'Satisfaction and performance: Causal relationships and moderating effects', *Journal of Vocational Behavior*, **1**(3), 263–9.

Steers, R.M. and L.W. Porter (1991), *Motivation and Work Behavior*, New York: McGraw-Hill.

Taylor, M.S. (1985), 'The roles of occupational knowledge and vocational self-concept crystallization in students' school-to-work transition', *Journal of Counseling Psychology*, **32**(4), 539–50.

Taylor, M.S. (1988), 'Effects of college internships on individual participants', *Journal of Applied Psychology*, **73**(3), 393–401.

Yamasaki, Y. and D.C. Kayes (2004), 'An experiential approach to cross-cultural learning. A review and integration of competencies for successful expatriate adaption', *Academy of Management Learning and Education*, **3**(4), 362–79.

PART III

THE RELATIONSHIP BETWEEN ENTREPRENEURIAL UNIVERSITIES AND ENTERPRISES: TECHNOLOGY TRANSFER, VENTURE CAPITAL AND SPIN-OFFS

14. The potential of and framework for promoting a business angel university and intellectual property exploitation: a case study from Wales
Simon McCarthy, Gary Packham and David Pickernell

INTRODUCTION

Universities have had long experience of directly utilizing internal knowledge to turn discovery and technology into application. Their strategic resources provide support for commercialization and technology transfer to industry through the use of physical spaces including equipment, laboratory space, human resources, and to utilize investment capital derived from outside sources (Bird et al., 1993). Higher Education Institutions (HEIs) have, however, also increasingly been encouraged to take a larger role in local economic development (e.g., see Lazzeretti and Tavoletti, 2005; Lenger, 2008) particularly through innovation (Boucher et al., 2003; Benneworth, 2007). Increased government policy efforts have therefore been focused in many countries to more directly commercialize the outputs of university research in some way.

Authors such as Lambooy (2004) have examined the transmission of university-created knowledge to their surrounding regions via a network approach. Wright et al. (2004) also suggest a range of formal and informal mechanisms in which knowledge creation and dissemination can be encouraged more widely through, for example, licensing and technology transfer. The arguments surrounding this can be seen as strongly related to the knowledge spillover theory of entrepreneurship (Acs et al., 2004). This argues, essentially, that knowledge developed in one institution may be commercialized by others, and that entrepreneurship is one way that the 'economic agent with a given endowment of new knowledge' can best appropriate the returns from that knowledge.

The complexity of knowledge-intensive entrepreneurship often creates barriers for firm creation. This may result from (1) failure of private firms and public institutions to generate new knowledge; (2) failure of that knowledge to be disseminated efficiently; (3) failure of individuals to exploit new knowledge; (4) a range of other factors that make entrepreneurship difficult (also see Audretsch and Lehmann, 2005). Any focus on knowledge creation (in universities, for example) therefore needs to be accompanied by the capabilities of knowledge users and effectiveness of knowledge transfer/translation (Cooke, 1997; Braczyk et al., 1998). Of central importance, therefore, is to link knowledge and innovation in the process of creation, with how it is then disseminated and commercialized in terms of new products, processes and capacities.

The commercialization of IP, however, can also be seen to be fraught with uncertainty and difficulty, with a so-called 'valley of death' between the stages of knowledge creation and exploitation, and knowledge-based entrepreneurship is often seen as high risk, as a result finding it difficult to raise the necessary finance. It is here that the role of informal investors or business angels can be important.

Wiltbank (2009) states that business angels are a key source of investment in very early-stage and high-risk companies with high potential for growth. In addition, however, the European Commission (2003), amongst others, also documents that business angels, as well as providing financing, also provide managerial experience, which increases the likelihood of start-up enterprises being able to survive. Numerous studies over the last three decades have supported the role of venture capitalists/business angels contributing to the success of their ventures in numerous ways other than simply providing finance (Berger and Udell, 1998; Harrison and Mason, 2000; Sörheim, 2005). In addition, Paul et al. (2007) found that new firms in particular often preferred equity to bank finance, specifically for reasons of minimizing personal liability, but also because of the additional business skills and social capital that could be accessed via equity.

Given the potential overlapping skills sets of universities, business angels and their networks, combined with simultaneous government policy focus in these areas, there does, therefore, seem to be potential to utilize business angels in university-derived IP exploitation. This is already being explored in the United States as an element contained within very recent programmes established at the University of Pennsylvania (Penn Communications, 2010) as well as at the Purdue Research Park (2010) university incubator. Their recently established angel investment network provides investment opportunity information and connections to firms or new technologies, but also provides capital for commercialization as well as access to three to four events per year, and online information. Their aim from this is to deliver IP to the marketplace on a much faster schedule, so that the market and economy will benefit through increased economic development.

More widely, this is also something already called for in Japan in Tsukagoshi (2008), but also in the Welsh context. The *Commercialization in Wales* report (Gibson, 2007, p. 18) noted that 'Experienced entrepreneurs working with academics undoubtedly form the best solution in understanding the dynamic nature of markets and in judging how to adapt intellectual property to create successful commercial enterprises'.

Overall, however, the US examples highlighted are very new developments in a different national context, and generally there appears to be a gap in the academic literature with regard to the analysis of the issues surrounding this possibility. This chapter aims to address this gap. In particular, this study evaluates if and how potential benefit could be delivered to university-generated IP by working with business angels and their networks to accelerate the commercial application of university research outputs within a UK and Welsh context, using existing university IP opportunities as initial examples.

The study was conducted as part of the Welsh government's EU-convergence-funded Academic Expertise for Business (A4B) research programme. Specifically, after an initial examination of the literature, the broad conceptual framework is established. Results are then outlined, followed by conclusions and a discussion of the need for further research.

BUSINESS ANGELS AND UNIVERSITY INNOVATION

The business angel, or informal venture capitalist, is a specific type of financial intermediary specialized in the financing of early-stage entrepreneurial ventures (Bygrave et al., 2003; European Commission, 2003). They can be viewed, however, as more important than venture capital firms (Harrison and Mason, 2000), as they can provide small amounts of external equity capital where others 'fear to tread'.

The British Business Angels Association estimates that each year private investors account for between £800 million and £1 billion of early-stage investment in the UK: the single largest source of early-stage capital in the country. Business angel investments can also have a leveraging effect for other sources of funding including bank loans and formal venture capital (European Commission, 2003).

Christensen (2007) has also highlighted potential roles and issues for venture capital at the regional economic development level, and Avnimelech et al. (2007) illustrated the role and potential benefits of venture capitalists in technological incubators. Entrepreneurial firms often struggle to obtain financing from banks when they are in the very early stage of development and lack a track record, accounts and often collateralizable assets.

Business experience is, however, also seen as necessary in order to build relationships with both experienced managers and equity investors. Business angels can also offer the benefits of their experience in these areas, with Langeland (2007) finding that venture capitalists had the potential to bring beneficial finance as well as knowledge to knowledge-intensive enterprises.

Large and Muegge (2008), for example, recently reviewed 20 empirical studies pertaining directly or indirectly to non-financial value-added (NFVA) by venture capitalists and attempted to identify areas of agreement and disagreement in the previous studies regarding NFVA. From this they created an eight-category typology of NFVA inputs that encompassed the findings of the previous studies. Two of the categories are external environment orientated and the other six have an internal environment orientation. The internal-orientated categories are recruiting activities (recruiting/advising on the recruitment of new employees), mandating activities (determining the management team's engagement), strategizing activities (contributing towards the overall strategy of the business), mentoring activities (providing informal guidance, mentoring etc.), consulting activities (providing arms'-length planned and structured knowledge) and operating activities (direct managerial involvement). The two external-oriented categories are 'legitimation' and 'outreach'. Legitimation is the process through which certain attributes such as credibility, reputation, validation and so on accrue to the venture from its association with the venture capitalist. Outreach encompasses activities that add value by establishing and developing connections to external stakeholders such as potential customers, marketing contacts and so on. Large and Muegge (2008) also state that the evidence to date suggests that operating and outreach are the most important categories of NFVA.

Related to this outreach role, business angels are also often known to co-invest and be active in several strategic and managerial activities of portfolio firms (Mayfield and Bygrave, 1999; Sörheim and Landstrom, 2001). This also makes them useful in linking firms and IP, as well as more likely to obtain growth because of such portfolio management expertise (Rosa and Scott, 1999).

A similar study by Politis (2007) reviewed previous studies relating specifically to business angel added value and broadly categorized the 'value-adding roles' as providing a sounding board/strategic role, providing a supervisory and monitoring role, providing a resource acquisition role and providing a mentoring role. Paul et al. (2007) summarize the traditional business angel investment process, as highlighted by Figure 14.1.

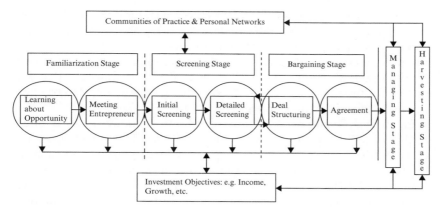

Source: Derived from Paul et al. (2007).

Figure 14.1 A model of the angel investment process

In analysing the potential role of business angels in university IP and subsequently developing an explicit model for their activity, it is therefore important to consider how the business angel-related factors indicated in Figure 14.1 might help stimulate, manage and diffuse university-generated knowledge and allow effective exploitation of innovation and IP. Owing to this, issues surrounding the management of networks, the structures and fora in which the actors operate and their absorptive capacity are important. What the university role (and the supporting government policies) should be specifically, however, is still the subject of much debate and uncertainty. The resultant perceptions have often dissuaded business angels from involving themselves in university IP commercialization.

The traditional view of a university's purpose and values includes knowledge for its own sake; making knowledge freely available to all (Behrens and Gray, 2001); organized scepticism (Kenny, 1987); and learning. The new entrepreneurial paradigm for universities, however, involves a focus upon direct value creation and academic freedom (Slaughter, 1988; Bird et al., 1993; Behrens and Gray, 2001; Harman, 2006). Shane (2002), however, found that academic spin-out (i.e., commercialization by the university itself) is a second best solution, behind licensing patented technology.

The university can utilize a range of structures including incubators, licensing and joint ventures, as well as start-ups and spin-outs (e.g., see Berggren and Dahlstrand, 2009). However, Birley (2002) highlights a number of potential university management and governance-related barriers that work against the new entrepreneurial-focused university paradigm (e.g., see Bok, 2003; Etzkowitz, 2003; Morrison, 2004). The university's management in relation to these structures, therefore, has the potential to enhance or inhibit firm innovation performance and growth (Carlsson and Mudambi, 2003). Chapple et al. (2005) also argue that university Technology Transfer Offices often lack the capability to be effective in commercialization strategies.

Frenz and Oughton (2006) also discovered that the level of direct UK-firm–UK-university cooperation is very low. They concluded more generally that firms must also have a certain level of absorptive capacity to provide legitimacy before entering into cooperation with a university. Kitagawa (2004) argues that that there is a need to examine the complementary relationships between university institutions, policy initiatives and other support organizations. Authors such as Potts (2002) also illustrate a regional dimension to these issues.

Reid and Schofield (2006) highlight the potential use of technology 'brokers' as conduits or fora through which knowledge and innovation transfer from academia can occur. It is here that the (non-financial) role of the business angel may come to the fore. Chemmanur and Chen (2003) argue, however, that for a financier to add additional non-financial value, he or she has to engage in costly effort, and they have to be given appropriate incentives to make these efforts on behalf of the firm.

The extent to which business angels can add such non-financial value in firms, whilst extensively documented, is still contentious to some. Harrison and Mason (1992, 2000), Berger and Udell (1998) and Sörheim (2005), for example, argue that the non-financial role can be important, but others (Prowse, 1998; Wong, 2001; Chemmanur and Chen, 2003) believe that the informal venture capitalist does not add significant non-financial value to their investee companies.

There is therefore a need for evaluation of a range of university and business angel-specific factors, in order to progress university IP opportunities (both current and future) at a range of stages of development. For example, technical development work of the initial IP itself may be needed to bring the knowledge to proof of concept stage. This may then need to be combined with enhanced connectivity with industry players in relevant markets, in order to overcome problems currently inherent in the process of bringing the IP to market. There is also an issue of a lack of market knowledge and business modelling expertise and a lack of appropriate commercial investment when the IP does come to market.

Business angels and informal investors are most obviously seen as potentially key in terms of accessing business networks, accessing markets, expertise in contract negotiations, in addition to access to finance.

Business angels also, however, have the opportunity to add value at earlier stages through investing (time and/or money) in IP opportunities.

There thus exist a range of potential inputs in the process, through developing the opportunity with the academic and university, taking that opportunity to market, developing the IP exploitation strategy, sharing in the financial returns, and as a result making a longer-term contribution to university research priority setting to build new opportunities. The review of the literature would suggest that the research questions fall into the following broad areas:

- the viability of the broad concept of business angel involvement with university IP, and identification of any problems with such involvement (from the university, business angel or business angel network perspective);
- the type of returns (consulting fees, licensing fees, management fees, equity, etc.) required by business angels, business angel networks and university academics to incentivize these relationships;
- the activities (financial, coaching, idea development, idea marketing, firm screening, deal brokering, firm management-related, network management-related) that business angels, business angel networks and university academics believe they should take part in and who they believe should lead these activities (from stakeholders including themselves but also universities, government and industry);
- what the university IP business angel commercialization framework and its mechanisms should look like.

METHODOLOGY

Obtaining a reasonably accurate estimate as to the number of business angels is problematic, with the European Commission (2003, p. 3) arguing that 'all inferences about the true and potential size of the angel investment market are based on guesswork'. In conducting a study of the role of business angels in university IP exploitation, therefore, there are a number of definitional issues (see, for example, Avdeitchikova, 2008; Mason and Harrison, 2008).

For the purposes of the study the definition of an active business angel was 'an individual who has previously made informal investments, either acting alone or in a formal syndicate, who invests their own money, directly in an unlisted business in which there is no personal or family connection' (Mason and Harrison, 2008, p. 309). For reasons of practicality this study therefore focused on business angels who have explicitly designated themselves as such via their participation in business angel networks. This is focused on members of the British Business Angels Association generally and Welsh Business Angels in particular, mainly through the business angel network explicitly created for Wales, Xenos Limited.

Xenos was incorporated in 1997 by the Welsh Development Agency as part of Finance Wales Plc. The network is wholly owned by Finance Wales Plc, an independently managed body that works in partnership with other public and private sector organizations to close the 'capital gap' from which Welsh firms suffer in comparison with those in more prosperous parts of the UK (Jones-Evans and Brooksbank, 2000).

Official records from Xenos indicate that there are presently 120 business angels registered with it (*Xenos Newsletter* 10). The median business angel investment made in Wales over the three years covered by the 2007 GEM Wales executive summary is the lowest of all UK regions at £3876. Jones-Evans and Thompson (2009) concluded, however, that Wales received more informal investment as a proportion of gross value-added than English regions such as London, though there was still an absolute concentration of investment in the prosperous areas of London and the South East of England. This highlights a need to examine the potential for business angel networks outside Wales to exploit IP created within it. This is justified given Lambert's (2003) evidence that universities often currently collaborate with firms outside of their localities.

In addition to the business angels themselves, there also seems to be a need to seek the views of two other sets of stakeholders. First there are the business angel network managers, who can act as gatekeepers of information to their wider network. Second, there is a need to examine the views of academics within the universities from which commercializable knowledge and innovations would need to come.

In terms of the techniques required, a mixed method approach was taken. This consisted of both quantitative methods (web-based questionnaires [see Yun et al., 2000] included within an e-mail, distributed to academics, business angel network managers and their business angel members) and qualitative methods (focus group interviews with those who attend the presentation of university IP ideas at a university-organized event) to develop an initial framework. This was then followed by a number of qualitative key stakeholder interviews carried out over a number of months following the event. These were used iteratively to determine what the university IP business angel commercialization framework and its mechanisms should look like.

The three questionnaires evolved from the existing literature, the authors' knowledge and informal discussions with a variety of stakeholders connected with the development and exploitation of IP, including business angels, business angel network managers and knowledge transfer experts. Prior to being distributed, the three questionnaires were piloted amongst a group that included both academic colleagues and also external contacts of the research team. In addition to looking at the questionnaires themselves, the pilot group completed it in order to ensure the questions were unambiguous, clear and relevant.

The decision was made to proceed with the online questionnaire using E-survey Pro. The three questionnaires were sent to business angel network managers, University of Glamorgan (now merged with the University of Wales to form the University of South Wales) academics and business angels in the Xenos network respectively. In addition, at the event that presented IP examples, focus groups that included these three groups plus other stakeholders from WAG government officials, Finance Wales, and university academics and TTOs from other parts of Wales were also conducted.

For the business angel network managers eight responses were received, representing a response rate of around 33 per cent. Whilst this can be considered good for this type of survey, the low numbers in the population obviously require caution to be applied to the results.

A questionnaire link was also e-mailed to academics in one university but across the full range of faculties and subject groups. In total, 13 responses were received, the academic respondents representing a range of specializations, but with a focus on engineering, technology and computing, as well as business and the social sciences.

Five respondents have previous experience of IP development activities and in total over half are currently involved or have been involved previously in IP development/commercialization activities. The vast majority of respondents have also taken part in paid consultancy activities, and a number of respondents had current or previous experience of small business ownership, small business or multinational employment, or working experience as a business professional.

All of this also supports the idea that these academics are a self-selected sample with valuable knowledge and insight, of use in developing IP pipeline-related processes. The low numbers compared to the potential population again obviously, however, require caution to be applied to the results.

For the business angels questionnaire, there were seven respondents. These were all located in Wales and members of the Xenos network, three also being members of the Beer and Partners private network, which covers Wales as well as other parts of the UK. This again suggests that respondents are likely to represent a small (though obviously important) sub-set of business angels. Even so, these results should also be treated with caution, and not seen as generalizable to business angels as a whole.

Indeed, in many ways the respondents can be seen as a self-selected purposive sample (e.g., Patton, 1990) offering insights from those most likely to engage in the activities proposed, though not allowing us to determine the potential size of this interest. As a result, for the data gathered from these three questionnaires, only univariate analysis is undertaken, the results used to highlight key areas for further investigation, and to allow better evaluation of the focus group event data.

This event was organized bringing together business angels, academics who had developed/were developing IP, business angel network managers and various other interested parties from three universities in South East Wales. Subsequent attendance at the event consisted of 31 people (all male) from each of the stakeholder groupings:

- ten academics presenting IP ideas;
- four university IP support staff (TTO etc.);
- seven business angels;
- three non-business angel finance providers;
- two business angel network managers;
- two Welsh Assembly Government representatives;
- four A4B research project facilitators/scribes.

Seven university IP ideas were presented from three universities located within 15 miles of one another, in an urban setting. This provided a full spectrum of ideas in terms of idea development and closeness to market, degree of pre-presentation assistance, and what they were seeking to obtain from the event and the business angels present. They also varied in terms of industry sector, whether they had already spun out of the university, were preparing to do so, or wanted to exploit IP in another way, had patents taken out, were seeking patents or wanted to protect their IP in other ways.

Following analysis of the questionnaires and focus group data gathered at this event, a number of interviews were subsequently carried out in the following six months with key 'gatekeeper' stakeholders. These were business angel network managers, University Technology Transfer representatives and external researchers. This was in order to further clarify the findings and determine what the university IP business angel commercialization framework and its mechanisms should look like. To complete this exercise, a 'focus group' that included these different groupings as well as Welsh Assembly Government representatives was also completed.

RESULTS

Online Questionnaire Summary Results

The networks the managers represent contain business angels from all the regions and nations of the UK, though, unsurprisingly, London (seven) and the South East of England (five) are best represented. Encouragingly, Wales and the surrounding regions of England (South West, East Midlands and West Midlands) also have four networks where business angels are represented in the network. This is encouraging for future activities, given that, from the literature, business angels usually prefer closer geographical distance to the firms they are investing in. This was a view supported by the fact that the network managers indicated that the business angels represented in their networks prefer the firms they invest in to be within 100 miles of their own location.

The opinions of the managers towards the use of business angels generally in university IP commercialization indicated that only a minority (three or 37.5 per cent) see this as an area of general interest. The reasons given were varied, the only common one being that it did not fall within the scope of what a business angel should do.

The network managers also believed that the concept as described appeared to require too much involvement from the business angel. Network managers are clearly important 'gatekeepers' to the network and the relevance of the concept needs to be clear to them to ensure access to the business angels themselves, particularly if the network managers also play a brokering role, determining which business angels might best be suited to particular IP opportunities. One of the business angel network managers also, however, commented that:

> [g]eneralizations where business angels are concerned are dangerous because they are not a natural affinity group. They all have different approaches, experiences and skills and whilst there is a significant overlap in these, they apply them in different ways. Some angels become significantly involved with the businesses they invest in and, therefore, may be similarly attracted to commercializing IP opportunities themselves. However, many are already involved with other projects and businesses and have no desire to commit significant amounts of their time to a single project.

These responses were also replicated when network managers were asked to discuss their own specific network. Only three of the network managers see this as something their own business angels would consider being involved in. The key reasons (expressed by at least two of the network managers) were uncertainty over the novelty of the ideas created by the academic, the lack of time business angels were likely to have to spend on such an activity and the physical distance between the business angel and the university (all but one of the business angel networks being outside Wales).

The network managers were then asked, if their members were to be involved in university IP exploitation, the importance of different types of returns that they might require. The results (shown in Table 14.1) indicated that network managers believe that their business angels will, as they would normally do, find an equity share in the company (adopting the IP) as of most importance, followed by a percentage of the IP-related income.

Greater importance was also attached to the university paying a brokering fee as compared with the other options of fees for advice and marketing. It seems, therefore, that network managers perceive the rewards as needing to be primarily equity based, though with importance also placed on IP-related income.

One of the network managers commented further that: 'The IPR MUST be owned by the investee and not by the university for a successful equity investment'.

These results suggest that business angel network managers, who often act as both gatekeepers and brokers for the business angels in their network, currently have a number of concerns and reservations about the use of business angels in university IP commercialization. These may partly be due to unfamiliarity with the concept and a consequent need to explain it more clearly.

Conversely, the results gathered for academics suggest that, unlike business angel network managers, academics are generally enthusiastic about the use of business angels in university IP commercialization. There also seems a consistent message that whilst academics see their role as generating and developing the IP, they also see an overlapping role with business angels in the commercialization of the idea with the firms.

They recognize the role of the business angel in the key area of finance. However, they also see their rewards being similar to the business angel in terms of equity in the firm licensing revenue from the IP.

Interestingly, the opinions of the responding business angels concerning business angels generally being involved in university IP commercialization are that only one saw this as an area of outside general interest (in the one case for a mixture of lack of apparent reward, time and being outside the business angel's perceived role). The responses were also unanimously positive when asked to discuss their own interest, with all the respondents being willing to be involved with commercialization of university IP.

These results, taken with those for business angel network managers,

Table 14.1 Business angel network manager opinions of returns required for business angel involvement

If members of your business angel network were to be involved in this type of activity, how important do you feel the following types of RETURNS are to their involvement?

	Unimportant	Of Little Importance	Of Some Importance	Important	Very Important	Number of Respondents
Fee from the academic/university for acting as advisor to the academic in developing the IP	14% (1)	14% (1)	42% (3)	14% (1)	14% (1)	7
Fee from the university for developing the marketing of the product	14% (1)	0% (0)	57% (4)	14% (1)	14% (1)	7
Fee from the university for acting as a broker for the university to potential firms	14% (1)	0% (0)	42% (3)	28% (2)	14% (1)	7
Percentage of the IP-related income from the firm adopting the IP	14% (1)	0% (0)	42% (3)	0% (0)	42% (3)	7
Equity share in the company adopting the IP	0% (0)	0% (0)	0% (0)	25% (2)	75% (6)	8
Number of respondents						8

reinforce the idea that the respondents are likely to represent a small (though obviously important) sub-set of business angels, who are likely to view involvement with university IP in a more positive light than business angels as a whole. Unsurprisingly all but two of these business angels were also university educated, and only one had no academic or other qualifications.

Business angels were then asked, if they were to be involved in university IP exploitation, the importance of different types of returns that they might require. The results are shown in Table 14.2.

The activities that business angels could be expected to carry out in return for these rewards were also examined. Interestingly, the business angels believed that the most important business angel roles were in assisting with broad management of the firm, coaching the academic in presentation, helping to utilize the idea, and initial screening of potential firms, rather than just a finance role. This reinforces the sub-set nature of business angels likely to be interested in this activity, but is also a clear difference with the network manager 'gatekeepers'. Again this highlights the need for clear articulation of the pipeline concept in order to attract this sub-set to the full range of activities potentially available.

This is crucially important, given that the network managers will be of key initial importance in information supply to business angels. This is demonstrated by the responses to the question regarding how business angels would like to receive information related to IP opportunities. Overwhelmingly, the responses focused on the business angel network, either via electronic or face-to-face methods.

Finally, in terms of who should lead activities, the preferred role of the business angel as the lead actor in investing equity was reinforced, with the business angel network also seen as playing a key role in organization of finance. In addition, however, the business angels also saw that they had a key role in screening potential firms and brokering deals, a response that differed from that of the network managers. Again this highlights that the business angels who were interested in involvement with university IP specifically were more likely to be willing to become more involved than business angels generally.

Business Angel Event Observations and Focus Group Results

Following the completion of the presentations and a working lunch, the attendees at the event were placed into five focus groups. Each group contained a mix of the different stakeholder groupings of persons at the event highlighted earlier. A member of the project team was placed with each grouping in order to gain feedback. This focused on what the attendees

Table 14.2 Business angel opinions of returns required for business angel involvement

If you were to be involved how important do you feel the following types of RETURNS are to your involvement?

	Unimportant	Of Little Importance	Of Some Importance	Important	Very Important	Number of Respondents
Acknowledgement of my role from the university, e.g., given Visiting Professor status	42% (3)	28% (2)	0% (0)	14% (1)	14% (1)	7
Allowed in my role within the university to develop future spin-outs in which I could take an equity share	0% (0)	0% (0)	42% (3)	28% (2)	28% (2)	7
Given option by the university to take a future equity stake in any early-stage IP I help to develop that eventually makes it to market	0% (0)	0% (0)	42% (3)	14% (1)	42% (3)	7
Fee from the academic/university for acting as advisor to the academic in developing the IP	0% (0)	0% (0)	42% (3)	42% (3)	14% (1)	7
Fee from the university for developing the marketing of the product	0% (0)	16% (1)	50% (3)	16% (1)	16% (1)	6
Fee from the university for acting as a broker for the university to potential firms	0% (0)	28% (2)	28% (2)	28% (2)	14% (1)	7
Percentage of the IP-related income from the firm adopting the IP	0% (0)	0% (0)	66% (4)	0% (0)	33% (2)	6
Equity share in the company adopting the IP	0% (0)	0% (0)	28% (2)	28% (2)	42% (3)	7
Number of respondents						7

wanted from the day, whether their objectives had been met and their views on future development of the concept.

The academics involved differed in terms of whether they were looking for funding, investment contacts, networking and one-to-one opportunities, ideas of how to exploit the IP, feedback on ideas, or someone to help share risk and so forth. These differences were related to whether their IP was at the pre-proof of concept stage (blue skies), proof of concept stage, or ready for market stage.

There was also a degree of uncertainty and nervousness from those academics at the pre-proof of concept stage about commercialization. Academic responses related to this included:

> It has been interesting to hear the different presentations here, patenting is being mentioned a lot and for a non-expert like me, a lot of advice is needed. [Pre-proof of concept stage]

> We have considered patenting but it appears problematic, the best idea protection we have is keeping it in our heads. [Proof of concept stage]

> We came today with the intention of seeing what others are doing and gaining contacts with big companies or intermediaries. [Ready for market stage]

The business angels also differed in terms of background and what they sought from the event. Some saw it as akin to a traditional *start-up stage* business angel event and thus saw the near to market concepts as most interesting. This group saw the university as needing to look at their processes before this in terms of mentoring and developing the idea through to this stage, and based their remuneration in terms of traditional equity in spin-outs. There was some consequent comment on the need for any future events to be more focused, presentations to be more focused on what the IP required in terms of resources for development (and what would be offered in return) and for the consequent role of the business angel to be spelled out more specifically within an explicit framework for engagement.

In terms of the presentations, one angel commented: 'There was too much technical content and not enough focus on what was wanted and why'. Others had, however, come to the event looking at earlier (seed-corn) stage involvement (pre-proof of concept idea stage, prototyping, etc.). They saw activities such as mentoring, business plan assistance and presentational coaching, as well as funding (both directly and supporting larger bids to government, etc.) to develop the idea, as ones where they might be prepared to become involved. These activities were also seen as needing to be incorporated within an engagement framework. Some of the specific business angel quotes included: 'Mentor support is needed to help IPR in presentation and maximising opportunities' and 'The event is what we wanted . . . identifying IP opportunities and how they may be funded . . . got three possible investment opportunities'.

The remuneration possibilities highlighted include 'options' to have equity at a later stage, direct financial remuneration from their time, explicit remit to develop ideas and students through incubators into spin-outs in which they would have a stake, and also 'status' rewards (e.g., Visiting Professor status). Broadly, the business angels who attended seemed to have a general focus on widening their network, curiosity about what types of ideas were being generated, a desire to tap into additional opportunities potentially available with the other stakeholders present, and a willingness to get IP out of universities in particular.

Overall this suggested, in support of the business angels survey, that whilst the feedback from the business network managers survey indicated that business angels as a group generally would not likely be interested in this activity, that there were a sub-set (self-selected in terms of the event) of the business angel community who were both able and willing to be involved with universities and these types of events generally, and at an earlier 'seed-corn' stage in the process in particular.

Most crucially, and again reinforcing the questionnaire-based evidence, there was also a general consensus that a more cohesive framework of engagement needed to be developed to get the ideas from the academics to the business angels, and that the mechanisms would need to be different depending on the stage of the IP (i.e., early, proof of concept, patent, spin-out etc.). The use of more focused industry-/technology-specific events and information and other 'filtering' devices (such as Technology Transfer Officers, business angel network managers, etc.) were also seen as necessary.

Some funders also stated that greater work on identifying the potential 'flow' of IP from universities might be advisable. Generally, an earlier engagement in the process was seen as generating a greater long-term potential benefit, by focusing the ideas at an earlier stage on the market, promoting relevant market research, marketing and better presentation of the ideas, with events providing detailed feedback on each presentation. There was no consensus, however, on what the framework should look like.

Key Stakeholder Interviews and Focus Group Outcomes

Taken together, the results suggest a need to more explicitly articulate the framework for engagement between universities, academics, business angels and their networks, with a range of incentives on offer to both academics and business angels. Given the heterogeneous nature of both business angels and academics vis-à-vis university IP, a more focused approach to identify the sub-sets most likely to be interested in creating as well as utilizing university IP would also seem to be necessary. For this, however, the roles of the business angel network manager (for business angels) and the Technology Transfer Office (for academics) are likely to be crucial. This suggests that support programmes and incentives for their involvement may also be required.

The study allowed the creation of a draft 'IP pipeline' process, utilizing the framework in Figure 14.1, but then building upon this using the results from the questionnaires and event focus groups in terms of stages, activities and rewards for universities, academics, business angels and angel networks. After creation of this basic draft pipeline, however, interviews and a focus group with the key 'gatekeeper' stakeholder groups of business angel network managers and university Technology Transfer staff, supported by interviews with relevant external governmental actors were also conducted. These focused on the best articulation of the pipeline, to establish a generally accepted terminology, as well as highlighting the key roles of each of the stakeholders. Issues raised for this included the overall name of the pipeline, which became broadened from IP to intellectual capital.

Renaming the types of business angels engaged at different stages of the pipeline also became necessary, as did renaming certain stages of the pipeline. A need was also identified for universities to complete a short initial IP pro forma to capture key information required by business angels in a form able to be disseminated easily via monthly newsletters and so on from which business angel involvement would then be stimulated. The final version of the resulting pipeline framework can be seen in Figure 14.2.

The diagram shows the pipeline, with intellectual capital moving horizontally from left to right, through the normal processes of commercialization (knowledge creation, dissemination, commercialization and exploitation), and the key milestones of commercialization (idea, proof of concept, ready for market vehicle, in the market). This part of the intellectual capital pipeline is not new and can be seen as linked to existing business angel processes highlighted in Figure 14.2. In addition, it can be, and is currently, 'fuelled' by a range of existing university and government support policies (such as the A4B's Scouting Project, Early Stage Development Fund, Patent and Proof of Concept and Feasibility Studies, and other university Technology Transfer activities). What is new is that within the existing pipeline's processes and milestones, there are five key stages (indicated vertically on the diagram and linked to the

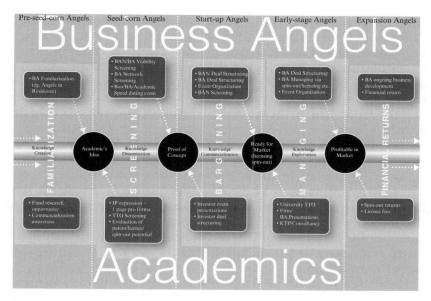

Figure 14.2   University intellectual-capital–business-angel commercialization pipeline

processes engaged in by both universities and academics on the one hand and business angels and their networks on the other) where business angels and their networks could become involved. Specifically, these stages are: familiarization, screening, negotiating, managing and financial returns.

The upper part of the diagram then indicates the roles of the business angel and business angel network at each of these stages, whilst the lower part of the diagram indicates the roles of the university's Technology Transfer Office and academics at each of these stages. In terms of the rewards that business angels could expect from their involvement, these would be a matter of negotiation, but would fall into one or more of the categories highlighted in Tables 14.1 and 14.2, with different mixtures of these depending on the point in the pipeline where business angels became involved.

CONCLUSIONS AND IMPLICATIONS

The recent economic downturn has seen business angels in the UK pulling back from funding university start-ups because of their inherent higher-risk nature, but also because the businesses created were not perceived as being sufficiently commercially focused (*Telegraph*, 2009a). As a result, *Telegraph* (2009b) reported a reduction in business angel-assisted university spin-outs and increased used of foreign funding. This study, however, has highlighted that there is potential for additional benefit to be delivered to university-generated IP by working with business angels and their networks to accelerate the commercial application of university research outputs within a UK and Welsh context. It is likely, however, to be a niche activity for only a small proportion of business angels willing and able to engage with university IP at a range of (mainly earlier) stages of development, for a range of different rewards.

Looking further ahead, it may be both possible and desirable for business angels to get together with policy actors, university managers, academics, students and alumni to create appropriate cooperative projects that include business angels and their networks to focus the initial ideas and innovation creation from the earliest stage possible. This, of course, would require new fora for engagement and again would likely be very much a niche activity.

The creation of an explicit framework of the processes involved appears to be vital. This is to clearly identify the stage of development of the ideas, the required activities of business angels, their networks and universities, and also the rewards on offer.

Ultimately, the aim must be to work towards extending and generalizing the benefits of these projects to other contexts, particularly other EU Member States. Such an aim would likely find favour given both the current focus of the European Commission, and the fact that the research discussed here was conducted as part of the Welsh Assembly Government's EU-convergence-funded A4B research programme.

In order to evaluate the success of this approach, however, and any changes or additions to it, there is a clear need for further research into the actual operation of this framework. This will need to determine the viability and sustainability of the processes involved for both universities and angels, the extent of the beneficial outcomes to be derived and the potential for this approach in different contexts and environments.

REFERENCES

Acs, Z.J., D.B. Audretsch, P. Braunerhjelm and B. Carlsson (2004), 'The missing link: The knowledge filter and entrepreneurship in endogenous growth', Discussion Paper No. 4783, December, London: Centre For Economic Policy Research.

Audretsch, D. and E. Lehmann (2005), 'Does the knowledge spillover theory of entrepreneurship hold for regions?', *Research Policy*, **34**(8), 1191–202.

Avdeitchikova, S. (2008), 'On the structure of the informal venture capital market in Sweden:

Developing investment roles', *Venture Capital: An International Journal of Entrepreneurial Finance*, **10**(1), 55–85.

Avnimelech, G., D. Schwartz and R. Bar-El (2007), 'Entrepreneurial high-tech cluster development: Israel's experience with venture capital and technological incubators', *European Planning Studies*, **15**(9), 1181–98.

Behrens, T.R. and D.O. Gray (2001), 'Unintended consequences of cooperative research: Impact of industry sponsorship on climate for academic freedom and other graduate student outcomes', *Research Policy*, **30**(2), 179–99.

Benneworth, P. (2007), 'Seven samurai opening up the ivory tower? The construction of Newcastle as an entrepreneurial university', *European Planning Studies*, **15**(4), 487–509.

Berger, A.N. and G.F. Udell (1998), 'The economics of small business finance: The roles of private equity and debt markets in the financial growth cycle', *Journal of Banking and Finance*, **22**(6/8), 613–73.

Berggren, E. and Å. Dahlstrand (2009), 'Creating an entrepreneurial region: Two waves of academic spin-offs from Halmstad University', *European Planning Studies*, **17**(8), 1171–89.

Bird, B.J., D.J. Hayward and D.N. Allen (1993), 'Conflicts in the commercialization of knowledge: Perspectives from science and entrepreneurship', *Entrepreneurship: Theory and Practice*, **17**(4), 57–76.

Birley, S. (2002), 'Universities, academics, and spin-out companies: Lessons from Imperial', *International Journal of Entrepreneurship Education*, **1**(1), 1–21.

Bok, D. (2003), *Universities in the Marketplace: The Commercialization of Higher Education*, Princeton, NJ: Princeton University Press.

Boucher, G., C. Conway and E. van der Meer (2003), 'Tiers of engagement by universities in their region's development', *Regional Studies*, **37**(9), 887–97.

Braczyk, H-J., P. Cooke and M. Heidenreich (eds) (1998), *Regional Innovation Systems: The Role of Governance in a Globalized World*, London and Pennsylvania: UCL.

Bygrave, W., M. Hay, E. Ng and P. Reynolds (2003), 'Executive forum: A study of informal investing in 29 nations composing the Global Entrepreneurship Monitor', *Venture Capital*, **5**(2), 101–16.

Carlsson, B. and R. Mudambi (2003), 'Globalization, entrepreneurship, and public policy: A systems view', *Industry and Innovation*, **10**(1), 103–16.

Chapple, W., A. Lockett, D. Siegel and M. Wright (2005), 'Assessing the relative performance of UK university technology transfer offices: Parametric and non-parametric evidence', *Research Policy*, **34**(3), 369–84.

Chemmanur, Thomas J. and Zhaohui Chen (2003), 'Angels, venture capitalists and entrepreneurs: A dynamic model of private equity financing', accessed 14 August 2013 at http://www1.fee.uva.nl/Fm/Papers/Chemmanur.Pdf.

Christensen, J. (2007), 'The development of geographical specialization of venture capital', *European Planning Studies*, **15**(6), 817–33.

Cooke, P. (1997), 'Regions in a global market: The experiences of Wales and Baden Wurttemburg', *Review of International Political Economy*, **4**(2), 349–81.

Etzkowitz, H. (2003), 'Research groups as quasi-firms: The invention of the entrepreneurial university', *Research Policy*, **32**(1), 109–21.

European Commission (2003), *Benchmarking Business Angels*, Brussels: The Commission of the European Communities, accessed 14 August 2013 at http://ec.europa.eu/enterprise/newsroom/cf/itemdetail.cfm?item_id=2053.

Frenz, M. and C. Oughton (2006), *Innovation in the UK Regions and Devolved Administrations: A Review of the Literature*, Final Report for the Department of Trade and Industry and the Office of the Deputy Prime Minister, London: DTI.

Gibson, S. (2007), *Commercialisation in Wales: A Report by the Independent Task and Finish Group, Independent Review of Publicly Funded Commercialisation Activities in Wales*, Cardiff.

Harman, G. (2006), 'Research and scholarship', in J.J. Forest and P.G. Altbach (eds), *International Handbook of Higher Education, Part One: Global Themes and Contemporary Challenges*, Dordrecht: Springer, pp. 309–28.

Harrison, R. and C. Mason (1992), 'International perspectives on the supply of informal venture capital', *Journal of Business Venturing*, **7**(6), 459–75.

Harrison, R.T and C.M. Mason (2000), 'Venture capital market complementarities: The links between business angels and venture capital funds in the United Kingdom', *Venture Capital*, **2**(3), 223–42.

Jones-Evans, D. and D. Brooksbank (2000), *Global Entrepreneurship Monitor: 2000 Wales Executive Report*, accessed 14 August 2013 at http://www.gemconsortium.org/docs/down load/674.

Jones-Evans, D. and P. Thompson (2009), 'The spatial dispersion of informal investment at a regional level: Evidence from the UK', *European Planning Studies*, **17**(5), 659–75.

Kenny, M. (1987), 'The ethical dilemmas of university–industry collaborations', *Journal of Business Ethics*, **6**(2), 127–35.

Kitagawa, F. (2004), 'Universities and regional advantage: Higher Education and innovation policies in English regions', *European Planning Studies*, **12**(6), 835–52.

Lambert, R. (2003), *Lambert Review of Business–University Collaboration: Final Report*, London: HM Treasury, London: HMSO.

Lambooy, J. (2004), 'The transmission of knowledge, emerging networks, and the role of universities: An evolutionary approach', *European Planning Studies*, **12**(5), 643–57.

Langeland, O. (2007), 'Financing innovation: The role of Norwegian venture capitalists in financing knowledge-intensive enterprises', *European Planning Studies*, **15**(9), 1143–61.

Large, D. and S. Muegge (2008), 'Venture capitalists' non-financial value-added: An evaluation of the evidence and implications for research', *Venture Capital*, **10**(1), 21–53.

Lazzeretti, L. and E. Tavoletti (2005), 'Higher Education excellence and local economic development: The case of the entrepreneurial University of Twente', *European Planning Studies*, **13**(3), 475–93.

Lenger, A. (2008), 'Regional innovation systems and the role of state: Institutional design and state universities in Turkey', *European Planning Studies*, **16**(8), 1101–20.

Mason, C. and R. Harrison (2008), 'Measuring business angel activity in the United Kingdom: A review of potential data sources', *Venture Capital*, **10**(4), 309–30.

Mayfield, W. and W. Bygrave (1999), 'The formation and organization of mega-angel syndicates', paper presented at the 1999 Babson College-Kauffman Foundation.

Morrison, D.A. (2004), *Marketing to the Campus Crowd*, Chicago: Dearborn Trade Publishing.

Patton, M.Q. (1990), *Qualitative Evaluation and Research Methods*, 2nd edition, Newbury Park, CA: Sage Publications.

Paul, S., G. Whittam and J. Wyper (2007), 'Towards a model of the business angel investment process', *Venture Capital*, **9**(2), 107–25.

Penn Communications (2010), 'UPenn unveils UPSTART program to nurture faculty start ups', accessed 14 August 2013 at http://techtransfercentral.com/2010/04/28/upenn-unveils-upstart-program-to-nurture-faculty-start-ups/.

Politis, D. (2007), 'Business angels and value added: What do we know and where do we go?' *Venture Capital*, **10**(2), 127–47.

Potts, G. (2002), 'Regional policy and the "regionalization" of university–industry links: A view from the English regions', *European Planning Studies*, **10**(8), 987–1012.

Prowse, S. (1998), 'Angel investors and the market for angel investments', *Journal of Banking and Finance*, **22**(6–8), 785–92.

Purdue Research Park (2010), 'Purdue Research Foundation establishes network for angel investors', accessed 14 August 2013 at http://eon.businesswire.com/news/eon/2010 0224006267/en.

Reid, P. and M. Schofield (2006), 'How a regional broker can improve industry demand for university interaction', *Industry and Higher Education*, **20**(6), 413–20.

Rosa, P. and M. Scott (1999), 'The prevalence of multiple owners and directors in the SME sector: Implications for our understanding of start-up and growth', *Entrepreneurship and Regional Development*, **11**(1), 21–37.

Shane, S. (2002), 'Selling university technology: Patterns from MIT', *Management Science*, **48**(1), 122–37.

Slaughter, S. (1988), 'Academic freedom and the state: Reflections on the uses of knowledge', *Journal of Higher Education*, **59**(3), 241–62.

Sörheim, R. (2005), 'Business angels as facilitators for further finance: An exploratory study', *Journal of Small Business and Enterprise Development*, **12**(2), 178–91.

Sörheim, R. and H. Landstrom (2001), 'Informal investors – a categorization, with policy implications', *Entrepreneurship and Regional Development*, **13**(4), 351–71.

Telegraph (2009a), 'Business angels turn backs on universities', 21 December 2009, accessed 14 August 2013 at http://www.telegraph.co.uk/finance/yourbusiness/6860442/Business-angels-turn-back-on-universities.html.

Telegraph (2009b), 'University spin-off activity collapses', 21 December 2009, accessed 14 August 2013 at http://www.telegraph.co.uk/finance/yourbusiness/6860435/University-spin-off-activity-collapses.html.

Tsukagoshi, M. (2008), 'The expected roles of business angels in seed/early stage university spin-offs in Japan: Can business angels act as saviours?' *Asia Pacific Business Review*, **14**(3), 425–42.

Wiltbank, Robert. E (2009), *Siding with the Angels: Business Angel Investing – Promising Outcomes and Effective Strategies*, London: Nesta, p. 10.

Wong, A. (2001), 'Angel finance: The other venture capital', unpublished working paper, University of Chicago, accessed 14 August 2013 at http://papers.ssrn.com/sol3/papers.cfm?abstract_id=941228.

Wright, M., S. Birley and S. Mosey (2004), 'Entrepreneurship and university technology transfer', *The Journal of Technology Transfer*, **29**(3/4), 235–46.

Yun, G., I. Woong and C. Trumbo (2000), 'Comparative response to a survey executed by post, e-mail and web form', *Journal of Computer Mediated Communication*, **6**(1), 36–9.

15. Commercializing science by means of university spin-offs: an ethical review
*Elco van Burg**

INTRODUCTION

Entrepreneurship within universities is important to exploit the full economic and social potential of university inventions. Without entrepreneurial individuals, and a university organization that supports those individuals, new research findings will probably be published and taught, but it is likely that broader value is not fully developed (e.g., Siegel et al., 2004, 2007). Entrepreneurship within universities, for instance in the form of university spin-offs – ventures founded to exploit university inventions – serves to transform technological breakthroughs from university research, which would probably remain unexploited otherwise (Shane, 2002; Meyer, 2006). Therefore, policy-makers have become very interested in university spin-offs and in the concept of an entrepreneurial university as a means for technology transfer and economic growth (Gilsing et al., 2010). Universities have established policies and support infrastructures to support entrepreneurship (van Burg et al., 2008), thereby moving in the direction of becoming entrepreneurial universities (Bramwell and Wolfe, 2008).

However, supporting entrepreneurial activities within universities creates several difficulties, such as the potential conflict of interest between commercial and academic work and the risk to university reputation if founders of spin-offs act inappropriately (Bird et al., 1993; Shane, 2004; Slaughter and Rhoades, 2004). Due to this debate in the popular press as well as within the university, academic entrepreneurs feel sometimes that their behaviour is not welcomed by the university. Therefore, there is a need to review the concept of an entrepreneurial university, and more specifically that creation of university spin-offs, from an ethical perspective. If one of the main goals of universities is to produce sound knowledge, would the usage of this knowledge for economic benefits not corrupt research 'objectivity'? On the one hand, faculty were proud of the success of the Stanford spin-off Google and were happy with the research funding of $US336 million that equity sales delivered to Stanford University. On the other hand, people asked what these unprecedented cases would imply for renowned universities. The benefits of commercializing science create what Roger Geiger calls the 'paradox of the marketplace':

> [T]he marketplace has, on balance, brought universities greater resources . . . and a more productive role in the US economy. At the same time, it has diminished the sovereignty of universities over their own activities, weakened their mission of serving the public, and created through growing commercial entanglements at least the potential for undermining their privileged role as disinterested arbiters of knowledge. (Geiger, 2004, p. 265)

Thus, the engagement of universities in commercializing research raises the question whether this engagement is good or bad.

This debate on the moral issues raised by the engagement of universities in commercializing of research has been lively, in particular since the 1980s (Feller, 1990). In addition, systematic inquiry of the phenomenon has started (e.g., Jensen and Thursby, 2001; Zucker et al., 2002; Perkmann and Walsh, 2008; Goldstein, 2010; Haeussler and Colyvas, 2011; Tartari and Breschi, 2012). Yet, in the debate on the moral side of commercializing research, empirical findings are often not taken into account. As a result, the empirical validity of some arguments is questionable. Moreover, many contributions to this debate have been remarkably one-sided. Therefore, this study aims to bring the debate an important step forward by collecting the arguments, evaluating them by reviewing the empirical findings and taking into account diverse stakeholders and different ethical perspectives. In this respect, this study goes beyond unproductive dichotomies between 'old-school Mertonian-style' and 'new-school profit-oriented' research (cf. Owen-Smith and Powell, 2001).

This study focuses on the ethical evaluation of university spin-off creation, as this way of commercializing university knowledge combines a number of important commercial activities, namely licensing, contract research and the transfer of personnel and students. First, a review of the literature collects the different pros and cons of the creation of university spin-offs. This inventory of arguments is, where possible, evaluated by a review of empirical studies that demonstrate the substance and signifi-cance of the arguments. Here, this study contributes to the debate on the commercialization of science by reviewing the advantages and disadvan-tages and showing that some of them are not empirically supported, while others are substantial. In this way, I extend earlier reviews that focused only on the (negative) effects of patenting activities (i.e., Thursby and Thursby, 2005; Baldini, 2008; Larsen, 2011). Second, deontological and teleological ethical perspectives are used to evaluate these arguments and create a synthesizing reflective equilibrium (cf. Rawls, 1999), thus extending previous reviews of the empirical evidence by performing an ethical evaluation. The reflective equilibrium balances current knowledge of advantages and disadvantages of university spin-off creation, evaluated by different ethical theories. As such, this reflective equilibrium provides a new foundation for the debate on the commercialization of science. This balance of different arguments and perspectives, while taking into account the empirical results, provides a moral criterion serving as an instrument to evaluate university spin-off creation. In addition, the review in this study contributes by specifying a number of directions for further inquiry.

ARGUMENTS IN SUPPORT OF UNIVERSITY SPIN-OFF CREATION

Knowledge Utilization

One of the main reasons to foster the creation of university spin-offs is the knowledge utilization objective (Bozeman, 2000; Siegel et al., 2004, 2007). Universities create new knowledge and produce inventions. Much of the research underlying these inventions has been paid for by taxpayers, at least in the case of public universities. Therefore, it is desirable that the benefits of this research feed back to taxpayers, to society. This is partly done by teaching students the results of the research and by publishing research findings in books and academic journals (Perkmann and Walsh, 2007). The value of inventions can be further unleashed by transferring this technology to the market, which may create more and better products and services, thus possibly increasing living standards for taxpayers. Thus, commercialization of science is justified by the benefit and use of the public (Powell and Colyvas, 2008).

Many inventions get to the market through established firms that acquire property rights of university inventions (Thursby et al., 2001). However, some inventions are not feasible for exploitation by established firms. This especially applies to inventions in early development stages and inventions that require the tacit knowledge of the inventors for their development (Thursby et al., 2001; Mitchell et al., 2002; Zucker et al., 2002). In these cases, exploitation by the inventor him- or herself in a university spin-off ensures the involvement of the inventor (Hsu and Bernstein, 1997; Shane, 2004). As such, spin-off firms are important catalysts in spurring technology flows (Rappert et al., 1999) and can serve to realize the commercial and social benefits of a discovery (Meyer, 2006).

Economic Growth

University spin-offs can contribute to economic growth, both locally and on a broader, national scale (Shane, 2004; Mueller, 2006; Gilsing et al., 2010). Although the relationship between university spin-off creation and economic growth is not linear (Mowery and Sampat, 2005), research results do imply that new high-tech companies such as university spin-offs contribute significantly to economic growth (Shane, 2004, 2009; Mueller, 2006). Support from universities helps these firms to grow (O'Shea et al., 2005; Powers and McDougall, 2005). For spin-off firms, maintaining the relationship with the university is important to obtain access to expertise, keep abreast of university research, get assistance and help with specific problems, and have access to public funding (Zucker and Darby, 1998; Zucker et al., 2002; Geiger, 2004). Thus, by enabling and supporting university spin-off creation, universities can contribute to economic growth.

Learning From Another 'Culture'

A popular idea is that faculty are too isolated in their ivory tower. Their tasks of independent observation and theorizing may have made them introspective with little attention for the outside world. One of the benefits of university spin-offs, as has been argued, is that they enable learning from the different culture of business (Welsh et al., 2008). Moreover, as there is no fundamental separation between the science and industry in terms of technology and research subjects, university spin-offs fulfil an instrumental bridging role (Powell and Owen-Smith, 2002). So, engaging in university spin-off creation can result in sharper market foci of faculty and the emergence of new research ideas (Feller, 1990).

A number of researchers have aimed to quantify this effect by examining whether academic researchers who engage in industry relationships in general and spin-off activities in particular have more research output in terms of published papers. Assuming that engagement in commercial activities spurs creativity and leads to potential new and fruitful research directions, higher publication rates are hypothesized. This hypothesis is confirmed by the finding that such inventor-authors publish at or above average publishing rates of faculty (e.g., Zucker et al., 1998; Lowe and Gonzalez, 2007; Larsen, 2011).

Revenue Generation

The generation of university spin-offs provides income for universities (Slaughter and Leslie, 1997; Jensen and Thursby, 2001; Colyvas et al.,

2002; Leute, 2005; Welsh et al., 2008). This income can result from patents or licences sold to these companies. Furthermore, many universities have policies to take equity in spin-off companies, which gives them the benefit of goal alignment and control, but also the ability to benefit from all the business activities related to the university inventions (Bray and Lee, 2000; Shane, 2004). Researchers report that some universities have positive revenues of technology transfer and in particular from equity holdings in university spin-offs (Bray and Lee, 2000; Chapple et al., 2005). Spin-offs may also bring complementary financial benefits because they often attract public funding, which is partly spent at the university. For instance, Hsu and Bernstein (1997) found that MIT spin-offs used grants to fund research at the university.

However, it is not evident whether there is always a net benefit for universities. For example, Stevens and Bagby state that it is 'unclear what benefits are distributed or what the incentives are for the instruction and service functions of universities; . . . there is no consensus regarding who benefits or should pay for knowledge creation and transfer' (Stevens and Bagby, 2001, pp. 264, 266). One of the main questions is whether more public money flows to private companies than the other way around. It seems that only a small number of top universities have net revenues from licensing and spin-off activities, but that the majority of the universities lose money on technology transfer (Geuna and Nesta, 2006; Klein et al., 2010).

ARGUMENTS AGAINST UNIVERSITY SPIN-OFF CREATION

Reduced Academic Commitment

The main reasoning opposing the commercialization of science and the creation of university spin-offs argues that conflicts of interest will arise. On the one hand, advancing academic knowledge is the primary goal of a university researcher. On the other hand, he or she is stimulated to engage in entrepreneurial activities that also need investment in time and effort. This could create a tension between the academic tasks versus the commitment to private entrepreneurship (Bird et al., 1993; Renault, 2006).

Empirical investigation of this topic, however, suggests that this tension is not very pronounced (Steffensen et al., 2000; Martinelli et al., 2008; Goldstein, 2010), as the portion of faculty expressing interest in licensing is remarkably low, indicating that faculty have not become too commercial (Thursby and Thursby, 2005), or because of effective 'conflict of interest' policies (Argyres and Liebeskind, 1998; Leute, 2005; Powell and Colvyas, 2008; Welsh et al., 2008). In addition, research on the relationship between patenting and entrepreneurship activities on the one hand and the publishing tasks on the other indicate that engagement in commercialization in general does not result in reduced academic research output (Zucker and Darby, 1998; van Looy et al., 2006; Lowe and Gonzalez, 2007; Baldini, 2008; Crespi et al., 2011). Moreover, results show a positive relationship between the quality of articles, measured by the number of citations, and the number of university spin-offs (Di Gregorio and Shane, 2003; Powers and McDougall, 2005). This indicates that entrepreneurial activities do not reduce academic efforts or vice versa; they rather tend to reinforce each other.

Research Direction Change

Related to the potentially reduced academic commitment is the objection that engagement in university spin-off creation will change research directions (Colyvas and Powell, 2007). As Feller states (1990, p.342), '[T]he institutional incentives to foster faculty research related to reducing technical and economic uncertainty increase as well, even when these lines of research diverge from "academic advances in knowledge"'. Whereas research output in quantitative terms does not change, the content of the research may change. Instead of executing fundamental research, faculty engaging in entrepreneurial activities and industry relationships may focus on research directions that have more commercial opportunities (ibid.). As a result, research that benefits the public interest but has no opportunity to contribute to a market solution could be abandoned (Krimsky, 2003). Instead, commercial success of particular research directions can lead to strengthening those directions, resulting in over-embeddedness that reduces both future academic and commercial success (Owen-Smith and Powell, 2003). Maintaining the focus on fundamental research will therefore be more beneficial over the long term, even in economic and commercial terms, because fundamental research can result in path-breaking innovations (Glenna et al., 2007; Lacetera, 2009). Moreover, as a result of growing commercial and monetary interests, the autonomy of researchers to choose their own direction could be lost (Kleinman and Vallas, 2001).

Empirically, the existence of changes in research directions is still indecisive (Larsen, 2011). Some researchers have observed that researchers involved in commercialization activities do more applied research (Godin and Gingras, 2000; Gulbrandsen and Smeby, 2005) or shift towards more applied research (Azoulay et al., 2009). Others, however, did not find a change in research directions (Ylijoki, 2003; Thursby and Thursby, 2005;

Martinelli et al., 2008). In addition, Thursby et al. (2007) show in a simulation study that a research shift is likely to occur not at the expense of fundamental research, but at the expense of leisure time.

Anti-commons Effect

One of the effects of having private parties such as spin-off companies commercializing university research could be that this research may not be shared freely. Because the rights on the intellectual property are sold and since commercial interests are involved, university researchers are not allowed to communicate openly about the research involved since competitors could be listening. As a result, only the research group that invented a certain technology can build on the research in follow-up research, but are not allowed to present their research results in the outside world, nor are they able to invite other researchers around the world to join their research direction. This effect is called the 'anti-commons effect': commercialization of research can restrict communication and exchange amongst scientists (Vallas and Kleinman, 2007; Welsh et al., 2008). Some argue that this is against one of the key values of universities (Krimsky, 2003; David, 2004), namely 'to create and sustain an "intellectual commons": a knowledge archive openly accessible to all members of society' (Argyres and Liebeskind, 1998, p. 428).

The existence of the anti-commons effect is empirically confirmed (Murray and Stern, 2007), although its impact does not appear to be very large or significant (Chang and Yang, 2008; Tartari and Breschi, 2012). Haeussler (2011) found that scientists are more likely to share information with others if they adhere to the 'open science' norm; Mars et al. (2008) report that communication of research results among students decreased if these students were acting as entrepreneurs commercializing the research results, and similarly Martinelli et al. (2008) reported some anecdotal evidence of decreased cooperation among faculty. Moreover, some studies have found that publications of which the intellectual property is protected by a patent receive slightly fewer citations than their unpatented pairs (Murray and Stern, 2007; Fabrizio and Di Minin, 2008).

Threats to Objectivity

Engagement of faculty in commercial activities such as spin-offs could result in research that becomes biased, because of the commercial interests. An example is the systematic bias that has been found in drug-testing studies that are sponsored by pharmaceutical companies (Krimsky, 2003; Lexchin et al., 2003). Many people argue that university research should be 'objective' and therefore free from (monetary) interest in the outcome of the research (i.e., Feller, 1990; Argyres and Liebeskind, 1998; Krimsky, 2003; Slaughter and Rhoades, 2004; Vallas and Kleinman, 2007). The empirical research of Colyvas (2007) has demonstrated that institutional change resulted in acceptance of commercial and monetary interests, which might indicate that the norm of monetary disinterestedness is eroding (see Kleinman and Vallas, 2001). In addition, a formal relation-ship of a university with a spin-off firm creates the risk of damage to the public reputation of the university's objectiveness if inappropriate or 'unscientific' behaviour of the spin-off company is directly associated with the university (Blumenthal, 1992; Shane, 2004).

Inequity Among Faculty

One of the potential side-effects of faculty's engagement in university spin-off creation could be that some faculty acquire a higher total income than other faculty that do not have these revenues. Differences in faculty pay because of entrepreneurship profits may cause envy (Slaughter and Leslie, 1997; Argyres and Liebeskind, 1998). Up till now, empirical research on university spin-offs did not report this inequity problem.

Departure of Faculty

In the case that university spin-offs are founded by university faculty, they will probably devote (part of) their time to this new venture and may eventually leave their academic careers. This could be a disadvan-tage, in the case that the university wants to keep this faculty longer on board. Slaughter and Leslie's (1997) research indicates that this issue is not perceived as problematic, nor is it reported in any other empirical study.

Unfair Competition by Spin-offs

Because university spin-offs typically exploit public-funded research and since they often receive support by the university, university spin-offs can be considered as 'state-sponsored' enterprises (Mars et al., 2008). This state sponsoring could create unfair competition relative to new ventures that have to arrange support themselves (Bird et al., 1993). The validity of this argument depends on the question of whether 'independent' ventures really do not receive support. In many countries and regions, entrepre-neurship is promoted and sponsored with incubators, funds, and so on, such as the SBIC grant in the US (Lundström and Stevenson, 2005). This implies that many 'independent' new ventures also can be considered to be to some extent state-sponsored.

DEONTOLOGICAL ETHICAL EVALUATION

To evaluate these advantages and disadvantages from a normative perspective, I will use two radically different ethical points of view, namely deontological and teleological ethics. Deontological ethics evaluates actions by assessing whether these actions conform to some specified set of rules. The foundations of this ethical philosophy are laid out by Immanuel Kant (Micewski and Troy, 2007). His basic rule to decide on just actions is: 'Act only on that maxim whereby you can at the same time will that it become a universal law' (Kant, 2005, p. 81 [421]). Based on this rule, specific deontological norms can be developed. For example, John Rawls advocated a contractarian approach, in which the Kantian maxim is translated as 'inherent moral standing of persons' articulated in a social contract (Lefkowitz, 2003). In this way, other ethical norms can also be considered as 'deontological', meaning that people have to adhere to these norms rather than base their evaluations on the consequences of their actions (ibid.).

I will discuss two deontological imperative approaches to evaluate university spin-off creation: the Mertonian ethos of science and the Kirznerian ethics of finders–keepers. The Mertonian ethos of science is relevant because it is the ethos most authors in the debate on commercialization of university knowledge refer to (e.g., Cook-Deegan, 2007). Although originally purely descriptive, the Mertonian ethos of science is often used as a (idealized) deontological norm for the appropriate behaviour of university scientists in the debate on university spin-off creation. On the other hand, the Kirznerian finders–keepers ethic is selected because in entrepreneurship theory the theorizing of Israel M. Kirzner is increasingly seen as one of the basics (Sarasvathy et al., 2003; Douhan et al., 2007; Foss et al., 2007). Moreover, Kirzner has developed a theory of distributive justice for an entrepreneurship context, which is similar to other emerging ethical evaluations of the specific distribution problems in entrepreneurial situations (cf. Dew and Sarasvathy, 2007). Thus, this Kirznerian finders–keepers ethic provides an important concept representing the entrepreneurship side of the debate on university spin-off creation. As such, these two perspectives provide extremes with regard to normative thinking about science and entrepreneurship, and are therefore likely to cover the continuum of perspectives on this issue.

Merton: Ethos of Science

The sociologist Robert K. Merton studied scientific practice to observe the 'normative structure of science' underlying the behaviour of scientists. Merton performed this research in the late 1930s and early 1940s; these studies are collected in *The Sociology of Science* (Merton, 1973). At the time of Merton's studies, the legitimacy of science was questioned because of developments that were not commonly accepted by the public, such as the German and Soviet Union ideological science and the scientific discoveries that were used to improve weapons. Merton sought answers to the question of how scientific knowledge can still be a source of universal truth if so many social structures are involved. To answer this question, he searched to identify the 'ethos of science', the social contract binding the behaviour of scientists. Merton identified four sets of 'institutional imperatives' (ibid., pp. 270–78):

Universalism means that science transcends the particularity of the investigator(s). *Communalism* (or communism) describes the common ownership of the goods produced by scientific investigation. *Disinterestedness* refers to scientific investigation without considerations of personal gain or other individual interests. *Organized scepticism* means a scientist employs 'temporary suspension of judgment and . . . detached scrutiny of beliefs in terms of empirical and logical criteria' (ibid., p. 277). These norms are tacit and also idealized. The latter can be illustrated with the norm of disinterestedness: for instance, each scientist is at least interested in getting publishable results. Merton acknowledged that these idealized norms of science were not always actually followed by scientists (ibid., pp. 383–412), which was also argued by other researchers (Mitroff, 1974; Montgomery and Oliver, 2009).

Regardless of the exact descriptive value, the Mertonian norms are often used as norms characterizing 'basic, fundamental or academic science and are distinguished from applied or industrial science' (Slaughter and Leslie, 1997, p. 178). Table 15.1 displays an evaluation of advantages and disadvantages of university spin-off creation according to the applicable Mertonian norms of universalism, communalism and disinterestedness. This makes clear that university spin-off creation in particular contradicts disinterestedness (Kleinman and Vallas, 2001; Owen-Smith and Powell, 2001; Krimsky, 2003; Vallas and Kleinman, 2007). When an individual researcher is involved in a university spin-off, this implies that he or she has an interest in the performance of this new venture. Because the venture is (partly) based on his or her research, this means that this research is no longer free from interest in the outcomes of the research. Furthermore, the anti-commons effect, implying that knowledge can no longer be shared

Table 15.1   Mertonian evaluation of university spin-off creation

Advantages	Evaluation	Disadvantages	Evaluation
Knowledge utilization	N/A[a]	Reduced academic commitment	N/A
Economic growth	N/A	Research direction change	Contradicts disinterestedness
Learn from other 'culture'	N/A	Anti-commons effect	Contradicts communalism
Revenue generation	Contradicts disinterestedness	Threats objectivity	Contradicts universalism
		Inequity among faculty	N/A
		Departure of staff	N/A
		Unfair competition	N/A

Note: [a] The Mertonian norms are not applicable to evaluate these advantages and disadvantages.

openly and freely, does contradict the norm of communalism (Argyres and Liebeskind, 1998; Krimsky, 2003). In addition, the threat to objectivity contradicts the norm of universalism, as the essence of the universalism norm is that research should be objective and transcending the particularity of the investigator (Slaughter and Rhoades, 2004). In sum, evaluating university spin-off creation by means of Mertonian scientific ethos shows that university spin-off creation to a large extent contradicts these three norms.

Kirzner's Finders–Keepers Ethics

Kirzner's (1989) theory is based on the Austrian School of Economics, which provides a different perspective on the market than mainstream neoclassical economics. For this study one particular consequence of Kirzner's theory is of interest, namely the implication for the division of profit in the market (Kirzner 1989; Burczak, 2002). Kirzner considers knowledge of economic opportunity, technology, potential market demand and resource availability as subjective. This knowledge depends on individual perception and can be wrong or can be right. Entrepreneurs use their subjective knowledge to discover economic opportunities. This discovery, thus, is dependent upon the individual; it is possible that no other person has the knowledge required to discover a particular economic opportunity. Because of this subjective perception involved in the discovery of an opportunity, the opportunity can be treated as if it does not exist without that person. Stated differently, it can be said that the entrepreneur creates products 'ex nihilo' (Kirzner 1989, p. 13). As a consequence, the output created by the entrepreneur is *discovered* output. According to Kirzner, in this case a so-called 'finders–keepers ethic' 'is consistent with what appear to be widely shared moral intuitions' (ibid., p. 17). Kirzner (ibid.; original emphasis) sees this finders–keepers ethic as different from a first-claimant ethic:

> One who finds a beautiful, previously unowned seashell and takes possession of it is entitled to that seashell, we interpret the finders–keepers ethic to mean, not because he was the first to register a claim to it, but because he found it. Not only was the seashell unowned and unclaimed before he found it, but it was in fact undiscovered as well. In other words the seashell had, insofar as human awareness goes, no *existence* prior to its discovery. By finding it, the seashell's discovery has, in a sense, *created* it.

The consequence is that because the finder of an entrepreneurial opportunity is more entitled to it than anybody else, he or she also has more right on the profits of the discovery. A fundamental condition to assign the property of the entrepreneurial opportunity to the finder is that the opportunity itself was 'not fabricated out of prior inputs, it was not the result of a deliberately undertaken research programme' (ibid., p. 152). But even in the case where prior inputs play a role in the discovery, as in a university spin-off based on the findings of a systematic research programme, still the ultimate discovery of the entrepreneurial opportunity as existing outside the immediate results of the research programme is attributable to the discoverer (Shane, 2000). As a result, simple distributive justice rules appear not to apply because 'naive applications of the contractarian framework to innovations assume novelties instantaneously reveal their full consequences to decision makers, at least probabilistically', as Dew and Sarasvathy (2007, p. 274) have argued.

Employing this finders–keepers ethic enables evaluating the advantages and disadvantages of university spin-off creation from a different perspective. Table 15.2 summarizes this ethical evaluation. Fundamental in the Kirznerian discovery justice is that discovering an opportunity is different from the inputs in the research and discovery process (cf. Dew and Sarasvathy, 2007). Thus, it can be argued that the commercialization of research results involves a different realm than the research realm. Knowledge utilization therefore is not linearly connected with the academic research underlying this commercialization. Depending upon the efforts from the university side into the commercialization (and the search for entrepreneurial opportunities), the discovery of the ultimate opportunity is at least partially owned by the entrepreneur. As a result

Table 15.2   Kirznerian evaluation of university spin-off creation

Advantages	Evaluation	Disadvantages	Evaluation
Knowledge utilization	Yes: Is a different discovery	Reduced academic commitment	N/A
Economic growth	N/A[a]	Research direction change	Research differs fundamentally from entrepreneurship
Learn from other 'culture'	N/A	Anti-commons effect	No: Knowledge is subjectively owned
Revenue generation	Yes: For discoverer	Threats objectivity	N/A
		Inequity among faculty	No: Revenues created by entrepreneur
		Departure of faculty	N/A
		Unfair competition	No: Opportunity created by entrepreneur

Note: [a] The Kirznerian norms are not applicable to evaluate these advantages and disadvantages.

of this distinction, there is a natural boundary between entrepreneur and inventor (in the case these two are different people) and at least between the entrepreneur and the other research group members. In this line of reasoning revenues from the university spin-off are also legitimate, and at least partially entitled to by the entrepreneur. This can create income differences among faculty, but these are legitimate because no one else (could have) discovered this opportunity. In sum, evaluating university spin-off creation from a Kirznerian discovery ethics results in an evaluation that is supportive for 'academic entrepreneurs'.

TELEOLOGICAL EVALUATION

Evaluating actions by a teleological ethical theory means that we focus on the consequences of the actions. Teleological ethics, also known as consequentialism or utilitarianism, assumes that something is done for personal or collective benefit, and not necessarily because it is the right thing to do (Frankema, 1973). Teleological ethical theory argues that an action is good if it produces the greatest amount of good for the greatest number of

Table 15.3   Teleological evaluation of university spin-off creation

Advantages	Evaluation	Disadvantages	Evaluation
Knowledge utilization	AS: Neutral EG: Positive	Reduced academic commitment	N/A: Not supported
Economic growth	AS: Neutral EG: Positive	Research direction change	AS: Moderately negative: sometimes changes EG: Moderately negative: Sometimes changes
Learn from other 'culture'	AS: Neutral EG: Positive	Anti-commons effect	AS: Moderately negative: to some extent existing EG: positive
Revenue generation	AS: Positive if existing EG: neutral: ambiguous	Threats objectivity	AS: Moderately negative: to some extent existing EG: neutral
		Inequity among faculty	N/A: Not supported
		Departure of faculty	N/A: Not supported
		Unfair competition	AS: Neutral EG: Potentially negative if existing

people (DeConinck and Lewis, 1997). This evaluation depends obviously on how we define 'good'. For our purposes, let us consider the consequences for two different goods: the first is the advance of fundamental science, the second is economic growth (cf. Bozeman, 2000). I discuss the consequences of university spin-off creation for these two different goods. Here, the review of empirical results as discussed in the literature review section provides insight into the *consequences*, whereas the deontological evaluation only focused on the *norms* and thus did not take into account the consequences observed in empirical studies. Table 15.3 presents an overview of the evaluation, whereby 'AS' refers to the good of 'advancing fundamental science' and 'EG' refers to the good of enhancing 'economic growth'.

With regard to the advantages of university spin-off creation, advancing fundamental science is not hindered substantially, whereas economic growth is generally fostered. The literature review showed that knowledge utilization, economic growth and the effect of learning from the business culture are enhanced by university spin-off creation. With regard to revenue generation for the university, research results were ambiguous. Moreover, it is unclear whether revenue generation for the university would foster economic growth. Considering the goal of advancing fundamental science, revenue generation for the university – if any – is likely positive, because it provides funding to perform fundamental research.

The evaluation of the disadvantages of university spin-off creation shows more mixed results. First of all, a number of disadvantages were not supported by the reviewed empirical research and are therefore excluded from the evaluation (indicated by 'N/A' in Table 15.3). With regard to the potential change in research directions, empirical studies have observed this change in some cases. The shift from fundamental to more applied research, if existing, is obviously detrimental to advancing fundamental research. Moreover, a change towards applied research is possibly also detrimental to long-term economic growth, as radical innovations by fundamental research results are more likely to generate sustainable competitive advantage (Owen-Smith and Powell, 2003; Glenna et al., 2007; Lacetera, 2009). Regarding the anti-commons effect, the goods of advancing fundamental science and economic growth result in different evaluations. Research findings indicate a small anti-commons effect, which could reduce the efficiency of fundamental academic research because research results are not openly shared. On the other hand, it is often stated that economic growth is enhanced by well-functioning markets and sustainable businesses. One of the means to create a sustainable business is by protecting the intellectual property, which potentially results in an anti-commons effect. With regard to the threat to objectivity, research results show that this threat exists and that the objectivity of research is sometimes undermined. For advancing academic science, this is obviously negative. On the other hand, it is not clear whether this has an impact on economic growth. Finally, unfair competition created by supporting spin-off creation could have a detrimental effect on economic growth, assuming that economic growth is fostered the most by fair competition in the market. The literature review, however, showed that it is unclear whether university spin-off support really creates unfair competition. Moreover, the unfair competition neither appears to harm nor to foster science.

In sum, the teleological ethical evaluation of university spin-off creation shows a number of elements that enhance both the goods of advancing academic science and economic growth. On the other hand, a number of elements were identified that likely harm these goods. In general, the effect of university spin-off creation is likely advancing the greatest amount of good for most of the people (assuming that the distribution of profits in the society is reasonably equal). If the remaining disadvantages of university spin-off creation could be reduced, the advantages clearly outperform the disadvantages.

A REFLECTIVE EQUILIBRIUM

The inventory of advantages and disadvantages of university spin-off creation provides the arguments to evaluate the commercialization of university knowledge by means of university spin-offs. The deontological and teleological perspectives show different evaluations. Now these evaluations will be integrated in a reflective equilibrium. Subsequently, I draw the contours of an ethically sound university spin-off policy.

A reflective equilibrium means that we come to a judgement that is aligned with a balance of the different principles we adhere to (i.e., the equilibrium), and that at the same time takes into account the current knowledge of conditions and outcomes (i.e., reflective) (Rawls, 1999). In this study, I have explored two very different sets of normative principles under the heading of a deontological evaluation. The consequences of university spin-off creation are reviewed under the heading of a teleological evaluation. The review of empirical results for each of the advantages and disadvantages shows that some of them are not significant, while others are actually substantial.

The arguments that are not consistent with the empirics can be taken out of the equilibrium. On the advantages side, the aspect of net revenue generation required is not supported. Regarding the disadvantages, the issue of reduced academic commitment is not consistent with data on publication results. As this could be the result of having the right incentives and structures in place, as some authors have argued (Ambos et al., 2008; Chang et al., 2009), universities should be careful not to neglect this disadvantage, but it does not play a role in our equilibrium. Furthermore, the disadvantage of inequity among faculty because of unequal benefits is not supported by the empirical evidence, which is also the case for the departure of faculty. In sum, the equilibrium includes three remaining advantages of university spin-off creation: (1) knowledge utilization, (2) economic growth, and (3) learning from the other 'culture'. Also, three disadvantages remain: (1) the research direction change, (2) the anti-commons effect, and (3) the threat to objectivity.

An equilibrium of these advantages and disadvantages, aligned with the ethical evaluations from different perspectives, tends towards the judgement that university spin-off creation is desirable if detrimental effects can be mitigated as much as possible. The balance of this equilibrium is constructed as follows. On the one hand, according to Mertonian norms, furthering university spin-off creation is not desirable. On the other extreme, according to Kirznerian logic, nothing is wrong with university spin-offs and private benefits from public-funded research. Furthermore, from a teleological perspective, the three supported advantages are contributing to economic growth and not reducing the advancement of science, whereas the change in research directions and the threat to objectivity are evaluated as negative for both advancing science and economic growth, and the evaluation of the anti-commons effect differs per defined good. Because economic growth is probably creating a good for more people than advancing science as such, the teleological evaluation tends towards the judgement that university spin-off creation is desirable. Moreover, the objections from a Mertonian viewpoint can be mitigated to some extent by designing the right structures governing the creation of university spin-offs, which reduces the disadvantages. Under the condition that these detrimental effects can be mitigated, the benefits of university spin-off creation, especially from a Kirznerian and teleological evaluation, appear to outweigh the disadvantages.

This reflective equilibrium is subject to mitigating the three disadvantages while conserving the already existing instruments that reduce the other disadvantages. The three disadvantages that need attention are: the research direction change, the anti-commons effect and the threat to objectivity. For (university) policy-makers, faculty and academic entrepreneurs the awareness of these three potential disadvantages is important. The change in research directions can probably be reduced by incentivizing not only the quality of the research but also the direction of the research (Thursby et al., 2007). The anti-commons effect is more difficult to deal with, although developments in the direction of open science appear to be driven by the intention to enhance the free sharing of academic knowledge (David, 2004; Rhoten and Powell, 2007). This direction is one that provides potential (David, 2004) and needs more attention, in particular in combination with commercialization of this knowledge (cf. Bozeman, 2007; West, 2008). An effective way to reduce the threat to objectivity is to increase the transparency of funding flows (Smith, 1998; Krimsky, 2003) as well as the enhancement of formal conflict of interest policies (Argyres and Liebeskind,1998; Leute, 2005; Powell and Colyvas, 2008; Welsh et al., 2008). In general, one of the important design principles to enhance both fundamental science as well as to stimulate university spin-off creation is the creation of a 'dual' structure. In this structure, the commercial activities are separated as much as possible from fundamental research, both in a managerial and a physical sense. Of course, especially in early stages of the development of the spin-off company, the scientific endeavour and the commercial path intermingle and boundaries have to be negotiated (Rappert et al., 1999). But in the long term, as well as in the formal rules, these two activities have to be separated to be able to enhance both fundamental science and spin-off creation (Debackere and Veugelers, 2005; Ambos et al., 2008; van Burg et al., 2008; Chang et al., 2009).

LIMITATIONS AND FUTURE RESEARCH DIRECTIONS

This ethical review of the university spin-off phenomenon and the construction of a reflective equilibrium make an important contribution to a more constructive debate, based on valid arguments and different perspectives. To advance this debate even more, important research questions have to be answered. First, the created equilibrium is 'reflective' in the sense that it is dependent upon the current state of knowledge regarding university spin-off creation (Rawls, 1999). Future research can discover other disadvantages or can show that disadvantages are increasing over the long term, for example by eroding the still existing Mertonian norms (Slaughter and Rhoades, 2004; Rhoten and Powell, 2007). Therefore, systematic enquiry is required to update the equilibrium and to enable decision-making based on sound knowledge. Second, the reflective equilibrium in this study is based on two deontological perspectives and two teleological evaluations. More perspectives could be added, in order to challenge or strengthen the constructed equilibrium. Third, an issue that becomes more important when commercialization practices are more and more replicated around the world is the study of the diverse legal and social regimes regarding universities and entrepreneurship. Most literature, including this review, implicitly assumes uniformity in practices around the world. Most research has focused on the USA and to a lesser extent on Western Europe. To develop policy and make normative recommendations, an understanding of the national, local and regional context is needed. Fourth, the literature review showed that it is necessary to study the net revenues from university spin-offs as well as other commercialization practices such as licensing. Fifth, the issue of potential unfair competition needs further research. Many new companies are supported by government and support organizations. It is worth considering whether this creates inequality in open market systems such as in the USA or in Europe.

CONCLUSION

The concept of the entrepreneurial university has raised lively debates around the moral question: is the increased role of commercial activities in the university good or bad? This study integrates the different lines of reasoning regarding the moral issues generated by establishing more entrepreneurial universities in general and the commercialization of science by means of university spin-off creation in particular. As such, an important contribution to this debate is the construction of an integral and balancing reflective equilibrium that can be used as a moral criterion. I conclude in this review that commercializing science by means of university spin-offs is ethically desirable on the condition that disadvantages can be mitigated by designing appropriate organizational structures. This has important implications for the organization of entrepreneurial universities. Essential design principles need to focus on creating incentive structures that support the pursuit of fundamental research alongside more applied research, supporting open science where possible, and separating commercial activities as much as possible from fundamental research. Future work and debates need to generate continuous attention for issues such as research objectivity and the contribution of science to society to update the reflective equilibrium and to notice whether unintended long-term effects on changes in the value system of scientists occur. In this respect, this study provides a basis for a continued discussion that draws on sound arguments.

NOTE

*   I am grateful to Lambèr Royakkers and Georges Romme for their helpful suggestions and comments. Financial support for this research was provided by the TU/e Innovation Lab at Eindhoven University of Technology. The usual disclaimers apply.

REFERENCES

Ambos, T.C., K. Mäkelä, J. Birkinshaw and P. D'Este (2008), 'When does university research get commercialized? Creating ambidexterity in research institutions', *Journal of Management Studies*, **45**(8), 1424–47.
Argyres, N.S. and J.P. Liebeskind (1998), 'Privatizing the intellectual commons: Universities and the commercialization of biotechnology', *Journal of Economic Behavior and Organization*, **35**(4), 427–54.
Azoulay, P., W. Ding and T. Stuart (2009), 'The impact of academic patenting on the rate, quality and direction of (public) research output', *Journal of Industrial Economics*, **57**(4), 637–76.

Baldini, N. (2008), 'Negative effects of university patenting: Myths and grounded evidence', *Scientometrics*, **75**(2), 289–311.

Bird, B.J., D.J. Hayward and D.N. Allen (1993), 'Conflicts in the commercialization of knowledge: Perspectives from science and entrepreneurship', *Entrepreneurship Theory and Practice*, **17**(4), 57–76.

Blumenthal, D. (1992), 'Academic–industry relationships in the life sciences', *Journal of the American Medical Association*, **268**(23), 3344–9.

Bozeman, B. (2000), 'Technology transfer and public policy: A review of research and theory', *Research Policy*, **29**(4–5), 627–55.

Bozeman, B. (2007), *Public Values and Public Interest: Counterbalancing Economic Iindividualism*, Washington, DC: Georgetown University Press.

Bramwell, A. and D.A. Wolfe (2008), 'Universities and regional economic development: The entrepreneurial University of Waterloo', *Research Policy*, **37**(8), 1175–87.

Bray, M.J. and J.N. Lee (2000), 'University revenues from technology transfer: Licensing fees vs. equity positions', *Journal of Business Venturing*, **15**(5–6), 385–92.

Burczak, T. (2002), 'A critique of Kirzner's finders–keepers defense of profit', *Review of Austrian Economics*, **15**(1), 75–90.

Chang, Y.C. and P.Y. Yang (2008), 'The impacts of academic patenting and licensing on knowledge production and diffusion: A test of the anti-commons effect in Taiwan', *R&D Management*, **38**(3), 321–34.

Chang, Y.C., P.Y. Yang and M.H. Chen (2009), 'The determinants of academic research commercial performance: Towards an organizational ambidexterity perspective', *Research Policy*, **38**(6), 936–46.

Chapple, W., A. Lockett, D.S. Siegel and M. Wright (2005), 'Assessing the relative performance of U.K. university technology transfer offices: Parametric and non-parametric evidence', *Research Policy*, **34**(3), 369–84.

Colyvas, J.A. (2007), 'From divergent meanings to common practices: The early institutionalization of technology transfer in the life sciences at Stanford University', *Research Policy*, **36**(4), 456–76.

Colyvas, J.A. and W.W. Powell (2007), 'From vulnerable to venerated: The institutionalization of academic entrepreneurship in the life sciences', in M. Reuf and M. Lounsbury (eds), *Research in the Sociology of Organizations*, Oxford: JAI Press, pp. 223–66.

Colyvas, J., M. Crow, A. Gelijns, R. Mazzoleni, R.R. Nelson, N. Rosenberg and B.N. Sampat (2002), 'How do university inventions get into practice?' *Management Science*, **48**(1), 61–72.

Cook-Deegan, R. (2007), 'The science commons in health research: Structure, function, and value', *Journal of Technology Transfer*, **32**(3), 133–56.

Crespi, G., P. D'Este, R. Fontana and A. Geuna (2011), 'The impact of academic patenting on university research and its transfer', *Research Policy*, **40**(1), 55–68.

David, P.A. (2004), 'Understanding the emergence of "open science" institutions: Functionalist economics in historical context', *Industrial and Corporate Change*, **13**(4), 571–89.

Debackere, K. and R. Veugelers (2005), 'The role of academic technology transfer organizations in improving industry science links', *Research Policy*, **34**(3), 321–42.

DeConinck, J.B. and W.F. Lewis (1997), 'The influence of deontological and teleological considerations and ethical climate on sales managers' intentions to reward or punish sales force behavior', *Journal of Business Ethics*, **16**(5), 497–506.

Dew, N. and S. Sarasvathy (2007), 'Innovations, stakeholders and entrepreneurship', *Journal of Business Ethics*, **74**(3), 267–83.

Di Gregorio, D. and S. Shane (2003), 'Why do some universities generate more start-ups than others?' *Research Policy*, **32**(2), 209–27.

Douhan, R., G. Eliasson and M. Henrekson (2007), 'Israel M. Kirzner: An outstanding Austrian contributor to the economics of entrepreneurship', *Small Business Economics*, **29**(1), 213–23.

Fabrizio, K.R. and A. Di Minin (2008), 'Commercializing the laboratory: Faculty patenting and the open science environment', *Research Policy*, **37**(5), 914–31.

Feller, I. (1990), 'Universities as engines of R&D-based economic growth: They think they can', *Research Policy*, **19**(4), 335–48.

Feller, I. (1990), 'University patent and technology-licensing strategies', *Educational Policy*, **4**(4), 327–40.

Foss, K., N.J. Foss and P.G. Klein (2007), 'Original and derived judgment: An entrepreneurial theory of economic organization', *Organization Studies*, **28**(12), 1893–912.

Frankema, W.K. (1973), *Ethics*, Eaglewood Cliffs, NJ: Prentice Hall.

Geiger, R.L. (2004), *Knowledge and Money: Research Universities and the Paradox of the Marketplace*, Stanford, CA: Stanford University Press.

Geuna, A. and L.J.J. Nesta (2006), 'University patenting and its effects on academic research: The emerging European evidence', *Research Policy*, **35**(6), 790–807.

Gilsing, V.A., E. van Burg and A.G.L. Romme (2010), 'Policy principles for the creation and success of corporate and academic spin-offs', *Technovation*, **30**(1), 12–23.

Glenna, L.L., R. Welsh, W.B. Lacy and D. Biscotti (2007), 'University administrators, agricultural biotechnology, and academic capitalism: Defining the public good to promote university–industry relationships', *Sociological Quarterly*, **48**(1), 141–63.

Godin, B. and Y. Gingras (2000), 'Impact of collaborative research on academic science', *Science and Public Policy*, **27**(1), 65–73.

Goldstein, H. (2010), 'The "entrepreneurial turn" and regional economic development mission of universities', *Annals of Regional Science*, **44**(1), 83–109.

Gulbrandsen, M. and J.C. Smeby (2005), 'Industry funding and university professors' research performance', *Research Policy*, **34**(6), 932–50.

Haeussler, C. (2011), 'Information-sharing in academia and the industry: A comparative study', *Research Policy*, **40**(1), 105–22.

Haeussler, C. and J.A. Colyvas (2011), 'Breaking the ivory tower: Academic entrepreneurship in the life sciences in UK and Germany', *Research Policy*, **40**(1), 41–54.

Hsu, R.C. and T. Bernstein (1997), 'Managing the university technology licensing process: Findings from case studies', *Journal of the Association of University Technology Managers*, **9**, 1–33.

Jensen, R. and M. Thursby (2001), 'Proofs and prototypes for sale: The licensing of university inventions', *American Economic Review*, **91**(1), 240–59.

Kant, I. (2005), *Groundwork for the Metaphysics of Morals*, Peterborough, ON, originally published 1785: NSW Broadview Press.

Kirzner, I.M. (1989), *Discovery, Capitalism, and Distributive Justice*, Oxford: Basil Blackwell.

Klein, R., U. de Haan and A. Goldberg (2010), 'Overcoming obstacles encountered on the way to commercialize university IP', *Journal of Technology Transfer*, **35**(6), 671–9.

Kleinman, D.L. and S.P. Vallas (2001), 'Science, capitalism, and the rise of the "knowledge worker": The changing structure of knowledge production in the United States', *Theory and Society*, **30**(4), 451–92.

Krimsky, S. (2003), *Science in the Private Interest: Has the Lure of Profits Corrupted Biomedical Research?* Lanham, MD: Rowman and Littlefield Publishers.

Lacetera, N. (2009), 'Different missions and commitment power in R&D organizations: Theory and evidence on industry–university alliances', *Organization Science*, **20**(3), 565–82.

Larsen, M.T. (2011), 'The implications of academic enterprise for public science: An overview of the empirical evidence', *Research Policy*, **40**(1), 6–19.

Lefkowitz, J. (2003), *Ethics and Values in Industrial-Organizational Psychology*, Mahwah, NJ: Lawrence Erlbaum.

Leute, K. (2005), 'Stanford's licensing and equity practices with biotechnology companies', *Journal of Commercial Biotechnology*, **11**(4), 318–24.

Lexchin, J., L.A. Bero, B. Djulbegovic and O. Clark (2003), 'Pharmaceutical industry sponsorship and research outcome and quality: Systematic review', *British Medical Journal*, **326**(7400), 1167–70.

Lowe, R. and C. Gonzalez (2007), 'Faculty entrepreneurs and research productivity', *Journal of Technology Transfer*, **32**(3), 173–94.

Lundström, A. and L.A. Stevenson (2005), *Entrepreneurship Policy: Theory and Practice*, Boston: Springer.

Mars, M.M., S. Slaughter and G. Rhoades (2008), 'The state-subsidized student entrepreneur, *Journal of Higher Education*, **79**(6), 638–70.

Martinelli, A., M. Meyer and N. von Tunzelmann (2008), 'Becoming an entrepreneurial university? A case study of knowledge exchange relationships and faculty attitudes in a medium-sized, research-oriented university', *Journal of Technology Transfer*, **33**(3), 259–83.

Merton, R.K. (1973), *The Sociology of Science: Theoretical and Empirical Investigations*, Chicago: University of Chicago Press.

Meyer, M. (2006), 'Academic inventiveness and entrepreneurship: On the importance of start-up companies in commercializing academic patents', *Journal of Technology Transfer*, **31**(4), 501–10.

Micewski, E. and C. Troy (2007), 'Business ethics – deontologically revisited', *Journal of Business Ethics*, **72**(1), 17–25.

Mitchell, R.K., L. Busenitz, T. Lant, P.P. McDougall, E.A. Morse and J.B. Smith (2002), 'Toward a theory of entrepreneurial cognition: Rethinking the people side of entrepreneurship research', *Entrepreneurship Theory and Practice*, **27**(2), 93–104.

Mitroff, I.I. (1974), 'Norms and counter-norms in a select group of the Apollo moon scientists: A case study of the ambivalence of scientists', *American Sociological Review*, **39**(4), 579–95.

Montgomery, K. and A.L. Oliver (2009), 'Shifts in guidelines for ethical scientific conduct: How public and private organizations create and change norms of research integrity', *Social Studies of Science*, **39**(1), 137–55.

Mowery, D.C. and B.N. Sampat (2005), 'Universities in national innovation systems', in J. Fagerberg, D.C. Mowery and R.R. Nelson (eds), *Oxford Handbook of Innovation*, Oxford: Oxford University Press, pp. 209–39.

Mueller, P. (2006), 'Exploring the knowledge filter: How entrepreneurship and university–industry relationships drive economic growth', *Research Policy*, **35**(10), 1499–508.

Murray, F. and S. Stern (2007), 'Do formal intellectual property rights hinder the free flow of scientific knowledge? An empirical test of the anti-commons hypothesis', *Journal of Economic Behavior and Organization*, **63**(4), 648–87.

O'Shea, R.P., T.J. Allen, A. Chevalier and F. Roche (2005), 'Entrepreneurial orientation, technology transfer and spinoff performance of U.S. universities', *Research Policy*, **34**(7), 994–1009.

Owen-Smith, J. and W.W. Powell (2001), 'Careers and contradictions: Faculty responses to the transformation of knowledge and its uses in the life sciences', *Research in the Sociology of Work*, **10**, 109–40.

Owen-Smith, J. and W.W. Powell (2003), 'The expanding role of university patenting in the life sciences: Assessing the importance of experience and connectivity', *Research Policy*, **32**(9), 1695–711.

Perkmann, M. and K. Walsh (2007), 'University–industry relationships and open innovation: Towards a research agenda', *International Journal of Management Reviews*, **9**(4), 259–80.

Perkmann, M. and K. Walsh (2008), 'Engaging the scholar: Three types of academic consulting and their impact on universities and industry', *Research Policy*, **37**(10), 1884–91.

Powell, W.W. and J.A. Colyvas (2008), 'The microfoundations of institutions', in R. Greenwood, C. Oliver, K. Sahlin and R. Suddaby (eds), *Handbook of Organizational Institutionalism*, London: Sage Publications, pp. 267–89.

Powell, W.W. and J. Owen-Smith (2002), 'The new world of knowledge production in the life sciences', in S. Brint (ed.), *The Future of the City of Intellect: The Changing American University*, Stanford, CA: Stanford University Press, pp. 106–32.

Powers, J.B. and P. McDougall (2005), 'Policy orientation effects on performance with licensing to start-ups and small companies', *Research Policy*, **34**(7), 1028–42.

Powers, J.B. and P.P. McDougall (2005), 'University start-up formation and technology licensing with firms that go public: A resource-based view of academic entrepreneurship', *Journal of Business Venturing*, **20**(3), 291–311.

Rappert, B., A. Webster and D. Charles (1999), 'Making sense of diversity and reluctance: Academic–industrial relations and intellectual property', *Research Policy*, **28**(8), 873–90.

Rawls, J. (1999), *A Theory of Justice*, revised edition, Cambridge, MA: Harvard University Press.

Renault, C. (2006), 'Academic capitalism and university incentives for faculty entrepreneurship', *Journal of Technology Transfer*, **31**(2), 227–39.

Rhoten, D. and W.W. Powell (2007), 'The frontiers of intellectual property: Expanded protection versus new models of open science', *Annual Review of Law and Social Science*, **3**, 345–73.

Sarasvathy, S.D., N. Dew, S.R. Velamuri and S. Venkataraman (2003), 'Three views of entrepreneurial opportunity', in Z.J. Acs and D.B. Audretsch (eds), *Handbook of Entrepreneurship Research: An Interdisciplinary Survey and Introduction*, Dordrecht: Kluwer Academic Publishers, pp. 141–60.

Shane, S. (2000), 'Prior knowledge and the discovery of entrepreneurial opportunities', *Organization Science*, **11**(4), 448–69.

Shane, S. (2002), 'Selling university technology: Patterns from MIT', *Management Science*, **48**(1), 122–37.

Shane, S. (2004), *Academic Entrepreneurship: University Spinoffs and Wealth Creation*, Cheltenham, UK and Northampton, MA, USA: Edward Elgar.

Shane, S. (2009), 'Why encouraging more people to become entrepreneurs is bad public policy', *Small Business Economics*, **33**(2), 141–9.

Siegel, D.S., R. Veugelers and M. Wright (2007), 'Technology transfer offices and commercialization of university intellectual property: Performance and policy implications', *Oxford Review of Economic Policy*, **23**(4), 640–60.

Siegel, D.S., D.A. Waldman, L.E. Atwater and A.N. Link (2004), 'Toward a model of the effective transfer of scientific knowledge from academicians to practitioners: Qualitative evidence from the commercialization of university technologies', *Journal of Engineering and Technology Management*, **21**(1–2), 115–42.

Slaughter, S. and L.L. Leslie (1997), *Academic Capitalism: Politics, Policies, and the Entrepreneurial University*, London: Johns Hopkins University Press.

Slaughter, S. and G. Rhoades (2004), *Academic Capitalism and the New Economy*, Baltimore, MD and London: Johns Hopkins University Press.

Smith, R. (1998), 'Beyond conflict of interest', *British Medical Journal*, **317**(7154), 291–92.

Steffensen, M., E.M. Rogers and K. Speakman (2000), 'Spin-offs from research centers at a research university', *Journal of Business Venturing*, **15**(1), 93–111.

Stevens, J.M. and J.W. Bagby (2001), 'Knowledge transfer from universities to business: Returns for all stakeholders?' *Organization*, **8**(2), 259–68.

Tartari, V. and S. Breschi (2012), 'Set them free: Scientists' evaluations of the benefits and costs of university–industry research collaboration', *Industrial and Corporate Change*, **21**(5), 1117–47.

Thursby, J.G. and M.C. Thursby (2005), 'Pros and cons of faculty participation in licensing', in G.D. Libecap (ed.), *University Entrepreneurship and Technology Transfer: Process, Design, and Intellectual Property*, Oxford: Elsevier, pp. 187–210.

Thursby, J.G., R. Jensen and M.C. Thursby (2001), 'Objectives, characteristics and outcomes of university licensing: A survey of major U.S. universities', *Journal of Technology Transfer*, **26**(1–2), 59–72.

Thursby, M., J. Thursby and S. Gupta-Mukherjee (2007), 'Are there real effects of licensing on academic research? A life cycle view', *Journal of Economic Behavior and Organization*, **63**(4), 577–98.

Vallas, S. and P. Kleinman (2007), 'Contradiction, convergence and the knowledge economy: The confluence of academic and commercial biotechnology', *Socio-Economic Review*, **30**(4), 1–25.

van Burg, E., A.G.L. Romme, V.A. Gilsing and I.M.M.J. Reymen (2008), 'Creating university spin-offs: A science-based design perspective', *Journal of Product Innovation Management*, **25**(2), 114–28.

van Looy, B., J. Callaert and K. Debackere (2006), 'Publication and patent behavior of academic researchers: Conflicting, reinforcing or merely co-existing?' *Research Policy*, **35**(4), 596–608.

Welsh, R., L. Glenna, W. Lacy and D. Biscotti (2008), 'Close enough but not too far: Assessing the effects of university–industry research relationships and the rise of academic capitalism', *Research Policy*, **37**(10), 1854–64.

West, J. (2008), 'Commercializing open science: Deep space communications as the lead market for Shannon theory, 1960–73', *Journal of Management Studies*, **45**(8), 1506–32.

Ylijoki, O.H. (2003), 'Entangled in academic capitalism? A case-study on changing ideals and practices of university research', *Higher Education*, **45**(3), 307–35.

Zucker, L.G. and M.R. Darby (1998), 'Entrepreneurs, star scientists, and biotechnology', *NBER Reporter*, Fall, 7–11.

Zucker, L.G., M.R. Darby and J.S. Armstrong (2002), 'Commercializing knowledge: University science, knowledge capture, and firm performance in biotechnology', *Management Science*, **48**(1), 138–53.

16. The meandering path: the university's contribution toward the entrepreneurial journey
Louise-Jayne Edwards and Elizabeth J. Muir

THE FIRST STEP ON A LONG PATH

This chapter uses the metaphor of a 'meandering path' to visualize the entrepreneurial journey of graduate entrepreneurs from education to business start-up. In our daily lives we are dependent on signposts and roadmaps to guide us; their clarity and direction enables us to avoid 'dead ends' and most importantly to reach our destinations. The 'signpost' provides a clear and accurate instruction and thus the authors propose that the entrepreneurial university should be envisaged as a signpost/road map for the student/graduate entrepreneur to follow. As per the theme of the meandering path, the authors interweave through extensive literature to uniquely bring together various fields: entrepreneurship, enterprise education, sociology, psychology and economics, to focus upon universities' contribution to future entrepreneurs.

The authors carried out a three-year qualitative study of graduate entrepreneurs in South Wales analysing their personal, educational and business journeys. The phenomenological research focused upon the subjective learning experiences of 16 graduates and the authors concluded that there is a gap between the academic offerings of universities and the actual requirements of the students as future entrepreneurs. This chapter analyses numerous ways in which universities can contribute to entrepreneurship development and the necessity of a clear strategy for staff and students to follow.

The university model of enterprise education is that of a series of core and optional enterprise (or enterprise-related) modules that contribute towards a qualification and a variety of experiential opportunities and support resources that the student may or may not access (Edwards, 2011). Within this model, the authors found that students 'meander' without clear signposting, whereby assessment is based upon traditional academic qualifications and outcomes are measured in terms of entrepreneurial intent. The main contribution of this chapter is the notion that if the entrepreneurial university model (the signpost) is converted into a coordinated framework and each student supported in developing a personal development plan to move through this, then the students can gain better knowledge, learning, skills development, experience, reflective practice, identity shift and access to the resources to become entrepreneurs. Additionally, the authors contend that the academic 'need' to seek a definition of an entrepreneur is no longer effective, as the concept is multifaceted, socially determined and changes over time. The authors move beyond the debates of 'What is an entrepreneur?', 'What is enterprise education?', 'What is it for?', and 'Can entrepreneurship be taught'? The effective focus is not about limiting the concept to a specific academic definition, but enabling students to enter the world of entrepreneurship on their own terms, to create successful and sustainable businesses that contribute to the economy and have social benefits for the community as well as psychological achievement for the individual.

TWO STEPS BACK – THE BACKGROUND

High rates of UK unemployment and more so 'under-employment' in relation to graduates (Rae, 2010), coupled with a rise in 'Graduate NEETs' (not in education, employment or training) implies that there is an economic and educational need to develop entrepreneurial people as well as entrepreneurs through all levels of education (Edwards, 2011). Despite a dearth of research in this area, particularly empirical studies of graduate entrepreneurs (Matlay, 2011), universities are encouraged to promote entrepreneurship as a viable option.

Such developments need to acknowledge the value of entrepreneurship for the economy and society, creating businesses and employment (Edwards, 2011). Garavan and O'Cinneide are in favour of policy-makers and political decision-makers who appreciate the 'role of the entrepreneur' and assert that entrepreneurs should be viewed 'as a possible solution to rising unemployment rates and as a recipe for economic prosperity' (1994, p. 3). This is a perspective supported in other countries such as Finland (Erkkilä, 2000) and Germany (Anderseck, 2004). In contrast, Wolf questions whether increasing government expenditure and enterprise education is the answer to promoting economic growth (2002). Whilst there is some evidence that enterprise education within universities is producing people who start their own businesses and contribute to the wealth of the nation (Kothari and Handscombe, 2007) there is much need for longitudinal evaluations that can capture data on growth levels, long-term incubation graduate entrepreneurs (Cox et al., 2002) and aspects of sustainability, serial entrepreneurs and portfolio entrepreneurs. Handscombe et al. (2005) identified that within universities there is concern that without such data, or evidence of long-term success, sources of funding for enterprise education might lapse.

Whilst policy-makers perceive that the outcome of enterprise education is to produce entrepreneurs (Edwards, 2011), evidence mainly supports the identification of individuals who have the *intention* to become business owners. There is a need for enterprise provision to move beyond entrepreneurial intention to measure entrepreneurial practice. One constraint to effective enterprise education is the development of appropriate enterprise educators (Hytti and O'Gorman, 2004). It is not always fully recognized that there is a disparity between their teaching skills in the subject matter and the learning needs of potential entrepreneurs. It is educators who establish the courses, the content, pedagogies and assessments and thus their understanding of entrepreneurs' needs and students' entrepreneurial learning journeys are paramount. Reluctance to move away from standard university assessments is evidence of a lack of understanding of these needs. Assessment needs to be inclusive of personal issues of identity development, clear linkage between theory and practice and critical reflection on practice. This means that evaluations of accredited enterprise courses need to take these factors into account and go beyond entrepreneurial intention, into entrepreneurial practice.

Furthermore, understanding that entrepreneurial activity is complex, varied and often a life-time commitment calls for long-term studies of entrepreneur alumni. Although this is a growing research area, there is little evidence to support the notion that enterprise education can actually impact upon entrepreneurial activity from initiation to exit (Matlay, 2008). Entrepreneur alumni growth and development patterns as microbusiness owners, fast-growth company leaders, portfolio entrepreneurs or serial entrepreneurs provide essential knowledge that feeds back into refinement of existing courses as well as the development of new ones. It also enables researchers to evaluate the long-term value of enterprise education in terms of its contribution to society, not just in economic terms of employment and national wealth creation, but also in wider concepts such as the environment, community and social enterprise, ethics and trading practices.

Promoting the notion that through enterprise education universities can produce entrepreneurs with merely the financial label attached to the concept, is limiting. If the aim of enterprise education is to enable individuals to become entrepreneurs and enact that identity through their value judgements, business acumen, social responsibility and personal achievements and satisfaction, then the authors conclude that evaluations of enterprise education need to expand to embrace (and recognize) the learning development of the whole person, as opposed to only measuring the economic outputs based upon quantitative data of the number of businesses and new jobs created.

One purpose of this chapter is to consider and question the role of universities in the development of 'future entrepreneurs'. The authors approach this from a teaching and learning perspective and propose that universities need to be entrepreneurial and advance their 'promotional strategies' (their signposts), whilst developing specific strategies that enable the student's entrepreneurial journey from university to business. As stakeholders, universities need to be reactive and responsible to nurture and develop graduate entrepreneurs as individuals, who can be guided to take advantage of appropriate teaching and learning opportunities, business mentoring and experiences, and university resources (including incubation centres, physical space and academic expertise), thus developing graduates *for* the economy.

The authors carried out research on a sample of graduate entrepreneurs from the University of Glamorgan in South Wales (UK) (now the University of South Wales) between 2009 and 2011. Their research comprised of 16 case studies of the life stories of graduate entrepreneurs, which re-told their business, education and personal journeys *towards* entrepreneurship since graduation. The businesses varied in terms of, sector, size of company and number of years that the business had been running. The longest-running business was five-and-half years and run by two university friends, who both came from families of entrepreneurs. Their parents invested in their business by giving them their start-up capital; based upon their own experiences of running businesses and strongly advising them against pursuing bank loans. Other businesses included a web design company, employing 20 staff within their first year of starting their business. A sports school established by two sport science graduates, running after-school clubs for hundreds of children in South Wales and a book publisher, running a social enterprise: 'I think we are doing a worthwhile job in the arts sector. We give new writers a start in the world which as a writer I know that is a hard thing, we don't do it for the financial reward' commented the research participant (Edwards, 2011, p. 175).

Following a constructivist philosophy, the aim of the study was to evaluate and present new meaning to the learning processes required on the path towards becoming an entrepreneur. One of the main research outcomes was the study group's disassociation with the term 'entrepreneur', which leads to the discussion in this chapter on identity. The second key finding was the lack of awareness and perceived value of accredited enterprise courses and extracurricular education by the university, to support them and signpost their journey to entrepreneurship. The authors contend that attention to a personal development plan, to guide and signpost students through a framework of university resources would most likely produce graduates who are practising entrepreneurship and developing their own businesses rather than graduates with the *possible intention* of becoming entrepreneurs, as conveyed by one of the research participants:

> Well, I finished my Masters and I'd had enough of learning for a while and thought what am I going to do now? I was 99% sure I was going to start my own business. I got to the point where I was thinking I'm going to do it in a year or two. (Edwards, 2011, p. 117)

THE INTERCHANGEABLE ENTREPRENEUR

Since the inception of research into the field of entrepreneurship, academics can neither agree on a definition of the term 'entrepreneur' nor the notion of 'enterprise'. An analysis of the literature confirms that a plethora of research on entrepreneurship exists, spanning some 40 years. However, the majority of research has a positivist approach and is concerned with finding answers as opposed to seeking and generating new meanings (Edwards, 2011). For example, the literature remarks upon the constant endeavours and frustrations to find a single definitive answer to the question of 'What is an entrepreneur?' As declared by Robson, 'positivists maintain that one reality exists and that it is the researcher's job to discover what it is' (2002, p. 27). Opposing the positivist stance, Rae states that 'The term "entrepreneur" is socially constructed and understood in different ways in different communities, and therefore does not hold the same implicit meaning in each of these communities' (2003, p. 3), this resonates with the authors' observations whilst attending enterprise and small business conferences and also from their research into graduate entrepreneurship, when they asked one graduate how they felt being labelled an entrepreneur, one research participant retorted: 'I don't like that word. It means "Richard Branson"; it means someone who is motivated by money. I'm more likely to say I run my own business. I don't think, I'd ever describe myself as an entrepreneur' (Edwards, 2011, p. 171).

However, the term 'entrepreneur' is widely used by the general public in the UK; the lives of entrepreneurs have been televised through programmes such as *Dragon's Den*, *The Apprentice*, *Mind of a Millionaire* and *Beat the Boss*, to name just a few. As Burns observes, '[entrepreneurs] provide the glamour pages for the business press with "against-all-odds" start-up stories and biographies of millionaire entrepreneurs guaranteed to sell well' (2001, p. 1). However, Rae's most recent research disapproves of media stereotypes of entrepreneurship and protests that 'they represent a kind of entrepreneurial pornography' (2010, p. 599), whereby the exploitation and grandiose glamorization of entrepreneurs through mass media does not represent a homogeneous group of entrepreneurs; it does create another level of research into entrepreneurship, particularly enterprise education.

With the marriage of media/marketing and enterprise brings a new level of entrepreneurship curriculum (moving away from business schools as the traditional home for such courses), with a rise in the creative industries developing undergraduate degrees that add enterprise education to fashion, design, film-making or journalism. However, in the context of this chapter, despite the upsurge in courses and despite the role that entrepreneurs play in the media, the underlying question remains 'What is an entrepreneur?' Definitions and traits of entrepreneurs are out of the scope of this chapter, but the point is that whilst researchers have endeavoured to find a single definition, the frustrations of not finding an agreeable definition creates paths for researchers to deviate away from the question. Of the 16 graduate entrepreneurs that the researchers interviewed, only one had studied an accredited business course; the participant expressed that he wanted to start a business before he started university, thus when questioned why he did not opt for an enterprise course rather than a general business degree, his response was that he viewed entrepreneurship courses as a 'finishing school', suitable for someone much older and who had been running a business for a number of years. His description of 'suitable candidates' for entrepreneurship courses is akin to the entry requirements of a standard MBA, for experienced managers. He perceived entrepreneurship courses to be for practising accustomed entrepreneurs, not as a place for aspiring young entrepreneurs and his lack of knowledge and experience deterred him from applying for the course. The researchers probed how he had reached this conclusion and it was through the flawed advice of a third party, in this case a school-based careers advisor. The careers advisor had a pre-conceived image of an entrepreneur and enterprise education and effectively gave the student incorrect information (Edwards, 2011). From the research carried out, it was compelling that whilst the remaining 15 research participants were from non-business-related subject disciplines, they still undertook a 'business module' as part of their degree. They reflected on the modules with great negativity; the modules often focused upon business planning, which the participants declared did not inspire them to start a business but instead gave them the impression that business was monotonous and boring. When further questioned as to who taught them the 'business modules' it was found that it was non-business-related staff and educators from within their own faculties (design/sport/technology). One graduate entrepreneur lamented:

> Well put it this way, my lecturers were really good at getting us to pass our coursework and pass our exams and yeah, I remember one used to be a rowing coach for Great Britain and she used to talk about that and one used to play rugby for England but there was never a positive message of 'you can do it, you can start a business'. We were never told the practicalities of how to do it, we were just told the theory about this and that. (ibid., p. 138).

Enterprise education has, for the most part, been developed upon academic Cartesian principles of defining the desired outcome (the entrepreneur) and generating programmes that teach the relevant knowledge and skills with some additional resources available. The understanding of what it means to be an entrepreneur has been limited to attempted definitions that focus upon economic need and business management skills, with little cognizance of the social context, psychological requirements and individual students' support that will enable them to take on the identity of being a practising entrepreneur. Thus, it is essential to identify what an entrepreneur is in terms of the economy and education but also in terms of personal identity – how do entrepreneurs label themselves?

Social scientists, psychologists and philosophers have attempted to define 'identity' and conclude that it is polymorphic, dynamic, influenced by many different aspects of life, and liable to change, and that individuals may hold multiple identities relating to differing groups (Burke and Stets, 2009). However, there is a consensus that 'identity' is both linked to and similar to concepts of the self and individual subjectivity (Elliott, 2008). Identity may be conceptualized as a construct of an individual that changes over time and that process of change is affected by social experiences and socialization (Burke and Tully, 1977; Ibarra, 1999). Jenkins confirms that identity is a 'process – *identification* – not a "thing". It is not something that one can *have*, or not; it is something that one *does*' (2008, p. 5; original emphasis). As a consequence of understanding their identity, individuals may attach meaning to their experiences, be cognizant of where they are within society and after reflection, develop guidelines for future action (Hoang and Gimeno, 2005).

The research findings for this chapter, based on 16 case studies of the life stories of graduate entrepreneurs have been linked to identity development (Edwards and Muir, 2012). Through the socioeconomic lens of identity the authors promote the notion that the evaluations of enterprise education need to expand and should encompass prime pedagogical objectives that education enables people to grow and develop, to shape their own new identities in the light of their learning experiences (ibid.). Linking professional identity to career self-efficacy leads to career change intention (Khapova et al., 2007). It is reasonable to determine that entrepreneurial identity and the extent to which an individual believes they are capable of *being* an entrepreneur is a fundamental driver for them to *become* an entrepreneur. Enterprise education needs to be positioned as a positive intervention within this development process. Noel (2001) found this to be the case in terms of intention to become an entrepreneur and Fayolle et al. (2006) confirmed that entrepreneurship graduates score highly in entrepreneurial intention, propensity to act as an entrepreneur and entrepreneurial self-efficacy.

The notion of an entrepreneur and how people identify with those who are entrepreneurs will vary according to one's position in society. Thus, the entrepreneurial identity may be viewed differently from the frame of reference of a specific discipline such as an academic, economist, psychologist, sociologist or philosopher. Similarly, how an entrepreneur is identified will vary through the lenses of the general public and specifically those who may be potential entrepreneurs, entrepreneurs themselves and those involved in providing enterprise support. Therefore, the label 'entrepreneur' has different meanings, both positive and negative (Howorth et al., 2005) and is borne out of some form of experience, whether it be research, close involvement with entrepreneurs or third-hand information via the media or peers. This then indicates that the purpose of enterprise education is to enable a student to further understand and hone their entrepreneurial roles.

Whilst the word and label 'entrepreneur' is familiar within academic circles and used frequently by researchers and educators, this is not necessarily the case in other institutions and organizations. In the researcher's study of graduate entrepreneurs, not one identified themselves in the sense of naming themselves as an 'entrepreneur' (Edwards, 2011). They either considered that they were business people or defined themselves by the business they ran, that is, web designer, marketer, crèche provider:

> Well I don't like the word entrepreneur, there is something snobby about it. If someone asks me what I do, I say I'm graphic designer, I don't say I'm an entrepreneur and I don't say I have my own company; in my line of business it's more relevant to tell people I'm a web developer because they might say 'Oh, I need a web developer' but they won't say 'Oh, I need an entrepreneur'. (Edwards, 2011, p. 94)

Further research could consider whether such 'labelling' affects the relationship between student and enterprise educators and subsequently whether it bears any impact upon the entrepreneurial identity formation of undergraduates. A person's identity is not static and people can have co-existent multiple identities. In the context of enterprise education it is important to focus upon two key identities: the student identity and the entrepreneurial identity. As found in the research, some of the graduate entrepreneurs identified early on in their lives that they were going to *become* entrepreneurs and their drive to achieve this was strong: 'I always wanted to start my own business and I started buying resources for the business in the January sales when I was at university' said one research participant (ibid., p.163). For them, going to university was part of the entrepreneurial action needed prior to entrepreneurial practice. They had clear, linear identities, there was no conflict, and one identity was a means to taking on the other. For some students, the emerging process of entrepreneurial identity had its beginnings during their time at university:

> I went to a careers fair with a friend from my course. The fair was depressing, 'Join the army' or become a supermarket manager. It completely put us off a career! We sat down and starting talking about what we would do in 'an ideal world' and that's how the business started, in the second year of our degree. (Ibid., p.174)

There may have been identity conflict or it may have been a smooth transition, managing dual identities and transferring from the student to entrepreneur identity. Motivation and belief in becoming an entrepreneur, although non-existent or weak in the beginning, strengthened over time. Finally, the demarcation was not so clear-cut. Entrepreneurship as a valid career option may have been latent during their time at university, but was not a strong or considered identity.

BEYOND IDENTITY

Williams suggests that enterprise has two separate meanings in Higher Education. On the one hand he suggests that enterprise is about developing an entrepreneurially focused university management team, which is 'inspired in part by financial stringency but mainly by the ideological changes about the provision of public services' (2003, p.15); and that the other stipulation by the UK government (and also some employers) is 'that in order to support a rapidly changing economy "enterprise" should become an explicit part of the higher-education curriculum' (2003, ibid., p.155). Questions arise as to what enterprise education is and how to embed enterprise into the curriculum. Yet the overarching question to pose is: 'Does every graduate need to be an entrepreneur?' Considering that the acclaimed traits of entrepreneurs are those of 'risk takers' and 'opportunists' that succeed despite occasional failure, what would the consequences of this have on society, education and economics?

The United States of America has a strong history of entrepreneurship and is a country that celebrates failure as part of the learning process, hence it is not a revelation that the routes of enterprise education germinate from the USA. But is the word 'enterprise' universal? Does it have the same meaning in Europe and America? Gibb suggests that the interpretation of words is culturally specific, noting that:

> the word 'enterprise' itself creates a problem because it is commonly used in the UK with several different connotations – for example: business enterprise (meaning business organisation); enterprise training (meaning small firms training); enterprise initiative (meaning a Department of Trade and Industry (DTI) scheme); and Training and Enterprise Council. (Gibb, 1993, p. 12)

Recognizing that standard business studies courses such as management, marketing and accounting are not the primary skills needed for an enterprising environment, Gunning notes that some institutions have addressed this 'by hiring faculty who are in some way associated with "entrepreneurship"' (1992, p. 195). Whilst Gibb (1994, p. 18) reflects that in the USA the term 'entrepreneurship' carries more excitement than 'small business', Anderseck (2004) contends that a new 'missionary' zeal has been built around the concept of entrepreneurship as a philosophy of life with subsequent notions of culture development beyond teaching.

The term 'small business' has been used more frequently in the UK, as it has not been hampered by the American perspective that 'small' somehow has less value than 'large' (Hills, 1988). However, aided by media flamboyancy and excitement associated with the term entrepreneurship, this term has now entered the world of academia. Universities face a complex situation. As institutions they have to be entrepreneurial as a means of survival and, as pointed out by Webb, Higher Education Institutions (HEIs) are 'business like', they are 'fully independent and are required – as is any private business – to fund their present and future capital requirements from the revenues they earn and the surpluses they can achieve' (2001, p. 4).

In terms of teaching future entrepreneurs and developing enterprise skills in their students, some would argue that support mechanisms are not needed for entrepreneurs, as it is presumed that they possess a 'get up and go' attitude. Nevertheless, Higher Education establishments need to be entrepreneurial themselves in order to provide properly funded chairs of entrepreneurship and research centres and to be able to exploit the latest technology, enabling efficient and effective research and teaching delivery (Edwards and Muir, 2005).

Handscombe et al. (2005), attribute the marked increase in enterprise education in the UK, between 2000 and 2005, to government enterprise support programmes supported by the Labour government, as well as a devolved Labour government in Wales. In March 2000, Prime Minister

Tony Blair addressed a conference by stating, 'I strongly believe that the knowledge economy is our best route for success and prosperity' (Blair, 2000). Webb echoed this, declaring that Wales needed to move beyond its historical coal mining and manufacturing era and that the 'generator of leading edge knowledge in Britain is Higher Education' (2001, p. 3), asserting that universities need to become more commercialized and widen their research activities away from the confines of their institutions, applying this knowledge and expertise to the economy. One means of achieving this is to engage academics with SMEs, either as an industry secondment or through consultancy.

Similar to the University Challenge and the Science Enterprise Challenge in England, as mentioned by Handscombe et al. (2005), the Welsh Assembly Government launched the Wales Spin Out Programme and the Knowledge Exploitation Fund to fill the niche, with the view that exploiting knowledge would lend itself to forming part of an 'enterprise culture in Wales', but this remit was far wider than increasing the number of SME start-ups in Wales. The creation and development of enterprises has been called the 'Third Mission' (Jones, 2002) and is about retaining and growing existing SMEs and creating entrepreneurial individuals as, 'we see "enterprise" as being about "empowerment" of individuals, by making them aware that they have choices, so that they have the opportunity to make them' (Jones, 1993, p. 45). The two elements, empowering individuals and making them aware of their choices, leads to self-actualization that entrepreneurship is a viable career option, which can also be interpreted as empowering individuals to develop enterprise skills. This fits within the debate of 'What are we teaching for?' Is it to give people the skills to be enterprising, regardless of their working environment, be it working for themselves or being employed? Or are we teaching them how to run their own businesses?

TOWARDS AN ENTREPRENEURIAL UNIVERSITY

Just as the 'What is an entrepreneur?' debate is inconclusive and has hindered progress, Watson (2001) notes that the divergent definitions of entrepreneurship have hindered the quality of research into (and the teaching of) enterprise education. Whilst 'clarification of the distinction between entrepreneurship and small business would improve the validity and reliability of entrepreneurship research' (ibid., p. 17) it would also enable educators and practitioners to distinguish between thinking and operating in an entrepreneurial manner as opposed to a business manner. Solomon et al. (2002) questioned whether entrepreneurship courses were not simply traditional management courses with a new label.

The discussion of whether it is business education, enterprise education or simply business education re-labelled stems from where entrepreneurship is 'housed'. Hills (1988) highlighted this as potential problem because enterprise may involve the capital exploitation of knowledge, skills and talents developed in any faculty. Entrepreneurship education must be inter-functional. Traditionally, entrepreneurship has been 'housed' within business schools, and this is possibly why the terms business education and enterprise education are coupled. Gibb maintains that:

> there is a need to develop understanding of where entrepreneurship education sits within the web of education theory and concept. It can be argued that entrepreneurship education can find its place comfortably within a number of well-established concepts broadly clustered under the umbrella of social constructionist theories of knowledge and learning. (2011, p. 154)

Whilst searching for the most appropriate 'home' for enterprise education, a growing number of enterprise educators within universities have endeavoured to separate themselves from business schools (and business subject disciplines) by establishing standalone enterprise centres. Such centres tend to focus on extra-curricular enterprise education as opposed to core formal teaching, and given the informality of such programmes they are perhaps not considered as 'worthy' in terms of academic rigour as business disciplines. Handscombe et al. also note that '[s]pecialist centres need institutional backing, without it, they tend to be funded as specialist initiatives and are vulnerable when the initial grant expires' (2005, p. 2).

Vesper and McMullen propose that enterprise education is different to business education because its purpose is 'to generate more quickly a greater variety of different ideas for how to exploit a business opportunity, and the ability to project a more extensive sequence of actions for entering business' (1988, p. 9), which suggests that enterprise education is the precursor to business education. It is important to recognize that much of the enterprise education that runs throughout universities in the UK is based on 'business studies', yet as Hall notes '[f]ew entrepreneurs have business school qualifications' (Hall, 1999 in Crainer and Dearlove, 2000, p. 77).

A report published by the European Commission, *Entrepreneurship in Higher Education in the EU*, specifies that enterprise education should not be confused with 'general business and economic studies, as its goal is to promote creativity, innovation and self-employment' (EC, 2008, p. 2). The report proclaims that enterprise education must contain the following points (p. 2):

- to develop the personal attributes and skills that form the basis of an entrepreneurial mindset and behaviour (ability to work in a team, self-confidence, creativity etc.);
- to raise the awareness of self-employment as a viable career option to students;
- to work on enterprise activities and projects;
- to provide business skills and knowledge of how to start and run a 'successful' company.

In the United Kingdom there has been a range of developments within universities that include the development of entrepreneurship teaching, specific moves towards consultancy, the development of science parks and various university business spin-out programmes. But there has not been a clear strategic framework for Higher Education. However, there has been a shift in a relatively short number of years, though 'the idea that supporting business and facilitating regional economic development should be a systematic process and strategic objective of Higher Education . . . is a commonplace assumption, but not yet delivered to anything like its full extent' (Webb, 2001, p. 5).

In terms of delivering enterprise education this leads to the ultimate debate of whether entrepreneurship can be taught? This is a recurring question that frequently arises in academic forums, conferences and in research papers. With the rise in the number of graduate start-ups, education is pertinent to them for starting a business, but whether this can be attributed to a form of 'enterprise education' is questionable.

Researchers in the 1990s started to dissect enterprise education, by questioning whether teaching was to develop entrepreneurs or individuals with enterprising skills. As Garavan and O'Cinneide observed in the 1990s, 'The debate on whether entrepreneurs can be taught still rears its head from time to time. Not everyone has what it takes to be an entrepreneur but, then, our society does not need everyone to be an entrepreneur' (1994, p. 3). Educators and researchers alike were conscious of the need to make the distinction between developing courses to start a business and developing courses to enable entrepreneurial skills. However, the recurring word between the 1970s and the 1990s was the word 'taught'. The authors' opinion is that asking whether entrepreneurship can be taught as an academic discipline is the wrong question and the question that should be addressed is 'Can entrepreneurship be learned?'

One of the earliest documents to address learning as opposed to teaching was an OECD publication, *Towards an Enterprising Culture*, which states that enterprise education 'does not just mean learning about enterprise, but learning through enterprise, as well as learning to be enterprising'

(Ball, 1989, p. 28). Subsequent research has led on from this publication and researchers have made distinctions by referring to courses *about* enterprise and courses *for* enterprise.

Courses *about* enterprise consider the importance and relevance of SMEs on the wider economic scale. Such courses should create an awareness of entrepreneurship through discussions and references to recognized entrepreneurs and how they contribute to the enterprise economy. Cresswell describes this as any educational activity that informs students about the nature of business (1999).

Teaching for entrepreneurship is attributable to those who wish to start a business and thus courses should focus on the stages of business start-up, how to put together a business plan, where to source funding and how to recruit and manage staff. Moreover, teaching *for* entrepreneurship should not merely be about economic development and enterprise creation, as one of the objectives of teaching *for* entrepreneurship should be the development of entrepreneurial individuals, that is, those who wish to become entrepreneurs and also developing individuals for enterprise skills, that is, those who do not want to run a business, but require the skills of an entrepreneur within their employment, for example an 'enterprising manager'. Cresswell describes this as a self-directed experiential learning activity that promotes the development of enterprise skills and behaviours in students (ibid.).

It is acknowledged that there is a process of becoming an entrepreneur and therefore courses about entrepreneurship are the basis for understanding the role of the entrepreneur and the relevance of entrepreneurship in society. Courses *for* entrepreneurship need to focus on identifying the attributes and characteristics that a person holds and more importantly what skills the person needs to develop to become an entrepreneur, essentially this can be termed as *applied entrepreneurship* (Levie, 1999) and thus *for* entrepreneurship is a means of allowing the student to practice entrepreneurship. Handscombe et al., summarize this by stating that:

> Students need to be taught *about* enterprise: to learn relevant knowledge and theoretical frameworks. They need to be equipped *for* enterprise such that they develop skills that they can apply in practice and they need a learning experience (education *through* enterprise) that gives them an understanding of the interpersonal and emotional issues. The challenge is to integrate enterprise into the student's overall learning experience, but not 'enterprise' at the expense of core discipline learning. The arguments for integrating enterprise raise the question as to where it should be taught. (2005, p. 3; original emphasis)

Whilst there is an acceptance that entrepreneurship can be taught, Levie's distinction between teaching *for* or *about* has not been fully evaluated and research questions have moved to consider how to 'improve the way we teach entrepreneurship' (Jack and Anderson, 1999, p. 2). Research based at Aberdeen University explores the tensions that exist in teaching entrepreneurship that is perceived as a process involving both 'art and science' (ibid., p. 1). Teaching the 'science' aspect of entrepreneurship is less problematic for it falls within a conventional pedagogic paradigm of subject teaching. This means that enterprise education now, for the most part, has developed to a level of competency teaching *about* entrepreneurship. This meets the needs of students who may develop managerial careers employed within SMEs, as well as those employed in SME research, academia and business support or business consultancy.

The ongoing political, social and economic drive to create an enterprise culture and expand the enterprising economy is forcing educational establishments at all levels to consider their roles and participation in such change. In Wales 'the essential contribution of Higher Education to the economic prosperity of Wales, and the need to increase that contribution has been remarked upon in countless reports over the last decade and more' (Davies, 2002, p. 1). Following reports focusing upon the economic shape and demands of Wales in 2010 (Jones, 1993), future skills requirements (MORI, 1998), the creation and utilization of knowledge within and for the economy (Jones and Osmond, 1999; Webb, 2001) and the development of the Entrepreneurship Action Plan for Wales (WDA, 2000) there can be little doubt that Higher Education has a growing responsibility to be involved in the education, motivation and support of individuals who are competent, capable and aspire to establish viable and sustainable enterprises.

There is little pedagogic debate on the goals within enterprise education for 'the question "What are we teaching for?" is surprisingly seldom posed or answered' (Ireson et al., 1999, p. 213). It is acknowledged that there is a process of becoming an entrepreneur, which involves an adjustment of a range of personal, professional and business relationships and the management of these (Muir, 1999). Similarly teaching and learning are not simply processes but 'a continuous social interaction between individuals, who are themselves products of interactions with the world around them' (Wankowski, 1991, p. 111) and in the case of enterprise education Hytti et al. affirm that social relationships are important for entrepreneurs as a means of acquiring information, seeking opinions on their ideas and to identify opportunities (2010, p. 592). At all levels, education can prepare individuals for venturing and entrepreneurship as the acquisition and development of relevant skills builds the individuals' entrepreneurial capacity (Gorman et al., 1997). However, the application of skills is always contextual (Jack and Anderson, 1999, p. 7) and the practice of entrepreneurial skills nearly always involves interpersonal skills (Gibb, 1997). The problem lies in determining the skills mix required, for there is variable need within enterprises (Freel, 1998) and entrepreneurship is a dynamic and changing process. Jack and Anderson purport that teaching the art of entrepreneurship is 'more problematic; it is experiential, founded in innovation and novelty' (1999, p. 2). This then is inclusive of the need for teaching *for* entrepreneurship, which is based upon heuristic practice and recognizably different from and beyond business management and process, for it is about creating something new. The focus of enterprise education here is not actually about business but about developing the individual, who will create, own and lead new enterprises. Thus Jack and Anderson's (1999) model of enterprise education embraces research findings integrated into theory, which then drives research and teaching. Crucial emphasis is placed on the development of students as reflective practitioners 'fit for an entrepreneurial career' (ibid., p. 10).

Moreover, Oleron (1978) purports that life comprises contact with other people and such relationships, however fleeting, take place within the framework of social organizations, institutions and habits. Certainly the requirement of self-awareness is vital for entrepreneurial behaviour and essentially is focused on what to do and how to do it, something that Farrell translates as 'corporate strategy' and 'corporate culture' (Farrell, 2001, p. 129). Farrell maintains that the 'classic model of entrepreneurship [is] – squarely based on the power of consequences' (ibid., p. 85) in that positive or negative consequences impact upon the entrepreneur and affect their behaviour.

In terms of self-reflection, a recent American study that focused upon the profiles of enterprise educators affirmed that educators need to ensure links between education specific to entrepreneurship and entrepreneurial outcomes (Kabongo and McCaskey, 2011), and furthermore asks 'are entrepreneurship educators actually entrepreneurs?' Kabongo and McCaskey (ibid., p. 32). The consequences of such behaviour result in performance outcomes that may be negative or positive, which then cyclically have further impact upon the entrepreneur. This may be considered to be one of the drivers of entrepreneurial behaviour in that non-risk-takers may not be so effectively influenced. Recent observations by Rae note that:

> Education is an important formative medium for influencing entrepreneurial culture and behaviours. The choices educators make when explaining enterprise have consequences, since popular messages, media stereotypes and summarised definitions of enterprise often perpetuate 'old entrepreneurship', while government agencies see the 'delivery' of an enterprise culture and the promulgation of a simplified ideology of enterprise to students as being the legitimate task of education. A critical academic stance on entrepreneurship education is

> needed to moderate such messages on the role and nature of entrepreneurship, which has the potential to create social good, as well as the destructive power to cause damage; a balanced approach to education should illustrate both sides of this argument. (Rae, 2010, p. 599)

In recent years the term (and function) of 'employability' has been incorporated under the enterprise education agenda and as such there is recognition that whilst developing entrepreneurial skills for self-employment, such entrepreneurial skills are also required for those seeking employment. Research carried out at the Northern Ireland Centre for Entrepreneurship (NICENT) found that courses labelled 'entrepreneurship' could have wide-ranging aims thus whilst:

> few programmes might have been aimed at learning to understand entrepreneurship, those aimed at helping students to become entrepreneurial and those aimed at helping students to become entrepreneurs were both being presented as entrepreneurship programmes. These two different approaches have been referred to by NICENT as 'enterprise for life' and 'enterprise for new venture creation'. (Bridge et al., 2010, p. 723)

The authors recognize that entrepreneurship can refer to business start-up, but also has wider connotations. To support this, Jones's research in Tasmania found that enterprise education does not directly lead to business start-up but can contribute to developing lifelong entrepreneurial skills (Jones, 2010). Researchers in the Netherlands have also focused upon the requirement of developing enterprise skills and maintain that 'enterprise education should aim to get people ready for a leading role in the enterprising way of life, rather than a supporting one' (van Gelderen, 2010, p. 712). Minniti and Bygrave describe the entrepreneurial learning process 'as the outcome of a sequence of choices' (2001, p. 4), therefore when pursuing an entrepreneurial career path or wishing to become an entrepreneur, it is important that the student or graduate exploit as many avenues as possible and that a choice of formal and informal enterprise education is provided.

THE MEANDERING PATH, A DESTINATION WITHIN REACH

Universities are faced with the challenge of finding innovative ways of teaching entrepreneurship whilst retaining rigorous academic standards of measurement and assessment. Gibb argues that only programmes delivered in an enterprising way can truly be labelled entrepreneurship programmes (1993). There is also a dilemma in that a first-class degree in entrepreneurship does not guarantee a successful entrepreneurial career or the development of an effective and efficient enterprise.

Current research expresses that universities need to move on in their thinking and development and move on from the traditional, historical university, steeped in research. Frade advocates that entrepreneurship is an absolute necessity and that:

> it is impossible for the universities to stay out of the creation of wealth or they cease to exist. Many factors improve entrepreneurship in the education system. Research into new methods of teaching is essential and I am sure there is not just one way of improving entrepreneurship. (2003, p. 172)

The infamous question 'What is an entrepreneur?' has fuelled debates concerning entrepreneurship as an academic discipline, questioning whether entrepreneurship can be taught (Hills, 1988), whether universities have a role in the teaching, development and creation of students as future entrepreneurs (Williams, 2003), determining whether the purpose of programmes is to be 'for' or 'about' entrepreneurship (Levie, 1999; Handscombe et al., 2005) and debates about differences between learning for the development of business skills and that of developing creativity, innovation and risk management (Watson, 2001).

Learning about enterprise and learning as part of the process of becoming an entrepreneur may be a formal, informal or social activity (Rae, 1999; Edwards and Muir, 2005). Social learning (Rae, 1999) is less placed in the university setting and whilst research has concluded that background and pre-entrepreneurial learning opportunities have an impact upon the propensity to become an entrepreneur (Edwards, 2011) little has been studied about the university role in this context. Universities in the main have focused upon the first activity (learning about enterprise) whereby teaching has focused upon the skills and understanding needed to run a small business – specific skills such as finance, leadership, managing change in larger businesses and more personal aspects of entrepreneurial practice (Gibb, 1994). Whilst there is debate as to whether *teaching enterprise* should be contained within business schools (Hills, 1988), be a university-wide initiative, embedded within the curriculum, or facilitated through a specific faculty/enterprise centre (Matlay, 2005), further discussions as to whether enterprise education (and in this case 'teaching enterprise') is best offered at undergraduate or postgraduate level have surfaced but not been expanded (Edwards, 2011) as well as the practicalities of teaching enterprise:

> The tension between the academic and the practical approach is only part of the story. Many researchers make the case for more flexible teaching methods

that stimulate the real world environment. They recommend learning by doing, encouraging independence and stimulating students to think for themselves, thus giving them ownership of their own learning. They also emphasize feelings, attitudes and values, thereby placing more importance on experiential learning. (Handscombe et al., 2005, p. 3)

The aforementioned 'learning by doing' approach is often within the remit of 'informal learning' (non-accredited/extra-curricular education) rather than formal (accredited) learning and thus educators exert caution over developing practical courses as 'the implications for educational establishments are how to accredit *applied* courses?' (Edwards, 2011, p. 48; original emphasis). Yet, regarding where and how enterprise education is taught, standard university evaluations apply: the focus is upon the number of students registered for courses, the pass rates and grades (Ireson et al., 1999).

In summary, universities privilege the development of specific knowledge and skills development for business management. Some enterprise/ entrepreneur education programmes give consideration to the understanding of the entrepreneur, entrepreneurial activity, opportunity evaluation and exploitation. On the other hand, less consideration is given to the development of the entrepreneur as a transformed being, journeying from roles of student to entrepreneur, through the process of being a potential entrepreneur and then becoming a practising entrepreneur (Edwards, 2011).

Thus, to return to Williams's earlier suggestion that enterprise has two separate meanings in Higher Education: the development of entrepreneurial management teams and second that 'enterprise' should become an explicit part of the Higher Education curriculum (2003, p. 155). The authors concur with Williams that they have separate meanings, however, in order for universities to create and enable *the entrepreneurial journey*, enterprise needs to become a core part of the curriculum that is driven by entrepreneurial managers (both at directorate level and scheme leader/ module leader level) and thus by implementing and initiating enterprise education university-wide strategies, such managers need to understand, support and comply with the following interlinked objectives: (1) the entrepreneurs' journey from university to business – strategies for entrepreneurship for students that wish to exploit the knowledge acquired at university to start a business; (2) the entrepreneurial journey from university to business – strategies to exploit entrepreneurial skills in individuals with a focus upon employability rather than business start-up. Both objectives are placed under the all-encompassing banner of 'enterprise education' and recent research by Rae acknowledges that there is an acceptance that enterprise education is more than running or managing a business and the trend is moving 'towards an intersubjectival relevance to a wider range of study programmes' Rae (2010, p. 601).

REFERENCES

Anderseck, K. (2004), 'Institutional and academic entrepreneurship: Implications for university governance and management', *Higher Education in Europe*, **29**(2), 193–200.

Ball, C. (1989), *Towards an Enterprising Culture*, Paris: OECD.

Blair (2000), Speech at 'Knowledge 2000', Conference on the Knowledge Driven Economy, accessed 16 August 2013 at http://webarchive.nationalarchives.gov.uk/+/http://www.dti.gov.uk/knowledge2000/blair.htm.

Bridge, S., C. Hegarty and S. Porter (2010), 'Rediscovering enterprise: Developing appropriate university entrepreneurship education', *Education + Training*, **52**(8/9), 722–34.

Burke, P.J. and J.E. Stets (2009), *Identity Theory*, Oxford: Oxford University Press.

Burke, P.J. and J.C. Tully (1977), 'The measurement of role identity', *Social Forces*, **55**(4), 881–96.

Burns, P. (2001), *Entrepreneurship and Small Business*, Houndmills, Basingstoke: Palgrave Macmillan.

Cox, L.W., S.L. Mueller and S.E. Moss (2002), 'The impact of entrepreneurship education on entrepreneurial self-efficacy', *International Journal of Entrepreneurship Education*, **1**(1), 229–45.

Crainer, S. and D. Dearlove (2000), *Generation Entrepreneur*, Harlow, Essex: Pearson Education Limited.

Cresswell, C. (1999), *A Review of Enterprise Education in Universities*, unpublished Welsh Enterprise Institute Report, University of Glamorgan, UK.

Davies, G.T. (2002), *Forward to the Third Mission: Creating a Business Culture for Higher Education in Wales*, Cardiff: Institute of Welsh Affairs.

Edwards, L-J. (2011), 'The entrepreneurial journey from university to business', unpublished doctoral dissertation, University of Glamorgan, UK.

Edwards, L-J. and E.J. Muir (2005), 'Promoting entrepreneurship at the University of Glamorgan through formal and informal learning', *Journal of Small Business and Enterprise Development*, **12**(4), 613–26.

Edwards, L-J. and E.J. Muir (2012), 'Evaluating enterprise education: Why do it?' *Education + Training*, **54**(4) 278–90.

Elliott, A. (2008), *Concepts of the Self*, 2nd edition, Cambridge, UK: Polity Press.

Erkkilä, K. (2000), *Entrepreneurial Education: Mapping the Debates in the United States, The United Kingdom and Finland*, New York: Garland Publishing, Inc.

European Commission (2008), *Entrepreneurship in Higher Education, Especially in Non-business Studies*, Final Report of the Expert Group, accessed 16 August 2013 at http://ec.europa.eu/enterprise/policies/sme/files/support_measures/training_education/entr_highed_en.pdf.

Farrell, L.C. (2001), *The Entrepreneurial Age: Awakening the Spirit of Enterprise in People, Companies and Countries*, Oxford: Windsor.

Fayolle, A., B. Gailly and N. Lassas-Clerc (2006), 'Assessing the impact of entrepreneurship education programmes: A new methodology', *Journal of European Industrial Training*, **3**(9), 701–20.

Frade, G. (2003), 'Entrepreneurship: A mega trend for nations, enterprises and universities', in G. Williams (2003), *The Enterprising University, Reform, Excellence and Equity*, Buckingham: The Society for Research into Higher Education and Open University Press.

Freel, M. (1998), 'Evolution, innovation and learning: Evidence from case studies', *Entrepreneurship and Regional Development*, **10**(2), 137–49.

Garavan, T.N. and B. O'Cinneide (1994), 'Entrepreneurship education and training programmes: A review and evaluation Part 1', *Journal of European Industrial training*, **18**(8), 3–12.

Gibb, A.A. (1993), 'The enterprise culture and education: Understanding enterprise education and its links with small business, entrepreneurship and wider educational goals', *International Small Business Journal*, **11**(3), 11–34.

Gibb, A.A. (1994), 'Do we really teach (approach) small business the way we should?' *Journal of Small Business and Entrepreneurship*, **11**(2), 4–27.

Gibb, A.A. (1997), 'Policy research and small business. From know what to know how', in M. Ram, P. Deakins and D. Smallbone, *Small Firms: Enterprising Futures*, London: Paul Chapman Publishing.

Gorman, G., D. Hanlon and W. King (1997), 'Some research perspectives on entrepreneurship education and its links with small business entrepreneurship and wider educational goals', *International Small Business Journal*, **15**(3), 56–78.

Gunning, J.P. (1992), 'The meaning of entrepreneurship in economic theory: Historical perspective', *Entrepreneurship, Innovation and Change*, **1**(2), 195–210.

Handscombe, R.D., E. Rodriguez-Falcon and E.A. Patterson (2005), 'Embedded enterprise learning: About, through, for and from', Proceedings of IMEC 2005, ASME International Mechanical Engineering Congress and Exposition 5–11 November, Orlando, Florida.

Hills, G.E. (1988), 'Variations in university entrepreneurship education: An empirical study of an evolving field', *Journal of Business Venturing*, **3**(2), 109–22.

Hoang, H. and J. Gimeno (2005), *Becoming an Entrepreneur: A Theory of Entrepreneurial Identity*, Paris: INSEAD.

Howorth, C., S. Tempest and C. Coupland (2005), 'Rethinking entrepreneurship methodology and definition of the entrepreneur', *Journal of Small Business and Enterprise Development*, **12**(1), 24–40.

Hytti, U. and C. O'Gorman (2004), 'What is "enterprise education"? An analysis of the objectives and methods of enterprise education programmes in European countries', *Education + Training*, **46**(1), 11–23.

Hytti, U., P. Stenholm, J. Heinonen and J. Seikkula-Leino (2010), 'Perceived learning outcomes in entrepreneurship education', *Education + Training*, **52**(8/9), 587–606.

Ibarra, H. (1999), *Working Identities: Unconventional Strategies for Reinventing Your Career*, Boston: Harvard Business School Press.

Ibarra, H. (2002), 'How to stay stuck in the wrong career', *Harvard Business Review*, **8**(12), 40–48.

Ireson, J., P. Mortimore and S. Hallam (1999), 'The common strands of pedagogy and their implications', in P. Mortimore (ed.), *Understanding Pedagogy and its Impact on Learning*, London: Paul Chapman.

Jack, S.L. and A.R. Anderson (1999), 'Entrepreneurship education within the enterprise culture: Producing reflective practitioners', *International Journal of Entrepreneurial Behaviour and Research*, **5**(3), 110–25.

Jenkins, R. (2008), *Social Identity*, 3rd edition, London: Routledge.

Jones, C. (2010), 'Entrepreneurship education: Revisiting our role and its purpose', *Journal of Small Business and Enterprise Development*, **17**(4), 500–513.

Jones, G. (1993), *Wales 2010: Creating Our Future*, Cardiff: Cardiff Institute of Welsh Affairs.

Jones, G. (2002), *The Third Mission: Creating a Business Culture for Higher Education in Wales*, Cardiff: Institute of Welsh Affairs.

Jones, G. and J. Osmond (1999), *Building a Knowledge-driven Economy*, Cardiff: Institute of Welsh Affairs.

Kabango, J.D. and P.H. McCaskey (2011), 'An examination of entrepreneurship educator profiles in business programs in the United States', *Journal of Small Business and Enterprise Development*, **18**(1), 27–42.

Khapova, S.N., M.B. Arthur, C.P.M. Wilderom and J.S. Svensson (2007), 'Professional identity as the key to career change intention', *Career Development International*, **12**(7), 584–95.

Kothari, S. and R.D. Handscombe (2007), 'Sweep or seep? Structure, culture, enterprise and universities', *Management Decision*, **45**(1), 43–61.

Levie, J. (1999), *Entrepreneurship Education in Higher Education in England: A Survey*, London: Department for Education and Employment.

Matlay, H. (2005), 'Entrepreneurship education in UK business schools: Conceptual, contextual and policy consideration', *Journal of Small Business and Enterprise Development*, **12**(4), 627–43.

Matlay, H. (2008), 'The impact of entrepreneurship education on entrepreneurial outcome', *Journal of Small Business and Enterprise Development*, **15**(2), 382–96.

Matlay. H. (2011), 'The influence of stakeholders on developing enterprising graduates in UK HEIs', *International Journal of Entrepreneurial Behaviour and Research*, **17**(2), 166–82.

Minniti, M. and W. Bygrave (2001), 'A dynamic model of entrepreneurial learning', *Entrepreneurship: Theory and Practice*, 25(3), 5–16.

MORI Research and Business Strategies Ltd (1998), *Future Skills Wales Project*.

Muir, E.J. (1999), 'Women entrepreneurs in the EU: Motivation and realisations for starting a business', paper presented at ICSB International Conference, Naples.

Noel, T.W. (2001), 'Effects of entrepreneurial education on intent to open a business', *Frontiers of Entrepreneurship Research*, Babson conference proceedings, accessed 18 August 2013 at http://fusionmx.babson.edu/entrep/fer/babson2001/XXX/XXXA/XXXA.htm.

Oleron, P. (1978), 'Development of cognitive skills', in A.M. Lesgold (ed.), *Cognitive Psychology and Instruction*, New York: Plenum Books.

Rae, D. (1999), *The Entrepreneurial Spirit*, Dublin: Blackhall Publishing.

Rae, D. (2003), 'Entrepreneurial identity and capability: The role of learning', PhD thesis, Nottingham Trent University.

Rae, D. (2010), 'Universities and enterprise education: Responding to the challenges of the new era', *Journal of Small Business and Enterprise Development*, **17**(4), 591–606.

Robson, C. (2002), *Real World Research*, 2nd edition, Oxford: Blackwell Publishing.

Solomon, G.T., S. Duffy and A. Tarabishy (2002), 'Entrepreneurship education in the United States: A nationwide survey and analysis', *International Journal of Entrepreneurship Education*, **1**(1), 1–22.

van Gelderen, M. (2010), 'Autonomy as the guiding aim of entrepreneurship education', *Education + Training*, **52**(8/9), 710–21.

Vesper, K.H. and W.E. McMullen (1988), 'Entrepreneurship: Today courses, tomorrow degrees?' *Entrepreneurship Theory and Practice*, **13**(1), 7–13.

Wankowski, J. (1991), 'Reflections and operational perspectives', in K. Raaheim, J. Wankowski and J. Radford (eds), *Helping Students to Learn: Teaching, Counselling, Research*, Milton Keynes: Open University Press, pp. 111–23).

Watson, C.H. (2001), 'Small business versus entrepreneurship revisited', in R.H. Brockhaus, G.E. Hills, H. Klandt and H.P. Welsch (2001), *Entrepreneurship Education: A Global View*, Burlington, VT: Ashgate Publishing Ltd.

Webb, A. (2001), *Knowledge and the Welsh Economy*, Cardiff: Institute of Welsh Affairs.

Welsh Development Agency (2000), *Entrepreneurship Action Plan for Wales*, Cardiff: WDA.

Williams, G. (2003), 'An honest living or dumbing down?' in G. Williams, *The Enterprising University, Reform, Excellence and Equity*, Buckingham: The Society for Research into Higher Education and Open University Press.

Wolf, A. (2002), *Does Education Matter? Myths About Education and Economic Growth*, London: Penguin Books Ltd.

17. Entrepreneurial learning and the IBM Universities Business Challenge: an experiential learning perspective

*Wim van Vuuren, Colm Fearon, Gemma van Vuuren-Cassar and Judith Crayford**

INTRODUCTION

The development and promotion of entrepreneurship have been strategic objectives of both the EU and Member State policies for many years. Key amongst the measures adopted is the building of a stronger culture of entrepreneurship and entrepreneurial capacities and mindsets. Education and training are key drivers in this process. Yet evidence of concerted attempts to establish entrepreneurship firmly within the structure and practice of national education systems has remained scarce (European Commission, 2010). The Final Report of the Expert Group (European Commission, 2008) concludes that the teaching of entrepreneurship is not yet sufficiently integrated in Higher Education Institutions' curricula and highlights the need for more experienced-based teaching methods, more interactive learning approaches and multidisciplinary collaboration, as essential elements in building entrepreneurial skills and abilities.

Industry and government are also calling for better enterprise and entrepreneurship education within university and Higher Education Institutions (Smith and Patton, 2011). However, when one examines entrepreneurship education to date, it has been accused of failing to deliver enterprising and innovative graduates (ibid.). In addition, there has been lack of sufficient research concerning the effectiveness and assessment of entrepreneurial education activities in the literature (Draycott et al., 2011; Jones and Jones, 2011).

In this chapter, we examine the role of the 'IBM Universities Business Challenge (IBM UBC)', which can be considered the UK's premier undergraduate business competition, as an example of an experiential learning environment for nurturing potential graduate entrepreneurs. We explore how business challenges such as this one can promote entrepreneurial and social learning, develop enterprise skills and competencies, as well as encourage an entrepreneurial mindset. We also discuss the role of the IBM UBC in emulating a community of practice and reflect upon the wider nature of entrepreneurial learning achieved.

ENTREPRENEURIAL LEARNING: THE 'ENTERPRISE' VERSUS 'ENTREPRENEURSHIP' EDUCATION DEBATE

Assessing the role and impact of entrepreneurial learning as part of 'enterprise' and 'entrepreneurship' education has been difficult in recent years (Pittaway and Hannon, 2008). The confusion over the terms 'enterprise' and 'entrepreneurship' education has led to much debate in the recent literature (Jones and Iredale, 2010; Draycott et al., 2011; Jones and Jones, 2011). Whilst the entrepreneurship education camp has generally considered entrepreneurial learning to involve 'acquisition and development of the propensity, skills and abilities to found, to join, or to grow a venture' (Hamilton, 2011, p. 9), there have also been arguments for fostering stronger enterprise skills and personal development for university students in a much broader sense. New ideas concerning the amalgam of entrepreneurial learning and enterprise education must involve more than just teaching students how to develop new business plans, or create and manage business start-ups within a business school setting (Crayford et al., 2012). Deacon and Harris (2011) highlight the problem of definitional ambiguity between entrepreneurship and enterprise education in relation to Higher Education (HE) and pedagogy. Jones and Iredale (2010, p. 10) suggested that enterprise education is more effective at developing general skills as part of an active learning environment, thus developing an enterprising individual, whether at home, work, or as a potential future entrepreneur.

There have also been recent calls from the UK's National Council for Graduate Entrepreneurship (NCGE) to help students develop stronger entrepreneurial mindsets. Taatila (2010, p. 51) noted the attributes of an entrepreneurial mindset: 'perseverance, trust, determination, risk management, a positive attitude towards change, tolerance of uncertainties, initiative, the need to achieve, understanding of timeframes, creativity, an understanding of the big picture'.

ENTREPRENEURIAL LEARNING AND ENTERPRISE EDUCATION

Draycott et al. (2011) consider entrepreneurial learning as a core tenet of the structure and context of a new type of enterprise education. Recent developments concerning the 'teacher–learner' experience, more general life skills and good citizenship are understood to be vital elements of the enterprise education perspective (Jones and Iredale, 2010; Draycott et al., 2011). In addition, enterprise education has been credited with helping to move enterprise skills out of the typical business school setting and into the wider realm of university education, forming a central part of the employability agenda for future graduates (European Commission, 2008; Crayford et al., 2012).

Exploring the nature of entrepreneurial learning as part of enterprise education as a vital social activity is important for exploring future pedagogic directions (Smith and Patton, 2011). In the following sections, we advocate the value of social learning and specifically the role of business challenges as a pedagogic vehicle for developing entrepreneurial learning in an environment that emulates the real-life experiences of the potential entrepreneur.

ENTREPRENEURIAL LEARNING AND BUSINESS CHALLENGE COMPETITIONS

There are increasing calls for a better understanding of entrepreneurial learning within social learning contexts (Cope, 2005; Hamilton, 2011). Based on ideas from situated learning theory (Hamilton, 2011), experiential learning takes students out of the classroom in order to develop core skills, experiences and personal development in an action-oriented environment. Situated learning theory helps us examine the impact of social and action-oriented contexts for promoting entrepreneurial learning together with implications for teacher–learner interactions and future pedagogy. We use a situated learning theoretical lens, along with the experience of the IBM UBC, to examine the nature of entrepreneurial learning and evaluate critical incidents from the participant (learner), as well as teacher (facilitator) perspectives.

Business challenge competitions have been cited as useful mechanisms for nurturing ideas, talent and future entrepreneurs (Russell et al., 2008; Jones and Jones, 2011). They help foster key enterprise skills, knowledge development, team building, mentoring, as well as, student/graduate competencies (Atchison, and Gotlieb, 2004; Der Foo et al., 2005; Russell et al., 2008). In terms of entrepreneurship education, business challenges enable a focus on: a structured knowledge base, with rich feedback from entrepreneurs and judging panels; the development of business planning skills as part of a shared and learned activity; interaction with other stakeholders, investors, partners and clients; and emulating the real world and life experiences of potential future entrepreneurs (Jones and Jones, 2011).

SOCIAL NATURE OF ENTREPRENEURIAL LEARNING

If we study how entrepreneurs learn, then better judgements can be made about the effectiveness of pedagogy (Pittaway and Cope, 2007). Increasingly, entrepreneurial learning focuses on understanding the impetus for cognitive action, as well as learning through shared experiences and personal development through reflection and discussion (Cope and Watts, 2000). There is an emphasis on learning from real-life experiences (Rae, 2000), in conjunction with problem solving, as well as risk and opportunity taking to help nurture real-world knowledge and skills (Cope, 2005; Pittaway et al., 2009). The literature often examines activities of students and combines this analysis with reflective research (Nikolou-Walker and Garnett, 2004). In the following sections there is a discussion concerning the role of the IBM UBC on entrepreneurial and social learning based on findings and reflections from recent exploratory research carried out in 2012.

RESEARCH DESIGN AND METHODOLOGY

Pittaway et al. (2009) discussed at length the role of entrepreneurial learning and the National Council for Graduate Enterpreneurship (NCGE) learning outcomes framework (see Box 17.1). Based on an analysis of over 40 focus groups in conjunction with the NCGE's entrepreneurial learning outcomes framework, a reflection and examination in the context of enterprise education was conducted. The authors (ibid., p. 76) noted: 'The eight areas [within the NCGE's entrepreneurial learning framework] as presented reflect changes in behaviours, empathy, values, motivations, awareness, competencies, venture creation knowledge and ability to manage relationships'.

Pittaway et al. (2009) used the framework (see Box 17.1) alongside the ISBE (Institute for Small Business and Entrepreneurship) conference (2005) as a guide for brainstorming sessions among academics,

---

BOX 17.1   NCGE'S ENTREPRENEURIAL LEARNING OUTCOMES FRAMEWORK

Key elements:

1   Entrepreneurial behaviour, attitude and skill development (Key entrepreneurial behaviours, skills and attitudes have been developed)
2   Creating empathy with the entrepreneurial life world (Students empathize with, understand and 'feel' the life-world of the entrepreneur)
3   Developing key entrepreneurial values (Key entrepreneurial values have been inculcated, e.g., strong sense of independence and ownership)
4   Motivation towards an entrepreneurial career (Motivation towards a career in entrepreneurship has been built and students clearly understand the comparative benefits)
5   Understanding the challenges of creating and maintaining businesses (Students understand the process [stages] of setting up an organization, role of business survival and helping students handle the challenges)
6   Supporting generic entrepreneurship competencies (Students have the key generic competencies associated with entrepreneurship and the generic 'how tos' – to find an idea; appraise an idea; identify key people to be influenced in any development)
7   Students grasping basic business 'how tos' (Seeing products and services as combinations of benefits; developing customer service orientation; pricing; product development etc.)
8   Managing stakeholder relationships (Students understand the nature of the relationships they need to develop with key stakeholders and are familiarized with them)

Source: Adapted from Pittaway et al. (2009).

---

stakeholders and practitioners using focus groups. Based on this NCGE framework, we will also be conducting exploratory focus groups and interviews that allow students to reflect and discuss their experiences of entrepreneurial learning in the context of the IBM UBC. The approach (agreed with Learning Dynamics, the company that designed and delivers the IBM UBC) is inductive in nature, similar in this respect to Pittaway et al. (2009). However, overall we employ a mixed methods approach, combining a survey of 125 IBM UBC students with evidence from focus groups among several competition teams, in order to examine and 'make sense' of the key areas of entrepreneurial and social learning identified within the NCGE framework (see Box 17.1).

CORE TENETS OF 'SENSE-MAKING'

'Sense-making' denotes a noticing or reflecting upon key events and activities to make sense of a complex of situations, in order to develop experiential learning and make situations more understandable for all participants (Weick et al., 2005). Sense-making is often guided and informed by one's own mental models, based on a participant's life and social learning experiences to date. Sense-making harnesses mental schemata for identifying highpoints as forms of participant learning relative to a social context, for example, when researching students on placement, or reflecting upon employee learning in the workplace (Walmsley et al., 2006; Shafari and Zhang, 2009). Sense-making also allows participants to develop new learned behaviours as response strategies in decision-making situations (Weick et al., 2005; Walmsley et al., 2006). However, sense-making is not so much about devising new interpreted frameworks (in a research context), as developing an interpreted or socially constructed understanding, based on post hoc reflections about what has happened within a learning situation from the participants' perspective, in order to develop and learn strategies for similar situations in the future (Rae, 2005; Walmsley et al., 2006).

Therefore, sense-making uses conversation and knowledge sharing to integrate intended cognitive actions with trusted mental frameworks and knowledge, thus co-managing retrospection with a desire for future action, as they duel in a reflexive context. This often involves the breaking down of existing mental frameworks and rebuilding them in a flux process of assimilation and new social learning (Weick, 1995; Weick et al., 2005). Frequent oral and written communication within a social setting such as IBM UBC can stimulate knowledge sharing and learning exchanges concerning important contextual events. Weick's naturalistic approach to sense-making (Weick, 1995; Weick et al., 2005) and application of narrated social construction is particularly useful, especially as it is fundamentally grounded in the data (Parry, 2003), thus uncovering the dynamics of entrepreneurial learning (Pittaway and Cope, 2007).

The discussion of findings in this chapter is also based on interpreting comments and findings from an exploratory survey (similar to Russell et al., 2008; Jones and Jones, 2011), as well as combining reflections from several focus groups, to better understand the wider process of entrepreneurial learning and social learning in the context of the IBM UBC as a competition. Constructing a sense-making narrative using these findings is useful because it allows organizers and participants to better understand the dynamic nature of entrepreneurial learning, which is similar to other recent entrepreneurship studies that use sense-making as a methodology (Rae, 2000, 2009; Mills, 2011), with the exception that we also incorporate additional survey findings for triangulation. Given the paucity of existing research concerning the role of entrepreneurial and social learning in the context of UK business challenge competitions, sense-making in this instance enables a useful macro-analytical approach for building upon exploratory research.

AIM OF THE STUDY AND RESEARCH QUESTIONS ASKED

No new frameworks are developed as part of this exploratory research. Instead the aim has been to draw upon key aspects of the NCGE's existing research framework (see Box 17.1) and develop insight for further investigation and potential avenues for related future research.

Based on Pittaway et al.'s (2009) framework, examples of research questions asked in the survey and during focus groups include: 'What were the main reasons for students joining the IBM UBC?', 'Has the Business Challenge Competition helped gain insight into the experiences of real-life entrepreneurs, or create empathy for an entrepreneurial life?', 'How has the competition helped students understand stakeholder relationships, or work as part of a team?' We also examine the extent to which the IBM UBC has helped students understand and empathize with the values and attributes required for becoming an entrepreneur, or indeed, a professional person. Finally, we ask about future career intent and discuss if the competition has made students think seriously about an entrepreneurial career.

DISCUSSION OF FINDINGS

The findings cover phase one of our exploratory study based on results from a combination of survey results and findings from focus groups from IBM UBC (2012). Drawing on NCGE's framework (see Box 17.1) and the questions above, we attempt to simply 'let the data speak'. The intention again is to draw reflections from focus group narrative in conjunction with analysis of relevant survey findings. A number of reflections and discussion points for entrepreneurial learning are subsequently discussed in light of the latest relevant literature and the NCGE framework (see Box 17.1), culminating in suggestions for further research.

Background Profile of Respondents from the IBM UBC (2012) Survey

The IBM UBC is now in its fourteenth year, with 304 teams participating from 75 faculties of 68 universities. One hundred and twenty-five student respondents completed the online questionnaire (58 per cent male and 42 per cent female). Regarding background characteristics, 57 per cent of respondents had been studying general Business and Management, 22 per cent of respondents Finance, Accounting and Financial Management, and 12 per cent Economics and Mathematics.

The majority of students (41 per cent) were in year two of their degree programme, 22 per cent were in year three (final year) and 12 per cent were in year four (final year). In terms of progression, 46 per cent reached round two of the competition (semi-finals) and 14 per cent reached round three (the grand final). Fourteen per cent of respondents had competed in the IBM University Business Challenge (UBC) competition in a previous year, but for the majority of students (86 per cent), it was their first experience. In a related question, 14 per cent of respondents had also taken part in other university business challenge competitions at the time of completing the current survey.

In terms of other interesting background/profile characteristics, whilst only 10 per cent of respondents stated they had previous experience of running their own business before joining the IBM UBC, 46 per cent of respondents had also indicated they were considering starting their own business. In terms of family background, 29 per cent of respondents' parents ran their own business.

What were the main reasons for joining the IBM University Business Challenge? When asked about reasons for participating in the competition, the highest numbers of respondents agreed, or strongly agreed with the following benefits:

- adding the experience to student's curriculum vitae (94 per cent);
- improving employability skills (90 per cent);
- gaining a wider understanding of business (90 per cent);
- testing one's own capabilities (91 per cent);
- and getting an opportunity to meet real businesses (75 per cent).

Other reasons included: considering it would be fun (52 per cent) and meeting students from other universities (46 per cent). Comments from one focus group shed greater light on reasons for student participation in the competition:

> I think we knew previously the university had gone into the competition . . . and I think for me it was something to add to your CV, and because you knew it was a competitive environment, having something extra on your CV is a positive.

Most of the groups cited employability and the learning experience as major reasons for taking part in the competition. Interestingly, reflections also very much highlighted the importance of the social side of the learning experience:

> I think it was pretty much the same as Jack; I don't generally get involved in the social side of university just because of commitments outside of it, so something social within the university that relates to the area I'm studying and something again to put on CVs when looking for jobs and I suppose it's the overall experience of taking part and getting to know more people like James and Jennifer who I hadn't met before is really important. [Note: names of participants have been altered]

Entrepreneurial Behaviour, Attitude and Skills Development

From the survey it was clear most students either agreed, or strongly agreed that the IBM Challenge helped gain an insight into the life of entrepreneurs, as well as the skills and attitudes required to be an entrepreneur. Most respondents also agreed that the competition helped develop their overall entrepreneurial skills and abilities (Figure 17.1).

This was an important finding and fundamental to the value of entrepreneurial learning within the IBM UBC setting (based on the NCGE entrepreneurial learning outcomes framework; see Box 17.1). From the responses to the open-ended responses to the survey, and reflections on the competition, further insight revealed the interconnectedness of skills development in terms of 'grasping the business basic how-tos' (Box 17.1) in a dynamic learning context:

> It showed us how to run our own business . . . there are a lot of things you need to consider in the Challenge, if you spend a bit more on advertising and marketing that makes a difference, it increases your awareness, so it's not just based on price only or the product itself, there are actually other things surrounding the products that you need to consider, that are important as well, if you want to be successful.

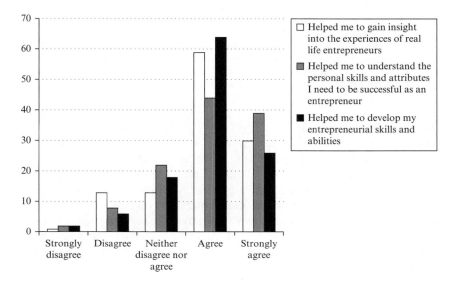

Figure 17.1   Contribution to entrepreneurial learning

Pittaway et al. (2009) suggested that an effective entrepreneurial learning outcomes framework must be action-oriented and that critical learning events are important, thus allowing transformative learning to occur. Many of these aspects are present in the IBM UBC, not least the element of social competition among participants, who actively become aware of the need to compete in order to win, or at the very least, progress to the next stage of the competition:

> At the start, from my perspective, I came in with quite a frivolous attitude and I didn't really take the UBC very seriously and it was spearheaded by the rest of the guys, but once we did get into the semi-finals, and thinking that we could actually have a chance, I took an interest in it and I think at the semi-finals we found we worked really well as a team.

Creating Empathy with the 'Entrepreneurial World'

The emphasis on real-life learning and emulating the periphery of a community of practice is a key element of IBM UBC. A key part of this is the development of an integrated and complex social learning situation that attempts to create dynamic learning through social interactions, emotional experience and reflexive support (Hamilton, 2011). One of the participants reflected on the complexity of the social learning environment created:

> We can compare UBC to [other simulations], where the concept of internationalism is truly experimented, or rather applied in simulated business scenarios. UBC works on a multitude of facets that, in effect, allows you to go through the essential steps to get you prepared for the real world. The thought of interacting with teams of various intellectual levels (in latter rounds) is what intrigues us, and we believe that this is vital for the simultaneous development of our skills. [Group 2]

The 'emulation capacity' (Fearon et al., 2012) within a community of practice arises from the interaction of a variety of components that make up a social learning situation. Emulation helps bring students as new entrants, or 'novices' from the periphery towards the centre of a community of practice through a process of 'local' and 'global' interactions, as part of an evolving joint enterprise (Wenger, 1998, 2000). Emulation is also informed by the situated nature of new learning environments, that is, the process of interweaving individual and group learning experiences within different and challenging social settings (Altrichter, 2005; Fearon et al., 2012). This can be illustrated through the views of a participant:

> The format of the competition, where a different company sponsors each round will expose us to different industries and further our understanding of the corporate environment. Also it allows us to network with senior figures and ask questions of potential employers.

We argue, in terms of social learning, that the emulation effect of a business challenge competition helps build 'social containers' (Wenger, 2000) of tacit knowledge that can be harnessed by individuals, or team members within the competition, as part of that legitimate community of practitioners (Altrichter, 2005). Complex business simulations and scenarios can then be dealt with effectively in a socially situated learning environment. This is demonstrated through the reflections of various focus group participants:

> It's the closest you probably can get without actually going to work in a business, because there's decisions that you've got to make and they've got repercussions, so with no risk it's probably the closest you'll get to a business situation, which was quite good.

> It really gave an opportunity for us to put ourselves in the shoes of like corporate people actually going through it day-in/day-out . . . just like to put yourself in one of these companies and experience what they go through, and again just something different, a lot of team work and involvement with other people that you just meet upfront and just getting to bounce off other people's ideas, and establish your communication and social skills.

Whilst there are many complexities associated with developing and measuring entrepreneurial learning, the role of community of practice as a lens on empathizing with the life of the entrepreneur is becoming increasingly important (Hamilton, 2011).

Key Entrepreneurial Values

Embedded in the various scenarios, action-oriented learning stems directly from engagement through negotiating, influencing and decision-making as part of the situational context in each of the simulations. As each round progressed, the stakes became higher and the intensity of social competition increased between the groups. Being able to harness a structured knowledge base, quickly develop financial strategies, apply intuitive decision-making skills and engage in necessary risk-taking are all entrepreneurial qualities, and a key part of entrepreneurial learning associated with a business challenge/competition environment (Atchison and Gotlieb, 2004; Russell et al., 2008). Interesting entrepreneurial values were reflected upon and explicated around the notion of 'risk':

> I think the main thing for me . . . was I think 'entrepreneurism is risky', and like I said before the risky decision we took paid off and again in the semi-finals we played quite a risky game in that we were playing a diversification strategy, but again that paid off as well. So, I think it showed me that in entrepreneurship you've got to take risks . . . that is the main thing!

Sense-making was useful in the understanding of the role of cash in the competition, how and where it is important:

> It basically teaches you, because if you think about what you're learning, in theory, in university, but then here you have to apply it and you have to have some accounting skills and you have to have some knowledge about cash flow. You actually find out that cash is very important, and you're not necessarily being taught about it in lectures . . . but here you see well it's everything about cash . . . because you have to apply for loans.

Interestingly, a vital personal quality attribute, which improved for many during the competition, was self-confidence developed through experience and participation, as part of a business team:

> I would probably say individually, after the whole experience, I probably feel a lot more confident in my own abilities . . . I know I can be given a situation, think about it, and make decisions that will give us a good outcome.

This finding was echoed by Russell et al. (2008), who suggested that motivated by team interaction and mentoring/coaching from tutors,

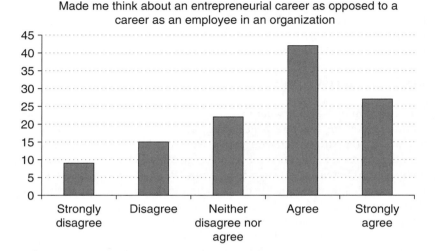

Figure 17.2   Impact on entrepreneurial intent

self-confidence grew along with a greater sense of achievement and efficacy for students. The role of a social learning environment and nurturing
of self-efficacy approaches towards inclusive learning are important in
enabling a sense of joint purpose in a community of practice environment
(Hamilton, 2011).

Motivation Towards an Entrepreneurial Career

The enterprise skills gained during IBM UBC could equally apply to
future corporate and professional careers, as well as entrepreneurial ventures. Therefore, disentangling social learning for general employability,
as opposed to intent to have an entrepreneurial career, is difficult. The
survey also highlighted conflicting results on this issue (Figure 17.2).

When directly asked the question: 'Has the competition made you think
seriously about an entrepreneurial career, as opposed to a career as an
employee?', an interesting discourse developed between two focus group
members, possibly depending on the viewpoint of each participant, and
their understanding of the term, 'entrepreneurial career':

> I don't think I got too much entrepreneurial stuff out of it, because the way it
> was designed . . . like we're trying to impress those companies basically, in order
> for us to get a job in those companies, so that's the way I saw it . . . I didn't see
> it as them giving us the skills to do what we want, they're trying to see skills that
> they want, so we can apply for their jobs.

Adding to what Chris was saying, I haven't been an entrepreneurial guy, but I think I agree with him in the sense that it gave us confidence, to think ok – I know it was a simulation – but we can actually make decisions that will positively affect the business and we, sort of our reasoning, if you want to start you own business, you've got confidence to undertake something. We're working as a team but when you pitch your ideas to each other, and the vision of the business or where you want to go, probably you got that from this Challenge.

Whilst there is considerable evidence supporting entrepreneurial learning and development of enterprise skills, establishing the extent to which the IBM UBC and other business competitions contribute to wider entrepreneurial intent would arguably be difficult to achieve. It may be more prudent to state that the emerging evidence suggests that business competitions such as the IBM UBC are likely to contribute to enterprise skills development. However, further empirical research is required.

Supporting Generic Competencies and Grasping the Basic 'How Tos'

Similar to Pittaway and Cope (2007), there are arguments that support an action orientation for entrepreneurial learning. There was strong reflection on the value of the financial, strategic and marketing skill sets acquired, as well as the value of simulation in a social environment that mimicked real-life trading:

There were a lot of external influences, so say every trading period you get like a scenario update about the environment, like predictions, and trends. In class you don't really get that. There's not much about an external environmental influence on your work that you're doing, so you don't base kind of group work and all that kind of stuff or decisions that you make in the group on what's happening on the outside, it's quite interior, so the IBM Challenge helped us to kind of take an external trend and then apply our strategy to it.

What came across in an emerging narrative was the sense of lived experience required for entrepreneurial learning (Rae, 2000, 2009; Rae and Carswell, 2000). In addition, a sense of emotional learning (Pittaway and Cope, 2007), learning and fun in particular, were frequent reflections:

It was good fun, enjoyed being in my team. This competition has taught me many things and I am aware of the financial side of the business better than before.

Being part of the social environment and business team has also helped develop and reinforce skills and identity in the learning group:

Yeah, that was just a good experience to meet new people and just kind of con-solidate those skills socially.

That was actually quite interesting how we came together as a group, because we didn't know each other . . . not everyone knew each other before, for instance I knew Gemma and I knew Sue, but I didn't know Bob and Stacey, while Sue knew Bob and Stacey. So Anneka and I, we said well we should do this IBM Business Challenge and so Sue said well I know two good people who would like to participate as well and I said well I know a very good person as well for whom it would be interesting and so we mixed together and we didn't even have an initial meeting because it was quite early in the beginning and everyone was quite spread out.

Similar to other studies (Russell et al., 2008), being part of a UBC team helped encourage a sense of participation and engagement:

I found, when you sometimes work in a group at university, not everyone's totally committed to doing something, whereas the nature of the competition is that people have applied for it from all over the university, so already they're showing willingness to take part in it . . . and working with a team that wants to do well, and take part.

Based on community of practice ideas (Wenger, 2000; Hamilton, 2011), legitimate participation, leveraging social capital and 'esprit de corps' become important aspects in renegotiating the fabric of joint enterprise and entrepreneurial learning:

If someone's struggling with it then you actually get the chance to say . . . well actually this bit goes there, and that bit goes here and that helps with this, it's a just a lot more friendly place to learn, rather than being put on the spot going, oh, I don't know.

Specific skills and competencies included decision-making and influenc-ing skills within a dynamic learning setting are particularly important for entrepreneurial learning (Cope and Watts, 2000; Cope, 2005; Russell et al., 2008):

I think what is also quite interesting is that you're doing something, you're gathering information, you're making decisions because the normal studying does not involve decision making . . . but here you have to gather your informa-tion, you have to discuss it, you have to make decisions, and then you actually see the outcome of your decisions, so that is something which you don't have in your normal student life.

For a small number of students, it was their second time in participating in the IBM UBC. For others, they heard about the experience within their university from previous students and staff members:

From speaking to previous students who took part in this Challenge, we learned that it is an exciting, realistic and fun way to gain an incredible insight into the running of a business and a practical way to apply our theoretical knowledge. The fact that all of the students we spoke to had positive experiences to share adds to our eagerness to participate.

Within the group, we have experienced similar challenges such as the ABC scheme providing us with additional experience relevant to the competition.

The willingness of students to participate twice, or enter into multiple competitions helps the process of spreading general enthusiasm, legitimizing business competitions as a valued form of entrepreneurial learning and enterprise education.

Managing Stakeholder Relationships – Interaction Between International Teams

Whilst the IBM UBC was based on the participation of leading UK universities, the actual composition of team members and nature of business scenarios were international and global in nature. The international make-up of team members and the social learning context a business challenge competition provides is important. Intercultural negotiation and student participation helps emulate a sense of international cooperation and develop experiences of working with different people in different ways:

It was also nice to have such an international team, because there were some teams they just applied with only Germans, or only the one nationality . . . and I wanted to be in an international team.

We are a diverse group of individuals with complementing skill sets ranging from organizational skills to leadership qualities. Having come from different cultural, religious and ethnic backgrounds, we are confident we can adapt our business ideas globally.

The unified structure of our team, which stems from multiple nationalities, gives us a good opportunity to network with our colleagues/competitors, and real world consultants. It is exciting to be competing with students who just might be future financial moguls.

Team structures are important for entrepreneurial business competitions, as more diverse team memberships lead to greater access of ideas and information (Der Foo et al., 2005). An innovative and entrepreneurial mindset must become increasingly global, and the intercultural community of practice ethos most Higher Education students are now operating in, must reflect dealing with greater cultural diversity.

DISCUSSION: IMPLICATIONS FOR ENTREPRENEURIAL LEARNING AND PEDAGOGY

The following sections recognize and discuss the need for understanding pedagogical advances in entrepreneurial learning and business competitions, as part of a possible wider research agenda.

Towards a Complementary 'Blended/Reflexive' Approach

There are implications for developing a co-learning pedagogy and entrepreneurial learning approach where both participant and educator both learn together. We draw upon the work of Hannon et al. (2005) and recent work of Deacon and Harris (2011), who suggest working with the lecturer as facilitator/mentor and using a team approach for entrepreneurial learning. Business challenge competitions are developmental and provide a useful research context for unpicking the social dynamics of entrepreneurial learning. The idea of blended pedagogy uses a mix of methods to create a 'specialist learning environment' (van Tassel-Baska, 1994; Deacon and Harris, 2011). Social entrepreneurial learning is thus strengthened through socialization, reciprocal exchanges and team bonding among the student participants during key team activities, which was evident from the IBM UBC (2012) study already discussed.

There is also further reflexive support and reciprocal exchanges from tutors who nurture through periods of reflection in order to support fledgling ideas, new skills and personal development. Gibb (2011) interestingly examines the role of 'personal entrepreneurial educator capacity' within traditional entrepreneurial education settings, suggesting that tutors may have little power, or resources to animate, or make things happen within a traditional classroom. Perhaps business challenge competitions can offer something different, a complementary approach, by nature of learning context and a wider social environment for students to participate and interact.

Towards Reflexive Complementarity

From the survey, it was evident that a majority of respondents believed that the IBM UBC provided a learning experience that could not be achieved in the classroom alone. There was also a perception that UBC complements existing skills and learning already being taught in class (Figure 17.3).

The complementary sense of learning from enterprise courses at univer-

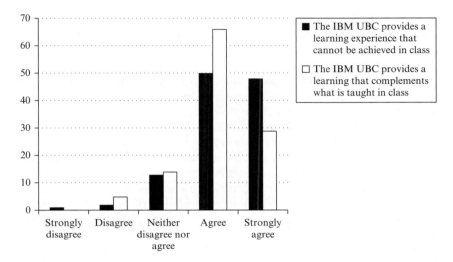

Figure 17.3 Complementing class-based learning

sity and the perception of applying entrepreneurial learning in a socially situated learning context was evident:

> I think this is why we're saying it complements the course nicely, because this comes up so much across all of the business strategy and entrepreneurship modules, it's the core really, so that's why I think it's a very positive experience and it fits very nicely with our course.

> It's a lot more practical, hands on, rather than just sitting in a classroom going, oh well this theory you can add to this, and that goes to there, it actually helps you understand what you're doing it for.

However, the sense of reflexive support and facilitation from tutors was also clearly evident:

> I think it's nice to know, with a class your lecturer, or seminar leader actually has to be there . . . with the IBM Challenge we had sort of dedicated lectures and people like Jane Doe, were just there if we needed them, and we could say . . . 'Could you help us?'

NEW DIRECTIONS FOR RESEARCH AND PEDAGOGY

More empirical case-based research is required to examine the role of business challenges through the lens of entrepreneurial communities of practice, which would be useful for establishing a more comprehensive understanding of entrepreneurial learning from a socially situated learning perspective (Gibb, 2011; Hamilton, 2011). Whilst of interest, there are still many weaknesses with the application of a 'communities of practice' ethos to entrepreneurial learning, not least a lack of understanding of the power mechanisms associated with the process of 'legitimacy', for example, when deciding who can and should participate in UBC teams, negotiating member roles and influence within the team and wider competition community. In addition, there is an argument that stable communities of practice and competition teams can provide a powerful mechanism for replication and entrepreneurial learning, but over time learning may in fact become static and the tacit knowledge base become too structured. A weakness of legitimized and stable communities of practice is the lack of flow, regarding new ideas, or member turnover, which can contribute to an overall loss in the transformative and entrepreneurial learning capability of the participating teams and wider community (Roberts, 2006; Hamilton, 2011).

Also of interest is Gibb's (2011) recent research regarding the International Entrepreneurship Educators' Programme (IEEP), a UK-based programme focused on staff in Higher Education and Further Education. Developed under the umbrella of two key UK organizations, NCGE and the Entrepreneurship Educators UK, the programme originally sought to widen entrepreneurial education in a cross-university developmental context. This may be a useful thread of research from a policy perspective to examine the wider trends in co-pedagogy and educator development in the UK. Matlay and Carey (2007) performed a similar study that was useful from a longitudinal perspective and perhaps it is time to carry out further work to establish what is happening in terms of entrepreneurial education initiatives among leading UK and international universities.

Gibb (2011) also discusses possible futures for entrepreneurship education and makes worthy suggestions for entrepreneurial pedagogy including the greater promotion of social interaction and reciprocal exchange (Bandura, 1977) as well as social learning through communities of practice. He also suggests a greater understanding of the conative and cognitive aspects of personal development. Furthering Gibb (2011) and indeed Bandura's ideas, we suggest that more research on the role of social interaction and reciprocal exchange for promoting both self- and group efficacy as part of entrepreneurial learning may also be a useful thread of future research, especially within a university business challenge setting, from social constructionist and human agency perspectives.

CONCLUSION

There have been increasing calls for further research into the contribution of business challenges, social learning and entrepreneurial learning for understanding pedagogic development from the student perspective (Jones, 2010; Jones and Jones, 2011). We are arguably at a turning point within entrepreneurial education, with less funding resources and a greater emphasis on developing inclusive, integrated approaches to pedagogy, as well as the need for evaluating impact, and devising usable mechanisms for assessing entrepreneurial learning outcomes (Pittaway et al., 2009; Jones and Matlay, 2011).

Given the paucity of existing research, the exploratory study of the IBM UBC (2012) represented an opportunity for educators and students to reflect and speak about the role of business challenge competitions for entrepreneurial learning as well as implications for entrepreneurial education. These discussions highlighted the value of business competitions as an experience-based form of entrepreneurship education. The majority of the respondents believed that the IBM UBC helped develop their overall entrepreneurial skills and abilities, and that it provided a learning experience that could not be achieved in the classroom alone. They also stated that involvement in the competition got them as close as possible to running a real business in a safe and controlled environment and therefore helped to emulate communities of practice (Fearon et al., 2012).

These findings support calls from policy-makers (European Commission, 2008, 2010) to make experiential learning methods such as business competitions an integral part of the curriculum, as opposed to an extra-curricular 'add-on', in order to develop entrepreneurial skills and abilities, raise entrepreneurial awareness and promote self-confidence and independence. Embedding business competitions in the curriculum also supports the employability agenda, as it provides students with an experience to evidence learning of key skills and abilities.

Finally, the results strengthen the call for crossing boundaries and multi-disciplinary collaboration, taking business competitions beyond the typical business school environment and inviting participation from students across the university. More diverse (international) team memberships lead to greater access of ideas and information, helps emulate a sense of international cooperation and intercultural negotiation, and develop experiences of working with different people in different ways.

NOTE

*   The authors would like to thank Peter and Deborah Cardwell of Learning Dynamics for their support in this research project.

REFERENCES

Altrichter, H. (2005), 'The role of the "professional community" in action research', *Educational Research Action*, **13**(1), 11–25.
Atchison, M. and P. Gotlieb (2004), 'Innovation and the future of cooperative education', in R. Coll and C. Eames (eds), *International Handbook for Cooperative Education: An International Perspective of the Theory, Research and Practice of Work-integrated Learning*, Boston, MA: World Association for Cooperative Education, pp. 261–9.
Bandura, A. (1977), 'Self-efficacy: Toward a unifying theory of behavioral change', *Psychological Review*, **84**(2), 191–215.
Cope, J. (2005), 'Toward a dynamic learning perspective of entrepreneurship', *Entrepreneurship: Theory and Practice*, **29**(3), 373–98.
Cope, J. and G. Watts (2000), 'Learning by doing: An exploration of experience, critical incidents and reflection in entrepreneurial learning', *International Journal of Entrepreneurial Behaviour and Research*, **6**(3), 104–24.
Crayford, J., C. Fearon, H. McLaughlin and W. van Vuuren (2012), 'Affirming entrepreneurial education: Learning, employability and personal development', *Industrial and Commercial Training*, **44**(4), 187–93.
Deacon, J. and J. Harris (2011), 'A longitudinal reflection of blended/reflexive enterprise and entrepreneurial education', *Reflective Practice*, **12**(5), 599–613.
Der Foo, M., P.K. Wong and A. Ong (2005), 'Do others think you have a viable business idea? Team diversity and judges' evaluation of ideas in a business plan competition', *Journal of Business Venturing*, **20**(3), 385–402.
Draycott, M., D. Rae and K. Vause (2011), 'The assessment of enterprise education in the secondary education sector', *Education + Training*, **53**(8/9), 673–91.
European Commission (2008), *Best Procedure Project: Entrepreneurship in Higher Education, Especially in Non-business Studies*, Final Report of the Expert Group, Brussels: EC.
European Commission (2010), *Towards Greater Cooperation and Coherence in Entrepreneurship Education*, Report and Evaluation of the Pilot Action High Level Reflection Panels on Entrepreneurship Education, Brussels: EC.
Fearon, C., E. Tan Yoke and H. McLaughlin (2012), 'Using student group-work in Higher Education to emulate professional communities of practice', *Education + Training*, **54**(2/3), 114–25.
Gibb, A. (2011), 'Concepts into practice: Meeting the challenge of development of entrepreneurship educators around an innovative paradigm: The case of the International Entrepreneurship Educators' Programme (IEEP)', *International Journal of Entrepreneurial Behaviour and Research*, **17**(2), 146–65.
Hamilton, J. (2011), 'Entrepreneurial learning in family business: A situated learning perspective', *Journal of Small Business and Enterprise Development*, **18**(1), 8–26.
Hannon, P.D., L.A. Collins and A.J. Smith (2005), 'Exploring graduate entrepreneurship: A collaborative co-learning-based approach for student entrepreneurs and educators', *Industry and Higher Education*, **19**(1), 11–24.
Jones, A. and P. Jones (2011), 'Making an impact: A profile of a business planning competition in a university', *Education and Training*, **53**(8/9), 704–21.
Jones, B. and N. Iredale (2010), 'Enterprise education as pedagogy', *Education + Training*, **52**(1), 7–19.

Jones, C. (2010), 'Entrepreneurship education: Revisiting our role and its purpose', *Journal of Small Business and Enterprise Development*, **17**(4), 500–13.

Jones, C. and H. Matlay (2011), 'Understanding the heterogeneity of entrepreneurship education: Going beyond Gartner', *Education + Training*, **53**(8/9), 692–703.

Matlay, H. and C. Carey (2007), 'Entrepreneurship education in the UK: A longitudinal perspective', *Journal of Small Business and Enterprise Development*, **14**(2), 252–63.

Mills, C. (2011), 'Enterprise orientations: A framework for making sense of fashion sector start-up', *International Journal of Entrepreneurial Behaviour and Research*, **17**(3), 245–71.

Nikolou-Walker, G. and J. Garnett (2004), 'Work-based learning: A new imperative: developing reflective practice in professional life', *Reflective Practice*, **5**(3), 197–212.

Parry J. (2003), 'Making sense of executive sense-making: A phenomenological case study with methodological criticism', *Journal of Health Organization and Management*, **17**(4), 240–63.

Pittaway, L. and J. Cope (2007), 'Simulating entrepreneurial learning: Integrating experiential and collaborative approaches to learning', *Management Learning*, **38**(2), 211–33.

Pittaway, L. and P. Hannon (2008), 'Institutional strategies for developing entrepreneurship education: A review of some concepts and models', *Journal of Small Business and Enterprise Development*, **15**(1), 202–26.

Pittaway, L., P. Hannon, A. Gibb and J. Thompson (2009), 'Assessment practice in enterprise education', *International Journal of Entrepreneurial Behaviour and Research*, **15**(1), 71–93.

Rae, D. (2000), 'Understanding entrepreneurial learning: A question of how?' *International Journal of Entrepreneurial Behaviour and Research*, **6**(3), 145–59.

Rae, D. (2005), 'Entrepreneurial learning: A narrative-based conceptual model', *Journal of Small Business and Enterprise Development*, **12**(3), 323–35.

Rae, D. (2009), 'Connecting entrepreneurial and action learning in student-initiated new business ventures: The case of SPEED', *Action Learning: Research and Practice*, **6**(3), 289–303.

Rae, D. and M. Carswell (2000), 'Using a life-story approach in researching entrepreneurial learning: The development of a conceptual model and its implications in the design of learning experiences', *Education + Training*, **42**(4/5), 220–27.

Roberts, J. (2006), 'Limits to communities of practice', *Journal of Management Studies*, **43**(3), 623–40.

Russell, R., M. Atchison and R. Brooks (2008), 'Business plan competitions in tertiary institutions: Encouraging entrepreneurship education', *Journal of Higher Education Policy and Management*, **30**(2), 123–38.

Shafari, S. and M. Zhang (2009), 'Sense-making and recipes: Examples from selected small firms', *International Journal of Entrepreneurial Behaviour and Research*, **15**(6), 555–70.

Smith, A.M-J. and R.A. Patton (2011), 'Delivering enterprise: A collaborative international approach to the development, implementation and assessment of entrepreneurship', *International Journal of Entrepreneurial Behaviour and Research*, **17**(1), 104–18.

Taatila, V.P. (2010), 'Learning entrepreneurship in Higher Education', *Education + Training*, **52**(1), 48–61.

van Tassel-Baska, J. (1994), *Comprehensive Curriculum for Gifted Learners*, 2nd edition, Boston, MA: Pearson.

Walmsley, A., R. Thomas and S. Jameson (2006), 'Surprise and sense-making: Undergraduate placement experiences in SMEs', *Education and Training*, **48**(5), 360–72.

Weick, K.E. (1995), *Sense-making in Organizations*, Thousand Oaks, CA: Sage.

Weick, K.E., K.M. Sutcliffe and D. Obstfeld (2005), 'Organizing and the process of sense-making', *Organization Science*, **16**(4), 409–21.

Wenger, E. (1998), *Communities of Practice: Learning, Meaning and Identity*, New York: Cambridge University Press.

Wenger, E. (2000), 'Communities of practice and social learning systems', *Organization*, **7**(2), 225–46.

18. Where do academic entrepreneurs locate their firms? How to access the development of entrepreneurship education at university level*

Christos Kolympiris, Nicholas Kalaitzandonakes and Ken Schneeberger

INTRODUCTION

University faculty members who engage in entrepreneurial activity mainly via firm creation are crucial to the effort of the entrepreneurial university in narrowing the gap between academic science and commercial applications. Accordingly, a considerable body of literature has studied these so-called academic entrepreneurs by focusing on research that has largely revolved around two general lines of inquiry: first, which academic scientists start a firm and what are the specific personal and contextual characteristics (affiliated university, social norms etc.) that influence such entrepreneurial behaviour; and, second, how academic entrepreneurs balance their academic- and business-related responsibilities (e.g., Stuart and Ding, 2006; Jain et al., 2009; Krabel and Mueller, 2009; Landry et al., 2010; Lam, 2011). This literature has advanced new knowledge that, for instance, highlights the impact of intellectual capital, workplace attributes, prior career experience and the availability of financial resources in determining whether a given academic scientist decides to enter entrepreneurship and meet both academic and business duties (Shane and Khurana, 2003; Zucker et al., 2002; Landry et al., 2006; Stuart and Ding, 2006).

What has gone largely unexamined in the relevant literature is where these faculty members choose to start their firms. Academic entrepreneurs typically start their firms from research that originated at university premises. However, it is not clear that such firms are always located close to the affiliated university. Indeed, a significant percentage of spin-offs, not necessarily from academic entrepreneurs, locate far from the parent organization (Egeln et al., 2004; Berchicci et al., 2011). In fact, in one of the few studies that focused on the firm location choice of academic entrepreneurs, Audretsch and Stephan (1996) reported that for their sample of university-based firm founders over 40 per cent started their biotechnology firms at a distance from their academic institution.

Upon reflection, such statistics may not be surprising. Given their high human capital and expertise, local firm creation is only one of the many options for academic entrepreneurs and their firm location choice is likely influenced by personal, environmental and institutional factors. On one hand, academic entrepreneurs may be inclined to start their firm locally to ensure close proximity to their academic duties and maintain their social ties (Dahl and Sorenson, 2012). On the other hand, they could be motivated to start their firms outside their current location when proximity to larger specialized labour pools, venture capital pools or agglomerations of similar firms can improve their chance of success (Zucker et al., 1998, 2002; Egeln et al., 2004; Kolympiris et al., 2011). Indeed, some of those factors, such as venture capital, have been found to attract firms to their locations (Samila and Sorenson, 2011). Hence, the academic entrepreneur's firm location choice maybe a complex decision that depends on a number of potentially counteracting factors.

Prompted by such considerations, in the present study we analyse the firm location choice of academic entrepreneurs employing a case study design. Sixteen in-depth interviews with US-based academic scientists who started life sciences firms from 1996 to 2008 allow us to provide novel insights in the factors that shape the decision of faculty members on where to locate their firm. Insights that derive from asking academic entrepreneurs not only what factors contributed to their firm location choice but also on the relative weight that each relevant player (academic scientist, funding sources etc.) had on that decision.

Our interest in the question at hand is, primarily, motivated by the complexity of factors that can influence the firm location choice of a given academic entrepreneur. However, addressing that complexity goes beyond academic curiosity. Many universities in the USA and elsewhere have embraced a fourth mission besides research, teaching and service; that of local economic development (Goldstein, 2009; Atkinson and Pelfrey, 2010). Newly founded firms that originate from university-based research tend to bring about benefits to the regions that host them such as increased employment and value creation (Chrisman et al., 1995; Huggins and Cooke, 1997; Etzkowitz et al., 2000; AUTM, 2001; Goldstein and Renault, 2004; Shane, 2004; Bramwell and Wolfe, 2008) perhaps because they tend to exhibit more persistent periods of success when compared to non-university-based ventures (Dahlstrand, 1997; Mustar, 1997; Nerkar and Shane, 2003; Degroof and Roberts, 2004; Shane, 2004).[1] In fact, the likelihood that such firms indeed experience long-term success is often heavily determined by the different kinds of support (provision of laboratory facilities, access to research equipment, consultation on intellectual property issues and the like) provided by the affiliated institution (Steffensen et al., 2000). Accordingly, the relationship between universities and their role in promoting firm creation has strengthened over the years and by extension understanding the factors that shape the firm location choice of academic entrepreneurs can inform policy-makers, university administrators and other interested parties as to the measures they need to devise and implement in order to promote local firm creation and accordingly allow the entrepreneurial university to act as a local growth engine.

We proceed with the rest of the chapter as follows: in the next section we review the relevant literature on the factors that affect firm location choice. In the third section we outline our methodology and in the fourth we present our results. In the fifth section we summarize and conclude.

BACKGROUND LITERATURE

Starting from the premise that location is a key determinant of the success rate of newly founded firms (Decarolis and Deeds, 1999; Fotopoulos and Louri, 2000; Strotmann, 2007) a number of researchers have sought to explain observed start-up rates or the probability that a given entrepreneur starts his or her firm at a certain location. This research has grown around three main traditions: the neoclassical, the institutional and the behavioural (Hayter, 1997). In the neoclassical tradition the behavioural postulate is that economic agents choose the location that they expect will maximize their net profit. Accordingly, the analysis typically focuses on the effects of regional characteristics, such as agglomeration externalities and proximity to customers, which minimize transportation and other costs and advance the firm's efficiency often through knowledge spillovers (Guimarães et al., 2000; Figueiredo et al., 2002; Audretsch et al., 2005). Works in the institutional tradition also place their attention on regional characteristics but more so on those that allow the development of networks of economic relationships among closely located organizations. Such characteristics may involve taxes, local wages or other factors that form the regional economic environment and provide monetary gains that may assist the formation of sustained supplier and client networks (Carlton, 1983; Bartik, 1985; Coughlin et al., 1991; Glaeser and Kerr, 2009). Finally, the starting point of research in the behavioural tradition is that the preferences of the individual shape the firm location choice. In this vein, the focus is on the characteristics of the individual such as age and previous experience that are expected to influence his or her preferences (Wright et al., 2008; Dahl and Sorenson, 2012). Collectively, research in all three traditions has shown that agglomeration effects, desire to stay close to family and friends, ability to exploit financial opportunities as well as entrepreneur-specific considerations are among the key drivers of firm location (Deeds et al., 2000; Figueiredo et al., 2002; Michelacci and Silva, 2007; Dahl and Sorenson, 2009; Arauzo Carod et al., 2010). However, the above-mentioned research has employed samples that do not focus on firms founded by academic scientists, which makes it difficult to identify the factors that shape the firm location choice of academic entrepreneurs.

Consequently, our knowledge on the drivers of firm location by academic entrepreneurs rests largely upon only a handful of studies (Audretsch and Stephan, 1996; Zucker et al., 1998; Egeln et al., 2004). The findings of these studies are generally in line with the insights of the studies in the neoclassical, the institutional and the behavioural literature on firm location. More specifically, Audretsch and Stephan (1996) estimated the probability that the academic scientist and the firm he or she is involved in share the same location and highlighted the impact of the scientist on location choice by reporting that compared to scientists that assume mainly an advisory role, firm founders are more likely to start their firm locally. Egeln et al. (2004) stressed the significance of urbanization and localization economies when they estimated the probability that a given firm founded based on public research locates at a distance from the parent institution. Finally, Zucker et al. (1998) studied the regional start-up rate of biotechnology firms and demonstrated that academic founders tend to exhibit a drawing power under which such firms (not necessarily started by academic scientists) often locate close to where influential scientists are employed.

There are at least two observations from those studies that we find particularly interesting. First, these studies do not incorporate simultaneously the impact of founder and contextual characteristics in the analysis, which leaves the reader wondering just how the two sets of factors interact and what weight they carry separately in the firm location decision. Second, the analyses do not take into account the impact of the funding sources of the firms started by academic entrepreneurs. This is curious because firms founded by academic entrepreneurs operate mainly in high-technology industries where intellectual property is typically easier to monetize largely because of the close ties between basic research and commercial applications. It is in these industries and often in those firms that venture capitalists and other private investors tend to invest and empirical evidence suggests that venture capitalists attract firms close to them (Samila and Sorenson, 2011) mainly in order to better monitor and guide their investment targets.

Prompted by such considerations in the present research we study the location choice of firms started by academic entrepreneurs and venture capitalists. In order to assess how contextual and founder-related characteristics influence location choice we employ a case study design, which we describe in the next section.

METHODS

To analyse the firm location decision of academic entrepreneurs we interviewed faculty members who had started life sciences firms in the USA. We focused on entrepreneurs in life sciences because it is a knowledge-based field with close ties between basic science and commercial applications (Shane, 2004). Accordingly, many academic entrepreneurs originate from that field, which then suggests that we target a sample we expect to be representative in terms of the industry where academic scientists materialize their entrepreneurial intentions.

Our sample was constructed as follows: because we were interested in venture-capital-funded firms, as a first step we sourced the full list of life sciences firms that received venture capital funds from ThomsonReuters' SDC Platinum™ Database. This list included 817 firms out of which 315 had an academic scientist and a venture capital firm listed as a (co-) founder. We visited the website of each of the 315 firms as well as the websites of the listed founders and venture capital firms to verify that information and identify the contact information. From the list of the 315 firms we drew a random sample of 100 firms. From the list of the 100 firms we purposefully selected 30 firms so that we had a sample of firms located across the country, started at different time periods and being affiliated with renowned as well as lesser (in terms of reputation) academic institutions. This purposeful selection was made in order to ensure that our findings are representative of both rural and urban areas, to time periods that exhibit different degrees of venture capital activity or opportunities for communication across space and to academic institutions that offer varying degrees of academic recognition and accompanying opportunities. From the 30 initial contacts we were able to conduct interviews with 16 faculty members[2] who had started life sciences firms between 1996 and 2008. The initial interviews were conducted by phone, took place between September 2009 and August 2011 and lasted from 30 to about 45 minutes. Whenever needed, we had follow-up interviews with entrepreneurs in the summer of 2012.

As seen in Table 18.1, three of the 16 firms were located in the traditional 'biotech hubs' in coastal cities such as San Francisco, CA and Cambridge, MA. Four firms were located in (smaller) interior life sciences clusters in Durham, NC and in the vicinity of Denver, CO and nine firms were located in non-traditional life sciences clusters mainly in the interior USA in Texas, Colorado and Wisconsin. Four firms were founded before or in 2000, three firms between 2001 and 2004 and nine firms after 2004. Approximately one-third of the firms were founded by academics affiliated with prestigious universities such as Harvard, MIT and Duke. The average distance between the firm and the university of the affiliated faculty was eight miles with 14 of the 16 firms located up to 10.7 miles from the affiliated university and only two firms located at larger distances. These statistics indicate the general propensity of firms to be located close to the academic founder. As we explain in the next section, the notion of proximity can differ across different states in the USA where, for instance, in rural areas even 20 miles distance is considered fairly proximate.

At the beginning of each interview the founders were asked to give a brief history of their company and identify the decision-makers of the firm location choice. Then, an open-ended question on the reasons that prompted them to start their firm at a certain location was used as the primary way to identify what factors shaped that decision. Whenever more than one reason was provided to explain why a given location was chosen, we asked academic entrepreneurs to rank these reasons in terms of importance in affecting firm location choice.

To help entrepreneurs freely address our questions we assured them that neither their identity nor that of their company would be disclosed. As such, we proceed with the discussion of our findings in the following fashion: first, we discuss our general findings that summarize the 16 interviews and then we succinctly present three cases that are representative of the rest. In these cases the names of the entrepreneurs and their companies are kept confidential.[3]

RESULTS

General Findings

In all the interviews the interviewees clearly indicated that the location decision was determined jointly by the academic entrepreneur and the funding venture capital firm. In particular, while the venture capital firms often made the final decision, in all the cases in our sample the chosen location was within a less than 30 minutes' drive from the academic institution where the chief scientist was based. Going back to Table 18.1, even in the two cases where the distance between the academic founder and the firm

Table 18.1   *Firm-specific information and factors undermining the choice of firm location for academic entrepreneurs*

Firm	Firm-specific information					
	Firm city/ neighbour hood	Firm state	Found- ing year	Number of founders	Affiliated university of the closest to the firm academic firm founder	Distance from firm to affiliated university (miles)
A	Broomfield	CO	2005	3	UNIVERSITY OF COLORADO DENVER/ HSC AURORA	20.2
B	Madison	WI	2001	2	UNIVERSITY OF WISCONSIN MADISON	3.2
C	Durham	NC	2004	2	DUKE UNIVERSITY	9.6
D	Cambridge	MA	2008	3	HARVARD UNIVERSITY (MEDICAL SCHOOL)	1.8
E	Austin	TX	2007	1	UNIVERSITY OF TEXAS AUSTIN	8.7
F	Watertown	MA	2005	3	MASSACHUSETTS INSTITUTE OF TECHNOLOGY	3.6
G	Austin	TX	2006	1	UNIVERSITY OF TEXAS AUSTIN	8.7

Primary and secondary reasons for choice of location		Ranking of reasons for choice of location						
Primary reason(s) for chosen location	Secondary reason(s) for chosen location	Proximity to academic scientist/ founder	Proximity to VC	Proximity to labour pool	Proximity to firms in the same industry	Low rent or other reduced costs of operations at incubator	Low rent or value added services at incubator	Social bonds
Proximity to academic scientist/ founder	Proximity to labor pool	1		2		3		4
Proximity to academic scientist/ founder	Proximity to VC	1	2				4	3
Proximity to academic scientist/ founder	Proximity to VC	1	2	5			3	4
Proximity to academic scientist/ founder	Proximity to VC	1	2		3			
Proximity to academic scientist/ founder	Proximity to VC	2	1		4		3	
Proximity to VC	Proximity to academic scientist/ founder	2	1	3				
Proximity to VC	Proximity to firms in the same industry	3	1	5	2		4	

Table 18.1 (continued)

Firm	Firm-specific information					
	Firm city/ neighbour hood	Firm state	Found-ing year	Number of founders	Affiliated university of the closest to the firm academic firm founder	Distance from firm to affiliated university (miles)
H	South San Francisco	CA	2003	3	UNIVERSITY OF CALIFORNIA SAN FRANCISCO	8.9
I	Cambridge	MA	1999	5	MASSACHUSETTS INSTITUTE OF TECHNOLOGY	1.1
J	Louisville	CO	1996	3	UNIVERSITY OF COLORADO DENVER/ HSC AURORA	26.4
K	Austin	TX	2006	2	UNIVERSITY OF TEXAS AUSTIN	8.7
L	Austin	TX	2007	2	UNIVERSITY OF TEXAS AUSTIN	8.7
M	Aurora	CO	2005	3	UNIVERSITY OF COLORADO DENVER/ HSC AURORA	4.1
N	New York	NY	2006	3	CITY UNIVERSITY OF NEW YORK	2.2

Primary and secondary reasons for choice of location		Ranking of reasons for choice of location						
Primary reason(s) for chosen location	Secondary reason(s) for chosen location	Prox-imity to academic scientist/ founder	Prox-imity to VC	Prox-imity to labour pool	Prox-imity to firms in the same indus-try	Low rent or other reduced costs of operations at incubator	Low rent or value added services at incuba-tor	Social bonds
Proximity to VC	Proximity to academic scientist/ founder	2	1					
Proximity to academic scientist/ founder	Proximity to VC	1	2		3			
Proximity to academic scientist/ founder	Low rent or other reduced costs of operations	1	3			2		4
Proximity to VC	Proximity to firms in the same industry & Proximity to academic	3T	1		3T		2	
Proximity to VC	Low rent or other reduced costs of operations	3	1		4		2	
Proximity to academic scientist/ founder	Low rent or value added services at incubator	1				3	2	4
Proximity to VC	N/A		1					

Table 18.1   (continued)

Firm	Firm-specific information					
	Firm city/ neighbour hood	Firm state	Found- ing year	Number of founders	Affiliated university of the closest to the firm academic firm founder	Distance from firm to affiliated university (miles)
O	Morrisville	NC	1999	4	DUKE UNIVERSITY	10.7
P	Boulder	CO	2000	1	UNIVERSITY OF COLORADO- BOULDER	1.0

exceeded 20 miles, the driving time is indeed less than 30 minutes because the firms are located in geographically widespread cities with strong road infrastructure where a 20-mile distance is a common commuting distance. The last seven columns of Table 18.1 include the list and the ranking of the reasons that academic entrepreneurs mentioned to have influenced their choice of firm location. We discuss the findings of these seven columns in the following paragraphs.

In all the cases the primary reason for the choice of firm location was either the proximity to the VC or the proximity to the academic founder. In fact, in nine out of the 16 cases proximity to the VC and proximity to the academic founder were listed together as the primary and secondary reason for the chosen location. With or without the proximity to the VC listed as secondary reason, proximity to the founding scientist was listed as the primary reason in nine out of the 16 cases we examined. Interestingly, in the seven cases where proximity to the VC alone was listed as the primary reason for the chosen location, the distance between the firm and the affiliated university was relatively short, ranging between 2.2 and 8.9 miles. This observation emanates from the fact that in the majority

Primary and secondary reasons for choice of location		Ranking of reasons for choice of location						
Primary reason(s) for chosen location	Secondary reason(s) for chosen location	Proximity to academic scientist/ founder	Proximity to VC	Proximity to labour pool	Proximity to firms in the same industry	Low rent or other reduced costs of operations at incubator	Low rent or value added services at incubator	Social bonds
Proximity to academic scientist/ founder & Proximity to VC	N/A	1T	1T					3
Proximity to academic scientist/ founder	Proximity to VC	1	2			4		3

of cases the firms in our sample had sourced funds from VCs who were already close to the affiliated academic institution.

In roughly one-third of the cases, the chosen location was at an incubator space, office park or a similar facility maintained by the affiliated institution. As shown in Table 18.1, for nine out of the 16 firms in our sample the low rent or/and value-added services offered at incubators were factors that influenced firm location even though, mostly, as secondary reasons. Overall, the findings with regard to the influence of incubator facilities on location choice indicate that such types of infrastructure tend to facilitate the growth of agglomerations of life sciences firms.

For seven firms in our sample the location choice was, in relatively small part, driven by the preferences of founders to stay close to family and friends (what we include under the heading 'social bonds' in Table 18.1). Note that all of these cases were observed in areas such as Morrisville, NC and Boulder, CO, which are either suburbs of urban areas or rural areas. While suggestive, this observation implies that the significance of social ties in affecting firm location is more pronounced for a certain cohort of academic entrepreneurs who show a general preference for living in non-dense regions where social bonds are often stronger when compared to the social bonds in metropolitan areas.

Notably, only a small portion of the academic founders indicated that proximity to larger labour pools was influential in the location decision. Even in the cases where proximity to labour pools was listed as a factor underpinning firm location, it was mainly ranked as having low importance. This low ranking of a local labour pool can be largely explained by the fact that academic entrepreneurs are often able to recruit employees whom they already know or have already worked with (e.g., former PhD students, post-docs etc.) and hence they rarely resort to potential employees with whom they are unfamiliar. Finally, proximity to firms in the same industry was ranked as mostly the third or the fourth reasons that influenced the location decision in six out of the 16 cases. All of these six cases came from firms that were located in an incubator or a similar facility, which potentially echoes the gains that firms collocated in such facilities often realize (Kolympiris and Kalaitzandonakes, 2012).

Upon reflection, the key role of the academic entrepreneur in influencing the location decision likely arises from his or her importance for the newly formed firm. The companies we studied had been operating for as little as three years up to 11 years. In all cases except one, the intellectual property (IP) upon which the company was founded continued to be central to the strategic direction being pursued by the company. It was common for the scientist upon whose IP the company was founded to have spent more than ten years (and millions of grant dollars) testing and perfecting the IP before the investors decided to support founding a start-up company. In more than 75 per cent of the cases there have been internally developed modifications to the original IP and/or purchases of complementary IP from external sources. To quote one of the individuals we spoke to: 'You start with the best science you can get and realize the science of biotech/biomedical is rapidly expanding; new insights require adapting to the new knowledge'. Indeed, in 14 of the 16 cases, the scientist who was central to developing the IP upon which the company was founded continues to be either the chief scientist or member of the Scientific Advisory Board of the companies studied. In one of the two cases where the scientist is not involved, it is because the original start-up company has been merged into another start-up company. The scientist is now involved in the merged company.

Compared to earlier literature, our findings side with previous research in demonstrating that the location of newly founded life sciences firms hinges upon the location preferences of the academic founder (Audretsch and Stephan, 1996; Zucker et al., 1998). Importantly, we also reach the novel finding that, whenever applicable, such preferences are commonly subject to accommodation by the funding investors who seem to agree to the preferences of the founding scientist perhaps because they realize the vital role that academic scientists play in the newly founded firm.

On a related topic, the conventional wisdom in the relevant literature is that agglomeration economies can drive location choice in life sciences (Deeds et al., 2000). Our findings support that proposition because different measures of agglomeration economies were listed by the academic entrepreneurs as factors influencing location choice in nine out of the 16 cases we analysed. However, our findings can also clarify the influence of agglomeration economies on location choice. Agglomeration economies such as proximity to larger labour pools that lead mostly to a reduction of production costs appeared to have only a minimal influence in the choice of location. On the other hand, agglomeration economies that relate more to improvements in the knowledge base of a given firm such as proximity to like firms appeared more relevant. Therefore, our results indicate that different types of agglomeration economies have a different effect on location choice.

Illustrative Cases

Case 1

This is a Colorado start-up, founded in 2005, located equidistant between the University of Colorado Health Sciences Center (UCHSC) in Denver and Boulder, CO mainly because (1) the location is less than a 30-minute drive for the chief scientist, and (2) laboratory and office rent is 'significantly less' at the site chosen for the business than at either the area close to UCHSC or in Boulder. In this case, the scientist who developed the IP upon which the start-up firm was established made the decision where the firm would be located, with the investors accommodating his decision.

In addition to the factors that determine the choice of location, this firm is representative of the cycles many biotech start-ups experience where at first there is enthusiasm associated with the establishment of a firm based on locally developed intellectual property and the firm or its founders may receive accolades and honours and attract the attention of additional angel investors and/or venture capitalists who invest tens of millions of dollars. However, if the long and resource-demanding research cycles of biotechnology (DiMasi and Grabowski, 2007) do not yield the expected outcomes the focal firm faces significant financial difficulties, which can force it to embark on a crash course of (1) belt-tightening, (2) merger with a stronger, better-financed partner or (3) outright closure. For the case at hand, the firm downsized to a sustainable, survival mode. The founding scientist became more heavily involved and a strong relationship with an international health association has provided a focus that suggests the firm will survive to rise again. Importantly, the location of the firm was not altered at any point during the life cycle of the firm. All in all, the history of this firm reiterates the significance of the academic founder for the firm and perhaps more importantly it illustrates that firm location is a crucial decision for the firm as it often stays the same despite potential ups and downs the firm may face.

Case 2

Founded in June 2006 in Austin, TX, this new firm exemplifies the significance of the venture capitalist for the firms at hand and is an example situation where the venture capital firm decided where the start-up would be located. This VC is focused on licensing novel biomedical/biotechnology IP at the major universities and research hospitals in a two-state region. The VC proactively scans new IP licence postings and in an attempt to identify licensing options that might (1) be synergetic with existing portfolio companies, (2) allow them to exploit their managerial expertise and/or (3) achieve a first-mover advantage. This VC has an innovative model of owning and operating its own incubator-accelerator, in addition to being a venture capitalist. In this start-up case the VC identified researchers who had been pursuing similar research goals and who knew each other because of their common research interest. Although the scientists were geographically separated by 400 miles the VC licensed the IP of each scientist and involved each of them as scientific advisers, but allowed each to remain at his research institution. The VC then used its managerial expertise and incubator facility to establish the new firm. The VC was able to spread its expertise, facilities and laboratories over multiple start-ups in an attempt to achieve economies of scope/scale.

Case 3

This start-up case is illustrative of the common situation of the VC wanting the new firm close so that monitoring and oversight become easier. Although the IP that was the basis of the start-up was developed over a ten-year period by two New York medical researchers and a colleague at Harvard, the lead VC investor (who supplied $2 million in Series A funding) was based in California. Because of the funding provided, and also bringing other VCs, the VC was able to dictate that the new firm would locate in San Francisco. Roughly two years later, the VC decided that the distance between the start-up and the scientist who was providing the intellectual capital was hindering the growth of the new firm and the decision was made to relocate. By relocating to New York City the firm qualified for funding from the New York City Investment Fund. In conjunction with the move to NYC, the original VC investors launched a $30 million Series B funding round. A New York City VC firm that specializes in health care investing entered Series B and $18.9 million was raised.[4] This case highlights that in the rare cases that a firm relocates, the decision rests typically upon the venture capital firm and it is primarily driven by the preference to locate close to where the academic founder resides.

CONCLUSIONS

Universities across the world are confronted with declining financial support from government sources and increasing calls to incorporate regional economic development in their traditional 'Mertonian' (Merton, 1968) role of teaching, research and service (Smilor et al., 1993). As a response, many research universities have embraced a new entrepreneurial role (Etzkowitz, 1998) under which they have intensified their efforts to generate revenues from research conducted at university premises and in the process become engines of local economic growth (Etzkowitz, 1998; Goldstein, 2009; Atkinson and Pelfrey, 2010). One way that universities promote such development is by encouraging the creation of local firms by faculty members whose research has commercial potential (O'Shea et al., 2007). Indeed, promoting the creation of new firms is increasing in popularity as a means to transfer technology from the university to the market (Blumenstyk, 2012) and subsequently allow the entrepreneurial university to promote local economic growth. Further, the steadily declining financial support prompts universities to secure funds from diverse sources and taking equity in university spin-offs has been, in large part, a fruitful means towards that end (Bray and Lee, 2000; Jensen and Thursby, 2001). Accordingly, shedding new light on the firm decision process of faculty members can potentially assist the entrepreneurial university in increasing its revenues and in aligning the incentives provided to scientists between academic and business duties.

In light of the scant evidence on the factors that shape the decision of a focal academic entrepreneur to start his or her firm at a certain location, the present study comprises a novel approach to better understand how the firm location decision is influenced by the academic founder and the funding venture capitalist. Our interviews with academic entrepreneurs revealed that, whenever applicable, the location choice is mainly determined by the venture capitalists who tend to accommodate the location preferences of the scientists, who in turn often decide on the basis of social ties and the presence of incubators and similar facilities in the affiliated university. This is a conclusion with a number of implications for the entrepreneurial university, for policy-makers as well as for academic research on location choice.

For instance, our findings imply that attracting and maintaining strong human capital is a necessary but not sufficient condition for universities that aspire to act as engines of local economic growth via boosting the local rate of university-based start-ups. Such firms are often investment targets of venture capitalists, business angels and other investors who commonly have the final say in the choice of location for a particular firm. Therefore, practitioners such as university administrators and policy-makers need to maintain ties that can strengthen the links between the investment and the academic community in order to boost the effectiveness of attracting and maintaining human capital in a particular region as a means to increase the rate of local start-ups. Such links may take the form of guest professorships for members of the investment community, student internships at venture capital firms, guest lectures from venture capitalists and so on.

Further, our results suggest that the creation of resource-demanding incubation facilities and research parks appears to pay off in terms of encouraging academic entrepreneurs to stay local. This is an important observation not only because it indicates that investments of this kind can assist local economies and the entrepreneurial university but also because it suggests that such facilities may assist universities in maintaining high human capital in the face of continuous competition among academic institutions for talent that can attract research funds, send signals of quality in the academic community and other benefits along these lines.

From a managerial perspective, the present research suggests that universities as well as remaining actors that aim at contributing to local economic growth should pay increased attention to the incentives of the academic entrepreneurs that establish new firms. As such, our findings may be relevant to the ongoing debate about policies designed to create 'entrepreneurial' local environments. As already discussed, broad capital investments in local research infrastructure may help to generate some new firms; nevertheless, our results imply that the various incentives academic entrepreneurs face may be equally important for the creation of local firm growth. As a case in point we refer to the BioRegio contest that was launched in 1995 by the German government in order to strengthen the biotechnology industry of that country, partly via the creation of local biotechnology firms. Briefly, under this contest different regions competed for a common pool of funds towards biotechnology; as explained in detail in Dohse (2000) the criteria for picking the winners focused solely on the institutional infrastructure of each region such as the number and scale of existing biotechnology firms. Notably, the characteristics and incentives of potential (academic) entrepreneurs were not taken into account when selecting the winning regions and this might have hampered the efficacy of the programme to promote sustainable high-growth start-ups (Champenois, 2012). Accordingly, our results indicate that policies that target the responsive cohort of academic professionals may have high payoffs not only by increasing the regional rate of new firm creation but also by promoting firms with strong growth potential.

It is important to note that because of our interest in contrasting the impact of funding sources with that of the academic founder, we focused solely on firms that received funds from venture capital firms. Venture capital firms are very selective in the firms they invest in and as such our results are difficult to generalize for other, perhaps lesser, firms that have not been successful in attracting external funds. Further research can shed new light on the types of firms that are not covered in our sample. On the other side, because venture capitalists are associated with firms with higher chances of success compared with other firms (Bertoni et al., 2011) the firms we study are likely to be among those with high growth potential; the firms that Shane (2009) argues that public policy needs to pay attention to as they are the ones that bring about the most economic benefits. Therefore, understanding the decision process for a crucial element of firm formation (i.e., location choice) can be informative for understanding how these types of firms are created and how the agents that create them interact.

In a more long-term scholarly implication, examining the effects of funding sources and in particular venture capital on location choice appears a fruitful avenue for research on location choice. Somewhat surprisingly given the general preference of venture capital firms to invest locally, the evidence of the location effect of venture capital is scant and based solely on large-scale aggregated data (Samila and Sorenson, 2011). The qualitative nature of our work can complement the existing quantitative evidence in gaining a finer-grained understanding of that process.

NOTES

*   Research funding provided by the Ewing Marion Kauffman Foundation Strategic Grant #20050176 is gratefully acknowledged.
1. In a study that reached different results, Ensley and Hmieleski (2005) discovered that in their sample university-based start-ups had lower net cash flows when compared with non-university-based new ventures.
2. In one case the academic founder directed us to an executive who was knowledgeable of the location decision and as such the interview was conducted with the executive.
3. In all the interviews, the academic founders stressed that disclosure of information about the funding venture capitalist should be as limited as possible. Accordingly, particularly in Table 18.1 as well as throughout the chapter we limit the presentation of such information.

4. The economic conditions prevailing in the US economy in 2009 were given as a reason for not meeting the $30 million funding goal. The firm has been growing more rapidly in NYC than in California, but it is difficult to infer with certainty that the growth can be attributed to close proximity between the founding scientists and the relocation to NYC.

REFERENCES

Arauzo Carod, J.M., D. Liviano Solis and M. Manjón Antolín (2010), 'Empirical studies in industrial location: An assessment of their methods and results', *Journal of Regional Science*, **50**(3), 685–711.

Atkinson, C.R. and A.P. Pelfrey (2010), 'Science and the entrepreneurial university', *ISSUES in Science and Technology* (Summer 2010), accessed 17 August 2013 at http://www.issues.org/26.4/atkinson.html.

Audretsch, D.B. and P.E. Stephan (1996), 'Company–scientist locational links: The case of biotechnology', *American Economic Review*, **86**(3), 641–52.

Audretsch, D.B., E.E. Lehmann and S. Warning (2005), 'University spillovers and new firm location', *Research Policy*, **34**(7), 1113–22.

AUTM (2001), 'Association of University Technology Managers: The AUTM Licensing Surveys; University start-up data', Norwalk, CT, accessed 17 August 2013 at http://www.autm.net/Licensing_Surveys_AUTM.htm.

Bartik, T.J. (1985), 'Business location decisions in the United States: Estimates of the effects of unionization, taxes, and other characteristics of states', *Journal of Business and Economic Statistics*, **3**(1), 14–22.

Berchicci, L., A. King and C.L. Tucci (2011), 'Does the apple always fall close to the tree? The geographical proximity choice of spin-outs', *Strategic Entrepreneurship Journal*, **5**(2), 120–36.

Bertoni, F., M.G. Colombo and L. Grilli (2011), 'Venture capital financing and the growth of high-tech start-ups: Disentangling treatment from selection effects', *Research Policy*, **40**(7), 1028–43.

Blumenstyk, G. (2012), 'Universities report $1.8-billion in earnings on inventions in 2011', *The Chronicle of Higher Education*, 28 August, accessed 17 August 2013 at http://chronicle.com/article/University-Inventions-Earned/133972.

Bramwell, A. and D.A. Wolfe (2008), 'Universities and regional economic development: The entrepreneurial University of Waterloo', *Research Policy*, **37**(8), 1175–87.

Bray, M.J. and J.N. Lee (2000), 'University revenues from technology transfer: Licensing fees vs. equity positions', *Journal of Business Venturing*, **15**(5), 385–92.

Carlton, D.W. (1983), 'The location and employment choices of new firms: An econometric model with discrete and continuous endogenous variables', *The Review of Economics and Statistics*, **65**(3), 440–49.

Champenois, C. (2012), 'How can a cluster policy enhance entrepreneurship? Evidence from the German "BioRegio" case', *Environment and Planning C*, **30**(5), 796–815.

Chrisman, J.J., T. Hynes and S. Fraser (1995), 'Faculty entrepreneurship and economic development: The case of the University of Calgary', *Journal of Business Venturing*, **10**(4), 267–81.

Coughlin, C.C., J.V. Terza and V. Arromdee (1991), 'State characteristics and the location of foreign direct investment within the United States', *The Review of Economics and Statistics*, **73**(4), 675–83.

Dahl, M. and O. Sorenson (2009), 'The embedded entrepreneur', *European Management Review*, **6**(3), 172–81.

Dahl, M. and O. Sorenson (2012), 'Home sweet home: Entrepreneurs' location choices and the performance of their ventures', *Management Science*, **58**(6), 1059–71.

Dahlstrand, Å.L. (1997), 'Growth and inventiveness in technology-based spin-off firms', *Research Policy*, **26**(3), 331–44.

Decarolis, D.M. and D.L. Deeds (1999), 'The impact of stocks and flows of organizational knowledge on firm performance: An empirical investigation of the biotechnology industry', *Strategic Management Journal*, **20**(10), 953–68.

Deeds, D.L., D. DeCarolis and J. Coombs (2000), 'Dynamic capabilities and new product development in high technology ventures: An empirical analysis of new biotechnology firms', *Journal of Business Venturing*, **15**(3), 211–29.

Degroof, J.J. and E.B. Roberts (2004), 'Overcoming weak entrepreneurial infrastructures for academic spin-off ventures', *The Journal of Technology Transfer*, **29**(3), 327–52.

DiMasi, J.A. and H.G. Grabowski (2007), 'The cost of biopharmaceutical R&D: Is biotech different?, *Managerial and Decision Economics*, **28**(4–5), 469–79.

Dohse, D. (2000), 'Technology policy and the regions – the case of the BioRegio contest', *Research Policy*, **29**(9), 1111–33.

Egeln, J., S. Gottschalk and C. Rammer (2004), 'Location decisions of spin-offs from public research institutions', *Industry and Innovation*, **11**(3), 207–23.

Ensley, M.D. and K.M. Hmieleski (2005), 'A comparative study of new venture top management team composition, dynamics and performance between university-based and independent start-ups', *Research Policy*, **34**(7), 1091–105.

Etzkowitz, H. (1998), 'The norms of entrepreneurial science: Cognitive effects of the new university–industry linkages', *Research Policy*, **27**(8), 823–33.

Etzkowitz, H., A. Webster, C. Gebhardt and B.R.C. Terra (2000), 'The future of the university and the university of the future: Evolution of ivory tower to entrepreneurial paradigm', *Research Policy*, **29**(2), 313–30.

Figueiredo, O., P. Guimarães and D. Woodward (2002), 'Home-field advantage: Location decisions of Portuguese entrepreneurs', *Journal of Urban Economics*, **52**(2), 341–61.

Fotopoulos, G. and H. Louri (2000), 'Location and survival of new entry', *Small Business Economics*, **14**(4), 311–21.

Glaeser, E.L. and W.R. Kerr (2009), 'Local industrial conditions and entrepreneurship: How much of the spatial distribution can we explain?' *Journal of Economics and Management Strategy*, **18**(3), 623–63.

Goldstein, H. (2009), 'What we know and what we don't know about the regional economic impacts of universities', in A. Varga (ed.), *Universities, Knowledge Transfer and Regional Development*, Cheltenham, UK and Northampton, MA, USA: Edward Elgar.

Goldstein, H. and C. Renault (2004), 'Contributions of universities to regional economic development: A quasi-experimental approach', *Regional Studies*, **38**(7), 733–46.

Guimarães, P., O. Figueiredo and D. Woodward (2000), 'Agglomeration and the location of foreign direct investment in Portugal', *Journal of Urban Economics*, **47**(1), 115–35.

Hayter, R. (1997), *The Dynamics of Industrial Location: The Factory, the Firm, and the Production System*, New York: Wiley.

Huggins, R. and P. Cooke (1997), 'The economic impact of Cardiff University: Innovation, learning and job generation', *GeoJournal*, **41**(4), 325–37.

Jain, S., G. George and M. Maltarich (2009), 'Academics or entrepreneurs? Investigating role identity modification of university scientists involved in commercialization activity', *Research Policy*, **38**(6), 922–35.

Jensen, R. and M. Thursby (2001), 'Proofs and prototypes for sale: The licensing of university inventions', *American Economic Review*, **91**(1), 240–59.

Kolympiris, C. and N. Kalaitzandonakes (2012), 'Geographic scope of proximity effects among small life sciences firms', *Small Business Economics*, 1–28, doi:10.1007/s11187-012-9441-0.

Kolympiris, C., N. Kalaitzandonakes and D.J. Miller (2011), 'Spatial collocation and venture capital in the U.S. biotechnology industry', *Research Policy*, **40**, 1188–99.

Krabel, S. and P. Mueller (2009), 'What drives scientists to start their own company? An empirical investigation of Max Planck Society scientists', *Research Policy*, **38**(6), 947–56.

Lam, A. (2011), 'What motivates academic scientists to engage in research commercialization: "Gold", "ribbon" or "puzzle"?' *Research Policy*, **40**(10), 1354–68.

Landry, R., N. Amara and I. Rherrad (2006), 'Why are some university researchers more likely to create spin-offs than others? Evidence from Canadian universities', *Research Policy*, **35**(10), 1599–615.

Landry, R., M. Saïhi, N. Amara and M. Ouimet (2010), 'Evidence on how academics manage their portfolio of knowledge transfer activities', *Research Policy*, **39**(10), 1387–403.

Merton, R.K. (1968), *Social Theory and Social Structure*, New York: Free Press.

Michelacci, C. and O. Silva (2007), 'Why so many local entrepreneurs?' *The Review of Economics and Statistics*, **89**(4), 615–33.

Mustar, P. (1997), 'Spin-off enterprises: How French academics create hi-tech companies: The conditions for success or failure', *Science and Public Policy*, **24**(1), 37–43.

Nerkar, A. and S. Shane (2003), 'When do start-ups that exploit patented academic knowledge survive?' *International Journal of Industrial Organization*, **21**(9), 1391–410.

O'Shea, R.P., T.J. Allen, K.P. Morse, C. O'Gorman, and F. Roche (2007), 'Delineating the anatomy of an entrepreneurial university: The Massachusetts Institute of Technology experience', *R&D Management*, **37**(1), 1–16.

Samila, S. and O. Sorenson (2011), 'Venture capital, entrepreneurship, and economic growth', *The Review of Economics and Statistics*, **93**(1), 338–49.

Shane, S. (2004), *Academic Entrepreneurship: University Spin-offs and Wealth Creation*, Cheltenham, UK and Northampton, MA, USA: Edward Elgar Publishing.

Shane, S. (2009), 'Why encouraging more people to become entrepreneurs is bad public policy', *Small Business Economics*, **33**(2), 141–9.

Shane, S. and R. Khurana (2003), 'Bringing individuals back in: The effects of career experience on new firm founding', *Industrial and Corporate Change*, **12**(3), 519–43.

Smilor, R., G. Dietrich and D. Gibson (1993), 'The entrepreneurial university: The role of Higher Education in the United States in technology commercialization and economic development', *International Social Science Journal*, **45**(1), 1–11.

Steffensen, M., E.M. Rogers and K. Speakman (2000), 'Spin-offs from research centers at a research university', *Journal of Business Venturing*, **15**(1), 93–111.

Strotmann, H. (2007), 'Entrepreneurial survival', *Small Business Economics*, **28**(1), 87–104.

Stuart, T.E. and W.W. Ding (2006), 'When do scientists become entrepreneurs? The social structural antecedents of commercial activity in the academic life sciences', *American Journal of Sociology*, **112**(1), 97–144.

Wright, M., X. Liu, T. Buck and I. Filatotchev (2008), 'Returnee entrepreneurs, science park location choice and performance: An analysis of high-technology SMEs in China', *Entrepreneurship: Theory and Practice*, **32**(1), 131–55.

Zucker, L.G., M.R. Darby and M.B. Brewer (1998), 'Intellectual human capital and the birth of U.S. biotechnology enterprises', *American Economic Review*, **88**(1), 290–306.

Zucker, L.G., M.R. Darby and M. Torero (2002), 'Labor mobility from academe to commerce', *Journal of Labor Economics*, **20**(3), 629–60.

19. How to access the development of entrepreneurship education at university level: the case of Denmark

Kåre Moberg, Lene Vestergaard,
Casper Jørgensen, Elisabeth Markussen and
Sose Hakhverdyan

INTRODUCTION

The Danish government has during the last decade been focusing on transforming the country's universities into entrepreneurial institutions (Blenker et al., 2006; OECD, 2008). A large range of state-sponsored initiatives has been launched, all with a purpose of supporting various entrepreneurial activities, such as student incubators, tech transfer offices and entrepreneurship programmes (ibid.). This is much in line with what has happened in other European countries as the process has been driven by pan-European strategies from the EU level (Geuna, 1998; Kyvik, 2004; European Commission, 2011). The goal of these governmental strategies has been to adapt the Higher Educational sector to the changing needs of society and the economy (Etzkowitz et al., 2000). Universities today are requested to focus on the diffusion of knowledge and research findings as well as commercialization of new research. Universities are also, to a larger extent, expected to obtain their own funding by capitalizing on these activities, which is made possible by an increased autonomy for the universities (Etzkowitz et al., 2000; European Commission, 2011).

The educational activities have proven to play an important role in this process (Gibb, 1987), but these are often less prioritized than more visible investments in infrastructure (Heinonen and Hytti, 2010; Nygaard, 2010). This is somewhat puzzling as the field of entrepreneurship is recognized to have its roots in educational activities (Brush et al., 2003). According to Katz (2008), we have experienced an immense dissemination of entrepreneurship education into departments outside of the business school, and we are now just beginning to see its effect on the overall entrepreneurial activities of the universities. The educational orientation of universities and student activities has, however, during the last decade been recognized as an important tool for universities to establish industry collaboration and increased overall entrepreneurialism (Davis and Diamond, 1997; Nygaard, 2010).

In this book chapter we present a study of how the eight universities in Denmark have transformed towards becoming entrepreneurial institutions. The focus is primarily on how these institutions have developed courses and programmes in entrepreneurship education. However, entrepreneurship education does not equal start-up training, especially not seen through the lens of the entrepreneurial university perspective, which recognizes a broad scope of activities as being entrepreneurial (Etzkowitz, 2003). As the focus of entrepreneurship education is on skills, competencies and attitudes, activities such as innovation within established organizations is viewed as being equally important as new venture creation (Solomon, 2007; European Commission, 2012). In order to capture the broad scope of entrepreneurship education in an inclusive, yet specific way, we have developed a categorization model that allows us to measure how the universities have developed their entrepreneurship education regarding focus on different type contents and stages in the entrepreneurial project. The model also allows us to capture which types of pedagogical methods are being used. This model's theoretical foundations will be thoroughly described in the following.

THEORETICAL FRAMEWORK

As described in the introduction to this anthology, it is evident that there has been an immense focus on transforming universities into entrepreneurial institutions. The dual process of cutbacks in public funding of universities (Geuna, 1998; Kyvik, 2004; UNESCO, 2004; OECD, 2005) in combination with an increased pressure of dissemination of research results and society's demand on universities to play a more active role in the regional economy, has been a real challenge to many universities (Etzkowitz et al., 2000; OECD, 2001; Etzkowitz, 2003; Debackere and Vaugler, 2005). There are, however, many universities that are not active within research fields with a potential to generate innovations and growth companies (Jensen et al., 2003; Debackere and Vaugler, 2005). Many universities have, thus, chosen different strategies than the typical so called 'Stanford Model' (Etzkowitz, 2003); instead of establishing new organizations such as Technical Transfer Offices, incubators and science parks, they have relied on their managements' networking capital and the entrepreneurialism of their researchers in order to establish industry collaboration and retrieve funding from external sources (Davis and Diamond, 1997). What is often forgotten in this process is the role that the educational activities play (Heinonen and Hytti, 2010; Nygaard, 2010).

In the holistic process of transforming the university into an entrepreneurial institution, the educational activities are of major importance (Etzkowitz, 2003). The students play an important role in building the entrepreneurial culture at universities and connecting their activities to the industry in many different ways, for example, through practice-based educational activities, internships and, naturally, as employees (Pittaway and Cope, 2006; Gibb, 2011). The field of entrepreneurship has its roots in teaching (Brush et al., 2003) and entrepreneurship education is thus a natural component of the entrepreneurial university (Heinonen and Hytti, 2010), as it has been seen to produce new ventures as well as innovative employees (Gibb, 1987; Charney and Libecap, 2000), but also because entrepreneurship programmes and centres have proven to have a positive effect on industry funding (Zeithaml and Rice, 1987).

During the past decades, researchers have used many different models in order to measure the development and spread of entrepreneurship education (cf. Solomon and Sollosy, 1977; Solomon, 1979, 2007; Vesper, 1985, 1993; Solomon and Fernald, 1991; Katz, 1994, 2003, 2004, 2008; Solomon et al., 1994; Vesper and Gartner, 1997). According to Katz (2008), we are reaching consensus within the field regarding what entrepreneurship programmes should contain, but we need better models to capture the wide scope of entrepreneurship education, both regarding the content and the teaching methods. Entrepreneurial activities come in many forms, and if we only focus on new venture creation we miss out on many entrepreneurial activities that take place within established firms (Kuratko, 2005; Foss and Klein, 2012). In the next section we will present our categorization model and how it is based in the broad scope of content and pedagogical dimensions that is included within the field of entrepreneurship education.

How to Measure the Development of Entrepreneurship Education

Our categorization model of entrepreneurship education is developed as a tool to be used in the process of transforming universities into entrepreneurial institutions. The model is based on the systems of innovation literature (Lundvall, 1992; Cooke, 2002) as well as the policy oriented Triple Helix research (Etzkowitz et al., 2000). These research streams recognize the systemic character of entrepreneurial activities, which not only include venture creators, but also specialists within other fields such as finance (for example, venture capitalists) and law (patent experts, etc.). Our model aims to connect the macro-level (political policy) with the micro-level (student competencies), by focusing on the mezzo-level (university education). In order to assure that universities take a holistic approach to entrepreneurship education and develop students with the various skills needed, we have included four content dimensions (entrepreneurship, intrapreneurship, finance and law) in our model. We have also included the specific pedagogies needed to teach entrepreneurship as well as the different stages that are included in a venture project, as different competencies are needed in each. The model, with its holistic approach to entrepreneurship, will be described more thoroughly in a later part of this chapter, but first we will describe how our systemic-oriented model is anchored in the entrepreneurship literature.

Entrepreneurship education is a topic with a broad scope regarding content and teaching techniques (Brush et al., 2003). Different stages in the venture project require different types of activities (Stevenson et al., 1985; Bhave, 1994), and depending on industry sector and other types of context, these projects can be very dissimilar and have very different skill requirements (Aldrich and Baker, 1997; Davidsson and Wiklund, 2001). Entrepreneurship education can further be divided into two major categories: specialized entrepreneurship courses and courses with integrated entrepreneurial elements (Blenker, Korsgaard, Neergaard and Thrane, 2011). The latter do not have venture creation as their major focus, rather these courses aim to alter the attitudes of the students and strengthen their entrepreneurial competencies in order to make them more employable and oriented towards entrepreneurial activities within established organizations (ibid.). It can be said that these courses rather focus on corporate venturing (Burgelman, 1983, 1984, 1985; Zahra, 1991; Block and MacMillan, 1993), or what has lately been termed strategic entrepreneurship (Hitt et al., 2001; Foss and Lyngsie, 2011), which within the policy world is often termed intrapreneurship (NIRAS et al., 2008). Regardless of the focus being on new venture creation or strategic entrepreneurship within established organizations there are common skill demands when it comes to understanding financial and legal issues (Foss and Klein, 2012). The extent to which this is necessary depends of course on the specific venture activity and the industry sector (Vesper and McMullen, 1988). Some industries, such as biotech, require a thorough understanding of venture capital and IPR, whereas more mundane venture activities only require very basic financial and legal skills.

The broad scope of knowledge, skills and competencies that a venture process requires has to be taken into account in the course design. The context within which entrepreneurs operate frequently spans over many boundaries (West, 2003; Lazear, 2004, 2005) and is often internationally oriented (McDougall et al., 1994; McDougall and Oviatt, 2000; Jonsson and Jonsson, 2002; Rialp et al., 2004). The entrepreneur frequently has to take on the role as a 'jack-of-all trades' (Lazear, 2004, 2005), that is, he or she has to be able to perform many of those activities that are separated by division of labour in larger companies (ibid.). A multidisciplinary course design in which the instructors make an effort to situate the content in an international or global context is a fruitful way to cover the complexity of a venture process (Brush et al., 2003; Klapper and Neergaard, 2012).

In order to navigate effectively in society of today, it is important that you are able to leverage uncertainty and adjust to input signals from the environment (Gibb, 1987). This can only be done through an iterative process in which the information and knowledge is practically applied and tested (Biggs and Tang, 2007; Loyens et al., 2008). Entrepreneurship education has always been viewed as a practical topic that needs different pedagogical methods in order to be taught effectively (Johannisson, 1991; Sarasvathy, 2004; Politis, 2005; Kyrö and Niemi, 2007). Ideally it should simulate the real-life processes of an entrepreneur (Gibb, 2002, 2011; Hannon, 2005; Pittaway and Cope, 2007). However, this might not always be feasible in all courses (Klapper and Neergard, 2012). Creative and practically oriented teaching methods are needed in order to infuse entrepreneurial attitudes and mindsets into students, as the students have often adapted to the job-taker mindset that the university setting is typically oriented towards (Blenker et al., 2011). Mind-changing teaching methods are only possible if the students actively participate and take responsibility and ownership of the learning process, which takes place both within and outside the walls of the university (Biggs and Tang, 2007). In order to effectively teach entrepreneurship-oriented content, there is thus much to take into consideration regarding teaching methods. A measurement model that aims to assess the development of entrepreneurship courses should therefore not only be specific and inclusive regarding the course content but also with regard to teaching methods. In the following a categorization model that satisfies these requirements will be described.

A Categorization Model for Entrepreneurship Education

The model is divided into three main categories: content, teaching methods and stages. On the horizontal axis, the model is divided into eight categories, four content categories and four pedagogical dimensions. The four content categories are: entrepreneurship, intrapreneurship, finance and law. The four pedagogical dimensions are: practical dimensions, student participation, multidisciplinary dimensions and international dimensions. On the vertical axis the model is divided into four different stages that resemble the different stages of the entrepreneurial project: idea, beginning, growth and running. Depending on the focus of the course, it can get a score from 0 to 3 in all these categories. It is thus possible to

Table 19.1   The categorization model

Stages/ Categories	Intrapre- neurship	Entrepr- eneurship	Finance/ VC	Law	Practical Dimen- sions	Student Partici- pation	Inter- disciplinary	Interna- tional Dimen- sions
Idea								
Beginning								
Growth								
Running								

categorize on which stage of the venture process the course has its focus as well as which content and teaching methods it focuses on. In Table 19.1, an overview of the model is presented.

There must be a clear focus on the content and the phase of the venture process in order for a course to get a star in one of the content categories. Two stars means that the course focuses heavily on the topic and three stars means that the course specializes in the topic, both practically and theoretically. The same logic applies to the pedagogical categories, but with some natural differences. In order to get one star, there should be a clear focus on the teaching method, whereas two stars means that it is used in the majority of the teaching situations and three stars requires that the course specializes in this specific teaching method. A course can, however, be categorized with three stars in more than one content and pedagogical category, as it is possible to specialize in more than one field and phase of the venture project. In the following sections we will describe thoroughly how each of these categories is assessed.

The content dimensions
Assessing the content is a fairly straightforward process. In this part of the text we will describe which type of content is included in each of our four venture stages. When it comes to entrepreneurship in the first stage it is about coming up with an idea for a venture. A course that focuses on entrepreneurship in this stage is typically about creativity and involves different idea generation exercises. The content is fairly similar to courses that focus on intrapreneurship, finance and law in this stage. When it comes to intrapreneurship the focus is on idea generation in established organizations. A course that gets scores in the finance/idea category focuses on the economic sustainability of the idea and when it comes to law, methods such as browsing patent databases are central.

A course that scores in the entrepreneurship/beginning category typically focuses on the act of starting up a new venture. Marshalling of resources and managing ambiguity is of central importance at this stage (Sarasvathy, 2008; Baron, 2012). The content of the courses is typically iterations and test of ideas, business planning and presentation skills such as elevator pitching. A course in intrapreneurship in this stage is fairly similar, but the focus is on established organizations as the context. A finance/beginning course focuses on the financial aspects of the activities in this stage, such as the financial analysis and market analysis for the new venture. A course that gets scores in the law category in the beginning stage typically deals with the legal processes of starting a company, how to file a patent, and so on.

In the growth stage, much focus is on developing and growing the venture. Internationalization and employment growth brings managerial as well as legal and financial challenges to the table. Courses in this stage often focus on best practice strategies for growth and internationalization, as well as mass marketing and human resource management.

According to Davidsson (2012), the entrepreneurial activities end when the venture has reached a break-even result. However, when it comes to education in the topic, there are many aspects and dimensions that can still be of interest for the student in the running stage. Continuous innovation, diversification and segmentation as well as serial and portfolio entrepreneurship and exit strategies are typical topics in this stage. In Table 19.2 an overview of what is included in the content dimensions related to the stage in the entrepreneurial project is presented.

The pedagogical dimensions
The pedagogical dimensions naturally follow the content dimensions and the stage categories, but there are many different ways to teach this content. Practical dimensions can be taught by either taking the students out of the classroom (e.g., field studies, real projects and interaction with the local industry), or by bringing the practice into the classroom (e.g., guest lectures, case competitions and prototype development). The practice dimension is often related to the student participation dimension. Entrepreneurial activities require proactive students who take an active role as learners rather than a passive role as listeners. A high degree of practical dimension in a course often implies that the students have to take a proactive role in performing the activities and assignments. However, if the practical elements of the course are only provided by guest lectures, the student participation will remain low.

As innovation and new economic activity often take place in the intersection between sectors, and entrepreneurs often perform many different roles, it is important to integrate multidisciplinary dimensions in the classroom.

Table 19.2   The content dimensions: examples of course content in the different stages

Stages/ Categories	Intrapreneurship	Entrepreneurship	Finance/ VC	Law
Idea	Idea generation and creativity exercises in the context of established organizations	Idea generation and creativity exercises targeted to new venture creation	Financial feasibility plans	Search in patent databases
Beginning	Marshalling of resources; iterations of new business ideas; elevator pitches; business plans	Marshalling of resources; iterations of new business ideas; elevator pitches; business plans	Financial analysis; market analysis; seed capital	Legal processes related to start-up activity; filing a patent
Growth	Human resources management, internationalization	Human resources management, internationalization	Financial analysis for growth; venture capital; acquisition	International law, IPR; employment legislation, in the context of growing a venture
Running	Continuous innovation, product diversification and segmentation	Serial entrepreneurship; portfolio entrepreneurship; exit strategies	Financial analysis; valuing the company; selling a company; acquisition	International law, IPR; employment legislation, in the context of running a company

Again, this can be performed in many different ways. One possibility is to have students with different disciplinary backgrounds, and actively work with their different competencies in the course assignments. Another possibility is that the educational team comes from different disciplinary backgrounds, and actively works to combine their competencies in the classroom.

Our last pedagogical category, international dimensions, can in some ways be seen as a content category. However, as the globalization process is accelerating, it is important to focus on international aspects, regardless of it being entrepreneurship or law that is taught. Entrepreneurs will have

Table 19.3   The content dimensions

Practical Dimensions	Student Participation	Interdisciplinary Dimensions	International Dimensions
Take the students out of the classroom to the real world or bring the real world into the classroom	Encourage being proactive. Student-centred exercises in order to create active and responsible learners	Working with the different disciplinary backgrounds of the students or the teaching team, or both	International cases; born globals; the globalization process

to relate to this dimension, either as competition in their home market or when deciding to internationalize their activities. The use of international cases, the focus on the internationalization process or discussions of new technology that enables 'born globals', that is, companies that internationalize from day one, can be good techniques to teach this dimension. In Table 19.3 an overview of our four pedagogical categories is presented.

METHODOLOGY

The data have been collected on a yearly basis for all universities in Denmark by the organization the Danish Foundation for Entrepreneurship – Young Enterprise, since 2010. The research team is led by a senior data analyst who has collected similar data by using the model on different universities since 2007. The data collection is performed by browsing of web pages where keywords such as entrepreneurship, business planning, intrapreneurship, corporate venturing, innovation, idea generation, creativity and patent (in both Danish and English languages) are searched for. Key personnel at all of the universities are also contacted in order not to miss any courses, especially those that have recently been developed.

Four employees of the research team at the Danish Foundation for Entrepreneurship – Young Enterprise analyse each course description individually and assess it according to the criteria in the categorization model. At a minimum two team members assess each course in order to secure an objective categorization. The course coordinator is contacted in order to double-check the evaluation and to assess the number of participants.

The data in this article are analysed with descriptive statistics as there are only eight units of analysis (the eight universities in Denmark), and because we have access to the complete population.

ANALYSIS

In this section we will present the results of our analysis. We will, however, first start off with a presentation of the Danish context and how it has developed over the past three years at university level.

The Danish Context

During the past decade there has been a large variety of state-sponsored initiatives in Denmark that all had the goal of initiating more entrepreneurial activities at the universities (Blenker et al., 2011; OECD, 2008). This has led to a significant overlap of activities. In 2010, the Danish government decided instead to channel their resources through one single coordinating organization that should be responsible for developing entrepreneurship education at all educational levels, from ABC to PhD, so to speak (Danish Agency for Science, Technology and Innovation, 2009). This organization became the Danish Foundation for Entrepreneurship – Young Enterprise.

The Danish government also decided to allocate 6 million euros over a three-year period for entrepreneurial activities, which was structured as a competing fund that should be granted to the university with the best strategy for transforming into an entrepreneurial university. There were three finalists for the grant. Aarhus University and the University of Southern Denmark applied as single institutions whereas Copenhagen Business School, the Technical University of Denmark and the University of Copenhagen, all located in the capital of Denmark, applied for the grant as a troika. At the end of 2010, Aarhus University won the grant but the Copenhagen troika was also awarded a smaller amount of funding (0.6 million euros). During 2011 and 2012 the universities have started up their activities.

The Copenhagen troika also managed to get funding from the EU, which enabled them to start the Copenhagen Innovation and Entrepreneurship Lab (CIEL) initiative. CIEL's goal is to establish a world-class entrepreneurial eco-system at the three universities through collaboration at student and teacher level as well as research level and by establishing partnerships with industry (ciel-lab.dk). At the University of Southern Denmark there is a long-standing initiative called the International Danish Entrepreneurship Academy (IDEA). IDEA, which was established in 2005, is a teaching and research-oriented entrepreneurship initiative, where industry collaboration is one of the most important ingredients (idea-denmark.dk). The entrepreneurial university initiative at Aarhus University started its activities in 2011 and has a clear goal of establishing AU as the leading entrepreneurial university in Denmark. The focus is on establishing entrepreneurship courses in all faculties, which are aligned with the specific context of the faculties' students. Ten new core courses in entrepreneurship will be established and seven programmes will be tuned towards entrepreneurship, by the end of 2013. The focus is just as much on student employability and innovation in established organizations as it is on new venture creation (eship.au.dk).

Other noticeable initiatives at universities in Denmark are the Centre for Social Entrepreneurship (CSE) at Roskilde University, which has been operating since 2008 and is focusing on research and education within the field of social entrepreneurship. The centre also has a strong focus on collaboration with the civil society (ruc.dk/cse). At Aalborg University they have just expanded their campus in Copenhagen, which started up its activities in the fall of 2012. The goal is to have an extensive focus on entrepreneurship in the educational programmes at this campus (aau-cph.dk).

The Development of Entrepreneurship Education at Denmark's Eight Universities

In order to analyse how entrepreneurship education has developed at the eight universities in Denmark it is natural to start by looking at the number of courses and participants at each university. This is, however, dependent on the size of the individual university. In Table 19.4 the number of students attending each university in the semesters of 2009/10, 2010/11 and 2011/12 are presented. In Figures 19.1 and 19.2 the number of entrepreneurship courses and the number of entrepreneurship students for the three years are presented.

We can clearly see that the three universities involved in the competition for the entrepreneurial university grant are well ahead of the other five

Table 19.4   The number of students enrolled at the eight universities in Denmark, 2009–12 ('000s)

	2009/10	2010/11	2011/12
Copenhagen Business School (CBS)	13.440	14.476	15.617
Danmarks Tekniske Universitet (DTU)	7.608	8.269	8.873
IT-Universitetet (IT-U)	1.116	1.398	1.667
Københavns Universitet (KU)	40.486	39.562	40.712
Roskilde Universitet (RUC)	7.398	7.657	7.982
Syddansk Universitet (SDU)	15.536	16.760	18.763
Aalborg Universitet (AAU)	11.959	13.039	14.702
Aarhus Universitet (AU)	32.024	34.126	36.093
In Total	129.477	135.287	144.409

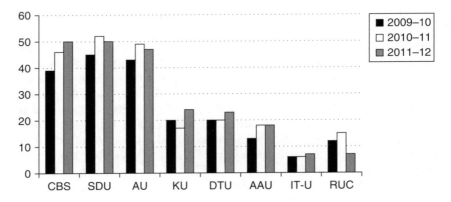

Figure 19.1   Number of entrepreneurship courses at the eight universities 2009–12

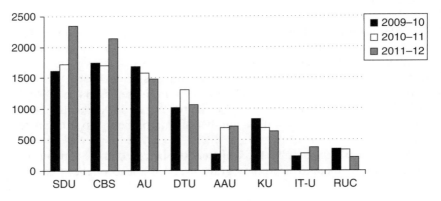

Figure 19.2   Number of entrepreneurship students at the eight universities 2009–12

universities. The highest number of courses is found at Copenhagen Business School (CBS) and the University of Southern Denmark (SDU), closely followed by Aarhus University (AU) (see Figure 19.1). These three universities have increased the number of courses compared to 2009/10, but both the University of Southern Denmark and Aarhus University has decreased their number of courses compared to 2010/11. It is also noticeable that the number of courses at Roskilde University has decreased significantly.

In Figure 19.2 we see that the universities that have experienced the most positive development regarding the number of students attending the

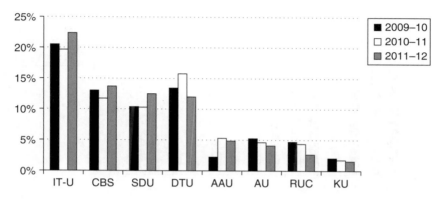

Figure 19.3   The percentage of entrepreneurship students at Denmark's eight universities 2009–12

courses are the University of Southern Denmark (SDU) and Copenhagen Business School (CBS), which both manage to increase their numbers significantly. At most of the other universities this number has been decreasing. The most significant decrease can be seen at the Technical University of Denmark (DTU) and Roskilde University (RUC). It is also noticeable that the number of participants in entrepreneurship education at Aarhus University, the entrepreneurial university, has decreased. As the universities vary much in size (Table 19.4), we have calculated the percentage of students subject to entrepreneurship education at the eight universities, which is presented in Figure 19.3.

When we take the number of students of each university into account we see that both the IT University of Copenhagen (ITU) and the Technical University of Denmark (DTU), two rather small universities, are doing fairly well, whereas Aarhus University (AU), which is Denmark's second largest university, falls to the level of Roskilde University (RUC) and that the University of Copenhagen (KU) is performing really badly.

In Figure 19.4 the number of ECTS credits (the European standard for comparing study achievement), is presented as a measure of how extensive the focus of the entrepreneurship courses are at the eight universities.

Here we see a rather stable and positive development for most of the universities. It is, however, noticeable that there has been a large decrease of ECTS credits in entrepreneurship at Roskilde University (RUC) and a fairly significant increase at Copenhagen Business School (CBS).

In order to investigate what content the universities are focusing on we have looked at how the individual university has developed in our four content dimensions over the three years. The number is calculated by the

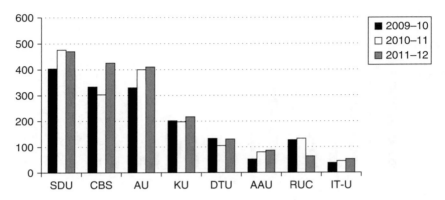

Figure 19.4   The number of ECTC credits in entrepreneurship education at Denmark's eight universities 2009–12

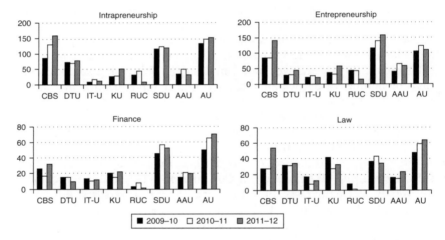

Figure 19.5   How Denmark's eight universities have developed regarding entrepreneurial content dimensions 2009–12

percentage of the maximum score the aggregated number of courses can get. In Figure 19.5 the results are presented.

We clearly see that entrepreneurship and intrapreneurship are dominating the curricula in entrepreneurship education in Denmark, over the more specialized content dimensions finance and law. Copenhagen Business School (CBS) has progressed very positively in all categories. The entrepreneurship courses at both the University of Southern Denmark (SDU) and Aarhus

University (AU) have a high specialization in the content categories. We see that most of the universities have either improved or remained stable on the content categories, which is positive as this means that the courses overall have improved and deepened their focus. The exceptions are Roskilde University that has experienced a negative development in all the content categories, and the IT University of Denmark (ITU) and Aalborg University (AAU), which have decreased regarding the content dimensions intrapreneurship and entrepreneurship. It should, however, be said that these universities are fairly small and have a limited number of courses, so a small change in the course supply comes out with a major impact in our model.

In order to analyse how the eight universities have developed regarding pedagogical methods, which also gives us an approximate measure concerning whether the courses are *about*, *through* or *for* entrepreneurship, as well as how well the content is taught, we have looked at each university's aggregated score on our four pedagogical dimensions. In Figure 19.6 the results of this analysis are presented.

Here we see fairly positive results as more or less all universities have improved in these categories. The pedagogical dimension that seems to be most problematic for the universities is the multidisciplinary dimension. Again, we see that the smaller universities, the IT University of Copenhagen (ITU), Aalborg University (AAU) and especially Roskilde University (RUC), have experienced a negative development on these dimensions. The troika from Copenhagen, that is, Copenhagen Business School (CBS), the Technical University of Denmark (DTU) and University

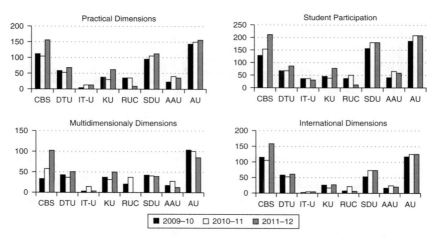

Figure 19.6   How Denmark's eight universities have developed regarding entrepreneurial teaching dimensions, 2009–12

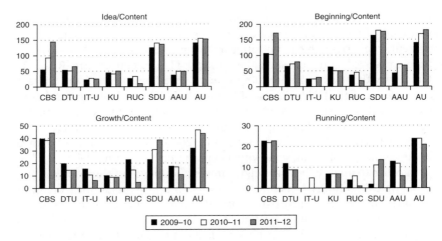

Figure 19.7a   How Denmark's eight universities have developed regarding stages in the entrepreneurial project, 2009–12 – content

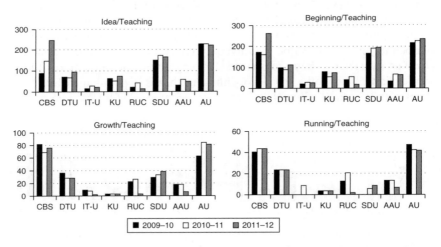

Figure 19.7b   How Denmark's eight universities have developed regarding stages in the entrepreneurial project, 2009–12 – pedagogical dimensions

of Copenhagen (KU), have managed to improve their entrepreneurship education on all categories in the pedagogical dimensions.

We have also investigated which stages in the entrepreneurial project that the entrepreneurship courses at our eight universities are focusing on. In Figure 19.7a and b, the results of this analysis are presented.

We see clearly that the main focus is on the idea and the beginning stages, which is quite natural as entrepreneurship is often synonymous with start-up activities. However, it is somewhat worrisome that there is such little focus on growth, which is a category often emphasized by policy-makers (EBST, 2011). Regarding the pedagogical categories we see that these naturally follow the content categories; however, we see that they have developed more positively than the content dimensions regarding the idea and the beginning stages, but decreased more than the content dimensions in the growth and running stages. It seems that the universities thus have had a strong focus on the two first stages in the entrepreneurial project, and that these courses on average are more *through* and *for* entrepreneurship, whereas the courses that focus on the later stages are more *about* entrepreneurship.

In order to analyse if there is a trend of entrepreneurship education developing outside of the business schools in Denmark, which according to Katz (2008), would be a measure of the field reaching maturity, we divided the universities into two groups, those with a business school and those without a business school. There are three universities in Denmark that have a business school, Aarhus University (AU), Copenhagen Business School (CBS) and University of Southern Denmark (SDU). Aalborg University (AAU) recently established a management and business department (2011), which is organized as a collaboration between the social science department and the engineering department, but it is still in its developmental phase (www.aau.dk). In Figure 19.8a the aggregated results of Figures 19.1 to 19.3 are presented, and in Figures 19.8b and c the aggregated results of Figures 19.5 to 19.7 are presented, for the two groups.

Even though the number of courses has decreased slightly at the three universities with business schools, we see that they have increased regarding the number of participants and the number of ECTS credits. What is also noticeable is that the courses have improved in quality, both regarding content and pedagogical methods. The courses thus focus more intensively on the topic and are becoming increasingly *for* and *through* entrepreneurship, rather than *about* entrepreneurship. The development of entrepreneurship education, at the universities without a business school, looks completely the opposite. Even though the number of courses has increased slightly, the number of ECTS credits and the number of participants at these five universities have decreased. We cannot see any real progress in either the content or the pedagogical dimensions, rather we see that the intrapreneurship category, a topic that should be especially suitable to universities without a business school, is decreasing.

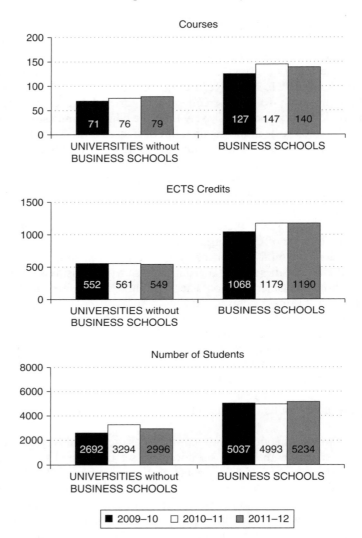

Figure 19.8a   Courses, ECTS and number of students

DISCUSSION AND IMPLICATIONS

Overall, our analysis of the development of entrepreneurship education at the eight universities in Denmark identifies a small but positive development. It looks like the efforts of the Danish government to transfer

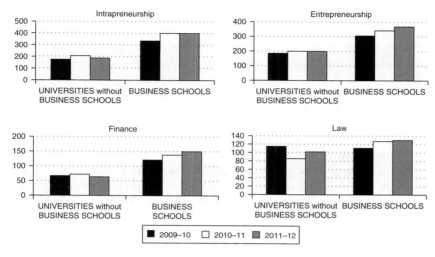

Figure 19.8b *Comparison between Danish universities with and without a business school – content*

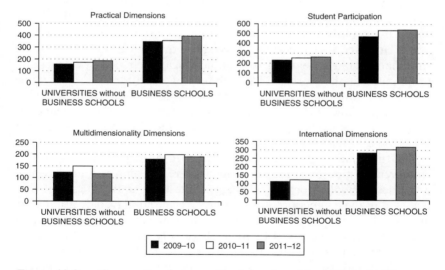

Figure 19.8c *Comparison between Danish universities with and without a business school – pedagogical dimensions*

the country's universities into entrepreneurial institutions through educational development are working. Our categorization model gives us a good overview of how the field has developed at the individual university and it enables us to identify strengths and weaknesses. It is positive to see that the universities are developing regarding pedagogical methods, as this implies that the courses are focusing more on teaching *through* and *for* entrepreneurship rather than *about* entrepreneurship. The analysis does, however, show that a couple of the universities, especially the smaller ones, have developed negatively, that is, they have not been able to sustain the supply of entrepreneurship courses.

The development of entrepreneurship education at universities with a business school compared to the universities without a business school looks very different. Regarding the question posed by Katz (2008), if the next paradigm of entrepreneurship education is developing outside of the business school, this does not seem to be the case in Denmark. What this implies is that the field is far from being mature in Denmark. As the field is still in its early stage we are bound to see a dynamic development with new course content and pedagogical methods being tested and restructured. Endurance is of importance in this process. It is clear that the government of Denmark with its investment in entrepreneurship education recognizes that the field of entrepreneurship has its roots in education and that innovation in established organizations is just as important as new venture creation. However, it is important to recognize that we need to focus on the sustainability of the field and not just the development of new courses and programmes in the short run. Development of education takes a long time and the real results only materialize in the long run. The data presented in our analysis show that the universities without business schools seem to be struggling with sustaining the supply of courses. This is a challenge that needs to be solved.

The three universities that have developed most positively regarding entrepreneurship education in Denmark are the universities at which a business school is located. It is also these three universities that participated in the competition for the entrepreneurial university grant. Our analysis shows that the initiative called the Copenhagen Innovation and Entrepreneurship Lab (CIEL) might be a way to develop and sustain entrepreneurship education at the weaker (regarding entrepreneurship education) universities. There is a lot of potential in using Copenhagen Business School's knowledge within the field in order to develop the field at the other two partnering universities, the Technical University of Denmark and the University of Copenhagen. CIEL has, however, just recently started up its activities, but it will be interesting to follow what effect this will have in later surveys, especially at the University of

Copenhagen, which is the largest university in Denmark and which today has very little focus on entrepreneurship education.

The result of our analysis also supports the choice of Aarhus University as the future entrepreneurial university of Denmark. We see that the development of entrepreneurship education at Aarhus University has been fairly stable even though the number of courses and participants has decreased slightly; they have managed to improve the courses regarding content and teaching methods. The results in Figure 19.3 show that there is great potential to increase the number of students targeted by entrepreneurship education at this university, as it is Denmark's second-largest university and fewer than 5 per cent of the students are presently involved in entrepreneurship education. We cannot yet see any positive results of the entrepreneurial university initiative regarding entrepreneurship education, but as the strategy is very clear on what will be accomplished by the end of 2013, it will be interesting to see how the university has developed by the next year. Hopefully, they will be able to sustain the courses they already have and not just replace them with newly developed ones.

Our categorization model has proven to be an effective assessment tool when evaluating the supply of entrepreneurship education on an aggregate level at universities. It gives us a good picture of how the field has developed both regarding content, focus on different stages in the entrepreneurial project and which pedagogical methods that have been used. The assessment of teaching methods is especially important as it gives us a good picture of whether the courses are *about*, *for* or *in* entrepreneurship.

CONCLUDING REMARKS AND SUGGESTIONS FOR FUTURE RESEARCH

The investment by the Danish government in entrepreneurship education as a means to transform the universities into entrepreneurial institutions is moving in the right direction. Our analysis shows that the universities that received the latest government investment have developed positively and have great future potential within the field, but the real results have yet to materialize. The entrepreneurship education field in Denmark is far from mature, as our analysis shows that the universities with a business school are far ahead within the field compared to universities without a business school. The smaller universities are struggling with sustaining their supply of entrepreneurship education, and our results show that it is just as important to focus on how to solve this problem as it is to develop new courses and programmes.

Our assessment model of entrepreneurship education has proven to be an effective tool in analysing the supply of courses and programmes on an aggregated level. As the model has its roots in the systems of innovation literature it takes a holistic and systemic approach to entrepreneurship education. It can thus be used by policy-makers who wish to assess where investments in the field will have largest effects, as it reveals potential gaps in the supply of entrepreneurship education. The model can also be used to assess single programmes regarding strengths and weaknesses, in order to understand how to adjust the courses involved. In order to assess entrepreneurship education at other levels of the educational system, it might be the case that the model needs to be altered regarding its content dimensions, but the overall structure should function well whether it is the supply of entrepreneurship education at elementary level or at PhD level that is being assessed as it is both inclusive and specific.

REFERENCES

Aldrich, H.E. and T. Baker (1997), 'Blinded by the cites? Has there been progress in the entrepreneurship field?' in D. Sexton and R. Smilor (eds), *Entrepreneurship 2000*, Chicago: Upstart Publishing Company, pp. 377–400.

Baron, R. (2012), *Entrepreneurship: An Evidence-based Guide*, Cheltenham, UK and Northampton, MA, USA: Edward Elgar.

Bhave, M.P. (1994), 'A process model of entrepreneurial venture creation', *Journal of Business Venturing*, 9(3), 223–42.

Biggs, J. and C. Tang (2007), *Teaching for Quality Learning at University: What the Student Does*, 3rd edition, Buckingham: Open University Press.

Blenker, P., S. Korsgaard, H. Neergard and C. Thrane (2011), 'The question we care about: paradigms and progression in entrepreneurship education', *Industry and Higher Education, Vol. 25*, No. 6, Dec 2011, pp. 417–27.

Block, Z. and I.C. MacMillan (1993), *Corporate Venturing – Creating New Businesses within the Firm*, Cambridge, MA: Harvard Business School Press.

Brush, C.G., I.M. Duhaime, W.B. Gartner, A. Stewart, J.A. Katz, M.A. Hitt, S.A. Alvarez, G.D. Meyer and S. Venkataraman (2003), 'Doctoral education in the field of entrepreneurship', *Journal of Management*, 29(3), 309–31.

Burgelman, R.A. (1983), 'A process model of internal corporate venturing in the diversified major firm', *Administrative Science Quarterly*, 28(2), 223–44.

Burgelman, R.A. (1984), 'Designs for corporate entrepreneurship', *California Management Review*, 26(3), 154–66.

Burgelman, R.A. (1985), 'Managing the new venture division: Research findings and implications for strategic management', *Strategic Management Journal*, 6(1), 39–54.

Charney, A. and G.D. Libecap (2000), *The Impact of Entrepreneurship Education: An Evaluation of the Berger Entrepreneurship Programme at the University of Arizona, 1985–99*, Tucson, AZ: Ewing Marion Kauffman Foundation.

Cooke, P. (2002), 'Regional innovation systems, clusters and the knowledge economy', *Industrial and Corporate Change*, 6(4), 945–74.

Danish Agency for Science, Technology and Innovation (2009), Strategy for Education and Training in Entrepreneurship. Rosendahl-Schultz Grafisk, Albertslund.

Davidsson, P. (2012), 'Entrepreneurial opportunity and the entrepreneurship nexus: A reconceptualization', conference paper presented at the Academy of Management Meeting 2012 in Boston.

Davidsson, P. and J. Wiklund (2001), 'Levels of analysis in entrepreneurship research: Current practice and suggestions for the future', *Entrepreneurship Theory and Practice*, **25**(4), 81–99.

Davis, H.G. and N. Diamond (1997), *The Rise of American Research Universities: Elites and Challengers in the Post-war Era*, Baltimore, MD: Johns Hopkins University Press.

Debackere, K. and R. Veugelers (2005), 'The role of academic technology transfer organizations in improving industry science links', *Research Policy*, **34**(3), 321–42.

EBST (2011), *Iværksætterindex 2011 – Vilkår for iværksettere i Danmark*, Erhvervs- og Byggestyrelsen.

Etzkowitz, H. (2003), 'Research groups as "quasi-firms": The invention of the entrepreneurial university', *Research Policy*, **32**(1), 109–21.

Etzkowitz, H., A. Webster, C. Gebhardt and B.R.C. Terra (2000), 'The future of the university and the university of the future: Evolution of ivory tower to entrepreneurial paradigm', *Research Policy*, **29**(2), 313–30.

European Commission (2011), *European University Funding and Financial Autonomy: A Study on the Degree of Diversification of University Budget and the Share of Competitive Funding*, EUR 24761 EN – 2011.

European Commission (2012), *Effects and Impact of Entrepreneurship Programmes in Higher Education*, DG Enterprise and Industry, Brussels: EC.

Foss, N.J. and P.G. Klein (2012), *Organizing Entrepreneurial Judgement: A New Approach to the Firm*, Cambridge, UK: Cambridge University Press.

Foss, N.J. and J. Lyngsie (2011), 'The emerging strategic entrepreneurship field: Origins, key tenets, and research gaps', in D. Hjorth (ed.), *Handbook of Organizational Entrepreneurship*, Cheltenham, UK and Northampton, MA, USA: Edward Elgar.

Geuna, A. (1998), 'The internationalization of European universities: A return to medieval roots', *Minerva*, **XXXVI**(3), 253–70.

Gibb, A.A. (1987), 'Designing effective programmes for encouraging and supplying the business start-up process: Lessons from UK experience', *Journal of European Industrial Training*, **11**(4), 24–32.

Gibb, A.A. (2002), 'In pursuit of a new entrepreneurship paradigm for learning: Creative destruction, new values, new ways of doing things and new combinations of knowledge', *International Journal of Management Reviews*, **4**(3), 233–69.

Gibb, A.A. (2011), 'Concepts into practice: Meeting the challenges of development of entrepreneurship educators around an innovative paradigm – the case of International Entrepreneurship Educators' Programme (IEEP)', *International Journal of Entrepreneurial Behaviour and Research*, **17**(2), 146–65.

Hannon, P. (2005), 'Philosophies of enterprise and entrepreneurship education and challenges for Higher Education in the UK', *International Journal of Entrepreneurship and Innovation*, **6**(2), 105–14.

Heinonen, J. and U. Hytti (2010), 'Back to basics: The role of teaching in developing the entrepreneurial university', *Entrepreneurship and Innovation*, **11**(4), 283–92.

Hitt, M.A., R.D. Ireland, S.M. Camp and D.L. Sexton (2001), 'Guest editors, introduction to the special issue. Strategic entrepreneurship: Entrepreneurial strategies for wealth creation', *Strategic Management Journal*, **22**, 479–91.

Jensen, R.A., J.G. Thursby and M.C. Thursby (2003), 'Disclosure and licensing of university inventions', NBER Working Paper No. 9734.

Johannisson, B. (1991), 'University training for entrepreneurship: Swedish approaches', *Entrepreneurship and Regional development*, **3**(1), 67–82.

Jonsson, C. and T. Jonsson (2002), 'Entrepreneurial learning – an informed way of learning: The case of enterprise and business development', Växjö University.

Katz, J.A. (1994), 'Growth of endowments, chairs, and programs in entrepreneurship on the college campus', in F. Hoy, T.G. Monroy and J. Reichert (eds), *The Art and Science of Entrepreneurship Education, Vol. 1*, Cleveland, OH: Baldwin-Wallace College, pp. 127–49.

Katz, J.A. (2003), 'The chronology and intellectual trajectory of American entrepreneurship education', *Journal of Business Venturing*, **18**(2), 283–300.

Katz, J.A. (2004), *2004 Survey of Endowed Positions in Entrepreneurship and Related Fields in the United States*, Kansas City, MO: Ewing Marion Kauffman Foundation.

Katz, J.A. (2008), 'Fully mature but not fully legitimate: A different perspective on the state of entrepreneurship education', *Journal of Small Business Management*, **46**(4), 550–66.

Klapper, R. and H. Neergaard (2012), 'Five steps to heaven: From student to entrepreneur – an agenda for innovative pedagogy', conference paper presented at the European Summer University in Kolding, Denmark, 19 to 25 August, 2012.

Kuratko, D.F. (2005), 'The emergence of entrepreneurship education: Development, trends, and challenges', *Entrepreneurship Theory and Practice*, **29**(5), 577–97.

Kyrö, P. and M. Niemi (2007), 'Advancing business planning – from planning to entrepreneurial learning', in G. Blauen (ed.), *Twente Case Study-book*.

Kyvik, S. (2004), 'Structural changes in Higher Education systems in Western Europe', *Higher Education in Europe*, **XXIX**(3), 393–409.

Lazear, E.P. (2004), 'Balanced skills and entrepreneurship', *American Economic Review*, Papers and Proceedings, **94**(2), 208–11.

Lazear, E.P. (2005), 'Entrepreneurship', *Journal of Labor Economics*, **23**(4), 649–80.

Loyens, S.M.M., J. Magda and R.M.J.P. Rikers (2008), 'Self-directed learning I: Problem-based learning and its relationship with self-regulated learning', *Educational Psychology Review*, **20**(4), 411–27.

Lundvall, B-Å. (1992), 'Introduction', in *Towards a Theory of Innovation and Interactive Learning*, London: Frances Pinter Publishers Ltd, pp. 1–19.

McDougall, P.P. and B.M. Oviat, (2000), 'International entrepreneurship: The intersection of two research paths', *The Academy of Management Journal*, **43**(5), 902–6.

McDougall, P.P., S. Shane and B.M. Oviatt (1994), 'Explaining the formation of international new ventures: The limits of theories from international business research', *Journal of Business Venturing*, **9**(6), 469–87.

NIRAS et al. (2008), *Survey of Entrepreneurship in Higher Education*, for the European Commission.

Nygaard, C. (2010), 'A learning strategy as a possible vehicle for branding universities?' CBS Working Paper, CBS Learning Lab.

OECD (2001), *Benchmarking Industry–Science Relationships, Science, Technology and Industry Outlook 2000*, Paris: OECD.

OECD (2005), *University Research Management. Developing Research in New Institutions*, Paris: OECD.

OECD (2008), *Entrepreneurship Review of Denmark*, Paris: OECD.

Pittaway, L. and J. Cope (2006), 'Entrepreneurship education: A systematic review of the evidence', National Council for Graduate Entrepreneurship, Working Paper No. 002/2006.

Pittaway, L. and J. Cope (2007), 'Simulating entrepreneurial learning: Integrating experiential and collaborative approaches to learning', *Management Learning*, **38**(2), 211–33.

Politis, D. (2005), 'Entrepreneurship, career experience and learning: Developing our understanding of entrepreneurship as an experiential learning process', doctoral thesis, Ekonomihögskolan vid Lunds Universitet.

Rialp, A., J. Rialp and G.A. Knight (2004), 'The phenomenon of early internationalizing firms: What do we know after a decade (1993–2003) of scientific inquiry?' *International Business Review*, **14**(2), 147–66.

Sarasvathy, S.D. (2004), 'Making it happen: Beyond theories of the firm to theories of firm design', *Entrepreneurship Theory and Practice*, **28**(6), 519–31.

Sarasvathy, S. (2008), *Effectuation: Elements of Entrepreneurial Expertise*, Cheltenham, UK and Northampton, MA, USA: Edward Elgar.

Solomon, G.T. (1979), *Small Business Management Resource Guides, Vols 1–6*, Washington, DC: US Small Business Administration.

Solomon, G. (2007), 'An examination of entrepreneurship education in the United States', *Journal of Small Business and Enterprise Development*, **14**(2), 168–82.

Solomon, G.T. and L.W. Fernald (1991), 'Trends in small business management and entrepreneurship education in the United States', *Entrepreneurship Theory and Practice*, **15**(2) 25–39.

Solomon, G.T. and M. Sollosy (1977), *Nationwide Survey in Course Offerings in Small Business Management/Entrepreneurship*, Washington, DC: International Council for Small Business.

Solomon, G.T., K.M. Weaver and L.W. Fernald (1994), 'Pedagogical methods of teaching entrepreneurship: An historical perspective', *Gaming and Simulation*, **25**(3), 338–52.

Stevenson, H.H., M.J. Roberts and H.I. Grousbeck (1985), *New Business Ventures and the Entrepreneur*, Burr Ridge, IL: Richard D. Irwin.

UNESCO (2004), 'Changing structures of the Higher Education systems: The increasing complexity of underlying forces', UNESCO Forum Occasional Paper Series Paper No. 6, Diversification of Higher Education and the Changing Role of Knowledge and Research Papers presented at the Second Scientific Committee Meeting for Europe and North America.

Vesper, K.H. (1985), *Entrepreneurship Education 1985*, Babson Park, MA: Center for Entrepreneurial Studies, Babson College.

Vesper, K.H. (1993), *Entrepreneurship Education 1993*, Los Angeles: Entrepreneurial Studies Center, UCLA.

Vesper, K.H. and W.B. Gartner (1997), 'Measuring progress in entrepreneurship education', *Journal of Business Venturing*, **12**(4), 403–21.

Vesper, K.H. and W.E. McMullen (1988), 'Entrepreneurship: Today courses, tomorrow degrees?' *Entrepreneurship Theory and Practice*, **13**(1), 7–13.

West, P.G. (2003), 'Connecting levels of analysis in entrepreneurship research: A focus on information processing, asymmetric knowledge and networks', in C. Steyaert and D. Hjorth (eds), *New Movements in Entrepreneurship*, Cheltenham, UK and Northampton, MA, USA, pp. 51–70.

Zahra, S.A. (1991), 'Predictors and financial outcomes of corporate entrepreneurship: An exploratory study', *Journal of Business Venturing*, **6**(4), 259–85.

Zeithaml, C.P. and G.H. Rice (1987), 'Entrepreneurship/small business education in American universities', *Journal of Small Business Management*, **25**(1), 44–50.

Index